Practicing Ethnohistory

PATRICIA GALLOWAY

Practicing Ethnohistory

Mining Archives, Hearing Testimony, Constructing Narrative

UNIVERSITY OF NEBRASKA PRESS • LINCOLN & LONDON

Library of Congress Cataloging-
in-Publication Data
Galloway, Patricia Kay.
Practicing ethnohistory : mining
archives, hearing testimony,
constructing narrative /
Patricia Galloway.
p. cm.
Includes bibliographical
references and index.
ISBN-13: 978-0-8032-7115-9
(pbk. : alk. paper)
ISBN-10: 0-8032-7115-8
(pbk. : alk. paper)
1. Ethnohistory—Methodology.
2. Ethnohistory—Research.
3. Choctaw Indians—History.
4. Louisiana—History—To 1803.
5. Mississippi—History—To 1803.
I. Title.
GN345.2.G35   2006
909'.04—dc22   2006000820

Contents

Practicing Ethnohistory

1. Introduction

How Deep Is (Ethno-)History?
Archives, Written History,
Oral Tradition

In the Beginning Was *Mississippi Provincial Archives: French Dominion*

In 1979 I came to Mississippi to revive a ghost: I was hired to edit and take through production the final two volumes of *Mississippi Provincial Archives: French Dominion* (MPA:FD), a collection of translated French documents pertaining to the eighteenth-century colonization of the lands that would become Mississippi.[1] The project had been prepared in typescript in 1932 and then set aside and eventually misplaced for forty years; the decision was made to publish it after it was rediscovered in 1974.[2] My qualifications for this job ostensibly included an undergraduate degree in French, an MA in comparative literature specializing in the eighteenth century, plus some rigorous exposure to textual criticism and historiography as a result of a PhD in comparative literature/medieval studies that nevertheless did not seem immediately relevant at the outset. What I found, however, was that, as is axiomatic of the multifarious qualifications of archivists in carrying out their jobs, this task of historical documentary editing and the path it started me on would call on everything I had learned to that point and would require the expansion of my theoretical and subject-area knowledge and of several areas of practice as well. In addition, the project itself was situated in the intellectual history of archival practice, historiography, ethnography, and ethnohistory, and the state of research in all of these fields would frame it and provide a starting point for all the ethnohistorical work that would flow from it. In a very substantive sense the essays here, covering some twenty years of my work in ethnohistory, track my intellectual autobiography; hence, in this introduction I will attempt to make that frame visible.

I knew next to nothing about the history of the French colony of Louisiana or of those of its inhabitants who lived in what would become the state of

Mississippi. I was also unaware that the MPA:FD project itself represented the continuation of an early-twentieth-century effort by Dunbar Rowland and the board members of the Mississippi Department of Archives and History (MDAH) designed to prove the depth and duration of early European involvement in the state's history and to make available to the public a selection of documents portraying Mississippi's French colonial history. But I apparently seemed intelligent enough to be up to the job of editing for publication two volumes of French documents that had already been translated and documented with scholarly comment. It didn't hurt that my great-grandfather had served on the founding board of trustees of the MDAH and had known Dunbar Rowland well. There was a poetic closure in the return to Mississippi of a "daughter of the regiment."

The original estimate was that, working with an excellent typist with a vast experience in preparing materials for publication, the task would take me six months. That estimate would not have been correct even had the task as defined not been problematic, but it soon became clear that there was nothing simple about the project. First and axiomatically to me, the very texts from which the original translator had had to work were inadequate simply as a consequence of the time in which he worked. The department had acquired twenty-six volumes of handwritten copies of French colonial documents about the region, dating from the 1680s to 1763, from the French Archives nationales on the basis of a protocol devised by Dunbar Rowland, the director of the department, when he visited the French archives in 1904. Although at that time the freelance copyists who made a living at the Archives nationales doing this work were very good at their jobs, were familiar with the material, and wrote in very clear scribal hands, they were subject to the same problems that medieval copyists had experienced. That at least was something I was qualified to detect, and it soon became obvious to me when I began comparing the handwritten copies with microfilm copies of the original documents, which had been obtained in 1970 as part of a consortium effort that included the Library of Congress. So initially it was clear that the underlying French text versions would have to be checked very carefully.

Nor could I trust the translations as they stood, not because they were not competent but because they were competent with respect to the standards of their time, and standards were not the same fifty years later. The translator, Albert Godfrey Sanders, a very scholarly professor of French language and literature at Millsaps College and the father of one of my own father's lifelong friends, had aimed for a sober literal translation, but there were numerous characteristics of the subject matter and its presentation that he did not and, in the state of knowledge at the time, could not know. We forget just how little was known from original documents at the turn of the twentieth century, but that very time was the one that saw the significant work done on calendaring the French documents by Nancy M. Miller Surrey (whose calendar, never properly published, remains the best brief description of what must be nearly all the relevant documents) and the acquisition of copies of the documents for the first time by American repositories, all thanks to the organizational work of the Carnegie Institution.[3] During that time also ethnographer John R. Swanton was in the process of laying the foundations for the ethnohistorical study of Indians of the greater Southeast, including those who appeared in the documents to be edited. In fact, in the person of Dunbar Rowland the original project interacted directly with both of these historical and ethnographic projects and participated in this first flush of work that opened up the European archives to American historical and ethnographic study.

Since that time, unfortunately, little more had been done with the French colonial history of the Southeast, at least not in the region itself. The first third of the century had indeed seen the editing and publication of a considerable body of primary source material from the period, but in a region still obsessed by the Civil War and the economic changes that followed, the major topics of discussion had been the Confederacy and the New South, not that which was very old. Several periodicals, most notably the *Louisiana Historical Quarterly*, had nevertheless published a mine of primary materials. There were a few excellent secondary studies, but they were a tiny handful and in general either inaccessible due to language reasons or not considered "mainstream" enough to affect the writing of Louisiana colonial history significantly.[4] The chapter on the French colonial history of Mississippi in the two-volume set brought out with such fanfare by the MDAH in 1973 ("the first comprehensive history of Mississippi in fifty years") was written by a nonspecialist.

On the anthropological side, Swanton's work from 1932, when the typescript of the materials I was working with seemed to have been completed as it stood, to his death in 1958 had added significantly to the foundation ethnography of the southeastern Indians, although his work had also been so exhaustive that it had daunted further researchers. In addition, the emergence of an interdisciplinary practice of ethnohistory had taken place in connection with research done under the Indian Claims Act of 1946 and had crystallized in the formation of the precursor to the American Society for Ethnohistory in the 1950s; its journal *Ethnohistory* had existed since 1954. There was therefore a body of ethnographic work and perhaps more relevant ethnohistorical practice to draw on.

Clearly, it would be necessary to do additional work over and above copyediting the existing typescript. I would need to do some serious research, because in the light of current editorial practice and historical trends in the direction of social history it was evident that the scholarly apparatus provided in the Rowland/Sanders typescript was quite inadequate, especially in view of one extremely salient fact: most of the people who resided on the lands that would later become the state of Mississippi during the period 1699–1763 were not Europeans but Indians. I therefore set for myself the goal of expanding the biographical notes already provided, which had been confined to the leading French figures in the colony and a very few Great Red Men. I would attempt to identify everyone (Indian, African, Englishman, and Spaniard as well as Frenchman), drawing on the documents themselves and the various censuses and service records that were available either in the collection or published elsewhere. In addition I would try to elucidate references in the documents that were not explained by other documents in the published MPA:FD collection so that the reader would not be obliged to look elsewhere in order to make sense of what was on the page. The resources already mentioned could be drawn upon, and in addition I could seek out archival sources in Mississippi and the surrounding states, notably Louisiana and Alabama; in fact, I made visits to archives in both states in pursuit of original materials. Finally, I would attempt to represent more equitably the actual population of the region by seeking out and publishing additional documents pertaining to the Indian history of the period.[5]

Tanselle and the Text

"Historical editing" was the rubric under which my work would fall, and it was obvious to me that even though I was preparing translations I would need to investigate the state of historical editing to see if there was anything that I needed to know beyond what I already understood as a result of my acquaintance with literary editing. To my amazement, I found that I had stepped into the field just in time to encounter a major scandal of historical editing, then being exposed by G. Thomas Tanselle. Tanselle wrote a very influential essay in which he described the common practices of the many editing projects, mostly sponsored by the National Historical Publications and Records Commission (NHPRC), producing modern editions of the papers of Great White Men Important in Political History in which the editors chose to clean up the spelling and even the language of these admired gentlemen without concern for faithfulness to the original manuscripts or the fact that people who used the editions would be unlikely ever to consult the originals. Tanselle compared this kind of practice, for a discipline that was ostensibly concerned with accuracy and truth, to the literary editing that had been going on at the same time under the aegis of the Center for Editions of American [literary] Authors, where common practice was if anything punctilious to a fault in reproducing the texts of the original manuscripts, warts and all. Tanselle pointed out the significant work of twentieth-century literary editors in building upon the long toil of classical and biblical textual criticism and the failure of historical editors to profit from this example. Having surveyed historical editing practice in the major NHPRC projects, he concluded that "the difference between the way American statesmen and American literary figures have recently been edited is a striking illustration of how two closely related fields can approach the basic scholarly task of establishing dependable texts in two very different ways, one of which [historical editing] seems superficial and naive in comparison to the other [literary editing]."[6]

With a background in medieval literary history, I was certainly predisposed to be persuaded by Tanselle's argument that the literalist literary standard was far preferable to what seemed to be the Whiggish bias of the historical standard.[7] My most recent background had included work on computer-aided medieval manuscript filiation, which was essentially invented by Dom Froger in the late 1960s to take advantage of the computer in order to establish relationships among manuscript copies with the intention of establishing authoritative texts with variants.[8] I was well acquainted not only with the literature pertaining to this new approach (some of which I had myself created) but with the underlying theory about information transfer *before* the age of mechanical reproduction that informed this literature: that of codicology, or the making of manuscripts and books, and that of diplomatics, or the establishment of authenticity in manuscript sources. This neighborhood of textual criticism was especially relevant to the French colonial documents, I believed, because, first, they were in fact manuscript documents, and, second, many of the "original" documents were not originals at all but official copies made under specific circumstances and for specific purposes. Ignoring those purposes would prune significant meaning from the text.[9]

In addition to the discipline of textual criticism per se I also drew upon long-honed practices of comparative literature. The subdivisions of that discipline that had occupied me were, first of all, the establishment of sources for written material. I had the good fortune to be trained by Werner P. Friederich, the doyen of comparative literature studies in the United States, and Papa Friederich brought intertextuality to life (*avant la lettre*—or at least he never used the term) by first showing his students how interlaced and interdependent all the literatures of Europe were and then requiring us to track down every last allusion and influence we could find, drawing upon information about the author's education and biography, his friends and enemies, people who might have been his friends and enemies, lists of books in his library, lists of books in his friends' libraries, and so on.[10] Working as a scholar primarily in the period from the twelfth to eighteenth centuries, I had also fortuitously studied the gradual emergence of the genre of history in European writing as separate from fiction and was therefore aware of the degree to which this was still a matter of serious debate in the eighteenth century.[11] Finally, having sat in on courses given by the eminent twentieth-century specialist Eugene Falk, I had read reader-response theory and imbibed the beginning of a concern with the author's intention for the work, the reader's reception of the work, and the notion of a text as something mutually constructed between author and reader; this approach had partly informed my 1974 dissertation and became an important part of my computational work with texts.[12]

One other element was blended into this mix: in 1966, before I went off to become a comparatist, I spent the summer at Indiana University as a Summer Folklore Fellow, and I was introduced to the study of folklore and the mysteries of tracing oral traditions in the spirit of the gatherers and classifiers of encyclopedic collections of folktales and traditions who had worked under the leadership of Stith Thompson.[13] Under the supervision of Linda Degh we all fanned out to gather folk traditions from informants in the region to add to the local collection, and I not only had the opportunity to see an entirely different side of my grandparents' lives as country people (they formed the key informants of the snowball sample I pursued) but gained a first understanding of how an official literate discourse can mask a world of tradition and practices unrepresented in the literate culture. Just gaining the attention of students at that time were the work of Marshall McLuhan on alterations in communication, the first translated writings of Claude Lévi-Strauss on oral tradition and its structural analysis, and the structural linguistics of Ferdinand de Saussure, the latter two of which influenced my dissertation power-fully and would continue to provide a frame for my understanding of positive evidence.[14]

In short, I was bound to be concerned with presenting through my transla-tion and editing activities something as close to the original as I could get (knowing only too well that most of my readers would never read the original French) and with contextualizing those texts as well as I could, given what I could learn of the people who wrote the texts, the people the writers wrote about, and what all of their situations were. And naive though that hope now seems and unprepared as I then was, MPA:FD was the gateway through which I stepped to practicing ethnohistory.

Part I: Taking Historical Text Production Seriously

Building on the bases just discussed, always aware of the production process behind any text, I have always been concerned with the contingency of the historical sources I had to deal with, and I have struggled—some would say too hard—with trying to wring blood from the stones of European incompre-hension and representation of Native behavior and testimony. This position has not been unusual in the context of contemporary developments in histo-riography. The influence of the French Annales school of structural history has been especially important, with Fernand Braudel's distinctions among temporal scales: the very long term of geological and climatic change; eras of the medium term shaped by the evolution of human systems like government and demography; and the small-scale events consisting of the actions of indi-viduals (generally only of interest to Annales if they included all classes and ranks and could be summed to larger patterns of social, economic, and cul-tural history).[15] Annales structural methods offered to the ethnohistorian the tools of the eighteenth-century mathesis of counting and classifying in their focus on repetitive records that allow statistical treatment to discern especially economic patterns over the long term.[16] They were also helpful in addressing with some effectiveness the clashes and mis-fits of culture contact as they expressed themselves in structural patterns.[17] Annales methods are positive in their conviction that in the reductive treatment of the record—documentary, material—an adequate account of the shape of what happened can be found.

At the same time, through decades of development of the social history that Annales work reinforced and sometimes inspired, the doubt that history itself could be seen as an objective positive science emerged along with the Marxist critique of capitalist liberal democracy as the universal goal of human striving.[18] As history writing was critiqued in this same vein, and with a significant four-hundred-year *longue durée* to serve as perspective, it was observed by Hayden White and others that historical *representation* was always of its time, not only in terms of writing style but also in choice of subject and manner of presentation. Whether presented as moral discourse or not, postmodern historiographical critique has shown how history always *was* moral discourse.[19]

Ironically, this in fact represents the only answer to Keith Jenkins's question "Why history?"—stripped of pretension to universalizing (Orientalizing) objectivity written from a "nowhere" standpoint, history can honestly be what it of necessity is and take its moral discourse seriously and reflexively.[20] This is especially important when it comes to the writing of ethnohistory, by definition written by people (even people sharing the same *ethnos* as their subjects) who experience themselves as "in history" about people who may not, or at least not in the same sense. From the outset the writing of ethnohistory was a moral/ethical exercise, and over its own history of practice ethnohistorians have grappled with such problems. How to deal with biased-observer sources? Such sources are always all there is, and even for externally observable fact they see what they look for. How to understand and perceive thoughts and intentions absent verbal externalization in text or spoken word? For that matter, what might count as externalization of thought in verbal production or in deeds? Assigning significance to events rests on constructing an understanding of what is going on from the perspective of now; thus even understanding European intentions as recently as a generation ago is a nontrivial exercise.

Here anthropology enters the picture. As the study of such Others by Western European Selves, anthropology itself has had an increasingly contested history. But for the ethnohistorian its power lies in providing a way of "defining the situation" in which events and interactions took place using its social, political, and cultural constructs.[21] For a long time anthropology has had increasing influence on the writing of ethnohistory precisely because it made this kind of contextualizing possible. Anthropology, however, was just as much a "noble dream" (or perhaps "colonialist nightmare," depending on perspective) as was "objective" history. From the beginning of European writing about indigenous people, those same people have objected to being misrepresented or even represented at all, and at the end of the twentieth century strong indigenous voices began to be heard not only on the political stage but in the academy.[22]

I have, as I said, spent a lot of time worrying about the usefulness of Euro-American texts for writing the history of Native American people. My interest in ethnohistory was piqued in the first place because as I edited French documents of the eighteenth century it simply became plain that the social and political activities of Native people represented the most important things going on in that time and place, the poorly described ground against which the more familiar figure of European colonization was constructed. Even where the Native population had been seriously damaged by the effects of European disease, until the very end of the eighteenth century in the interior of the Southeast, Native people dominated in every way, and Europeans had to behave with circumspection or achieve none of their ends at all. This was very frustrating to some, while others were oblivious, but in general Native people and their affairs were not known in detail because the only Europeans they welcomed to live among them frequently "went native" themselves and began to practice the same reticence about their affairs as the hosts who had often reared them.[23]

Nevertheless, these partial views are the only ones we now have, and so we need to devise better ways of interrogating them to try to understand at least what the witnesses thought they saw. The first step in this direction is achieving usable texts to work with, and especially attempting to establish the context in which the texts were written so as to be able to weigh them. As I was editing the documents in MPA:FD I realized that while the standard of documentation that the original editors thought adequate worked well enough for the writing of French colonial political history, they were inadequate to support the social and economic history of the French colony and sometimes worse than useless to support the writing of ethnohistory. Without special efforts in supplying background and context, it seemed to me, historians using these materials would continue to concentrate on the French part of Louisiana colonial history and miss such complexity and detail as did begin to emerge when adequate context was presented. Although since I was editing and producing translations I was not in a position to do nuanced textual work, I attempted to bring the importance of this kind of practice to the attention of historical editors in general in the essay "Dearth and Bias: Issues in the Editing of Ethnohistorical Materials."

I was also especially interested in finding some way of discovering the completeness status of the record we now have at our disposal, because we have also learned from the historiographers that the historical record itself is and has been manipulated and constructed at several levels and that construction constrains what can be done with it. The appearance in print of Bill Barron's calendar of the correspondence in the Vaudreuil Papers at the Huntington Library provided the occasion to investigate such lacunae in detail in the context of a carefully maintained eighteenth-century gubernatorial letter-book.[24] This analysis, written up as "Louisiana Post Letters, 1700–1763: The Missing Evidence for Indian Diplomacy," allowed me to explore a method influenced by Western archival practice that I have come to use with all kinds of evidence that can be seen as a body constrained by some kind of unity of provenance, namely, always making a preliminary attempt at inventorying and describing the whole original body of evidence as defined in terms of a specific record-keeping practice, looking for any principles of exclusion operating alongside principles of inclusion.

This issue of principles of exclusion operates *within* sources as much as it does in the process of making up groups of sources, and it requires no less understanding of the context of creation. In the early 1990s I investigated examples of this issue in terms of what voices were being articulated in any source we might use and how authoritative for the purpose in hand the identified voice might make the information to be found in the source. In the course of analyzing the evidentiary value of the sources used to write the history of early Spanish exploration in the Southeast I kept encountering what I felt was, all around, an extremely uncritical use of a source written for an entirely different purpose, and I investigated it in "Agustín Dávila Padilla's Fabulous History of the Luna Expedition: Ideology in Two Centuries." I also had occasion to examine one of the most revered sources for eighteenth-century Louisiana history, the *Histoire de la Louisiane* of Antoine Simon Le Page du Pratz, in beginning to prepare a translation.[25] I found that Du Pratz's apparently straightforward account of things he witnessed must have been profoundly influenced, particularly in matters pertaining to women (for which Du Pratz is unusually helpful for a patriarchal colonizing male of the eighteenth century), by the testimony of a young Chitimacha woman who was his servant, first as a slave and then as a sort of adoptee. I treated part of that analysis in "Natchez Matrilineal Kinship: Du Pratz and the Woman's Touch."

Finally, I was especially interested in what we might be able to do as historians to understand what European observers would not be likely to notice at all (and therefore would not report) and how anthropological methods might be used to do a better job of defining the situation in which the observations took place. I made use of both narrative analysis (to discover what the writer of narrative sources wanted the reader to notice) and a critique of the method christened "Direct Historic Approach" by archaeologists and "upstreaming" by ethnohistorians, which aims to describe past lifeways by analogy with practices observed in the more recent past by ethnographers, to suggest a range of behavioral phenomena that Europeans would not notice or would misdescribe. That analysis became "The Unexamined Habitus: Direct Historic Analogy and the Archaeology of the Text."

These essays suggest that the sources of historical data for Native history in the Southeast continue to be limited for the colonial period. There are clearly several reasons for this: Europeans did not witness or notice important phenomena or did not choose to write about them; they did notice and write, but we now fail to understand what they meant to say; they did notice and write, but their writings are now lost. I will have a great deal more to say about this last and far too frequent case of missing records at the end of this essay.

Part II: Archaeology, Computing, and Positive (Information) Science

Although dealing harshly with written text makes it possible to find ways to hear the voices of Native people themselves through it, too many of these techniques were too sidelong and tenuous for trying to get at many of the conditions of Indian life that had nothing to do with war, diplomacy, or trade. I needed methods that could look beyond the judgment of European witnesses to query and critique their direct observations about Native people. I needed methods that didn't require European witnesses and their tunnel vision at all. I needed positive methods that could accumulate comparable information in enough quantity that it could be queried for pattern, pattern that might be the direct reflection of lives and practices. In four years spent as a medieval archaeologist in England and Norway I had gained experience with the realia of medieval (and postmedieval) European life, learning also just how little information textual representation generally even attempts to deliver about material culture. Archaeology is thus one way to get at patterns left behind by living people—not the patterns of every activity, not evidence for every thought, but partial evidence of how people dwelt with each other on the land. Repeated Annales-like evidence pulled from documentary sources is, for all its failings, another way. Patterned evidence from both sources may be manipulated to discover how they fit with one another to construct yet more kinds of evidence.

All of these methods of historian and archaeologist strive to "discover" evidence and then to locate it as to where and when. Archaeological evidence is usually very clear as to the where—it is minutely located by being found buried in the earth—but struggles mightily to establish the when by constructing sequences ("space-time systematics") and attempting to tie them to datable objects or absolute dating techniques. (Although these latter become less and less reliable as one approaches the present, the more frequent appearance of European objects, often very tightly datable, comes as some compensation.) Documentary evidence, on the other hand, is usually very clear on the when—leaving aside the problem of the reuse of written materials—but is disappointingly vague about the where, as Euro-American observers were all too often much more interested in the who and why. Using both kinds of evidence, it is sometimes possible to mitigate the shortcomings of one by the strengths of the other, bearing in mind at all times that the archaeological evidence is no less constructed by the situatedness of its research designs, recovery techniques, and analytical modes than the historical evidence is.[26]

Nevertheless, archaeological evidence indisputably represents some of the traces left behind where people lived and used the land. In 1994, as I was attempting to establish for a museum exhibit the population of Indians in the state of Mississippi over time, I had only one reasonable set of figures available from documentary sources drawn from the late seventeenth century forward. To reach farther back in time I had only the archaeological sites in the state's site file to proxy for the numbers I sought, though at the historic end of the scale I could calibrate that evidence by the better-established historic numbers. The failings of the site-file data were enormous, ranging from the bias introduced by the easy driving distance from state universities that taught archaeology courses to specific survey projects (one of which I had directed) to fads in the characterization of temporal periods, yet in "Prehistoric Population of Mississippi: A First Approximation" it was—just—possible to pull a trend out of those very compromised and heavily constructed numbers, simply because it was so obvious, and to suggest broader implications of that trend.

Another sort of canonical archaeological evidence, the definition of pottery types, became the support of an investigation of interethnic influence, both Indian-Indian and European-Indian. Pottery typology is a notoriously questionable form of evidence for establishing ethnicity in the past, and almost no archaeologist will argue for its certainty where it is not possible to connect types or styles to living people or indisputable populations from the recent past. It is, however, sometimes possible to correlate pottery types with other evidence. In "Technical Origins for Chickachae Combed Ceramics: An Ethnohistorical Hypothesis" I brought to bear a range of pottery type definitions for "Bayougoula Incised" and "Chickachae Combed" and related types of pottery, a well-documented population movement, and a specific type of well-attested European trade object, the boxwood comb, to offer a suggested explanation for the apparently sudden distinct appearance of a specific decorative motif for Choctaw pottery in the eighteenth century. The explanation was one possibility, certainly not proved, but it was strengthened by the convergence of several lines of evidence.

Convergence of another kind is important in taking advantage of the observations of places by eighteenth-century European observers. The information that European travelers recorded when they described journeys or made maps was not a set of "floating signifiers" for them or those who lived in the region, but today we find it very difficult to connect places they described with places we can identify and to make the specific locations on maps they drew tally with the results of our very different imaging methods. Part of this is due to the specific observational habits they brought to their observations and mapping; part is due to the inaccuracy of their instruments and observational practices; part is due to the "changes in the land" that have taken place since they made their observations.[27] Yet these observers provided us with detailed though distorted maps (distorted, we can see, with respect to the watercourses we know have not changed *that* much) and a tantalizing series of lists and itineraries that name the places they mapped. Lists of names—of people, inhabited places, and landmarks—appeared especially in the early and late eighteenth century for the very reason that we now attempt to exploit them as we do: they were part of the anatomizing of the world that served emerging nation-states to classify and manage their holdings, and they were made at times when those holdings were being explored or were threatened. Several of these lists and maps are of particular interest, and I have revisited them repeatedly. In "Multidimensional Scaling for Mapping Ethnohistorical Narrative: Choctaw Villages in the Eighteenth Century" I made use of a method I had used successfully to provide names for the known locations of medieval Trondheim churches, exploiting the links between them provided by a thirteenth-century itinerary used by nightwatchmen.[28] We had several maps to check configurations against and two significant itineraries to provide linkages—via traveled paths—between Choctaw villages. The evidence was not systematic, and in the end it told us less about actual locations and more about perceived relationships, but the attempt provided an interesting and better understanding of the data.

I undertook a more systematic investigation of the location of Choctaw villages as part of a National Endowment for the Humanities (NEH) grant-funded project to study Choctaw landholding.[29] In this project I followed earlier studies in choosing to "rectify" Bernard Romans's 1772 map of Choctaw country, based upon actual travel among villages, using a method borrowed from geographical information system (GIS) capabilities called "rubber sheeting," which allows a map to be transformed in a uniform way about a series of fixed points; an historical map can thus be adjusted to a now better-known topography of rivers and relief features. The resulting paper is "Choctaw Villages and Rubber Sheets: A GIS Application to Historical Maps," and in writing it I meant to bring to the attention of archaeologists and ethnohistorians this potentially very useful method for working with historical maps. I also hoped that archaeologists who had been essentially doing the same thing by hand and without formalizing their practice might experiment with this method (and incidentally make their decisions explicit) to provide provisional results for locating sites for testing in the field.

As part of the same grant project we were interested not only in where but why: how could we find out why Choctaws ceded some areas of their land in treaties before they were willing to cede others? I thought it might be worth taking the same lists of names and looking at them not only from a locational but also from a semantic point of view. Could the names placed on the land tell something about how it was regarded? The result was the paper "A Storied Land: Choctaw Place-Names and the Emplotment of Land Use," which sought to construct an image of Choctaw land use on the basis of toponyms.

The lists that I had worked so diligently also supplied a host of personal names, which had been used long ago by John Swanton to suggest office titles, warrior classes, and, to a more limited extent, clans. In the work I had done on the critical apparatus for MPA:FD, since I vowed that I would try to identify every named person, I had done a lot of disambiguation of names, attempting to be sure whether the same name actually applied to the same person in all cases. I had discovered that the previous editors had mostly assumed that they did, but my work began to reveal the fact that there were probably more office titles than Swanton had identified on the basis of a smaller body of information: I had not only the lists but also the "action contexts"; I was able, on the basis of a database containing each separate occurrence of a named individual, to begin to construct identities in a "thicker" way than had been possible before. In "Choctaw Names and Choctaw Roles: Another Method for Evaluating Sociopolitical Structure" I used those data to confirm the existence of the Fanimingo title and to explore other possibilities, including two possible lineage or clan names. As will be clear to readers who continue to the end of the book, this kind of granular analysis, akin to linguistic distinctive feature analysis and clearly inspired in my case by my background in languages and my interest in structuralist methods, has grounded much of my work.

Part III: Interpretive Moves

The limitations of positive methods lie in their advantages, that they provide only iteration and pattern. To go beyond such methods and achieve the kind of understanding ethnohistory claims to attempt, to try to reach even into the realm of "ethno-ethnohistory" and "nonevents" described by Ray Fogelson in a notable American Society for Ethnohistory presidential address, it is necessary to take the interpretive turn to a microhistorical, ethnographic concern with thickly described incidents.[30] This is not to say that in our case we are likely to indulge in the sin of "event history" decried by Annales or to be under any illusion that what we can construct is anything like what "really happened": through the eyes of alien observers we almost never have that much detail at our disposal. Instead, what we address is most frequently moments of the *conjoncture*, those medium-term processes of portentous change/interaction (or what Europeans saw as portentous enough to pay attention to) when grave decisions were made and individual acts were picked out from the undescribed quotidian. Such "moments"—which are, as Fogelson noticed, not usually the moments that Native people would have chosen to represent their history—may nevertheless, if we can understand them as process and look for the patterns in that process, allow us to propose a reading of the experience of all parties involved.

In the work I have done along these lines I have usually tried to address a few themes, and they will be obvious in the papers gathered here. First, I have been interested in language, rhetoric, and etiquette as displayed in specific formal settings for what they can tell, interpreted as symbolic action, about what was considered proper behavior in certain ceremonial circumstances. Relations between Native people and Others—whether Native Others or Europeans—had formal protocols that we need to understand in order to recognize the meanings of variant performance within them and thus to have a chance of explaining why subsequent actions were taken. Issues can be as substantive as what language medium was used for communication in the first place. I have discussed this issue and explored further my interest in the interpreters of colonial Louisiana in engaging with the scholarship on the so-called Mobilian trade language and its function during the eighteenth century in the essay "The Currency of Language: The Mobilian Lingua Franca in Colonial Louisiana." More recently, I have addressed the complexities of a specific drama of treaty making in " 'So Many Little Republics': British Negotiations with the Choctaw Confederacy, 1765," where who spoke and the histories and situatedness of individuals were as important as what they said.

Second, I have always been interested in understanding the power of Native agency and resistance, not only because of trends in decolonizing anthropological research but because it was so obvious in the French-Choctaw case that I first encountered. During the period of French occupation of the Louisiana colony these Europeans really only controlled small regions around focal settlements like New Orleans and Mobile and outposts like forts Toulouse, Tombecbé, Rosalie, St. Pierre, and aux Akansas. Native people called almost all the shots in the region, so from the beginning of my background research on MPA:FD I had been struck by the ludicrous acceptance by so many conventional historians of the convenient declension story of Native dwindling. Russell Thornton's general demographic research and Peter Wood's detailed focus on the colonial period have revealed what was obvious to anyone who had read the French documentation of their relations with the Choctaw. By the eighteenth century the large confederations of the Southeast, of which the Choctaw was one, were beginning to increase in population: it was, starkly, the reason they had to be Removed, but it was also, equally starkly, the reason why the French in particular had to comply with Native convention when pressed.[31] In this volume I gather several essays that explore *conjonctures* when Choctaw power was at issue. Two hinge on what John Phillip Reid called the "law of blood."[32] In "The Barthelemy Murders: Bienville's Establishment of the Lex Talionis as a Principle of Indian Diplomacy" I looked at how the French need for Choctaw support in their war on the English-allied Chickasaw drove the establishment of a principle of equal treatment under law for Choctaw victims in capital cases. In "Choctaw Factionalism and Civil War,

1746–1750" I explore the history of a painful internecine struggle among the Choctaw that resulted from French failure to understand their role as the Choctaw's allied-Other and from an internal Choctaw contestation for leadership. Finally, a specific instance of symbolic actions on both sides of the Choctaw-French relation, turning on an exchange of objects that explicitly symbolized that relation, is explored in "The Medal Chief's *Grosse Lettre*: A Chapter in French-Indian Management Policies."

A third central theme that has interested me more recently (especially as I gray) is the issue of the life course and how its stages were navigated by Native people during the colonial period. This is a difficult area to work because it moves over the line into "ethno-ethnohistory," and the evidence to support the interpretive contortions required to even glimpse it is very thin indeed: Europeans, for this as everything else, tended simply to map their own categories onto what they saw and thereby to mask what was going on. I touched on this topic in " 'So Many Little Republics,' " but I reworked some of that evidence more explicitly in a biographical sketch of one of the most attractive Choctaw individuals of the eighteenth century in "Four Ages of Alibamon Mingo, fl. 1700–1766," in which I also attempted to pay attention (as well as I could through several layers of European interpreting) to the rhetoric and pragmatics of his self-presentation on a sequence of public occasions. Written near to that essay in time, an additional piece, "Dual Organization Reconsidered: Eighteenth-Century Choctaw Chiefs and the Exploration of Social Design Space," explores more speculatively some of the larger patterns of the inhabiting of roles of power and its practice among Choctaw chiefs of the middle to late eighteenth century in an effort to question what has become received wisdom about the attractions of the market economy in mobilizing Native desires during that period. It should come as no surprise that I come down rather on the substantivist side of that argument.

Part IV: Whose Identity Is at Stake?

Part of the reason why I do take the substantivist position is that I insist on reading non-Native sources, whether from the eighteenth century or now, as compromised and suspicious. The emergence of the discussion of a "market revolution" in colonial North America, for example, complete with the acceptance of a derivative and uncritical economic discourse about rational acting, correlates all too well with the ascendance to political dominance of a discourse that sees capitalist markets as the solution for and cause of everything.

Yet although this discourse might ask or attempt to find out whether this is how the participants actually saw things, as long as it applies a positivist historiography to external observation of their actions it is extremely difficult to arrive at any other results. Awareness of this kind of situatedness for historical discourse itself becomes self-awareness for the historian when it is necessary to act apart from the academy in the world where one's discourse has to compete with many others and has to be accountable to the people whose history (and identity) one claims to describe. Most of the work here was produced while I in fact did work outside the academy, and although I have aspired to the serious acceptance of my work by others who were insiders, yet on many occasions the work I was called on to do has had to answer to a wider audience; I have included here two essays from those contexts. The first, "Mississippi 1500–1800: Revising the South's Colonial History for a Post-colonial Museum Audience," was presented at a meeting of the Organization of American Historians but described the establishment of a participatory process for construction of a discourse of objects and texts in a historical museum, reporting on the creation of the permanent exhibit Mississippi 1500–1800 at the Mississippi state historical museum. The second essay, presented at a public symposium addressing the controversy over the Columbus Quincentenary, discussed how Euro-American treatment of and assumptions about dead bodies (theirs and Others') were confronted by the Native American Graves Protection and Repatriation Act (NAGPRA). In "Blood and Earth: European Use of North American Native Remains from Contact to the Present" I attempted to show how contradictory and hypocritical the selective application of Euro-American discourses about the sacredness of the dead and the scientistic right to access to the dead has been and remains.

Time and Memory

The issues raised for me by this more public work were part of my own growing awareness of the responsibility the historian always takes on with respect to identities affected by historical discourse. As ethnohistorians we all must feel that we have a special responsibility to the Native communities whose histories we investigate. I think we must also recognize that if we do not belong in every way to those communities, their histories are ours to tell only in a limited sense. It is heartening to hear in the last couple of decades a strong emergence to audibility of Native voices in the historical chorus, too long dominated by Euro-American voices. It is even more heartening to see in the last few years stronger gestures being made by Native historians and archivists both to preserve the materials of Native history by actively recording them and to reclaim control of them and the discourse about them.[33] The actions of the Bureau of Indian Affairs, in concentrating official U.S. government records of interactions with Indian tribes in a single underground repository operated by the National Archives and Records Administration in Lenexa, Kansas, and supporting an archival training program at nearby Haskell Indian Nations University, do certainly bring these materials nearer to most of those whose lives they document.[34] But this gesture is a little too late: tribal archivists with established programs are insistent on tribal rights to hold these materials themselves, and they know that Euro-American archival practices are no more universally applicable to all needs than are Euro-American historical practices.[35]

This issue and those raised by Native people around NAGPRA make unavoidable the question of whether an ethnohistory primarily practiced by Euro-Americans, however focused on ethno-ethnohistory, however concerned to reveal "the concrete, the unexpected, and the puzzling," can exist without power relations coming into play.[36] Europeans and Euro-Americans still physically control the majority of the written historical materials that ethnohistorians use. Is it useful (or necessary) for Euro-American ethnohistorians of good will to "spend privilege," as, for example, Larry Zimmerman has done in archaeology, by continuing to practice sensitive observation and self-critical analysis and to advocate for a more active view of Native history in support of Native people? Some have taken a collaborative path and shown that this can be viable. To ask whether European-defined history is a useful model for expounding the past of Native people at all is a question many are beginning to explore, though not always with support from the mainstream. Is there, might there be an "indigenous mode" for practicing history or something like it? If there are plural histories, as Fred Hoxie asserts, are there also plural historiographies? *Is* there after all an ethno-ethnohistory, and should non-Native people aspire to practice it?

I pointed earlier to the notion that history is and must be a moral practice; I had to address this issue head-on when I branched out ten years ago to explore the history and anthropology of medical education. Others had already tackled the inevitably Whiggish history of medical education written by practitioners, with its familiar triumph of Science over Ignorance, so I did not have to do that particular heavy lifting, but it was remarkable to see the degree to which the perceived importance of medical practice by the public (and the power accrued by the medical profession over the twentieth century) nearly demanded that it be seen as uniformly beneficent and deserving of its triumph. This in spite of the scandalous revelation in the 1970s of the Tuskegee experiment, which observed black men with untreated syphilis for some forty years after there was an effective treatment, ostensibly to see whether the disease followed a different course among African Americans. Yet in spite of such excesses of arrogance, what might have been the therapeutic good that came of the institution built on those years of triumphalist rhetoric? In the case of an ethno-ethnohistory, Hoxie has urged the need to leave behind the kind of advocacy and romanticizing history that idealizes its subjects. We might, however, listen to William McNeill, doyen and exponent of the broader canvas of world history, who suggests that all human history is really "mythistory" and that an idealizing history has its uses: "An appropriately idealized version of the past may also allow a group of human beings to come closer to living up to its noblest ideals. What is can move towards what ought to be, given collective commitment to a flattering self-image. The American civil rights movement of the fifties and sixties illustrates this phenomenon among us."[37] McNeill's observations, to be sure, are made from a "nowhere" that is quite sure of at least its present standards of historical objectivity, but his vantage point somewhere on the moon looking down at the whole world permits a wider view of local historicities, as we have increasingly come to recognize anthropologies and identities in general as local phenomena. Taking that kind of view, we have to ask ourselves what the materials for an ethno-ethnohistory would look like and how they would be used in practice. Would the answer be radically different from the answer we would give for the history of Europeans? Some are very sure that it would indeed be radically different and not worthy of being called history at all.

The signing of the Native American Graves Protection and Repatriation Act by George H. W. Bush in 2000 was a blow to archaeologists and museum curators who had assumed that their control of Native American remains, justified by arguments of scientific value and their own barely completed enterprise of institution building, would continue indefinitely. They were especially offended by the stipulation that in establishing claims to the remains in question, Native Americans' own traditional histories, either entirely oral or based upon oral histories, would be accepted as evidence on an equal footing with written Western-style document-based history. They proceeded to argue, often and in many venues, that Indians, in Eric Wolf's ironic and inaccurate phrase, were "without history": what they had was "myth" or "tradition," but it certainly was not history, and it certainly was not as good:

> Knowledge transmitted solely by word of mouth undergoes substantial changes in the course of a few generations because, as Marcel Detienne points out, each person "selects 'facts' and produces an account in terms of the way in which his social sphere organizes spoken memory." Memory, selection, and the cultural context of a body of oral tradition alter accounts of events over time. Moreover, a storyteller often embellishes and redacts for purely narrative purposes; thus aesthetic and dramatic motives also alter content.[38]

This argument obviously depended upon an outdated commitment to a positivist historical "truth" that contemporary historians have themselves mostly discarded, with a growing understanding that Western historical modes have been subject to their own discursive distortions.[39] But it also drew on a long-running discussion of orality and literacy that ran the gamut from assertions that literacy is the only royal road to real humanity through its fundamental alteration of human cognition to a recognition that what literacy offers is simply a technology that permits the preservation over time of longer and more complex textual materials.[40] This discussion joined that of especially Africanist historians who were concerned to define how oral history materials could be used to write European-style positivist history. This historiographical writing argued generally that nonliterate cultures produce their history differently from literate ones in that they edit out generations to accommodate the limitations of human memory, maintaining the depth of their traditional history, from the present to the founding ancestor, constant. This phenomenon was called (by Africanist Jan Vansina) "telescoping."[41]

Vansina's earliest formulation of these ideas observed three significant historical scales found in the experience of oral cultures: the "ecological time" of the natural setting (cyclical natural phenomena); the "sociological calendar" of regular human activities with a social setting (recurrent social practices); and the "whole of the past" structured in terms of "structural relations actually obtaining between groups."[42] All three of these systems of time measurement are normally coexistent, but the whole past articulation dominates the distant past, while the sociological calendar and ecological time govern the middle period. Limitations of memory lead to a "history" that consists of a mythic distant past of one or more etiological eras that found the sociological calendar, followed by a more detailed citation of significant events taken from actions on the sociological calendar, with the most recent past consisting of whatever detailed memory people might have of the daily performance of ecological and sociological facts—or, in Western terms, myth, history, and gossip.

Vansina elaborated this scheme later, listing ecological time, a time signposted by extraordinary events, calculation by "domestic genealogies," and the sociological calendar. He then explored how memory played upon these materials, organizing them into epochs (e.g., the reigns of kings) and then bundling epochs into eras (e.g., creation, historic time) that may be successive or coeval, and how events may be moved toward the future or the past to make them more convincing or important.[43] David Henige discussed in greater detail special genres related to the construction of temporal sequence, like lists and genealogies and the many specific ways they may be altered, notably by telescoping. Henige observed that "the process of telescoping—shortening or omitting entire portions of a society's past—is a classic characteristic of the collective memory. Most often, the part of the past that is forgotten is the period between the time of origins and the recent past. That genealogical forgetfulness should assume this form stems from the demands of myth on the one hand and increased ability to remember the past few generations on the other."[44] We are dealing here, of course, with a historiography built on a naturalized, positivist Western practice, which constructs oral historical practice as marked in all categories so as to devise means to "correct" it. To their credit, however, Africanists have focused on oral sources as seriously primary, a recognition that has not obtained in mainstream American history or archaeology. Thus Vansina, sounding remarkably postmodern himself in places:

> Oral traditions are not just a source about the past, but a historiology . . . of the past, an account of how people have interpreted it. As such oral tradition is not only a raw source. It is hypothesis, similar to the historian's own interpretation of the past. Therefore oral traditions should be treated as hypotheses, and as the first hypothesis the modern scholar must test before he or she considers others. To consider them first means not to accept them literally, uncritically. It means to give them the attention they deserve, to take pains to prove or disprove them systematically for each case on its own merits. . . . In short, the historian must justify his interpretation. Why should it be better than the local one? That is the question he must address. He must continue the historiological process that has been underway.[45]

The anthropological literature on literacy, which has been used so frequently to circumscribe and judge this "historiology" of oral cultures, devotes far too little of its attention to the actual behavior of *literate* people with respect to history. In fact, it is clear that ordinary people in literate societies (and note that most people in Western literate societies come from families in which literacy itself is only a few generations deep), people whose literacy is of the "lay" variety, tend to "telescope" history in exactly the same way, both in the case of their own family histories and in the case of the history of the wider world, as we recognize all too well while laughing helplessly at Walter Carrithers Sellar and Robert Julian Yeatman's send-up of ordinary historical knowledge, *1066 and All That*.[46] In fact, most people in literate societies have never behaved literately most of the time.[47] Some would even argue that the growing dominance of electronic media as information sources is returning Euro-American cultures to nonliterate practice with respect to communication modalities.[48]

It may be argued that this is irrelevant, since in a complex society with division of labor we need only be concerned to examine the behavior of those who specialize in studying and preserving history and who are unlikely to give up their literacy any time soon: historians and archivists. I would like to suggest, however, that even among these practitioners there are unavoidable effects of power distorting the preservation of the "historical record," creating as an end product what might equally justifiably be referred to as a temporally telescoped end product.

The key to this behavior in all these cases—literate and nonliterate, layperson and specialist—is the *relevance* of history and historical meaning. Relevant to what? On the individual level, relevant to whatever depth of historical rootedness makes one feel sufficiently situated in time that it does not represent a source of crippling anxiety. On the societal level, the construction of a "good enough" history is measured by the success with which the society is able to reproduce itself without alarming disruption—hence McNeill's observation about the inevitability of mythistory in all identifiable societies. These issues are common to preservation of traces of the past in nonliterate, literate, and "postliterate" societies alike, as the informal comparison in Table 1.1 suggests.

Readers unfamiliar with the concerns of archival preservation and the details of archival practice (and this includes many historians) may find it novel to consider that the decay of human memory just happens to be a little

Table 1.1. Informal comparison of nonliterate, literate, and "postliterate" societies

Feature	Oral Tradition	Paper Literacy	Digital "Postliteracy"
Division of labor	Specialists: singers of tales, griots, etc.	Specialists: historians, archivists	Specialists: historians, digital archivists
Methods of preservation	Mnemonic techniques that group words meaningfully	Original order/*respect des fonds* practices that group documentary materials meaningfully (and permanently)	Metadata that group materials meaningfully but virtually (other groupings possible)
Change in the record over time	Using algorithmic modification over time that maintains time depth and breadth of coverage constant ("telescoping," "fusion")	Using algorithmic means of winnowing materials that maintain breadth (and temporal depth?) of coverage constant ("disposal," "weeding," "deaccessioning," arrangement, and description)	Potentially may use algorithmic means of modifying materials that maintain breadth (and temporal depth?) of coverage constant (appraisal/selection and migration/emulation)
Contingent pressures on shaping of the record	Responsive to context of performance	Responsive to context of use	Must meet presentation demands of new contexts of use
Goal and justification	Sociocultural reproduction takes place without serious disruption	Sociocultural reproduction takes place without serious disruption	Sociocultural reproduction takes place without serious disruption

faster than that of paper, but the eventual decay of the latter is no less sure (and it is a truism that a copy of a paper original made for preservation is always degraded in quality to some degree). Anyone who owns and uses a computer will doubtless have learned how fragile the digital record is— certainly, without the investment of time and expense, far *more* fragile even than human memory. Thus it is *always* necessary to build an institution of some kind to preserve a record of the past, and because the operation of that institution incurs real and open-ended costs in time and space, it requires the will to continue making that investment. Justification of expenditure being what it is, unlimited funds are not available for the perpetuation of all possible records of the past: something—indeed, in modern Western government records management practice, close to 95 percent of it—has to go. The reality of the case is that in spite of ethnocentric rationalizations by European and Euro-American archivists, decisions about what to keep and what to let go are nearly always made or influenced by the powerful, even if only by the denial of adequate resources. Nobody, therefore, has a complete record of any past. The chief must be flattered; the king must be portrayed as kingly; the president will seek an archivist of state who agrees with him about keeping secrets.

Perhaps most interesting of all, at least in the trajectory of Western European and especially North American archival history, archival practices of removing "unneeded" materials in an orderly fashion from especially government and business records (sometimes raffishly referred to as "weeding" but generally and preferably justified by a formal though poorly theorized practice of "appraisal" before acquisition ever takes place) have the effect of telescoping history in substantially the same way as oral transmission, while their effects are misrecognized as harmless by practitioners who are making their own rationally justified moral choices:

- Current records are retained by the creator for as long as their original purpose is being served;
- Records past their period of usefulness for their original purpose are subjected to reduction by 95 percent (case files being a particularly favored target of destruction);
- So-called vital records—the Whiggish pronouncements of policy and procedure, foundation myth and staffing requirements; in short, those records that would be required to reconstruct the institution in case of disaster—are preferentially and unquestioningly kept even though all actual evidence (including primary financial records) of whether these idealist statements were ever carried out may be destroyed as irrelevant.

Taking these facts together with my earlier discussion of the Annales temporal frame (*longue durée, conjoncture,* and *histoire événementielle*) and including the temporal formulations of oral historians, the discussion of how to evaluate and put together the materials of history begins to take on a rather different complexion. In fact, historical sources of any kind cannot be unbiased, must always be partial, and are never representative of perfect recall of the facts. We know and accept this (after all, we don't want to have to deal with a record of *everything,* even though in a panoptically digital world that might be much more possible than it yet is), but as literates we do not apply it uniformly to our assumptions about the record we actually have. Furthermore, a

Table 1.2. Comparison of temporal formulations discussed

Annales time	Archival time	Traditional time
Longue durée	Vital records	Mythic foundations
Conjoncture (valorized)	Historical performance (weeded)	King lists (telescoped)
Histoire événementielle	Current records	Gossip

good deal of the notion that oral-traditional sources are somehow less "reliable" than written-modern sources is dependent upon different formulations of concepts of temporality and chronology by the society that produced the source and the historian trying to understand it. If we try to compare the temporal formulations just mentioned, it is possible to lay out a simple parallel, not precise but to my mind quite suggestive.

What we see from this perspective is that the historical product of oral tradition is not after all so incompatible with the historical scales theorized by Braudel and made available by the reductive practices of archivists, although the discourse about it has implied something different and has ignored entirely the archival shaping of the Western historical record. And what is the result of this shaping by archival choice? A revered and perfect past of glorious Founders, little detail of practice over time, and a gracious plenty of information about the immediate past, *very like the kind of evidence seen in nonliterate and lay literate settings*. Over time, the effect becomes even more similar: the majority of the records of government agencies become reduced to a sequence of policy statements—in effect, a telescoped king list. This is a real part of the reason why mythistory is as inevitable to the literate as to the nonliterate: none of us could write a perfect account of what happened if we tried. We are back to the recognition that we get the history we construct, with the addition of just a little more insight into the contribution of literate preservers of historical materials and a new awareness of how the temporal space of literate societies is also constructed and selectively telescoped.

In the essays in this book I do not practice an indigenous historiology, but perhaps it can be called a kind of ethno-ethnohistory. At any rate, it is historiography of some kind, and I hope that it offers a suite of "technologies of the word" that can be used to get closer to at least hearing echoes of Native words and seeing outlines of Native actions in the kinds of European documents that record the specific past I have studied for twenty-five years. I have tried to credit real sources and to take specific kinds of Native tradition about the past seriously, but there is always more to learn in order to treat this complex past with adequate seriousness.[49] If we are to go on practicing "ethnohistory" at all, and if by that we mean trying to write something we call history on the basis of incomplete and biased testimonies that we only partially understand, then we need to recognize that there is really no history that is *not* ethnohistory for a species whose daily personal communication is a clash of idiolects.

Notes

1. The first three volumes of *Mississippi Provincial Archives: French Dominion* are edited by Rowland and Sanders; the final two are edited by Rowland, Sanders, and Galloway. Hereafter they are cited in the text and notes as MPA:FD.

2. Capers, "Foreword," xi–xiii.

3. Miller Surrey, *Calendar of Manuscripts*. This calendar is extraordinarily accurate in its reportage of names and its understanding of the relevance of evidence in the documents. It has not been superseded by another (still useful) calendar specifically calendaring only the Louisiana general correspondence (AC, série C13A), published for the Bicentennial by the Archives nationales: Menier, Taillemite, and Forges, *Inventaire des archives coloniales*.

4. Marcel Giraud's multivolume *Histoire de la Louisiane français* had begun to be published in France in 1953, but its French print run was small, it was not easily available in the United States (we forget what amazon.com has done for the international traffic in books—how many scholars in foreign languages remember running a tab with Blackwell's in Oxford?), and its first volume had only been published in translation in 1974. The five volumes that had been completed at the time of Giraud's death only reach to 1731, and so far only three of them have been published in translation.

5. In this work I received the warm encouragement and assistance of Milo Howard at the Alabama Department of Archives and History, Archbishop Oscar Lipscomb of the (then) Diocese of Mobile, and Michael Scardaville and Stanley Hordes at the Louisiana State Museum. I am especially grateful for the introduction to ethnohistory, and especially the ethnohistory of the Choctaw, that I received from John Peterson at Mississippi State University, and I am thankful for the graciousness with which the Mississippi Band of Choctaw Indians accepted my interest in their history.

6. Tanselle, "The Editing."

7. It is interesting to reflect, in the light of the rather later modern versus postmodern argument in the history profession about the ontological status of documents as evidence, how clearly historical editing practice of this era reflected historians' assurance that they knew better how to represent what had been said in the past than did those who wrote the words.

8. Froger, *La critique des textes*. I had got into the act myself with an example from Old French literature (Galloway, "Clustering Variants").

9. In the language of diplomatics these were "copies in the form of originals" and occupied a specific category of evidentiary value.

10. Friederich's masterly grasp of the entire early modern to modern Euro-American world as an enormous intertextual field can be seen in *Outline of Comparative Literature*.

11. I remain tremendously indebted also to Frederick Behrends for his courses in medieval history and historiography, which I audited when I didn't have time to take them formally. His work in historical editing and translation (e.g., Fulbert of Chartres, *The Letters and Poems*) partook of the European medieval critical tradition, making another reason why I was surprised that American historical editors were so heavily into reputation grooming.

12. Falk, *Types of Thematic Structure*, gives a glimpse of Falk's grounding as a phenomenologist and formalist. My dissertation was "Transaction Units"; my interest in reader-response theory began to be fully expressed in "Testing a Theory of Narrative Analysis."

13. Thompson, *The Folktale*. I came within an ace of becoming an anthropologist at that point but did not do so. Nevertheless, my studies at Indiana were responsible for opening my eyes to the complexities of making meaning and for beginning a legitimate interest in anthropology.

14. McLuhan, *The Gutenberg Galaxy*; Lévi-Strauss, *Structural Anthropology*; Saussure, *Course in General Linguistics*.

15. Burke, *The French Historical Revolution*; Bintliff, *The Annales School*; Stoianovitch, *French Historical Method*. Note that the name of the school is taken from its journal, *Annales d'Histoire Économique et Sociale*, which suggests the focus. Dissatisfaction with the exclusion of the experiences of individuals in favor of a rather determinist structural bias by Braudel was countered by a new emphasis on the evolution of *mentalités* in the work of Emmanuel Le Roy Ladurie: see Galloway, "Conjuncture and Longue Durée." It could be said that Michel Foucault's project of uncovering the archaeology and genealogy of knowledge represents a parallel reaction; see Dreyfus and Rabinow, *Michel Foucault*, 104–25.

16. Foucault, *The Order of Things*, 46–77. The use of these tools, however, was not problematized by the first-generation Annalistes. For Foucault on history see *The Archaeology of Knowledge*, 3–17.

17. For an overt example see Sahlins, *Islands of History*. Charles Hudson has also aligned his work on the Soto expedition with the Annales approach.

18. Novick, *That Noble Dream*.

19. White, *Metahistory*, *Tropics of Discourse*, and *The Content of the Form*.

20. Jenkins, *Why History?*; Said, *Orientalism*; Nagel, *The View from Nowhere*.

21. McHugh, *Defining the Situation*. From the perspective of postmodern historiography, the combination of synthetic empirical facts of historical documentation with the analytical assertion of anthropological constructs to make a hybrid representation simply substituted one set of analytic eternalities (tribes, kinship structures, etc.) for another (historical periods, classes, etc.); see Keith Jenkins discussing Frank Ankersmit's interpretation of Quine in *Refiguring History*, 49–53.

22. How easy it is to slip into the Greek analytic frame in discussing rhetoric!

23. See Galloway, "Talking with Indians."

24. Barron, *The Vaudreuil Papers*.

25. Du Pratz, *Histoire de la Louisiane*.

26. Reviews of these issues can be found in Trigger, *A History of Archaeological Thought*, and Wylie, *Thinking from Things*. My own efforts on these lines, questioning the situatedness of archaeological research designs, are in the essay "Where Have All the Menstrual Huts Gone?"

27. The phrase is due to Cronon, *Changes in the Land*.

28. Galloway, "Restoring the Map of Medieval Trondheim."

29. In this project I partnered with Clara Sue Kidwell.

30. Fogelson, "The Ethnohistory of Events."

31. Thornton, *American Indian Holocaust*. Thornton pays attention to overall trends rather

than local recoveries and thus sees the major recovery as occurring after 1900, but it is clear that during the eighteenth century there were considerable local recoveries that were not wholly canceled out by continuing disease episodes and client warfare. See Wood, "The Changing Population": "It is clear . . . that the rate of decline within the southern Indian population slowed during the eighteenth century and eventually reversed itself, achieving a slight net increase in the era of the Revolution after centuries of decline" (91). Wood attributes this effect to the shift in disease environment as contagious diseases that were cataclysmic to so-called virgin-soil populations began to become diseases of childhood as immunity built up ("The Changing Population," 92).

32. Reid, *A Law of Blood*.

33. When I made a statement to that effect twenty years ago to an NEH-sponsored teacher workshop, an outraged gentleman said he supposed I thought women ought to do women's history, too. Well, yes! White men have always been content to focus on their own history, so why should that change?

34. I am not sure whether the heavy irony of the records being Removed west of the Mississippi 170 years after the Indians was grasped by the National Archives or how many considered that the United States did not even *have* a national archives until a hundred years after Removal!

35. Thanks to the Society of American Archivists' Committee on Diversity, the 2004 annual meeting of that body included sessions entitled "Documentation Issues Concerning Tribal History and Recognition" and "Native American Perspectives on the Treatment and Usage of Tribal Materials in Archives," which addressed an emerging practice of defense of intellectual property in traditional knowledge from a Native point of view, based upon the power and danger of the words being defended.

36. The phrase is taken from Hoxie, "Ethnohistory for a Tribal World," in which Hoxie advocates for abandonment of polemical, romantic, and "cookbook" ethnohistory in favor of narratives that "teach the viability of a complicated, plural past by defending ambitious, multi-faceted, and self-critical scholarship that focuses on differences rather than commonalities" (613).

37. McNeill, "Mythistory," 15.

38. See Custred, "Oral Traditions."

39. White, *Metahistory*; Cohen, *Historical Culture*.

40. The extreme position of cognitive revolution has been argued by Ong, *Orality and Literacy*, and Goody in *The Domestication*: both claim antecedents in the structuralism of Lévi-Strauss and the insights of Marshall McLuhan. For a gamut of opinions, some critical of this position, see Olson and Torrance, *Literacy and Orality*.

41. Vansina, *Oral Tradition*, 100–102. Vansina's *Oral Tradition as History* is a thoroughly revised and reconsidered version of the earlier work. David Henige's briefer handbook of field practice in collecting oral history is *Oral Historiography*.

42. Vansina, *Oral Tradition*, 101.

43. Vansina, *Oral Tradition as History*, 174–78.

44. Henige, *Oral Historiography*, 80–105; see also Henige, *The Chronology of Oral Tradition*, 27–38.

45. Vansina, *Oral Tradition as History*, 196.

46. Sellar and Yeatman, *1066 and All That*. For a study of the uses of history by the U.S. general public see Rosenzweig and Thelen, *The Presence of the Past*.

47. This observation is discussed interestingly by Illich, "A Plea for Research." Illich makes the useful distinction between "clerical literacy," or that of people who make a living in working somehow with written texts, and "lay literacy," the kind of functional literacy of people who never

envision making any texts themselves but whose living and assumptions are informed by the pervasiveness of literacy in their culture. He also despairs for the future of lay literacy in an increasingly computerized future.

48. This was a central argument of McLuhan's *The Gutenberg Galaxy*.

49. The work is a lifetime's investment, as Raymond DeMallie makes clear in " 'These Have No Ears.'"

1. *Historiography*

Deconstructing the Text

2. Dearth and Bias

Issues in the Editing of Ethnohistorical Materials

In North America the work of ethnohistorians interested in reconstructing the history of Native American groups prior to European contact must concentrate on the evidence from the period just before and during the earliest contact, before the native peoples themselves began to leave surviving verbal records of their own. For this reason the only documentary sources for precontact North American ethnohistory are the accounts of European-Indian relations written by European explorers and colonists. For North America these resources are not negligible, but neither are they vast; most Indian activities were, after all, tangential to the central concerns of colonial governments. Nor can such material usually be easily segregated from the mass of colonial paperwork. The South Carolina "Indian Books" and the Jesuit Relations are exceptional in their focused concern, and even they do not contain all the relevant information for the periods they cover.[1] Memoir accounts, such as those of Adair and Du Pratz for the Southeast, are so rare that they treat only a tiny fraction of the number of tribes extant when European explorers entered North America.[2] More usually, material of ethnohistorical interest is embedded in governmental and commercial papers, where it is not always easy to find or even to recognize. The first factor defining the plight of the ethnohistorian with references to sources, then, is dearth. The shortage of information is only made worse by the lack of an overall guide to existing materials.

As for the documents that exist and can be found, they embody the ethnohistorian's second nemesis: bias. Indian societies and Indian activities were described by Europeans whose attitudes usually ranged from fear and hatred

This chapter was originally published as "Dearth and Bias: Issues in the Editing of Ethnohistorical Materials" in the *Newsletter of the Association for Documentary Editing* 3, no. 2 (1981): 1–6. It is reprinted by permission of the Association for Documentary Editing.

to loving contempt, and only rarely were Indian lifeways described by observers who even began to understand what they were seeing. Inevitably, their ethnocentrism made it impossible for them to ask the right questions of their observations, even when they were otherwise inclined to do so. This means that when the ethnohistorian does find one of these windows on Indian life and history, he also finds that it is covered by a far from translucent film.[3]

It is in these two problem areas, lack of material and ethnocentric bias, that the historical editor can best offer help to the ethnohistorian. The importance of any single early colonial document containing a description of preliterate peoples in North America is almost incalculable. In some few instances our knowledge of the very existence of individual tribes rests upon such a single document.[4] For this reason the historical editor should consider the needs of ethnohistory when he is choosing documents to edit for publication. The modern growth of interest in social history has broken the hold of the "Great White Men" bias in historical editing, and Native Americans are among those groups that have suffered from this kind of neglect in the past. But just as is the case with documentary materials that give us more information about the lives of women, blacks, and the poor, ethnohistorical materials make a solid contribution to a more complete history, and this reason alone offers adequate justification for paying special attention to them.

While the editor's options permit him to make selections of documents that can be helpful, his responsibilities do not end with selection. The ethnohistorian's other difficulty, bias, can also be approached by the historical editor through the choices he makes with regard to annotation. By and large the ethnohistorian, though he is obliged to be concerned with the veracity of the author-observer of an ethnohistorical description, will not possess as thorough a knowledge of the context of the document as does the historical editor.[5] Issues of attitude and reliability of observation can best be addressed in the first instance by the editor, whose acquaintance with what is actually a far more vast collection of documents than those that will actually be published places him in a unique position to evaluate those issues. Though modern standards of annotation and the realities of publishing budgets argue against extremely elaborate scholarly annotation, it is still possible for the editor who has an eye to the ethnohistorian's needs to render significant interpretive aid in a small space.

For a closer look at these problems and the solutions sought for one project, I will draw upon my experience as editor of the *Mississippi Provincial*

HISTORIOGRAPHY

Archives: French Dominion (MPA:FD) project at the Mississippi Department of Archives and History. The prehistory of the project goes back to 1906, when the first director of the department, Dunbar Rowland, began the collection of transcripts from European archives. The considerable body of transcriptions obtained from the French archives consisted primarily of selections from the Archives des colonies C13A series of reports, sent from the Louisiana colony to the minister of the colonies in France between 1694 and 1819. From these transcriptions Rowland selected and A. G. Sanders translated three volumes of documents covering the years 1701–43. These three volumes were published from 1927 to 1932.[6] Another two volumes were planned and a rough translation was completed when the means required to publish them failed, and during the ensuing years the typescript was lost. Found again in 1974, it was discovered to be in need of extensive editing. This provided the opportunity for bringing the selection of documents and the annotation into line with modern practice and also for amplifying the volumes' emphasis on the ethnohistorical materials in which the documents are so rich.

There was already an established principle for document selection used in the first three volumes and intrinsic to the thematic intention of the series: the documents selected had to bear in some way upon the history of the lands and peoples that were finally to become the state of Mississippi. Since the most numerous residents of the state's area in the French period were the Choctaw, Chickasaw, and Natchez Indians, an increased ethnohistorical focus was obviously justified; the first volume of the series, indeed, had concentrated on Indian diplomacy. The only geographic extension of the original principle of selection was the decision to include reports of Indian activities beyond the bounds of Mississippi when the Indians in question were the aboriginal inhabitants, no matter how far-ranging their travels might be.

Another principle that was consciously adopted as a result of this decision to highlight ethnohistorical data was that primary reportage of events involving Indians would be selected wherever found in preference to secondary summaries. Finding it, however, proved to be rather difficult. The reasons for the rarity of such accounts can be explained through a description of the process involved in the creation of the C13A collection. Commands and royal policies were dictated from France and communicated to the governor and commissary general by the minister of marine and colonies (these documents appear in a separate series with which we shall not be concerned). These two highest officials in turn formulated their commands and policies in local terms and sent them out either directly to the post commanders and warehouse-keepers or through the higher level district commanders at the Illinois post and Mobile (these documents are lost or irretrievably scattered except in one unusual case, that of Governor Vaudreuil's letterbooks). Reports of actions taken would then come back to the governor and commissary general from their subordinates at the posts (these documents are mostly lost), and, completing the cycle, the governor and commissary general would write the reports that were sent to France, basing them upon the reports received from the field.

Had this system worked in a regular way there would be almost no direct reportage of Indian affairs from Louisiana at all except for the events directly observable by governor and commissary general and such items as they chose to incorporate verbatim from the field reports. But fortunately conflicts of personality and the hazardous contingencies of colonial settlement did not allow the system to work regularly. The actual interface between the French colony and most of its Indian neighbors was made up of the personnel of the smaller and more distant posts among the Indians, of missionaries living in their villages, and of deerskin traders traveling and living among them. These are the people who were most ideally situated to report valuable observations on Indian life and behavior, and, thanks to difficulties and rivalries, some of these reports attained to inclusion in C13A. There could be several reasons for this: a governor forwarding a firsthand report of a military disaster in order to disculpate himself; a dissatisfied post commander writing directly to the minister, bucking for promotion; a missionary writing to a superior in France; a trader complaining to the minister about government-supported monopolies. In some instances whole journals were sent in this way. An understanding of this system and how it did or did not work, vital to an editor of these documents, also provides crucial insight into the reliability of the reports themselves. For where a choice between two documents reporting Indian activities must be made, reliability of observation should be the deciding factor.

The level of reliability in these matters is at least partly a function of the system itself. The first consideration is directness of reportage. Obviously the report of a subaltern who accompanied an Indian war party on an expedition has a better chance for accuracy than a governor's two-sentence summary of the expedition. This is clearly demonstrated by a journal from August 1742, written by the cadet Canelle reporting on his participation in a raid on the Chickasaw Indian villages by the French-allied Choctaw.[7] The journal details the stages of the attack, casualties, taunts hurled at the Choctaw by the Chickasaw, the political currents within the Choctaw force. This journal was sent to Paris by the district commander at Mobile, Louboey, in December; the cover letter gives the background of the attack and offers an evaluation of it but counts on the journal to provide specifics of the circumstances.[8] It is also evident in Louboey's letter that the background details had been supplied by Canelle's commander at Fort Tombecbé, a post near the Choctaw nation, though his letter is lost. Later on, Louboey even sent a list of casualties drawn up by Canelle.[9] In contrast, the governor's summary does actually take only two sentences.[10] As a rule of thumb, then, the firsthand report will always be preferable to any other, but if this is lost, the nearest version to that of the original testimony, in terms of both rank and function of the witness, is to be preferred.[11]

A second factor, ideological bias, also must be taken into account in judging reliability. The larger the political investment a commentator has in a set of events, the more likely he is to view them from a fixed and inflexible position, and it was very easy for a European to get away with reporting almost anything of Indian peoples because of their accepted strangeness to the European view. In 1746 Governor Vaudreuil reported to the French authorities that three Frenchmen had been murdered at the behest of the Choctaw chief Red Shoe in order to restore his credibility with the English after three of their Chickasaw allies had been killed while on an embassy by pro-French Choctaw.[12] What he does *not* say, and what is revealed in his correspondence with the posts and in Adair's *History of the American Indians*, is that one of the murdered Frenchmen had been accused of raping Red Shoe's wife and that Vaudreuil had not only not bothered to investigate but had merely suggested that the subaltern in question be more circumspect in his conduct in future.[13]

A similar case of bias obtains when the viewpoint is a religious one, so that missionary observations, though they will usually be richer in commentary on ethnohistorical matters, will view them from an angle that suffers from predictable blind spots and that must itself be evaluated.[14] Crosscutting both reliability factors, nearness of testimony and ideological bias, is the problem of personalities, the degree to which a description of events may itself be a weapon in its author's pursuit of private purposes. This is a particular problem with presentations of data gathered by someone other than the writer, which are almost never reported gratuitously.

Selection and annotation can both be brought to bear to deal with these problems. In the new MPA:FD volumes the principle of selection for ethno-historical materials is clearly biased in favor of firsthand accounts, including restatements or elaborations of these reports only when they add to or contrast significantly with the eyewitness observations or when they occur in a document that includes an expression of official reaction to the events. Annotation is used for further clarification in several ways that simultaneously serve other editorial purposes. First, as far as is possible, all persons who write or appear in reports are identified in terms of their rank and their position in colonial hierarchy or tribal structure. Second, any known personal affinities or dislikes that may influence interactions between persons portrayed in the documents are mentioned when they are not made obvious by statements in the document texts. This is possible because in many cases these prejudices will be more clearly stated in some document that could not be chosen for publication. Finally, the experience that forms the background of a person's actions is briefly indicated where known, again appealing to other documentary materials. In this way it is possible to contextualize documentary evidence for Indian history in the brief space of a biographical note without indulging in lengthy genealogical or psychological speculation. Such a focus helps direct the choice of materials for annotation so that a picture of the European and Indian intentionalities that meet in the context of an event can emerge. Similarly, in the case of the author of a document, such annotation aids in the reconstruction of the attitude the author brings to his material. None of this goes beyond what the historical editor would normally expect to make clear, but its special importance in the case of ethnohistorical observations cannot be stressed too much.

Once the reliability of a document has been established by means of such annotation, there are several other problems that must be dealt with in the same way but that spring from cultural rather than individual bias. For the purposes of this discussion I will use the example of linguistic problems because they can be treated in a highly specific manner. The first of these has to do with the large issues of orthography and phonetic systems. Whenever the European came into contact with a native culture, his first problem was to assimilate its language or at least to learn enough of it to get along in whatever capacity he had to serve. The difficulty was that of two phonetic systems in confrontation. It is a truism of phonetic observation that an adult learner of a foreign language is distinctly handicapped because not only does he have difficulty in pronouncing some of the new phonetic combinations, but it is always the case that the expectations of his own phonetic system prevent his even hearing many distinctive features in the new one, some of which may be crucial for distinguishing meaning in the target language. When he attempts to write the native words he hears, he will usually write them in the phonetic system of his own language, which will be the best that one can hope for but which one can expect to be inconsistent not only from writer to writer but within the writings of a single observer. There will be three reasons for this variability: the orthographic system of the observer himself may be none too firmly fixed; the observer may improve in his hearing of the language; border-line phonemes may be heard one way at one time, another at the next.

French colonial policy was actually quite aware of at least the language-learning problem, and it was usual to send very young cadets, often less than twelve years old, to live in Indian villages and learn the languages. Young boys sent out in this way at the beginning of the Louisiana colony would later serve for many years as the first generation of interpreters.[15] But only very rarely do we have documents written by the interpreters themselves.[16] Most usually, the documents that record Indian words for us were written by officers who used these interpreters. Such is the case of a subaltern ordered to travel among the Choctaw and set up trade with them between 1729 and 1732, Régis du Roullet. Régis was so totally ignorant of Choctaw that he was unable to judge his interpreter's competence, and he certainly must have had an extremely bad ear for languages in any case, since his spellings of Choctaw village names vary wildly and include phonemes that did not exist in Choctaw.[17] Yet his lists of village names, as found both in formal lists and in the texts of his journals, constitute the most complete source for such names at that period.[18]

Lack of familiarity with Indian languages is a problem with documents like these, and it can be increased when the documents we have are not the originals written by the men in the field but copies made by secretaries sitting safely at home in the colony. In all these cases, however, if the historical editor has provided enough annotation for the linguist to estimate the writer's acquaintance with the language and the document's distance from the original transcription, his only other obligation will be to provide the original trans-literations exactly as found in the documents so that the linguist can disentangle the phonetic interference of the writer's mother tongue. It is worth remarking here that the linguist is often able to reconstruct the original Indian phonetics on the basis of a consensus of variant spellings.

There are certain items of Indian vocabulary to which the historical editor should pay special attention because they are connected with deeply important issues in cultural anthropology and ethnohistory, and his vigilance may bring a valuable item to light. Under this head comes first the abstract terminology of kinship systems, social organization, and the sacred. These components of "cognitive anthropology" are normally inaccessible *except* through early documentary accounts. A neat example of the ethnographer's need for editorial aid in this regard is shown in John Swanton's interpretation of Governor Kerlérec's honorary title, Youlaktimataha, given him by the Choctaw in 1753. The governor reports that the meaning of this title is "the greatest of the first race" (le plus grand de la première race).[19] Swanton, without reference to the context of the naming, supplied Dunbar Rowland, the original MPA:FD editor, with the comment that it really means "the chief who is a support," taking the Youlakt- (*oulacta* or *holahta*) element to mean "chief."[20] Yet this word is also the name of one of the moieties of the Choctaw, and this moiety had dominated the pro-French faction that won the Choctaw civil war that ended in 1751. There is an additional statement, made by a leading Choctaw chief of this moiety, that the two moieties are "the two first races" (les deux premières races) of the Choctaw; the *oulacta* is named first of the two.[21] Swanton did not refer to and indeed at that time could not have known about the details of the civil war, since most of the documents were not then available. But its result would make Kerlérec's interpretation de facto correct in 1753, and this would have serious implications for the effect of the war on Choctaw social structure.

The concrete terminology connected with subsistence and lifeways is also important, but as such practices are susceptible of reasonably accurate description on the part of the European observer, terms with concrete referents are not so desperately sought as those from the abstract conceptual vocabulary. It should be stressed that terminology of either sort is equally interesting, though more difficult of interpretation, when it occurs in loan translation, which will be more frequent by far. This is the case in a document of 1756 in which the chiefs of the Quapaw, a nation long associated with the French, asked for clemency for some French deserters whom they were returning to French custody. Through an interpreter who was a Fleming by birth, they claimed that the deserters, who had managed to take refuge in the Quapaw "sacred cabin, where they practice their religion" (cabanne de Valeur, ou ils exercient leur culte), had thus come under the protection of the "chief of the sacred cabin" (chef de la cabanne privilegiee) and were entitled to sanctuary.[22] The reader should know additionally that French missionaries had been instructing the Quapaw for more than fifty years by that time and that the earliest reports of the Quapaw claimed that they had no institutionalized religion. The context, however, suggests that however influenced by Christian teachings this concept of sanctuary may have been, the religion being practiced was an Indian one. There is no other such report extant regarding the Quapaw; the historical editor, by noting facts like these, can help to rescue them from obscurity by pointing out such loan translations. It is up to the specialist to discern the details of the meshing and overlap of the European and Indian category sets, but if the editor does not call attention to the presence of the words, the specialist may have nothing to work with.

What all the foregoing observations come down to is the assertion that the historical editor who is faced with documents rich in ethnohistorical data should be aware first of the importance of the data and then of his need to familiarize himself with some of the problems and methods of ethnohistory in order to do justice to it. This is not to say that he should become an ethnohistorian or cultural anthropologist but simply that by bearing in mind the questions that such scholars will ask of his documents he can help them to estimate the reliability of the testimony. The continuing argument over the appropriate scale of annotation for historical documents seems to have settled for the present at a reasonably explicit level, but there is also agreement that the historical editor's task is not preinterpretation.[23] I would argue that the sort of attention to ethnohistorical materials I have advocated does not fall under this ban. I would term the procedures *pro*-interpretation, and I would stress again the serious need that exists for more of it.

Notes

1. McDowell, *The Colonial Records of South Carolina*, vols. 1–3; Thwaites, *The Jesuit Relations*.

2. Adair, *History of the American Indians*; Du Pratz, *Histoire de la Louisiane*.

3. Hagan, "Archival Captive," 137.

4. Swanton, *Indian Tribes*, 274.

5. Pitt, *Using Historical Sources*, 46–62; see also Vansina, *Oral Tradition: A Study*.

6. The first three volumes of the *Mississippi Provincial Archives: French Dominion* are edited by Rowland and Sanders; the final two are edited by Rowland, Sanders, and Galloway. Hereafter they are cited in the text and notes as *MPA:FD*.

7. Archives des colonies (AC), série C13A, 27:176–77. Most of the documents cited in these examples are in the *MPA:FD* volumes.

8. Louboey to Maurepas, December 7, 1742, in AC, série C13A, 27:142–43, 148–49.

9. Louboey to Maurepas, February 8, 1743, in AC, série C13A, 28:140–43.

10. Bienville to Maurepas, February 4, 1743, in AC, série C13A, 28:31–39. The two sentences: "In the month of last September [*sic*] as they had promised me our allies raised a force of fifteen to sixteen hundred men to go and cut the grain of the enemies. They ravaged more than a league of country, killed six men, took thirteen prisoners and carried off twenty horses" (MPA:FD, 3:774–75).

11. The terms "testimony" and "witness" are used as they are developed in Vansina, *Oral Tradition*, except that here we are generalizing to include the eyewitness account not as a pro-tototestimony but as a testimony and to treat, obviously, written accounts. This traduces Vansina in a sense, but his theoretical treatment of reliability and the context of different versions seems so pertinent that it is hard to resist using the notions.

12. Vaudreuil to Maurepas, November 20, 1746, in AC, série C13A, 30:76–84.

13. Post correspondence is preserved in the Vaudreuil Letterbooks, vol. 3; Adair, *History of the American Indians*, 313–19 (Adair was a trader among the Chickasaw at this time); see "Louisiana Post Letters: The Missing Evidence for Indian Diplomacy," in this volume.

14. And those blind spots might not always be so predictable. During his nearly twenty years as missionary to the Choctaw Father Baudouin never seemed to make any appreciable number of conversions, but he was a very effective spy and kept a warehouse of trade goods in the Chickasawhay village where he lived.

15. Boys were sent to live among the Indians in Louisiana as early as 1700. See Giraud, *A History of French Louisiana*, 1:84–85.

16. There are a few documents extant by the interpreter Huché; the "Anonymous Relation," included by Swanton in *Source Material*, 243–58, is doubtless by an interpreter-trader.

17. See Régis du Roullet, Journal, 1729, in AC, série C13A, 12:67–99, translated in MPA:FD, 1:21–54. The passage confirming his inability to judge his interpreter's competence is in MPA:FD, 1:21–22.

18. Compare the two lists of village names given by Régis in Journal, 1729 (list in MPA:FD, 1:41–44), and Journal, April–August 1732, in Archives du service hydrographique, vol. 67^2, no. 14-1, portefeuille 135, document 21, translated in part in MPA:FD, 1:136–54 (list in MPA:FD, 1:150–54), for the variant spellings. For the importance of these lists see Swanton, *Source Material*, 58–76.

19. Kerlérec to Rouillé, August 20, 1753, in AC, série C13A, 37:66–76.

20. This is in accord with his judgment in *Source Material*, 120, on the longer version of the title in Kerlérec to Machault d'Arnouville, December 8, 1754, in AC, série C13A, 38:122–29.

21. Dupumeux to Beauchamp, June 18, 1751, in AC, série C13A, 35:354–60.

22. "Where they practice their religion" is probably a gloss by the interpreter, Grevemberg, who had been personally involved in trade with the Quapaw. Minutes of a Council of War, June 20, 1756, in AC, série C13A, 39:177–80.

23. Teute, "Views in Review."

3. Louisiana Post Letters, 1700–1763

The Missing Evidence for
Indian Diplomacy

Over the past eighty years the efforts of archivists and historians of the Mississippi Valley have made available to scholars and the general public a great deal of the source material in the French archives for the history of the Louisiana colony before 1763. By far the richest French source for citations and published documents has been série C13A, Correspondance générale: Louisiane, from the Archives des colonies.[1] Today some several American libraries have complete microfilm copies of this series.[2] Their availability has revolutionized the historiography of the period and challenged a one-sided British view of colonial America. I do not wish to disparage the value of C13A; indeed, at the moment I am editing translations of a selection from it relevant to the history of what is now the state of Mississippi.[3] But while the virtues of the collection are many, close acquaintance inevitably makes one aware that even this large body of documents is very incomplete for some aspects of the history of the Louisiana colony.

The point I am trying to make requires a brief review of what C13A is in order to clarify what it is not. Primarily, C13A contains reports to the minister of marine and colonies, sometimes only summaries of these reports prepared by ministry secretaries, from the governors and commissaries general and sometimes from other officers in the colony. In them the governors report on the events in the colony and their involvement in them, but since (except for Bienville) they rarely left New Orleans except to go to Mobile for the annual present giving to the Indians, by and large they depended for information

This chapter was originally published as "Louisiana Post Letters, 1700–1763: The Missing Evidence for Indian Diplomacy" in *Louisiana History* 22, no. 1 (1981): 31–44. It is reprinted by permission of the Louisiana Historical Association.

upon written reports from the commanders of posts in the colony and from missionaries, traders, interpreters, and subalterns on missions among the Indians. When some particularly interesting information came in this way to the governor or the commissary general (who received similar reports from the post warehouse-keepers and other civil personnel), and particularly when he needed to justify his course of action, he might enclose one or more of these letters with one of his own, and in this way C13A also came to include a small selection of such documents.[4] "Minor" reports sometimes sent to the minister of marine by the commandants of the district posts of Illinois and Mobile, which are also included in C13A, depend in a similar way upon reports from the field and sometimes also forward such reports.[5] The true relationships among the governors' reports and their sources were not obvious, however, until Bill Barron's *The Vaudreuil Papers* made an accurate calendar of one governor's letterbooks widely accessible.[6] Using information from this additional source together with the Surrey *Calendar* we can show just how representative of the whole of the facts C13A is.[7]

Governor Pierre de Rigaud de Vaudreuil's letterbooks, especially the third one, clarify the process embodied in the correspondence between the colony and the mother country. The governor would receive orders and statements of policy from the minister of marine and other officials in France (in série B, Archives des colonies).[8] He would then reformulate these orders in terms of local policy and communicate his orders directly either to the commanders of the posts or to district commanders (in H M LO 9:III).[9] Commanders of the posts would attempt to carry out his orders, adapting them to local contingencies, and would report back to the governor on the results. (These reports are mostly missing but mentioned in H M LO 9:III by acknowledgments of letters received.) In the case of the district commanders, the same process would take place in miniature: they would write similar letters to the posts under their jurisdiction; they would then use the answering reports in turn as sources for their reports. (Some district commanders' letters preserved in C13A contain such references.[10] Many explicit references to post letters are also found in the letters in H M LO 9:III.) The governor would then prepare his report, using the post letters selectively as sources for fact and adding his own interpretation of events, and send it to the minister of marine (C13A). The governor would also sometimes send reports to the court directly (H M LO 9:II). This statement of procedure shows that C13A with few exceptions does *not* contain just those documents that constitute primary reportage of events in the field.[11] Nor, except for the remarkable series of letters from Macarty at Illinois and a few from various other western posts, do the Vaudreuil letterbooks.[12] If it were not for letterbook III, which contains all Vaudreuil's correspondence *to* the posts of the Mobile district from June 1743 to July 1747, in which he acknowledges receipt of most of the post reports for the period, we would not even be able to estimate their frequency.

The importance of these missing letters, especially for details of Indian diplomacy and evidence for the ethnohistory of the Indian tribal groups of the region, is considerable. I would like to look at a series of events as shown in one group of surviving letters from C13A and the Vaudreuil letterbook III to show how important they are. For this period C13A is at its most helpful, for Louboey, commander of the Mobile district, wrote numerous letters himself directly to the minister in France, frequently recapitulating letters he had received from officers in the field. The events in question occurred in the years 1745 and 1746, and they constituted the contributing causes of the Choctaw civil war, which resulted from the death of Soulouche Oumastabe, or Red Shoe, the famous war chief of the important town of Couechitto.

The story really begins in 1744, when two cadets, the brothers Dominique and Henri de Verbois, were assigned to detached duty among the Choctaw based in the village of West Yazoo, serving partly as distributors of trade goods and partly as spies while they ostensibly trained as interpreters.[13] At that time the Chickasaw Indians, against whom the French had been making war since they gave refuge to the Natchez in 1731, were trying to make peace with the French and the French-allied Choctaw. But they refused to expel English traders from their villages, and when war was declared between France and England in 1744, one Verbois brother and another cadet, Canelle, were sent to persuade the Choctaw villages to attack the Chickasaw.[14] The following year, in August, a Verbois was an observer at an assembly of chiefs to debate the question of war with the Chickasaw, and he submitted a written report of the allegiances of the various Choctaw chiefs.[15] At the same time or shortly thereafter the Choctaw seem to have complained to the commander of Fort Tombecbé (Erneville) or to their missionary (Father Baudouin) or both that the younger Verbois and Chambly, another young subaltern, were guilty of raping Indian women. We know this because Vaudreuil wrote to the commander and the missionary, declining to believe the accusation and ordering that the younger Verbois continue his mission among Red Shoe's faction, keeping a low profile.[16]

Meanwhile, Vaudreuil received at least one letter from a Verbois, written on October 2, reporting an attack on the English trading convoy by a pro-French village, Blue Wood (Iteokchako).[17] In December Vaudreuil directed Beauchamp, second-in-command at Mobile, to use Verbois's evaluation of the chiefs' loyalty to decide on the apportionment of presents.[18] In the following year, in August, Vaudreuil approved Verbois's handling of Red Shoe in supplying him with munitions for expeditions he promised to undertake against the Chickasaw.[19] At the end of the same month Vaudreuil received news of the death of the younger Henri de Verbois, also known as Henri de Baussière, and two traders from the western villages at the hands of minions of Red Shoe. This made it necessary for Vaudreuil to order Beauchamp into Choctaw country to deliver a demand for the heads of the perpetrators, Red Shoe's included.[20]

Now we can look at the report Vaudreuil sent on all this to Maurepas.[21] He says that Red Shoe had not appeared at the present giving at Mobile but instead had gone to the Chickasaw to contrive a separate peace with them. When the loyal Choctaw returned from Mobile, Red Shoe argued with them to accept the peace and to treat some expected Chickasaw deputies well. But a loyal contingent led by Choucououlacta attacked this embassy and killed three of the four of them. At this juncture, Vaudreuil says, he ordered Louboey, commander at Mobile, to withdraw the "cadets and traders who were within reach of this rebel" (fol. 77v), but Red Shoe had Verbois and two traders killed in order to restore his credibility with the English. As a result, it was necessary to send Beauchamp into the nation with a demand for the heads of the guilty parties.[22] The letter closes with details of various economic sanctions invoked against Red Shoe to decrease his power in the nation. Vaudreuil's letter to the court is even less specific.[23] He states that the western faction of the Choctaw nation was pro-English and that the eastern faction had decided to kill Red Shoe in order to retain the favor of the French.

Now it is clear, even given the fact that we have no primary sources for these occurrences as they happened, that a great deal of distortion of objective fact entered into Vaudreuil's presentation of these events to the government at home. For a start, there is no mention of the alleged rapes, although Beauchamp's journal, sent to France as a supporting document, contains the following statement by Tatoulimataha, Red Shoe's elder brother:

He added that if his brother had committed this evil act, it was only from the despair of seeing that the promises that had been given him in the past at Tombecbé had not been kept, together with the bad treatment that he had received, both personally and in the matter of his wives. He [Tatoulimataha] even asked me [Beauchamp] if it was by order of the governor that the chiefs [officers] and other Frenchmen [traders] who are in the nation were sent, who behaved badly towards them and their wives; that we ought to know that that gave them much pain and that red men would kill one another for such things. (fol. 238v)

Even in this statement, however, there is nowhere an indication that one of the murdered Frenchmen had been specifically so accused. Another factor that is ignored is the activities of the Verbois brothers as informers and spies among the Choctaw and the participation of one of them in war parties that attacked the Chickasaw and the English, though the Beauchamp journal (fols. 238v, 239) states that the English had originally demanded only the death of one Frenchman "for an Englishman who had been killed by the Choctaw of the village of Blue Wood." Neither of these items is important in the context of international politics, however, and certainly they are not the sort of thing that Vaudreuil's superiors would necessarily consider important, but when it comes to the warning that he claims to have sent for the removal of the cadets and traders from the nation, careful examination of the third letterbook offers no evidence that this is anything but an outright lie. The only specific orders regarding these personnel are the ones of a year earlier, stating that they should stay in the nation, and the ones that came after the fact, telling Beauchamp to pull them out if possible.

Thus we do not know much from French archival sources about the real relationships that existed at this time between the Choctaw and the French traders and young cadet-interpreters who lived among them, nor do we know what these men knew about the personalities of the Indians involved in the pro-French/pro-English power struggle within the Choctaw nation. The elitist bias of the governors' reports, evident here in the fact that we do not even have the name of one of the two traders who were killed, skews the evidence even further. In this incident C13A offers only the hint of these relationships contained in Tatoulimataha's speech to Beauchamp, and that only fortuitously. C13A cannot tell us that such complaints had been registered almost a year before, as we see from the third letterbook, and even it does not give us direct reportage of these complaints but only Vaudreuil's unbelieving reaction to them. Yet these relationships between the Indians and the Frenchmen whom they knew best were crucial to the attitudes of the Choctaw toward their French allies, perhaps even more so than the constant lack of trade goods suffered by the French during King George's War. There is ample evidence to show that the English were never able to supply the Choctaw adequately with the goods they needed due to the difficulties of the long overland trail.[24]

Another side of the story is preserved in this instance in an account of these events by James Adair, English trader to the Chickasaw, in his *History of the American Indians*.[25] We have noted above Verbois's report of October 2, 1745, of an attack made by warriors of the village of Blue Wood, an attack in which Verbois was probably involved. The English convoy was, in fact, led by Adair's partner, who was killed in the attack (313). Adair soon heard of the rape incident, however: "It happened . . . that one of the French of Tumbikpe-fort, being guided by Venus instead of Apollo, was detected in violating the law of marriage with the favourite wife of the warlike chieftain of Quansheto, *Shulashhummashtabe*, who by his several transcendant qualities, had arrived to the highest pitch of the red glory" (313). Upon receipt of this news Adair sent Chickasaw deputies to the injured chief to propose peace and English trade. "The sharpness of his own feelings for the base injury he had received from the French, and the well-adapted presents we sent him and his wife and gallant associates, contributed greatly to give a proper weight to our embassy. Such motives as these are too often the mainsprings that move the various wheels of government, even in the christian [*sic*] world" (315). Adair in fact seized upon this incident and gave it a prominent place in his speeches of persuasion to the Choctaw as an object lesson in French contempt for them. He states that he urged the Choctaw to kill and scalp "the dangerous French snakes" to prove that they had declared war on them (318–19). Adair's final statement on the subject of the murdered Frenchmen is: "These opulent and mercenary white savages being now dead, I shall not disgrace the page with their worthless names" (319). From this account, which is not without its own self-interest, it seems that Adair was able to combine his own revenge with that of Red Shoe, and although we do not know which brother participated in the raid on the English convoy, at least this seems to be one explanation for the death of Henri de Verbois in particular. It may be worthy of note that Chambly, the other subaltern accused of rape, was not mentioned at all in connection with the attack on the English convoy.

It is true, of course, that the events just discussed fit into a much more complex picture and that an adequate account of the political rivalry between the French and English in the Old Southwest can be written from the French and English sources that we already have.[26] It is also true that the radically different ways in which government business was conducted in the opposing colonies make it inevitable that the South Carolina "Indian Books" are a mine of on-the-spot reportage, while it is only through the lucky preservation of the Vaudreuil letterbooks—and that by an Englishman—that we even have any notion of the richness of the corresponding material for the French colony.[27] Perhaps we should not wish for more. But the fact is that the topics most frequently discussed in these lost letters will have been Indians and Indian diplomacy, discussed by the men who were most closely concerned. We know so very little about this earliest period in the documented history of many of the tribes in question, so little about how their social organization was affected by their involvement in French-English rivalry. For ethnohistory this is a great loss. Adair's repeated praise of the Frenchman's uncanny skill at Indian diplomacy (see 288 for one of Adair's numerous remarks to that effect) and our nearly complete lack of documentation from the French side intensify the mystery.

Letterbook III's particular importance is that its detail permits us to form rather precise notions of the nature and quantity of the lost material. The most prominent category of documents is, of course, letters from the commanders of the posts. Letterbook III covers the district of Mobile, including the four posts of Mobile itself, Tombecbé, the mission post at Chickasawhay, and Fort Toulouse. Vaudreuil wrote 135 letters to the three forts over a period of fifty months, and, according to my calculations, based upon the stated acknowledgments of letters received, he received 194 letters from the post commanders or their seconds-in-command. These were not the only letters received by Vaudreuil, however; though, for example, he wrote only twelve letters to the Jesuit Baudouin living in the Choctaw village of Chickasawhay, Baudouin sent him twenty-three. And he received at least eleven letters directly from traders and subalterns, to only two of which he sent replies. In addition, the letterbook cannot take into account the large number of inter-post letters, usually sent by Indian runners or traders, whose existence is revealed constantly, for instance, in Beauchamp's account of his journey to the Choctaw from C13A, mentioned above.[28]

We may grant that this period of French-Choctaw relations was an especially tense one, but it would be equally valid to ask what period did not offer some tension in Indian-French diplomacy. The period to follow, of course, was worse; the period that preceded contained two Chickasaw wars. In fact, it seems safe to say that the volume of such letters must have been nearly constant from the time of the Natchez rebellion in 1729 until the end of the French and Indian War some thirty-odd years later. And if this may be accepted as the case, there are at the very least fifteen hundred letters for the Mobile district alone that remain unaccounted for. This is not counting the intradistrict correspondence, whose volume cannot begin to be estimated without a district commander's letterbook. Nor does it attempt to go beyond the period or the district in question. In such an extended context we are talking about several thousands of letters that remain to be unearthed.

Thus we come to the main question: where are these letters? Even a few of them would be invaluable, and more than a few would be well worth the considerable effort that searching for them would be likely to entail. Our first impression is that they ought to be found, at least some of them, in the governors' letterbooks. Yet the evidence of the Vaudreuil papers shows that such is not likely to be the case. The letters from Macarty at Illinois and the western posts that are preserved among these papers are preserved as just that—miscellaneous papers. The fact that they are preserved at all reflects Vaudreuil's sense of the relative importance of the parts of his colony. The contest for the Ohio Valley loomed larger for him than did that for the southern Indian trade, and his interest in it eventually won him the governorship of Canada. We would be far more likely to find the material we are searching for among the papers of Bienville, who prided himself on Indian diplomacy; Périer, who seems to have had some personal interest in the Indian trade; and Louis de Kerlérec, whose strategies in the south would have won the Creeks and the Cherokees wholly to the French side had support from home not been so dilatory. Perhaps even D'Abbadie, though governor for only a short time, might furnish us with information, for by his time interest other than local was manifestly futile.

Searching for these letterbooks, however, is not so simple. Bienville's papers were supposedly destroyed with those of his family in Canada, but this seems rather hard to believe, since he never set foot in Canada again once he had come to Louisiana. It is more likely that his papers reside somewhere in

France, perhaps in the family papers of his heirs.[29] As for Périer, once he left Louisiana, returned to France, and came out again to Santo Domingo there seems to be little knowledge of his fate.[30] Kerlérec certainly kept a letterbook; it is mentioned in C13A, 42:55v.[31] Marc de Villiers du Terrage, a descendant, used a collection of family papers for his book *Les dernières années de la Louisiane française*, but it must be admitted that that book does not give evidence that those family papers contained material of the kind that interests us. Finally, John Francis McDermott has pointed out the possibility that D'Abbadie's correspondence, carried back to France by his wife, might turn up someday.[32]

I suspect, however, that such sources may take years to appear, if they are found at all. There is, fortunately, another possibility, one that requires no less exhaustive search but that promises more prompt success, if only because it lies, at present or potentially, in our own state and university archives. I refer to family papers belonging to descendants of the various post commanders, traders, and interpreters. For one thing, many of these people, unlike their more exalted superiors, had found a home in the Louisiana colony, and numbers of them stayed on to found families, even after the loss of the colony to England and Spain.[33] And why would these letters still exist? In the first place, officers were as likely as governors to keep copies of the letters they sent, if only as insurance against accusations of malfeasance (e.g., this was true of Diron d'Artaguette when he was commander at Mobile, and the copies stood him in good stead in a quarrel with Périer).[34] The same would be true of interpost correspondence of a military nature, though social correspondence between posts was probably rare in any case.[35] After the passing of the French colony, the families of these men could mostly be counted upon to keep these letters as evidence of rank, pride, or property.

What is needed, then, is a careful study of the families who actually remained in Louisiana after the colony was ceded to Englishman and Spaniard, with a view to isolating and identifying surviving families of men who were directly involved in Indian diplomacy. It may be that such families have preserved nothing earlier than their first antiquarian ancestor.[36] But it also may be that one or two of them still possess a small packet of letters or journals about an ancestor's activities on missions to the Indian nations, and the worth of the few such documents that we have is ample justification for such a search.

Notes

1. Beers, *The French in North America*, 12–13, gives a brief summary of the topics covered and the nature of the series. Examples of publications of C13A documents are Pease and Jenison, *Illinois*; Rowland and Sanders, *Mississippi Provincial Archives: French Dominion*, 3 vols.; Thwaites, *The French Regime*. All of these are based on transcripts obtained from France.

2. Brasseaux's *A Comparative View* was based on microfilm of C13A.

3. Rowland, Sanders, and Galloway, *Mississippi Provincial Archives: French Dominion*, vols. 4 and 5. All five volumes are hereafter cited in text and notes as MPA:FD.

4. A sampling of years shows the following figures for letters from governor and commissary versus letters from all others: 1725, 23 (Superior Council) versus 17; 1737, 63 versus 6; 1752, 91 versus 9. These figures exclude the occasional long memoirs on colonial development and various inventories that also appear in C13A, but they include the "minor" or district reports from district commanders. The figures support the general assertion that for the earlier period, until Bienville took office the second time, numerous people competed with the government for the minister's attention. The same seems to have been the case during Périer's rather weak administration. Vaudreuil and Kerlérec, however, ran a tighter ship, and few letters were sent independently during their administrations. During no administration were letters sent to the minister directly from any post besides New Orleans except Mobile or Illinois.

5. An example of such a report from Mobile is Diron d'Artaguette to Maurepas, October 24, 1737, in Archives des colonies (AC), série C13A, 22:233–43. Diron mentions the use of Indian runners to carry his letters to Chickasawhay and Tombecbé (fol. 233v), receipt of letters from his post commanders (fols. 234, 237–43; the latter long passage, which has several textual difficulties, was probably mostly transcribed from the field report), and the forwarding of documents relevant to his capture of an English ship (fol. 236v). This and most of the other C13A examples cited in these notes appear in MPA:FD.

6. Barron, *The Vaudreuil Papers*. Vaudreuil's letterbooks are the only known examples that survive, though he was not the only governor who kept them. Letterbook III has great importance because it is the only extant compendium of a governor's orders over an extended period. Scattered examples, the orders received by one officer during much of his career, are preserved in Works Progress Administration, Historical Records Survey, *The Favrot Papers*; a few scattered orders to various officers appear in the Parsons Collection held by the Humanities Research Center, University of Texas at Austin.

7. Miller Surrey, *Calendar of Manuscripts*. This calendar, though lacking an index, is the most complete guide to the relevant documents.

8. These appear in AC, série B. For further details see Beers, *The French in North America*, 12.

9. The third letterbook is cataloged in the Huntington Library as Huntington Manuscript Loudoun (H M LO) 9:III. The other two letterbooks are cataloged as H M LO 9:I and H M LO 9:II. These abbreviations will be used throughout. See Barron, *The Vaudreuil Papers*, xxvii–xxix.

10. See the example from Diron d'Artaguette mentioned above, note 5. For the Vaudreuil period numerous letters from Louboey at Mobile contain such references; for example, Louboey to Maurepas, December 7, 1742, AC, série C13A, 27:142–49 for only one of them, which mentions forwarding the journal of Canelle cited in note 11 below. There is a rule of thumb for determining on internal evidence whether a letter was sent to the minister in France or to the author's Louisiana superior: the minister is always addressed as "Monseigneur," while others are addressed as "Monsieur."

11. These exceptions are nearly all single isolated documents, like the young subaltern Canelle's journal of a small Choctaw campaign against the Chickasaw in 1742 (AC, série C13A, 27:176–77)

and the 1746 letter from Hazeur at Tombecbé to Louboey cited below, note 28. An exceptional series of letters from the commandant (Gamon de La Rochette) and the commissary (Layssard) of the Arkansas Post to Bobé Descloseaux, acting commissary general of New Orleans, consisting of thirty-four pieces of correspondence from January 9, 1758, to February 13, 1759 (AC, série C13A, 40:291–395), is mainly concerned with squabbles over jurisdiction.

12. Most of the Macarty letters are published in Pease and Jenison, *Illinois*.

13. Louboey to Maurepas, October 6, 1745 (AC, série C13A, 29:190v), states that they were living in the village of West Yazoo; H M LO 9:III, 31, places them among the Choctaw in 1744. The elder of the brothers, Dominique, had been serving in this way and leading Choctaw attacks on the Chickasaw for at least two years. See Father Baudouin to Louboey, May 20, 1742, AC, série C13A, 27:131; and Journal of Cadet Canelle, August 17–29, 1742, AC, série C13A, 27:176–77. He had been serving in Louisiana since 1736 (Maurepas to Bienville and Salmon, September 19, 1736, AC, série B, 64:506). On officer lists of 1742-43 (LO 16 and LO 19) both are listed as cadets, but Dominique was promoted to ensign in 1746 (Maurepas to Vaudreuil, June 1, 1746, AC, série B, 83:323).

14. H M LO 9:III, 117.

15. Mentioned in H M LO 9:III, 179, but the report itself is lost.

16. H M LO 9:III, 178, 180. This had been a recurrent problem; Vaudreuil chides La Houssaye for similar behavior in H M LO 9:III, 28. Ten years earlier Diron d'Artaguette had accused Le Sueur and his officers of the same offense. Diron to Maurepas, April 29, 1735, AC, série C13A, 20:267–72.

17. H M LO 9:III, 182. Louboey to Maurepas, October 6, 1745, AC, série C13A, 29:194, has a brief notice of this attack, in which the Englishman killed was probably James Adair's partner.

18. H M LO 9:III, 184. Doubtless this is the report made in August; see note 15 above.

19. H M LO 9:III, 199. This is probably Henri, who was earlier mentioned as working with the rebel faction.

20. H M LO 9:III, 207, 213, 215, 217.

21. H M LO 9:I, 188; Vaudreuil to Maurepas, November 20, 1746, AC, série C13A, 30:76–84.

22. Beauchamp's report on this journey was also sent to Paris on August 28, 1746 (see AC, série C13A, 30:222–40). It is translated rather carelessly in Mereness, *Travels*, 261–97. A new translation appears in the final volumes of the MPA:FD.

23. H M LO 9:II, 38.

24. For the failure of the English effort to trade with the Choctaw before and during their civil war (pro-French versus anti-French Choctaw) see Atkin, "Historical Account." The situation as seen by the French in August 1748: "The partisans of the English were in such great need of powder and bullets that they loaded their guns with small pebbles and walnut and oak knots dried over the fire" (Beauchamp to Maurepas, October 24, 1748, AC, série C13A, 32:215v).

25. Adair, *Adair's History*, 313–19. Hereafter cited in the text. All page references will be to the original pagination of Adair's book, which the editor, Samuel Cole Williams, indicates.

26. Crane, *The Southern Frontier*; Alden, *John Stuart*. It should be noted that Vaudreuil's letter reporting the death of Verbois and the two traders was only one of fifteen letters written by him to France in the same week; the other fourteen were concerned with colony affairs, fortifications, relations with the Spanish, English military movements, and events in the Illinois country.

27. The "Indian Books" are edited in three volumes by William L. McDowell as *The Colonial Records of South Carolina*, series 2, vols. 1–3. The volume titles are *Journals of the Commissioners of the Indian Trade, 1710–1718* (1955), *Documents Relating to Indian Affairs, 1750–1754* (1958), and *Documents Relating to Indian Affairs, 1754–1765* (1970).

28. Beauchamp's journal of his journey to the Choctaw, August 28, 1746, AC, série C13A, 30:222–40; references to interpost letters on fols. 223, 226v, 227v, 229, 229v, 234, 238, 239v. During the

month that he stayed in the Choctaw nation Beauchamp kept in constant touch with Louboey at Mobile, Hazeur at Tombecbé, and Le Sueur at Fort Toulouse. A copy of a letter from Hazeur to Louboey of November 11, 1746, a month after Beauchamp's departure, preserved as AC, série C13A, 30:183–86, illustrates the potential value of these letters, as in the space of eight pages it recounts an abortive attempt on Red Shoe's life and in passing contributes a valuable item of ethnographic information on warrior classes and tattooing.

29. King, *Jean Baptiste Le Moyne*. On page i of her preface King asserts that no papers of Bienville are known to exist. O'Neill, in "The Death of Bienville," discusses the procès-verbal of Bienville's death, and no papers were found at his residence at that time (1767), though ample reference to relatives suggests that such papers may have been in other hands.

30. Careful perusal of série C9, correspondance générale, Saint-Domingue, might reveal more, but Périer himself stated to the Abbé Raguet, early in his administration, that he was not inclined to keep a journal of his activities because he could not spare the time; presumably, this attitude might well extend to the keeping of an orderly letterbook (Périer to Abbé Raguet, March 28, 1729, AC, série C13A, 12:5). In any case, a 1758 statement by Kerlérec implies that Périer was back in France (Kerlérec to Massiac, December 12, 1758, AC, série C13A, 40:152).

31. Registre de correspondance; Kerlérec even gave each of his letters a number in this register. It is not clear, however, if post letters were included in this letterbook, since there are many gaps in the numbered series attributable to losses in encounters with English privateers.

32. McDermott, "Some Recent Books."

33. It seems quite possible that this was the case with the family of the surviving Verbois brother, Dominique, mentioned above. He is mentioned in 1754 as serving on detached duty among the Tunica (Kerlérec to D'Arnouville, September 15, 1754, AC, série C13A, 38:98); he was married to Marguerite Chauvin DeLéry and must have died by 1759 when she married again (Cruzat, Dart, and Prichard, "Records of the Superior Council," 573; Arthur and Huchet de Kernion, *Old Families of Louisiana*, 244). A Nicolas de Verbois served in the militia under the Spanish government (Holmes, *Honor and Fidelity*, 226), and this Nicolas had two sons, Jean-Baptiste Dominique and François, and lived with his family in Iberville, dying in 1824. It is probable that Nicolas, born in 1756, was the son of Dominique. To cite another who is directly involved with the events discussed, Joseph Louis Boucher de Grandpré, who was credited with bringing an end to the Choctaw civil war in 1751 as commandant of Tombecbé, was the father of Carlos (Charles) de Grandpré, who was commandant of Natchez for the Spanish.

34. See Diron to Périer, October 1, 1729, AC, série C13A, 12:l43–47. Copy of documents concerning proceedings between Périer and Diron, July–October 1729, AC, série C13A, 12:l59bis–61; Diron to Superior Council, September 5, 1729, AC, série C13A, l2:l7lv–72; Diron to Superior Council, October 1, 1729, AC, série C13A, 12:176v–80. These constitute a dossier of copies of letters sent back and forth between Diron and Périer in 1729.

35. Beers, *The French in North America*, 5. But a striking example of friendly correspondence from Terisse de Ternan in Illinois to Rossard in New Orleans is found in the Judicial Records of the Superior Council held by the Louisiana Historical Center, Louisiana State Museum (see April 14, 1730).

36. One such collection, the Favrot papers, chronicles the career of a family whose first Louisiana founder arrived in 1732, but most of the documents are copies made by his son from missing originals. See Works Progress Administration, Historical Records Survey, *The Favrot Papers*; also Parkhurst, "Don Pedro Favrot"; and Náñez Falcón, *The Favrot Family Papers*.

4. The Unexamined Habitus

Direct Historic Analogy and the
Archaeology of the Text

Ethnographic analogy has long been the archaeologist's mainstay for the interpretation of patterns emerging in material remains. Although great care has not always been shown in its use, many archaeologists, by virtue of their training as social scientists, assume that they know how to accord proper evaluation to ethnographic evidence gathered in the modern period. Where difficulty arises and is seen to arise, as it must in the case of peoples now extinct or heavily acculturated, is in the case of "ethnographic" evidence taken from historical sources rather than living peoples. In spite of the fact that this is recognized as a special case with special problems, archaeologists often abandon the evaluation of such sources to historians, accepting their judgments at face value even in the absence of critical historical work in the relevant field. But although it is part of the historian's task to have a broad knowledge of the cultural and social contexts of his subjects, historians who are competent to handle both sides of a culture-contact situation that occurred in the past are few and far between; most frequently, they only interpret the European view of events, while the "Natives" remain "people without history."[1] Nor in this context is the problem of narrative history—either that written by modern historians or the narrative sources on which they depend—addressed, though among historiographers it is as hotly debated a problem as are Western interpretive frames in anthropology. Because the issues involved in the use of historical ethnographic analogy have been so little discussed from a theoretical standpoint, I have chosen to examine the documents portraying early

This chapter was originally published as "The Unexamined Habitus: Direct Historic Analogy and the Archaeology of the Text," in *Representations in Archaeology*, edited by Jean-Claude Gardin and Christopher Peebles (Bloomington: Indiana University Press, 1992), 178–95. It is reprinted by permission of Indiana University Press.

contact between European and Native in the southeastern United States as an example of the problem, with a view toward the suggestion of at least a partial solution.

The Southeastern Problem

The meeting of European and Indian in the southeastern United States in the fifteenth and sixteenth centuries occurred so relatively recently that the outcome of this meeting in the shape of European accounts has exercised an irresistible fascination for students of the prehistory of the region ever since. However embarrassed we may be by the fact that we have met the enemy and he is us, Western anthropologists dealing with the testimony of sixteenth-century Spaniards have presumably felt that their guilty kinship of Western-ness and conquest made the narratives of the early explorers transparent and therefore usable without question. If Hernando de Soto and his men were our cultural brothers, their hypocrisy in relating what they saw would be the same as our own, and we could make up for it. This is a fairly commonplace problem in the social sciences. What is not commonplace is the apparently willed blindness with which southeastern archaeologists have ignored it. Here I will set aside the really serious purely archaeological questions that remain unanswered in the region to focus on just this problem.

Fifty years of archaeological research suggest that the social geography of the southeastern region in the sixteenth century, when it was first penetrated by European explorers, was a patchwork of varied social organization: agri-cultural chiefdoms, where floodplain widths and richness permitted the so-called Mississippian adaptation that depended upon maize, beans, and squash supplemented by hunting and fishing; possible chiefdoms, where gathered resources were rich enough to support elites and minor horticulture was sufficient to make up the difference; and segmented tribal organization, where the land did not favor full sedentarism and at least seasonal displacement was necessary to subsistence on hunted and gathered materials. The correlation between organizational complexity and the horticultural or agricultural sub-sistence base is a real one, based upon settlement pattern studies at macro- and microlevels.[2]

By the fourteenth century there were several sites assumed to represent multilevel Mississippian chiefdoms situated at strategic points across the Southeast. They were characterized by major centers surrounded by minor centers and small settlements, both thought to be in some sense dependent upon the major centers. These centers all showed evidence of social ranking in the population they served, residence by the society's elite, and craft specialization of some degree.

It is clear that these chiefdoms did not exist in a vacuum and that they communicated with one another. The keystone of this observation is the appearance across the region of a set of artifacts and motifs so mysterious in connotative content that they have been grouped under the rubric of "Southern Cult" or (more "objectively") "Southeastern Ceremonial Complex." Soberer researchers have suggested that these materials represent not a belief system but prestige goods trade, but all agree that they indicate that contact between chiefdoms in the Southeast, by whatever mechanism it was achieved, was widespread and sustained.[3]

Yet these chiefdoms were not all contemporary; they could reach the end of a "natural" lifespan without the help of Europeans, and many of them had done so by the time of contact. All over the Southeast they were dispersed and their "ceremonial" centers abandoned at a dateline that is too ill defined to permit the assignment of a unitary cause but that lies in the near temporal vicinity of the first period of European contact. It is tempting to wish for a unitary cause, and there are those who think they have found it in the diseases brought to the New World by Europeans.

Clearly, European disease attacking the vulnerable populations of the New World was a major factor in the reduction of aboriginal populations in morale as well as in numbers. The reduction in numbers is now seen to have been dramatic, as the work of historical demographers shows that a large aboriginal population for the Americas was likely.[4] But several very big and important questions remain. Just when and in what order did disease reduce the aboriginal populations? Epidemiological speculation still remains just that in the region. Did European disease cause the reduction of the southeastern chiefdoms to the more familiar tribes of the eighteenth century, or was some other factor at work? The notable lack of models for social devolution makes this a crucial question for the region that must be accommodated by anthropological theory. And (although this question is not so mysterious in the Southeast as it is in Mexico and Peru) why did the Indians let the Europeans get away with abuse? This serious problem of the meeting of two very disparate cultures and the communication process between them has been dodged repeatedly as archaeologists reduced it to one of "acculturation" without asking what made acculturation begin and whom it happened to.

These questions are hard to answer in the Southeast because many of the answers to them are to be found, if at all, in the period 1550–1680, between the major inland incursions of Europeans. The implied changes happened, in other words, "behind the scenes" of European expansion, and the only evidence for them is in archaeological remains that are so far largely unknown (survey coverage in the region is shockingly poor given the rate of site destruction) and that in any case cannot be reliably dated by any absolute method. Sequence alone will not suffice because drastic population movements apparently occurred, and social organization took no single form across the region.[5] It is for these reasons that the accounts of the earlier incursion are considered so important for a reconstruction of the "protohistory" of the region.

In general terms, this protohistoric period can be divided into three phases. The first saw an incursion by the Spanish expedition led by Soto upon a relatively untouched inland population. This episode was followed by nearly one hundred years during which the inland Southeast is a black box for which even historical knowledge of inputs and outputs is limited. This "blank" period was in turn followed by full and continuing contact initiated by the journeys of La Salle and his Spanish and British rivals. Thus we know what things looked like at the end, and from three different and competing points of view, but historical knowledge of the conditions that obtained at the opening of the drama is basically dependent upon the evidence of a single expedition. It is true that there were several other expeditions—those of Juan Pardo and Tristán de Luna being most important—that caught glimpses of what was going on in the interior after Soto, but their contacts were limited in time and area and do not offer the kind of panorama the Soto accounts seem to make available, nor can their evidence always be securely linked with that of the earlier expedition.[6]

Hence archaeologists have felt that it is vitally important to pay the closest attention to what information there is to be had from the first incursion. The promise is a very tempting one: if the living groups observed by Soto and later explorers can be identified with specific archaeological "cultures," then we will presumably know what they thought and how they arranged their lives as well as how they made pottery and traded in exotic metals. Then, of course, we will have no difficulty charting their trajectory into Western history.

The Direct Historical Approach

In the United States the attempt at a solution to difficult problems of late prehistoric social evolution and culture change through the use of historical documents has been called the Direct Historical Approach. Its goal is to connect named Native tribes of the historic period with protohistoric and prehistoric archaeological remains, and this is generally held to be a simple matter of moving from the known to the unknown backward in time while moving at the same time from document to material artifact. Julian Steward dates its beginnings with archaeological work in the Southwest and New York around 1915, but its real application came as a response or a corrective to the Midwestern Taxonomic System with its "set of timeless and spaceless categories"; it was, ironically, an attempt to deal with such cultural intangibles as were ignored in that formalist approach.[7] The Direct Historical Approach has been applied to two main problems: the location and identification of archaeological sites and the explanation of social organization. For finding and identifying archaeological sites information like travel time, distance estimates, and topographic features mentioned in early accounts are of interest, while for social organization the archaeologist turns rather to the behavior and lifeways of the aboriginal people as recorded by Europeans.

In the Southeast the Direct Historical Approach has been the basis for a good deal of research into the cultural dynamics of the late prehistoric period. First in this field as in many others was the Lower Mississippi Survey, beginning with the work of Philip Phillips, James A. Ford, and James B. Griffin in 1951. These three scholars tried to approach the late prehistory of the segment of the Mississippi River valley of interest to them through the documentary evidence generated by both the Spanish expedition of Soto (1539–42) and the French expeditions that followed more than a hundred years later, intending to bracket the period with these two baselines. Continuing this tradition has been the work of Jeffrey P. Brain, who with various collaborators has been pursuing for nearly twenty years the historical and physical trajectory of the Tunica people, who became eponymous of their ancestors in the eighteenth century.[8] The hope of this long-range project has been to study culture change through the study of a people who may have been pioneers of the Mississippian culture complex in prehistory and who certainly were successful assimilators of certain aspects of European cultures after contact. In the process of pursuing it, Brain has paid some considerable attention to the theoretical underpinnings of what he terms "ethnohistoric archaeology" without really facing the shaky historical ground on which it is often built.

Charles Hudson and his students have been pursuing the eastern path of Soto for many years and have recently turned to the task of taking on the remainder of the route of that expedition. This effort has had two goals. The first is the locational one: using the routes of Soto, Pardo, and other early explorers to put a name and cultural affiliation to known archaeological sites.[9] The second has been the use of that identification to anchor and thus make exploitable the cultural observations that can be teased out of the exploration accounts. So far this latter line of research has been most clearly exemplified in the team's account of the Coosa chiefdom.[10] These researchers have been especially interested in the work of the Annales historians without being aware of how seriously such a position should indict their favorite narrative sources.

The Problematic of the Contact Situation

Although the practitioners of the Direct Historical Approach in the Southeast have made use of European historical materials, and although Phillips, Ford, and Griffin warned of archaeological naïveté in the face of historical documents well over thirty years ago, archaeologists have never actually questioned more than the observational ability of these documents' authors. There has been no indication that their sincerity or indeed the historical status of their entire testimonies might be in doubt, and no effort has been made to examine these questions. Presumably because they have judged these Europeans to be like themselves as inheritors of the Western tradition, anthropologists have abandoned the cautions of their own discipline (and ignored the fact that the area and period have received no attention from modern historians) and accepted the transparency of these texts. Clearly, this is a mistake, for historical evidence is never Direct.

Sixteenth-century Spaniards were not like us. Although no real anthropological study of the personnel of the conquest of the New World has been made, quite adequate data exist for doing so, and social historians have made a beginning in this direction with their "group studies" of conquest expeditions in Central and South America.[11] Such studies have shown that the *mentalité* of the conquistador was peculiar to him and emerged from his unique historical formation.

Spaniards of the sixteenth century in Spain had barely emerged from feudalism and were still bound by the rigidities and limited horizons of a society based upon local manors farmed by peasants. Another important element in the immediate past history of the conquistador or his father or elder brother is that he had just completed the Reconquista, expelling the Moors from the southern part of Spain and taking over the lands they dominated by handing out their manors as *encomiendas* to the victorious *reconquistadores*. The pattern of the Reconquista, more than one observer has remarked, was repeated in the New World—and this new conquest served to occupy warriors who found life a little tame at home.

Variations were introduced into the successful strategies of the Reconquista by the experience of the New World, and each new area of conquest entered by the Spaniards taught a new lesson. To take only the experiences of Soto, he made a beginning in Nicaragua with Pedrarias and learned there to deal with heat and swamp and more dispersed populations than Cortés had found in Mexico. It is often unremarked that Soto was also one of the Men of Cajamarca, that elite led by Pizarro who shared both the honor and the spoils of the conquest of the Inca. This experience was significant not only because it enabled Soto to finance his Florida expedition; it also taught him much about the organization of New World states and how to exploit that organization for the purposes of conquest.[12]

As the conquest of the Americas began with heroic and epic expeditions led by charismatic individuals, so it was recorded by and large in the genre of the individual narrative account so closely related in theme and structure to the chivalric romance that was popular during the age. One author of a Soto account (Garcilaso de la Vega) was a literary man by profession.[13] The editor of another (Oviedo) repented the frivolous romance he wrote in his youth.[14] No rational case can be made for the independence of these narratives from the literary traditions of their age. Such texts are thus already two removes from "what happened."

If the "thoughtworld" of the sixteenth-century Spaniard was peculiar to his own place and time and quite different from that of a modern Western anthropologist, that of the protohistoric native of the Americas can by no stretch of the imagination be thought to be much like anything we know. One need only rethink the contact situation itself as a cognitive problem to apprehend the difficulties it presents for obtaining a true account *of* either side *from* either side. The contact situation should be viewed as the meeting of cognitive styles supporting very different social formations, and nothing in it is more certain than mutual misunderstanding, as Tzvetan Todorov's analysis has suggested.[15] Before tackling an analysis of the record of the ensuing interaction, I want to approach a more detailed formulation of this model of the contact situation. I am going to try to formulate in the same terms all of the various forms of discourse that meet in the "ethnohistoric archaeology" construct.

Anthropologists and archaeologists have found in Bourdieu's concept of the habitus a fruitful notion that has helped them recognize both nonlinguistic modes of culture transmission and nonlinguistic messages in the resulting material patterns.[16] But although Bourdieu has phrased and rephrased definitions of the habitus, he has not precisely come out and said what it is and where it resides; even his examples amount more to examples of the functioning of the habitus than to a description of the structure actually orchestrating behavior. If, however, one can suggest a close analogy between the many facets of habitus as defined by Bourdieu and recent mentalist schemes of knowledge acquisition and representation as proposed by cognitive scientists, it is possible to arrive at a model that retains all the generative capacity and improvisational virtuosity of Bourdieu's concept but that is far less impressionistically expressed. I am going to give a fairly detailed outline of this model just because I am going to use it later in formulating the problem of historical narrative.

The model to which I am referring has roughly two categories of elements. First are the declarative data structures that contain the system's world knowledge—its semantics or memory—organized in more or less static structures called "frames," which may include situational frames or scripts (knowledge including sequences of normal actions about frequently encountered situations), state frames ("commonsense" knowledge about physics and psychology—"ethnoscience" in some senses), and object/person frames (permissible predications belonging to classes of objects and persons). Such frames are generalized structures containing "slots" that are filled in (instantiated) by the specific occurrences. They are built through repeated exposure to the kinds of entities they represent, and they may be altered, expanded, or newly generated in response to new experience.

The active, syntactic, and pragmatic side of the model is represented by the procedures that operate on the frames. At lowest level is a set of linguistic parsing procedures that refer both to input and to established knowledge in the shape of the currently instantiated frame(s) to comprehend what is happening and predict what will happen next. This pragmatics, to go beyond language understanding, must include procedures to decide what frame to instantiate and must also be able to "parse" nonlinguistic behavior. It also incorporates goal orientation by including procedures for "planning" or pre-

HISTORIOGRAPHY

dicting a course through contingencies without benefit of scripts, attempting to realize such goals as may apply.

An individual's practical knowledge of how to conduct himself in the world, then, amounts to a set of frame-based knowledge structures and the procedures for manipulating them. It is not claiming much more to characterize an individual's competence in his culture as the sum or the average of these representations of knowledge about it. If cultural competence can be formulated as a set of frame-based knowledge structures coupled with capacities for "planning" or orchestrating low-level frames containing commonsense knowledge to maximize performance in novel situations, we arrive at a model that can explain more clearly how the real behavioral flexibility of humans depends on what they know.[17]

If the introduction of this model seems extraneous, bear with me; like others here, I wonder why behavioral sciences other than psychology have not yet made more use of the findings of cognitive science, and I personally find it helpful to use its language as a lingua franca to mediate between anthropology and the "textual sciences" of literature and history. Structuralist and hermeneutic interpretations of texts and other semiotic structures often seem to me to drown in an indefensible self-referentiality, and I am afraid I am not satisfied with Barthesian *jouissance* as an adequate analysis of any discourse.

Using the equation of habitus with a set of scripts and a competence for planning, it is possible to describe the contact situation in a way that more directly addresses the internal social processes on both sides. Spaniard and Indian alike were faced at contact by novelty and the necessity for improvisation. The cognitive view of human interaction asserts that for each participant the first step in dealing with any situation is to attempt to find an appropriate script to instantiate, since the use of an already-learned structure reduces the effort required. The sort of structure that might come to mind on both sides can be suggested informally to give an idea of what I mean here. Clearly, very different intentions may have been at work, and these intentions would lead to the selection of very different script structures.

For the Spaniard, "conquest" might have meant carrying out relatively newly developed scripts that—after Cajamarca—might include such variations as duplicitous seizure of a ruler to coerce the cooperation of his subjects. For the leader of a multilevel southeastern chiefdom, "contact with powerful strangers" might mean extension of hospitality and the signs of kinship. But if human beings learn by modifying old frames and adding new ones, and if that means instantiating old ones until they start to go wrong and planning one's way out when they do, then there is room for improvised solutions to be introduced on both sides. It is, of course, quite probable that in unprecedented situations script selections may go disastrously wrong, as would be the case when the Spaniards adopted patterns of a conduct that had been successful in dealing with social formations that granted leaders such monopolistic control over symbolic capital that the man who controlled them thus easily dominated that capital and its implied obligations. This same conduct could not be very effective when the chief's leadership rested less on a set of institutions than on a more constant day-to-day maintenance of obligation through the distribution and transmutation of real capital; imprisonment of such a leader stops the maintenance of his leadership and weakens it. Southeastern Natives, too, seem to have been more or less bound by their own cultural conventions to choose initially an inappropriate "hospitality" script for coping with these marauding intruders (but not, one should stress, apparently a fully instantiated one), but this "mistake" is easier to understand in terms of a notion of obligatory choice subsumed under a dominant goal structure that classifies various "greeting" script choices as more or less honorable in a given situation.

But neither side was required to adhere to any first choice. In many cases the explorers appear to have been dealing with ranked societies: chiefdoms or the dependencies and devolved remnants of chiefdoms. Although at such levels an institutionalization of structures of dominance can be assumed to have taken place to a modest degree, manifested in terms of detailed obligatory scripts for some aspects of social life, chiefdoms were in some ways prepared to cope with novelty. By definition, some members of a ranked society must transcend the face-to-face habitus characterized by Calvin Martin as the "bio-logic" of hunters and gatherers and must undertake to specialize in managing not animals and the nonhuman world but people.[18] That is, elites become so and stay so because they have developed the knowledge to manipulate the habitus of other people and the flexibility to modify their techniques as their power grows and their trading networks expand. So even though their position and many of its appurtenances become institutionalized, their function as problem solvers and appliers of the society's theories to reality actually makes them expert in the generative capacities of the habitus. The notion that Native peoples of the Southeast met the intrusive Europeans trapped in the set habits of tradition like flies in amber simply does not take account either of the relative recency of parts of that tradition or of its potential ad hoc malleability in the shock of novel situations.

Other aspects of the contact situation are external to these considerations. Its brevity has been underemphasized. Soto and his men observed individual southeastern groups for at most a few continuous months, but that was the rare exception, and in most cases those observations lasted no more than a few days. In addition, in spite of the arguments of Henry Dobyns for the early spread into the Southeast of epidemic disease, there is no documentary evidence and certainly as yet no archaeological evidence to show that it definitely had or had not yet affected the groups of the interior.[19] If it had, or if it had differentially, what the first interior expedition saw had already been altered radically: the likelihood that the bearers of the framesful of esoteric and other specialized knowledge had died means that the repertoire of knowledge possessed by the community would have been reduced to the common denominators of subsistence and kinship rules that would permit only partial reproduction of complex late prehistoric societies.

Thus in many respects the contact situation is by its nature one that cannot tell the archaeologist much about the cognitive implications of precontact archaeological remains simply because the entire situation is novel and it warps behaviors on both sides accordingly. Unless we assume that Native peoples naturally prostrated themselves before the obviously superior European, it is necessary that we admit that they might equally well have reacted creatively and interestedly and that by doing so they altered "traditional" behavior. The story of Cortés's being "mistaken" for the god Quetzalcoatl and his exploitation of such a belief is taken by Todorov as a successful manipulation of the situation by Cortés, but it certainly also represents a novel and creative manipulation by the Aztecs of their belief system to accommodate an unprecedented situation; Cortés could not have forced the belief on anyone.[20] A very similar situation, in which Captain Cook was taken also for a god who returned but who had to die ritually soon after, shows that such "mistakes" can be quite effective in coping with novelty.[21]

The Texts

In spite of the foregoing pessimistic analysis there was certainly much of value to be observed in the contact situation, but the problem lies in identifying and extracting it. This information is preserved embedded in the texts produced by the European participants in the contact (Todorov offers an exceptional close reading of such texts).[22] These texts lie at the heart of the enquiry here because as long as their status as evidence is in doubt, any linking of that evidence with archaeological referents is a futile exercise. As I have said, these texts are for the most part cast in the form of historical narratives; the specific narratives I will discuss here are those that pertain to the Soto expedition, since not only are they the earliest and most detailed and therefore the most interesting to archaeologists, but their status is also the most questionable.

Because it is of first importance to know the source of information, the initial problems are raised by unresolved questions of authorship. Of the extant four narratives of Soto, only one (Biedma) comes to us directly. Of the others, in order of presumed authenticity, the first (Ranjel) has been included with commentary in another man's history; the second (Elvas) leaves its authorship anonymous; while the third (Garcilaso) claims to represent mostly the direct testimony of a second anonymous participant. In no case except possibly the first can anyone be sure that the actual words of an expedition participant are thus made available.

It is almost as hard to find out why the narratives were written. The first of the four cited above was an official report, and the second is supposed to have been, but the other two could have been written to satisfy any of a number of motives. This is a serious issue because narrative is an artistic form: it picks and chooses the things it will represent and the ways it will represent them simply because there is not enough paper in the world to represent everything, even if an informant could remember it. Most archaeologists who have dealt with these sources have treated them as though they were simply compilations of discrete observations, without attention to the communicative purpose and overall structure of the text; much has been said about the necessity for reconstructing the whole of the expedition's route, but nothing at all about the necessity for grasping the import of the texts as a whole. But these texts are meaningful not piecemeal but whole—and to swallow one item from such a text is also to accept the assumptions that inform it, which could well invalidate the desired item if made explicit. Such problems can be clearly exposed in a closer examination of the use that has been made of the textual evidence.

Locational Evidence

These narratives have been minutely studied in order to settle the apparently simple question of where Soto went across the Southeast. Although American

Babbitry has found almost no more fertile outlet than the Soto route question, several quite serious efforts have been made to study the possibilities. In this research several kinds of evidence have been pulled from the texts to be intercollated, weighed, and erected into a unified route structure. Perhaps the most carefully studied of this evidence has been the portrayal of time and distance. Lengthy debates have raged over the measurement of a Spanish league and the distance that could have been covered by the expedition in a day. Direction estimates and accuracy have been equally hotly debated without, to my knowledge, any careful enquiry about the availability of adequate instrumentation. Finally, detailed note of the landforms observed and described by the Spaniards has been taken, and taken to signify more or less precise observation of the topography the explorers passed through. All of this discussion has led to characterizations of the authors themselves as "careless in their observation of direction" or guilty of giving "exaggerated distances"—phrases that suggest that the scholars themselves have rather prejudged the data.

From the beginning of serious study of the route for ethnographic purposes it has seemed obvious to researchers that they would have to reconstruct the whole of the route before any part of it could be counted as reliably identified. John R. Swanton and the De Soto Expedition Commission met with local experts in the location of "Indian trails" and walked all over the Southeast in carrying out their task for the U.S. Congress, constructing at last a route that represented a consensus of many theories current in their day and that gave about equal weight to time, distance, direction, and topography.[23] Their work was doomed from the outset to a certain extent, however, since the archaeological chronology of their time was so compressed that they were satisfied if their route crossed almost any kind of evidence of aboriginal occupation.

Charles Hudson and his colleagues have been particularly concerned to be sure that their findings coincide with archaeological remains that at least stand a chance of being the right age, and they have made drastic revisions of the route by being more concerned with time, distance, and especially topography than with direction. Jeffrey Brain and his coworkers have similarly depended more on distances and topography and upon likely archaeological correspondences than they have on direction. The fact that the routes recommended by Hudson and Brain differ radically at several points, however, suggests what must be admitted about any such efforts: the evidence hardly supports replicable scientific research.

Cartographic theorists are acerbic in their strictures against the suitability of the narrative form for conveying spatial information.[24] Although some of this aversion is attributable to a rather odd application of Piaget's discredited developmental topological-to-Euclidean space sequence, there are real cognitive problems with the reconstruction of maps from narrative sources. As numerous observers have pointed out, the fundamental sequentiality of narrative implies more than it can deliver in spatial terms; this is especially true of a narrative whose main focus is not spatial information. To avoid this problem, a document would have to approach the equivalent of "annalistic" form; that is, it would have to be a simple list of places and distances from which a reasonable map could in fact be constructed, depending upon the accuracy of the data.[25] But the narratives of Soto cannot be so characterized, and their capacity for representation of spatial information must be low, even if it can be assumed that they were *intended* to represent spatial information.

It is obvious that this must be so if we merely consider the information actually available to the explorers. In simply moving through the landscape they encountered serious perceptual problems familiar to psychologists who study the human capacity for getting around in a strange place. Soto's expedition was perhaps most nettled by the rank and rampant vegetation they encountered in the uninhabited borderlands between groups, which often made it difficult to see the way ahead even for men on horseback. The topography of the southeastern coastal plain is not unduly challenging (except for the numerous watercourses that had not at that time been subjected to the tender mercies of the U.S. Army Corps of Engineers), but there are several difficult obstacles farther inland: the southernmost salient of the Appalachians, the Tombigbee-Alabama watershed, and the Mississippi River valley. The mountains would not have presented an undue problem to men who had tackled the Andes, but the rivers were another matter: the Guadalquivir is the best simile the authors can manage, and it was certainly no match for the Mississippi.

Both of these difficulties, joined to the problems of supervising reluctant bearers and a large herd of pigs and to concerns as to where food, booty, and women might next be found, were bound to affect the Spaniards' estimates of time and distance, both notoriously difficult for humans to encompass. Time could certainly be measured pretty accurately in days (though the narratives do not agree), but distance is the only important datum to be taken from such evidence, and there is no assurance that travel could have been at all constant in speed over different topographies or with different burdens of numbers or baggage. Hence the distances in which archaeologists have been so interested require a much more critical analysis than they have so far seen.

But these are subjective issues. There are other issues that must also be raised, and they have to do with the mental and physical tools the Spaniards might have used to improve their grasp of spatiality. As adult Europeans the members of the expedition presumably possessed a commonsense model of hydrological behavior that included the facts that rivers flowed down from mountains and toward the sea. Probably many of them, and certainly their leaders, were familiar with the portolan charts of the Gulf of Mexico that had been made by Spanish pilots and that indicated the mouths of several rivers on the Atlantic and Gulf coasts. They would therefore expect that the sources of these same rivers would be found inland, probably in mountainous or hilly regions.

There is no indication in any of the narratives that the expedition possessed even a compass, but it seems astounding that it would not have had one, and it is not beyond the bounds of credibility that someone may also have possessed a portable astrolabe, according to Garcilaso and his own independent testimony.[26] But clearly, readings of position were not the matter of course that they would be even a century later, as the importance of accurate observations to scientific mapmaking began to be appreciated.

Doubtless the Spaniards' perceptions were also shaped by what they hoped and expected to find in the way of portable wealth. Among the most important of these things were gold, for which they sought mountains, and pearls, for which they learned to seek rivers. And to these ends they certainly questioned Indian informants, but here again systems of spatial perception and representation are likely to have clashed, even when the Indian informants were not being purposefully misleading in their information.

In fact, it would be very surprising if the members of Soto's expedition had had a clear notion of where they were, since contemporary mapmakers who not only spoke their language but had the opportunity to question expedition members themselves were confused. The so-called De Soto map made around 1544 by Alonzo de Santa Cruz, chief cartographer of the Casa de Contratación in Seville, is an excellent example of this misunderstanding.[27] In order to square the number of rivers the explorers said they crossed with the number of mouths on the portolan charts, he had to wander them back and forth across multiplied tributaries. It is worth noting that Santa Cruz paid almost no attention to the distance and direction reports in the accounts; it is odd that we would give them so much more credence today.

More than 150 years later the confusion about Soto's route had not abated, and the Delisle family, cartographers to the king of France, spent much time considering the accounts and attempting to map them.[28] This was the first critical examination of these data of which evidence survives, and it is interesting to see what kind of route is constructed when a professional cartographer attempts to pay serious attention to the distance and direction estimates of the exploration narratives. The Delisles themselves saw that the results of such a practice were ludicrous, and they made notes to that effect. Hence on their published maps they mostly expunged the names that contemporary explorers were telling them were not relevant anyway, eventually adopting a route constructed as much by guess (dependent upon the eighteenth-century locations of the few Indian groups that had not changed their names) as by anything else—a route that is not so different from the modern one supposedly reconstructed by careful scholarship.

Finally, there is very good reason to discount the entire procedure of using multiple narratives to construct a composite route. First, only one of the narratives (Biedma) can even possibly be assumed to have been written with the *intention* of portraying where the expedition went. The rest of them offer this information no more seriously than as transitional phrases between portrayals of events and observations; we have no way of deciding now if the narrator mentions crossing a swamp between two named towns because there was one exactly there, or there was one in the vicinity, or there was difficulty getting from one town to another and a swamp sounded a likely obstacle, or the swamp represented some sort of moral turbidity in the decision making of the expedition leadership. Each account needs to be evaluated for the structure that it creates, and mutual agreement says nothing at all about the reliability of any of the narratives where they do not agree. The point is that, as we shall see in the subsequent discussion, these narratives are not obliged to present fact as we understand fact at all and certainly not to present it uniformly.

"Ethnographic" Evidence

The major interest in these narratives is not in the locations, however—that information is only of interest so far as it can tie observations to specific archaeological remains. The goal of the whole exercise is to extract "ethnographic" information from the narratives. If there are serious problems with narrative as a vehicle for spatial information, the serious problems do not cease when we pass to the descriptive information, in spite of a nearly universal tendency to accept whatever descriptive data seem to suit the explanatory preferences of the researcher. Hayden White has examined the problem of historical narrative in great detail and has described the writing of it as the imposition on a sequence of events of a story or plot recognized as acceptable by the culture of the writer.[29] It is this culture-specific pre-interpretation that opens the problematic of the narrative form itself for conveying historical ethnographic description.

What are these plots? If, as White suggests, they are patterns of event sequences that make sense, that have explanatory force, then they are quite easily equated with certain of the scripts that make up the writer's cultural repertoire. Since such scripts have a generative capacity, their slots may be instantiated in nearly infinite combinations and different stories generated (hence fiction, when the slots are instantiated with characters and things known to be imaginary). White does not mean to suggest that just any story will be used to mold the shape of a historical narrative, for this will not be the case. There are unspoken *topoi* at work in historical writing, which would not be taking place at all if it did not take its task as the presentation of the most important events. Likewise, the canons of tragic drama, for example, indicate to us that cultures have certain scripts that embody their most significant cultural themes, certain habitus that are ignored at peril of cultural disintegration.[30] These "master scripts" (or "cultural root paradigms") will be the ones that serve the historian as interpretive templates.[31] It is worth remarking also that this frequently tends to mean that historians write the same history over and over, clothed in different instantiations.

Perhaps a more serious problem for the archaeologist is the fact that narrative is of its nature selective in terms of the information it will present. It is instructive to look at some of the considerations that govern that selectivity. Because a story is being told, because a script is being instantiated, facts that do not conduce to the telling of the story are omitted. White remarks that "the social system . . . alone . . . provide[s] the diacritical markers for ranking the importance of events" and thus their suitability for being chosen, but it is the social system of the *observer* that dictates these choices, not that of the people whose social system actually interests the archaeologist.[32] The unfolding of every script is limited in the possible sequences it can support, and events may be shifted around or omitted if they do not fit the sequence. Finally, the authors of narratives choose their materials for relevance to the communicative situation of the telling itself. The prominent inclusion of an episode in which a detachment is sent to look for the gold that so obsessed the Spanish Crown appears in all the narratives, but in each one it is attributed to a different point in the journey.

Above all, the particular situation of narrative plots as the master scripts of their cultures raises the ideological question that has impelled Western historians to write antihistory: that the very genre of connected linear narrative governed by a plot has a teleological force that binds it to Western ideologies, that makes it an expression of the master scripts of Western culture in particular. Calvin Martin and those Indian historians who find narrative history alien in kind from what counts as history among nonliterate peoples have been vehement in their agreement with this assertion, claiming that narrative is of its nature incapable of rendering the thoughtworld of their subjects.[33]

But I would say that such a question is irrelevant here. Unlike the emerging state societies of Mesoamerica and South America, the southeastern chiefdoms at their height did not require more than pictographic literacy and thus did not pass down a written record of what they thought their history was. Whenever it happened, the drastic wasting of disease must certainly have wiped out any esoteric traditions nurtured by elites, leaving behind as tradition only those mnemonic devices—scripts—known to the largest number of people, things like subsistence patterns and the gross rules of kinship. Hence it is useless to quibble over the fact that the narrative history we have does not represent the thoughtworld of Native peoples: we know it doesn't. What we need to agree is that it does represent the thoughtworld of the teller. If there is any way to correct for that, it may be possible at least to observe some of the things he or his informant saw. The way to apply such a corrective is to exploit what is known of narrative as a linguistic object to neutralize the cultural specificity of the form and a good deal of the content.

Both of these are very much ruled by the meaning to be conveyed, the story to be told. To decide what this story is one must first know who is telling it and for whom it is being told. Concerns with authorship are of the first priority, as are bibliographic and codicological matters that further situate the event of the telling and identify the person—and thus possibly the concerns and predispositions—of the author. Unfortunately, so far few literary scholars have turned their interest to what they view as bibliographical donkeywork for the sake of only marginally literary works (even more unfortunately, the exception to this is the very literary Garcilaso), while historians have been very little concerned with the details that would reveal Spanish bias in portrayal of the Indians, since Indians are of marginal interest to them. But further information is available in the text. One school of poststructuralist literary criticism, taking its cue on the one side from the phenomenological *epochē* and on the other from linguistic pragmatics, has come to be called "reader-response" literary criticism: it envisions the narrative as a cooperative venture entered into by the mutual participation of writer and reader and thus has attempted to deconstruct the interlocking strands of narrative that define the presence of an implied author, an implied audience, and perhaps also a narrator. This model of textual structure offers the tools for separating the habitus of teller and occasion from the tale, and its constructs fit very well with the cognitive model that has already been introduced in discussing the contact situation.

I have detailed elsewhere a mapping onto the cognitive process model of the version of reader-response theory advanced by Wolfgang Iser and will only summarize it here.[34] Iser's model of what happens as a reader apprehends a narrative is very detailed and includes the manipulation of the reader's apprehension process by the writer as well as the creative role of the reader's own activity: the reader brings to the narrative his world knowledge in terms of schemata or frames and a set of procedures for processing the text that are analogous to the procedures he uses in everyday life to call up frames matching real situations, instantiate their slots, and thus arrive at his options for what to do next, only in the case of reading he undertakes to plan what the characters will do next. The author, possessing the same competences and aware of what the reader will be doing, orchestrates the reader's experience by manipulating the way he processes the text: a blatant example is the author's trickery in persuading the reader to instantiate an erroneous frame in a mystery story so that he can resolve the reader's growing confusion by leading him to the correct frame in the denouement.[35] There is a higher level of this processing model that is directed at least partially by the reader's model of story reading itself, which includes a story grammar that would indicate the kinds of master scripts that the reader could expect. The goal of this higher level is the reduction of the sequence of instantiated frames encountered in processing the narrative to a single structure that Iser refers to as the "primary gestalt" but that will be in our terms one of the master scripts or in White's the culturally approved story.

The point of all this is that the author so directs the reader's activity that he arrives at the same story or overall cultural meaning from the narrative that the author wants him to perceive *and that this intention pervades the author's presentation of the events of the narrative.* But since we are not the author's or reader's contemporaries it is likely that the modern reader of an older text will not be receptive to this manipulative intention in the same way. Thus it must be the cultural context of the telling that offers additional clues for deciding what master script is being invoked. It is imperative that the literary context be examined here for judging historical texts: in the period in question (and to the present, it might be added) historical discourse was judged by the same canons as other products of literary art, and it is just as legitimate to compare sixteenth-century historical narratives with fictional ones as it is to compare them with contemporaneous narrative histories (which were few in any case). Indeed, in a sense it is fiction that most clearly demonstrates in its choice of script/plot what contemporaries (the implied reader) viewed with interest and favor and hence what kind of habitus the culture aspired to reproduce, for the New World was as much a flight of the imagination for the sixteenth-century Iberian as was the court of the Grand Turk, and the historical claims of chivalric romance were so seriously taken that some of them are only now being shown false.[36] What I am arguing is that the whole import of the narrative may have nothing at all to do with what actually happened: if we decide, for example, that Garcilaso's *La Florida* has much in common with chivalric romances that portray the triumph of the hero over adversity (evil Moors, rapacious barons) through knightly conduct and piety, then we will begin to understand why conflict between Indian and Spaniard is portrayed as chivalric tournament.

Having identified the script that provides the plot of the narrative, the task that remains is to "read out" the cultural preinterpretation of the narrative: to return the sequence of events to a relatively neutral annalistic format of "this happened and then this happened." For although in this format the sequential bias still remains, at least it can be made to bear no more than the implication of causality.

Here we come to the point where we have to bite the bullet and decide what shall be allowed to count as fact. Archaeologists have always done this with these texts as they selectively picked "descriptive" passages over the awkwardly inconvenient distances and directions as offering the unmediated reality the Spaniards saw; the difference here is that I am trying to make this process explicit and repeatable. The constructs of narrative theory make this possible. The task is simply to remove the interpretive apparatus constituted by all modifiers that express the narrator's and/or implied author's judgment of object, person, or action, to make conscious and thus to discard the frames that constitute the author's situational expectations and classificatory apparatus.[37] In semantic terms this means simply the removal of modifiers. To say, for example, that "the cacique approached boldly" is first to judge that the individual in question did actually hold and maintain any of a range of positions of dominance, which the Spaniard could not know. It is also to say that characteristics of the Indian's bearing and stride seem to have been read by the Spaniard as having an aspect of the masculine pride he understood, but again, neither he nor we could know that this was an appropriate reading of the Native's postural code. This sentence, then, can only validly yield "the man who, by virtue of sumptuary distinction and his treatment by others, we assumed was the leader, approached." Not very colorful or exciting, perhaps, but when such a process is carried out in extenso for one of these texts, an amazing thing happens: the story of Indian actions in response to invasion emerges from these tales of Spanish heroism like the transposition of figure and ground in a visual perception experiment. The resulting story of what the Indians did is still not comprehensible, nor should it be: we do not see all of it, and it does not match our own or the Spaniards' master scripts. But at least this version of events can be clearly seen to be incomprehensible in our terms, and we are no longer deluded by plausibility.

Limitations of the Direct Historical Approach

The Direct Historical Approach in archaeology, then, has serious limitations that are a direct consequence of the preinterpretation of the narrative sources used by the method. If the goal of such an effort is to wrest a nonmaterial interpretation from such archaeological cultures as can be tied to early contact documents, it must be recognized that an understanding of the document as an artifact of a process is indispensable and that the archaeology itself is going to have to help judge its truth.

Thus the archaeologist who has access to such materials will have to work harder than if he had none. He will have to find structure and implication in material remains that match what he finds in the "subtext" of the documents before he can use them with confidence. And above all, he will have to do some anthropology to the Europeans before he can understand the narrative artifacts they left. These Europeans, after all, were not participant observers. They wrote stories with themselves as the heroes and the Other as antagonist and background. They wrote stories for self-justification and glory; it was not necessary that they portray the places they went and the people they saw accurately—just that they do it convincingly. Unfortunately for archaeology, they succeeded.

Acknowledgment

I would like to thank the Hermon Dunlap Smith Center for the History of Cartography, Newberry Library, Chicago, for a short-term fellowship in 1987 that provided time and access to research materials for a good part of the work on this essay.

Notes

1. Wolf, *Europe.*
2. Smith, *Mississippian Settlement Patterns.*
3. Galloway, *Southeastern Ceremonial Complex.*
4. Cf. Dobyns, *Their Number Become Thinned.*
5. Smith, "Depopulation."
6. Pace Hudson, "The Uses of Evidence."
7. Steward, "The Direct Historical Approach."
8. See especially Brain, Toth, and Rodriguez-Buckingham, "Ethnohistoric Archaeology"; Williams and Brain, *Excavations*; Brain, *Tunica Treasure*; Brain, "The Archaeology of the Hernando De Soto Expedition."
9. DePratter, Hudson, and Smith, "The Hernando de Soto Expedition"; Hudson, Smith, and DePratter, "The Hernando de Soto Expedition."
10. Hudson et al., "Coosa."
11. Lockhart, *The Men of Cajamarca.*
12. Lockhart, *The Men of Cajamarca.*
13. Henige, "The Context."
14. Merrim, "The Castle of Discourse."
15. Todorov, *The Conquest of America.*
16. Bourdieu, *Outline*; Hodder, *Reading the Past.*
17. Schank and Abelson, *Scripts Plans Goals and Understanding*; Schank, *Dynamic Memory*; Minsky, *The Society of Mind.*
18. Calvin, "Introduction" and "Epilogue."
19. Dobyns, *Their Number.*
20. Todorov, *The Conquest of America*, 116–19.
21. Sahlins, *Historical Metaphors.*
22. Todorov, *The Conquest of America.*
23. Swanton, *Final Report.*
24. Robinson and Petchenik, *The Nature of Maps.*
25. For example, Kendall, "Construction of Maps."
26. Weddle, "Soto's Problems of Orientation."

27. Boston, "The 'De Soto Map.' "

28. Boston, "The Route of de Soto."

29. White, *Tropics of Discourse*, 81–99.

30. Lévi-Strauss, *Structural Anthropology*, 202–28.

31. For "cultural root paradigms" see Turner, "Social Dramas," 154.

32. White, *The Content of the Form*, 10.

33. Martin, *American Indian*.

34. Galloway, "Narrative Theories."

35. See Galloway, "Yngve's Depth Hypothesis."

36. Henige, "The Context."

37. Galloway, "Transaction Units."

5. Agustín Dávila Padilla's Fabulous History of the Luna Expedition

Ideology in Two Centuries

Nothing can be more risky than the attempt to distinguish jest from earnest in the literature of the distant past, for we are aliens to the culture and insensitive to its nuances.

WILLIAM NELSON, *Fact or Fiction: The Dilemma of the Renaissance Storyteller*

From 1559 to 1561 Tristán de Luna y Arellano tried in vain to establish a permanent Spanish settlement in the middle South starting from a base on the Gulf Coast. Although that expedition was amply recorded in the voluminous papers of several lawsuits arising from the colony's failure, recent reconstructions of the actions of the colonists and the routes of their explorations have made frequent and crucial use of an account embedded by the Dominican friar Agustín Dávila Padilla in his history of the Dominican order in Mexico, based in a complex way upon the eyewitness account of Domingo de la Anunciación, one of the Dominicans who accompanied Luna. In this paper I will discuss the relationship of this source to the historical context in which it was written and to the writing of providential history, compare its evidence to that offered by other documentation of the expedition, and argue that several extraneous agendas, rather than what actually happened, drove both its portrayal of a crucial incident in the Luna expedition and modern acceptance of that portrayal.

Background of the Expedition: Ongoing Conquest and the New Laws

The first of the successors of Hernando de Soto, Tristán de Luna y Arellano, was sent in 1559 to the Florida coast. Motivations for the expedition were

---

The material in this chapter was presented at the Gulf Coast History and Humanities Conference in Pensacola, Florida, on October 5, 1991. It has been revised for this volume.

already mixed. It was undertaken at the behest of Philip II of Spain to establish a haven for the Spanish treasure fleets at the height of Spain's "corsair war" against French pirates; supported by the viceroy of Mexico to find occupation for the sons of conquistadors seeking land and riches; and urged by the Dominican order of preachers and teachers, which, as the last order to come to Mexico, was eager to carve out for itself a larger region for conversions than was available to it there. Luna's mission was to establish a base on the Gulf of Mexico and then to find an overland route through the allegedly rich lands of Coça reported by Soto to establish another base at Santa Elena on the Atlantic. Luna himself had exploration experience with Juan Vásquez de Coronado and was a favored friend of the viceroy, Luis de Velasco.[1]

The expedition drew what profit it could from Soto's failure. Information about Soto's expedition was clearly available, and its more than 250 survivors were the reason why. Many had settled in Mexico and might be willing to return to Florida.[2] Luna's expedition included at least one man, Alvaro Nieto, who had certainly survived Soto's march, and two others, Rodrigo Vazquez and Juan de Vargas, whose names had appeared on the list of Soto's survivors or in accounts of the expedition.[3] Although Luna was as well informed as was possible, and two special coastwise explorations by Guido de Lavazares and Juan de Rentería had established in advance the place where he would land, his mission lay in the interior.[4] Because the Spaniards still did not know which rivers debouching on the Gulf Coast led to which Indians inland, exploration of the interior was an indispensable first task of the expedition, and the Soto survivors were counted on to lead it.

While Soto had been busy with his rape and pillage of the interior, however, the "Protector of the Indians," Dominican friar Bartolomé de las Casas, had succeeded in promoting the adoption in Spain of the so-called New Laws of 1542, which provided for radically better treatment of the native inhabitants of the new lands. No longer were Indians to be treated as though they had no right to govern themselves or hold lands. No longer were they to be made slaves or subjected to the bondage of *encomienda* tribute, which compelled them to labor for a Spanish overlord and served to finance the Spanish system of colonization. Existing *encomiendas* were to revert to the Crown on the death of the holder, effectively making the Indians direct tributaries of the Spanish king. From 1526 every expedition sent to explore had been obliged to be accompanied by at least two religious, who were empowered to consent to the granting of Indians in *encomienda* if they judged it was "for their own good."[5] Now they would be obliged to see that the Indians received fairer treatment.[6]

After the promulgation of the New Laws led to revolt and civil war by the *encomenderos* in Peru, some of these requirements were abated. Mexican ecclesiastics, who depended themselves on *encomienda* tribute to support their missions, were among the most avid in their opposition to these reforms, and the whole of Mexico had rejoiced when in 1545 the law limiting existing *encomienda* grants was revoked. Viceroy Velasco, when named to his post in 1550, had been charged particularly with the enforcement of the New Laws in Mexico, but in order to finance the colony and attract settlers he had asked the king to allow *encomienda* tribute in Florida from uncooperative Indians to begin as soon as the land was laid under conquest and settlements were established and to make even peaceful Indians pay *encomienda* tribute after some time. Velasco made these requests before he ever knew what application of the *encomienda* system would be recommended by the religious accompanying the expedition.[7]

There was in fact still one loophole that allowed immediate new *encomienda* grants: the "natural law" notion of a "just war" (still being used, we should remember, in our own country's war making). The ordinances of 1526 stated that a "just war" could be undertaken by the Spaniards to subjugate native peoples who refused to accept Christianity and acknowledge the sovereignty of the Spanish Crown or who were already at war among themselves; twenty years later were added as just causes for war the practice of human sacrifice or other cruelty and the incapacity for self-governance.[8] The purported idea was that by bringing indigenous people to submission, the conquistadors would bring about the good of a "Pax Hispanica" and stop them from killing each other. The original ordinance of 1526 stated that the two ecclesiastics accompanying expeditions had to approve in writing of the waging of war, or the responsible conquistador's contract would be revoked.[9]

Las Casas carried on a great debate with Juan Ginés de Sepúlveda on this very topic before Spanish jurists and ecclesiastics for four months in 1550 and 1551, arguing that there was no ground in natural law for the conquest of free people. The result was inconclusive, although Sepúlveda's writings were suppressed and those of Las Casas were published.[10] There was still no outright prohibition in law of a just war, nor was much done to ensure that the project of a just war would not be undertaken cynically simply to subjugate natives, since this was now the most certain way to appropriate their land and labor. It was in this legal context with reference to the region's inhabitants that the Luna expedition was undertaken.

Outline of the Expedition's Activities

The story of the expedition is quickly told. Initially, it made its landfall at Mobile Bay, where the reconnaissance of Lavazares had recommended that it land, but it returned eastward to establish its base at what was said to be the better anchorage of Ochuse, or Pensacola Bay, on August 14, 1559.[11] Early on, a hurricane destroyed the ships and much of the supplies, and the expedition was quickly thrown upon the resources of the countryside, which meant that, like Soto, it had to find Indians to find food.

Shortly after landing Luna had sent a party of men led by Soto veteran Nieto to explore the river emptying into the bay of Ochuse. These men returned after the hurricane with the news that they had found but one small village in 20 leagues' travel.[12] By September 24 Luna had sent another party of some two hundred men out overland under the military commander Mateo del Sauz to find the provisions that were now desperately needed. This time they met with success, finding "towns, a moderate number of people, and some provisions" in what was apparently the Mobile-Tensaw delta.[13] Although the Indian reaction to their presence was less than enthusiastic, Nieto and his men behaved with restraint, made friends of the natives, and sent word to Luna to join them in the town of Nanipacana. Luna moved the main settlement to Nanipacana in February 1560.

With the influx at the end of winter of nearly fifteen hundred expedition-aries to a village of no more than eighty small houses, all provisions were shortly exhausted. A detachment of a hundred men went 70 leagues up Nani-pacana's river in boats but found the populated lands vacated and empty land beyond.[14] The Spaniards were desperate for food, and once more a detach-ment of some two hundred men was sent forth, this time with the goal of seeking the concentration of Indian towns and Indian wealth that they imag-ined would provide the expedition with a sufficiency of provisions: Coça.

This polity had been remembered and described by the survivors of Soto's expedition as the richest that had been seen, and there were high hopes for it as a colony: Velasco's letters to Luna repeatedly referred to "the good country where Soto was" and identified it with Coça, urging Luna to find and exploit the riches there.[15] Velasco himself was familiar with available information about the Soto expedition; he mentioned sending to Luna "the memoir given me by Alvaro de la Torre, the cleric who was with Soto in those provinces," and referred to a "painting and description" of the region that he possessed.[16] Certainly, the Soto survivors Alvaro Nieto and Rodrigo Vazquez, who were a part of the detachment, would have recognized a place where they had spent more than a month.[17]

Having found Coça but reluctant to report that it was not all that had been hoped for, the party sent word to Luna to come and examine the land for himself. This word arrived in Nanipacana too late to be of use, for the starving thousand there, already seriously dissatisfied, formally refused to follow Luna deeper into the wilderness in search of food. After weeks of charges and countercharges, the main camp in Nanipacana was broken up on June 24, and the people returned to Mobile Bay to subsist on the seafood to be found there.

Some meager supplies had arrived at the port of Ochuse from Mexico, but royal orders were included to found a post at Santa Elena on the Atlantic Coast without further delay. Luna sent a party in that direction by sea, but it was thwarted by storm and shipwreck. When reports at last arrived from the party at Coça, he determined to approach the project by returning inland to Coça to establish a settlement, thence to proceed to the Atlantic Coast to found Santa Elena. This proposal precipitated the last pathetic act of this particular tragicomedy, when everyone from soldier to captain to clergyman entered into a massive lawsuit against their commander, maintaining not only that the men were unfit for such an expedition but that the commander was unfit to lead them. In the end, a small contingent was sent to Coça to recall the detachment to the port of Ochuse, and Luna was replaced by Villafañe. Little save the gathering of intelligence about the interior had been accomplished.

Source Materials for the History of the Expedition

What intelligence was in fact gathered is the issue that historians, anthropologists, and archaeologists have been grappling with ever since, for the simple fact is that the historical evidence represents many voices that do not agree. Herbert I. Priestley has noted that "it is a matter of more than ordinary interest that none of the contemporary documents collected and preserved by Luna himself mention any of the exciting incidents which the garrulous Dominican historian [Dávila Padilla] obtained some thirty years later from his coreligionist Father Anunciación."[18] This lack of corroboration is an initial warning that it is necessary to examine the evidence critically, not simply to use it to construct a single account that glosses over its inconsistencies. This is especially important because the conflict between these two kinds of sources mirrors perfectly the tension being discussed at the time between the value of scholarly authority (especially that of religious writers) and that of sworn judicial testimony.[19]

What is known about the history of Luna's expedition is based on the two major sources mentioned by Priestley, both ultimately focused on the actions and interests of the Spaniards rather than the Indians, both concerned in different ways with Indians only as means to Spanish ends. The first source is the one we are examining, a narrative account composed on the basis of the thirty-year-old reminiscences of one of the expedition's clergymen, Fray Domingo de la Anunciación and included in Fray Agustín Dávila Padilla's 1596 *Historia de la fundación y discurso de la provincia de Santiago de México.*[20] The second source is a dossier of letters and legal papers assembled in the course of the lawsuit issuing from the expedition's failure, translated and edited by Priestley as *The Luna Papers.*[21] There are certainly further undiscovered relevant materials in the Spanish and Mexican archives, but Priestley's work has seemed so definitive that it has tended to discourage further research. My concern in this paper is to discuss the work of Dávila Padilla, but *The Luna Papers* material offers crucial comparative perspective with a judicial-evidentiary focus.

The Dávila Padilla history of the expedition is of particular interest today because it seems to provide such a wealth of detail about the Indian societies of the interior that ethnologists and anthropologists have been eager to use it to understand the otherwise very poorly documented period during which many Indians of the Southeast were undergoing a transition from centrally organized chiefdoms to confederations of autonomous towns. Because there is such a dramatic difference between the Indians Soto saw in 1540 and those whom Iberville met in 1699, anthropologists who seek to understand the processes of social change find this particular transition of great interest. The only problem is that most of the apparently richest data on the southeastern Indians from the sixteenth century come from narrative accounts like this one, which do not adhere to the same conventions of historical objectivity that modern readers assume. Thus it is particularly important to examine this narrative and others like it with great care to discover what kind of primary reportage it actually provides.

For Dávila Padilla the account of the Luna expedition is only a part of a much longer general account of Dominican activities in New Spain. It has much the character of the many other epic narratives of conquistador activity in the New World: it purports to represent eyewitness testimony, although it is a secondary historical synthesis; it portrays the events of the expedition selectively to achieve rhetorical aims other than the relation of an "objective" history; and it is contradicted or at least uncorroborated by the "better" evidence of *The Luna Papers*. Robert Weddle has remarked upon Dávila Padilla's "lack of reportorial skills and geographical knowledge."[22] Priestley observed that its status of oral history thirty years after the fact caused the work to fall "into the class of memoirs or reminiscences rather than that of contemporary narratives."[23] In evaluating its worth to him in writing a modern history of the Mexican missions, Robert Ricard remarked that as a source the account "would be even more valuable if the author had been less stingy with chronological facts and less prodigal with edifying proverbs and anecdotes, as well as if, preoccupied to the point of exaggeration with extolling the personal virtues of his brothers of the order, he had not frequently relegated the collective work [of the order] to the background"—and Ricard, a Dominican friar himself, was a sympathetic reader of the work.[24]

Dávila Padilla was born in Mexico in 1562, studied and eventually taught theology at the University of Mexico, and joined the Dominican order in 1580. He had taken up the task of compiling an account of the activities of the Mexican Dominicans at the order of the General Chapter of Mexico in 1589. At that time he was given a manuscript and papers from a project that had been started in the middle 1550s by Andrés de Moguer, added to by Vicente de las Casas and Domingo de la Anunciación, and translated into Latin by Tomás Castellan.[25] By the time Dávila Padilla began to work on the history, Anunciación had long returned from Florida, had been an active evangelist among the Indians of Mexico, had become blind, and had retired to the Dominican convent. Indeed, the second part of the history contains an account of Anunciación's saintly life, which Dávila Padilla describes as marked by a history of self-discipline with a hair shirt and an iron chain, several episodes of destruction of pagan idols, devotion to Mary and the rosary (which enabled him to raise the dead on one occasion), and devotion to a fragment of the True Cross, which accounted for the miracles he performed in Florida and after his return.[26]

Dávila Padilla says he worked from manuscripts and from oral interviews with his confreres, and he explicitly mentions having heard some incidents of the Luna expedition from Anunciación's own lips.[27] He completed the work by 1592, when many of the necessary approvals for printing the work were secured, but could not have it printed in Mexico for lack of paper.[28] When he was sent to Spain in 1596 to represent Mexican Dominicans at the Chapter

General meeting in Valencia and subsequently to serve as procurator of his order at court, he was able to have his *Historia* printed by the house of Pedro Madrigal in Madrid. He became known and respected in Spain, was named chronicler of the Indies by Philip II after dedicating the *Historia* to the king, and was chosen to preach the sermon at Philip's funeral mass in 1598. Named archbishop of Santo Domingo, Dávila Padilla there ironically confronted serious depopulation from the same pirate activities that the Luna expedition had been meant to address. He died there in 1604.[29]

But clearly what Dávila Padilla and his predecessors were writing was providential history, history interpreted as evidence for the truth of Christian teachings and the continued action of God in the world.[30] It was also important for Dávila Padilla to represent Mexican Dominicans favorably so that Spanish authorities would support the continued work of the order and even its expansion. It was not (and is not) unusual for ecclesiastical writers to claim special evidences of holiness and even of the enactment of miracles for their own order or church, for obvious reasons; in the case at hand the Dominicans of Mexico had to establish a holiness track record that could compete with that of the Franciscans and the Augustinians.

In addition, in the context of the Counter-Reformation and the Inquisition as well as the serious discussions about the rights of conquered peoples that surrounded the New Laws, Philip II had been suppressing the publication of accounts of the conquest of the Americas for forty years.[31] Yet the king approved this history that highlighted the conquest as part of a sacred mission, and this seems to be how the publication was received at the time. In the second printing of the *Historia* in Madrid the title was changed to emphasize the Dominican connection with Florida and the attraction of its sensational subject matter: *Varia Historia de la Nueva España y Florida, donde se tratan muchas cosas notables, ceremonias de Indios, y adoracion de sus idolos, descubrimientos, milagros, vidas de Varones ilustres, y otras cosas sucedidas en estas Provincias*.[32] This rather less sober title also suggests that Dávila Padilla had taken his superiors seriously in their request that he "gather all the documents and write the history as a romance, and it is necessary to find out as much as possible from living observers, because of the brevity with which things are presented in the documents."[33] The word "romance" is a clue to the context of Renaissance historiography in which Dávila Padilla wrote, in which ethics and artistry were accorded as much worth as facts because of the edifying purpose that histories were supposed to have.[34]

The proof that Dávila Padilla was arguing for a specific view of the events in question can be seen in the Luna expedition account. Although Dávila Padilla's separate biography of Anunciación argues for the friar's saintliness and speaks particularly of his modesty, the account of the Luna expedition drawn from his testimony gives a central place to his own actions. I think it very likely that this story of the Luna expedition, otherwise very out of place in the history of the Mexican order, was put together by Anunciación's successors for a purpose more relevant to their own day. To the critical secular eye Dávila Padilla has assembled in the *Historia* a sort of mass hagiography so full of miraculous events that it soon becomes difficult to separate the real from the supernatural, and it is only the lack of an English translation of the entire history that has kept this fact from being blatantly obvious to modern English-speaking researchers. Dávila Padilla's narrative of the Luna expedition has never been evaluated for its historical value since the ethnologist John Swanton gave it his imprimatur by drawing on it verbatim for evidence about Creek towns, and Priestley himself drew upon it profusely for his introduction to *The Luna Papers* and his popular history of the Luna expedition.[35] But among historians of ecclesiastical writings in sixteenth-century Mexico Dávila Padilla's work is recognized as incorporating miracle narratives familiar from medieval times in compendia of exempla used for preaching and "as legitimating evidence for local saints and shrines."[36]

Dávila Padilla's *Historia* is divided into two books. Book I, which consists of 107 chapters, treats the actual roughly chronological history of the Dominican order in Mexico, including some lives of men prominent in that history, and the account of the Luna expedition has a dominant place in it, its fourteen chapters (chapters 58–71) accounting for 13 percent of the entire story. Book II is ninety-two chapters long, and it is made up of the life stories of significant Dominicans of the Mexican chapter; in this segment the life of Domingo de la Anunciación (chapters 73–83) occupies nearly 12 percent of the whole. This sheer numerical significance reflects, I think, the importance of the Florida project to the Mexican Dominicans.

The Dávila Padilla account of the Luna expedition would not have been included in the book at all if the expedition had not been an important project of the Mexican Dominican order. Dávila Padilla tells this tale to magnify Dominican holiness as he does all the other stories in his book. And the story of the Luna expedition is strongly structured by that intention, as the theme of Dominican steadfastness against evil is reiterated with nearly every chapter.

One need only enumerate the miracles performed by Anunciación to get the supernatural flavor of the whole:

1. Anunciación and Domingo de Salazar prayed chestnuts into ripeness on the way to Olibahali.
2. God caused a poisonous caterpillar crawling on the chalice of the mass to drop dead at Anunciación's request.
3. Observing the Coça chief make a pact with the devil for his people to defeat the Napochies, and failing to persuade them to eschew killing, Anunciación prayed on it—and God told the Napochies to flee and escape the Coça surprise attack.
4. Anunciación finally broke Luna's stubborn resistance to advice, after five months of praying, when God spoke through him to chastise Luna.
5. Anunciación then correctly predicted the very day that relief ships arrived.
6. For the last five months of the colony's ordeal God multiplied a tiny quantity of flour for Anunciación to be able to prepare the Host for the mass and make gruel for the sick.

Cheek by jowl with supposedly accurate ethnographic observation, these calmly accepted evidences of supernatural causation are bound to raise questions about the events themselves, and just as calmly scholars have weeded them out in their uses and citations of these materials. Swanton silently eliminated most of the supernatural apparatus from the segment he quoted.[37] Hudson mentioned only the caterpillar story in his retelling of the raid on the Napochies, ignoring the fact that these events form the central episode of the story precisely so that the teller can focus on how Anunciación, to thwart the Coça pact with the devil, was able to call on God to deliver the Napochies and thus save the Coças the sin of killing them.[38] But is it possible to take the good and leave the bad? Is it possible to weed out the unbelievable and leave only facts? I want to argue here that the author's purpose in creating the larger narrative history of the Dominican order in Mexico has so shaped the materials he used in telling the constituent stories that it is not now possible to depend upon any part of it as literal truth without specific kinds of external corroboration.

The Napochies Incident as Propaganda

I am not going to be concerned here with where Luna's expedition or any of its detachments went from Pensacola; that is another task. What I am concerned with is a specific incident portrayed only by Dávila Padilla and not mentioned at all by the other papers of the expedition because I think that incident casts into sharp relief two very relevant phenomena: (1) the Dávila Padilla account's reflection of his order's claim to the mission to the Indians of the interior Southeast and (2) its justification of just war and the granting of Coça people (defined as broadly as possible) in *encomienda*. The incident in question is a side trip supposedly made by a part of the detachment sent by Luna to Coça during which the Spaniards allegedly helped the Coça people subjugate rebellious tributaries, the Napochies.

The story surrounding this incident can be reconstructed from *The Luna Papers* alone. It begins with the departure from Nanipacana of the detachment to Coça. Led by Mateo del Sauz, it included Soto veterans Alvaro Nieto and Roderigo Vazquez, Luna's nephew Cristobal de Arellano, three other captains (two of infantry and one of cavalry), and the Dominican friars Domingo de la Anunciación and Domingo de Salazar, together with some fifty horsemen and one hundred infantry. This is the best reported of all the detached explorations, described by four letters dispatched from the Coça region (two to Luna, one to Velasco, one to a friar), two transcribed oral testimonies, and additional oral information from participants incorporated into the lawsuit against Luna, in addition to the narrative of Agustín Dávila Padilla.

The expedition departed on April 15 and had some forty days of hard going until it reached a town named Caxiti in the province of Taxcaluça, where enough food (35–40 or 80 fanegas of corn) to be worth sending was sent down the river they had been following on rafts with Juan de Porras and nine men.[39] Beyond Caxiti some ten days was Onachiqui (or Talis), believed by them to be the first Coça town.[40] From this point on they found the Indians at least nominally in residence (though women and clothing had been taken away), food for the asking, and crops ripening in the fields. Rations were short, since the first crop was not yet ready, but especially in Coça food was willingly sold to the Spaniards. They passed through two further named towns, Apica and Ulibahali, before reaching the main Coça town on August 1, where three of the letters were completed and carried to Luna by his nephew, Cristobal de Arellano, and twelve horsemen. Their accounts suggest that although there were roads and communication and trade between the Nanipacana-Atache-Upiache region and the Coça towns, settlement was scattered and cleared fields were few.

The Spaniards' characterization of what they found in the two populated areas was conditioned by what they were looking for: places to plant Spanish towns where they could be supported by *encomienda* labor, clearly stated over and over as being most desirably based upon field agriculture and broad pasturage for cattle.[41] To the Spaniards the Indian fields looked meager and poor, and the depth and impenetrability of the forests made the Indians themselves able to escape Spanish observation—and thus also domination—at will. The marginal superiority of the Coça region and the apparent exploitability of its population were offset by its large population's full utilization of its resources: if Spaniards settled, Indians would have to be ejected, for both populations could not be supported.[42]

In the Coça region the detachment found a large population in small towns of forty to fifty houses clustered along river floodplains. All the towns had a public space (*placa*) outside the town containing a sort of post set up in the middle of it, and some had walls for defense and temples for worship, though no specifics were described.[43] The Spaniards observed both winter and summer houses. They remarked that the very limited cleared lands in the floodplains barely sufficed to feed the Indians themselves, but in default of corn the Spaniards had been able to subsist on nuts, berries, and acorns.

As for the main Coça town and its leader, a great deal is implied and inferred about his power. Upon entering the Coça "province" the detachment was sent a *prencipal* to serve as guide and messenger, and burden-bearers served willingly in consideration of payment in trade goods. Sauz worried that after the harvest the Indians might be less obliging, but he grimly soldiered on to Coça town to carry out his mission. Reaching Coça and settling their camp on cleared land outside the town, members of the detachment learned what they reasoned must be the cause of the cordial reception they had received.

The chief of Coça was said to have willingly placed his people and lands under the protection of the Spanish king in order to obtain relief from "certain Indians" who had encroached upon Coça lands and cut off trade and communication routes.[44] It is interesting to note what source gives us this information: the first joint letter from all the expedition leaders, including Anunciación, to Luna. It is equally interesting to note that these same people wrote a second letter on the same day to Viceroy Velasco that repeats many details from the first but only says that the Coça chief "submitted himself to the protection of the king" without saying why.[45] Furthermore, the expedition's military leaders *did not report any follow-up by the Spaniards*. The only source that elaborates on the incident is Dávila Padilla, allegedly reporting a story told by Anunciación. Depositions made in Hispaniola by two soldiers of the detachment after the failure of the expedition also did not mention the encroaching Indians or any Spanish efforts to eject them.[46]

A closer look at the incident as described by Dávila Padilla shows that it incorporates both literary borrowings and rhetorical devices that alone move it some considerable distance from any direct portrayal of actual events. To begin with, it is obvious from a simple analysis of the structure of the tale that the Napochies incident is seen as important by us as readers because Dávila Padilla has foregrounded it structurally. The account of this episode occupies three of fourteen chapters and fully 25 percent of the space he devoted to the entire Luna expedition. Second, a major miracle performed by Domingo de la Anunciación, the prevention of actual bloodshed in the proposed attack by the Coça people on the Napochies, is accomplished by God's warning as a direct result of the friar's prayer—a prayer elicited as much by his revulsion for a ceremony that he interpreted as a devilish pact entered into by the Coça chief to guarantee victory as by his concern for the health of the Napochies. The fact that the Napochies were somehow warned and then fled is taken as proof of the efficacy of the friar's prayer, of God acting in the history of the expedition.

The story itself is full of epic touches. According to Dávila Padilla, the Coça people had ancient rights of domination over the Napochies, but of late years, as their own numbers waned, they found the Napochies, who were growing in numbers, less willing to pay the accustomed tribute, until at last they refused. Since the Coça people were unable to defeat the Napochies in battle, they asked the men of the Spanish detachment to help them do so in consideration of the hospitality they had provided. The Spaniards consulted together and decided to send one troop of horse and one of foot, to a total of fifty men, along with one friar to make up an army with the Coça people. This decision handily made Anunciación into the only witness of events. The Coças were said to be delighted and assembled three hundred bowmen for the expedition (thus providing the occasion for a classical digression on native weaponry).

The actual expedition is related not as a series of events but as a series of set pieces. First we see a description of the Coça marching order, which is likened to that of the children of Israel. Then there is a curious ceremonial in which the chief of the Coça army mounts on a sort of scaffold built in an open plain, carries out a threat pantomime in the direction of the Napochies, and then chews up and spits out seeds that he likens to the Napochies. Anunciación, we are told, considered this a pact with the devil, which implies that neither he nor Dávila Padilla recognized it as anything they had ever heard of. Next, as the Spaniards prepared to spend a hungry night, as no one had brought food, they were attracted by sounds of great celebration in the Coça camp, where they were able to see the leader encouraging his men with a vigorous talk, reminding them of the seriousness of the venture. Dávila Padilla remarked that the resemblance between the Indian captains' feudal oath sworn to their leader and that of the ancient Romans must have been due to the commonalities of war in all places and times.

The following day the army reached the country of the Napochies and decided to wait until night to attack; the same ceremonial was repeated, with the men swearing fealty to their captains. Spies sent into the Napochie town found it very quiet, and Anunciación, worried about the potential for so many unbaptized deaths, pleaded in vain with the Coça people not to kill the Napochies but only to take them prisoner. Failing in that, he prayed to God, who warned the Napochies to vacate their village. Thus the next morning the Coça people found only an empty village, but they were so enraged when they found the scalps of their people on display that they tortured a completely innocent prisoner left behind by the Napochies, and Anunciación was unable to manage a deathbed conversion. The friar was able to thwart the burning of the village, however, by persuading the Spanish captain to threaten to leave if the Coça people did not extinguish the fire. After this the Coça chief took possession of the village with great ceremony and sent all its corn back to his town.

The Napochies had still not been found, and as they were not in evidence anywhere the Coça people left a small garrison in the town and led the Spaniards to a large river they called Oquechiton, which Dávila Padilla tells us was what the Spaniards called the River of the Holy Spirit. There they found two recently vacated villages and took possession of their corn. Pursuing the fleeing Napochies across the great river (Anunciación remained with the cacique dry and safe on the near side) and with the benefit of a demonstration of Spanish marksmanship with a gun, the Coça people ran the Napochies to ground on a spit of land, and the Napochies surrendered. At the request of the Spaniards they were treated graciously and received back into their former position of subjection after promising to pay a tribute of hunted and gathered foods. The Spanish-Coça army returned to the first Napochie village, rested for three days, and then returned to Coça.

Whether all this happened or not, not a word about the Napochies incident appears in any other papers of the expedition. Why would Anunciación so magnify this particular incident in the context of his own eventful life of service in Mexico or Dávila Padilla so emphasize Luna's failed project as part of Mexican Dominican history?

After the collapse of Luna's colony under Mexican administration, the next colonization project was administered directly from Spain, and Pedro Menéndez de Avilés succeeded in founding San Agustín in 1565. Like Velasco, Menéndez had an ambition to conquer all the land north of Mexico, and he began by missionizing Florida Indians with the help of the Jesuits. In 1573 he introduced Franciscans to this work, but their efforts were still limited to the Atlantic coast and peninsular Florida by 1589, when Dávila Padilla began his work. Thus the interior mission field was still open to claims by Dominicans.

In addition, the Napochies incident is almost a textbook example of the application of the "just war" doctrine, so happily and repeatedly used as an excuse by the Soto expedition and so exhaustively argued by Las Casas and Sepúlveda. Anthropologists have interpreted the incident as suggesting both that paramount chiefdoms were under stress and using violence to maintain the subordination of tributaries and that one polity might use the Spaniards as a tool against another (both of these arguments support another for the existence of paramount chiefdoms by presupposition). In the actual documents, however, there is conflicting evidence as to the political situation the Spaniards saw in Coça.

Dávila Padilla portrayed a clear-cut case of a feudal subordinate, the Napochies polity, being returned to its tributary status, but with a twist: although the presence of the two priests in Coça meant that with their approval the war could take place, thanks to the prayers of Anunciación no war was actually conducted. Spanish participation in this action, however, constituted a claim of sovereignty over the reestablished paramount as well as the rebellious subordinate, and the argument could be made that Anunciación's role in it meant that the Dominicans had already begun the evangelization of the Coça people. The broader the claims for the control of people and lands by the Coça chiefdom, the broader the region over which the Dominicans might have authority.

The letters sent from Coça by the Spanish detachment leaders, on the other hand, indicated that the Coça chief was complaining of another who had "usurped" and "made demands" upon his people, who had cut off communication "with his own people," occupied roads, and stopped trade. He requested that the Spaniards aid him in restoring communication and trade with "his own natural lord."[47] This is a very different picture, suggesting that the Coça people themselves had a tributary status with reference to some other group and that the Napochies were possibly incomers to the area. It might even be taken to imply that the Coça people could not speak for the region in accepting Spanish sovereignty. And these letters do nothing to support a Dominican claim to the mission.

Making History

Why have scholars interested in the history of non-European people in the Southeast been so eager to make selective literal use of Dávila Padilla's *Historia* in spite of its distance from the events and the possibility that its portrayal of those events was influenced by a Dominican missionary agenda? One obvious reason is the lack of historiographical criticism of Dávila Padilla's book, which I hope this paper has at least pointed out. Second, authorities have accepted it: Priestley used it selectively to write both his introduction to *The Luna Papers* and his later popular account of the expedition, and Swanton not only used it without question but even published a handy translation of the passage on the Napochies, provided to him by Mrs. F. Bandelier.[48] Finally, most of the research carried out since both men wrote has been done for a focused purpose by researchers who appear not to have been familiar with the whole of Dávila Padilla's work (which has still not been translated into English) and who were thus unaware of how the story of the Luna expedition fit into his arguments for the saintliness of Domingo de la Anunciación, the worthiness of the Mexican Dominicans, and the solidity of their claim to Florida missions. Finally, the portrayal of Indian polities fit very well with a neat model of sociopolitical change in the interior Southeast that both affirmed the importance and geographical spread of the Coça chiefdom seen by Soto and witnessed its crumbling as a result of European contact.[49]

There is a significant problem here, too, that echoes the Renaissance discussions about authority versus eyewitnessing in historical evidence. In our time the "judicial" model for historical evidence has triumphed: German positivist historiography that valorized the use of first-person witness, written documents over any other kind of evidence underlies the historiographical model that supported the widespread establishment of archives that would legitimate nation-states and that encouraged the professionalization of history, turning it away from obvious moral exempla written well by respectable people and toward an ideal of the investigative discovery of "truth," however morally unedifying.[50] This kind of model, humanized by the interest of the Annales school and social historians in happenings among lowly as well as exalted people, has persisted in spite of growing questioning of the entire post-Rankean historical enterprise as anything much *other* than edifying exempla, ideology, and/or professional social-capital accumulation by historians.[51]

Where does this leave historical archaeology, whose material evidence is solid (to the extent that we are not made uneasy by the degree to which research designs are prey to the same concerns as those for history) but whose interpretation of that evidence is frequently dependent upon an equally solid and unproblematic historical record? If the historical record is called into question (and in the case of the historical record of colonized people written by the colonizers this is becoming more common every day), where can archaeologists go to find out what their evidence means? Uprooted in this manner, made uncertain as a coherent picture of indigenous life at any time before indigenous participation in the enterprise Europeans call history, what can archaeological evidence even be for?

Well, perhaps it can be for deconstructing colonialist history.[52] Dávila Padilla's version of the relations between Coça and its neighbors, the very idea that Coça had tributaries in 1560, is called into question by a more recent critical view of the archaeological evidence that suggests what the other Luna documents show: that Coça was not as impressive as it had been made out to be by the Soto survivors (and this included Roderigo Ranjel, who was involved in arguing for what became the Luna expedition).[53] Archaeological arguments have more recently pointed to a more nuanced reading of what "paramount chiefdom" might mean with reference to the sixteenth-century Southeast and more specifically to ranked societies in collision with new and dangerous intruders. They suggest that Coça's apparent importance at the time of the Soto expedition had itself perhaps been an artifact of the encounter, representing the visible part of a "mutual nonaggression pact" in which Coça was an important participant.[54] As is frequently the case with the increasing sophistication of archaeological recovery and analysis, it may be the interpretation of the archaeological evidence that urges us to look once more at the verisimilitude of a history. It could be that in this case such questions will turn us back once more to the sources and what they tell us about the concerns of Mexican Dominicans as they played their part in the clashes of empires and peoples.

Notes

1. For the political background of the expedition see Hoffman, *A New Andalucia*, chap. 7, "The Luna Expedition and European Diplomacy, 1557–1559."

2. Avellaneda, *Los sobrevivientes*, 73.

3. Weddle, *Spanish Sea*, 266.

4. Weddle, *Spanish Sea*, 257–60.

5. Simpson, *The Encomienda*, 70–71.

6. Hanke, *The Spanish Struggle*.

7. Hanke, *The Spanish Struggle*, 94–105.

8. See Adorno, "The Discursive Encounter," 213n14.

9. Adorno, "The Discursive Encounter," 111–12.

10. Adorno, "The Discursive Encounter," 116–31.

11. Priestley, *The Luna Papers*, 1:xxiv; Swanton, *Final Report*, 164; Weddle, *Spanish Sea*, 267.

12. Priestley, *The Luna Papers*, 2:302–3.

13. Priestley, *The Luna Papers*, 1:93.

14. Priestley, *The Luna Papers*, 2:290–91.

15. Priestley, *The Luna Papers*, 1:181.

16. Priestley, *The Luna Papers*, 1:75. It is unfortunate that neither of these sources appears to be extant.

17. Weddle, *Spanish Sea*, 266.

18. Priestley, *Tristán de Luna*, 129.

19. Adorno, "The Discursive Encounter."

20. Dávila Padilla, *Historia de la fundación*. I have personally struggled, with the considerable assistance of Anne Gilfoil, with translating the whole of the Luna segment and the biography of Anunciación but have examined the whole work for structure and emphasis.

21. Priestley, *The Luna Papers*.

22. Weddle, *Spanish Sea*, 250.

23. Priestley, *The Luna Papers*, 1:ix.

24. Ricard, *The Spiritual Conquest of Mexico*, 317. The translation here is mine.

25. Millares Carlo, *Cuatro estudios*, 189.

26. The biography of Anunciación is contained in Dávila Padilla, *Historia de la fundación*, 2:599–625.

27. Dávila Padilla, *Historia de la fundación*, 1:227. According to the biography, Anunciación died in 1591 at age eighty, three years after Dávila Padilla had taken up the writing task. This would imply that Anunciación had not in fact written a history of the expedition while he himself was working on the *Historia*, although Dávila Padilla credits him with the core of the history of the order up to the year 1580 (*Historia de la fundación*, 2:625). Clearly, Dávila Padilla had access to Anunciación as an informant, because the old friar lived in the Dominican convent for the last six years of his life.

28. Millares Carlo, *Cuatro estudios*, 183. The problems with printing the work are described in the "Prologue to the Reader."

29. Millares Carlo, *Cuatro estudios*, 173–80.

30. It can be argued that in the sixteenth century all history being written by Europeans—or even by aspirant Europeans like Garcilaso de la Vega el Inca—was written as providential history to some degree, but clearly this degree could be dramatically greater in the hands of an ecclesiastical historian like Dávila Padilla.

31. Adorno, "The Discursive Encounter," 219.

32. Millares Carlo, *Cuatro estudios*, 184, fig. 6. The text from *tratan* onward was paraphrased and elaborated by the printer from Dávila Padilla's prologue: "En el discurso de la lectura se tratan algunas cosas notables de pestes, ceremonias, ídolos, descubrimientos, milagros y otras cosas que han sucedido en la Nueva España y son dignas de saberse" (quoted in Millares Carlo, *Cuatro estudios*, 189–90).

33. The text: "Recoger todos los papeles y escrivir historia en romance, y fue menester averiguarse lo más con originales vivos, por la cortedad con que se hallan las cosas en los papeles" (quoted in Millares Carlo, *Cuatro estudios*, 189).

34. Dowling, "*La Florida del Inca*"; see 100–106 for a discussion of historiography in the late sixteenth century.

35. Swanton, *Early History*, 230–39 and passim; Priestley, *Tristán de Luna*.

36. See Burkhart, "'Here Is Another Marvel,'" 91.

37. Swanton, *Early History*, 231–39.

38. Hudson et al., "The Tristán de Luna Expedition."

39. Priestley, *The Luna Papers*, 1:224–25, 234–35, 2:290–91. The quantities vary in the sources.

40. Priestley, *The Luna Papers*, 1:224–25, 236–37, 2:290–91.

41. Priestley, *The Luna Papers*, 1:200–201, 206–7, 214–17, 220–21, 226–27, 240–41.

42. Priestley, *The Luna Papers*, 1:240–41.

43. Priestley, *The Luna Papers*, 1:338–41.

44. Priestley, *The Luna Papers*, 1:230–33.

45. Priestley, *The Luna Papers*, 1:238–39.

46. Weddle, *Spanish Sea*, 284.

47. Priestley, *The Luna Papers*, 1:230–33.

48. Swanton, *Early History*, 239n1. Remarkably, in *Conversations with the High Priest of Coosa* Charles Hudson has taken a postmodern approach to ethnohistorical writing by fictionalizing the background context of this very questionable source (and so arguably returning it to its fictional roots) in order to provide a setting for a revised and updated version of his work on southeastern myth.

49. For a summary of this research see Smith, *Coosa*. Throughout, echoing the historiographical confusion of much of this work, Smith cites Dávila Padilla as though he were an independant witness to these events.

50. This history of history is outlined in Novick, *That Noble Dream*.

51. See as outline and example Jenkins, *Why History?*

52. It should be noted, for those who may have a knee-jerk reaction to this word, that "deconstruction" refers to an attempt to *understand* that which is deconstructed together with the interests that went into making it, not necessarily to *destroy* it utterly except as ideology. To the extent that archaeologists pride themselves on being scientists, they should also accept the likelihood that anything they think they know may be fundamentally uncertain—Heisenberg, after all, lies as much at the heart of the dreaded postmodernism as does Heidegger or any Frenchman.

53. Hoffman, *A New Andalucia*, 147.

54. Smith, *Coosa*, 93. See also Hally, Smith, and Langford, "The Archaeological Reality."

6. Natchez Matrilineal Kinship

Du Pratz and the Woman's Touch

Kinship and Social Organization

In all societies kinship is one of the most powerful glues holding people together, and families are fundamental units of the social structure. But in spite of recent attempts to arrive at a very specific definition in our own society of what a family is, not only is it difficult to find many examples of any single narrow definition (particularly with a near 50 percent divorce rate), and not only are there many varieties of family structure in the past and in other places that differ dramatically from the so-called standard nuclear family consisting of a breeding couple and their children, but as soon as any such system is closely examined we learn that there are always myriad exceptions and adaptations to local conditions.[1]

Anthropologists who study the larger primates have shown that they clearly recognize those they grew up with and prefer to live with them. Among wild groups of our closest genetic relative, the chimpanzee, residential groups consist of related adult females and their young offspring that adult males may temporarily join if invited. In spite of attempts to romanticize the evidence, many researchers think that groups of our ancestor *Homo habilis*—made famous by the discovery of the bones of "Lucy" in Kenya—were organized in just this way as they began to exploit the East African savannah from the forest's edge, which is thought to be the course these ancestors took as they became *Homo sapiens*.

I take the liberty of starting thus "before the Flood" to emphasize the

The material in this chapter was first presented as a paper, "Natchez Matrilineal Kinship: Du Pratz and the Woman's Touch," at "Southern Women: 300 Years of Influence," the Natchez Literary Celebration in Natchez, Mississippi, February 1–3, 1996. It has been revised for this volume.

noninevitability of male-headed nuclear families. In fact, until recently, when life expectancy began to improve with the advances of modern medicine, it was the lineage—the expanded family of as many generations as anyone can manage to remember—rather than the actively reproducing couple that dominated as the conceptual family in most cultures. Further, until the Industrial Revolution drew the majority of workers away from farming (and immigration and pioneering fragmented extended European families as they stretched their boundaries to settle North America), extended multigenerational families represented the most important economic unit all over the earth, and in most parts of the world this is still the case in spite of globalization.

Matriliny

The question is, How shall such lineages be organized? There are only two choices that preserve lineages: the principle of kinship shall be traced either through the father (patriliny) or through the mother (matriliny). Our own system of bilateral kinship tends to fragment lineage groups because each generation introduces additional groups with a claim on family loyalties. This is not generally true of either pure patriliny or matriliny, although it is clear that one is stronger than the other. Perhaps surprisingly, it is patrilineal kinship that is the weaker of the two in keeping large corporate groups together in the absence of other social infrastructure apart from kinship. Historically, patriliny characterized hunter-gatherer groups that lacked permanent settlement and formed bands of no more than twenty-five people. Matriliny, on the other hand, was frequently characteristic of sedentary groups, mostly farmers, that lived in hamlets, towns, and even cities.

Another characteristic of kinship reckoned by matrilineal descent is that it is supported by the practice of matrilocal residence: this means that males marry *into* the matrilineage and either go to live with their wives' families or visit there periodically. Scholars have maintained that "matrilocality is a necessary but not sufficient condition for the development of matrilineal descent groups, which perhaps cohere about the control of resources worked by women, women's production, or their equipment."[2] This was the case with the mound-building southeastern Indians, of whom the Natchez have been considered to be a representative group. Scholars have pointed out that matrilines might also incorporate avunculocal (living in the household of the mother and her brother) or duolocal residence principles.

It should be stressed that although patrilineal kinship generally implies patriarchy, or rule by men, in general matriliny does not mean matriarchy but rather a more gender-equal social organization. The matrilineal family is relatively matrifocal, in our terminology. In the southeastern case, households were headed by the eldest woman and her brother. Husbands were visitors; men's primary duty was to the household of their sisters. Children were considered not to be significantly related to their fathers or their fathers' kin. Governance in such societies may *apparently* only include women in a minor way, but land and housing are usually the property of the matriline, and males involved in governance are frequently selected by the women of their matrilines.

The Natchez Example

The famous descriptions of Natchez kinship by eighteenth-century French observers—which really only offer details on the kinship practices of Natchez elites—have been discussed endlessly by anthropologists for many years. They apparently portray a quite exceptional variant of matrilineal kinship, created by overlaying on the basic matrilineal principle the special treatment accorded to the elites. John R. Swanton, who was among the first to study the matter in detail and comparatively, determined on the basis of French descriptions that the Natchez kinship system consisted of hierarchical classes of Suns, Nobles, Honored People, and "Stinkards" (or commoners). The three upper classes were all obliged to marry commoners, while commoners could marry anyone. Class membership depended upon the class of the mother unless she was a commoner and married above her class; men of the other three classes were obliged to marry commoner women, but their children only "descended" by one class level, not necessarily to commoner level. In other words, the matrilineal principle did not strictly hold for the children of the two highest classes, since their children moved "down" one class only, even if their mothers were commoners.

This alleged process of class variation occasions the so-called Natchez paradox. Some anthropologists have calculated that this system would have exhausted the supply of marriage partners available from the commoner class after ten generations.[3] This timescale conflicts with the archaeological dating of the Plaquemine archaeological manifestation of Natchez culture. As a result, many solutions have been proposed to explain these contradictions. One researcher even suggested that commoner women might have been more fertile than Sun women.[4] Others have seen the Natchez system as less complex than Swanton believed, consisting instead of only two classes, noble and commoner, where the Suns were a special "royal family" part of the nobility and "Honored" was only a nonhereditary status title for the sons of noble fathers or for commoners who had achieved that status.[5] Archaeologists have argued that all such theoretical discussions disregard the historical context and that the requirement for marrying commoners was likely a device for the assimilation of refugee populations fleeing the disaster of European disease epidemics in the sixteenth and seventeenth centuries.[6]

All of this discussion has been based in greater or lesser detail on French accounts of the Natchez. That of Antoine Simon Le Page du Pratz is the most complete and best known of these and is usually given pride of place, although, like all the rest, it has been observed to describe kinship from a male and patriarchal point of view.[7] Let us, therefore, hear what Du Pratz has to say about Natchez kinship.

> The Natchez nation is composed of nobility and common people [*du Peuple*]. The common people are called in their language Miche-Miche-Quipy, which signifies Puant, a name, however, that offends them and that no one dares to pronounce before them, for it would put them in a very bad humor. The common people have a language entirely different from that of the nobility, to whom they are submissive to the last degree. That of the nobility is soft, solemn, and rather rich. The substantives are declined, as in Latin, without articles. The nobility is divided into Suns, Nobles, and Honored men. The Suns are so named because they are descended from a man and a woman who made them believe that they came out of the sun, as I have said more at length in speaking of their religion.
>
> The man and woman who gave laws to the Natchez had children and ordained that their race should always be distinguished from the mass of the nation and that none of their descendants should be put to death for any cause whatsoever but should complete his days calmly as nature should permit. The need for preserving their blood pure and faithful made them establish another usage, of which examples are seen only in a nation of Scythians, of which Herodotus speaks. As their children, being brothers and sisters, were unable to intermarry without committing a crime, and as it was necessary in order to have descendants that they marry commoner men and commoner women, they wished in order to guard against the disastrous results of the infidelity of the women that the nobility should be transmitted

HISTORIOGRAPHY

only through women. Their male and female children were equally called Suns and respected as such but with this difference, that the males enjoyed this privilege only during their lives and personally. Their children bore only the name of Nobles, and the male children of Nobles were only Honored men.[8] These Honored men, however, might by their warlike exploits be able to reascend to the rank of Nobles, but their children again became Honored men, and the children of these Honored men, as well as those of the others, were lost in the common people and placed in the rank of commoners. Thus the son of a female Sun (or Sun woman) is a Sun, like his mother, but his son is only a Noble, his grandson an Honored man, and his great-grandson a commoner. Hence it happens, on account of their long lives (for these people often see the fourth generation), that it is a very common thing for a Sun to see his posterity lost among the common people.[9]

The women are free from this unpleasantness. From mother to daughter nobility is maintained, and they are Suns in perpetuity without suffering any alteration in dignity. However, they are never able to attain the sovereignty any more than the children of the male Suns, but the eldest son of the female Sun nearest related to the mother of the reigning Sun is the one who mounts the throne when it becomes vacant. The reigning Sun bears the title of Great Sun.

As the posterity of the two first Suns has become much multiplied, one perceives readily that many of these Suns are no longer related and might ally themselves together, which would preserve their blood for the most part without any mixture, but another law established at the same time opposes an invincible obstacle, namely, that which does not permit any Sun to die a violent death. It is this, that it was ordered that when a male or female Sun should come to die his wife or her husband should be put to death on the day of the funeral in order to go and keep them company in the country of spirits. That could not be carried out if the wife and husband were both Suns, and this blind and barbarous custom is so punctually observed that the Suns are under the pleasing necessity of making mésalliances. (2:393–97)

In a more general vein, Du Pratz offered additional remarks that clearly refer to the male head of a matrilineal household, what the Creek would call a "clan uncle": "An old man who is the chief of a family is called Father by all the children of the same household, be it by the nephews or grand-nephews; the natives often say that such a one is their father; he is the head of their family; and when they want to speak of their proper father they say that such a one is their true father" (2:313). And elsewhere on living conditions Du Pratz observes: "The same household ordinarily contains the same family" (2:321), that is to say, an extended family.

Du Pratz's account only gave details for the Natchez nobility. In addition, he was only interested in what happened to the male children, as we would expect from a European male from a patriarchal society. Yet how did Du Pratz learn this information, particularly when he says the Natchez were unwilling for outsiders to know about the class declension of Sun men's offspring? We know that he lived among the Natchez as the manager of his own plantation for eight years, from 1719 to 1728, during at least part of which time he was on friendly terms with the most important members of the Sun class. Most commentators reason that his experience and friendship with the Natchez nobility make his observations privileged, but nobody ever talks about how he established these friendly terms. The whole story of Du Pratz's knowledge of Natchez lifeways is not limited to his own skill as an ethnographer. As is very frequently the case when some historical fact is being ignored, it is necessary to *chercher la femme*.

The Chitimacha Slave Woman

In 1718 Du Pratz temporarily settled on the "Bayou Tchoupic" preparatory to establishing a plantation on Bayou St. Jean near the newly established New Orleans. At that time he "bought from a neighboring settler a native slave in order to be certain of a person to cook food for us. . . . We did not understand one another yet, my slave and I, but I made her understand by signs, which the natives understand easily; she was of the nation of the Tchitimachas, with whom the French had been at war for several years" (1:82-83). The Chitimachas were a small tribe, probably of the Tunican language family, living west of the Mississippi around Bayou Lafourche. Sporadic fighting had been going on between the French and the Chitimachas since 1707, and many Chitimacha people had been taken captive and sold as slaves among the French. Those who have read Du Pratz's *Histoire de la Louisiane* in French will know that although this young woman's story does not dominate the book, she is referred to several times as the source of information on Indian traditions. This information and much of the detail about her are missing from the 1774 English translation and so have been frequently overlooked in the scholarship on Du Pratz.[10]

Although Du Pratz was handicapped by lack of a knowledge of Indian languages at first, he said that this young Chitimacha woman learned French "rather well" within something over a year, while Du Pratz learned what he referred to as "the vulgar language of the country" (1:90), probably not Natchez but the Mobilian trade language that seems to have been a kind of Choctaw pidgin.[11] At any rate, he seems *not* to have learned Chitimacha. He asked her to translate and explicate for him when in late 1718 he observed a calumet ceremony in New Orleans in which peace was cemented between the French and the Chitimachas. The minute detail of his ensuing account of the speeches at the ceremony implies that she did an excellent job (1:107–14).

Du Pratz's Chitimacha slave woman was also instrumental in his decision to make the move to the Natchez country. She argued for its beauty, healthfulness, and fertility, but she also said that because she "had relatives who retired there during the war that we [the Chitimachas] had with the French, they would bring us things that we need" (1:91). These relatives were more important than Du Pratz initially expected. At the Chitimacha calumet ceremony he learned that her father was a "relative to the sovereign" of the Chitimachas through an elder daughter, who was the chief's wife. Her father was also the hero of the day among the French for having killed the murderer of the missionary St. Cosme. He had thought his daughter dead and visited Du Pratz to express his delight in finding her and his wish that she should return to her nation.

Du Pratz worried that her father's heroism and its appreciation by the French might force him to return his slave, although the conditions of the peace that had been made explicitly exempted the French from returning Chitimacha slaves.[12] But the young woman "declared that she did not wish to leave me. I had the happiness to find in her an excellent creature. I had treated her with much gentleness; she had become attached to me and had lost the custom of going nearly naked, as in her country" (1:115). She explained that with her mother dead and her father in peril from the revenge of his victim's relatives, both of them would be more secure if her father went to Natchez to join "their relatives of that nation." Her father agreed that his great age made this a realistic plan, and Du Pratz described how the old man "granted me his rights over his daughter by placing her between the two of us, carrying my right hand onto her head, and putting his own on top of it. He then pronounced several words that signified that he gave her to me for my daughter after this ceremony and after having spent a week at my house" (1:116). In the event, the old man died only a few days after his arrival in Natchez, but Du Pratz congratulated himself on having "a faithful person attached to my interests" who could help him obtain laborers through her Natchez relatives. This supposed adoption ceremony does seem to have features that point to a formal transmission of authority over the young woman from the father to another. The incident suggests that she no longer held the status of slave, at least in her own and her relatives' eyes. It is arguable that her power to influence subsequent events in Du Pratz's favor would not have been so effective had she continued to be considered a slave.

Du Pratz's language acquisition did not include Natchez in the early days of his settlement in the Natchez country, since he purchased land from the Natchez by means of an interpreter. (He does not say who or indeed what language was used; it could have been the young woman using Chitimacha or Natchez [1:126–27].) And it was quite soon, within six months, that he found himself disabled with sciatica that kept him housebound and under her care for four months before he was persuaded (by her?) to try a native cure, which worked perfectly (1:135–36). In three more years, however, Du Pratz's position with reference to the Natchez elites was significantly altered. In 1723 he had to lead the colonists in defense against a minor Natchez uprising, and it was to him that the Natchez brought the calumet of peace instead of to the post commandant. Du Pratz portrayed himself discussing the outcome with Natchez war chief Tattooed Serpent, and this unmediated intimacy apparently continued. When next Du Pratz needed medical help, the Great Sun himself sent him his personal physician. From this point onward in Du Pratz's narrative we hear almost nothing of the Chitimacha woman. Had she provided him with the entrée he needed to establish close relations with the Natchez elites?

It is not precisely clear when Du Pratz began to learn something of the Natchez language or just how far he got with it, but he needed the help of his slave woman to get in contact with his first informants about Natchez history and culture. "Most of the Natchez," he reported, "speak the vulgar language [Mobilian]," but he wanted to learn Natchez so that he could learn Natchez history by questioning the women who brought food supplies. "I therefore told my slave to have one of her relatives among these people come to visit me," Du Pratz said, and his politeness so impressed this female relative that by her agency he was introduced to the leading temple guardian. It turned out that this man also had a good command of Mobilian and taught Du Pratz a good deal about Natchez religion. The temple guardian in turn introduced him to the Great Sun and Tattooed Serpent. In their company he reported that he "learned easily the language of the commoners, and was not laggard in understanding a little of that of the Nobles" (2:323). The difference between the two, it turned out, was in the expressions used for referring to the nobles themselves. Natchez women and men also spoke the same language, although by virtue of spending most of their time with Natchez women, Frenchmen learned an effeminate accent that Du Pratz was told was considered hilarious by Natchez men and women alike (2:325).

The temple guardian told Du Pratz it was no use talking to women to learn about history; on his authority Du Pratz reported that the Natchez selected only the most apt boys to be taught to preserve the traditional history. Yet in spite of Du Pratz's expressed prejudice in favor of the expert knowledge of the male temple-keeper, the evidence of his narrative shows that the Chitimacha woman's contribution to his understanding of the country and its people was considerable. On one occasion she demonstrated, to his amazement, how to kill an alligator with a club. On another she told a legend about a supernatural white deer that led deer herds (1:233–34), a tradition later confirmed by a male informant. As cook and housekeeper her knowledge must have been drawn upon by Du Pratz in writing the passages describing the preparation of corn-meal, the making of dried persimmon loaf, the use of the seeds of cane tops as a grain, the virtues of dye plants (2:62–63), and the use of herbal remedies for "female troubles" (2:56).

Finally, it is also quite likely (to come to the initial point) that her under-standing was crucial to Du Pratz's grasp of the Natchez kinship system. As Du Pratz describes Natchez marriage practices, decisions about marriage were made between the two old men who were the heads of the potentially con-tracting matrilines. But we are not told who actually preserved the detailed genealogical knowledge that would be required for what must have been a much more complicated system than Du Pratz described, and in other matri-lineal systems it was usual for women to be genealogical experts. We should note that the Chitimachas were also apparently matrilineal and matrilocal. They made a distinction between nobles and commoners, but their marriage rule apparently dictated marriage *within* the respective classes rather than outside them.[13] Remember first that the young woman's elder sister was mar-ried to the Chitimacha great chief; this endogamous rule would imply then that *her* family was of the Chitimacha noble class. Remember also that the young woman claimed that she and her father had "relatives" among the

Natchez and that these people were able to give Du Pratz the access he needed to make his famous friendships with the Natchez Suns. It is not at all impossible that one of these relatives was a woman married to a Natchez Sun.

It is probably safe to assume that some of the Chitimachas may have joined the Koroas, Tioux, and Grigras as refugees being assimilated by the Natchez. The Chitimacha origin myth pointed to a homeland in the Natchez country, they had long been Natchez allies, and they were even referred to as "brothers" by the Natchez.[14] If Jeffrey Brain is correct, all of these refugee Tunican groups might have been taken into the Natchez system as "commoners." But the Chitimacha woman's relatives' access to the noble class suggests otherwise (although these outsiders technically construed as "commoners" could possibly have been preferred as Natchez Sun marriage partners because of their noble standing in their own tribe), so Natchez male Suns could marry Chitimacha noble women, who as "commoners" could be subjected to widow sacrifice as Sun women could not. In any case, Du Pratz's young slave had access to female informants who knew very well how the Natchez commoner-Sun marriage system worked.

Conclusion

We must then ask ourselves what this might have meant for Du Pratz's understanding of the Natchez system. The best scholarship on the subject, as we have seen, has concluded that his description supports the following conclusions:

1. The Suns were a royal family rather than a separate class; the Natchez recognized two classes, noble and common, and the Suns were a special case of the noble class whose rank remained constant as reckoned through the mother.

2. Descent was not symmetrical for children of noble males, in that their female children would have the commoner rank of their mothers as expected, while the male children would decline one rank from that of their fathers.

3. The Honored category was a male honorific rank rather than a self-perpetuating class, and there were no Honored women.

This system does look much more Chitimacha-like than the baroque constructions of less well informed French writers than Du Pratz, but it also looks more generally southeastern. This view would simply suggest an exogamous moiety system in which a tribe was divided into two halves called moieties and marriage would have to be outside one's moiety to avoid incest. In most southeastern societies the moieties were ranked, one usually being referred to as "elder brother" to the other. In the seventeenth and eighteenth centuries this practice could accommodate very well the adoption of ethnically diverse populations as "younger brother" in order to fortify group numbers in the face of the disruptions of colonization. The only exceptional feature here would then be the fact that the Suns (as the more highly ranked moiety) were distinguished by very special privilege (including much greater power over their subjects than other southeastern leaders enjoyed): people they married were put to death when they died in order to serve them in the other world, and that meant that, like everyone else, Suns had to marry outside their class (into the "commoner" moiety) in order to avoid violent death to a Sun, as Du Pratz says. The fact that chiefly marriage rules were just the opposite for the Chitimachas, requiring endogamy within the higher-ranked moiety for chiefs, may be why Du Pratz has described in such detail a justification for the exogamous practice. It may be that it is the Chitimacha woman's perception of the Sun marriage customs as odd that we see here, not that of Du Pratz.

Du Pratz did not tell us what became of his adopted Chitimacha daughter when he left Louisiana. He even failed to mention her when he described his move back to New Orleans to undertake the management of the royal plantation when it reverted to the Crown from the Company of the Indies in 1728—but then he was rather cagey about his own motivation for this move, which implies that his affairs in Natchez were not going well.

Many things may have happened to her: in the worst case, she could have married among the Natchez and been killed for her links with the French in the course of the Natchez Revolt or the war that followed. If she stayed with the Natchez she might also have been captured with them by the French and sent into slavery in Santo Domingo, or she could have fled with the Natchez to settle among the Chickasaw, Cherokee, or Creek. We can hope instead that she simply returned to the Chitimacha. Whatever happened, she disappeared from view: she was "erased" from the record, even more so for the monoglot English reader. I think, however, that we must conclude that her legacy is found in the sensitive account of the Natchez that Du Pratz has left us, not least in the explanation of Sun kinship.

Notes

1. In response to all the uproar around this issue in our times the American Anthropological Association recently felt motivated to devote an issue of *Anthropology News* (45 [May 2004]) to marriage and family.

2. Aberle, "Matrilineal Descent," 659.

3. Hart, "A Reconsideration."

4. Fischer, "Solutions."

5. White, Murdock, and Scaglion, "Natchez Class."

6. Brain, "The Natchez 'Paradox.'"

7. Du Pratz, *Histoire de la Louisiane*, my translation. Hereafter cited in the text by volume and page number.

8. White, Murdock, and Scaglion, "Natchez Class," 375, observe that, from here on, by "children" Du Pratz means "male children"; they conclude that in fact Du Pratz says nothing about what happens to the female children of male nobles and hint that they must be considered commoners, thus making up the alleged shortage.

9. Footnote by Du Pratz: "The Suns conceal this degradation of their descendants with so much care that they never suffer strangers to be taught about it. They do not wish anyone to recognize them as being of their race, neither that they themselves boast of it nor that their people speak about it among themselves. It is much when the grandfathers say that such a one is dear to them."

10. Le Page du Pratz, *The History of Louisiana*.

11. See "The Currency of Language: The Mobilian Lingua Franca in Colonial Louisiana" in this volume.

12. Swanton, *Indian Tribes*, 339, quoting from Pénicaut.

13. Swanton, *Indian Tribes*, 348–49.

14. Swanton, *The Indians*, 23.

II. *Positive Methods*

Constructing Space, Time, and Relationships

7. Prehistoric Population of Mississippi

A First Approximation

> We have enough data now that our hypotheses should be based on what we
> have, not on what we haven't.
>
> THOMAS LYNCH, "The Peopling of the Americas—A Discussion"

Background of the Project

In 1988 the Mississippi State Historical Museum, mindful of the Columbus
Quincentenary initiatives announced by the National Endowment for the
Humanities, applied for a planning grant under the museum's program to
redesign its colonial period exhibits. Its existing exhibits, constructed in the
early 1960s, were textbook examples of triumphalist "great (white) man"
history, dreadfully in need of replacement. Grants for planning this replacement were duly received, consulting scholars were hired, and the entire process was brought in the spring of 1993 to the point of actually deciding what
would be put before the public.

The room to be used for these new exhibits is the former "Indian Room,"
and archaeologists will perhaps not be surprised to hear that prehistory has
been demoted from a whole room to half of it. In the new design half the
room is to be devoted to the development of Native societies up to the contact
period, with the exhibit dominated by the Swan Lake canoe and a huge
diorama of a Mississippian period settlement (based on Lake George).[1] The
other half of the exhibit room will tell the story of the encounter of three

This chapter was originally published as "Prehistoric Population of Mississippi: A First Approximation" in *Mississippi Archaeology* 29, no. 2 (1994): 44–71. It is reprinted by permission of the
Mississippi Department of Archives and History and the Mississippi Archaeological Association.

Table 7.1. Indian, European, and African population of Mississippi, 1685–1790

	1685	1700	1715	1730	1745	1760	1775	1790
Gulf Coast	4,000	2,500	1,000	750	500	350	225	150
Central Mississippi River	12,000	8,000	5,333	2,666	1,800	1,333	1,400	1,533
Chickasaws	7,000	5,000	4,000	3,100	2,300	1,600	2,300	3,100
Choctaws	28,000	21,000	16,800	11,300	12,200	13,300	14,000	14,700
TOTAL Indians	51,000	36,500	27,133	17,816	16,800	16,583	17,925	19,483
Europeans		100	300	1,800	4,000	4,100	10,900	19,900
Africans			100	3,600	4,100	5,300	9,600	23,500
TOTAL pop.	51,000	36,600	27,533	23,216	24,900	25,983	38,425	62,883

Sources: Data adapted from Wood, "The Changing Population," 66–79; Hall, *Africans in Colonial Louisiana*; and Usner, *Indians, Settlers, and Slaves*.

worlds—American, European, and African—and the development of a multicultural colonial society in Mississippi to 1800. One of the featured items will be a presentation telling the whole story of the human population of Mississippi from the advent of humans to 1800.

Recent work by Peter Wood and Dan Usner on the colonial period population of the Southeast and by Gwendolyn Midlo Hall on the African population of the Louisiana colony have made it possible to work out believable and usable figures for Indians, Europeans, and Africans living in what is now the state of Mississippi between 1685 and 1790 (table 7.1, figure 7.1).[2] Hall in particular has been able to make use of the techniques of historical demography developed in Europe since the 1950s, which use series of regularly kept records to carry out "family reconstitutions," tracing actual people through their births, marriages, and deaths in order to arrive at the statistics on fertility and mortality that make it possible to write relatively accurate histories of populations.[3]

For the prehistoric period, however, we are without conventional statistical data; from ca. 15,000 BP to AD 1700 only the archaeological record can help us. And in answer to the designers of the exhibit, it won't do to just throw up our hands and say, "We don't know enough"—that is why precolonial history has lost half of the room already. To ignore this chance is to risk completely failing to get the message about precolonial Indian dominance of the American continent to the public. There is a serious need to counter the "widowed land"/

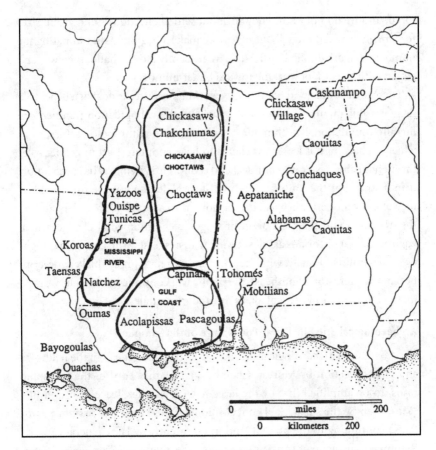

Fig. 7.1. Regions for derived historic period Indian population counts in table 7.1.

"howling wilderness" stereotype that constitutes the public's notion of what "colonists" and "pioneers" encountered, but, as I have learned from working with my museum colleagues, lengthy textual explanations are not an option. "Book-on-the-wall" is the direst condemnation in modern exhibit design.

Must we then just cut to ca. AD 1500, incorporate the new demographic scholarship about high numbers laid low by European disease, and let it go at that?[4] If so, then why have we all been gathering and systematizing archaeological site data for the last fifty years? These rhetorical questions are meant to suggest that I think we can usefully grapple with the problem, as the recent work by David Anderson and others to attempt to look at Archaic settlement models in the Southeast has shown.[5] Site file data are inevitably poorly structured, and we do not know enough about settlement models and group sizes for a really detailed model, but unless we make a beginning in estimating the numbers that are implied by the data we presently have in hand, then we can't get on with the task of working toward better numbers.

There are a lot of good reasons why working toward the goal of a believable demographic picture is important for archaeology. Population numbers are literally foundational to thinking about all of the anthropological issues in which archaeology at least now claims to have an interest, from gender roles through kinship systems to political and economic systems, as has been amply demonstrated by the contributions of historical demography to the social history of early modern Europe. Furthermore, they are crucial to understanding the dynamics and the scale of anthropogenic environmental change, which environmental historians are now trying to distinguish from changes wrought by climate shifts.[6] Finally, without such data as a base for a "thicker" description of the prehistoric Southeast, the public will continue to view our work, if they get a chance to view it at all, as dry and meaningless.

Archaeological Site File Data: The Nature of the Sample

The Mississippi archaeological site file saw its original genesis in the fieldwork and data collection by Moreau Chambers and James Ford in the 1920s and 1930s, to be amplified first by the large federal Natchez Trace project in the 1940s, then by the substantial contributions of the Lower Mississippi Survey (LMS) continuing to the present, and more recently by large federal Cultural Resource Management (CRM) projects like the Tennessee-Tombigbee Waterway in the 1970s. Additionally, a constant trickle of site reports has come from collectors. Until relatively recently the only physical form of the site file was file cards; in the middle 1980s computerization began, and as of this writing we are about to add Geographical Information System (GIS) capabilities to the system. All of which is to say that we are ready at last to reach for a return on our computerization investment, and this seems an ideal project to make generalized use of the data.

We begin with full knowledge that there are problems with these data. Nearly twenty years ago Fred Plog demonstrated, by comparing ordinary site file data like ours with systematic survey sampling, that "casual surveys miss a large number of the sites in an area and tend to locate the largest sites only"— what Flannery has referred to as the "Teotihuacan effect."[7] Site counts, Plog showed, needed to be subjected to transformations even if they could be thought reliably representative because (1) not all sites are where people lived and (2) sites vary in size. Plog, who had the luxury of dealing with southwestern sites with surviving architectural evidence, decided to count rooms and to depend on absolute dating through pottery series to arrive at population profiles for all sites instead of dating through coarser, less accurate, and logically circular phases. We do not have the same luxury.

Nor can we ever be so lucky in the Southeast, for we know our chronologies to be very much more relative, and most of our prehistoric peoples' houses were eaten by termites or slimed by fungus. Furthermore, if as in this case we want to extract an estimate for such a completely artificial topographical construct as "the state of Mississippi," sites are really the only proxy data that offer any semblance of reasonable coverage, since the site file itself does at least have a relationship to the state as an administrative entity. This is true even though the data in our site files are for the most part what Plog called "casually" gathered.

In Mississippi as elsewhere a lot of the data are very old, and uniform standards for recording data are still hard to enforce, which means that the data have many familiar problems: (1) they were gathered due to incommensurable research designs or individual interests or were simply chance finds; (2) they were recorded using different frames of reference and terminologies; (3) they were recorded to varying standards, mostly very low for early data, better for more recent data. Inevitably, then, bias has been introduced into the site file simply by the complexity and heterogeneity of its formation processes. Examination of the site counts from individual counties (figure 7.2) makes it obvious that high counts correlate with one or more of several factors:

1. Nearness to a university with an archaeological program
2. Presence of a state archaeological office
3. Subjection of the county to systematic county survey
4. Location of a large federal project (Natchez Trace, Tennessee-Tombigbee Waterway)
5. Location of a long-term archaeological research program
6. Presence of a conscientious amateur
7. Presence of significant agricultural activity

Additionally, when distribution of sites for individual periods is examined, patterns introduced by specific research interests also emerge in different regions.

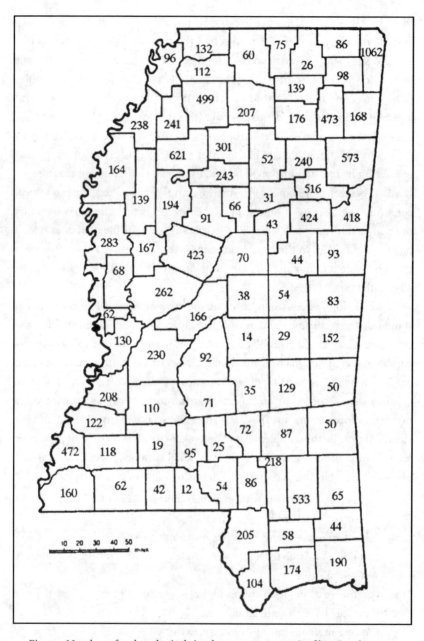

Fig. 7.2. Number of archaeological sites by county, MDAH site files, October 1993.
MDAH county surveys completed: Lowndes, Coahoma. Universities: Lafayette,
Oktibbeha, Forrest.

POSITIVE METHODS

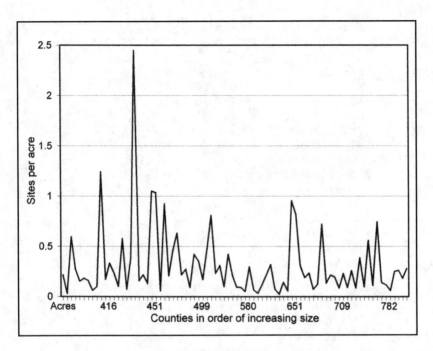

Fig. 7.3. County site densities in order of county size.

The Mississippi-Yazoo Delta, for example, is clearly characterized by many of these factors (specifically, 1, 2, 5, and 7 above), and there is no doubt that data from the Delta do skew the sample, although not perhaps as obviously as might have been thought; they account, for example, for only about 10 percent of specifically labeled Middle Mississippian sites. Fortunately, however, in most regions of the state one or more of these factors has been at work, so that the ratios of numbers of sites to numbers of acres, plotted in order of county size, show no discernable trend (figure 7.3); in other words, either a county has had a lot of attention or it hasn't, and whether it has or hasn't, it tends to have about as many sites per acre as others in the same situation. Which means that since the counties in the major physiographic regions have had about equal attention and inattention, it looks as though in the mass the numbers are likely to be reasonably representative.

Thus with over thirteen thousand recorded sites, it just may be that the broad outlines of the population of prehistoric sites in Mississippi are in fact reflected in this record. What can be done with these data as they stand will have to be rather simple-minded, but it will enable us to enter into dialogue

Table 7.2. Assignment of phases and date ranges to periods

Period	Date Range
Paleo-Indian	10,000–8000 BCE
Early Archaic	8000–6000
Middle Archaic	6000–3000
Late Archaic	3000–1200
Poverty Point	
Early Woodland	1200 BCE–AD 100
Gulf Formational	
Middle Woodland	100–500
Marksville	
Issaquena	
Miller I, II	
Late Woodland	500–900
Baytown	
Bayland	
Deasonville	
Miller III, IV	
Early Mississippian	900–1200
Coles Creek	
Kings Crossing	
Ballina	
Balmoral	
Middle Mississippian	1200–1350
Gordon	
Anna	
Late Mississippian	1350–1500
Emerald	
Protohistoric	1500–1700
Historic Indian	1700–?

Note: Phases shown are those that are actually recorded for sites in the Mississippi site file.

with the demographic literature and with settlement models for insight into improving our reading of the data and indeed into improving the future collection of data.

Temporal Segmentation

The first task, therefore, is to segment the data temporally in some reasonable way. We have the familiar problem here that while by now archaeologists have defined a contiguous series of periods and phases for which there are a few agreed-upon marker artifact types, this is a relatively recent achievement: for

Table 7.3. Number of sites by specifically labeled period

Period	Number of Sites
Paleo-Indian	179
Early Archaic	706
Middle Archaic	853
Late Archaic	1,789
Early Woodland	902
Middle Woodland	1,777
Late Woodland	1,996
Early Mississippian	269
Middle Mississippian	221
Late Mississippian	247
Protohistoric	433
Historic Indian	518

most of the lifetime of the site file, contributors simply wrote in whatever they wanted to write in, which might be a temporal segment, a period name, or a phase name. Or they did not place the site temporally at all. The realities of exhibit design and the relative inexactness of temporal assignment for much of the sample, then, dictate that the division into temporal segments should be relatively coarse. Subtlety is not what is called for here, and we know, after all, that a Madison point does not betoken a Paleo site. To bring labels other than our broad periods under control, I worked with Keith Baca, Sam Mc-Gahey, and Joe Giliberti to establish a list assigning phase names to temporal segments (table 7.2). Since for now it is not possible for us to establish the accuracy of the assignment of period names, we are simply sticking with the assignments made by site recorders.

Once the equivalences to coarse period designations were made for all sites where temporal information was present, it was possible to retrieve a count of sites assigned to temporal segments. Out of 13,714 sites in the site file at the time these data were sampled, only 9,890 components were unambiguously identified temporally; many sites are simply recorded as "unknown prehistoric" or by general period: "Mississippian," "Woodland," "Archaic." Unless we can decide how to use these other sites, the only sites we will have to work with are those yielding diagnostic finds. Still, it is very interesting to look at the numbers of actual component counts (table 7.3, figure 7.4). As raw numbers, these suggest all sorts of bias, ranging from the regional concentrations already mentioned to preferential lithic survival to difficulty of recognition of

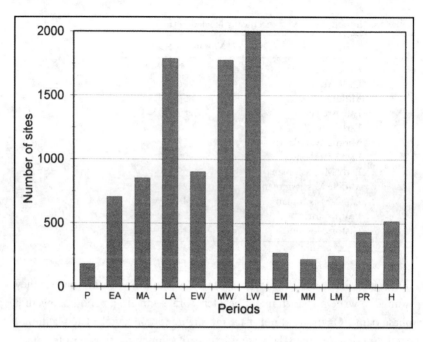

Fig. 7.4. Number of sites with specific period assignments. Key: P = Paleo, A = Archaic, W = Woodland, M = Mississippian, PR = Protohistoric, H = Historic Indian, E = Early, M = Middle, L = Late.

certain marker types to outright lack of good marker types at all. But as raw numbers they are unusable in any case.

First Transformation: Incorporation of Generalized Site Counts

It might seem to go without saying that we cannot incorporate sites with generalized period attributions into this study. If we do not do so, however, it turns out that we introduce different biases depending on period. This becomes obvious when we look at the numbers. For example, Archaic sites, which must be identified as such almost solely on the basis of intensively studied lithic materials, are relatively rarely given a general "Archaic" designation; out of a total of 3,894 Archaic sites of all periods, the 328 sites labeled merely as "Archaic" sites constitute only about 8 percent. General "Mississippian" site identifications, on the other hand, which can be identified on the basis of lithics but are far more regularly the product of finds of undiagnostic shell-tempered pottery, represent at 742 a whopping 46 percent of the 1,611

Table 7.4. Number of sites per period corrected for generalized period assignments

Period	Number of Sites
Paleo-Indian	179
Early Archaic	762
Middle Archaic	921
Late Archaic	1,932
Early Woodland	1,082
Middle Woodland	2,132
Late Woodland	2,395
Early Mississippian	393
Middle Mississippian	323
Late Mississippian	361
Protohistoric	433
Historic Indian	518

total sites attributed to the Mississippian period as a whole. The pattern for Woodland is somewhere in between, as one would expect: the 1,159 generalized "Woodland" sites are 20 percent of the total 5,834.

The bias here depends on the fact that lithic materials are much more easily classified than undecorated ceramic materials. Furthermore, that bias is not likely to go away if ceramic classifications get better; we will always have to ignore a disproportionate number of ceramic sites if we hold to a strict demand for period designation (and note that the later periods are briefer and briefer). What I suggest we do here, then, is to increase the site counts for each designated period by a percentage that corresponds to the "period specificity uncertainty factors" derived above: 8 percent for Archaic, 20 percent for Woodland, and 46 percent for Mississippian (see table 7.4).

Second Transformation: Sites per Generation

It does us no good to know how many sites were inhabited for the whole of a period; we need instead to know how many were simultaneously inhabited for some specific shorter time, something on the order of a "time slice." It makes sense to take a generation as the period of interest, particularly since the most spatially significant site formation processes are attributable to adults. I decided, therefore, to normalize on generations, so that for each time period I would arrive at a number of sites per generation.

Historical demographers have established several baselines: life expectancy

Table 7.5. Sites per generation for site file data with corrected period assignments

Period	Length	Generation Length	Number of Generations	Sites	Sites/ Generation
Paleo-Indian	2,000	25	80.0	179	2.2
Early Archaic	2,000	25	80.0	762	9.5
Middle Archaic	3,000	30	100.0	921	9.2
Late Archaic	1,800	30	60.0	1,932	32.2
Early Woodland	1,100	30	36.7	1,082	29.5
Middle Woodland	600	30	20.0	2,132	106.6
Late Woodland	400	35	11.4	2,395	209.6
Early Mississippian	300	35	8.6	393	45.8
Middle Mississippian	150	35	4.3	323	75.3
Late Mississippian	150	35	4.3	361	84.1
Protohistoric	200	35	5.7	433	75.8
Historic Indian	130	35	3.7	518	139.5

in medieval Europe to 1600 ranged from age twenty to forty, while it improved to thirty-five to forty during the eighteenth century and has since effectively doubled.[8] Hassan has suggested that for practical purposes a range between thirty and thirty-five is appropriate from the Neolithic to the eighteenth century, but he merely suggests that survivorship was less than that for hunter-gatherers.[9] I therefore rather arbitrarily set a generation at twenty-five for Paleo through Early Archaic, at thirty for Middle Archaic through Middle Woodland, and at thirty-five for Late Woodland through Late Mississippian. Protohistoric and Historic, with the presumed serious declines in population, are a problem, but as there is no indication that life expectancy was significantly reduced for those who survived disease, I have assumed that life expectancy is correlated with subsistence-settlement pattern and have left their generation length at thirty-five. I then divided the length of each time period by its assigned generational length and arrived at my first set of normalized numbers for sites per generation for each time period (see table 7.5). The distribution of the number of components per generation is beginning to look remarkably like what our intuitions have been telling us all along, except that the numbers diminish for the Mississippian, which doesn't fit the received wisdom at all.

Third Transformation: People per Site

So we move on to the third transformation, a commitment to the number of individuals represented by each site. The existing literature agrees on a "magic

POSITIVE METHODS

number" of twenty-five for band size of mobile hunter-gatherers. Hassan has pointed out that while this number seems reliable for hunter-gatherers, more sedentary subsistence-settlement systems are probably very much sui generis in site size, depending upon social organization and other factors, especially environmental ones.[10] Bruce Smith, in his "Dalton to de Soto" summary, refers only seldom to actual group sizes but suggests villages of about twenty-five to fifty in certain instances as early as the Late Archaic and villages more consistently around fifty people during the Woodland period.[11] Clearly this is a problem, because special-purpose extraction camps may be attributed to any period and probably represent the temporary activities of the same small numbers throughout. On the other hand, more permanent sites, like base camps, villages, and ceremonial centers, should be more significant for actually establishing population numbers, if we could be sure that they are likely to be found in representative numbers.

The work presently being done on Paleo and Archaic "pioneering" models may help with this problem of establishing numbers per site.[12] These researchers envision a small population coming into a region and exploring it for a short period of time, perhaps over a yearly round, during which it establishes certain reference locations for itself. But the exigencies of survival demand that these reference points—locations of preferred resources, safe and convenient camping places—be established as quickly as possible, and if this is carried out successfully, then the small population can settle into more established patterns and think about reproducing itself.

This one small group will presumably expand in this way, perhaps even through immigration from the parent group, to the "magic number" of twenty-five in reasonably short order, and these people will occupy and make use of a few main camping places and of many and varying extraction sites, depending on the mobility of the resource being extracted (hence the notion of populations "tethered" to lithic resources, water sources, or hardwood forests but more variably creating sites with evidence of butchering). Through a generation of twenty-five years they may create two or three major sites concentrating on specific parts of their foraging range, while they will create a larger number (but still not large) of "tethering" resource extraction sites and a significantly larger number of "mobile" resource extraction sites. However, given the routine seasonal scheduling of hunter-gatherers' activities in a known environment and even the seasonal routines of prey species, these sites also may be seen as "tethered" in a sense, as camps will probably be reused

Table 7.6. Population unit sizes assigned to sites by period

Period	Unit Size
Paleo-Indian	25
Early Archaic	25
Middle Archaic	25
Late Archaic	25
Early Woodland	35
Middle Woodland	45
Late Woodland	50
Early Mississippian	50
Middle Mississippian	75
Late Mississippian	100
Protohistoric	50
Historic Indian	50

unless and until human predation forces a change in prey species' behavior. But the crucial issue here is what is likely to be found in the ground. Clearly, we are more likely to find the main camps and the resource extraction sites tethered to extraction of resources leaving inorganic remains like lithics and mollusks; the other sites will be found only serendipitously if at all. And given the relatively sparse survey coverage statewide, I think it very unlikely that we will often find more than one site used by any single group.

Models for Woodland villages and extraction sites and for Mississippian extraction sites, farmsteads, villages, and polity centers may be similarly expanded, but in every case the sites found will be those exhibiting permanence of occupation or habitualness of use for extraction of items whose remains are likely to be preserved. In other words, the evidence of one person killing one deer is not likely to skew the sample because it will seldom be found. Furthermore, the problem of dealing with the Mississippian ceremonial centers (which of course do tend to be preferentially found) is not so serious for biasing the sample if we simply treat them as the large villages they effectively were. Many hundreds or thousands of people may have congregated at them periodically, but except in a few very exceptional cases that do not anyway occur in Mississippi, the permanent populations were probably not large, and if we treated them as such we would in effect be counting the general populace of the region twice. It might be argued that since the large ceremonial sites are virtually certain to be found, we should count them and ignore the rest, but I have not seen good arguments for actually defining the number of people for

POSITIVE METHODS

Table 7.7. Population represented by site file data by period, representing number of sites per generation times number of people per site

Period	Population
Paleo-Indian	56
Early Archaic	238
Middle Archaic	230
Late Archaic	805
Early Woodland	1,033
Middle Woodland	4798
Late Woodland	10,479
Early Mississippian	2,291
Middle Mississippian	5,647
Late Mississippian	8,414
Protohistoric	3,789
Historic Indian	6,973

whom a given Mississippian polity center is hegemonic, and I would suggest that each is a special case and would require a separate evaluation. This represents a problem that should be explicitly tackled in the future.

In the end, therefore, I have decided to make the general assumption that the sites counted for any period will represent the average size of the longest-term site inhabited by the average group during the period; in essence, this means that I am considering each site to represent the preferred local group size (table 7.6). Certainly, these numbers need a lot more discussion, and if it is possible to tease out consistent site-type distributions for each period, it would be preferable to construct a more complex mode. But when we quickly apply this conversion factor, all of a sudden we see numbers that begin to represent actual people, however crudely (table 7.7).

Fourth Transformation: Correcting for Sampling Error

Now that we have these numbers, which represent the number of people implied by the sample of sites actually in the site file and labeled as to period, we can make the final transformation from sample to total. Since we have a reasonably reliable number for the protohistoric period based upon documentary evidence (51,000), we simply derive another scale factor from it and multiply all of our numbers by 13.5 as a very crude way of running the sample up to 100 percent (table 7.8, figure 7.5). The scale factor of 13.5 is

Table 7.8. Population by period scaled by a scale factor of 13.5

Period	Population
Paleo-Indian	753
Early Archaic	3,207
Middle Archaic	3,100
Late Archaic	10,837
Early Woodland	13,908
Middle Woodland	64,584
Late Woodland	141,057
Early Mississippian	30,839
Middle Mississippian	76,008
Late Mississippian	113,266
Protohistoric	51,000
Historic Indian	93,864

Note: Based on the 51,000 Protohistoric period Indian population from Wood, "The Changing Population," table 1.

undoubtedly much too large, because protohistoric sites are probably under-counted in the site file. "Protohistoric" is a relatively new category and is probably not reliably applied similarly by everyone; in practice it usually means sites with late Mississippian ceramics (or even with plain shell-tempered ceramics) and early European trade goods, but deciding which European trade goods are early can be a problem.

Thus this result is nothing like a final answer. The conversion factors used were far too crude and did not take serious account, as was remarked, of observer bias, geographically skewed sample distribution, or site types. Nor was any attempt made to develop specific settlement models for different periods and subsistence modes; nor was this model structured according to environmental regions. The question is, Can these factors be dealt with, or are we stuck with data too bad to do any further work with at all?

Observer bias can in theory be explored by working with correlations between site recorders, sites, and date ranges, but we have to admit that in conclusive detail most of it will be irretrievable in practice. Skewed sample distribution is a real problem that is easy enough to see simply by looking at site counts broken down by county. For example, for the Protohistoric, where the shortfalls so crucially condition the final conversion factor for this analysis, it is clear that the bulk of reported sites in fact comes from a very few relatively recent projects by Marshall, Atkinson, Stubbs, Voss, and Blitz (figure 7.6). Middle Mississippian site counts by county show two trends: con-

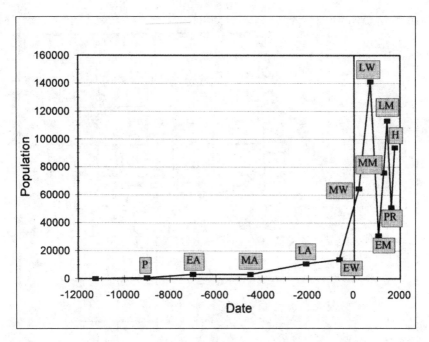

Fig. 7.5. Population by period after all transformations. See key to figure 7.4.

centration by the LMS on a few large sites in the Delta, as opposed to more concentrated coverage of many more sites with distinctive ceramics in the Natchez and Starkville regions, with very little really significant activity elsewhere (figure 7.7). But in principle such obviously skewed sample bias can be accounted for.

The data here raise other questions that can only be addressed in the design of future survey work. McGahey has dealt exclusively with actual counts of recorded lithics in building up a picture of man-land relationships in Mississippi from the Paleo through the Early Archaic periods.[13] These data powerfully suggest that the bulk of early settlement in Mississippi was in the northeastern and north-central regions, which McGahey reckons mark the entrance point for populations into the state. Yet a look at actual Paleo site distributions suggests that the apparent preponderance of evidence from these regions may be at least partially an artifact of the Tennessee-Tombigbee project, which affected the state's northeastern counties, and of research investigations in the vicinity of the University of Mississippi in the north-central region (figure 7.8). Although McGahey notes the existence of survey bias in individual

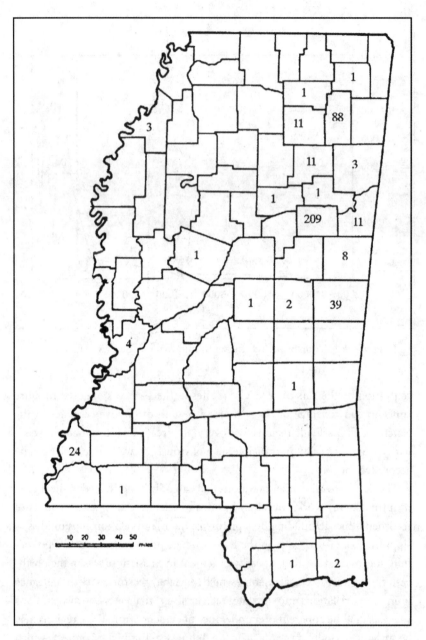

Fig. 7.6. Protohistoric site counts by county, MDAH site files, October 1993. Projects:
Blitz/Voss (Kemper), Stubbs (Lee, Pontotoc), Marshall/Atkinson (Oktibbeha).

POSITIVE METHODS

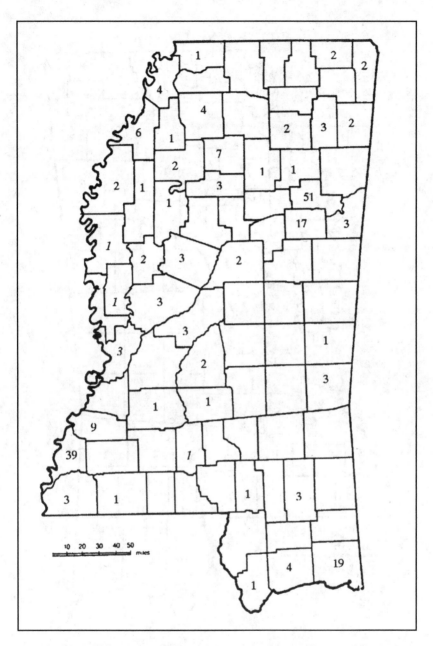

Fig. 7.7. Middle Mississippian sites by county, MDAH site files, October 1993.

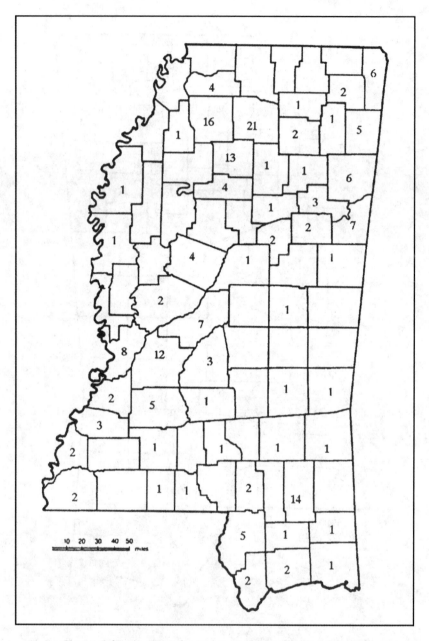

Fig. 7.8. Paleo site counts by county, MDAH site files, October 1993.

regions, it seems clear that we are seeing a basic survey bias across the whole state; it correlates too well with consistent patterns of the same kinds for site distributions from other periods.

There is much that can be done to improve survey coverage. This is obvious from the recent discovery of large numbers of Archaic sites in the south of the state and Woodland sites in the north, simply as a result of the Forest Service's action to put into place serious systematic survey programs in several forests across the state.[14] Lacking models of site distribution for most regions of the state, we cannot realistically compensate for these inequities of distribution with the existing site data, although we can incorporate correctives into the state plan for archaeology.[15]

The issue of site types has been ignored here because of the uncertainty of attributions (most sites in the file are unexcavated), the frequency of non-reportage, and the certainty that most small sites are simply not found. Yet much more can be done along these lines than I have attempted, at least for the Mississippian period and probably for the Middle and Late Woodland as well.[16] Again, there are problems with uneven coverage, but an approach focusing on regional settlement systems could address these problems and arrive at much better results (e.g., see the massive collection of studies that is eventuating from the Tennessee-Tombigbee Waterway archaeology).

While the model outlined here is at best crude, it can provide the basis for a better one, which should emerge through refinements suggested by new data and case studies of old data. We should continue to run the numbers through the model as new data are incorporated into the site file. And we can insist that the museum exhibit that motivated the enquiry be designed so that it can be changed as new data are seen to change our understanding significantly.

Issues Raised by the Derived Population Curve

In spite of all these reservations, the fact of the matter is that a graphical representation of these data (figure 7.5) corresponds very well with any number of models that have been built to describe the demographic expansion of human beings in the world, in the whole hemisphere, in the eastern woodlands, and indeed in the southeastern region alone.[17] Whatever may be the accuracy of these models, the adherence of the numbers in the present study to them is hardly likely to be due to research design bias, since there was no overall research design in the collection of these data. I believe that it is reasonable to assume that such a trend is so marked that it is bound to show

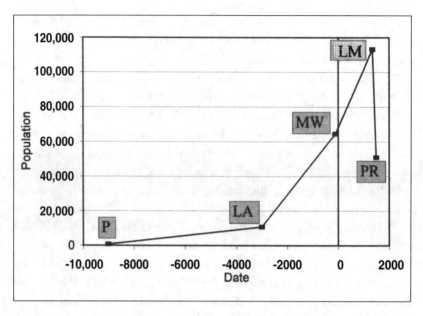

Fig. 7.9. Population by "superperiod." See key to figure 7.4.

through any sample this large, however "casually" it was obtained. As Ammerman, Cavalli-Sforza, and Wagener observed, "Population size may be more difficult to estimate than rates of growth," which is what this curve makes visible.[18]

Thus we see a small population at the outset, growing very slowly for a long time, achieving a dramatic "takeoff" in the Woodland period and further dramatic population growth during the Mississippian period, punctuated by a mysterious falloff in the Early Mississippian period. This "mysterious" falloff probably reflects the fact that most of the sites in the file were reported before Emergent Mississippian had had several symposia devoted to it, and nobody wanted to call anything Early Mississippian or indeed knew what to call Early Mississippian. A similar problem, not so visible because all the numbers are so small, lies at the other important transition points, Paleo to Early Archaic, Late Archaic to Early Woodland, and Late Mississippian to Protohistoric. For the purposes of representing these numbers to the public, then, I have decided to use the numbers for five "superperiods" only, and I have chosen just those for which the archaeological diagnostics are thought to be relatively unambiguous: Paleo, Late Archaic, Middle Woodland, Late Mississippian, and Protohistoric (figure 7.9).

POSITIVE METHODS

Further Steps toward "Thick Description"

Does this mean that running a spreadsheet or two on bad data is enough to salve our consciences, permitting presentation of a theory we were comfortable with already? The sites are real enough; the transformations that have been applied are, after all, very modest and conservative ones. No, the real importance of such an effort is the proof that the data can be put to such a use and that there are specific ways in which it can be improved upon; and if this is true, then we have the possibility of amplifying our thinking in significant ways about the social and environmental effects of the prehistoric peopling of Mississippi.

One issue worthy of consideration is that of population size and density effects. The influence of population density on the intensification of subsistence technologies and indeed on the emergence of agriculture has been heatedly debated.[19] Whether the argument in favor of its causative effects on subsistence has been discredited or not, the suggested population curve calls upon us to consider other less controversial effects. We might, for example, pay closer attention to the texture of everyday life suggested by the very slow population growth during the Paleo and Archaic periods. This kind of almost infinitesimal population growth over such a long period (not uniformly characterized by poor climatic conditions) suggests that perhaps some degree of intentional limitation of population is at work here. It contradicts the historian's received wisdom about rampant population growth in a population pioneering a region with apparently ample resources, suggesting that the explosive growth of the Euro-American immigrant "pioneering" population in North America in the nineteenth century was not based on "natural" population growth patterns but must be accounted for by other factors. It may be time for us to consider the possibility that the first American pioneers used practices familiar from Lee's work on !Kung hunter-gatherers: late start and end to childbearing, wide birth spacing, possible seasonal amenorrhea, possible infanticide or infant neglect, and even the social construction of sexual abstention practices.[20] We are therefore able to begin to integrate women into the Paleo picture as mothers as well as makers of spearpoints and subsistence providers.[21]

The population takeoff and sustained growth over the comparatively short period from Early Woodland to Middle Mississippian also suggests some provocative possibilities for the amplification of models for social structure and change. With the introduction of the bow and arrow subsistence may have become more secure, supporting the investment in additional children; this will have been promoted further by the increasing subsistence security offered by control over crops, which in its own turn may have affected the status of those who provided them. The constant and dramatic rise in numbers would have created a population structure that remained bottom-heavy: dominated by the young. Such a population structure is thought to be conducive to innovation, which certainly characterized the period, but it also has concrete implications for the lives of women.

Although an increasingly sedentary lifestyle may have been responsible for the survival of more children, it is also likely that female fertility was greater through the period than it had been before the Woodland takeoff. Again, referring both to Lee's work on the !Kung and Binford and Chasko's observations on the Nunamiut, which showed an increase in fertility with a reduced birth spacing among former hunters and gatherers who took up a sedentary existence, this would have meant more, and more frequent, pregnancies (and additional risk of death in childbirth) for Late Woodland and Mississippian women, but it would also have meant a larger family workforce for assistance with crops.[22] Here it is obviously appropriate to investigate the emergence of matriliny in terms of a possible effect of sedentarism plus population density.

The consideration of this expanding human population is not complete without consideration of known long-term climatic changes and their interactions with human populations in this region of the Southeast.[23] In Mississippi we have not asked to what degree prehistoric populations may have been responding to climatic changes or to what degree they may have been helping to create them. The likely correlation between the "Mississippian Decline" and the Little Ice Age deserves much more investigation. If Gunn and Adams are right about shifts in bands of precipitation with long-term fluctuations in mean temperature, then part of the Woodland-Mississippian takeoff may be attributable to the favorable conditions for corn agriculture provided by the dry subtropical climate that the Southeast would have enjoyed along with the Southwest ca. AD 900–1250. The extension of bald cypress dendrochronological sequences for the Southeast promises that in the future it will be possible to fill in more precise details for such fluctuations in the region for at least five thousand years before the present.[24]

Anthropogenic environmental changes, however, will have been far more significant over the period. We do not know exactly when southeastern populations began to manage forests with fire for better hunting conditions, but the routine adoption of such practices must surely have added to the global burden of carbon dioxide in the atmosphere being created by forest clearance and burning elsewhere. Such effects must have been increased significantly by the adoption of agriculture during the Mississippian period; although early travelers in the Yazoo Delta found dense forest there, and although the modern nearly complete deforestation of the region is due to post–Civil War clearance, European settlers took for "virgin land" what must often have been second-growth forest. Although there has been much evidence brought forward that the Protohistoric population crash was due to European-introduced disease, dated sites in the Delta indicate that the population there had already thinned by the time Europeans arrived.[25] The collapse of Cahokia in the fourteenth century, attributable at least in part to the increasing cold of the Little Ice Age, stands as an unavoidable suggestion that growing conditions in the northern half of the Delta may also have become unreliable. At the same time, modern agronomic literature is full of discussion of the falling productivity of fields repeatedly cropped in corn, but other significant environmental effects are the deforestation, erosion, and destruction of prey species habitat that must have resulted from field clearance and the cutting of wood for fuel and building purposes. Discussions of the so-called Mississippian Decline and various arguments that have been put forth for Late Mississippian, precontact chiefdom dissolutions in the region could make use of additional evidence from population profiles and global climatic variation to suggest new avenues of investigation.[26]

Most of these questions cannot be tackled without better samples of sites and additional data about already-known sites. I would like to suggest, however, that we can make our existing sample into a better one with a little additional planning and a novel application of sampling method. Obviously, it would have been better had the first European settlers drawn a stratified random sample of quadrats and only settled (and observed) there. But there is nothing to prevent our drawing such a sample today—a 20 percent sample of the whole state, stratified on soil association, physiographic region, elevation, distance from water, or a combination of factors. Then we simply lay the sample over our existing site collection, declare the sites that fall within the selected quadrats a part of the sample we are seeking, and proceed to encourage strongly an emphasis upon the remaining quadrats in future research- and mitigation-oriented work in the state. Of course, it may take a long time to complete such a sample, but it will be shorter than doing it haphazardly, as we do now. And will it be worth doing? I hope I have shown that it will, if only because this analysis of the existing sample has raised so many useful and serious questions.

Acknowledgments

I would like to thank the National Endowment for the Humanities for having funded the museum exhibit project that is at the base of this work; David Morgan and several student assistants for sticking faithfully to the task of getting the Mississippi site file data into the computer; Keith Baca, Sam Mc-Gahey, and Joe Giliberti for their help in narrowing some definitions and cleaning up the site file data; James Ware for assistance in restructuring the site file; and David Anderson for suggesting that this project might not be completely impossible. The impetus of Carole Crumley's human ecology class at the University of North Carolina was responsible for the project's emergence in finished form. Nobody but me should be blamed for rash claims.

Notes

Abstract: This paper describes an attempt to use data in the Mississippi archaeological site file to construct believable numbers that can be used in interpreting the prehistory of Mississippi to a general museum audience. It will also address the issues raised by such an effort and suggest directions that further work in Mississippi and the region might take to arrive at better demographic information for prehistory.

1. Fuller, *The Swan Lake Canoe.*
2. Wood, "The Changing Population"; Usner, *Indians, Settlers, and Slaves*; Hall, *Africans.*
3. See Flinn, *The European Demographic System.*
4. Dobyns, *Their Number Become Thinned*; Stannard, *American Holocaust.*
5. See Anderson, Sassaman, and Judge, *Paleoindian and Early Archaic Period Research.*
6. Crumley, *Historical Ecology.*
7. Plog, "Demographic Studies"; Flannery, *The Early Mesoamerican Village.*
8. Yaukey, *Demography.*
9. Hassan, *Demographic Archaeology.*
10. Hassan, *Demographic Archaeology.*
11. Smith, "The Archaeology."
12. Dincauze, "Pioneering in the Pleistocene"; Anderson, "The Paleoindian Colonization"; cf. Dillehay and Meltzer, *The First Americans.*
13. McGahey, "Paleoindian and Early Archaic Data."
14. Sam Brookes, Joe Giliberti, and Evan Peacock, personal communication, 1993; see Peacock, "Twenty-five Years of Cultural Resource Management."
15. McGahey, "Mississippi State Plan for Archaeology: Preceramic"; Morgan, "Mississippi State Plan for Archaeology: Ceramic Prehistoric"; Elliott, "Mississippi State Plan for Archaeology: Historic"; Galloway, "Mississippi State Plan for Archaeology: Protohistoric"; Joe Giliberti, personal communication, 1993.

16. See Brain, "Late Prehistoric Settlement Patterning."

17. Welinder, *Prehistoric Demography*, fig. 2.1-1 from Deevey, "The Human Population"; Butzer, "An Old World Perspective," 145, his "late Pleistocene population model"; Smith, "The Archaeology"; Anderson, "The Paleoindian Colonization."

18. Ammerman, Cavalli-Sforza, and Wagener, "Toward the Estimation," 40.

19. Boserup, *The Conditions of Agricultural Growth*.

20. Lee, *The !Kung San*; cf. Lienhardt, *Divinity and Experience*, 92.

21. For example, see Gero, "Genderlithics."

22. Binford and Chasko, "Nunamiut Demographic History."

23. Gunn and Adams, "Climate Change, Culture, and Civilization"; Gunn, "Analysis of Modern Climate Data."

24. Stahle, Cook, and White, "Tree-Ring Dating."

25. Dobyns, *Their Number Become Thinned*; Smith, *Archaeology of Aboriginal Culture Change*; Ramenofsky, *Vectors of Death*.

26. See Peebles, "The Rise and Fall."

8. Technical Origins for Chickachae Combed Ceramics

An Ethnohistorical Hypothesis

Chickachae Combed ceramics were identified as the diagnostic type for historic Choctaw sites by Henry B. Collins in 1927 (figure 8.1). Since Collins wrote and collected, the type has become recognized for what he said it was on a number of sites in east-central Mississippi and has been formally described by Haag.[1] In no case has it been possible, however, to date one of these sites securely in the French period (1700–1763) on the basis of the surface collections secured. Excavations have been carried out recently at the French Fort Tombecbé, which was established on the Tombigbee near present Epes, Alabama, in 1736 to provide close trade and diplomatic links with the Choctaw. No Chickachae Combed sherds were found on this site in securely sealed French period deposits, and this evidence first suggested unequivocally that the type was not characteristic of the French period, at least not in the eastern Choctaw region.[2] Further work carried out by John Blitz in Kemper County demonstrated that Chickachae Combed was indeed a minority ware in that area, and the European items found in conjunction with it were quite clearly to be dated no earlier than the eighteenth or early nineteenth century.[3] We know that the type continued in use in Mississippi around the time of Removal and was even made by Choctaw in Oklahoma later in the nineteenth century.[4] The nearest thing to the type that we have from the French period is the Bayou Goula Incised type (figure 1) from the eponymous site excavated by Quimby.[5] I would like to suggest here that the type is of relatively recent date in the Choctaw heartland and that its execution technique came from the west.

This chapter was originally published as "Technical Origins for Chickachae Combed Ceramics: An Ethnohistorical Hypothesis" in *Mississippi Archaeology* 19, no. 2 (1984): 58–66. It is reprinted by permission of the Mississippi Department of Archives and History and the Mississippi Archaeological Association.

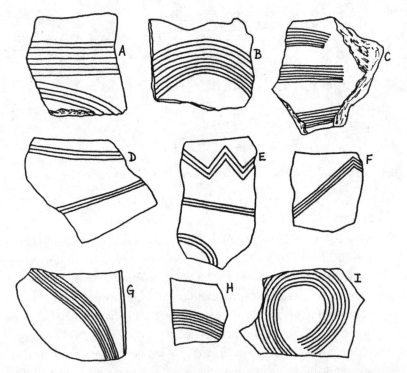

Fig. 8.1. Combed ceramics. A–C, Chickachae Combed from Clarke and Jasper counties. D–F, Chickachae Combed from Lowndes County reservation sites, ca. 1830. G–I, Bayou Goula Incised from the Bayou Goula site.

The first step in arguing this view is the suggestion of a technical hypothesis: ceramics with combed decoration had their decorative motifs executed using a broken piece of a European trade comb. As gratuitous as this remark may seem on the surface, I think there are sound arguments in its favor.

1. The absence of combing as a decorative technique, in the context of the astonishing variety of decorative techniques employed on Late Woodland and Mississippian ceramics, suggests that there was no natural floral or faunal material that enabled almost perfectly parallel, evenly spaced combed lines to be executed in an obvious way. Combed decorative techniques observed on types other than Chickachae Combed, especially the misleadingly named Bayou Goula Incised, occur only on sites known to have had contact with Europeans and producing ample evidence of this contact in French trade goods.[6]

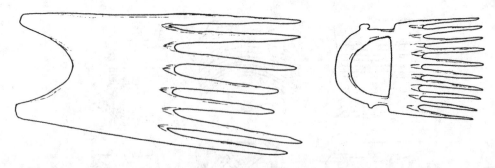

Fig. 8.2. Sketch of two combs from Fort Ancient aspect sites, Cramer (left) and Feurt (right).

2. Very few combs have been found on aboriginal sites in eastern North America. Those that are known are of a type that would not fit the requirement of closely spaced teeth needed for the historic combed ceramics (figure 8.2), nor is it easy to see how such combs could be made without metal tools.[7] Existing combs of certain Native origin without European influence come only from sites with a Woodland period component.

3. Lists of French trade goods from the earliest period always include gross after gross of boxwood combs; the French distributed combs to all their allies.[8] The Choctaw, who were known among the southern tribes for wearing their hair long, presumably were eager to acquire such combs.[9] But there was another more basic reason for the attraction of combs as trade items: their use in the eradication of fleas and lice. Certainly, the demand for them seems to have been continuous, since they appear on the trade lists down to the end of the French period.[10] And Romans, remarking on the skill of a Choctaw craftsman he observed, reports having seen a comb made in the 1770s.[11] In other words, Native groups had acquired these combs and were using them at the same time that combed ceramics appeared.

4. A wooden comb is made in such a way that the grain of the wood runs in the lengthwise direction of the teeth for the very good reason that if it is not, the teeth will break off almost immediately when the comb is used. When one of these combs breaks, then, it breaks along the vertical axis in such a way that a piece having some small number of intact teeth may be broken off. Wooden combs would have been especially prone to this kind of breakage when exposed to extremes of heat and moisture, normal in the Southeast. The same type of comb was issued to the French soldiers at the rate of

POSITIVE METHODS

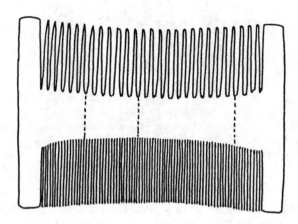

Fig. 8.3. The type of the standard French trade comb. These combs were made of boxwood, with the grain running vertically with reference to this drawing. Likely breakage lines are shown with dotted lines.

two per year; this does not argue for extreme durability.[12] A drawing of the type of comb in question and a suggestion of normal breakage patterns is shown in figure 8.3.

What we have, in short, is an object whose broken pieces are not very useful for its primary function. The object was in the right place at the right time, and the adoption of necessary techniques for its manufacture by the aboriginal population ensured that it would continue to be available.

What explains the apparent lateness of the appearance of combed ceramic decoration among the Choctaw? To tackle this problem we will look at the spatial distribution of Chickachae Combed and similar ceramic types (figure 8.4). First, however, we should examine the latest evidence on the Choctaw ceramic complex. Blitz, in his recent thesis, reanalyzed all collections of Choctaw pottery now available, including his own samples from a Kemper County survey, and reclassified the ceramics (table 8.1). He has separated the incised pottery from the combed instead of subsuming it as others have done, separated the combed pottery on the basis of paste, and demonstrated that combed pottery is associated with late British or American trade objects.[13]

Yet it is clear that elsewhere combing has earlier associations. The very similar Bayou Goula Incised, from a site on the west side of the Mississippi River south of Baton Rouge, is clearly associated with French trade materials and

Table 8.1. Classification of the Choctaw ceramics by John Blitz

Type	Temper
Mississippi Plain	coarse shell
Bell Plain	fine shell
Addis Plain	fine grog + fine sand and/or shell
Kemper Combed	fine grog + fine sand and/or shell
Fatherland Incised	fine grog + fine sand and/or shell
Unclassified Plain	fine sand
Chickachae Combed	fine sand

Fatherland Incised ceramics, while a type identified as Chickachae Combed is found extensively in the eastern part of the Mobile River delta, also in association with French trade goods.[14] We know that the Bayou Goula site was abandoned by 1721; cartographic evidence suggests that the Mobile River delta sites were inhabited into the British period. The key to a connection lies in identifying the inhabitants, and there is a possible link.

The French met the Bayou Goula as early as Iberville's first expedition in 1699, although La Salle in 1682 does not mention them.[15] The fortunate fact that Henry de Tonti left a letter for La Salle with the Quinipissa in 1686 allowed Iberville to learn that the Bayou Goula were newcomers to the site and that they had absorbed the remnants of a group identified as Mugulacha, who were somehow related to the Quinipissa. But by 1706 the Bayou Goula had been replaced by the Taensa, a tribe that had been found and traded with rather extensively by La Salle on Lake St. Joseph in 1682; Tonti saw and traded with them again in the same location in 1686 and 1690.

The Taensa spent ten years at the Bayou Goula site. In 1715 they requested of Bienville that he allow them to resettle on the eastern side of the Mobile River delta, which had been depopulated by Choctaw-related groups due to English-sponsored slave raids by the Alabamas around the turn of the century.[16] There they remained, giving their name to the eastern branch of the Mobile River. A few Taensa, however, apparently crossed the Mississippi to settle at Manchac.

It is possible that the peripatetic Taensa hold the clue to the transmission of combing as a technique for the execution of "Natchezan" decorative motifs. Little is known of Taensa pottery from their original home of 1682,[17] but the circumstantial evidence cited above does permit us to attribute combed ceramics, identical but for temper, to them in two other locations:

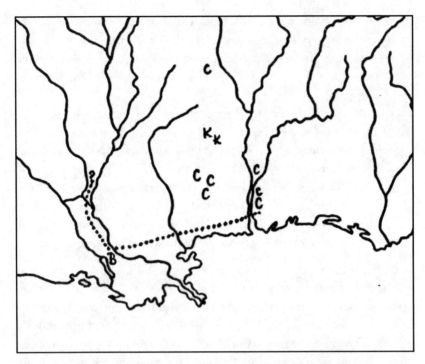

Fig. 8.4. Geographical distribution of combed ceramics mentioned in the text. B = Bayou Goula Incised; C = Chickachae Combed; K = Kemper Combed. The route of the Taensa's historic migration is shown with a dotted line.

1. At the Bayou Goula site, Bayou Goula Incised and Fatherland Incised ceramics are found together with French trade goods as the latest component on the site. We know that the Taensa were the last to inhabit the site and that they effected a mass removal eastward, thus justifying a large discard of damaged pottery. The paste of Bayou Goula Incised is apparently Addis: "very fine particles of grit, clay, shell, and unidentified organic matter."[18]

2. The Taensa, according to several French sources, spoke the same language as the Natchez (a language very different from that of any other group west of the Mississippi) and were on terms of alliance with them. Both their missionary, Montigny, and Antoine Simon Le Page du Pratz remarked upon their cultural similarity to the Natchez.[19] That they should share decorative motifs for ceramics (e.g., Natchezan scrolled motifs) would not be unexpected. The sparse ceramics from the Lake St. Joseph site are said to bear such motifs.[20]

3. Both Bayou Goula Incised and Chickachae Combed ceramics share decorative motifs very similar to Natchezan motifs and unlike those of the Alabama River phase ceramic tradition found east of the Tombigbee. Quimby recognized this long ago when he placed both within the "Natchezan culture type."[21]

4. Finally, the likelihood that the Taensa may have been responsible for the introduction of combing is favored by two facts: they were among the earliest to trade with the French and obtain combs, and the cultural disruption of their travels would favor innovation.

5. Even if the Taensa merely adopted the combing technique from their Bayou Goula victims, it is quite possible that they carried it eastward with them. The Bayou Goula were almost completely destroyed by the Taensa at an early date and could not have been responsible for such influence much later.

But what can be done to test these hypotheses? There are several suggestions that can be made for the technological hypothesis. First, if the combing technique of surface decoration can be paralleled from a prehistoric stratified context, the assertion of the hypothesis with regard to time of origin for the technique will be proved null. Positive verification that trade combs were used can be sought via a closer examination of the combing that occurs on the sherds. If double-sided simple combs were the tools used, then it is conceivable that one vessel might have two gauges of combing corresponding to the fine and coarse teeth of the double-sided comb; this would constitute a very circumstantial argument.[22] Finally, casts should be made and cross-sectioned so that the profiles of the combed lines can be compared to lines made in the same way experimentally using a similar wooden comb on a similar ceramic paste.[23]

The hypothesis that the Taensa may have invented and spread the technique of combing is less easy to test, but there are some suggestions for further research that can be made. First, there is a serious need for intensive survey and testing of the areas known to have been inhabited by the Taensa on Lake St. Joseph and at Manchac. We would expect that such research would at least establish Natchezan decorative motifs for Taensa ceramics and the presence of French trade goods. Next, there is a need for further detailed study of the Bayou Goula site ceramics, for survey of the site's catchment area, and for a careful review of the documentary evidence. Such study should establish the proportion of combed ceramics now called Bayou Goula Incised and show whether the type is confined to this site—as we would expect if only the

POSITIVE METHODS

transient Taensa had made it—or is to be found also on farmstead sites in the area—which would argue more for the Bayou Goula. The areas north and south of New Orleans said to have been inhabited by the Bayou Goula after their expulsion by the Taensa should be surveyed to establish their pottery complex with more assurance. Documentary review might be expected to reveal more about the complex relations among the Acolapissa, the Mugulacha, the Bayou Goula, and the Taensa, which would allow us to speak with more assurance to the sequencing of the site.

Work now in progress by Stowe and his colleagues should establish a similarly clearer picture of the Taensa east of the Mobile delta in the context of the cultures and tribes originally located there. We would, of course, like to know much more about the Choctaw and Choctaw-related groups in that area, not only to learn more about Choctaw-Taensa contact as it might relate to the transmission of the combing technique but to help solve the general puzzle of the relationship between Choctaw and Natchezan cultures.

Why do we need the Taensa at all for the explanation of combed ceramics among the Choctaw? As we have seen, the Choctaw had French combs at least from the first decade of the eighteenth century, and they could certainly have invented combing for themselves. The Bayou Goula are assumed to have been related to the Choctaw, though there is no direct evidence of direct contact between the two groups during the crucial 1682–1706 period. What we are trying to account for here, however, is the delay factor—the fact that so far we know of no combed Choctaw ceramics before the end of the eighteenth century. It would also be nice to account for the only other areal manifestations of combed ceramics at the Bayou Goula site and east of the Mobile River, and it seems more than coincidental that the Taensa have the only credentials to tie these areas together. If, after all this analysis, either or both of the hypotheses seem reasonable, it may alter our approach to tracing the origins of the Choctaw in the protohistoric period through their pottery. Blitz has pointed out that we should refocus our search for continuities of design by looking for general design themes rather than precise techniques of execution.[24] If we can firmly establish that this must be so in the case of the Choctaw, we may finally locate the earlier sites that have so far eluded us.

Notes

Abstract: This essay suggests two hypotheses about Chickachae Combed ceramics: that the tool used to produce the design elements was in fact a European trade comb and that the technique of combing may have been invented and transmitted by the Taensa.

1. Moreau B. C. Chambers, Field Notes, 1932–35, manuscript on file, Mississippi Department of Archives and History, Jackson; Ford, *Analysis*; Phillips, *Archaeological Survey*; Atkinson and Blakeman, *Archaeological Site Survey*; Penman, *Archaeological Survey* and "Historic Choctaw Towns"; Ward, "English Earthenwares"; Blitz, *An Archaeological Study*; Haag, "Choctaw Archaeology."

2. Parker, "Archaeological Test Excavations."

3. Blitz, *An Archaeological Study*.

4. Ward, "English Earthenwares"; Williams, "On the Location."

5. Quimby, *The Bayou Goula Site*.

6. Quimby, *The Bayou Goula Site*.

7. Galloway and Newcomer, "The Craft of Comb-making."

8. Rowland and Sanders, *Mississippi Provincial Archives: French Dominion*, 2:154.

9. Swanton, *Source Material*, 57.

10. Rowland, Sanders, and Galloway, *Mississippi Provincial Archives: French Dominion*, 5:231.

11. Romans, *A Concise Natural History* (1961 ed.), 56.

12. Rowland and Sanders, *Mississippi Provincial Archives: French Dominion*, 2:124.

13. Blitz, *An Archaeological Study*.

14. Quimby, *The Bayou Goula Site*; Noel Read Stowe, personal communication, 1984.

15. Le Moyne d'Iberville, *Iberville's Gulf Journals*, 58–64.

16. Rowland and Sanders, *Mississippi Provincial Archives: French Dominion*, 3:183.

17. Williams, "On the Location."

18. Quimby, *The Bayou Goula Site*, 126.

19. Du Pratz, *Histoire de la Louisiane*, 2:219; Shea, *Early Voyages*, 76.

20. Williams, "On the Location."

21. Quimby, "The Natchezan Culture Type."

22. Galloway, "Note on Terminology."

23. Since the publication of this essay such research has been carried out; see Voss and Mann, "Stylistic Variation."

24. Blitz, *An Archaeological Study*.

9. Multidimensional Scaling for Mapping Ethnohistorical Narrative

Choctaw Villages in the Eighteenth Century

The modern Mississippi Band of Choctaw Indians lives on four reservations of tribal lands and on scattered farms in ten Mississippi counties, with the administrative center of the tribe located in Pearl River Community near Philadelphia in Neshoba County. Not far away, in Winston County, lies the Nanih Waiya mound associated with the tribe's origin myths. Yet the evidence of the Soto narratives, reporting events in 1540–41, and that of recent excavation on the Tombigbee River suggest that some of the proto-Choctaw peoples lived rather farther east, on the Tombigbee watershed.[1] Between the time Hernando de Soto met them and the time they came into close contact with the French of the Louisiana colony 150 years later, the tribe moved westward into central Mississippi, perhaps pushed by the pressure of slave raids instigated by the English colonies to the east and carried out by their allies, the Creek and Chickasaw.

There is as yet only limited archaeological proof for this hypothesis; still less is there sufficient evidence of any kind to say what happened to cause the developed chiefdom societies Soto met to become the more loosely organized segmented societies that the French knew. The first step toward pushing the more secure later evidence backward is a thorough analysis of the French documents. The actual degree of organization of eighteenth-century Choctaw society is not clearly stated in these documents. By comparison with the highly organized Natchez society, with which the French had close relations

This chapter was originally published as "Multidimensional Scaling for Mapping Ethnohistorical Narrative: Choctaw Villages in the Eighteenth Century" in the *Proceedings of the Data Management and Mathematical Methods in Archaeology Section* by Commission IV of the Union internationale de sciences préhistoriques et protohistoriques in 1981, pp. 158–75. Reprinted courtesy of the UISPP.

for the first thirty years of their settlement and of which they wrote several detailed descriptions, the Choctaw social structure was apparently without much interest to French observers, so that what we have from them are only passing references from which to draw inferences. But it is clear from the French accounts that there were tribal divisions of some kind, certainly three and perhaps four, and that these divisions corresponded loosely to geographical regions.[2] It is also evident that during the French period there was movement of the villages themselves and that in many cases this movement had to do with shifts in the tribal power structure. A clearer picture, however, requires correlation of the documentary material with the archaeological evidence, and up to the present archaeological evidence remains sparse.

The first person to recognize Choctaw ceramics of the historic period was Henry B. Collins, who thus identified several sites.[3] Further survey in various areas has discovered more historic period Choctaw sites, but attempts to connect archaeological remains with the evidence of colonial maps, and therefore to put names to the sites, have been dependent upon relatively modern local tradition or late British accounts.[4] If Choctaw villages have been subject to movement as pronounced as the eighteenth-century evidence suggests, these identifications are bound to be distorted for earlier periods. Further, the closely datable European artifacts from Choctaw sites so far known are predominantly British and American and date from the 1770s on. We still do not know of a Choctaw village site with a significant concentration of French trade goods, perhaps because as yet no Choctaw site has been excavated. In order to gather sound evidence for the changes in Choctaw settlement patterns during the colonial period it will be necessary to undertake a much more comprehensive survey for sites and to use the evidence of colonial documentary sources to help identify some of these sites. In view of impending flood-control projects and strip-mining operations in the region, any aid to identifying likely survey targets must be helpful.

The colonial cartographic evidence, however, cannot be trusted in this regard, as Halbert has shown for the later Romans map.[5] Soto's party drew no maps; the sixteenth-century Spanish maps informed by the Soto narratives are schematic and just plain wrong.[6] The earliest French maps of any accuracy do not detail the Choctaw villages, nor do the British.[7] But beginning with the Barnwell and especially the Crenay map we begin to be shown what purport to be specific locations, though in both cases the locations are shown with reference to inaccurately drawn watercourses, in both cases the maps were not based upon accurate survey, and at least in the Crenay case it is certain that the map was not based upon the eyewitness observation of the mapmaker.[8] The later Romans and De Brahm maps, whatever the accuracy of their observation, were made after a major upheaval in the Choctaw nation, the civil war of 1746–51, and thus cannot give reliable representation of the situation in earlier periods.[9]

Close consideration should be given to the fact that the majority of the European maps were based upon narrative travel accounts and were not drawn up by those who reported the data. Since this was the case, it could be useful to attempt a modern reconstruction of some of the narrative evidence. It would obviously be of most interest to reconstruct a map from the earliest possible period. For the precontact period we have no account except the Native tradition reported briefly in eighteenth-century sources but only collected fully during the nineteenth century, and it does not mention village locations in any case. The evidence from first contact, the Narváez, Soto, and Luna y Arellano expeditions, consists solely of what I would call "one-way itineraries," that is, lists of villages passed through only once, with no indication of any connections between the villages except the single path taken.[10] We cannot be certain that any of these villages were actually proto-Choctaw. The earliest period from which we do have adequate narrative accounts is that of early French contact, or ca. 1700–1730; the termination date corresponds to the Natchez/Yazoo/?Chickasaw conspiracy to overthrow French rule, culminating in the Natchez/Yazoo rebellion of 1729, which led to ten years of war by the French and their Choctaw allies on the Natchez and Chickasaw Indians. The most complete accounts for this early period are from the end of it and stem from a concerted effort to establish trade with the Choctaw in order to bind them more firmly to the French cause. The accounts come from the subaltern Régis du Roullet, who set up a trading post in the southernmost Choctaw village after having traveled extensively through the nation.[11] Another officer, Jean-Christophe de Lusser, was sent out to help Régis set up the trading post and to travel among the Choctaw, and the journal of his travels provides a cross-check of Régis' data.[12]

In spite of the fact that only one of Régis' accounts was intended for use in map preparation, there is good reason to assume that these narratives provided some of the source material for the map drawn by the Baron de Crenay in 1733 (figure 9.1 shows a section of this map). Crenay, who had come to Louisiana for a punitive expedition against the Natchez in 1730 and who had

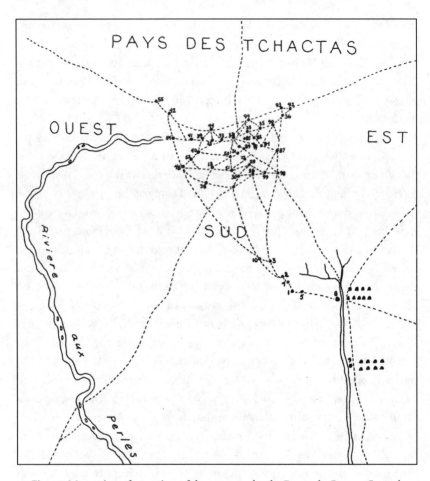

Fig. 9.1. My tracing of a portion of the 1733 map by the Baron de Crenay, Carte de partie de la Louisianne qui comprend le Cours du Missisipy depuis son embouchure jusques aux Arcansas celuy des rivieres de la Mobille depuis la Baye jusqu'au Fort de Toulouse: des Pascagoula et de la riviere aux Perles . . . Village names are replaced by numbers from the list in Swanton, *Source Material*, 59–75.

been assigned after a short time in the field to command the fort in Mobile, had never himself traveled among the Choctaw villages, so his map could not have been based upon personal knowledge. There is no direct evidence to show why the map was prepared, but it is obvious from its date that its purpose was the delineation of what was rightly anticipated as a future theater of war. Besides the information that could have been provided by Régis and

POSITIVE METHODS

Lusser, Crenay could also draw upon the knowledge of the interpreters and the traders who operated out of the Mobile district among the Choctaw and Chickasaw. A brief glance at the whole of Crenay's map, however, shows that its watercourses are distorted and that its Indian nations, particularly the Chickasaw, may be badly located. Thus, although the connections among the Choctaw villages on this map seem very tight and circumstantial, there is good reason not to trust it implicitly.

But between the narrative accounts and the map it may be possible to arrive at a better picture of the village configuration if we can derive a map from the narratives to compare with Crenay's map. A preliminary investigation can be made using the nonmetric multidimensional scaling technique developed by Shepard and Kruskal for the reduction of psychological data.[13] It has been used before for the construction of maps from several sorts of archaeological and historical data.[14] The method suggested here requires that a graph be derived from the narratives, in which the villages are the vertices and the paths taken between the villages are the edges. Since these paths are only inconsistently specified in terms of distances, actual distances are not used for the edges; instead, each edge is considered as a unit distance. The complete graph is expressed as a symmetric matrix with both rows and columns representing the same list of villages as in a highway distance table, such that the diagonal is filled with zeroes and the remainder of the matrix is filled with sums of unit distances. The distance between any two villages is the sum of the unit edges traversed in going from one to the other *by the shortest path*; these distances are computed from a list of the pairs of vertices defining the edges of the graph. Previous research by the author, following a suggestion by Kendall, has shown that maps reconstructed using such data agree substantially with maps reconstructed using actual distances if the underlying graphs are sufficiently connected.[15] Since in any case the environmental conditions encountered by our two narrators made accurate observation of distances nearly impossible, this handling of the distances was felt to be a reasonable compromise for the initial stage of analysis.

Once the matrix is constructed, the remainder of the procedure is simple. The lower half of the matrix, excluding the diagonal, is input to a computer program that will carry out a nonmetric multidimensional scaling algorithm (in this case, the Guttman-Lingoes smallest-space analysis of the MINISSA-I [M] suite was used, minimizing the Kruskal stress measurement), starting at a higher dimensionality than the desired two (five dimensions were used here) and iterating the analysis down to two dimensions to obtain a configuration of points in a plane.[16] If a sufficiently low stress measurement (0.05 or less) is obtained, then the resulting configuration can be considered a faithful representation of the data in the input matrix, though it is always possible that the configuration will be oriented in a different way or will be a mirror image of the "correct" configuration.[17] Either of these eventualities can be ignored and the plane of the configuration permuted to correct them, as long as the relationships between the points in the configuration are maintained.

For this study three matrices were constructed: one for the data from Régis du Roullet's journals, one for the data from Lusser's journal, and one containing combined data from both sources. The numbering of the villages and the spelling of their names are taken from Swanton's summary table, for the sake of uniformity.[18] This means that the village names are given the same number each time that they appear in order to simplify comparison of the resulting configurations. A list of these names with their corresponding numbers is given in table 9.1. A tracing of part of Crenay's map, using Swanton's numbers instead of village names, is shown in figure 9.1 for comparison with the computed configurations.

The first set of data is drawn from the narrative of Régis du Roullet, a young ensign who had served in Louisiana for five years before Governor Périer sent him, just before the Natchez rebellion of 1729, to make a tour of the Choctaw nation and to summon the chiefs to New Orleans for discussions on the prices of trade goods. Régis did not speak Choctaw, and some accounts suggest that the Choctaw did not think much of him, especially after he established a trading post in the Yowani village in 1730. But he did keep a detailed journal of his travels, and later, in 1732, he traveled from Mobile to Bokfoka in order to map the Pearl River from its source to the Gulf Coast. There are thus three batches of data that we have from Régis: the journal of his 1729 trip through the nation, a messy, on-the-spot manuscript full of scratchings-out and insertions; a compilation made at some time after the events described in the journal that summarizes his activities among the Choctaw in 1729–33 (we also have two reports that he sent to Périer in 1731 that apparently served him as source material for part of the compilation); and the 1732 itinerary, describing in detail—with compass bearings and estimated distances—his trip from Mobile to Bokfoka and thence down the Pearl. The last of these three sources was used to make maps, which also survive.[19]

Table 9.1. Names of Choctaw villages

0	Tohome	36	Skanapa
1	Nashobawenya	39	West Yazoo
2	Oskelagna	40	Imoklasha
3	Tala	41	Kashtasha
4	Siniasha	42	Kafitalaia
5	Boktoloksi	43	Abeka
8	Chickasawhay	45	Osapa chito
9	Yowani	48	Chanke
13	Bissacha	50	Itichipota
26	Kunshak	54	Bokfoka
29	Okalusa	58	Oka hullo
31	Iyanabi	60	Hashuk homa
32	Koweh chito	76	Nita asha
33	Boktokolo	82	Holihta asha
35	Lukfata	89	East Yazoo

Note: Code numbers from Swanton, *Source Materials*, 59–75.

Data for inclusion in the graph of villages were taken from all three of these sources. The bulk of the data comes from the journal and the itinerary. The compilation, due to its more general nature, supplies only a few links between villages. Only the villages actually mentioned as having been passed through or as being directly linked to such villages are included. The list of adjacent vertices of the graph, together with an example showing a part of the resulting matrix, appears at the head of figure 9.2, which represents the configuration obtained after twenty-one iterations in two dimensions (Kruskal stress 0.04564). The configuration as output by the program has been rotated counterclockwise 90 degrees and taken in mirror image to obtain a "north-south" oriented map with the eastern and western towns at their respective sides of the page. The edges connecting the vertices of the underlying graph have been drawn in.

A word should be said here about Swanton's grouping of the towns into divisions, which attempts to set up a static structure for what amounted, at least at the early French period, to political alignment superimposed upon some sort of "natural" divisions arising from geographical location and tribal structure. It seems to be the case, however, that the dominant towns of the divisions were Oskelagna (2) for the Sixtowns, Kashtasha (41) for the Western Division, and Kunshak (26) for the Eastern Division. The putative central division, with Koweh chito (32) as its dominant town, seems to have been not so much an autonomous division as the dominant town of the whole nation

Pairs of vertices defining edges:

0	9	8	76	32	43
1	2	9	26	32	60
1	8	13	54	39	41
2	3	13	76	39	43
2	4	26	31	39	60
2	8	26	32	41	42
2	50	29	31	41	45
3	8	29	32	41	54
5	9	31	32	42	54
8	9	32	33	45	54
8	26	32	36		

Partial lower half matrix:

	0	1	2	3	4	5
0	0					
1	3	0				
2	3	1	0			
3	3	2	1	0		
4	4	2	1	2	0	
5	2	3	3	3	4	0

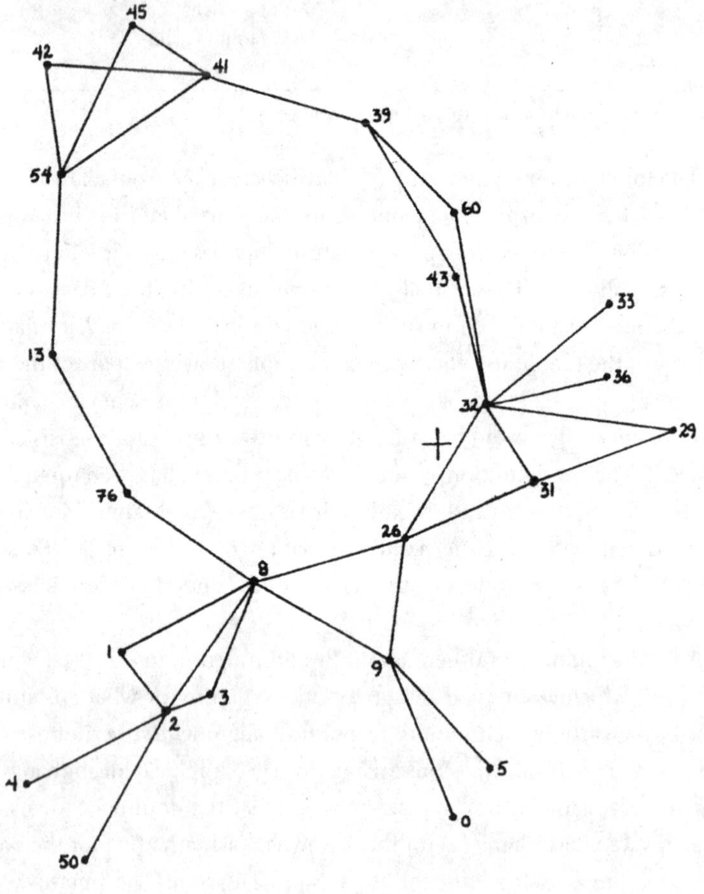

Fig. 9.2. Régis du Roullet data and configuration.

with dependent villages. Lusser, who seems to have been an altogether soberer and more experienced individual than Régis du Roullet, aligns it with the eastern towns, while Régis is the main authority for a separate central division.[20] These remarks should be borne in mind in considering the configurations derived from the testimonies of the two men.

To turn to an examination of the configuration from Régis' data, then, it will be seen that those points connected to only one edge of the underlying graph tend to be placed randomly in the vicinity of their single adjacent point (this applies to 0, 4, 5, 33, 36, 50), so all that can be said of them is that they belong somewhere in that vicinity. Leaving those points aside, we see that the configuration does not disagree badly with the Crenay map in figure 9.1, as far as the villages represented in that map are concerned, particularly in view of the fact that only unit distances were used. The great empty space in the center of the configuration reflects the fact that Regis' travels were limited to one tour of the nation (1729) and one "one-way itinerary" (1732); in fact, a good number of the cycles in the graph are the result of his having taken a different route on another occasion. As a result of the poor connectivity of the underlying graph, the subgraphs that are well connected are drawn together, while the loose connection to the "western" group centered on Kashtasha (41) distorts its relation to the other villages. The underlying graph has twenty-four vertices and thirty-two edges, with fully six vertices only connected to a single edge. A graph as poorly connected as this is not likely to yield a very accurate map, even if the edges are properly weighted as distances, since vertices adjacent to only two edges, particularly when a walk through the graph traverses a string of them, will merely be stretched out in a line.

It will be noted that Régis' perception of the village groupings as recorded in his 1732 village list is not reflected in the configuration, since in that list he includes the Sixtowns (1–5 and possibly 8 and 9) in the Western Division and since he does not record any travel through his small Eastern Division, which therefore does not appear on the map (Régis considers Kunshak [26] a central town). Instead, the configuration more clearly reflects a north-south dichotomy. This fact suggests that the strongest influence on the configuration comes not from the relationships that Régis perceived to exist between the towns but from the limitations of his travels. That is, all the links are physical rather than notional, though his travels themselves were doubtless influenced by the connections between closely related towns in that when he visited a division center he was quite likely to be invited to visit its dependencies.

Mapping Ethnohistorical Narrative

The second set of data comes from the 1730 journal of Jean-Christophe de Lusser, a Swiss captain of infantry based in Mobile whose journey through the Choctaw nation was to serve three purposes: to set up the new trading post at Yowani village that would be manned by Régis du Roullet; to evaluate the Choctaw attitude toward the French; and to urge the Choctaw to join the French in the war against the Natchez. The journal is a day-by-day account, very much a field notebook, although the copy that survives is a clean copy that was probably made especially to accompany the governor's reports to France. Because of the aims of his journey, Lusser made a rather carefully organized trip in which he visited all the major towns in the company of the two experienced interpreters, Huché and Allain.

The graph that can be derived from this data has twenty-three vertices and thirty-three edges, but it is better connected than the one representing the Régis du Roullet data, since vertices 4, 5, and 33, which were adjacent to only a single edge before, are now better connected, and only two vertices are left with but a single edge. Two edges present in this graph that are of particular importance for the resulting configuration are those between Oskelagna (2) and Kashtasha (41) and between Kashtasha and Koweh chito (32). The villages between 2 and 41 are thus pushed "westward" in the configuration. (Lusser did not record villages between 41 and 32, so no corresponding effect is visible as a result of this second new edge.)

The configuration obtained after twenty-eight iterations in two dimensions (Kruskal stress 0.02341) is shown in figure 9.3, rotated 180 degrees and taken in mirror image. Again, the effect of poor connection in the underlying graph can be seen to the "east" of the configuration, but the empty center space has been diminished considerably. Also once again the relative locations of village groups are roughly in keeping with the Crenay map. As far as the Eastern and Western Divisions on Lusser's town list are concerned, the configuration does reflect them to the extent that a line drawn through it to the left of 8 and 32 does divide the towns into the divisions that he indicates in the list, whereas on Régis' configuration the "central" clump cannot be divided off so neatly.

The justification for combining the two sets of data lies in the fact that they are strictly contemporary. In addition, in spite of the very different perceptions of the village groupings held by the two men, their data on the connections between villages do not conflict. The two sets of data produce a combined graph made up of thirty vertices and fifty edges, yielding a gratifying increase in the latter number; only two vertices besides the initial starting

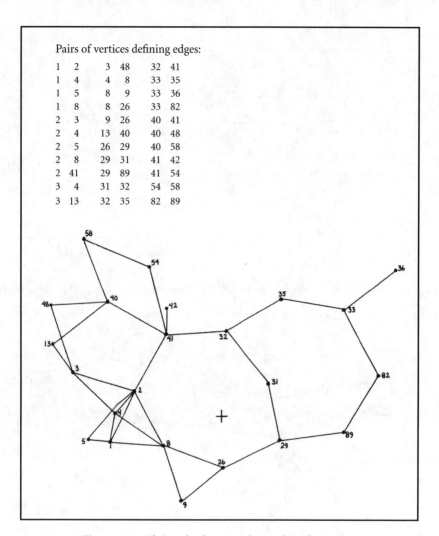

Pairs of vertices defining edges:

1	2	3	48	32	41
1	4	4	8	33	35
1	5	8	9	33	36
1	8	8	26	33	82
2	3	9	26	40	41
2	4	13	40	40	48
2	5	26	29	40	58
2	8	29	31	41	42
2	41	29	89	41	54
3	4	31	32	54	58
3	13	32	35	82	89

Fig. 9.3. Jean-Christophe de Lusser data and configuration.

point remain with a single-edge connection. The configuration derived from these data is shown in figure 9.4, after seventeen iterations in two dimensions (Kruskal stress 0.05291).

The considerable increase in connectivity of the underlying graph yields a configuration that is much more closely related to the Crenay map than either of the two sets of data has produced alone. Of course, it is increasingly clear that the use of unit distances produces serious distortion in the location of the

Pairs of vertices defining edges:

0	9	3	8	26	29	32	43	41	89
1	2	3	13	26	31	32	60	42	54
1	5	3	48	26	32	33	35	43	89
1	8	5	9	29	31	33	82	45	54
2	3	8	9	29	32	39	82	54	58
2	4	8	26	29	39	40	41	60	89
2	5	8	76	31	32	40	48		
2	8	9	26	32	33	40	58		
2	41	13	54	32	33	41	42		
2	50	13	40	32	36	41	45		
3	4	13	76	32	41	41	54		

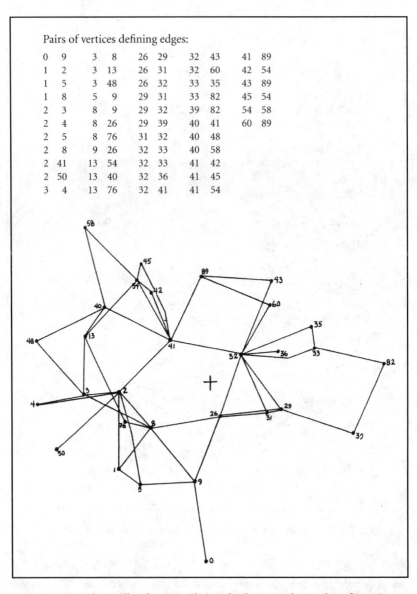

Fig. 9.4. Régis du Roullet plus Jean-Christophe de Lusser data and configuration.

Sixtowns group centered on 2 and of Chickasawhay (8) and Yowani (9), but the locations of the other three centers, 26, 32, and 41, now make much more sense when compared with Crenay. Something else, however, emerges in this configuration, and that is a conceptual map of the power structure involving the principal towns: the central pentagon defined by 2, 41, 32, 26, and 8 is made up of the principal towns of the Sixtowns, the Western Division, the central division or chief town of the tribe, the Eastern Division, and the French missionary post, respectively. Though it would be difficult to say what relationship this structure bears to the actual social structure of the tribe at this period, the evidence of the historical sources provides ample support for the assertion that it does reflect the French view of that social structure.

It is obvious that the foregoing exercise has not yet been useful in providing us with an accurate map of the Choctaw villages. At most we have established that the Baron de Crenay's map seems to be correct in its placement of at least the major villages. What we have done is to take a first step in the analysis of the data. To proceed further, several additional steps must be defined. First, the narratives we have used must be examined carefully for every possible hint of real distances, including both times taken and distance estimates mentioned, and further analyses should be performed using distances rather than unit edges, thus weighting the edges of the graph. To test the comparability of the narrative data with the Crenay map, another analysis should be performed to discover what sort of configuration would be generated from the data on that map, using the dotted-line paths indicated by Crenay for the edges of the underlying graph. Additional analyses should attempt to "tie down" some of the vertices of the graph. For example, it should be possible to specify coordinates for the three villages of Yowani, Chickasawhay, and Bokfoka, because their locations are pretty definitely known with relation to existing watercourses. The other points in the configuration would then be forced to take their positions with reference to these three. If survey subsequently defines sites that have a clearly distinct French component, and these sites can be identified because of their location in some topographically well defined place, then further points could be tied down. With improvements of these kinds the likelihood that fruitful areas for survey could be identified would be increased.

But it is also interesting to consider what has been learned from the results so far. First, we are able to define more clearly in graph-theoretic terms what kind of underlying graph will yield the most informative configuration. The graph should be as fully connected as is consistent with the data, and cycles should be especially sought, since with increase in connectivity comes a far less arbitrary placement of points in the final configuration. Second, we have seen that the map derived from narrative data using unit distances may be helpful in defining the prejudices of the observer, and in the colonial context such prejudices could and did have noticeable effects on official policy.[21] In dealing with the Choctaw the French attempted to establish influence through a redistributional system that depended upon a small number of chiefs to whom they gave medals. Régis lists five medal chiefs in his 1732 itinerary, and, not too surprisingly, they come from Chickasawhay (8), Kashtasha (41), Koweh chito (32), and Kunshak (26). He does not list the chief of Oskelagna (2) as having the medal, but this chief's prominence in other documents suggests that he may well have had one; in Lusser's list Oskelagna is shown with the same kind of dominance over the Sixtowns as Kashtasha is given over two other villages. The configuration in figure 9.4 may therefore be of intrinsic interest because of the possibility that it represents a version of the French redistributional system.

The Baron de Crenay, having come to Louisiana for the specific purpose of commanding an infantry unit in the punitive war against the Natchez in 1730, returned to France in 1732 and probably completed his map there as his last connection with the Louisiana colony. Régis du Roullet returned to France in the following year, also never to return to the Southeast. Lusser, after having helped establish Fort Tombecbé on the Tombigbee River as a forward post for the 1736 war against the Chickasaw, was killed in that war. Yet from the sojourns of these three men we have documents that represent a great deal of what we are likely to know of the Choctaw villages in their time until excavation can show more. Archaeologists have learned that the usefulness of colonial maps in locating and identifying aboriginal sites is limited. They have not yet attempted to extract all the information contained in narrative sources in any systematic way, except in the case of the Soto narratives. The method described here offers promise for exploiting the narrative evidence and the cartographic evidence together in such a way as to permit a more accurate identification of sites and site locations than has hitherto been possible. Further development should demonstrate whether the promise can be kept.

Acknowledgments

I would like to thank Dr. Christopher S. Peebles, director of the Moundville Archaeological Project, for having provided facilities for the completion of the analyses reported in this paper using the GTE/TELENET-MERIT network and the Michigan Terminal System under National Science Foundation grant BNS 78-07133-01.

Notes

Abstract: The French documents that emanated from the Louisiana colony from 1699 to 1763 contain a great deal of information about the largest and most important Indian nation with which they had to deal, the Choctaw. The French accounts, however, and the Spanish accounts that preceded them, suggest that during the colonial period the Choctaw suffered a serious dislocation in social structure that may have been mirrored by a noticeable change in settlement pattern. The aim of this paper is to begin the investigation of that change by analyzing the narrative evidence for the early French period. There are several French narratives describing travels among the Choctaw villages. Taking a group from the end of the earliest period, 1729–32, the study attempts to reconstruct a two-dimensional map of the data from the narratives. Using a graph model of the connections between locations, square matrices representing the number of graph edges traversed between villages are constructed for two groups of evidence and then for the combined data from both. These matrices are used as input to a nonmetric multidimensional scaling procedure in order to obtain two-dimensional configurations. The paper describes the method used to derive the configurations and discusses the results of the analyses as they relate to a French map of the period and to the known archaeological evidence. Suggestions for further analysis and for the application of the results to the needs of site survey are offered.

1. Bourne, *Narratives*; Peebles, *Prehistoric Agricultural Communities*.

2. For a discussion of tribal divisions see Swanton, *Source Material*.

3. Collins, "Potsherds."

4. Ford, *Analysis*, 40–49; Phillips, *Archaeological Survey*, 1:65–66; Penman, *Archaeological Survey* and "Historic Choctaw Towns"; Brown, "Antiquities"; Halbert, "Bernard Romans' Map."

5. Halbert, "Bernard Romans' Map."

6. Anonymous, Mapa del Golfo; Ortelius/Chiaves, *La Florida*.

7. Delisle, *Carte de la Louisiane*, Carte des environs, Carte du Canada, and *Carte du Mexique*; and Crisp/Nairne, *A Compleat Description*, see especially the Nairne inset.

8. Barnwell, untitled manuscript map; Crenay, Carte de partie.

9. Romans, A Map of Part of West Florida; De Brahm, A Map of the Indian Nations and A Map of the Southern Indian District.

10. Cabeza de Vaca, *La relación*; Bourne, *Narratives*; Priestley, *The Luna Papers*.

11. Régis du Roullet, Journal abstract, 1729–33, in AC, série C13A, 15:l97–211, translated in Rowland and Sanders, *Mississippi Provincial Archives*, 1:170–92.

12. Jean-Christophe de Lusser, Journal, January 12–March 23, 1730, in Archives des colonies, série C13A, 12:l00–134, translated in Rowland and Sanders, *Mississippi Provincial Archives*, 1:81–117.

13. Kruskal, "Multidimensional Scaling."

14. Kendall, "Maps from Marriages," "Construction of Maps," and "Review Lecture"; Tobler and Weinberg, "A Cappadocian Speculation"; Cherry, "Investigating the Political Geography"; Galloway, "Restoring the Map."

15. Kendall, "Construction of Maps"; Galloway, "Restoring the Map" and "Producing Narrative Maps."

16. See Guttman, "A General Nonmetric Technique"; Lingoes and Roskam, *A Mathematical and Empirical Study*.

17. Kendall, "Review Lecture," 578.

18. Swanton, *Source Material*, 59–75.

19. Régis du Roullet, Journal, April–August 1732, in Archives du service hydrographique, vol. 67^2, no. 14-1, portefeuille 135, document 21, translated in part in Rowland and Sanders, *Mississippi Provincial Archives*, 1:136–54.

20. Lusser, Journal, 134; Régis du Roullet, Journal, April–August 1732, itinerary; see Swanton, *Source Material*, 56.

21. Watson, "The Role of Illusion."

10. Choctaw Villages and Rubber Sheets

A GIS Application to Historical Maps

Ethnohistorians have little access to colonized peoples' own view of their history; they are usually limited to European views of the extraordinary events that characterized the inevitable social change brought on by the shocks of culture contact. Consequently, ethnohistorians attempting to reconstruct the history of non-European and nonliterate peoples are compelled to focus importantly on long-term historical trends and the kinds of evidence for them that can be deduced from archaeological remains. Fundamental aspects of such trends depend upon demographics and the man-land relationship, so the single fact of settlement location is very important for establishing how a people interacted with the natural world and how that interaction may have changed over time under conditions of demographic and social change.

In Europe, where nearly every square meter has been occupied by so many for so long, evidence for settlement locations of many sequent cultures has had plenty of time to come to light. In relatively sparsely settled areas like the Americas or many parts of Africa, however, simply finding settlement locations is an enormous task impossible to complete by carrying out complete survey of the surface; one of the archaeologist's most painful tasks is the revision of failed predictive hypotheses of settlement pattern, especially when he is dealing with a region whose natural richness makes many areas appropriate and favorable for settlement by humans practicing a variety of subsistence strategies. Hence the persistent fantasy, epitomized in the Indiana Jones films and secretly shared by the most sternly scientific of professional archae-

The material in this chapter was first presented as a paper, "Choctaw Villages and Rubber Sheets: A GIS Application to Historical Maps," at the International Conference on Computers in the Humanities in Tempe, Arizona, March 17–21, 1991.

ologists, of finding some kind of ancient treasure map that will literally tell him where to dig. Yet in certain cases, although treasure is seldom what their use can yield, there actually are such maps, if only we can find a way to make use of them. These maps are the ones drawn by European explorers and cartographers during the early stages of contact with colonized peoples.

If European maps of the Age of Exploration were actually reliable guides to any real geography, they would clearly have been used long before now, and the archaeologists would have no further need for settlement-pattern hypotheses. But European cartography only began to come of age, to portray what we understand as a scientifically measured view of the earth's surface, during the eighteenth century, and as cartographers perfected their methods the Native people they mapped in colonized areas were being wiped out by disease or removed to other areas; in any case, their lives were being dramatically altered. These facts set an immediate temporal limitation on such cartographic evidence.

From the technical side there are limits too. The historian is concerned to know such things as the reliability of the observer who made the map or supplied the information and the likelihood that his information is sound in any modern sense. He needs, in short, to be able to judge the value of map evidence. So although it may be technically possible to "do something" with a historical map, we must first determine whether something is worth doing—even before we decide what to do.

Eighteenth-century observers gathering data on the ground (even in wilderness) had reasonably accurate equipment in the shape of compass and astrolabe to establish direction and distance, and hence their mapping of limited areas is likely to be quite accurate. Many of these men had training in engineering or navigation. They were specifically commissioned to explore, and in nearly all cases they depended on Native guides and informants as well as their own observation. The best of them used informant data only as a guide and checked everything on the ground themselves. But it is clearly important to distinguish, where possible, directly observed from informant data, especially since in the case of informant data it is highly unlikely that distance measures or directional data will have been accurately conveyed across cultural boundaries. If we can be reasonably certain that a map embodies mostly evidence from direct European observation, then it can be a candidate for the kind of analysis we are discussing here.

POSITIVE METHODS

What we want to do to make such maps usable for finding actual locations or analyzing settlement patterns is to "correct" them, to render them as distortion free as possible with reference to modern coordinate systems. Modern cartography has long referred to such a process as "rectification," and it has a distinguished history comfortably predating computers (by roughly a hundred years) in the practice of aerial photogrammetry, or the use of aerial photographs for topographic mapping. Because it is nearly impossible to obtain a perfectly vertical aerial photograph, it has long been recognized that to obtain accurate topographic mapping data from such photographs there would have to be some way to correct for such problems as angle of tilt from the vertical or altitude from which the photograph was made. Accordingly, almost from the earliest days of aerial photogrammetric work the mathematics of photogrammetric rectification have been developed and elaborated, and optical instruments were devised to perform this rectification virtually automatically by reexposing the original image through suitably angled lenses.

With the advent of computer-based geographical information systems (GIS), the task of rectification was almost infinitely simplified because it now had become possible to correct distortion not by direct optical means, which limited the variability that could be dealt with, but by applying mathematical transformations directly to the digitized image itself. In principle its variability was limited only by the resolution of the data.

The task of rectification of distortion in a GIS is quite simply described. The data in a GIS are accumulated in "horizontal" layers, called coverages, all of which are referenced to a single basic absolute topographic grid system. Where a coverage is known to have distortions, it is possible to align specific points on the coverage to known absolute grid points and then to apply transformations to fit the coverage's surface to the fixed known points, stretching some areas and shrinking others to an ideal "flat" surface. This technique is called, vividly enough, "rubber sheeting."[1]

The specific project described here, funded by an NEH grant for the historical study of Choctaw settlement patterns, took advantage of the existence of the Mississippi Automated Resource Information System, a state government GIS aimed at the management of resources in the state and therefore already equipped with the relevant coverages for making rectifications for the alignment of historical maps.[2] The process was rather simple: the historical map was digitized, specific points on it were identified as being linked with specific reference points on the coverage for rivers and streams, a transformation was constructed to deform the historical map surface so that the linked points were aligned, and the resulting historical map layer was plotted as an overlay to the political boundary coverage and the rivers and streams coverage. The simplicity of this statement belies the many considerations that lay behind the choices of link points.

To begin with, I was fortunate in the fact that two previous projects had attempted to plot the region of interest on the basis of historical maps, both of them working with multiple historical maps and both of them simply working by eye to estimate the proper plotting of locations. The first, a BA honors thesis at Harvard by Paul Millhouser in archaeology, used river similarities and known properties of the region's topography to arrive at probable locations of eighteenth-century Choctaw villages in terms of large circles plotted on modern topographic maps (see figure 10.1).[3] The second, an MA thesis at the University of Georgia by Kenneth Carleton in anthropology, sought to reconstruct Indian trails of the eighteenth century and, incidentally, the location of Choctaw villages, resulting in a very small scale map of trails and rivers with the villages fit to both by eye (see figure 10.2).[4] Both projects took existing archaeological identification of Choctaw village sites into account, and both made useful strides in the identification of the actual rivers portrayed in specific historical maps. In addition, both offered useful impressions of the accuracy and skills of specific cartographers. Both of these studies came to the obvious conclusion that the group of maps underlying the several large maps of the southeastern region made in the 1770s under the supervision of John Stuart, British superintendent of Indian affairs for the region, provided the most detailed and accurate information on contemporary Indian settlement patterns.

The map used for this experiment was a draft of the Tombigbee River watershed, probably prepared by Bernard Romans around 1772 and contributing to the masterful Stuart-Purcell map of 1775.[5] It is known to have been based upon actual survey carried out by Romans in the region together with materials provided by both cartographer George Gauld for the coast and Indian agent David Taitt for the interior.[6] It had been acquired in photostatic form in the 1970s for the collections of the Mississippi Department of Archives and History from the British Public Record Office. Its author, Bernard Romans, was a cartographer and naturalist who traveled over the region in 1770, personally navigating the Tombigbee and traveling overland among its tributaries with Native guides. Historical geographers have accorded Romans high praise

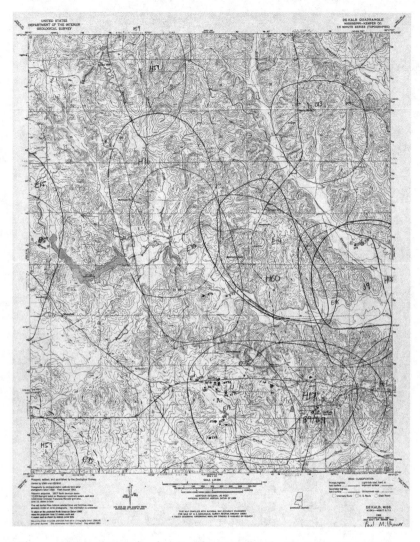

Fig. 10.1. Manuscript overlay showing Choctaw village locations fitted to USGS map, 1988. Courtesy of Millhouser, "A Map Method"; scan created by Tozzer Library of Harvard College Library.

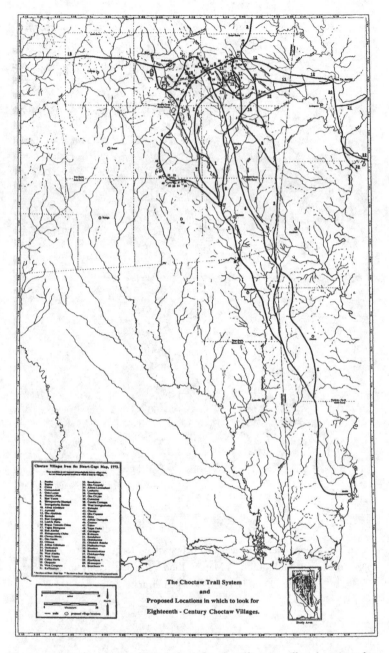

Fig. 10.2. Map of east-central Mississippi showing Choctaw village locations from Romans's cartography fitted to rivers in the region, 1989. Courtesy of Carleton, "Eighteenth-Century Trails."

for his cartographic work, and the details that he recorded, particularly of hydrography, are quite impressive given the available instrumentation.[7]

However excellent the cartographer, digitization of his map with the intention of identifying it with real coordinates requires that several assumptions be made explicit and problems be solved. We bother to analyze his map in the first place because we judge his information to be accurate, and to a degree there is a circularity to this judgment. Clearly, we can see by inspection that the gross features of Romans's river systems are quite accurate in proportion to the actual systems. Close inspection reveals, as it had as early as 1902 to the historian and amateur ethnographer Henry Halbert, that Romans's portrayal of the fine details of river systems west of the Tombigbee, especially the tributaries of the Chickasawhay/Pascagoula, incorporated several confusions that caused the conflation of several creeks. We know from the early cadastral surveys of the 1830s that the hydrography of these particular small creeks has not changed substantially enough that these were not errors, so we had to decide how to deal with them. This specific problem, thanks to the nature of the rubber-sheeting process, could basically be ignored: all we had to do was decide how to map the main river forks onto the modern map, not how every digitized point would subsequently fit.

A second consideration was the need to decide on the degree of accuracy we expected for the location of the Choctaw villages. The explicit assumption here was that we expected all the villages to be placed relatively accurately with reference to vertical distance from referenced watercourses, however inaccurate the watercourses might be themselves. This assumption was based on the notion that Romans himself actually visited many of the villages he mapped and had the opportunity to check in the field the accuracy of distance estimates given him by his informants. We accordingly wished to maintain the location of each of the village sites constant with respect to its nearest watercourse.

Because the scale of the original map from which we were working was a bit larger than 1:250,000, we began the task of fitting the digitized image by establishing peripheral control points on very well defined features at the edges of the area of interest (the mouth of the Pearl River, the headwaters of the Pearl River, the mouth of Mobile Bay, and the junction of the Tombigbee and Black Warrior rivers) to shrink the digitized image uniformly to fit that scale.

Fixing the points that we wanted to link between the historical map and the underlying coordinate plane was relatively simple: we concentrated upon the

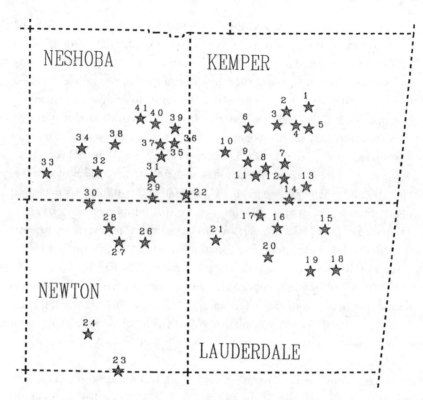

Fig. 10.3. Synthetic map showing Romans's 1772 village locations fitted to modern USGS map, large plot.

junctions of river and stream branches. We had prior scholarship available to help identify which minor creeks were being portrayed, and the initial plot of results was quite encouraging. But it was clear that if we wanted a better fit we would have to link more points, so we decided to include headwaters for rivers and most creeks and additional branch junctions. The final plot of our results achieved what we felt was a very respectable fit with the hydrography of the area of interest (figures 10.3 and 10.4).

From the point of view of our initial aim the results were equally interesting. Prior scholarship had indeed suggested similar patterns for eighteenth-century Choctaw settlement patterns, but we felt that our results reflected more accurately the data of the particular map we worked with. And the pattern itself was of interest because comparison with the patterns derived from Choctaw land claims data dating from about a hundred years later

POSITIVE METHODS

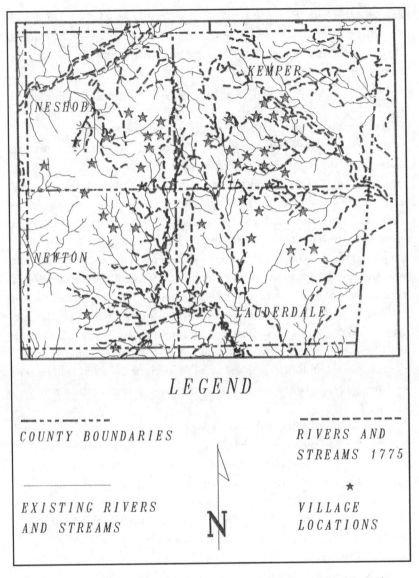

LEGEND

- - - - COUNTY BOUNDARIES

——— EXISTING RIVERS AND STREAMS

N

- - - - - - RIVERS AND STREAMS 1775

★ VILLAGE LOCATIONS

Fig. 10.4. Synthetic map showing Romans's 1772 village locations fitted to modern USGS map, showing details of streams.

indicated that patterns had not changed significantly during the interval, even though other evidence had suggested that Choctaw tribal life had indeed changed under the influence of Christian missionaries and the secular pressure of Mississippi state government. This evidence joins with a good deal of additional new evidence to suggest that indeed many fundamental elements of Choctaw culture have survived into the present virtually unchanged in structure, even if their surface appearance suggests the contrary.

So how accurate is this plot of village locations? Although it is a trivial matter, once the rubber-sheeting transformation has been effected, to obtain absolute geographical coordinates for each village site, certainly we do not expect these coordinates to yield eighteenth-century villages invariably (see table 10.1). The region was thickly populated, and there were many villages, so some of them will at least be close; but what is more important is the ability simply to project an historical map with its features of interest onto a modern map in a perfectly specifiable way, sparing the student the necessity of laborious hand work that will yield transformations in the data that cannot be precisely described. This particular exercise was superfluous to a certain degree because prior studies had carried out the same task by hand, but at least one of these studies suggested that a computer should be used for the task in the first place, and it is to be hoped that in future this method will be used as a first approximation for studying settlement patterns rather than as a last step.

Having achieved a degree of success working with the Romans map, I think it is possible to generalize on the use of this technique with other historical maps. Obviously, the application will not be successful if the historical map is not based upon the same assumptions as modern cartography (e.g., maps made by Native Americans use very different conventions for representing space and features, so any attempt at direct rectification of this kind would be nonsense). But what about less accurate European maps? I think the answer must be that we need to go very carefully with them, since there is some evidence to suggest that where maps are based upon informant evidence without field check and thus upon the mental map of the mapmaker, they may portray more metaphor than fact as the mapmaker uses other knowledge to load his distance and direction portrayals.[8]

One reviewer of the abstract to this paper said that it had nothing earth-shaking to say about geographical information systems or the techniques involved in their use. I am not apologetic; I have never expected to teach

Table 10.1. UTM coordinates for projected Choctaw village locations

Index Map Identification Code*	X-coordinate (meters)	Y-coordinate (meters)
1	348,884.781	3,627,886.250
2	343,626.094	3,626,857.250
3	341,367.906	3,623,723.250
4	345,839.563	3,623,629.000
5	348,883.750	3,622,882.750
6	334,533.250	3,623,136.750
7	343,136.500	3,614,715.250
8	338,641.969	3,613,774.500
9	334,359.188	3,615,219.250
10	329,040.469	3,617,562.500
11	336,235.688	3,611,967.500
12	342,986.938	3,611,258.750
13	348,207.563	3,609,429.250
14	344,117.031	3,606,380.750
15	352,440.313	3,599,502.000
16	341,252.469	3,599,944.250
17	337,164.594	3,602,380.250
18	354,890.438	3,590,204.750
19	348,946.406	3,590,085.500
20	339,015.938	3,593,294.500
21	326,595.063	3,597,241.000
22	319,636.844	3,607,652.750
23	303,236.625	3,567,442.000
24	296,144.625	3,576,001.000
25	333,167.375	3,555,220.500
26	309,720.938	3,596,809.250
27	303,792.750	3,596,936.000
28	301,400.625	3,600,107.000
29	311,689.000	3,606,993.000
30	296,782.469	3,605,859.250
31	311,531.375	3,611,797.500
32	298,935.031	3,613,243.500
33	286,664.500	3,612,954.000
34	295,083.625	3,618,670.500
35	313,842.031	3,616,652.500
36	316,969.656	3,619,697.000
37	313,634.156	3,619,542.000
38	303,029.344	3,619,524.000
39	317,201.844	3,623,078.500
40	312,507.031	3,624,239.000
41	308,967.656	3,625,448.000

Note: Index map identification numbers correspond with the location ID numbers on the index map.

computer scientists their business. The real audience for this paper consists of historians and archaeologists of European colonialism and of the "people without history" that it affected; of historical geographers interested in the cognitive process of mapmaking; of demographers; of ecologists; of cultural and natural resource managers. There are, in short, many disciplines address-ing a time depth that makes this technique interesting, and I will be pleased to solve this problem for them so easily with existing technology that I think it unlikely most users of GIS systems would ever think of applying to such problems.

Acknowledgments

I would like to thank the staff of the Mississippi Automated Resource Infor-mation System, especially its director, Paul Davis, who supported the project, and resource analyst Neal Smith, who digitized the historical map and facili-tated this analysis. Paul Millhouser and Kenneth Carleton were kind enough to share their work. The research project of which this work was a part was carried out with Clara Sue Kidwell under grant no. RO-21631-88 from the National Endowment for the Humanities. I also want to thank Dr. Irwin Scollar of the Labor für Feldarchäologie, Rheinisches Landesmuseum Bonn, for having introduced me to photogrammetry.

Notes

1. ESRI, "Rubber Sheeting."
2. Galloway and Kidwell, "Choctaw Land Claims."
3. Millhouser, "A Map Method."
4. Carleton, "Eighteenth-Century Trails."
5. Halbert, "Bernard Romans' Map."
6. Ware, "Introduction."
7. DeVorsey, "Early Maps."
8. Gould and White, *Mental Maps*.

11. A Storied Land

Choctaw Place-Names and the
Emplotment of Land Use

Most modern discussions of the southern North American landscape deal with landscapes that are in some sense accessible; that is, they are preserved in some way—by literary description, cartographic or representational image, or even material reality. I want to talk about recovering landscapes that no longer exist, except perhaps partly in memory. This is the land as it was known and lived by its first inhabitants, the Indian groups who populated what Europeans so conveniently and inaccurately chose to call "wilderness." Since my own work has focused upon the late prehistory and early history of the Choctaw, I have drawn my examples from the Choctaw's early descriptions of their land, but the Choctaw were not exceptional. As we shall see, the land was everywhere an integral part of the stories of Native nations, woven into history, cosmology, and moral discourse—hence "emplotted": constructed cognitively as an active participant in the drama of human life. This seems to be a feature of the human relation to the land everywhere, even where humans have imposed upon it several layers of self-constructed virtual realities like systematic landownership, a lasting "built environment," and (certainly most important) lives consisting primarily of tasks unconnected with the land.[1] The way the land is emplotted mediates our relation to it, makes it more or less direct. But without an understanding of the systematics and pragmatics of this emplotment, it is not possible to begin to grasp non-European concepts for the man-land relation. As a practical matter, lack of this kind of under-

---

The original version of this chapter, "Toponymy of the Choctaw Homeland," was presented at the American Society for Ethnohistory conference in Chicago in November 1989. A revised version was presented at "The South: Its Land and Its Literature," the Natchez Literary Celebration, June 4–6, 1998. The material was further revised for inclusion in this volume.

standing has denied Native people their rightful claims on the land. As a historical matter, it has prevented us from being able to detect climatic and ecological "changes in the land."[2]

What ethnohistorians would most love to know is how this land appeared to the first humans who saw it ten or twelve or twenty thousand years ago. But although archaeology has begun to tell us something of how the early Indians used the land, we cannot learn from material remains much beyond a hint of what they thought about it; "the [archaeologist's] desire to fill the empty signs with meaning almost invariably leads the analyst to create a surrogate discourse" on the basis of patterns discerned using contemporary Western-constructed categories.[3] To avoid this conundrum we really need words, so we are forced to skip forward to the seventeenth and particularly the eighteenth centuries, to begin to hear Indian people characterize the land through the reportage of Europeans attempting to learn about it. And what we can now hear depends upon what the Europeans of that era wanted to know.

We should not imagine that the land so described was in any sense "virgin" land except in the fevered dreams of Europeans. Archaeology, again, reveals that Native people made several drastic subsistence shifts over time, some dictated by climate change and some by their own alteration of the landscape. As populations grew, the latter factor became more important. Thus intensive hunting led to management of the land for hunting, particularly controlled burning of forested lands. The shift to agriculture around twelve hundred years ago led to land clearance that further acted to create the "parklike" appearance so admired by sixteenth-century Spaniard and eighteenth-century Englishman. All these things the scientist can tell us; but to know how Indian people related to the land, placed themselves in it, and understood themselves as part of it, we are constrained—apart from guesses—to the last period of Indian control, before the land was taken by people who had significantly different ideas about it. Debates about all of these issues have been drawn from myths and legends and from European-observed practice.[4] Recently, however, scholars have begun to look at place-name evidence and to take "landscape ethnography" seriously.[5] Here I am most interested in clues to how the Choctaw of the eighteenth century may have inscribed their values with respect to the land and the way they dwelt on it in names and stories that made the land an actor in their lives and a part of Choctaw identity.

POSITIVE METHODS

Purpose of the Investigation

My research on the ethnogenesis of the historic Choctaw tribe has suggested very strongly that the Choctaw were a protohistoric, multiethnic confederacy and that most of the constituent Choctaw population of the eighteenth century had probably begun to settle the modern homeland beginning in the late sixteenth century.[6] Evidence from archaeology allows the assumption that the region of east-central Mississippi was mostly unpopulated in late prehistory (though not before) because its lack of a major river floodplain suitable for maize agriculture to support large populations meant that while hunters could make good use of it, agriculturists would not consider it the best land.

It is unlikely, however, that these particular lands were entirely unused or "unimproved" during that time, since they offered (and still do offer) excellent habitat for wild game and sources for many materials used in Choctaw subsistence activities, clothing, shelter, and ceremonials. It seems reasonable to propose that the large populations in the delta of the Mobile and Tensaw rivers to the east, populations that would later comprise most of the Eastern Division of the tribe, made use of the region as a hunting ground and resource area, which they reached via Sucarnoochee Creek, a major western tributary of the Tombigbee. It is also likely that the core of the Western Division, inhabiting the region just north of the Pearl's headwaters near the Nanih Waiya mound, also hunted here, as did the future Sixtowns people, then located in small farmsteads and hamlets in the Leaf River drainage. Thus the region was probably very well known, was probably also managed by burning, and had at least several hundred years of potentially memorable events connected with it even before it became the location of a large proportion of the fifty settlements of the Choctaw confederacy during the late sixteenth and seventeenth centuries.

The French colonials who had most contact with the Choctaw in the eighteenth century described the three divisions of the tribe that were important during that period as localized on the three watersheds of the Pearl, Chickasawhay/Pascagoula, and Sucarnoochee/Tombigbee. It is arguable that this localization reflected the constituent ethnicity of the confederacy and even the geographical origin of the constituent groups. It is possible that three groups all using the same region for hunting could easily divide it up so as to avoid hostilities by referring themselves to specific watersheds. When they later saw advantages in inhabiting the same region permanently, each group would choose the watershed with which it was most familiar, whose resources it best understood.

Almost all of this, however, is hypothesis, and apart from the evidence of archaeology, which so far is suggestive but not conclusive, it seemed to me that place-name evidence might offer an additional way of looking at the Choctaw relationship to the land, a way that might begin to sketch the lands of the new confederacy as a cognitive space so that we might recover hints of how early Choctaws inhabited, used, and imagined the land.

What do I mean by cognitive space? We all carry around maps in our heads, consisting of several culturally specific grids—not all of them very regular—with specific images, names, events, and particularly routes tagged more or less tightly to them.[7] We inhabit several cognitive spaces, really, since there are usually several distinct scales. First, at the most "intimate" scale we have a very specific map of our living space and perhaps a similarly complete one of our workspace. Second, we know a "local" map of the parts of our community with which we are familiar, usually structured in terms of familiar routes and neighborhoods and highlighted with well-known "landmarks." Finally, we conceive of larger and far more general "country" or "world" maps in which all of this is situated. The parts of this cognitive space that we know best, where we spend time instead of traveling through, are heavily embroidered in memory with images and events, while less well known regions are a virtual blank often eliciting fear, much like the terrae incognitae of medieval maps that mapmakers liked to populate with monsters; such whole regions may be characterized by monster *stories* (like "evil empires").

None of these "maps" should be thought of as static two-dimensional representations, however; in the case of eighteenth-century Choctaws it is likely that very few thought of the "bird's-eye view" then not even familiar to most Europeans. Such groupings of geographical information really serve rather as productive arrangements of relationships used to navigate both physically and metaphorically. They may include visualization but are not limited to it, and they may simply be ways of expressing how spaces become articulated by human meaning and serve as mnemonic and "structuring structures" that may be involved in the constitution of kinship, identity, morality, or any number of elements of the social. We cannot say that we are going to be able to understand fully how eighteenth-century southeastern Indians gridded their larger cognitive space (although there are a few Native-made maps from which we can make inferences),[8] but it may be possible to find in place-names some references that can help us bring an apparently familiar countryside alive with some of the images and events belonging to

POSITIVE METHODS

Choctaw people of an earlier time for whom east-central Mississippi was a very different cognitive space.

Landscape Ethnography

During the 1990s a number of trends in history, geography, anthropology, linguistics, and archaeology began to converge on an interest in "man-land relationships." Certainly, this focus was related to growing environmental concerns. But it is likely that in most of the fields mentioned these trends were at least nudged by the emergent power of indigenous voices in a discourse that combined a demand for decolonization and human rights with a critique of the Western market-oriented commoditization of land and eviction of both European peasantries and colonized indigenous peoples in a process of laying all the land of the earth under discipline, all of which has come to be referred to by critical anthropologists as "enclosure." The constituent fields had various relations to this critique: American "environmental history" (cf. White; Cronon; Silver) aimed at framing the declension of North American Native occupancy and the emergent hegemony of European land use ("Euroforming," to borrow a science-fiction name for Crosby's argument about intentional modification) in a detailed manner that focused on land use rather than ideology.[9] Another branch of this discussion cared very much about ideology and argued over the quality of Native environmental stewardship (Martin; Krech) in an ironic reversal of the original European argument that inadequate stewardship meant *not* "taming" the land.[10] Much of this discussion was also related to contemporary Native claims on resources, and this aspect of the discussion was of interest to geographers. Architects and urban planners (Alexander; Hillier and Hanson), seeking to understand the principles of spatial organization that made unplanned villages and houses more "livable" than dying urban centers and soulless suburbs, turned to a study of village and dwelling plans that had long histories of clear functionality.[11]

Among anthropologists certain ethnographers had always been interested in the relation of peoples to the land, especially when those peoples were primarily hunter-gatherers. Nowhere had these complexities been more elaborately traced than in Australia, where no issue involving Aboriginal people could ignore their fundamental relation to the land and its contribution to their cosmology and identity.[12] Because the persistence of indigenous peoples and their claims on the land and its resources led to their management by nation-states that had engulfed them, anthropologists in Australia and elsewhere (especially in the Northwest and Southwest of the United States) were increasingly in demand to interpret the meaning of those claims (and hopefully to find them meaningless). Studies on the ground especially called upon linguists to develop an understanding of place-names and naming systems as enduring manifestations of the meaning and use of land to indigenous people who had no societal requirement for a European system of land discipline. Archaeologists came into the picture as subdisciplinary interests began to focus on the contingency of archaeological interpretation, based on Western perceptions of patterning upon the land.

Linguists, for whom place-naming systems have long been a routine part of systematic language study, have pointed out that the linguistic features of place-names may be different in different cultures. Bright, for example, suspects that many cultures have an adverbial as well as a nominal function for place-names, like that which survives in English in the generic word "home" when used in "he went home."[13] Other issues include the degree to which a toponym is meant to name in the sense of "identify as unique" and how we may tell whether a place-name that can't be etymologized is actually a much-compressed story. In general, the naming of places has been much taken for granted, but, as Keith Basso strikingly showed in his work on Western Apache place-naming, linguistic systematics, without pragmatic knowledge of language use, would simply miss fundamental dimensions of place-naming.[14]

Several commonalities became clear in at least the anthropological approaches to this man-land relationship, which emerged from linguists' awareness of issues around the question of what names actually are and how the names themselves are related to places and the people who named them. Place-names, whatever their function, must signify intersubjectively; that is, they must be known by more than one person in order to communicate at all, and the numbers and kinds of persons who may or must know them are dependent upon what and why they signify.[15] For non-Western people, many studies showed, the so-called Western gaze that was concerned with controlling and administering land uniformly was simply irrelevant.[16] Place-names could be used for marking boundaries and wayfinding, but there were many other and richer ways that names could signify and many more complex man-land relationships that they could facilitate.[17]

As anthropologists began to argue, then, "social landscapes," embroidered by and indeed partly embodied in place-names, were important *actants* in the

POSITIVE METHODS

practices of dwelling that were fundamental to cultures. Indeed, as Bourdieu had long before suggested, they provided habitus-like "structuring structures" that taught members of a culture how to interact with the land and offered a discourse in which new interactions could be articulated.[18]

I will outline two examples briefly here just to point to the richness of meaning possible when the testimony of members is available. The first is the well-known Australian Aboriginal case mentioned above. For Aboriginal people the landscape is densely figured with the stories of the creation era called the "Dreamtime," when by their actions in moving across the land the creator beings (generally conceived of as animals or insects) created all the features of the land and, in addition, by merging with the earth at the end of their "track," sowed it with all the souls that would be needed for an entire population forever. Aboriginal identity is constructed from the identification of kinship groups with individual beings and with named sites and groups of sites along the track they followed across the landscape. Aboriginal groups so identified are morally bound to maintain the landscape as it was in the Dreamtime in order to guarantee an inexhaustible supply of resources. Stories of the events along the tracks created in the Dreamtime constitute moral exempla that speak to human interaction with the land, animals, and each other in ways favorable to survival in a harsh landscape.

In this context Mark Harvey carried out a recent analysis of the system of place-naming in several areas of Australia.[19] He found that the "language names" that distinguish "tribal" groups are congruent with the land where European impact has not been damaging to Aboriginal land use but not where the reverse is the case. A second class of names, exclamations ritually associated with specific territories and specific contexts of use, has the effect of relating the bodies of the persons owning these names with the lands to which they refer. Finally, a third class of names is specifically devoted only to the naming of land and only reflexively to those who have ritual relationship to that land. In this Gun-mogurrgurr naming system (or "landscape content names" in Harvey's terminology) name elements and construction vary from language group to language group, but elements may include the place-name of a prominent feature, the name of a generic landscape type of plant species characteristic of the region, or a noun referring (generally briefly) to a significant Dreaming-event site. Unlike the other two types, which refer to broad groups of sites, landscape content names are specific to individual sites or by extension to the sites of an "estate" that includes the named site. The connections between people and land as mediated by these names remain strong in Australia.

The second example is taken from Keith Basso's study of Western Apache place-naming. Basso found that some Apache place-names are minutely descriptive of individual places, and those names are also the names of the clans that dwell nearby. Another type of place-name, however, alludes to events along the trail or path of Apache history, in which time is expressed spatially and all historical events are seen as present for consideration. Events commemorated by such names always point to a moral lesson about appropriate conduct. Apaches well versed in this nomenclature and its significance can have nuanced discussions about moral issues or events in the past by alluding to these events through the place-names. Such rehearsal of the names and their lessons is an important element of social regulation and reproduction: a special discourse of speaking the names alone is characteristic of specific contexts in which one person reminds another of these important moral lessons with a view to advising politely on the amendment of conduct.[20] Further, because the names link lessons to places, the landscape itself speaks moral lessons to a traditionally educated Western Apache.

Basso's work reveals the social pragmatics of place-naming and place-name use among the modern Western Apache; Harvey's work on Australian place-name systems exposes something of their systematics for Aboriginal people. Both examples suggest possibilities far beyond the presumed significative function characteristic of the "Western gaze." In attempting to understand something of the eighteenth-century Choctaw place-naming system and practice, these two examples can open up many new possibilities for interpretation.

Method

For the historical evidence to be of most use in reconstructing this space as the early Choctaw lived it, it would have to come from the earliest possible sources. Europeans did not, however, bother to map the Indian-dominated interior in any detailed way except during periods when they were convinced that internal Choctaw politics were crucial to their own purposes. There are two periods from which evidence is particularly detailed. During the early 1730s French maps and documents reflect *their* profound concern with Choctaw attitudes following the Natchez revolt of 1729. During the late 1760s and early 1770s British maps and documents reflect *their* intention to inventory and begin to make use of the spoils of their victory in the French and Indian War in the Southeast, which gave them the entire region east of the Mississippi.

The evidence in question comes both from maps and from other documents. Map evidence would seem to be the most desirable because it actually labels a location with a name, while textual mention of a toponym is bound to be much less exact. Unfortunately, textual mention of toponyms is far more frequent than their appearance on maps; map evidence usually includes nothing but town names and (infrequently) river names. Fortunately, the men who mention them in texts are frequently the same ones who drafted the maps, so there is fair adequacy in their reference to features that were in fact mapped.

There are specific and inevitable spatial biases to the European evidence. Its particular strength lies to the south and east of the Choctaw villages, since the routes traveled by Europeans lie in these directions (especially the Mobile-Choctaw paths).[21] Hence we know nearly nothing about the lands to the north and west of the central region the Choctaw inhabited. To a certain extent this reflects a reality, since for at least the earlier period of the 1730s the Choctaw would not have spent much time in the area to the west controlled by the Natchez or the area to the north used by the Chakchiuma and the Chickasaw. But from that time onward the west was virtually clear, while after the incorporation of at least a part of the Chakchiuma in the 1730s and the Chickasaw wars of the 1730s and 1740s the Choctaw had little to fear toward especially the northwest, where we know they frequently hunted in the Yazoo basin during the early nineteenth century, naming and "emplotting" what would later become William Faulkner's Yoknapatawpha country.[22] Neither the French nor the British, however, paid significant attention to the Choctaw presence in those regions during the eighteenth century, so there is no early Choctaw place-name evidence for them.[23]

I should state here that while town names, the names applied to active dwelling places of human beings, are not entirely excluded here, my central interest focuses on names given to features in the "landscape," that is, the land beyond the boundaries of human habitation, where generally sedentary peoples like the Choctaw carried out extractive activities of various kinds. Town names can reflect or seem to reflect descriptive intent, but, like the "language names" of Australia and the descriptions of physical features of the Apache, they can also be entangled with and become ethnonyms, identifying their inhabitants—note the frequency with which Choctaw town names incorporate the "ogoula" element, meaning "people." The spaces "between" are also unlikely to be understood very well by other methods (e.g., few or no artifacts will be discovered in them even by archaeologists), yet they are very important in the way they provide a setting that makes "settlement" visible. Place-names applied to features in these spaces can perhaps thus make us more aware of what went on there in ways that archaeological method cannot, not only because archaeological culture borders are defined by the falloff in artifact frequencies and the presence of "empty" space but because place-names introduce the kinds of other levels of meaning we have just discussed.[24]

In the evidence I will consider here we only hear of locations that were on or near paths to or between towns. Carson has observed that during early European contact, as interior tribes adopted the horse, "footpaths became horsepaths."[25] This may be true in a larger sense, as pre-European trading paths were apparently so converted, but the evidence here is not so clear. The Europeans whose evidence we examine, all of them entering the nation from the south, were all using horse transport for themselves and at least some of their party, so the paths they used would have had to be negotiable to some degree on horseback. Clearly, the paths were not optimized for travel on horseback by the 1730s, since both Régis du Roullet and Lusser reported many crossings of bayous and swamps that were exceedingly difficult for horses. Heavy rains even forced them to make part of their journeys on foot, and they reported almost no fords at river crossings and many necessary detours. French plans for supplying a trading post in the southern part of the Choctaw nation thus included transport by boat up the Chickasawhay River, not horse trains like the English used to reach the Chickasaw and Choctaw overland. Horses were certainly used by the Choctaw in open country, however: when Lusser rode from Caffetalaya to Cushtusha, he said they rode "at a gallop in the Indian fashion" through open hills and prairies.[26]

Such evidence as we have is also highly dependent upon the individuals who elicited and offered the information in question and the social setting in which it was obtained. If a Choctaw guide declined to offer toponymic information or was not familiar with the region and hence did not know it, none could be recorded. Similarly, if a traveler's curiosity did not run to place-names, then he would never ask about them. Further, the capabilities of the recorder as a linguist are also relevant, for although most European travelers had an interpreter at their disposal, they also had as part of their traditional

POSITIVE METHODS

European intellectual equipment an unfortunate tendency to etymologize, which may have totally obscured real evidence by forcing it to harmonize with preconceived notions.[27]

Finally, it is very difficult to know how a Choctaw guide would have understood a request for place-names. If there were no specific Choctaw name for a place, he might, like many an anthropological informant, have supplied a simple description, just to be obliging: it now looks to us like a descriptive name. When there was a name, it might actually be a few brief words standing for a fuller name or an entire story—like Apache and Aborigine historical event names—well known to other Choctaws but a complete mystery to the European visitor. So it would not be wise to assume that we know how these toponyms were used or understood, whether in fact they were actually fixed place-names, unless similar names were collected in the same place by several observers, mutually ignorant of one another's work. Fortunately, such is the case with the French and British observers who visited the Choctaw homeland in the eighteenth century.

Case Study No. 1: French Panic in the 1730s

In 1729 the Natchez Indians, who saw the integrity of at least one of their sacred sites threatened, rebelled with the help of some enslaved Africans against French occupation and killed all the French males they could lay hands on in the Natchez region, taking women, children, and the remainder of the black slaves as hostages. Most alarming to the French colonists, the evidence of an ill-coordinated uprising of the Yazoo Indians led to the inference that the Natchez might have colluded with all the Indians of the region. Thereafter for several years the French waged direct war against the Natchez, forcing them from their lands, and then the French undertook to wage war on the Chickasaw for having taken the Natchez in. Two major campaigns against the Chickasaw were launched in 1736 and 1740, both with the aid of the Choctaw. All of these events and projects pointed to the need for better maps of the interior of Louisiana east of the Mississippi, and a number of mapping projects were carried out in the early 1730s in conjunction with several efforts to evaluate and assure Choctaw loyalty.

One of these efforts was carried out by the Swiss officer Jean-Christophe de Lusser, who was sent from Mobile into the Choctaw nation in 1730 to retrieve black slaves and French women and children who had been liberated from the Natchez by the Choctaw but not yet returned to the French settlements.

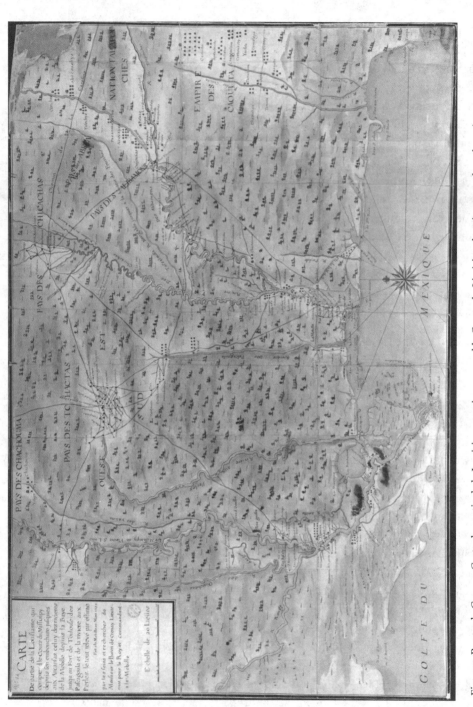

Fig. 11.1. Baron de Crenay, Carte de partie de la Louisianne qui comprend le Cours du Lississipy depuis son embouchure jusques aux Arcansas celuy des rivieres de la Mobille depuis la Baye jusqu'au Fort de Toulouse, des Pascagoula de la riviere aux Perles . . . , 1733, Archives nationales, Dépot des fortifications des colonies, no. 1A, Louisiane. Courtesy Centre historique des archives nationales, Paris.

Lusser's travel diary, although it was not accompanied by any sketch of the region it describes, probably served as a source for the regional map made by the Baron de Crenay in 1733, the first map to show the Choctaw villages in detail (figure 11.1).[28] But Crenay did not by any means exploit the sum of the information in Lusser's diary, which names many watercourses and a few other landmarks.

It is somewhat difficult to decipher Lusser's place-names, since for the most part he offered no translation and his spellings often did not segment Choctaw phrases in any helpful way (see table 11.1). I say "for the most part," since for the initial segment of the journey into the nation, when he had a competent French interpreter with him, Lusser did suggest translations of the names. For the rest of his itinerary after reaching Chickasawhay, which includes his tours of nineteen Choctaw villages, he gave no explanations of the names either of towns or of watercourses. Some of these can be compared to names given by others, but some can only be guessed at. Poor Lusser seems to have been ill with a persistent nosebleed during this time and was not an explorer in any case, so his lack of attention is understandable. What we can tell from this list, however, is that the names of places he was given (he lists thirty-nine nonvillage names) fall into two classes: those that are strictly descriptive of a natural feature ("nine springs of water," "cold waters") and those that seem to refer to some event that took place at a given location ("buffalo bones," "alligator hole," "hurricane-flattened plain"). Lusser's testimony is especially valuable because he described a route from Mobile to the Choctaw homeland, then through the homeland, and back by virtually the same route. He thus provided a list of place-names, relatively sparse though it is, against which other descriptions can be placed in an attempt to discern which place-names do not vary but *are* actual place-names—publicly agreed identifiers of specific places—and not simply ad hoc descriptions.

A second Frenchman who provided us with a significant amount of place-name data is Régis du Roullet, a young officer who was sent into Choctaw country in 1729 to divert English trade back to the French and to propose setting up a French trading post to be controlled directly from New Orleans. He returned to set it up in 1730 and was sent back in 1732 with several purposes, among them to map the trail from Mobile into the Choctaw nation and the course of the Pearl River.[29] Although Régis seems in some respects to have been a poor linguist himself, the list of place-names he supplied in his diaries and reports from Choctaw country is by far the richest of the

Table 11.1. Jean-Christophe de Lusser itinerary toponyms, 1730

[Northward into the Choctaw nation:]
Mobile
Chactaele
Bouchitto bayou
Loucfeata bayou
Kintabouc (beaver bayou)
Petit Scatape bayou
Grand Scatape bayou
Iteokchaco (blue wood)
Inafalacto (two roads)
Yanache Founichinya (buffalo bones)
Kalebichakale (nine springs of water)
Ouctaaymontalanya (trembling prairie)
Chouchoubachoufoue (alligator hole)
Bacatane River
(bayou of bad water)
Yowani village
Oskichitto (big canes)
Yayabouc
Oskelagna bayou
Apeleboucouchi (hurricane-flattened plain)
Octibia River (cold waters)
Chacchibou bayou
Acchouchy bayou

[Tour of eastern villages:]
Chickasawhay River and villages
Cipsi bayou
Ouscoubo bayou
Chaoucha bayou
Accipanya bayou
Concha village
Okalusa bayous and village
Jachou village
Oulicatacha village
Chukinatcha bayou
Bouctoucoulou village
Loucfeata village
Couechitto village
Yanabe village
Okalusa village
Concha village
Bachaloucha bayou
Accipanya bayou

Etechouca River (wood rat)
Apelle bayou
Inalecha bayou
Little Octibia
Great Octibea
Chickasawhay village

[Sixtowns village tour:]
Nitabouc [nita, bear; bouc, stream]
Nachabaouenya bayou and village
Cheniacha village
Oskelagna village
Ouchouty bayou
Boucfilame
Tala bayou and village

[Tour of western villages:]
Foketlapale bayou
Okeata bayou
Tchianke bayou
Bistacha bayou and village
Mongoulacha village
Chanke village
Fokettelalape bayou
Okeata bayou

[Sixtowns villages again:]
Tala village
Cheniacha village
Chickasawhay village
Cheniacha village
Oskelagna village
Nachoubaouenya bayou and village
Nitabouc [nita, bear; bouc, stream]
Chickasawhay village
Oskichitto (big canes)

[Southward out of the Choctaw nation:]
Yowani village
[L]oucfeata (?bayou)
Bacatane River
(trembling prairie)
(blue wood)
Grand Scatape
Petit Scatape
Bouchitto

Source: Journal of Jean-Christophe de Lusser accompanied by Sieurs Duché and Régis, January 12–March 23, 1730, AC, C13A, 12:100–134, translated in Rowland and Sanders, *Mississippi Provincial Archives: French Dominion*, 1:81–117. Meanings of the names given in parentheses are from the original document.

POSITIVE METHODS

eighteenth century (see table 11.2). He recorded a name for practically every watercourse he saw on the overland journey into the nation and included French translations for most of them; his French interpreter on the 1732 expedition was capable, and his Choctaw guide seems to have been particularly voluble and well informed. In addition, because he made what amount to several strip maps documenting his journey, we have at our disposal at least his idea of the placement of his streams and villages where they intersected with his path. Finally, since a major part of his route was nearly the same as the one Lusser took, the two can be compared to see if names repeat.

In fact, the two French observers agree fairly well for the Mobile-to-Choctaw country path, which had been well known to the French for years since Henri de Tonti first traveled it in 1702.[30] Yet there are differences that may be significant. Régis du Roullet reported many more names than Lusser, suggesting that he was attempting in prose a complete description of what he would later attempt to capture as a mapmaker, possibly for mnemonic purposes: the path, with features seen alongside or passed through.[31] Lusser listed only the most important features along the way, which makes it all the more interesting that he listed two apparently "story-based" place-names that Régis did not list ("trembling prairie" and "alligator hole"), whereas for the same stretch Régis listed three *different* such places ("bayou of two mortars," "small canes where a horse died," and "bayou where wolves chased [them] away"). Perhaps the routes taken differed slightly; perhaps their guides were of different ages or came from different tribal divisions. There may be any number of explanations here, but where they agree we can be sure that, for example, "like a beaver foot" and "bayou of buffalo bones," which both Europeans reported along the portion of the trail between the town of Blue Wood and the Bakatané River, were agreed-upon names of specific places. It is also well that the disagreements include toponyms that seem to have attached stories, because these especially were clearly not merely descriptions of visible natural features.

It is unfortunate that the Choctaws who accompanied Régis on his journey down the Pearl River were not equally informative. Régis remarked upon every stream he saw emptying into the Pearl, but his guides apparently had no names for most of them. This may not be surprising; indeed, it may reflect one of the aspects of Choctaw cognitive space we are trying to understand. The two creek names given were for tributaries near the source of the Pearl, deep in the western Choctaw heartland that may have been the only region

Table 11.2. Régis du Roullet itinerary, 1732

[Journey into the nation:]
Bouq ou Poulou (bad bayou)
Bouc ouakapouka (bayou where cows pasture [*wak*, cow])
Boukaille (death bayou [*ailli*, death])
Boukouma (red bayou [*ouma*, red])
cypress swamp
Kale (spring [*kali*, spring])
Bouk Tchakale (nine bayous [*chakali*, nine])
Bouktiak an tchaba (bayou where a pine tree serves as a bridge [*tiak*, pine, *achaba*, footbridge])
Boukouchi Tapunta (two little twin bayous [*ushi*, child, *tapa*, divided in two, *chipunta*, little])
Quinta ouba yllie (like a beaver foot [*kinta*, beaver, *holba*, like, *iyi*, foot])
Bouk Chikachoa ajouetta (bayou of Chickasaw[hays?] hunting ground [*aiowata*, hunting ground])
Boukchancoulou (cypress bayou [*shankolo*, cypress])
Boukoufoubé (deep bayou [*hofobi*, deep])
Skatape bayou ("a proper name")
Battcha albina (place of camping-huts, sleeping-place [*bina*, camp])
Ite Ouktchaco Tchitou (great blue wood [*iti*, wood, *okchako*, blue, *chito*, large])
Conchak ouéchakché (end of the great canebrake [*conchak*, canebrake, *wishakchi*, end])
Bouk janache founi atcha (bayou of buffalo bones [*yannash*, buffalo, *foni*, bone, *hacha*, river]: "the Indians formerly killed buffaloes there whose bones are still visible")
Katbitchakale (nine springs [*kali*, spring, *bicha*, to spout, *chakali*, nine])
Bouk kité toucoulou (bayou of two mortars [*kitti*, mortar, *tuklo*, two])
Tiakouillé (pine bayou of the low valley [*tiak*, pine])
Conchak oufoube (deep bayou among small canes [*hofobi*, deep])
Conchak ou soubaille (small canes where a horse died [*isuba*, horse, *ailli*, death]: "there is a large hole in the midst which is filled with water, where a horse that fell in stuck fast in the mud such that the Indians could not pull him out")
Bouk yte achiché (bayou of tree roots [*iti*, wood, *akshish*, root])
Bouk outakou jakené (bayou where the earth shakes [*oktak*, prairie, *yakni*, earth)
Bouk oka atchokema falacto (bayou of fork of good water [*oka*, water, *achukma*, good, *falakto*, fork])
Conchak opotale (little canes where there are two double bayous [*pokta*, grow together)
Bouk nachouba atchafu (bayou where wolves chased [them] away [*nashoba*, wolf, *achafa*, pursue])
Bouk yte ane (bayou of tree-seed [*iti*, wood, *ani*, fruit])
Bouk tchitou (great bayou)
Bakatané River
Bouk ouchane ou lafu (bayou where the otter lives [*oshan*, otter])

Table 11.2. *Continued*

Bouk oke oullou (bayou of scarce water [*oka*, water, *ullohchi*, drawn water]: "it has no water at all during the hot season")

Bouk fala noce (bayou where crows roost [*fala*, crow, *nusi*, roost])

Sakté coutchouaka (bluff barred with various colors [*sakti*, bluff])

Bouk tapunkcha (bayou of grey clay)

Bouk yté tchuie souba (bayou where there is a log serving for a horse track [*iti*, wood, *isuba*, horse])

Bouk tiak yté ilbucha (bayou of the bare pine tree [*tiak*, pine, *iti*, wood, *ilbasha*, poor, meager])

Bouk chankoulou (cypress bayou)

Bouk Loukfeata (bayou of white earth [*lukfi*, clay, *hata*, white])

Conchak tchitouka (great clump of small canes: "in the midst of this conchak there is a hole always full of water")

Yowani village

Bouk tiakillé (bayou of the dead pine tree [*tiak*, pine, *ailli*, death])

Bouk tale ouaktche (bayou where one throws stones [*tali*, stone, *kanchi*, throw])

Bouk tale okabenille (bayou where the stone lies in the water [*tali*, stone, *oka*, water, *binili*, settled])

Bouk okapotala (bayou of low water [*oka*, water, *patala*, flat])

Bouk atcha bakaloue (bayou of the strong bridge [*achaba*, footbridge, *akallo*, strong])

Bouk loksouche a alemon (bayou where one gathers the *real* Tamon?)

Tale pouktalé (bayou of two joined stones [*tali*, stone, *pokta*, grow together])

Yowani village

Boukouchi (sons of the bayou)

Joukatte bayou (interpreter could give no meaning)

Kapinapa (bayou where one eats small tender nuts [*kapun*, shagbark hickory nut, *apa*, eat])

Yutchoubaté bayou (interpreter could give no meaning)

Boukouma

Soulaoue bayou

Bouk Chikeuchi (bayou of carrioncrow/vulture feathers [*sheki*, vulture, *hushi*, feather])

Bouk sapoutak (bayou of the mosquitoes [*isapuntak*, mosquito])

Chickasawhay village

Bouk oské tchitou (bayou of big canes [*uski*, cane])

Bouk hoktak (bayou whose water has no current [*oka takba*, bitter water])

Bouk bes Tchakko (bayou of green blackberries [Régis has *murs de hoy vertes*, correctly *mûres de haie vertes*] [*bissakchakinna*, green thorny vine with berries])

Chickasawhay River ("there is even a waterfall over stones")

Nitache village (*nita*, bear, *hacha*, river)

Three bayous ("of which I do not report the names at all, the Indians who were with me not knowing how to tell me them")

Bisacha village

Okeoullou village (village of scarce water [*oka*, water, *ullohchi*, drawn])

Table 11.2. *Continued*

[Tour of villages:]
Boucfouca village
Cushtusha village
Jachou village
Jakene atchoukima village [*yakni*, land, *achukma*, good; Régis gives no translation]
Couechitto village
Abika village
Jachou village
Cushtusha village
Boucfouca village
Sapatchitou village

[Trip down the Pearl:]
Ecfinatcha (pearl river)
. . .
Taskalamita bayou
Jakene oukoue bayou (*yakni*, land)

Source: Régis du Roullet, Journal, April–August 1732, in Archives du service hydrographique, vol. 67², no. 14-1, portefeuille 135, document 21, translated in part in Rowland and Sanders, *Mississippi Provincial Archives,* 1:136–54. Place-name translations in parentheses are given in the original document, followed by relevant Choctaw words from Byington, *A Dictionary,* in square brackets.

occupied by a component of the historic Choctaw before the coming of Europeans. At least the Middle Pearl farther south was protohistorically inhabited by Natchezan peoples, however, yet Régis gave no names for the region. Although some of these peoples probably joined the developing Choctaw confederacy as the Sixtowns people, Régis' guides were from the Western Division and may not have been so well acquainted with the region. It is significant that the only landmark specifically cited by Régis on the trip down the river was a sunken trace he saw crossing the river at a ford, which he described as the "road to the Natchez used by the Choctaw." We now believe that that trace crossed the Pearl just south of Monticello, where in 1977 a major mound site that we now believe to be of Natchezan cultural affiliation was reported, overlooking the river but not seen by Régis (and too ancient to have been actively occupied at the time).[32]

With the considerably amplified list of toponyms and translations offered by Régis (seventy-seven names, of which only fifteen are villages) it is again apparent that there are two kinds of names: names descriptive of the land ("deep bayou" in "small canebrake") and event labels ("small canebrake where a horse died"). With Régis' more profuse list we can now see that descriptive names and event labels are about equal in number. Descriptive names most often refer to some remarkable natural feature that could provide a permanent or temporary landmark ("variegated bluff," "dead pine bayou"), while event labels can be subdivided into memorable events ("vulture feathers bayou," "two mortars bayou," "bayou where wolves chased [them] away"), human alteration of the environment ("cabin place," "bayou with pine footbridge," "cow pasture bayou"), or—most frequently—an observation relevant to human comfort or subsistence ("crows' roost bayou," "good water fork," "Chickasawhay hunting ground bayou," "mosquito bayou").

This rich list of names exhibits only limited spatial patterning apart from the notable lack of names for Régis' trip down the Pearl River. There does seem to be a clear reflection of major physiographic features and resource locations, whatever else the names may mean. The low swampy ground southeast of Régis' crossing of the Bakatané River (i.e., preceding it in the list) is characterized by numerous canebrake names ("end of the great canebrake," "deep bayou among small canes," "small canes where a horse died," "little canes where there are two double bayous"), and these names are noticeably clustered. As those familiar with the remarkable art of Choctaw cane basketry may have already thought, these names probably point to prominent sources of cane for the making of baskets, mats, wall hangings, and roof coverings. Between the crossing of the Bakatané and Yowani village, the names "bluff barred with various colors," "bayou of gray clay," and "bayou of white earth" probably reflect the geological feature of the Pleistocene clays that underlie that region. Again, these names may also point to Choctaw use of them for pottery making; it would be interesting to test these particular clays' chemical constituents to see if they were so used. The next stretch of the journey, from Yowani to Chickasawhay through a region where streams cut across stone outcrops, shows three related names: "bayou where one throws stones," "bayou where the stone lies in the water," and "bayou of two joined stones." This particular interest corresponds well with historic Choctaw use of these same materials for projectile points and other tools and eventually for musket flints.

Case Study No. 2: British Stocktaking in the 1770s

With the end of the French and Indian War in the Treaty of Paris of 1763, the Louisiana colony east of the Mississippi River was ceded to Britain. The British were not slow to take advantage of the lands they had thus acquired, and in spite of the creation of the Proclamation Line that was to forbid English settlement west of the Appalachians, efforts to inventory the new lands and to advertise their advantages to prospective settlers were soon under way. Difficulties were experienced at first with the Indians, who did not understand what the treaty had to do with them and certainly objected to the notion that they and their lands could be handed over by virtue of such a paper. But by the 1770s a modus vivendi of sorts had been reached through treaties and agreements with the several tribes of the region, and European travelers began to cross and recross the land.

In 1771 surveyor-cartographer Bernard Romans traveled a route from Mobile into and through the Choctaw nation and on to the Chickasaw, returning down the Tombigbee River.[33] As far as his published narrative records, he followed a rather odd itinerary, starting from Mobile and then following the Bakatané to skirt the towns on the Chickasawhay, visit the eastern villages (many noted as deserted because of an ongoing war with the Creek Indians), and then loop back down to Chickasawhay and Yowani villages before traveling north to the Chickasaw. His route after reaching Yowani seems to have been rather different from that of Lusser or Régis forty years before, probably because of the war.

Romans reported plentiful horses among the Choctaw by 1771 but claimed that these horses, like their owners, were unable to swim.[34] Because he was much more interested in scouting out the land than in meeting with any people, he frequently avoided villages, reporting only seeing paths leading to them. Romans actually made use of specific trails or paths, and although he still reported some difficulties in finding fords, he had fewer problems than French witnesses, so these paths may indeed have to some degree become horse paths by his time. A comparison of the village names of the Eastern Division in Lusser and Romans appears to suggest that some considerable changes may also have taken place in the settlements in forty years: only two or possibly three of the names match (see table 11.3: Blue Wood, Blackwater [Okalusa], possibly Yanabe). In addition to effects of the Creek war, we know and Romans noted that villages had been outright destroyed as a result of the Choctaw civil war of 1746–50.[35] Neither of the lists appears to be exhaustive, however, since both the Romans 1772 map and the Crenay 1733 map, depending on Lusser, include additional villages, so the changes at least in names may not have been major.

POSITIVE METHODS

Table 11.3. Bernard Romans itinerary, 1771

Mobile
Dog River
Pine Log Creek
Coosak hattak falaya (large cane branch)
Pasca Oocoloo river
Bogue Hooma (red creek—Choctaw boundary)
Poos coos Paahaw (? a savannah)
Bogue aithee Tanne / Bakkatane
Hoopab Ullah (noisy owl)
Oku Ullah (noisy water)
Pancha Waya creek
Paonte village
Haanka Ullah (bawling goose) village (road to)
Sock han Hatcha river
Sapa Pesah village (deserted)
Hatchatikpe river
Etuck Chukke village (Blue Wood—deserted)
East Abeka
Soohanatcha river
Ebeetap-Oocoola village
Chooka-hoola village
Oka-hoola village
Hoola-tussa village
Ebeetap-oocoolo Cho village
Moka-lassa village
Haanka Ullah village
Oka Loosa village
Okaattakkala village
East Congeata village (ruins)
Yanatoe (Yanabe?) village
Bague-fooka creek
Poreetamogue creek
Bogue Chitto creek
Coosak Baloagtaw village
Pooscooste Kale village (deserted)
Talle Hatta creek (branch of Chickasawhay
Aitheesuka creek (branch of Chickasawhay)
Chickasawhay village
Owhan lowy creek (branch of Chickasawhay
Yoani village
Abeeka village
—————————going toward Chickasaws
Nashooba river
Oka tebbe haw river
—————————coming down Tombigbee

Table 11.3. *Continued*

Noxshubby / Hatcha oose river
Eetombgue be (crooked creek—source of Tombecbe fort name)—on west of river
Tombecbe fort ruins
Chickianoee (?white bluff)
Tuscaloosa river
Sookhavatcha river
Suktaloosa (black bluff)
Coosada town
Occhoy town
Abeshai creek
Bashailawaw creek
Nanna Falaya (hills)
Batcha-Chooka (hill)
Nanna Chahaws (hills)
Teeakhaily Ekutapa (settlement of Chickasawhays, deserted)
Yagna-hoolah (beloved ground; ceremonial?)
Isawaya creek
Senti Bogue (snake creek)
Atchatickpe creek/lagoon (British boundary with Choctaws)
Ape Bogue oose creek (salt spring)
The Forks:
   Ape Tonsa
   Beelosa
   Caantacalamoo
Tomeehettee bluff (former home of Tomeh)
Naniabe (fish killer) island
Alibamo river
Nita Abe (bear killer) bluff

Source: Romans, *A Concise Natural History of East and West Florida*, Braund ed., 305–33.

Romans's observations of the effects of the Creek war introduce another element of spatial marking. Romans noted a "heiroglyphick painting" that he saw by a path east of the Pascagoula River that commemorated a successful Choctaw war party against the Creek. This painting was placed at "the first publick place in their territories where they arrived with the scalps," so it may have marked the customary southern boundary of the Choctaw lands.[36] Romans reported arriving at the newly negotiated Choctaw-English boundary, Bogue hooma (Red Creek) some 17 miles farther on. Near the road to Chickasawhay he also saw the severed head of a warrior on a pole "with many other marks of our being in the theatre of war."[37] All of this suggests that the eastern region had become a liminal buffer zone as a result of the Creek war, but it is also of interest precisely because it may suggest an initial step in the creation of event-related place-names.

If Romans disappoints for the region for which we could compare him with his French predecessors because his place-names are heavily dominated by village names only, the description he offers of his trip down the Tombigbee confirms the same kind of pattern demonstrated by Régis' description of his path to Chickasawhay. Here also there are striking natural features ("white bluff," "black bluff," "long hills"), descriptions ("strong-smelling water"), and reminiscences of events ("snake creek," "bear killer bluff"), but only the event names are likely to have been drawn from his guides. Romans's spelling of the Choctaw words is often bizarre, but the persistence of this pattern is obvious, and a comparison with the 1733 Crenay map shows that many of these names had been around for at least a generation.

Conclusions

The first conclusion that may be drawn from this brief look at place-name studies and Choctaw place-names in particular is the counterintuitive fact that because of the scale and purposes of European maps, for place-name studies *narratives* by mapmakers rather than their resulting maps provide the fullest data. On reflection this is not surprising, since the narratives constitute a record of the observers' actual physical experience of the terrain and at least the Europeans' understanding of the social context in which information was obtained, while the maps can offer only a comparatively small-scale and conventionalized summary. The maps used in this study were indispensable for locating the general trajectories of the itineraries they reflect, but they do not record significant additional authentic names—they just permit us to compare the names from different narrative sources.

A great deal of information about the fauna of the Choctaw natural world at the time of the observations is directly present in the place-names. Beaver, "wood rat," bear, buffalo, wolf, and otter; crow, vulture, goose, and owl; alligator and snake; mosquito and flea—all appear in the place-names, most of them names apparently memorializing specific encounters. It is puzzling that these lists do not include the two major meat animals, deer (*isi*) and turkey (*fakit*): did European observers pass through no especially good hunting lands? Was there some prohibition on naming these animals? From what we know of the symbolism and legends of the Choctaw in particular and south-eastern Indians in general, we know that most of the animals that were mentioned had particular symbolic significance, and some were clan relatives that could not be hunted by clan members.

In the case of two animals we can also already observe European impact by the 1730s. The Choctaw distinction between European cattle (*vaca*) and buffalo (*yannash*) allows us to hypothesize that the introduction of European cattle to the Piney Woods region of the Gulf Coastal Plain was contemporary with at least the memory of use of the area for the hunting of buffalo. The relatively frequent occurrence of place-names mentioning horses by the 1730s (two mentions by Régis) confirms that horses had begun to be a significant part of Choctaw life by that time; indeed, on Régis' water-borne trip down the Pearl River he observed a branded Choctaw horse, property of the chief Red Shoe, corralled on an island.[38] The evidence at hand does not, however, permit us to decide whether the routes of well-used trails had been altered to favor horse traffic, since Romans's route differed so much from that of the French officers.

It may also be significant that the flora other than cane mentioned in these names are only trees or large shrubs: pine, cypress, and holly. Romans, with his interest in botany, reported many tree species of direct interest to potential European settlers from his personal observation, but he gave no Choctaw place-names incorporating them. There are no domesticates here, but none of the Europeans encountered many planted fields on their journeys, and since planting locations changed, they would ordinarily make poor place-names. Although we know that Choctaws made wide use of gathered plant materials for herbal medicine and their locations should have been preferentially marked, none were reported in place-names, suggesting perhaps that such knowledge may have been limited to specialists (as we know it was later) and closely guarded.

The names we have seen here do not offer any evidence for the kinds of power-laden landscapes created by European planters as they tamed their new world and subdued its people. That is not to say that Native societies were edenically egalitarian—their public and private spaces were densely gendered and demarcated by lines of clan and moiety—but simply that the present evidence is at the wrong scale and in the wrong place to reveal such spatial reflections of social realities. All these Europeans were transiting the larger landscape of a "greater Choctaw territory," and most of the place-names offer guidance *outside* the intimate community groupings. As such they tell obviously what Choctaws knew about the *extra*social world, even if we cannot interpret the additional content that event-based names might add. The naming of the landscape, dimly reflected as it is by these kinds of data, still stands as ample evidence of the exploitation by southeastern Indians of the full range of subsistence sources available for the gathering throughout the region, in spite of some seven hundred years' practice of agriculture. Male hunting and female gathering activities seem to be about equally represented. Hunting and food preparation technologies are also evident in the mention of a specific range of minerals.

The impression left by these names is of a cognitively well mapped living world in which, with specific exceptions, the frequently used sources of gathered materials were cataloged. This was not a "wilderness" at all but a land where every economically significant resource had its place in the cognitive maps of the people who used them and who altered the landscape to make their use more effective. In this landscape unusual natural landmarks served as waymarkers along established trails. The *descriptive* names for resource locations are sometimes so generic that they could not identify a specific feature to someone who did not have in mind a larger connected sequence into which it fit: evidence again that the region was well known to the European reporters' Choctaw informants. The *event-based* names, on the other hand, obviously did not refer often to any material residue at the given location; instead, we can suggest that they were shorthand references to stories that had a place in the mnemonic schema of the path, referring to an event in the past that the European travelers could not actually observe:

Alligator hole
Bayou of two mortars
Hurricane-flattened plain
Bayou of buffalo bones
Small canes where a horse died
Bayou where wolves chased them away
Bayou of vulture feathers

Behind each of these phrases lies a story, a memorable event; if analogies may be drawn with the Aboriginal and Apache examples, they might have been stories with moral force, evidence of a speaking and teaching landscape. Perhaps the death of a still rare and valuable horse, for example, taught something about the path itself and cultural change.

The Choctaw place-name evidence from these three observers, then, may certainly be seen as reflecting how Choctaw people used the land in the eighteenth century; they may even hint at how the land was imagined. It can be suggested that the sum of these added dimensions may point to their mode of inhabiting or dwelling on the land and can help to interpret, for example, decisions made by Choctaws in land cessions and treaties. It is unlikely that at this distance in time we can recover the full meaning of the eighteenth-century Choctaw landscape, but it is important that we realize that the Choctaw names still remaining upon the land today are but the merest hint of the landscape that helped "Choctaw" mean what it meant.

Notes

1. Worster, "Transformations of the Earth."
2. Cronon, *Changes in the Land*.
3. Layton and Ucko, "Introduction," 12.
4. See Martin, *Keepers of the Game*; Krech, *The Ecological Indian*.
5. Cf. Basso, *Wisdom Sits in Places*; Field and Basso, *Senses of Place*; Hirsch and O'Hanlon, *The Anthropology of Landscape*; Ucko and Layton, *The Archaeology and Anthropology of Landscape*.
6. Galloway, *Choctaw Genesis*.
7. Hall, *The Hidden Dimension*; Gould and White, *Mental Maps*; Hillier and Hanson, *The Social Logic of Space*.
8. Cf. Lewis, *Cartographic Encounters*; also Warhus, *Another America*.
9. White, *Land Use, Environment, and Social Change*; Cronon, *Changes in the Land*; Silver, *A New Face on the Countryside*; Crosby, *Ecological Imperialism*. A review of much of this literature is available in the articles, arguments, and references of a group of papers published in the 1990 *Journal of American History*.
10. Martin, *Keepers of the Game*; Krech, *The Ecological Indian*.
11. Alexander, *The Timeless Way of Building*; Hillier and Hanson, *The Social Logic of Space*. Some of this work seems to have been inspired by Martin Heidegger's account of human relations to space in the essay "Building Dwelling Thinking"; some of it also echoes Bourdieu's account of the Kabyle House in *Outline*.
12. See, for example, Morphy, "Landscape"; and Layton, "Relating to the Country."
13. Bright, "What is a Name?" 678.
14. Basso, *Wisdom Sits in Places*.
15. Layton and Ucko, "Introduction."
16. For the phrase see Bender, "Subverting the Western Gaze."
17. For examples taken from European contexts see Gould and White, *Mental Maps*.
18. Bourdieu, *Outline*; Sahlins, *Islands of History*.
19. Harvey, "Land Tenure."
20. One cannot help observing how similar, in the socialization of young historians and the honing of practice among older ones, is the practice of providing a reference without comment in a footnote.
21. Compare this situation to the bias in known archaeological sites due to the physical locations of archaeologists and major projects; see my "Prehistoric Population of Mississippi: A First Approximation" in this volume. We can only see what we look for.
22. Choctaw *yakni* (land) *katapa* (divided); Chickasaw *yaakni* (land) *kashapa* (divided). See Doyle, *Faulkner's County*.

23. There is, however, some sparse Spanish evidence for Choctaw habitation in this area from the end of the century, chiefly because the Spanish were so interested in the establishment of Fort Nogales where the French had abandoned Fort St. Pierre at the Yazoo-Mississippi confluence. See Weeks, "Searching for Straight—and White—Paths."

24. For the significance of "empty" space see Hodder, *The Spatial Organization of Culture*.

25. Carson, "Horses," 498.

26. Jean-Christophe de Lusser, Journal, January 12–March 23, 1730, in Archives des colonies, série C13A, 12:l00–134, translated in Rowland and Sanders, *Mississippi Provincial Archives*, 1:81–117, citation on 99.

27. Cf. Bright, "What is a Name?"

28. Lusser, Journal.

29. Régis du Roullet, Journal, 1729, in AC, série C13A, 12:67–99, translated in Rowland and Sanders, *Mississippi Provincial Archives*, 1:21–54, Journal, April–August 1732, in Archives du service hydrographique, vol. 67^2, no. 14-1, portefeuille 135, document 21, translated in part in Rowland and Sanders, *Mississippi Provincial Archives*, 1:136–54, and Mission among the Choctaws, February 21, 1731, in AC, série C13A, 13:173–80, translated in Rowland, Sanders, and Galloway, *Mississippi Provincial Archives*, 4:58–72.

30. Galloway, "Henri de Tonti du village des Chacta."

31. One is struck in reading this minute account of every small stream, matched by no other reporter, by the notion that the young officer, like an ethnographer first entering the field, was writing down everything he could, not yet knowing what might be useful. In the end he drew quite detailed sketch maps incorporating these names and showing the Mobile path and a strikingly detailed Pearl River; see Carte de Chemin du Fort de la Mobille aux villages des Tchaktas levée par estime en 1732 le 14 juillet par Monsieur Regis du Roullet officier dans la Colonie and Carte du cours de la Riviere aux Perles depuis Boukfouka jusqu'a son embouchure qui est à la passe a Dion vis a vis l'Isle aux Oyes levée a l'estime le 14 juillet 1732 par Monsieur Regis du Roullet, officier dans la colonie.

32. Galloway, *Choctaw Genesis*, 53. Patrick Livingood's report of subsequent investigations is in "Investigation of Mississippian Mounds."

33. Romans, *A Concise Natural History*; the account of his travels on Choctaw lands can be found on 305–33 (Romans's pagination, which is henceforth cited).

34. Romans, *A Concise Natural History*, 86; horses are not particularly good swimmers in any case.

35. See my "Choctaw Factionalism and Civil War, 1746–1750," in this volume.

36. Romans, *A Concise Natural History*, 102.

37. Romans, *A Concise Natural History*, 306.

38. See Carson, "Horses," 497–98.

12. Choctaw Names and Choctaw Roles

Another Method for Evaluating
Sociopolitical Structure

The Context of the Problem

Any student of the ethnohistory of the Choctaw during the colonial period must pay special attention to their social organization in order to understand the motivations for their actions as a group as they moved into the historical arena. Yet the scholarship available to the late-twentieth-century scholar did not really have much to say on this topic for the eighteenth century. John R. Swanton's work, important though it is, tended to amalgamate without distinction information from a much longer period and in any case was written without full access to all the relevant European documents.[1] And aside from the work on the Choctaw kinship system by Fred Eggan and Alexander Spoehr, both of whom derived their evidence for the colonial period from Swanton, very little further exploration of Choctaw social organization had been made.[2] The assumption seemed to be, as Spoehr famously quoted from Swanton, that there was a "powerful indefiniteness" not only about the Choctaw as a people but about their social organization, and their later, apparently rapid acculturation was in part thought to be due to the informality of this organization.[3]

The picture Swanton assembled was a simple one, but it was unfortunately made up of anomalous parts. Following the eighteenth-century French "Anonymous Relation" that he had had translated and published separately, Swanton saw the forty to fifty Choctaw communities in his village lists as "constituting small States, each with its chief, war chief, two lieutenants of the war chief, or Taskaminkochi, and an assistant to or speaker for the town chief,

The material in this chapter was presented at the American Society for Ethnohistory annual meeting at Williamsburg, Virginia, in 1988. It was revised for inclusion in this volume.

the Tishu minko."[4] Individual kinship, on the other hand, was defined by Swanton in terms of the named matrilineal clan, crosscut by moiety divisions; most of this information Swanton drew from informants born in the nineteenth century, many of them still living to be interviewed by him. What is wrong with this picture? Not only is it seriously incomplete in some respects, but in other respects it overspecifies the precolonial Choctaw case by relying upon data collected in the nineteenth century with no sense of how problematic that might be.

Several rather important problems of social organization have either not been addressed or have been passed over in a swath of assumptions. In fact, we do not really know how dual organization worked among the Choctaw: we do not know how the moieties were distributed or how—or whether—they mapped isomorphically onto the dual "red" versus "white" divisions.[5] We do not have unequivocal information about clans *that dates as early as the eighteenth century*: we need to know if there were named matrilineages, how prominent they were, and whether they governed the inheritance of political power. Finally, we know very little about the allocation of power in general: we do not know how the influences of village chief and division chief impinged upon one another or to what degree—if at all—either or both owed any kind of homage to a central chief. It may be impossible to resolve these problems unequivocally, but at least an effort to solve them requires that the evidence to solve them be made explicit and then gathered together. Analogy from "better-documented" other tribes is not sufficient, nor is it necessarily even applicable apart from the suggestion of possibilities for interpretation.

Two factors account for the anachronistic amalgam that Swanton offers. The first is the poor availability of perspicuous observations of Choctaw social structure under the French regime. The only Frenchmen who spent a great deal of time among them were the traders and subalterns operating out of Mobile and the Tombecbé fort, who often did not live permanently among them and who revealed little when they did, and the missionary who lived at Chickasawhay. Apart perhaps from the "Anonymous Relation," printed in part and insufficiently identified by Swanton in his book on the Choctaw, there is very little in the way of commentary on the Choctaw by the French traders and subalterns, due to the failure of their reports to survive in the French colonial system of paperwork.[6] Loss of documentation is also partly the reason that we have so little information from Father Baudouin, their Jesuit missionary, but in any case it is worth remembering that the mission only persisted from 1727 until 1746, and its location at Chickasawhay was not among the main body of towns.

The second factor that may account for Swanton's "powerful indefiniteness" is that the Indians who seemed thus "indefinite" were not the same in the early eighteenth century as they had been even a century before. Aside from the fact that no society remains static for centuries under any conditions, it is known that the Choctaw had undergone a massive transformation from Late Mississippian times into the eighteenth century. Their forebears had abandoned hierarchical chiefdom organization for a variety of reasons, including both population pressure *and* subsequent decimation by European disease and warfare, the latter of which had set several of their ethnic components adrift to join in a protohistoric confederacy.[7] In the seventeenth century the Choctaw were a new people, completing the synthesis of Moundville and Plaquemine cultures, and in the eighteenth century some of the seams still showed. One of them may have been ripped again when the Choctaw suffered a serious civil war from 1747 to 1750 in which "80 chiefs" and an uncounted number of other warriors were killed. I have argued that this civil war was not merely between pro-French and pro-English factions but that it was also between the moieties of the tribe, and this fact alone if proved could account for a great deal of dislocation in the earlier social organization.[8]

The fact is that for the earliest period of contact with the French we have very little in the way of a clear-cut "ethnographic" account of the Choctaw, which we might have expected to receive had they had a missionary that early. Even in the case of the scattered and voluminous references to the actions of the Choctaw in their alliance with the French we can find no witness whose observations are complete enough or reliable enough to present us with sufficient direct evidence to draw confident conclusions about social organization. The author of Swanton's "Anonymous Relation" reveals himself upon close reading as an observer who had limited direct experience of Choctaw lifeways and whose presentation of his own observations of Choctaw personal habits is laced with a scornful attitude that must make us question their accuracy. Internal evidence suggests that the relation was written in the early 1730s, just as the French were beginning to pay serious attention to the Choctaw, and the rest of the document that Swanton did not publish is by no means concerned with the Choctaw alone.[9] We may even wonder if the French mind-set, prepared to see noble savages behind every pine tree or to appreciate the Natchez Suns as they appreciated their own Sun King, did not

POSITIVE METHODS

to some extent actively prevent such observation.[10] Certainly it is the case that they tried to force Choctaw tribal structure into a hierarchical redistributive model, and their reports suggest that they came to see it that way, however little success they had had in the attempt.[11]

The Evidence and Methods of Dealing with It

The evidence we seek, then, must be looked for in a disappointingly small number of documents, none of them intended to convey such information. The approach suggested here to getting around the problem of bias is to use evidence of a kind that presents no particular opportunities for ax grinding and whose major drawback comes from the simple ignorance of the reporter: names of Choctaw people. The European tendency to inventory is of great value here. At several times in the history of Choctaw contact with European colonials, lists of villages, important men connected with those villages, and presents given to those men were made.[12] In addition to these formal lists, other documents also contain narrative enumerations that are no less useful for the same reasons.

We must be concerned here, of course, with the notion of naming people in the first place and how naming practices vary with culture. Naming people, like naming places, permits talking about them when they are not present, but there may be elaborate etiquettes of name bestowal or name usage that are ill understood by those who are not members of the culture, and this may seriously affect data collection. Swanton provided in his ethnography of the Choctaw a section on personal names in which he distinguished between personal names given to children and war names earned later.[13] Of the latter, of which he listed nearly a hundred gathered from different sources, he observed that they frequently consisted of two elements, the first related to some incident of war, while the latter might represent "rough categories" or "classes" of warriors: *humma, holahta, imastabi, imataha, hacho*.[14]

In another segment under "government" Swanton also spoke of political titles that might be borne by men involved in the governance of villages or kinship groups.[15] He observed, however, that certain difficulties in gathering names intruded: Choctaws did not like to give their own names and refused to speak the names of the dead. Further, he said nothing about why he had collected almost no women's names. Was he right about male names and changes in them as a result of war prowess? Was this the only thing that affected naming? What about the names connected with governance? In fact,

Swanton did not really define a specific unitary understanding of the personal name and its involvement with Choctaw identity at all.

Such problems are familiar to lexicographers working with indigenous languages in which whole classes of words cannot be spoken at all to outsiders or cannot be spoken at all except by certain people.[16] The major Choctaw dictionary assembled by Cyrus Byington and edited by Swanton and Henry Halbert was much influenced by the purpose to which Byington intended to put the data he assembled: the translation into Choctaw of Christian evangelical literature.[17] And although a Mississippi Choctaw community project has been at work on a modern dictionary of Choctaw for some years, we as yet do not have access to a more systematic lexicon of the Choctaw language to even make sense of some of the vocabulary items that make up the names, and it is certain that nuances and meanings will have changed in three hundred years.[18]

The observational difficulties in these contexts are also, of course, many. Most of the names were recorded by officers who had very little understanding of the people whose names they were or of the relation between the name itself and its bearer. The context in which most of the lists were recorded was one in which the French were attempting to impose a hierarchical order they understood upon a more complex heterarchical reality through the creation of a redistributional system of presents.[19] Bienville invented the role of great chief of all the nation in about 1710, where clearly it did not exist before.[20] Eventually, the existence of major political divisions within the tribe was recognized by the creation of a medal chieftainship for each of three division chiefs.

To retain the favor of the Choctaw through their leaders, the French instituted an annual occasion for present giving that was generally held at Mobile. On this occasion the Choctaw leaders came to Mobile with, over time, a larger and larger entourage. They brought presents for the French chiefs and were given presents in return, but these presents were not given to everyone. Initially, they were given to the great chief; then to the great chief, division chiefs, the chief of Chickasawhay, and a "national" war chief; then finally to all these and village chiefs as well.[21] In addition, warriors who had performed unusual service might receive presents from time to time. But the original intention, which was that the presents would be given to one or a restricted number of men and shared with their adherents, thus binding them all to the French, ran up against all the difficulties one might expect when important leaders accustomed to articulating their power through generosity are put into a competitive situation. Yet in spite of these problems the French persisted in seeing the nation in terms of this structure, so that, for example, it is now impossible to determine the personal name of the nation's great chief from the 1720s to the 1750s.[22]

Whatever may have been their understanding of the meaning of the names, the French still often recorded them. Because they had no written form, they were simply written down as heard. The observer's knowledge of the Choctaw language was frequently minimal, and to complicate matters he would be hearing the information from informants who spoke several dialects, at least one of them (that of the Sixtowns) apparently significantly divergent. Since even French spelling was not fixed in the eighteenth century, spelling and segmentation of the names could thus vary wildly. And while rare references indicate directly that some of the names were in fact role titles, there was no systematic attempt by the European observers to define all names that functioned in this way, nor with their assumption of Choctaw governmental simplicity did they seem concerned to define more than a very few roles. Finally, many of the sources we must use come to us as copies made by contemporary scribes, not as originals, and this compounds the difficulties of interpreting unfamiliar scripts.

Even a brief perusal of one of the French lists is enough to show that several of the names must be function titles and that some of them seem to incorporate moiety designations (see table 12.1). Such observations are not new; Swanton made several casual suggestions regarding the meanings of proper names but did not pursue the patterns in which they occurred.[23] It is, however, possible to go beyond the lists and the French view of the village and nation power structure reflected in them. One can correlate the narrative accounts of the actions of name-bearers in observed political activities with the intention of matching classes of names with behavioral patterns in specific "action contexts."

The French reports of the Choctaw do not appear to portray a complete picture of Choctaw life but rather a limited repertoire of the structural poses that the social organization might take. As was the case with Fred Gearing's work on the Cherokee, and for similar reasons, there is very little account of subsistence or domestic activities or the activities of women, since the contact that literate Frenchmen had with the Choctaw was primarily of a political nature.[24] The most frequently depicted structural poses, as in the Cherokee case, are therefore those of the war and council organizations. The war

Table 12.1. Régis du Roullet's first list of chiefs and villages

Aloue (Couechitto), Village of the Great Chief

1	Mingo Tchito, Great Chief	Coat
2	Capitane	Coat
3	Oulatimataha	Coat
4	Soulouche oumastabe	Coat
5	Atakabe mingo	Coat
6	Pakana oulacta	Coat, son of the Great Chief
7	Mingo tchito ouchi	Coat
8	E yachoumataha	Coat

Bouktoukoulou

1	Atache Mingo	Coat
2	Chikacha oulakta	Coat
3	Tascanangouchi	Coat
4	Soulouche mastabe	
5	Souakabe Tachka	
6	Pacana oulacta	

Ayanabe

1	Atatchichkaa	Coat
2	Tachickiaoulakta	

Okeloussa

1	Mingo pousecouche	Coat
2	Oulatouktale	Coat
3	Taskanangouchi	

Youane

1	Opae mingo	Coat
2	Niougouchi Chtaboka	Coat
3	Tchoukouaala	

Tchikachae

First, Patlako		Coat
2	Capitane	Coat
3	Mingo Emitta	Coat
4	Taskanangouchi Taboka	Coat
5	Ougoulabyssenya	
6	Taskanangouchi	
7	Sonakabe mingo Taskanangouchi	
8	Mongoulacha mingo	

Kastacha

First, Atkabe oulakta capitane		Coat
2	Ounatokelo	Coat

Kaffetalaya

1	Taskanangouchi Taboka	Coat
2	Soulouche mastabe	

Table 12.1. *Continued*

Abeka

First,	Tachka oulakta	Coat
2	Tichou mingo	

Concha

1	Asatchioullou	Coat
2	Alibamon mingo	Coat
3	Taskanangouchi	Coat
4	Tichou mingo	Coat

Yte Tchipota

First,	Opatchi mingo	Coat
2	Tachka mingo	

Ckanppa

1	Mingo E'mitta	Coat
2	Tachka mingo nak fich	Coat
3	Tachka oumma	Coat
4	Taskanangouchi	Coat

Nachoubaouanya

1	Oulactacheo	Coat

Oskelagana

1	Fani mingo Tchaa	Coat
2	Oulabessenya	Coat
3	Mingo pousecouche	Coat
4	Mongoulacha mingo	

Tala

1	Tchikacha oulakta	Coat
2	Oulactabeneya	Coat

Boukfouka

1	Opaemiko	Coat
2	Atakabe oulakta	Coat
3	Taskanangouchi	

Source: Régis du Roullet, Journal, 1729, AC, série C13A, 12:67–99 (see 89–90), translated in Rowland and Sanders, *Mississippi Provincial Archives*, 1:21–54.

organization acted in external wars against enemies of both the Choctaw and the French, and it may also have been partially operative in the extraordinary internal civil war. Council activities seem to have been similarly subdivided into external councils or parleys held with the French and other tribes and internal councils held within the nation and only rarely observed by the French (or other tribes). There are of course all sorts of problems with these generalizations, particularly in the extraordinary situations called forth by

Choctaw dealings with the French and by the civil war and factionalism, but the point that the French were only exposed to a limited range of the repertoire is clearly valid.

Another problem we would hope to address in a longer study of this kind is to add something to what is known of Choctaw kinship. In the narrative contexts there is sometimes mention of kinship relationships between named individuals, and it may sometimes then be possible to infer transivity in these relationships to third parties where other relationships are known. In the case of immediate kinship the major problem in interpreting the terms of relationship is to locate *ego*—to know who is using the term. The second aspect of kinship, about which much less is known, is lineage. Swanton claimed that the named matrilineal clan was characteristic of Choctaw society, but his evidence was obtained from living informants; we shall have to see whether there is evidence for it from the earlier date.

The Data

Gathering data for such a study is more time-consuming than complicated. Obviously, an exhaustive search of all possible documents might take years, but there are some shortcuts to assembling enough data to work with. The lists are obvious and easy, but they are relatively few. The narrative sources are too many if all are to be considered, but there are certain narrative sources that may be easily targeted as being literally thick with names: these generally include treaty occasions or ambassadorial visits. There are also certain periods that, because they were times of "Indian troubles," yielded increased attention to Indian affairs. All of the sources are biased in favor of leading males, which does no harm for an analysis of political structure but will skew the information available on kinship relations.

A good limited sample to use for this analysis, from a period during which a reasonable degree of uniformity can be assumed, is the French documentary sources dating to the period between the Natchez rebellion of 1729 and the outbreak of the Choctaw civil war in 1747. Up until 1729 the French archival materials made practically no mention of individuals, far less their names, but after the deaths of several hundred colonists it became clear to the French that they would have to make a far more careful evaluation of at least the men who led the most powerful Indian groups. It is no accident that the three maps that for the first time show details of Choctaw villages (Anville 1732, Régis du Roullet 1732, Crenay 1733) date from this period.

There are clearly some leading sources that cover the period. In 1729 the French governor, Périer, sent one of his own henchmen, Régis du Roullet, among the Choctaw to choose a site or sites for a trade house and to evaluate the mood of the nation, followed in the next year by the Swiss infantryman Jean-Christophe de Lusser to tour the nation and evaluate its loyalty. This whole episode generated two lists and several lengthy journals, the latter amply supplied with proper names (see tables 12.1, 12.2, and 12.3). At the same time, written reports from interpreters began to be passed on for the first time, and the proprietor of the still new mission, Father Baudouin, offered his own evaluations. Governor Périer and his *commissaire-ordonnateur*, Edmé Gatien Salmon, wrote to France summarizing further letters, while Bienville, sent to replace Périer and make something of the shambles of Périer's Indian policy, made his own reports. On one occasion Bienville's nephew Gilles Augustin Payen de Noyan was sent to consult with Choctaw chiefs and provided a particularly informative account. A really striking document is the journal of Jadart de Beauchamp, major of Mobile, in which is recorded his consultation with Choctaw leaders in 1746 in an attempt to avoid war.[25]

I gathered 267 names from these sources and related narrative sources dated 1729–46 and placed them in a simple database table containing name, date, documentary source, affiliation(s) (village, division, moiety, lineage) where known, and a context note including why the individual was mentioned, whom he was with if relevant, and what he was represented as doing. Spelling variations made it difficult to determine whether names were the "same" (i.e., if they designated the same person or were made up of the same words designating different persons), but more than seventy different names were represented. Such data can be sorted and correlated in a number of ways to attempt to establish continuities and discontinuities in identity and thus to try to separate role from personal name. It should be possible to distinguish the recurrence of names as names of abstract persons (roles) from that of names as labels for specific individuals and further to discern functional regularities if such regularities exist. This is the task that I shall undertake here, to demonstrate the possibilities for enriching our concept of Choctaw social organization.

Some Results

There had to be some ground rules for what would be considered to count as evidence of a specific kind. Proper names could not be distinguished by

Table 12.2. Régis du Roullet's second list of chiefs and villages

1732

Western part, or Goula falaya, "Friends of the Great Band"

Youannes	Mongouchi Tabaka
Chikachoe	Great Chief and Medal
Boukiouloukchi	No chief, dependency of Yellow Canes
Chenouk Tchaukelisa	No chief
Nachou baouania	Oulakta ejo
Oske Laguna	Ougoula Bersenia
Seneacha	Fanimingo Tchaa
Tala	Oulakta benia
Tala poukta	No chief, dependency of Tala
Nitacha	abandoned
Besacha	
Poucecoutte Takale	Chouastabe
Abesa	
Bouktchiou	No chief
Boukfalaya	No chief
Itechipouta	Coupatchimingo
Baloupouka	No chief
Oke oullou	No chief
Boukfouka	Pacuuko
Mongoulacha	Souloute ou mastabe
ite ousano	No chief
Fany tallemon	No chief
Tchanke	No chief
Jachou	Ounatikillou, at present Tchacta oulakta
Castacha	Great medal chief and great chief of the western part
Caffe talaya	Fani mingo
Jakene atchoukema	No chief
Fany Yakera	No chief
Ounitalemon	No chief
Achouk Tchouka	Taskanangou Tchiarta
Abeka	Taskalonia
Outapoucha	No chief
Kintaoke	No chief
Noucekoutchitou	No chief

End of the part of the Great Band or western part

Villages of the center of the nation, or Goula Tchitou, "the Great Friends"

Concha	Alibamon Mingo, Great Medal Chief
Okeloussa	Mingo Poucecousse
Ayanabe Ayoutaka	Tacheka oulakta
Coue tchitou	The Great Chief of the Choctaw nation by right of birth, who has the medal

POSITIVE METHODS

Table 12.2. *Continued*

In this village besides the Great Chief of the nation there are three other chiefs who are some of the principal men of the nation, two of whom are great war chiefs and the other is the one who distributes the employments. Their names are:

	1 Chikacha oulakta, uncle of the Great Chief of the nation
	2 Mingo ou Mustabe, he has the medal
	3 Captain Taboka, who gives employment
Loukfeata	Taskamingo
Bouk toukoulou	Atachimingo
Schkannapa	Mingo Emitta

End of the center of the nation or of The Great Friends

Eastern part, or Goula Tennap, "Friends of the Other Side"

Pante	No chief
Ouatouloula	No chief
Ite oukchaka	No chief
Pattachanouce	No chief
Caffetaloya	No chief
Mongoulucha	Honored Man
Jachou	
Oulitacha	Oulaka Taska, Honored Man
Abeka	No chief
Ayepata	Couchiou mingo, Honored Man
Ebitoupougoula	Honored Man, he is the same as Ayepata

Last of the villages of the "Friends of the Other Side"
End of the villages of the Choctaw nation.

Source: Régis du Roullet, Journal, April–August 1732, in Archives du service hydrographique, vol. 67^2, no. 14-1, portefeuille 135, document 21, translated in part in Rowland and Sanders, *Mississippi Provincial Archives*, 1:136–54.

capitalization alone, as the French more or less consistently capitalized anything they used as a name, including obvious function titles. A personal name, referring to a single individual, had to identify one person from one village in more than one instance and preferably more than two instances. The most obvious example of this is Alibamon Mingo of Concha, whose name means "chief of the Alabama" but who did not share this name with anyone else among the Choctaw and who was probably the single most important Choctaw leader of the whole colonial period.[26]

To be considered as a possible title of office or function, on the other hand, a name would have to appear in several different villages in a single year. Not surprisingly, it was clear to see from the accumulation of names that Swanton—or rather his eighteenth-century French informant—was correct in

Table 12.3. Régis du Roullet's 1729 journal references to proper names

Name	Affiliation	Source	Remarks
Taskanangouchi	Boucfouca	12:95v	
Atachimingo	Bouctoucoulou	12:91	chief
Taboka	Caffetalaya	12:95v	taskanangouchi
Patlaco	Chickasawhay	12:71	apparently chief
Mingo Emitta	Chickasawhay	12:87v	third chief
Great Chief	Couechitto	12:72v	medal from Diron: speaks first
Red Shoe	Couechitto	12:79	speaks third
Captain Taboka	Couechitto	12:94	
Oulactaeo	Nachoubaouenya	12:96v	chief
Tagoula Bessenia	Oskelagna	12:94	chief
Mingo Pousecouche	Oskelagna	12:95	third chief, nephew of Tagoula Bessenia
Mongoulacha Mingo	Oskelagna	12:96v	chief
Mingo Emitta	Scanapa	12:73	village chief, speaks second
Taskanangouchi	Yanabe	12:72v	
Opatchi Mingo	Yte Tchipota	12:96v	chief

abstracting several function titles from his observations: not only are *tichou mingo*s and *taskanangouchi*s cited from many different towns in the same year (see table 12.1 for examples), but clearly several of the taskanangouchis are also known by individual proper names: Taskanangouchi Chaoulacta from an unknown village in 1730, Taskanangouchi Arta from Achouk tchouka in 1732, and Taskanangouchi Atlako from Yazoo in 1746. Sometimes the French sources make it apparent that a title rather than an individual is meant by preceding the title with the definite article.

Identifying the function that the title was intended to define, however, is more difficult, particularly if the function is not well defined elsewhere. The only way to do this is to observe the described behavior of the named individuals, and this may or may not be "official" behavior inhering in the function. Behavioral observations were only complete enough to confirm the role of the tichou mingo. The different tichou mingos are almost invariably mentioned as having been sent to carry messages or to bring back observations, and the "Anonymous Relation" states that they served as the chief's speaker.[27] Mentions of the taskanangouchis are much more varied, suggesting only that they were in general important men and sometimes raised war parties (although others who did not bear this title did so as well), which squares with the observation in the "Anonymous Relation" that they were the war chiefs' assistants.[28]

POSITIVE METHODS

There are two other possible function titles that Swanton did not apparently recognize as such but that appear when any summary of names is considered. The first is one I have discussed elsewhere: the *fanimingo* (squirrel chief). Although these men apparently served as village chiefs, they also seem to have had another function, that of peacemakers or peace preservers. Elsewhere I have cited Thomas Nairne's description of the Chickasaw "Fane Mingo or Squirrel king," and I repeat his duties here: "His bussiness is to make up all Breaches between the 2 nations, to keep the pipes of peace by which at first they contracted Freindship, to devert the Warriors from any designe against the people they protect, and to Pacifie them by carrying them the Eagle pipe to smoak out of."[29]

Such fanimingos as appear in the documents referring to the Choctaw are specifically shown carrying out similar tasks. In 1730 the fanimingo of Concha said that he had authority to restrain some aggrieved persons of Okeloussa from vengeance against the chief of Yowani. In 1730 also Lusser referred to the fanimingo of Bouctoucoulou as "calumet chief of this nation" and said that he was especially concerned to maintain the peace with the Chickasaw. In 1746 the fanimingo of Seneacha opposed the killing of Choctaw by Choctaw to satisfy the French for three murdered men because he feared the dangers of internal strife to which the nation would be thus exposed. Both the fanimingo of Oskelagna in 1729 and that of Seneacha in 1732 and 1746 were referred to as Fanimingo *tchaha*, which strongly suggests that they may have given such service on behalf of whatever faction of the nation considered itself "Tchaha" at the time. It may be worth considering, since the Choctaw were clearly multiethnic, whether the multiple fanimingos also played a role in smoothing over divisional differences and ensuring Choctaw solidarity.

This is not the last of the function titles that emerge from the analysis of names. Swanton noted a number of names that contained the component *hopaii* and identified it with Choctaw missionary Alfred Wright's help as "prophet" or "war-prophet," but he did not identify it as a function title.[30] There is, I believe, enough evidence to suggest that it was one. In the names that I collected there were an Opae mingo from Yowani in 1729, an Opaemiko from Boucfouca in 1729, a Paymingo from Boucfouca in 1730 (presumably the same man), a Paymingo from Chickasawhay in 1742, and a Paemingo from Cushtusha in 1746. Interestingly, these men seem to share some rather anomalous behaviors. The paymingo of Chickasawhay stole the wife of a young warrior in 1742 and participated in the killing of his own chief when objection was made. In 1746 it was the paymingo of Cushtusha who proposed a conspiracy of several lineages to murder Red Shoe and thus give the French the vengeance they were requesting. All of them were clearly important men, and these two examples, while not conclusive, do suggest that they were feared men and perhaps men of unpredictable temper as well. The degree to which this particular function title was dependent upon personal qualities, however, is an open question.

Of course, the most notorious of eighteenth-century Choctaws also bore a function title: Red Shoe, or Soulouche (shulush) oumastabé.[31] It was my own attempt to identify this man in his various daring activities, complicated as it was by the fact that his village was seldom indicated, that led me to an awareness that he was not the only one to bear this name or title. The French documents identified several *souliers rouges*, from Couechitto in 1737, Cushtusha in 1738, 1739, and 1740, Yanabé in 1746, and Tombecbé in 1746. Additionally, they mentioned soulouche oumastabés from Bouctoucoulou, Caffetalaya, and Couechitto in 1729 and from Mongoulacha in 1732. Clearly this was *a* title if not *the* title for a war chief, as nowhere was there a suggestion that any of these men were village chiefs or higher, except for the individual who made the name famous, and in 1732 the war chief of Couechitto (probably Red Shoe) was referred to specifically as Mingo oumastabe.

This issue of the war chief's name also brings up the problem of the red = war/white = peace dichotomy. Soulouche oumastabé is imprecisely translated as "Red Shoe"; in fact, *oumastabe* apparently contains the elements *ouma* (red) and *abe* (to kill), and the whole name is probably somehow connected with the wearing of red moccasins in the initiation ceremony for a new warrior observed among the Chickasaw.[32] Certainly, red is thus connected with blood and war, but there are two questions to be answered here: did a war chief invariably have the *ouma* element in his name, and how likely was it that the war chief was a member of the red/war moiety (if there actually was such a thing)?

French documents referred often to the "red chief" from a village but puzzlingly spoke far less often of a "white chief." It has been argued that the red chief dealt with the affairs of war and the white chief with those of peace, that white stood higher in rank than red. It might then be the case that "white" was actually the unmarked feature and was assumed of village chiefs. Where we can look at a list that ranked more than one chief to a village this seems to fit, since no "first" chief had the *ouma* element in his name (e.g., see

POSITIVE METHODS

table 12.1). But on that list there were few other "red" chiefs either—Tachka oumma of Scanapa in addition to the soulouche oumastabes. The Mingo ou Mustabe mentioned at Couechitto in 1732 and 1737 was probably the notorious Red Shoe, leaving only a brace of mingo oumas from Nachoubaouenya and Chickasawhay in 1746 to suggest that more commonly at least Beauchamp simply used the term *chef rouge* to refer to a village "red" chief and that the "red" chief need not bear the *ouma* element in his name either.

Can anything be said about the linking of moieties with the red/white dichotomy? Swanton, quoting from a transcript of the 1771–72 Choctaw-British congress at Mobile, noted that the Choctaw chief Concha Oumanstabe was "of the Immongoulascha or Peace Family of the Town of Chickasawhay" and thus assumed that the Inholahtas were connected with war.[33] Either this was an error or drastic change had taken place in twenty years; I have suggested elsewhere that the assignment in the 1730s and 1740s was probably the reverse.[34] Certainly, through that period the general impression was that the "red chiefs" sided with Red Shoe and the British, while the Inholahtas sided with Alibamon Mingo and the French. But the sides taken simplify the matter too much. A detailed reading of Beauchamp's journal of 1746 shows that though those chiefs who were identified as of the "caste" of Red Shoe were automatically suspected of favoring him and the English cause, those who were not so identified were not so much pro-French as opposed to precipitate action—desirous, in fact, of mature consideration of the moral dilemma created by the killing of three Frenchmen.[35] This is the kind of behavior that a "white" or "peace" chief should demonstrate, yet the group with these sentiments included red chiefs, taskanangouchis, and Itemongoulacha of Chickasawhay.[36] In other words, the kind of evidence offered by names is probably not going to solve this problem, and indeed the problem itself has probably been stated too simplistically. What the evidence does show is that dual organization is not a matter of neat categories among the Choctaw.[37]

A final type of name that I will consider here is akin to the function title, for it implies that the bearer does perform a function but for a kinship group rather than a political one; it may be referred to as a classificatory or genealogical name. To my knowledge there has been no effort to identify such names or to see kinship functions in them, and admittedly it is a very difficult task with the information available, but if such names can be identified we may begin to solve these more complex and less visible problems of kinship organization. In such names one may identify a term referring to moiety or perhaps named lineage as part of the name, and behaviorally the bearer may seem to speak or act in behalf of such a segment. We know from Swanton's research that the two Choctaw moieties were known as the Inholahta ("oulacta" in the French spelling) and the Imoklasha ("mongoulacha" in the French spelling); we do not know names for lineages, or at least we have not recognized them.

Still, the moiety names are not a bad place to begin, since presumably an individual would not be given such a name at random. Swanton derives the Inholahta moiety name from the Choctaw "esteemed man" or Apalachee "leading man, chief." Imoklasha, he says, contains the *okla* (people) root followed by a verb meaning "to dwell."[38] Even if Swanton's etymologies are not precise, it is clear that the two moiety names probably have different semantic origins and that the former is itself a word that has a separate meaning, while the latter seems to be a compound whose applicability may be more restricted in its usage.

In fact, the usage of these two words as parts of names would seem to bear out this assumption. The former, in its French oulacta form, appears much more frequently than the latter and may take the prefix or postfix position (see table 12.4). The mongoulacha name element also shows positional variety, but the list of names is much more restricted. This evidence would suggest the hypothesis that the oulacta element is not necessarily connected with the moiety name and may simply mean "leading man" when used in names, while the mongoulacha element actually may indicate moiety membership. Certainly in the case of the violent Mongoulacha Mingo of Chickasawhay there is a chain of inference that would seem to establish his membership in that moiety: he stated that he was of the same "caste" as Belle Dent of the Tohome while claiming that the latter had been victimized, and Beauchamp called upon another Choctaw, stated to be of the Imoklasha caste, to contradict Mongoulacha Mingo and tell the true story.[39]

There are several other name elements that appear with fair frequency and wide distribution, do not seem to have any direct interpretation in terms of ideal career trajectories, and may thus have some possibility of indicating named lineages. Swanton, in his dependence upon complexly conflicting evidence from many Choctaw remnants of the nineteenth century, concluded that the Choctaw were organized below the moiety level into clans and local groups, though he was frank in admitting that the information he could get was a welter of confusion. The French documents do suggest the possibility of something other than moieties, but both the descriptions and the terminology

POSITIVE METHODS

Table 12.4. Oulacta and Mongoulacha names in the French documents

Oulacta

Atakabe oulacta	Cushtusha 1729; Boucfouca 1729
Chicacha oulacta	Couechitto 1731, 1732; Bouctoucoulou 1729; Tala 1729
Choucououlacta	Yowani 1729; village unknown 1742–46
Oulacta benia	Tala 1729, 1732
Oulacta ejo	Nachoubaouenya 1729, 1732
Oulacta taska	Oulitacha 1732
Oulactimataha	Couechitto 1729
Pacana oulacta	Bouctoucoulou 1729
Tach[e]ka oulacta	Abeka 1729; Yanabe 1729, 1732

Mongoulacha

Itemongoulacha	Chickasawhay 1746
Mongoulacha mingo	Chickasawhay 1729, 1745, 1746; Oskelagna 1729
Mongoulacha tchactas	Couechitto 1732

used (both *race* and *cast[r]e* are used in the French to refer to moieties, but it is not clear whether one or both may refer to other units as well) are also somewhat confusing. Father Baudouin was reported by the *commissaire* Salmon to have said: "All the Choctaw come from two principal races, namely: from the Inoulakta, which is the most numerous and the most noble, and from the Eukatatlape, which is less numerous and less distinguished. . . . [T]he first race is divided into seven different classes and the second into five, which forms twelve different bands. . . . [E]ach of these races has a separate chief."[40] This seems straightforward enough, until one takes into account the report of Bienville's nephew Noyan, who referred to the strongly pro-French Alibamon Mingo and the then (1738) chief of the Chickasawhay as having a high rank in the nation, "being of the highest caste." Opposed to them was Red Shoe and the "ten village chiefs who, being of the same caste as he, appear to be attached to his interests." Noyan also referred, however, to "the six different castes that compose the nation"; in each case the same word was used, yet two kinds of groupings seem to be referred to, the latter perhaps reflecting moieties parsed across three divisions.[41]

In Swanton's treatment of the submoiety *iksas* there is little system, as there apparently was little in the contemporary data he was able to obtain. He thought that "it will always be impossible in the present decadent condition of the old organization to distinguish the true local groups" and pointed out that many of the names he collected varied little or not at all from those of the towns.[42] Yet he did not really attempt to look any earlier, nor did he attempt to find evidence in proper names. I have found what may be two possible candidates in the recurrence of two name elements: *pakana* and *taboka*.

There are several tabokas who appear in different towns, three taskanangouchis with that "surname" from Yowani, Chickasawhay, and Caffetalaya in 1729, and a very active captain of that name from Couechitto mentioned in 1729, 1730, and 1732.[43] Swanton, in discussing the village list in the "Anonymous Relation," noted that *taboka* may mean "noon" or "south" and may be linked with the central Choctaw towns, but there is no such linkage with the distribution of taboka names.[44]

There is a similar kind of distribution for the pakanas: two pakana oulactas named in 1729 for Bouctoucoulou and Couechitto. Pakana is also found as a name element among the related Alabama Indians. A leadership role is indicated for men with both pakana and taboka names, but neither name element seems to be exclusively associated with any specific role. I am frankly pessimistic that any certain identification of named lineages will ever be achieved for the eighteenth century, but I would think that this is one way such a grouping might show itself in the evidence.

Concluding Comments

The work reported above is not intended to be exhaustive; to achieve better results one should include data from the whole of the colonial period and profit from the possibility of using French, English, and Spanish sources as checks on each other. I think it is safe to assert, however, that a close examination of the "proper names" reported in the documents is worth carrying out. The process simply of bringing together the contexts in which the names occur is helpful for the behavioral consistencies it sometimes shows, as is particularly striking in the case of the tichou mingo. This is especially important because we lack usable pragmatic contexts for the use of these names. I am satisfied that placing this kind of grid over the data has also been helpful in confirming the fanimingo and paymingo role names. There is much more to be done, of course, both in terms of an incorporation of additional data and of a closer examination of behavioral patterns attributed, for example, to individuals simply referred to as "chief." But the exercise has been far from fruitless, and the attention it has forced to the complexity of both behaviors and naming conventions has strengthened the conviction that Choctaw social organization was far from "powerfully indefinite."

Acknowledgment

I would like to thank the National Endowment for the Humanities for grant RO-21631-88, which I shared with Clara Sue Kidwell, to study Choctaw land use; it has contributed to the research reported here.

Notes

Abstract: Choctaw personal names, or what Europeans took to be personal names, were recorded frequently in the papers that document European-Choctaw contact in the eighteenth century. A careful analysis of these names and the historical contexts in which they appear reveals patterns that may be of material relevance in the reconstruction of functional roles and kinship. In this paper I describe a sample of the evidence taken from French sources and outline some conclusions that can be drawn from it.

1. Swanton, *Source Material*. When Swanton wrote, he was still confined to hand-copied texts gathered by the Library of Congress and the Carnegie Institution in the first quarter of the twentieth century.

2. Eggan, "Historical Changes"; Spoehr, *Changing Kinship Systems.*

3. Spoehr, *Changing Kinship Systems*, 200.

4. Swanton, *Source Material*, 95.

5. For more on this subject see my "Eighteenth-Century Choctaw Chiefs, Dual Organization, and the Exploration of Social Design Space," in this volume.

6. Swanton, *Source Material*, 243–58; and my "Louisiana Post Letters, 1700–1763: The Missing Evidence for Indian Diplomacy," in this volume.

7. For more detail on this process see Galloway, *Choctaw Genesis.*

8. See my "Choctaw Factionalism and Civil War, 1746–1750," in this volume.

9. The original document is in the Ayer Collection, Newberry Library.

10. Jaenen, *Friend and Foe.*

11. For the deep effects that this kind of prejudgment might have on documented observations see my "Multidimensional Scaling for Mapping Ethnohistorical Narrative: Choctaw Villages in the Eighteenth Century," in this volume.

12. In addition to the French materials analyzed here, there is a notable list made by the English in 1765 ("An exact list of Warriors belonging to the Chactaw Nation who are entitled to Presents," Colonial Office 323/23, fols. 193–201; I am indebted to John Juricek for bringing this document to my attention and for supplying me with a copy of it) and another, less detailed list of treaty signers made by the Spanish in 1784 ("Tratado de alianza entre España y los indios Chactas y Chicasas o Chicacas, Movila, 14 de julio de 1784," in Serrano y Sanz, *España y los indios*, 82–85; I am indebted to Charles Weeks for bringing this source to my attention). I hope to analyze both of these lists at a future time.

13. Swanton, *Source Material*, 119–24.

14. There may have been others: John Dyson has suggested that the name Sonakabetaska means "he who kills someone wearing metal" and may be partly derived from the Spanish word *sonaja*, referring to small metal tinklers but generalized to cover all metal (and thus European armor) by Indians (Dyson, "Kettles, Metals and Killing").

15. Swanton, *Source Material*, 90–102.

16. See Frawley, Hill, and Munro, "Making a Dictionary," 13.

17. Byington, *A Dictionary.*

18. Linguist Pat Kwachka has been involved with this project since the late 1990s, but the project is primarily staffed by Mississippi Choctaws under the leadership of Roseanna Nickey; it is broadly aimed at language preservation, and its purpose is to produce not only a dictionary but a broad range of language-learning materials. See "Choctaw Language," retrieved from http://www.choctaw.org/culture/choctaw_language.htm on November 4, 2005.

19. For the term "heterarchy" see Crumley, "Three Locational Models."

20. Rowland and Sanders, *Mississippi Provincial Archives*, 1:156.

21. Rowland and Sanders, *Mississippi Provincial Archives*, 1:195.

22. Galloway, "Multidimensional Scaling."

23. Swanton, *Source Material*, 119–24.

24. Gearing, *Priests and Warriors*.

25. Most of these sources are to be found in the French Archives des colonies, série C13A, which contained the correspondence coming from Louisiana, and are published in the five volumes of the *Mississippi Provincial Archives: French Dominion*.

26. For my attempt at a biographical sketch see "Four Ages of Alibamon Mingo, fl. 1700–1766," in this volume.

27. Swanton, *Source Material*, 91. Dale Nicklas (personal communication, 2004) points out that the root *ticho* is present in the Choctaw verb "to translate."

28. Swanton, *Source Material*.

29. Galloway, "The Chief Who Is Your Father"; Nairne, *Nairne's Muskhogean Journals*, 40.

30. Swanton, *Source Material*, 122–23.

31. Or, more accurately, *shulush huma isht abe*, "red shoes he took and killed" per Swanton or "he killed wearing red shoes." See Richard White's biographical sketch, "Red Shoes."

32. Adair, *History*.

33. Swanton, *Source Material*, 78; Mississippi Department of Archives and History, RG 25, vol. 5.

34. Galloway, "Choctaw Factionalism."

35. Rowland, Sanders, and Galloway, *Mississippi Provincial Archives*, 4:269–97.

36. See Gearing, *Priests and Warriors*, 37–46 for the Cherokee; Nairne, *Nairne's Muskhogean Journals*, 38–39 for the Chickasaw.

37. See my "Eighteenth-Century Choctaw Chiefs" in this volume.

38. Swanton, *Source Material*, 76–77.

39. Rowland, Sanders, and Galloway, *Mississippi Provincial Archives*, 4:273.

40. Rowland, Sanders, and Galloway, *Mississippi Provincial Archives*, 4:125–26.

41. Rowland, Sanders, and Galloway, *Mississippi Provincial Archives*, 4:161–62, 165, 166.

42. Swanton, *Source Material*, 83.

43. For the significant career of a Taboca from West Yazoo in the latter half of the century see O'Brien, *Choctaws in a Revolutionary Age*.

44. Swanton, *Source Material*, 56.

III. *Essays in Ethnohistory*

Making Arguments in Time

13. The Currency of Language

The Mobilian Lingua Franca in Colonial Louisiana

Colonizers need tools for the control of colonized populations, and it is a truism that where those tools do not lie ready to hand, the colonizers will invent them or at least strongly influence their invention. In the case of colonial Louisiana, James Crawford has argued, the Choctaw-like "Mobilian" trade language, possibly originating modestly on the fringes of Choctaw lands before the coming of the French in 1699, was adopted by them as a semiofficial Indian lingua franca and thus elevated to a role that it did not attain in prehistory and would not have attained had Europeans not so used it. But is this an adequate account of the facts?

Whatever its merits on linguistic grounds, the reliability of this historical interpretation is initially suspect because the evidence is so sparse. Although some early French observers claimed that the Mobilian language was so widely understood that learning it was of great advantage in dealing with Indians throughout the colony, the sample of the language now available for study is very small and except for a few tiny fragments does not date from the eighteenth century. Crawford began collecting his sample of Mobilian, often as isolated words, almost exclusively from the few living speakers remaining in the late twentieth century, all of them of Alabama-Koasati affiliation.[1] Crawford's original sample was discussed by Mary R. Haas in an article that presented the results of her "preliminary investigation" of Mobilian. Haas's analysis concluded that the sample represented a "jargon" or grammatically and lexically simplified language whose vocabulary and morphemic elements

The material in this chapter was presented at the annual meeting of the French Colonial Historical Society in Martinique and Guadeloupe in May 1989. It was revised and updated for this volume.

appeared to be a mixture of Choctaw and Alabama, while its grammar borrowed pronouns and modifiers from both in order to avoid the more complex Western Muskogean use of affixed particles for verb conjugations and negatives.[2]

Haas's very brief paper hinted at one result that became more obvious when Crawford undertook an extended analysis of the data Haas had used together with an additional sample: the resemblance of especially the lexical elements of the Mobilian sample to other languages (Choctaw, Alabama) was strongly correlated with the native linguistic background of the speaker offering the data.[3] Crawford argued, however, that Haas had been in error when she emphasized the Alabama language so strongly as the source of personal pronouns, finding that they showed a closer resemblance to Chickasaw.[4]

But all that modern evidence can directly demonstrate is that in the middle and late twentieth century a few people spoke a nearly vanished pidgin seeming to be a hybrid of Choctaw, Chickasaw, and Alabama, and sometimes they identified that pidgin as Mobilian (actually, they most often identified it as "Indian"). For evidence on the origin of the jargon and the details of its existence and spread Crawford had to turn to historical sources. Since these sources, with a tiny number of exceptions, offer no more than a passing word in any Native language and were certainly not authored in the main by linguists, they are open to interpretation. I wish to argue here that although Crawford may have been right in raising doubts about the widespread use of a Mobilian jargon before the coming of Europeans (or, given the ambiguity of the evidence, Emanuel Drechsel may have been right in arguing for it), his and Drechsel's further interpretation of the documentary evidence to make arguments about the uses of Mobilian by the Native peoples and French officials of colonial Louisiana was at best incomplete and at worst wrong.

Crawford's and Drechsel's Arguments

The Hernando de Soto expedition, which represented the first lengthy contact of Europeans with speakers of the Western Muskogean family of languages to which the languages of interest belong, resulted in several accounts that Crawford believed did not support an argument for the existence of a specific lingua franca east of the Mississippi.[5] Crawford seems to have been in error in taking as literal truth Garcilaso de la Vega's description of a chain of thirteen interpreters needed to talk with tribes of the interior; Garcilaso's account is the only one to envision such a stratagem, yet close reading of all the accounts makes it very unlikely that this large number of Indians remained constant through the long march of the expedition.[6] There may be, for example, good reasons to believe that the Chicasas (probably Chickasaws) were spoken to through an Apalachee interpreter: the first village of that polity that the expedition encountered was deserted, and *chicasa* is attested as a seventeenth-century Apalachee word for "abandoned village."[7] This interpreter would have been with the expedition for nearly a year, since it had left the Florida Gulf Coast. The accounts do suggest, however, in their clear implication that Indians at least from Coosa (northwest Georgia/northeast Alabama) to Chicasa (east-northeast Mississippi) were in communication with one another (since the Spaniards found that new groups they met had been consistently warned of their coming all the way to the Mississippi-Yazoo delta region), that a more limited claim for some sort of communication medium for this region must be made.

Such claims, by no means limited but taking a lingua franca almost as given, were made by Albert Gatschet and John Swanton in their works, citing as evidence the Muskogean names of non-Muskogean peoples and places used by the Spaniards of the sixteenth century and given to the eighteenth-century French by non-Muskogean informants.[8] Crawford pointed on the contrary to the many observations by early French explorers—Marquette and Jolliet, La Salle, Tonti, Joutel, and various missionaries—of the diversity of Indian languages. He argued that their observation of Native interpreters living among adjacent tribes was evidence that a widespread trade language did not exist in the seventeenth century and that even among tribes of the Tombigbee Basin north of Mobile, where we know Western Muskogean languages were spoken exclusively at the time, there was need for such interpreters.[9]

But oddly, Crawford did not conclude from these facts that interpreters were used by the French for individual Native languages. Remarking on the French policy to train and make use of interpreters, Crawford suggested that most of the French interpreters actually learned Mobilian and concluded that late-eighteenth-century and early-nineteenth-century accounts showing frequent mention of Mobilian, together with the evidence of the language collected by him in 1970, supports an argument that it was official French use of Mobilian that promoted and popularized it to the rank of a true lingua franca in the space of less than a century.

Crawford's argument was really quite simple: if early Spanish and French explorers did not report use of a lingua franca in the lower Mississippi valley, and if American observers of the nineteenth century did report such a jargon, then the jargon developed or at least spread in the interim, and the European newcomers may well have been responsible for its spread. But I think Crawford's account of the development of Mobilian ignored some specific southeastern Indian sociopolitical practices and historical realities with respect to language and made an unjustified leap in its assumption that the French actually used Mobilian in a systematic and official way. This is because he also failed to consider, except from the French point of view, the social contexts of the occasions that offered French observers the opportunity to learn, use, and hear spoken Indian languages.

Several of these criticisms have been articulated in some detail by Drechsel, who has refuted each of Crawford's arguments. Drechsel, however, wants to argue for a very deep past for Mobilian, making the even more serious claim that Mobilian may have been the vehicle for the prehistoric spread of certain linguistic and cultural features throughout the Mississippi valley and the Southeast.[10] Drechsel's dissertation and the subsequent monograph developed from it, which constitutes the most thorough study of Mobilian jargon now available, made the important point that Mobilian is not merely a broken-down version of one of the Western Muskogean languages but rather has its own quite distinctive grammatical structures that mark it clearly as a pidgin language, suitable specifically for use in interlingual contact situations.[11] He further argued that Mobilian, with its vocabulary of synonyms with a broad range of the Muskogean languages, would have been easily understood by speakers of Western Muskogean languages after they learned something of its syntactic conventions.[12] But Drechsel, too, believed that the young Frenchmen placed among the Indians by Iberville and his successors to learn to be interpreters were learning Mobilian and "undoubtedly" employed it.[13] He assumed without detailed analysis of ethnohistorical sources that Native diplomatic conventions would accept the informality of a pidgin, when in fact their seriousness and emphasis on conventions of diplomatic speech by proxy speakers present serious problems for such an interpretation.[14] He also failed to take into account the tremendous upheavals in Indian life that took place as a result of sustained contact with Europeans, especially after the end of the European colonial period. As I will show, there are many reasons to suspect that these more recent events in themselves may have offered the most powerful impetus to pidgin usage, because the real question here is not whether a Mobilian pidgin developed—Crawford, Haas, and Drechsel have amply established that it did—but when it developed and why.

Historical Evidence for Native Contexts of Interaction

I think the work I have been carrying out for a number of years on the ethnic origins of the Choctaw can be of some help here. All the tribal groups whose languages appear to be most closely related to Mobilian—Choctaw, Chickasaw, Alabama—are also tribal groups that were somehow related to the regional hegemony of the complex prehistoric chiefdom whose ceremonial center was at Moundville (Tuscaloosa, Alabama), which in its turn had been the outcome of cultural developments in place that had been going on for many hundreds of years.[15] The historic Chickasaw tribe was apparently an autonomous countrified neighbor to the west of Moundville that had developed independently from a highly similar underlying cultural stock in a region whose relative lack of rich agricultural land limited the Chickasaw of prehistory to less concentrated populations and less complex organization.[16] The Chickasaw may, however, have been involved as middlemen in the trade between Moundville and the Tunican and Siouan populations of the central Mississippi valley.[17]

The Chakchiuma tribe, not usually mentioned at all in the Mobilian language discussion because its language did not survive for comparison, was quite likely a closer dependent of Moundville, living slightly southward of the Chickasaw and sharing many cultural features with them but so much more closely connected culturally with Moundville that it may represent an early spin-off from the Moundville chiefdom while it was still fully functional.[18] Finally, there was clearly a population centered on the ceremonial center of Bottle Creek in the Mobile-Tensaw delta above Mobile Bay, and this population, very much influenced by Moundville, was probably its close ally.[19]

The Moundville chiefdom, limited to the agricultural potential of the Black Warrior River floodplain, apparently began to outgrow its resources sometime in the fifteenth century. As population grew surpluses became more meager, so that eventually the administrative overhead of the complex chiefdom was too great, and the population of the Moundville chiefdom dispersed before European contact.[20] Some of that population moved eastward into the Alabama River valley, where it settled to become the historic Alabama tribe. A good part of the rest moved down into the lower Tombigbee valley and Mobile delta.[21] When in the sixteenth and seventeenth centuries this population underwent violent contact with Spaniards and then harassment in the form of slave raids promoted by Englishmen, a substantial part of it moved onto familiar hunting lands in east-central Mississippi, to be joined by Natchezan people from the southwest and possibly some Chakchiumas from the north in the formation of the confederacy that became known as Choctaw.[22] That part of the population that remained in the Mobile delta, which probably consisted primarily of the "native" population that had dwelt there in amicable relations with Moundville before the dispersal, became known to history as Naniabas, Tohomes, and Mobilians.

If this scenario is even partially correct it is obvious that several of these groups must have spoken substantially the same language at one time in this temporal sequence. Linguistic differences among Chickasaw, Choctaw, Mobilian, and even Alabama were not so great as to create complete mutual unintelligibility. Although some dialects were apparently harder to understand than others, no interlanguage would have been required for basic communication.[23] Where a pidgin would have been of most use was in dealing with tribes on the fringes of the Western Muskogean area, if they could only be persuaded to learn it. Yet Crawford observed correctly that the early French explorers and settlers remarked on no such pidgin. What they did observe (and what the Spanish explorers had observed a hundred years before) was what they described as Native interpreters.

I have written elsewhere of the importance of the *fani mingo*, or "Native ombudsman," institution as it was observed among the Chickasaws and Choctaws in the early eighteenth century: tribes would adopt an advocate within a neighboring tribe, and it would be his duty to argue in favor of his adopted tribe whenever war threatened to break out.[24] It is nowhere specifically stated that the adopted fanimingo would also be capable of speaking the language of the tribe whose interests he represented, but there are several instances in which this is implied. This institution and several others bear discussion at some length, since their existence demonstrates the fact that Native cultures, like the cultures of their European contemporaries, provided quite adequate formal mechanisms for linguistic accommodation without the development of interlanguages or pidgins.

These institutions all fall under the heading of fictive kinship structures. Since in nonstate societies kinship is the chief underlying organizational mechanism, all other relationships within the society are defined in terms of or as analogues of kinship, and this seems also to have been the way neighboring groups managed to deal with competition and differences. I have mentioned the fanimingo institution, and I have suggested elsewhere that under other names it may have been widespread throughout at least the Southeast and the lower Mississippi valley.[25] The calumet ceremony, that very visible trapping of intertribal diplomacy throughout the eastern woodlands, is now thought to have marked the creation of fictive kinship for its European participants with the tribe offering the ceremony, and presumably it functioned in the same way when it was used intertribally.

It is worth remembering how willingly the Louisiana tribes accepted the French notion of placing young boys in Indian villages to learn languages. This was not a case of Indians acceding to French suggestions only, although the French had already had experience with this policy in Canada and did suggest it; Indian leaders in the Southeast actively sought these young French boys and almost certainly adopted them formally. In 1700 Iberville left a young French boy with the chief of the Bayou Goulas and promised the same to the Natchez chiefs.[26] Two years later, when the Chickasaw chief asked for a young boy, Iberville sent with him little St. Michel, who had already learned something of the Houma language, which Iberville said was "the same language as Chickasaw or very close to it."[27] The Choctaw alleged the following year that St. Michel had been killed, but in spite of a Choctaw attack on the Chickasaw, the boy was kept safe and brought back to Mobile not only unharmed but fluent in Chickasaw.[28] These boys did not just go into the Indian towns and hang around observing like a modern ethnographer; instead, they were fostered for years, as young boys still were in noble Europe, handed over to leading Indian men who would stand in loco parentis and see that they were properly educated in the language as well as the culture.[29] The proof of this lies in the fact that so many of them also married within their adopted culture and founded métis families.[30]

What this phenomenon says to me is that we may connect the early observations of Native interpreters and Thomas Nairne's description of the fanimingo institution to suggest that Nairne's description was incomplete: fanimingos were not just adopted randomly; important tribal groups' leaders, contrary to the routine southeastern practice of matrilocality in marriage, certainly married their sisters off into neighboring tribes for alliance purposes, and their sons, retaining the mother's ethnic identity, held rank in both tribes.[31] Such young men would also have dual language proficiency, and in several instances they became prominent men: one very obvious example is

Alibamon Mingo, "Chief of the Alabamas," of the Choctaw Concha village and eventually the entire Eastern Division, who was said to hold the same rank in both tribes.[32]

A second example is particularly striking because it occurred at such a dramatic juncture, the outbreak of the Choctaw civil war in 1746. After the murder of three Frenchmen, Jadart de Beauchamp, major of Mobile, was sent to reason with the Choctaw and demand vengeance. All the chiefs came to meet with him at the town of Chickasawhay, but Beauchamp needed all the influence he could get. Knowing the one root cause of the outbreak was the blandishments of English traders, he had asked an Alabama chief, who was friendly with the Choctaw but stood neutral between the two European groups, to attend as well. And when the chief Tamatlémingo arrived, he was accompanied by his son, the nephew of the Choctaw war chief of Yanabé village. When Tamatlémingo rose to speak, he apologized for not speaking the Choctaw language well but said that he would explain himself the best he could. The young man spoke in his turn, basically repeating the arguments of his father and emphasizing his credibility as an ethnic Choctaw. Clearly he was, then, also the son of the Yanabé war chief's sister, and he had already attained to some rank or he would not have spoken.[33]

There is another piece of evidence that fits well with the hypothesis of the Native importance of interpreters. Complaints were offered by the *commissaire-ordonnateur* Edmé Gatien Salmon in 1731 that traders and hunters were being used as interpreters and that this offended the Indians. Apparently, they had voiced concern that whereas the speaker for any chief was a man of rank and dignity, the interpreters used by the French were of low rank and lived by somewhat questionable trading practices. The suggestion made was that the interpreters be given officer rank.[34] It is not by any means certain that the speaker for a chief—an officeholder in the tribe and the village who presented the chief's speeches at home as well as among foreigners—had also to be an interpreter, but this example does suggest that the Indians had a model for what rank an interpreter should have and that they saw it as comparable with that of a chief's speaker.[35]

The assumption by Crawford and Drechsel that the young boys sent to learn Indian languages would thenceforth converse in Mobilian is controvertible by many examples; this was clearly neither the intention of the French government nor the result it obtained from this practice. From the beginning specific tribes—Choctaw, Chickasaw, and later Natchez, Alabama, Tallapoosa

ESSAYS IN ETHNOHISTORY

—were chosen to receive these boys, and they were chosen because of their perceived importance to French policy (or their possible threat to it).

I have already cited the examples of young boys sent to the Bayou Goula, Natchez, and Chickasaw. The official position was made clear when in 1708 Bienville reported sending one boy to the Chickasaw and one to the Choctaw.[36] Pontchartrain replied, "You have done well to send two young boys to the Chickasaw and to the Choctaw to learn their language. It is necessary to have some likewise among the neighboring nations whose languages are unknown to the French."[37] That specific languages were to be learned is emphasized by an incident of 1742 in which the young soldier Laubelle was sent back by the Tallapoosa chief when he proved incapable of learning Tallapoosa.[38] Three years later a younger, eleven-year-old boy was sent.[39] And because the Choctaw proved so important strategically, there was an ongoing policy of placing young boys among them. In the early 1730s, as the first crop of interpreters who had begun as children—Huché, Bromets, and Allain *dit* Rousséve —reached maturity, Bienville, returning to Louisiana to reorganize the colony under the Crown, was ordered to send a new batch of boys—"those whom he thinks most intelligent"—among the Indians "in order to learn the Indian languages so that they may be able someday to serve as interpreters and to win the confidence of the Indians."[40] Of four chosen, the cadets Mouy and Vauparis were sent to the Choctaw.[41] And again in 1745 Governor Pierre de Rigaud de Vaudreuil sent several cadets, among them the nephew of Father Baudouin, to be assigned to the Tombecbé post on the Tombigbee River but to live among the Choctaw to learn their language.[42]

The evidence that the boys were sent to learn specific languages and that they thus fit into a preexisting Indian model for diplomacy supported by the formal politeness of using one another's language is compelling, and it supports an emphasis on language differentiation. There are good reasons to argue that such emphasis was in the interest of historic southeastern Indian groups. After the holocaust of European disease and the subsequent population movements and reorganizations in the sixteenth and seventeenth centuries, newly formed groups would seek ways to mark their distinctiveness, to emphasize their boundaries.[43] This is the argument that has been offered for the rapid spread of one pottery type among the groups belonging to the Upper Creek confederacy, and language would serve as an even more obvious marker of identity.[44] It was only in the eyes of uninformed Europeans that Native people of the Americas were undifferentiated "Indians," not in their own eyes.

Thus I would argue that widespread use of Mobilian was not officially fostered by the French in the Louisiana colony at least partly because during that period Europeans did not enjoy dominance over their Indian allies and had to comply with the conventions of intertribal diplomacy, whose protocol demanded the use of speaker-interpreters as a mark of the rank of the negotiator and of respect for the negotiating partner. Apart from this, it was in the Indian interest to retain these marks of tribal uniqueness, while the military orientation of the French colony and its lack of manpower made the French interest coincide with a policy of respect for the Indian interest. This reading of the evidence, therefore, would invalidate the suggestion made by Crawford and Drechsel that official French efforts were instrumental in the spread of Mobilian before 1763.

Of course, we have no way of estimating the amount of informal use of Mobilian that may have taken place, but it should be remembered that a good deal of the credit for good French relations with large groups like the Alabama and the Choctaw goes to the fact that the French were not their close neighbors and, except for interpreters (who had been raised to speak the target language anyway), did not indulge in the kind of daily informal contact that leads to the need for an interlanguage.[45]

The Function of Mobilian in French Colonial Louisiana

But if Mobilian did not play the role Crawford and Drechsel mapped out for it, we are still left with the task of answering the questions both posed: what was its origin and what role if any did French colonials have in its spread?[46] It is obvious that Frenchmen who had to interact with Indians on a daily basis and in less rarefied ways than diplomacy would need to "pick up the language," and there is plenty of evidence that they did. Jean-Baptiste Le Moyne de Bienville was himself the first example of this practice, and he prided himself in serving as a model to his officers. Arriving in Louisiana in 1699 with his brother, Iberville, who had been sent to establish a colony, he began right away to attain a working knowledge of the vocabulary of the language he perceived as being that spoken by the greatest number of Indians of the region.[47] This may have been the Mobilian jargon, for under Drechsel's analysis the few vocabulary and textual samples reported by Father Du Ru, who was learning under the same circumstances, does seem to be so.[48] But Bienville's case offers clear evidence that the influence of Mobilian did not go very far; in 1716, when he was being sent by Antoine Laumet de La Mothe, sieur de

Cadillac to suppress the Natchez, he wrote to Pontchartrain to justify his using an interpreter, since "all the Indian nations on the St. Louis River [Mississippi] speak languages quite different from those that I know and . . . it would be very necessary for me to have an interpreter, . . . without whom I cannot get along, to manage the Indians."[49]

Not everyone was eager to learn the difficult Indian languages, either. There are repeated complaints in the French records that both missionaries and officers were failing to learn the Indian languages and that they needed interpreters to carry on their work. In 1699 Iberville lamented his reluctant Recollect missionary, saying that if he had brought a Jesuit, the language would have been learned quickly.[50] Apart from the Choctaw mission, Indian missions in Louisiana were not in the end staffed by Jesuits, and the complaints continued.[51] As early as 1707 Bienville complained that although all the Indians were asking for missionaries, the only one available was laughed at for his attempts at the language.[52] In 1714 Father Le Maire, a missionary who had had difficulty learning Indian languages, wrote to advise Pontchartrain that any missionaries should be young so that they could learn the languages.[53] Two years later Cadillac was still complaining that the missionaries did not know any Indian language.[54] Apparently, this was a trend that could not be fought, for in 1725 Father Raphael wrote to his friend the Abbé Raguet asking for three or four Indian missionaries and saying that at first they would each require an interpreter.[55] There are very logical reasons, totally apart from the difficulties of learning or the reluctance to do so, why this situation should persist. There is no indication that mastery of a Mobilian jargon alone would have been adequate for the teaching of spiritual subtleties; in fact, Le Maire despaired of the possibility even when missionaries used the individual languages after years of study.[56] Furthermore, apart from a few cases—the Choctaws' Father Baudouin being one—the missionaries tended to be subject to transfer at more frequent intervals than the adequate learning of a specific language would require. The complaints listed confirm that they did not in fact take the expedient step of learning Mobilian for the purpose.

A similar problem beset the officers: there were specific military requirements for the regular rotation of officers and men from post to post, and they might find themselves among the Alabama one year, the Natchez the next, and the Quapaw the next. Had they set themselves to learn the local Indian language, they would have had to learn at least three. Officers thus were sometimes forced to the expedient of hiring interpreters themselves. I have already cited Bienville's request for reimbursement for the interpreter he needed at Natchez in 1716. In 1725 both Desliettes, who had commanded at Natchez, and Boisbriant, who had commanded at the Illinois post, petitioned the Superior Council of Louisiana for reimbursement for interpreters they had hired.[57] Over time it was established that each post kept an interpreter on staff, but officers who did succeed in mastering Indian languages were invariably praised for it: St. Denis on the lower Mississippi in 1708; Delery among the Choctaw in 1736; Le Sueur at Tombecbé (Choctaw) in 1742; Canelle among the Choctaw in 1744; d'Erneville at Fort Toulouse (Alabama) in 1760.[58] The lavishness of praise for these officers suggests that their accomplishment was quite unusual.

The competence of these officers, however, because it was so specifically recognized, permits us to point again to the ceremonial importance of interpreters, since in spite of their acknowledged competence in specific languages, some of these very officers were reported as having used interpreters on important occasions. In 1738, when the Choctaw were uneasy as English and French traders competed for their trade and urged them to kill their respective European competitors, Le Sueur traveled through the nation with the interpreter Allain and had Allain speak for him on several occasions.[59] On an even more important and public occasion, that of the annual present exchange with the Choctaw in Mobile, Bienville used the interpreter until an insolent speech from an Indian angered him (implying that he either understood enough Choctaw or understood enough of Choctaw body language to be offended), at which point he said, "I replied myself for fear that the interpreter might not render well what I wished to say to him," which was in fact rather intemperate.[60] The use of interpreters in both cases would of course offer assurance that accurate translation was achieved, but it also quite clearly served the ceremonial purpose of demonstrating both the importance of the man who used the interpreter and his consideration for his interlocutor. For this reason governors other than Bienville did not make a serious effort to learn Native languages but depended upon skilled interpreters in the different languages to present their speeches.

There was one very good military reason that the French would not encourage the learning of an Indian lingua franca by soldiers and even young officers. Desertion was a common and serious problem at the posts.[61] Since the Indians, not understanding why soldiers did not have a perfect right to go where they wished when they wished, frequently helped them desert, it would hardly have been a military advantage to the French to promote the use of Mobilian either by soldiers or among all the tribes of Louisiana. An excellent example of the fact that even this policy could be ineffective is provided by Governor Vaudreuil's cousin, Antoine Adhémar de Lantagnac. Assigned to Fort Toulouse among the Alabama at the age of thirteen in 1745, Lantagnac claimed that he got lost in the forest and was captured by Chickasaws, who spoke to him by signs after their language was not understood and subsequently carried him off to South Carolina, where he found favor with Governor Glen (with whom he spoke in French) and was set up as a Cherokee trader.[62] Lantagnac returned to the French colony in 1755 with a Cherokee wife and a fluent command of Cherokee and apparently several of the Upper Creek languages, never having developed a need for Mobilian.

Official policy, in fact, was clearly opposed to the use of a pidgin language for several more strategic reasons. Throughout the history of the financially struggling colony, interpreters were maintained on the payroll of both financier and king. Explicitly voiced policy was cast in the formula of "divide and rule," and one persistent goal was to encourage separateness among the tribes. Fostering of Mobilian or any such pidgin would also have been unlikely in an atmosphere of distrust toward the African slaves imported to do the work of the concessions; in fact, the French purposely encouraged the belief among their black slaves that the Indians would kill them hideously if they got the chance and in one instance had a company of black slaves massacre a small tribe, the Chaouacha, that had been giving trouble.[63] In at least one instance where a slave rebellion was feared, explicit statements make it clear that enslaved Africans were not encouraged to learn much of any language but their own. In this instance the French congratulated themselves that the revolt was confined to slaves of Bambara origin, because their language was said to be incomprehensible to other Africans.[64]

Clearly, enslaved Africans did learn something in the way of an Indian language, but although it could have been Mobilian it was quite likely whatever dialect they were exposed to. After the Natchez revolt in 1729 Choctaws helped the French obtain the release of French women and children and African slaves, and most of the slaves ended up in the possession of the Indians, who demanded a reward for their return. Blacks held by the Indians later reported that a Chickasaw chief had visited the villages where they were held in order to argue the advantages of slavery under the British but had had to depart dissatisfied.[65] As there were no French interpreters on hand at the time, Choctaw, the mutually intelligible Chickasaw, or Mobilian must have been used to speak to the slaves.

I have already mentioned that the Indians complained of the use of traders as interpreters, which raises the real question of Mobilian as a trade language in colonial Louisiana. The colonial government tried to control the trade as well as everything else, very much more strictly than was done in the English colonies, which means that there was thus further restriction of the need for Mobilian. This was done by the simple expedient of entrusting the trade either to the official interpreters themselves, who we have seen did actually learn specific languages, or to the post commanders, who also kept interpreters on staff. The most significant opportunities for trade, however, were even more tightly controlled by the government and consisted of the annual present-giving ceremonies in Mobile, to which the Indians brought reciprocal presents for French officials and which were also the occasion for trade. Again here the official interpreters played a leading role.[66]

Doubtless there were other less formal—even less legal—occasions for trade between Indian and Frenchman and African that might in some instances have provided a context for the use of a pidgin language. Such would not have been true of the families that settled around some of the posts and even in the coastal hinterlands, since often these families consisted of a retired French soldier and his Native wife. The one context where it is likely that some form of interlanguage was often used was in food provisioning. When Indians brought their wares to the growing French settlements, especially New Orleans and Mobile, it is likely that enslaved Africans sent to market for food would have been exposed to some Indian language.[67] When Indians undertook contract hunting work for the French settlers, which was apparently a common occurrence, there was another opportunity for such interaction. An incident of 1738 suggests Mobilian: a Choctaw couple, doing contract hunting around the Pascagoula, obtained transportation to Mobile to sell their share of the hunt with two young Frenchmen and their family's black slave. Spending the night on an island, the younger Frenchman murdered the Indians after the elder had failed to persuade the black to do so; the slave had said the Choctaws "had done him no wrong."[68] No specific mention of a communication medium was made, but in the triracial context it is quite possible that an interlanguage would be used.

Conclusions

Surely there were all kinds of efforts at communication among Indians, Frenchmen, and Africans in the Louisiana colony, and it is likely that, as the nineteenth-century records show, Mobilian came to be a significant vehicle used for informal communication. As contacts of all kinds increased among these three populations, and wherever people with an Indian heritage were involved, it may have been Mobilian that offered a kind of neutral ground. It should be remembered that the French colony itself was not monoglot, since it had Frenchmen, Flemings, and German-speaking Alsatians and Swiss; the African slave population spoke several mutually unintelligible languages from regions as far apart as the Bight of Benin and the Senegal-Gambia area; and the Indians of the colony—which, it should be remembered, stretched from Texas to Illinois to Montgomery, Alabama, to Mobile—were in the same situation.[69] But the bulk of the colony's population and the center of its administrative gravity rested in and on the borders of lands inhabited by Western Muskogean–speaking Indians, Indians for whom a Mobilian lingua franca would have been easy to learn and use. It is therefore likely that Mobilian did become a favored medium for unofficial Indian/non-Indian communication, but apart from the very early comments on the existence and usefulness of Mobilian made by Iberville and Pénicaut, there is little else to document its use during the French colonial period. "Unofficial" communication was most often also "undocumented."

I would suggest, however, that it was not the usage of Mobilian during the French colonial period that gave it enough currency to survive into the twentieth century but its use in the population movements that followed the loss of the French colony in 1763. As tribal remnants like the Tunica, Houma, Biloxi, and Pensacola moved west of the Mississippi to escape the English in 1763, to be followed in the first half of the following century by removed groups like the Alabama, Choctaw, and Kasihta, a melting pot of tribes developed in Louisiana and east Texas consisting of tribal remnants or fragments cut off from larger tribal populations, a majority of which were Western Muskogean speakers.[70] Deprived of the ceremonial panoply that demanded speaker-interpreters, compelled to deal with one another frequently, these groups had recourse to the neutral jargon, Mobilian. Drechsel's analysis of the social context in which Mobilian was used suggests that no one was demeaned by its use, as they would be by ungrammatical speech in a Native language.[71] Their French and black neighbors, too, were probably already conversant with it through its use by the Choctaws who hunted annually west of the Mississippi in the early nineteenth century.[72]

I do not mean to say that Mobilian was only used in this late multiracial context but that this was its period of greatest efficacy and importance to Indian people for whom, as Drechsel has pointed out, it served as a buffer protecting their culture from outsiders. In the French colony, in official dealings with individual Indians and Indian groups at a time when Indians and not Europeans held the balance of power, politeness and diplomatic advantage demanded the use of what amounted to the host's language, as had been the case in Indian diplomatic practice before the coming of Europeans (and, it may be worth observing, as was the case in European diplomatic practice among peers in Europe). Mobilian thus remained the jargon of marginal, unofficial, and even unsanctioned relationships and transactions down through the end of the eighteenth century. But when the balance shifted and the Indians became marginal, there was no longer any reason for the newly dominant American culture to take the trouble to master the niceties of myriad languages and dialects. From that time, Mobilian sufficed on the Euro-American side, while on the Indian side it became an indispensable tool of survival.

Acknowledgments

I would like to thank Emanuel Drechsel, Pat Kwachka, and Dale Nicklas for commenting on this essay; although I have not agreed with every comment, they have aided me immensely in strengthening my argument. The original idea for this paper goes much farther back, to my thinking about the implications of Kennith York's brief paper on Mobilian written with the insight of a sophisticated native speaker of Choctaw.[73] None of these scholars is responsible for any errors or wrongheadedness that remains.

Notes

1. Crawford, *The Mobilian Trade Language*, 60–62.

2. Haas, "What Is Mobilian?"

3. This has remained true in Emanuel Drechsel's further collecting work, although he has made it into an advantage, attributing it to the flexibility of the Mobilian pidgin in absorbing vocabulary items from whatever environment it has found itself in through relexification; see Drechsel, *Mobilian Jargon*, 157–200.

4. Crawford, *The Mobilian Trade Language*.

5. Crawford, *The Mobilian Trade Language*, 16–17.

6. See Booker, Hudson, and Rankin, "Place Name Identification." These authors argue that the original interpreter of the Pardo expedition (a French captive) worked with a limited number of others by virtue of the fact that he commanded a Muskogean language and could speak to designated interpreters met with in the towns the expedition passed through, and they see a similar pattern with the Soto expedition.

7. "The native name applied to the site of an abandoned village and to its surrounding lands. It probably is an Apalachee term" (Hann, *Apalachee*, 401). Hann found the term turning up frequently in Spanish documents of the seventeenth and eighteenth centuries in a context of Spanish reoccupation of abandoned villages and their lands by Spanish ranches.

8. Gatschet, *A Migration Legend*; Swanton, *Final Report* and *Indians*.

9. The tribes of the region were the Chickasaw, Choctaw, Chakchiuma, Mobilian, Tohome, and Naniaba. The evidence for the latter four languages is only indirect. In one French document the Mobilian, Tohome, and Naniaba were referred to as "Choctaws established on the Mobile River" (Jean-Christophe de Lusser, Journal, January 12–March 23, 1730, in Archives des colonies, série C13A, 12:l00–134 [see 134], translated in Rowland and Sanders, *Mississippi Provincial Archives*, 1:81–117), and in the course of the eighteenth century the Chakchiuma settled with both the Choctaw and the Chickasaw.

10. Drechsel, *Mobilian Jargon*, 286 ff.; I will refer here to this work as reflecting Drechsel's most recent thinking. The dissertation is Drechsel, "Mobilian Jargon: Linguistic, Sociocultural, and Historical Aspects of an American Lingua Franca."

11. Drechsel, *Mobilian Jargon*, 73–135.

12. Drechsel, *Mobilian Jargon*, 193–99.

13. Drechsel, *Mobilian Jargon*, 258–59.

14. Though not directly relevant to my argument here, it is important to point out that Drechsel's arguments based on archaeological evidence suffer from a lack of exposure to the most recent work, which is understandable, since there is often such a time lag in the publication of archaeological work.

15. Drechsel referred to Moundville as "Muskogia's heartland" and argued that Mobilian probably served as the tool for the "sociopolitical integration of paramount chiefdoms" (*Mobilian Jargon*, 293–94), both of which assertions are problematic in view of the recent scholarship on sociopolitical complexity in the Southeast.

16. Johnson and Sparks, "Protohistoric Settlement Patterns."

17. Sheldon and Jenkins, "Protohistoric Development."

18. See Atkinson, "A Historic Contact Indian Settlement"; Marshall, "Lyon's Bluff Site." The name of the tribe, of course, is apparently Choctawan, "red crayfish."

19. Stowe, "The Pensacola Variant"; Fuller, "The Bear Point Phase."

20. Peebles, "Paradise Lost, Strayed, and Stolen."

21. Sheldon, "The Mississippian-Historic Transition."

22. Galloway, "Confederacy as a Solution."

23. Nicklas (personal communication, 2004) observes that Choctaw and Chickasaw are today mutually intelligible, that it is likely that some degree of understanding between both and Alabama exists today, and that similar conditions could have obtained between them in the eighteenth century as well. I have personally observed examples of the mutual intelligibility of Choctaw and Chickasaw, at least.

24. Galloway, "The Chief Who Is Your Father."

25. Galloway, "The Chief Who Is Your Father."

26. Pénicaut, *Fleur de Lys and Calumet*, 25, 30.

27. Le Moyne d'Iberville, *Iberville's Gulf Journals*, 176–77.

28. Pénicaut, *Fleur de Lys and Calumet*, 67–68, 73–79; Galloway, "Talking with Indians," 114.

29. As Drechsel describes the upbringing of Joseph Pierite, Sr., among the Choctaw-Biloxi of Indian Creek, Louisiana, "one would expect Pierite as a child . . . to have acquired Choctaw proper rather than Mobilian Jargon" (*Mobilian Jargon*, 246n32). It is inconsistent, then, that Drechsel resists the idea that young French interpreter trainees learned the language of their adopted tribe.

30. See Galloway, "Talking with Indians."

31. Nairne text in Nairne, *Nairne's Muskhogean Journals*.

32. See my "The Four Ages of Alibamon Mingo, fl. 1700–1766," in this volume.

33. Jadart de Beauchamp, Journal, September 16–October 19, 1746, in Archives des colonies, série C13A, 30:222–40 (see 236–37), translated in Rowland, Sanders, and Galloway, *Mississippi Provincial Archives*, 4:269–97. The first three volumes of the *Mississippi Provincial Archives: French Dominion* are edited by Rowland and Sanders; the final two are edited by Rowland, Sanders, and Galloway. Hereafter they are cited in the text and notes as MPA:FD.

34. Salmon to Maurepas, December 9, 1731, AC, série C13A, 13:124–25, translated in MPA:FD, 4:99–100.

35. Ethnographer Jason Jackson (personal communication, 2004) notes that among the modern Creek, Yuchi, and Seminole in Oklahoma the function of speaker is equated with that of town diplomat and interpreter. Dale Nicklas (personal communication, 2004) points out that in fact the term *tichou* shares the same stem as the verb *tisholi*, to translate.

36. Bienville to Pontchartrain, October 12, 1708, AC, série C13A, 2:183–84, translated in MPA:FD, 2:37–44.

37. Pontchartrain to Bienville, July 11, 1709, AC, série B, 30:181–83, 182, emphasis added, translated in MPA:FD, 3:127–29.

38. Vaudreuil to La Houssaye, November 2, 1743, Vaudreuil Letterbooks, Huntington Manuscript Loudoun (H M LO) 9:III, 16.

39. Vaudreuil to Hazeur, June 11, 1745, H M LO 9:III, 159.

40. Bienville and Salmon to Maurepas, May 7, 1733, AC, série C13A, 16:31, translated in MPA:FD, 3:585–86. Note that of interpreter Allain *dit* Rousséve it was explicitly observed that he had been reared among the Choctaws and knew their language perfectly; see Louboey to Maurepas, October 6, 1745, AC, série C13A, 29:189–95, translated in MPA:FD, 4:233–42.

41. Bienville and Salmon to Maurepas, April 15, 1733, AC, série C13A, 18:95.

42. Vaudreuil to D'Erneville, March 7, 1745, H M LO 9:III, 156.

43. See Dobyns, *Their Number Become Thinned*.

44. Smith, *Archaeology of Aboriginal Culture Change*.

45. The one significant exception is the case of the garrison at Fort Toulouse among the Alabamas, where the families and especially the children were referred to by the Alabamas as their adopted children—again emphasizing the closeness of the relationship.

46. The details cited in this section are drawn from a database of document summaries from AC, série C13A, prepared as part of research on Choctaw landholding under NEH grant RO-21631-88.

47. See Le Moyne d'Iberville, *Iberville's Gulf Journals*, 59, 126. It should be noted that according to his brother Iberville it was more than a year later that Bienville was beginning to make himself understood in the languages of the lower Mississippi valley.

48. Drechsel, *Mobilian Jargon*, 139, 217.

49. Bienville to Pontchartrain, January 2, 1716, AC, série C13A, 4:766–67, translated in *MPA:FD*, 3:191–97.

50. Le Moyne d'Iberville, *Iberville's Gulf Journals*, 93.

51. If the Jesuit missionary to the Choctaw did become proficient in that language (and he did live alone among them), he did not so far as is known produce any translations, grammars, and so on that survive.

52. Bienville to Pontchartrain, February 20, 1707, AC, série C13A, 2:16–17, translated in *MPA:FD*, 3:35–46.

53. See Delanglez, "M. Le Maire on Louisiana"; document in the Ayer Collection, Newberry Library.

54. Cadillac to Pontchartrain, January 23, 1716, AC, série C13A, 4:542.

55. Father Raphael to Abbé Raguet, May 15, 1725, AC, série C13A, 8:404v, translated in *MPA:FD*, 2:470–92.

56. Drechsel's suggestion (*Mobilian Jargon*, 262) that it would have been adequate cannot be taken seriously, as Le Maire's reports on the difficulties of expressing doctrine without years of study attest (see Delanglez, "M. Le Maire on Louisiana," 152–53). Eighteenth-century missionaries were just as aware as later ones that translating the spiritual was a subtle task. The example of Father Paul Du Ru, who may have provided the earliest attestation of Mobilian, is not useful as evidence on this point, since Du Ru did not anticipate a permanent assignment in Louisiana.

57. Minutes of Superior Council, March 20–May 24, 1725, AC, série C13A, 9:84, translated in *MPA:FD*, 2:416–57.

58. See AC, série C13A, 5:29; Bienville to Pontchartrain, February 25, 1708, AC, série C13A, 2:114, translated in *MPA:FD*, 3:111–24; Bienville to Maurepas, June 29, 1736, AC, série C13A, 21:184v, translated in *MPA:FD*, 3:685–90; Bienville to Maurepas, March 28, 1742, AC, série C13A, 27:66 (Bienville observes that Le Sueur knows Choctaw perfectly); Vaudreuil to Baudouin, July 30, 1744, H M LO 9:III, 95 (Canelle was directed to deliver a formal speech to the Choctaws on Vaudreuil's behalf); and D'Erneville to Berryer, March 15, 1760, AC, série C13A, 42:184v, translated in *MPA:FD*, 5:242–50.

59. Salmon to Maurepas, November 26, 1738, AC, série C13A, 23:145, translated in *MPA:FD*, 1:374–75; Louboey to Maurepas, November 28, 1738, AC, série C13A, 23:169v, translated in *MPA:FD*, 4:154–59; Noyan to Maurepas, January 4, 1739, AC, série C13A, 24:225v, translated in *MPA:FD*, 4:160–68.

60. AC, série C13A, 18:158v.

61. See Thomas, *Fort Toulouse*, 18–21 for mutinies and desertions at one post.

62. Petition of Lantagnac to Kerlérec, AC, série C13A, 39:40–44, translated in *MPA:FD*, 4:161–66.

63. Willis, "Divide and Rule," 106–7.

64. Périer to Maurepas, December 10, 1731, AC, série C13A, 13:64, translated in *MPA:FD*, 4:101–10.

65. Régis du Roullet to Périer, March 16, 1721, AC, série C13A, 13:189v, translated in *MPA:FD*, 4:64–72.

66. Galloway, "Talking with Indians."

67. Usner, *Indians, Settlers, and Slaves*, 258–59, accepts the arguments of Crawford and Drechsel uncritically in assuming that Mobilian was the preeminent medium of trade, and this may indeed have been the case with reference to the urban settings that were the focus of Usner's interest. Yet more sources may be worth seeking; an account notebook kept by George Rapalje at the turn of the eighteenth century at his trade house on the Big Black River, where triracial relations were the norm, contains page after page of undoubtedly Choctaw vocabulary items relevant to trade; see Rapalje, Rapalje/Rapalji (George) Notebook.

68. See my "The Barthelemy Murders: Bienville's Establishment of the Lex Talionis as a Principle of Indian Diplomacy," in this volume.

69. We should perhaps also ask ourselves how those heterogeneous Europeans communicated among themselves, or how Africans managed to communicate in imagining freedom. In the latter case the Louisiana Creole language, with a French vocabulary and African grammatical structure, which emerged soon after the arrival of enslaved Africans in Louisiana, may have been derived from a Portuguese pidgin developed in Africa and relexified with French and will apparently outlive Mobilian; see Hall, *Africans in Colonial Louisiana*, 187–200.

70. Kniffen, Gregory, and Stokes, *The Historic Tribes*.

71. Drechsel, *Mobilian Jargon*, 244–49, 266–70.

72. White, *The Roots of Dependency*.

73. York, "Mobilian."

14. The Barthelemy Murders

Bienville's Establishment of the
Lex Talionis as a Principle of
Indian Diplomacy

As editor of the *Mississippi Provincial Archives: French Dominion* series at the Mississippi Department of Archives and History, I have been working to prepare translations of French documents from the Louisiana colony, 1730–63, to complete the series started more than fifty years ago by Dunbar Rowland and Albert Godfrey Sanders.[1] In the course of this work it became obvious that one crucial factor for the colony's survival, both for this period and for the earlier one, was success in Indian diplomacy, and the documents reflect this by their interest in such matters. The French, by the testimony of their English adversaries and by the evidence of history, were remarkably skilled in dealing with the American Indian tribes.[2] Part of this skill came from their general attitude toward the Indian, but an important contributing factor in terms of local application of imperial policy was the influence of the governor of the colony.[3]

The Louisiana colony did not always have governors who were skilled diplomatists, but for most of its early history it benefited from the guidance of the most skilled of them all: Jean-Baptiste Le Moyne, sieur de Bienville. The Canadian seemed to have an intuitive grasp of the Indian concept of honor and to understand tribal power structures as no other governor did. In addition, he made it his business to learn and use Choctaw or the Choctaw-like Mobilian trade language in his dealings with the Indians—the only governor to do so.[4] What Bienville seems to have been trying to do in general was to

The material in this chapter was previously published as "The Barthelemy Murders: Bienville's Establishment of the *lex talionis* as a Principle of Indian Diplomacy" in the *Proceedings of the Eighth Annual Meeting of the French Colonial Historical Society, 1982*, edited by E. P. Fitzgerald (Lanham MD: University Press of America, 1985), 91–103. Reprinted by permission of University Press of America.

replace certain Indian institutions by others, French controlled but morphologically similar. These replacement institutions were intended to fit into Indian custom and move it in the direction of changes that would accommodate European patterns.

An example of such policy can be seen in Bienville's initial success with the Choctaw. Living in a wide area of what is now east-central Mississippi, the Choctaw were the most powerful tribe within the bounds claimed by the colony and always its most important ally. They were first won over to French allegiance when Bienville armed them against the Chickasaw of northern Mississippi and the Creek of central and eastern Alabama, tribes that had terrorized and enslaved them using English-supplied firearms.[5] This original success was played upon throughout the history of the colony. Whenever the allegiance of the Choctaw wavered, a reminder of this "restoration of manhood" by Bienville was always proffered by French officials and always acknowledged, even if grudgingly, by the Choctaw.[6] In this instance Bienville had understood the insecurity that would be experienced by a southeastern Indian male when he found himself not only unable to protect the persons of his wife and children but even unable to compete successfully for the wild game to feed them.[7] He had thus redeemed the dignity of Choctaw males by replacing the traditional weapon with another whose effectiveness altered the very nature of intertribal warfare.

Chapman Milling, in his study of English interaction with the Indians of the Carolinas, stated that he had "failed to discover a single recorded instance of a white man's suffering either death or penal servitude as a sentence meted out to him by a colonial white government for the murder of an Indian."[8] This was the case with the English, whose official policy was to offer material compensation for the death of an Indian, but it was certainly not so with the French in Louisiana, and it was Bienville who took the initiative to establish equality of punishment as a legal principle.[9] Although the principle did not quite coincide with the Indian concept of blood revenge, it seemed to be close enough to achieve the same kind of success as the supplying of firearms had done.

In the most fundamental sense, of course, the lex talionis in the case of death is blood revenge. The eighteenth-century French version of it called for the death of a murderer, but the rendering of justice was vested in a tribunal representing the polity, and the penalty could not be borne by anyone except the murderer himself. On the side of the Choctaw and indeed for all of the

ESSAYS IN ETHNOHISTORY

tribes of the Southeast, the available evidence points to blood vengeance as the accepted response to homicide, but there was no governmental institution to carry it out, so the responsibility for the execution of a murderer fell upon the relatives of the victim.[10] If the murderer had escaped or indeed if one of his relatives were willing, the death of that relative could be substituted for that of the murderer to satisfy the victim's relatives.[11] A comparison of the two approaches to the punishment of murder shows quite clearly that the European notion depended upon handing over regulatory powers to a legal institution; the Indian notion, on the other hand, assumed that familial sanctions would keep individuals in line, and when they failed, then the family itself was held responsible for the aberration of one of its members. These two notions were superficially compatible in terms of penalty unless a Frenchman should murder an Indian and subsequently be removed from reach. At a deeper level, however, a fundamental incompatibility lay in the identification of the entity that was to take responsibility for carrying out the punishment of the murderer. For among the things that Europeans found most "savage" about the Indian was that inflicting death in this way actually provided a good deal of consolation to the executioners.[12]

There was a further complication in that the procedure Bienville was trying to set up was meant to deal with international incidents so as to avert war. While it is true that both the French and the Choctaw punished domestic murder as a capital crime, an examination of the way intertribal murders were treated by the Indians of the Southeast shows that unless there were some prior will for peace prevailing at the time of an intertribal murder, the most likely outcome was war. Although within one Indian nation a retaliatory killing was privileged and did not lead on to an infinite chain of retaliations, this was not generally true of retaliatory killings between tribes. Two tribes could agree to let equal numbers of deaths on both sides be set off against one another, however, once a peace process began.[13] Certainly, cases in which one tribe executed one of its own to satisfy another were exceedingly rare, and for good reason: the one who carried out the execution would then be liable to punishment within his own tribe by the relatives of the victim.

When the murders that occasioned Bienville's application of the lex talionis principle occurred in 1738, there was strong motivation for the French to seek to maintain the allegiance of their Choctaw allies. After the failure of Bienville's first campaign against the Chickasaw in 1736, it was realized that another had to be mounted soon in order to reestablish French authority and military reputation. Accordingly, during the years 1737 and 1738 Bienville was occupied with gathering the resources of the colony and making painstaking plans for such an expedition. Among the difficulties he faced at this time was the fact that the English traders among the Creek and Chickasaw were offering to trade with the Choctaw at half the prices asked by the French. The wisdom of adopting such an advantageous trade had been seen by Red Shoe, a young Choctaw war chief who was beginning to build a strong factional power base within the tribe.[14] In pursuit of this goal he had orchestrated a peace with the Chickasaw that was guaranteed by the presence among them of a number of important Choctaw visitors, and he had himself traveled to Carolina to work out the details of the trade with the English. The climate of opinion among the Choctaw was so unsettled that any untoward action by the French could have serious consequences.[15] The French colonists, well aware of the situation, were in an equally unsettled and apprehensive state of mind.

Such was the atmosphere when the most unfortunate of possible events occurred. Two Choctaws, a man and his wife, were murdered by two French creole youths. The sources for this incident and its background are the documents from the colony in the French archives and local records of the parish of Mobile, to which the two youths belonged.[16] Referring to these two sources, we may first obtain some information about the people involved in the event.

The documents tell us that the Choctaw victims had been employed in hunting to provide meat for the French settlers in the Pascagoula area. They came in contact with the youths, who had come to the area from Mobile to buy foodstuffs, because they wanted to go to Mobile to sell some deerskins and bear oil from their hunt.[17] We do not have sufficient evidence to tell us if such connubial hunting teams were common, but we do know that it was fairly common for Choctaws to hire out as hunters to the colonists. The usual division of labor between the sexes among the Choctaw would make such a team a convenient one, particularly if they intended to profit twice over from their labors by handing the meat over to the colonists while preparing the skins and oil to sell on their own account.

As for the youths, we are told that they were maternal half-brothers in one document and in another that their family names were Alexandre and Barthelemy. They were, respectively, twenty-four and fifteen or sixteen years old.[18] A search of the census and church records reveals that Jean-Baptiste Alexandre, a master joiner, married Marie-Marguerite Dufresne, one of the original "Pelican girls," in 1704, and that she bore him four sons, François in

1708, Philippe in 1710, Antoine in 1715, and Pierre in 1717.[19] Jean-Baptiste Alexandre must have died and his wife remarried by 1720, for in that year Balthazar Barthelemy and his wife, Marie-Marguerite Dufresne, had a son Henri, and in the next year Barthelemy is listed as a settler in Mobile having a wife, four children, and one Indian slave.[20] It seems then that Barthelemy took Alexandre's sons under his protection but that by 1721 one of them had died. The elder of the two young men involved in the murder must have been Philippe Alexandre. In 1723 Barthelemy and his wife had another son, not named in the records, who was probably the younger of the brothers.[21] In 1726, on another census, Barthelemy is listed with a wife, four children, and an Indian slave—presumably one of the other children had died between 1721 and 1726, a common occurrence in the early days of the colony.[22] By 1738 the family must have prospered, because the two half-brothers were accompanied at the time of the murder by a Negro slave.[23]

This Negro slave is of interest himself, since he refused to take part in the murders on the grounds that the Choctaw had never injured him. One would suspect, both because he was accompanying the young men on this trip away from home and because he was able to refuse to take part, that he was an older man and one trusted with some responsibility by the young men's father.

The Choctaw man and his wife, who are not named in the documents, had apparently spent the winter of 1737–38 as hired hunters, and the following spring they were looking to travel to the Mobile area. For the events that then took place we can do no better than to quote the colony's *commissaire-ordonnateur*, Edmé Gatien Salmon, who was present at the trial and who summarized the evidence from the questioning:

> They were two maternal half-brothers, the elder of whom was twenty-four and the younger fifteen or sixteen. They went in a pirogue from Mobile to the Pascagoulas with a Negro slave to look for some food supplies, and there they found a Choctaw and his wife who were proposing to go to Mobile to trade some bear oil and a few deerskins and who asked them for passage, which they granted them. Contrary winds having cast them ashore on some neighboring islands, they went hunting there. The elder of the two brothers proposed to the Negro that he kill the husband and wife, saying that the savages were dogs, and that if they ran across Frenchmen in the same straits in their country they would not object to killing them. The Negro having rejected the proposition, saying that he had no reason at all to kill them, that they had done him no wrong, the two brothers discussed the same thing, and the elder

told the younger that he would be doing a valorous deed, and that he would be regarded as a true man, if he made the attack; this child allowed himself to be so persuaded that on the following day at sunrise, while everyone was sleeping, or pretending to, the younger shot twice at the husband and his wife and killed them, the elder having taken care to put the savage's gun into the covered part of the pirogue under the pretext of putting it under cover.[24]

There was apparently no immediate reaction to the killings, nor is it known what was done with the bodies of the victims. After some months, when the two Indians did not return to their village from the winter hunt, doubtless their friends and relatives began to wonder what had happened to them. On his way to Mobile for the annual Indian present-giving ceremonies in November 1738, Bienville stopped at the Pascagoula settlement to drop off his nephew, Gilles Augustin Payen de Noyan, for a mission to the Choctaw. At that time both of them learned from the settlers that the two Choctaws had not been heard from since their departure with the young men. The French settlers were sure that the young men had killed them, and they thought that the Choctaw Indians also suspected a murder.[25] By the time Bienville arrived at Mobile, the Choctaw were there in some numbers to receive their presents. They were in a state of great expectation because the presents had been mishandled the previous year while Bienville was ill and because they were anticipating material encouragement to undertake a Chickasaw war. Several Choctaws, relatives of the victims, told him of the disappearance of their people and accused the young Frenchmen. The evidence, if only circumstantial, seemed to justify arrest, so the two Frenchmen and the Negro were arrested and indicted by the authority of the *commissaire* of Mobile, Bizotton de St. Martin.[26]

At this point a difficulty arose. Apparently, the intention was not to let the Choctaw know that the accused were in Mobile but to send them quickly to New Orleans for trial, since Bizotton maintained that only the Superior Council had sufficient authority to try a capital case involving civilians. But the Choctaw found out that the prisoners were being held in the prison of the fort, and they demanded that justice be done immediately, claiming that sending the accused to New Orleans was simply a ruse to allow them to escape. In line with the Choctaw notion of justice achieved through blood revenge, Bienville was told that if quick justice were not done, young warriors might simply take revenge on the nearest available Frenchmen.[27]

Although Bienville was nettled with Bizotton's punctiliousness and the delay it caused, he was able to calm the Choctaw somewhat by promising that justice would be done and would be carried out in Mobile before their appointed witnesses. Bizotton for his part offered to pay the expenses of such witnesses as the Choctaw wished to leave behind at Mobile to await the outcome of the trial. Delayed by contrary winds, the boat carrying the accused finally departed on December 24, and the trial took place on January 10. After the testimony reported above by Salmon, the two young men were condemned to die, while the Negro was dismissed as guiltless.[28] The original sentence called for hanging, but to spare the dignity of the boys' family it was changed to death by a firing squad.[29] Salmon reported that the younger brother had no notion of guilt and was convinced that in the dangerous times then prevailing he had performed a deed worthy of praise. Even Salmon believed that had the situation been different Bienville would have allowed the younger to escape death. But this was not to be, and the young men were returned to Mobile for execution, which took place before Choctaw witnesses on January 14.[30]

Before examining the results of these events, it is necessary to dispose of two points. There are no Superior Council records of the trial extant, either among the Superior Council records in the Louisiana Historical Center in New Orleans or in France, so the only existing report of the trial itself is the summary from Salmon.[31] This is not as suspicious as it may sound, since the damage of centuries has been particularly hard on the Superior Council records covering the years in question, but it does leave some unanswered questions about the questioning of the elder half-brother and about the arguments presented by members of the Superior Council. A much stranger occurrence involves the burial records of Mobile. An early entry for the year 1739 in the *registre mortuaire* shows "Philippe" and "Barthelemy" in the margin, but the entry is heavily crossed out, although it definitely includes two names.[32] There is no other record of the burial of the two young men, and the obliteration of the entry seems, without scientific analysis, to be contemporary with the entry itself. Further work, including perhaps X-ray examination of the record, would be needed to determine when the crossing-out actually took place and whether the contents of the entry might have some significance for understanding how the colony reacted to the execution.

It is hardly to be doubted that the colony's reaction to the sentence was unfavorable, but it is also clear that Bienville's decision to make an example of the young men had to be accepted as unavoidable. Both Salmon and the

Superior Council, who acted without Bienville's presence, realized as well as he had that there was no other solution. Noyan had been sent to encourage the Choctaw to break Red Shoe's peace with the Chickasaw while that chief was absent in Carolina, and he had returned to New Orleans with news that the promise of justice had helped motivate two influential Choctaws, Alibamon Mingo and the chief of the Chickasawhay villages, to take the field at the head of war parties against the Chickasaw. After the executions the witnessing chiefs also departed with the same purpose.[33] According to French report, Red Shoe had returned disappointed from Carolina even before the executions.[34] Whether this is true or not, it is clear that the consensus in the nation was such that Red Shoe felt that he also had to call for a Chickasaw war to remain in power. Certainly, the Choctaw seem to have been satisfied that justice had been done.

The executions also had a more immediate effect in that Bienville was able to obtain justice from the Tunica, a smaller tribe living just west of the Mississippi near Natchez, for a Frenchman murdered by them more than a year before. The way that this was done—the murderer's head was delivered to the French by "the principal men of the village who were for the most part his relatives"[35]—probably gave Bienville cause to expect that all the Louisiana tribes would react in this way: that they would integrate the French principle into their own laws of blood revenge by having murderers of Frenchmen killed by relatives too close to be held to account for their deaths.

But the Tunica, harried from one homeland to another by Indian adversaries, decimated in numbers over their years of contact with the French, and by 1739 not only heavily acculturated but at least partially dependent upon the French presence for protection, were not in the same position as the Choctaw.[36] Even after 1739 the Choctaw still numbered around fifteen thousand, their distance from most French posts and all French settlement had effectively protected them from acculturative influence, and it would be safe to say that it was the French colony that depended on the Choctaw, at least to secure its borders. Yet even in their power and importance to the colony it is evident that many Choctaws were in fact prepared to accept Bienville's principle, although not quite in the form that he proposed it. French insistence that the Choctaw adhere to the principle exactly as they themselves had done was partially responsible for the bloody events of the Choctaw civil war.

To discuss these effects upon the Choctaw we need to skip lightly over some seven years, years that were characterized by increasing Choctaw factionalism as French trade goods became harder and harder to obtain during the War of the Austrian Succession and as the French continued to demand war against the Chickasaw in spite of the failure of Bienville's campaign against them in 1739–40. During these years, remarkably enough, there was no international murder between French and Choctaw to call the principle into play.[37]

That state of affairs changed in 1746. Red Shoe's factional power base had been growing steadily, and for several reasons, among them a desire to maintain credibility with the English and to punish a Frenchman who had raped his wife, he had three Frenchmen killed within the territory of the Choctaw nation. The victims were two traders and a young subaltern on detachment from Fort Tombecbé as an observer in the Choctaw villages.[38]

By this time Bienville had been replaced, but Governor Pierre de Rigaud de Vaudreuil proceeded to apply the principle that his predecessor had established. He sent Jadart de Beauchamp, major of Mobile, into the Choctaw nation to demand restitution—a death for a death—and one of the first things Beauchamp did in his talks with the various village chiefs was to buttress this demand by citing the Barthelemy case: "We ask nothing of you but justice, since M. de Bienville had justice done you 1740 [sic] for a man and woman that some Frenchmen had killed."[39]

The trouble that the French encountered here in having their claim recognized lay in their failure to understand the distinction made by the Choctaw between domestic and international law in a homicide case. The evidence is quite clear that the Choctaw were prepared to accept the notion of setting off the French deaths by an equal number of Choctaw deaths, but they expected the French, as the injured party, to carry out the killings themselves. If the French wanted the Choctaw to carry out the killings, they said, the French would have to persuade close relatives of the required victims to do it, or else there would be an unending train of vengeance set loose in the nation.[40]

The French never really knew which individual Choctaws had killed their men, and in the beginning they simply asked for a life for a life. In the space of a few days, however, and doubtless on the basis of information received in conversation with the Choctaws he met, Beauchamp decided to demand the deaths of Red Shoe and the two chiefs in whose villages the two dead traders had lived.[41] This demand was superficially in line with the principle of permitted substitutions that the Choctaw understood in intertribal dealings, but it did not follow the spirit of traditional practice. The usual procedure in such cases was to substitute people who were of little use to the tribe or who for some reason already deserved death and who might even find importance or redemption of reputation in being so sacrificed.[42] The French were instead trying to lay responsibility at the door of politically important men and probably also to disorganize the pro-English faction by depriving it of its leaders.

Even this might have been encompassed had the relatives of these men been willing to undertake the task. It is not known if direct appeal was ever made to the relatives of the other two chiefs, but Beauchamp certainly spoke in this vein to Red Shoe's brother, Tatoulimataha, who refused to kill Red Shoe.[43] That refusal left the Choctaw unable to respond except with a more radical substitution: killings committed against a group that was the enemy of both French and Choctaw. Therefore, to set off the deaths of three Frenchmen at the hands of pro-English Choctaw, the pro-French Choctaw attempted to fulfill the French demands in part by killing English traders. This was done in a raid on an English convoy that was being escorted by Red Shoe. After Red Shoe was murdered by stealth, two Englishmen were killed in an open attack, making up the required three deaths.[44]

The French, however, completely missed the point of the Choctaw restitution and refused the two English scalps, insisting on two more Choctaw deaths. This demand was politically motivated, because instead of one of the village chiefs previously asked for, they now demanded the death of another of Red Shoe's brothers, who had in the meantime fallen heir to his influence with the English. The deaths of the Englishmen did not go without notice on the pro-English side. Doubtless as a result of a symmetrical demand by the English, the Choctaw killed five French settlers on the Mobile River. These killings were followed by retaliatory raids by French-allied Choctaws on English trade convoys, killing two more English traders.[45]

It is obvious that by these exchanges both factions of the Choctaw were trying to satisfy their respective allies by the deaths of mutual enemies, not Choctaws.[46] But this continual exchange could not go on indefinitely without loss of Choctaw life, and when a Choctaw chief was accidentally killed in one of the raids on an English trading convoy, the civil war was actually initiated. At first it was halfhearted, consisting of small retaliatory raids meant simply to claim vengeance, and the raids on European settlers and traders continued. Eventually, intertribal violence escalated, however, and the result was frightfully intense internecine warfare, which included the deaths of some eight hundred people and the total destruction of at least three villages.[47]

Yet in the face of all this carnage the French continued for two years to claim that they were not satisfied. In the end they finally realized that to end the terrible complex of blood revenge that had been brought on by the civil war they would have to take the field themselves, as they had been asked to do in the first place. Once this was done it was possible to arrive at a treaty in which Bienville's principle was at last officially enunciated as binding the Choctaw: (1) any Frenchman killed by a Choctaw must be avenged by the Choctaw; (2) English traders and their Choctaw sponsors were to be killed by the Choctaw, and these deaths were to be privileged, with no revenge obligation accruing to the victim's family.[48]

Presumably, the French failure to understand what Choctaw justice defined as their role had a great deal to do with French fear of war with the Choctaw. It also stemmed in part from the French failure to grasp the fact that revenge killings, even between nations, could be treated as privileged, but only when carried out by the injured party. There is some evidence that the Choctaw had, without the French realizing it, in a sense adopted their European neighbors as an additional, fictive division of their nation.[49] For purposes of punishing homicide the French were not only obligated to seek vengeance but were considered by the Choctaw to be shamed by their failure to do so.[50] The fact that the French took the field toward the end of the war and participated in the bloody suppression of several villages and that this did not precipitate war provides no definitive proof of this hypothesis, since by that time the pro-French Choctaw were so strong that retaliation against the French would have been out of the question. We will never know if such a solution would have worked when the pro-English faction was at the peak of its power, but certainly the French, with some thirty-five hundred colonists, were justified in hesitating to trust their luck with a potential enemy numbering over ten thousand.

This was, of course, only one of the myriad misunderstandings that arose between the Indians of the Southeast and the European newcomers, nor perhaps was it the worst of them. Bienville's intentions were good, and it is to the credit of the French that they carried out the execution of the half-brothers against their inclinations, because this was the kind of justice that the Choctaw understood. Nor are the French to be blamed for expecting the Choctaw to make the same kind of concession to their notion of justice. The tragedy arose not because the Choctaw did not want to render justice at all but because they had no vicarious legal mechanism to carry it out. In the end, therefore, they were forced into civil war because vengeance carried out by a

Choctaw on another Choctaw in behalf of a third party not a Choctaw did not leave the avenger free of punishment himself. Like other aspects of south-eastern Indian culture, this one was so inconsistent with European under-standing that it had to adapt or disappear, and although it did not actually disappear among the Choctaw themselves until 1823, the principle in dealings with white nations was firmly asserted in treaties from the time of the end of the Choctaw civil war.[51] The Choctaw had dearly bought comprehension of Bienville's principle with the weighty currency of culture change.

Notes

Summary: French and Indian interaction in the Louisiana colony was generally peaceful and nonexploitative by colonial standards, but this was mostly due to the policy toward the Indians pursued by a few enlightened Indian diplomatists like Jean-Baptiste Le Moyne de Bienville. An example of his efforts in Indian diplomacy is seen in his treatment of the Barthelemy murders: two creole youths guilty of the deaths of two Choctaws were executed for their crime. Bienville felt that such action on the part of the French would lead their Choctaw allies to apply the same justice on behalf of the French, but he reckoned without the conflicts that such action would create within the dynamics of the Indian system of justice. This paper discusses both the original case and the tragic outcome of the French attempt to force the Choctaws to accept the European notion of an institutionalized judiciary system.

1. The first three volumes of the *Mississippi Provincial Archives: French Dominion* are edited by Rowland and Sanders; the final two are edited by Rowland, Sanders, and Galloway.

2. Adair, *History*, 259–61, 284–85; Jacobs, *Indians of the Southern Colonial Frontier*, 6–13.

3. For the French attitude toward the Indians see Jaenen, *Friend and Foe*, 12–14. See also Berkhofer, *The White Man's Indian*, 127–29.

4. Duclos to Pontchartrain, October 9, 1713, AC, série C13A, 3:266, 272. Bienville had begun learning the language when he first arrived in Louisiana; see Le Moyne d'Iberville, *Iberville's Gulf Journals*, 126.

5. Bienville to Pontchartrain, September 14, 1706, AC, série C13A, 1:509.

6. Bienville to Maurepas, July 26, 1733, AC, série C13A, 16:279v; Jadart de Beauchamp, Journal, September 16–October 19, 1746, in AC, série C13A, 30:224v–225, translated in Rowland, Sanders, and Galloway, *Mississippi Provincial Archives*, 4:269–97.

7. Sexual division of labor was fundamental throughout the aboriginal Southeast, and males had primary responsibility for hunting and war. Henry de Tonti's report on the Choctaw and Chickasaw in 1702 (Archives du service hydrographique 115, 10: No. 20) shows that even this early the Chickasaws' guns were affording them superiority in hunting as well as war.

8. Milling, *Red Carolinians*, 282n50.

9. For official British policy see Reid, *A Law of Blood*, 103.

10. Swanton, *Source Material*, 104–10.

11. Swanton, *Source Material*, 104–10; cf. Reid, *A Law of Blood*, 80–82.

12. This point has only been treated in detail for the Indians of the Northeast (Jaenen, *Friend and Foe*, 137–48); but various details reported by Swanton (*Source Material*, 104–6) imply that this was the case, especially in conjunction with the many mentions in AC, série C13A, of "drying the tears" of the bereaved through the death of the responsible party.

13. For this concept of the "setoff" see Reid, *A Law of Blood*, 108, 169–70. For its application among the Choctaw see Bienville to Pontchartrain, February 25, 1708, AC, série C13A, 2:101; Bienville to Maurepas, August 18, 1739, AC, série C13A, 24:74–75.

14. For an outline of Red Shoe's career see White, "Red Shoes."

15. See Noyan's report to Maurepas, January 4, 1739, AC, série C13A, 24:224–235.

16. The C13A series cited above is held by the Archives nationales in Paris, while the Mobile Church Records are held by the Diocese of Mobile at the Catholic Center.

17. Louboey to Maurepas, January 14, 1739, AC, série C13A, 24:188–192; Salmon to Maurepas, January 12, 1739, AC, série C13A, 24:115–118.

18. Salmon to Maurepas, January 12, 1739, AC, série C13A, 24:116.

19. DeVille, *Gulf Coast Colonials*, 17. The fabled "Pelican girls" were the first women who came to the nascent Louisiana colony in 1704 onboard a ship named the *Pelican*. About twenty of them arrived, and most married and founded families.

20. Maduell, *The Census Tables*, 24.

21. Mobile Church Records, March 7, 1723.

22. Maduell, *The Census Tables*, 63.

23. Salmon to Maurepas, January 12, 1739, AC, série C13A, 24:116.

24. Salmon to Maurepas, January 12, 1739, AC, série C13A, 24:116.

25. Noyan to Maurepas, January 4, 1739, AC, série C13A, 24:224–235. The most important settlers on the Pascagoula were the Gravelines, who had close and friendly relations with the Choctaw.

26. Bizotton to Maurepas, December 15, 1738, AC, série C13A, 23:200–202.

27. Bizotton to Maurepas, December 24, 1738, AC, série C13A, 23:203–5.

28. Salmon to Maurepas, January 12, 1739, AC, série C13A, 24:117.

29. There is some ambiguity about this. Salmon states (AC, série C13A, 24:115v) that the sentence was to have "their heads broken" ("La tête cassée"—the same expression used by the French to describe tomahawking), but the report of the execution indicates that they were in fact shot (Bizotton to Maurepas, May 9, 1739, AC, série C13A, 24:246v). The change in manner of execution may have been made in view of its effect on the Indians or to make the deaths mercifully quick.

30. Bizotton to Maurepas, May 9, 1739, SCac, série C13A, 24:246v.

31. The Superior Council Records for 1738–39 were kindly searched for me by Stephen G. Reinhardt of the Louisiana State Museum, Louisiana Historical Center, with negative results (personal communication, March 11, 1982).

32. The original document is closed to public use, but a photostat exists at the Alabama Department of Archives and History in Montgomery. It was, however, not sufficient to determine any alteration of the record. The Most Reverend Oscar H. Lipscomb, archbishop of Mobile, kindly examined the original document visually and reported, "There is a definite entry for the two of them, the last names are sufficiently legible, and the whole has been deliberately crossed out." It is his opinion that such a thing could only have been done contemporarily by someone with sufficient access to the records or considerable influence over the curé who had custody of them (personal communication, April 3, 1980).

33. Bienville to Maurepas, March 25, 1739, AC, série C13A, 24:38v–41.

34. Bizotton to Maurepas, May 9, 1739, AC, série C13A, 24:248–49.

35. Bienville to Maurepas, June 15, 1740, AC, série C13A, 25:104–6.

36. Brain, *Tunica Treasure*, 265.

37. My reading of the documents in série C13A has revealed no such incident, although of course one could have occurred and failed to come to light.

38. Fort Tombecbé was located on the Tombigbee River near present-day Epes, Alabama. My "Louisiana Post Letters, 1700–1763: The Missing Evidence for Indian Diplomacy," in this volume treats the circumstances of this incident.

39. Beauchamp, Journal, 224v. With regard to the erroneous date it may be that Beauchamp was remembering the date of the execution of a French militiaman at Fort Toulouse for the murder of a Creek Indian (Adair, History, 294).

40. Beauchamp, Journal, 234v. See my "Choctaw Factionalism and Civil War, 1746–1750," in this volume for a detailed reconstruction of the historical sequence of these events.

41. Beauchamp, Journal, 227v.

42. The Choctaws reported that Red Shoe might hand over the actual killers in time (Beauchamp, Journal, 233), but Beauchamp had decided to hold the chiefs responsible, and even some Choctaws felt that this was justified.

43. Beauchamp, Journal, 238.

44. Atkin, "Historical Account," 6; Vaudreuil to Maurepas, September 19, 1747, AC, série C13A, 31:98–102.

45. Vaudreuil Letterbooks, Huntington Manuscript Loudoun (H M LO), 9:III, 268, July 8, 1747; Louboey to Maurepas, February 16, 1748, AC, série C13A, 32:211–213; Atkin, "Historical Account," 8.

46. See Reid, A Law of Blood, 99, 204; cf. Beauchamp, Journal: "They said they would do everything they could to avenge the death of the man named Petit, their trader, and that if they could not take revenge on the red men, they would do it on the English" (232v).

47. Vaudreuil to Rouillé, January 12, 1751, AC, série C13A, 35:61–69.

48. Vaudreuil to Rouillé, January 12, 1751.

49. This evidence is admittedly conjectural. It consists first of the Choctaw acceptance of the term "father" to refer to important French officials, second of the Choctaws' apparent expectation, throughout the colonial period, that the French would treat them with indulgence no matter what they did. In an exogamous matrilineal society like that of the Choctaw, a person's father was considered to be of another lineage and not related by blood; kinship terminology referred to nearly all the male members of the father's lineage as "father" and considered them similarly unrelated. The father's social role, and that of all persons called "father," was not authoritarian (that function was reserved for the mother's brother) but indulgent, much as that of the uncle in a patrilineal society. And a killing by a member of the mother's lineage of a member of the father's lineage, or vice versa, called for blood revenge to be carried out by members of the victim's lineage. See this argument developed in Galloway, "The Chief Who Is Your Father."

50. Vaudreuil to Rouillé, January 12, 1751, 68v, mentions the Choctaws' indebtedness to Grand-pré for having led the decisive final campaign against the pro-English faction.

51. Debo, The Rise and Fall, 45–46.

15. Choctaw Factionalism and Civil War, 1746–1750

This nation will not forget for a long time the civil wars which the projects of Red Shoe have caused it and which have been the source of the troubles that have prevailed among them for four years.

Vaudreuil to Rouillé, June 24, 1750,

Archives des colonies, Série C13A, 34:268v

Most previous treatments of the Choctaw intratribal war of 1746–50 have been brief, and few have gone further than to say that it took place and that it involved factions supported by the French and the English. The one really extended study of these events, a 1946 dissertation by William Paape, is an excellent analysis from the European point of view, but even this is generally unavailable, as it has never been published.[1] In this paper I will not have the space to present a thorough analysis of every facet of the conflict, but I would like to present here and argue for the thesis that this civil war, a response to the French version of the lex talionis, demonstrates Choctaw resistance to acculturation in the area of crime and punishment and their persistence in the belief that even an ally had to obtain justice through limited war.

The source materials for such a study, though of course they provide us with nothing obtained directly from Choctaw sources, are unusually rich for this period of Choctaw history. At the baseline is the French colonial correspondence contained in series C13A of the Archives des colonies; here we find not only Governor Pierre de Rigaud de Vaudreuil's official reports but also several field reports that he sent to supplement his own.[2] We are extremely

This chapter was originally published as "Choctaw Factionalism and Civil War, 1746–1750" in the *Journal of Mississippi History* 44, no. 4 (1982): 289–327. It is reprinted by permission of the Mississippi Historical Society.

fortunate that one of the volumes of Vaudreuil's private letterbooks, the one covering the Mobile District, also survives with the evidence for part of this period.[3] It contains all the letters written by Vaudreuil to his officers in the field in the Mobile District, which had jurisdiction over the Choctaw area. In most cases Vaudreuil acknowledges receipt of letters from his correspondents, and his answers permit us to reconstruct something of what the original reports must have contained.[4] Finally, there is an unusual abundance of English material, much of it of a polemic nature but still very useful. Edmond Atkin wrote a lengthy account of the Carolina traders' activities in the war in order to prove his own governor's self-interest, and James Adair's account of the southeastern Indians contains much mention of his own part in the events of the war.[5] In addition, the surviving Carolina "Indian Books" have some material relating to the traders' activities (though only in the aftermath of the war); and the journals of the Upper House, the Commons House of Assembly, and the Royal Council log the official actions of the South Carolina colony that bear upon the Choctaw.[6]

There is much bias in these European reports of the Choctaw conflict, but fortunately for us the bias sprang from internal squabbles in the French and English colonies, so that in a sense the facts emerge as the bias cancels itself out. It is clear that the French were much more concerned than the English about the effects of the war on the Choctaw themselves, but the English sources permit us to have an exceptional view of the attempt by one Choctaw faction to manipulate one European ally in order to gain independence from another.

If all we wanted to know about the Choctaw civil war was what happened, it would be sufficient to relate the sequence of events as we have them from the European accounts and leave it at that as the best that we could do. But this tragic conflict, which must have been the most momentous happening in Choctaw history from the beginning of European contact until Removal, deserves rather closer scrutiny not only because of its importance in this light but because of the fact that it represented the most serious stress that Choctaw society had had to face up to that point in the process of acculturation. Because of this, a closer examination of the events and the people who participated in them may permit us to learn more about the structure of Choctaw society before acculturation was too far advanced. By observing how the system performed under stress, we may be able to understand its structure better.

The Choctaw civil war looked momentous at the time not only to the Choctaw but probably also to everyone else in the Southeast. According to Vaudreuil, writing in 1751, more than eight hundred chiefs, honored men, and warriors of the western faction had lost their lives, and the villages of Couëchitto, Nushkobo, and West Abeka were totally destroyed.[7] Thereafter he was wont to reiterate what an extraordinary mark of loyalty this had been on the part of the Choctaw. Atkin commented in 1753 on the unprecedented lengths to which the Choctaw went in undertaking civil war; Adair called the war "bitter beyond expression."[8] We have little record of what other Indian groups thought of it, but we do know that the Abihka, an Upper Creek tribe that one faction turned to for support, found it horrifying.[9]

Such a reaction, by the French and English as well as the Abihka, cannot be justified by the number of dead alone. The Choctaw may have lost more lives in one year of the war to smallpox than to the hostilities of the whole of the civil war.[10] There is, on the other hand, much inferential evidence in the accounts to suggest that the war was not simply a factional struggle nor client warfare on behalf of the French and English allies but a conflict that cut far more shockingly into the fabric of Choctaw social life by involving the moieties of the tribe, eventually applying to them the sanctions of blood revenge usually reserved for external enemies. It is possible to show, however, that this was a situation into which the Choctaw were forced by the demands of their French allies for justice on the French model and that it was not continued once the French had realized that their justice could not be done in Choctaw terms.

It is admittedly very difficult to make sense of this evidence, since in the first place it is made up of tiny scraps and in the second place Choctaw sociopoliti-cal organization, which is so much at issue in understanding the problem, has never been well defined for the early contact period. For the latter reason it will be useful to review what is known about it on the several levels of village, division, and nation and at the same time to outline the French attempts to make use of what they perceived the organization to be.

To the French the Choctaw looked like a confusion of small polities with no clear-cut chain of command. Generally speaking, each village had its chief, although some few villages had smaller dependent villages without indepen-dent chiefs, probably as a result of the budding-off of populations that could not be supported on the land of a single locality.[11] Each chief had his staff of officials, numbering about five. These men can be detected in the documents, where there is no clear statement about such an office, through the repeated occurrence of what the French took for personal names but what are clearly functional titles, though the function in question is sometimes unknown. The *tichou mingo* was apparently the master of ceremonies or "waiter" to the chief; the *taskanangouchi* was his speaker. Many if not all villages had a war chief, and often his office carried the title of *soulouche oumastabé* (red shoe killer) or simply *mingo ouma* (red chief). The frequently mentioned *hopaii mingo* (prophet chief, spelled variously *pahémingo, paemingo, opayémingo*) was presumably the "war prophet," but this charismatic talent seems to have been a frequent attribute of the war chief as well. Finally, *fanimingo* (squirrel chief) is a name so often seen that it also seems to be a title, since it is nearly always qualified by village or other designation, but its function if it is a title is not known.[12]

Such a picture of a staff of men involved in village government is probably not so simple if Fred Gearing's notion of different "structural poses" for different village activities can be said to apply in a general way to the Choctaw.[13] It does seem reasonable to apply this model at least to the activities of peace and war, and here we encounter the problem of the moieties and their function. There is solid evidence for the existence of "red" and "white" chiefs from the same village. They are referred to thus generically from time to time in the French documents and indeed in scattered reports of Indian speeches.[14] John R. Swanton has cited the evidence of a late English document to the effect that "war" and "peace" and hence "red" and "white," respectively, do map onto the two moieties, called in the French documents the Oulacta (Inholahta) and Immongoulacha (Imoklasha) "races" or "castes."[15] There may be a problem with this mapping, since it is certain that the Choctaw moieties were traditionally ranked, the first-ranked moiety being the Inholahta. If the Inholahta were the moiety of war, this would run counter to the very strong southeastern preference for wise deliberation over individual brilliance and abruptness of decision.[16] Whatever may be the correct assignment, and the events of the war do not provide an unambiguous answer, it is likely that in the village context the red and white leaders were conventionally chosen from the two moieties and that their powers were quite differentiated.[17] Certainly, there are several instances in which the recorded speeches of such leaders do differ substantially in tone.[18]

There is also mention in the documents of "honored men" and "principal warriors," though we have no notion at all from these sources of what their roles were in Choctaw sociopolitical organization. It is likely that the honored men served as council to the white chief and that they were older men; the principal warriors were probably leaders among the red chief's following and were probably younger men—if we may assume an analogy with other southeastern tribes. The fact is that there was simply very little European observation of village government in action, and we are forced here to depend upon inference.[19]

The Choctaw villages were grouped into divisions. Swanton has discussed the number of divisions and the details of village membership in them, but there is now more evidence to which Swanton did not have access that allows us to assert that the number of three divisions was apparently constant throughout the historic period, though the village composition of the divisions might vary to some extent.[20] But in understanding the divisions it is necessary to distinguish between cultural-geographic and political aspects, since it seems to be the overlay of political factors that accounts for the shifting of villages from one division to another. The cultural-geographic divisions were pretty clearly based upon territories related to the three neighboring watersheds of the Pearl, Tombigbee, and Pascagoula rivers, and the cultural differences between them are reflected not only in stray references to oddities of dress and speech but also in the external alliances they maintained with other tribes: the Western Division with the Chakchuima and Chickasaw, the Eastern Division with the Alabama, and the Sixtowns (including Chickasawhay and Yowani) possibly with the small coastal tribes and the Choctaw-related tribes of the Mobile River.[21] The evidence of Henry de Tonti's journey among the Choctaw and the subsequent first French negotiations with them in 1702 shows that the three divisions existed by that time and could be represented in external negotiations by a single representative each.[22] Under Governor Périer the French tried to make use of this institution of representation by recognizing certain "division chiefs" as medal chiefs who would be granted large presents in order to strengthen their influence, but some of the problems the French encountered with the institutionalization of the division chiefs probably stemmed from the fact that originally the division representatives were not permanently appointed to the job.[23]

There are also problems with the relationship between the moieties and divisions. Because the moieties were distributed through all the villages it is very difficult to understand what is going on in terms of the influence of moiety affiliation upon political loyalty. It may, however, be possible to take an analogy from the white and red towns of the Creeks and to suggest that white and red towns were distributed among the divisions as the moieties were distributed among the villages. There is no evidence at all to prove that one or another of the divisions was dominated by either of the moieties, although it is possible to show that at least in the case of the civil war the leading men of the Eastern and Western Divisions were members of opposite moieties.[24] And although the evidence is not conclusive, the Eastern Division, which proved firmly loyal to the French, may at least have been strongly influenced by the Inholahta moiety, whose members avowed a continuous adherence to the French alliance.[25]

There is little doubt that no supreme chief over the entire Choctaw nation existed until Bienville created such an office for the purpose of establishing some kind of hierarchical accountability on the French model.[26] It is repeatedly obvious that the man recognized as supreme chief by the French held no such power in the nation; in fact, the apologetic tone taken by these chiefs in many of their public statements reported by the French suggests that they knew themselves to be a powerless anomaly.[27] Governor Vaudreuil himself was perfectly aware that this was the case with all the medal chiefs.[28]

The same thing is not true of the war chief of the nation. This seems to have been an office that existed at time of need and that was generally filled by some outstanding warrior whose charismatic qualities or luck in leading war parties made him able to gather large parties from the whole of the tribe under his leadership.[29] The fact that such an office should develop in advance of that of a supreme peace chief is not surprising if we consider that the historic tribes of the Southeast were born in the collapse of the Mississippian chiefdoms, which must have included warfare.[30] It was probably the current Choctaw war leader who was first recognized by Bienville as the supreme chief of the nation, and at least at first this created office seems to have devolved upon a lineage.[31] By contrast, the demand for charismatic qualities in a war leader made it certain that when the French-recognized supreme chief happened not to possess these qualities, a supreme war chief would be recognized separately in the nation. This is probably what made the French eventually recognize such a war chief.

It is not known with certainty how many medal chiefs were recognized by the French during the early years when their attempt at a system of governance was being built, but by 1732 five of them appear on the list made by Régis du Roullet, and at later times there are repeated references to the number six.[32] The distribution of the medals was never actually congruent with the power structure within the nation for reasons already discussed, but from the French viewpoint the medal was given to the supreme chief, the nation's war chief, and the three division chiefs. In addition, the medal was also held by the chief of Chickasawhay village, where the Jesuit mission was established, and it was apparently granted for support of that mission.[33] We shall see that at the beginning of the Choctaw civil war the picture was more complex, since the medal was held by a western chief, an eastern chief, the chief of Concha villages, the Chickasawhay chief with authority over the Sixtowns, the supreme chief, and the war chief.

It was through this superimposed system of medal chiefs and their subordinates that the French attempted to control the Choctaw by means of carefully graded and specified gifts. The largest gifts went to the medal chiefs, with the supreme chief distinguished especially above the others. Lesser gifts were given to the village chiefs and some of their officers. Finally, "extraordinary presents," which were one-time gifts ranked according to their correspondence with the permanently fixed gifts, were occasionally given to chiefs or warriors who had performed some unusual service. These gifts were intended not only to secure the loyalty of key men but to help them build their political power in the nation through redistribution of the gifts to their followers. By this means the French made a powerful if unknowing contribution to the spirit of factionalism among the Choctaw.[34]

At the time of the coming of Europeans, the Choctaw structural pose for war was a temporary seasonal change in the tribal structure, and even at first war leaders came and went with the fortunes of war. But possibly as early as the English slave-raiding period from before 1700 to about 1713 and certainly after the Natchez Revolt of 1729, the Choctaw were encouraged to stay on a nearly permanent footing of war with their Chickasaw neighbors. The old patterns persisted in that the Choctaw enthusiasm for war was directly proportional to the season in which the French wished it to take place. Nor could the French medals prevent the emergence of successful division or village war leaders or the refusal of the majority of the nation to follow the French-recognized war chief. The real influence of the medal and substantial present granted to the war chief began to be felt when a war leader emerged who had the talents and persistence to hold the office through sheer force of personality over a period of years. When Red Shoe rose to this level of importance in the Natchez and Chickasaw wars of the thirties, he was able to hold the office permanently and thus to build a powerful enough faction that he was recognized as supreme chief by the English and was able with their support to make a bid for independence from the French, setting off the chain of events that led to the civil war.[35]

A major part of the function of war among the tribes of the Southeast was the execution of blood revenge on whatever enemy had caused loss to the aggrieved tribe.[36] Long years of this between neighbors had created "traditional enmities" by the time Europeans arrived, but the Europeans' concept of total war made them unable to understand how an enemy in time of war could become a relative connected by marriage ties and thus much reciprocal obligation at a time of peaceful negotiation. The French could not comprehend the notion that vengeance did not require the death of the person directly responsible but could be satisfied by that of someone who could stand for him. But they had a perfectly lucid view of the meaning of the lex talionis as far as they themselves were concerned, and to give them credit it was two Frenchmen who were first put to death for the murder of two Choctaws in order to establish the principle in the French-Choctaw relationship.[37]

Among the Choctaw the principle of blood revenge as defined by the French was hedged around with difficulty. When a death occurred at the hands of another tribe, custom dictated that war was the answer, a limited engagement that could account for enough death to assuage the tears of the bereaved. Yet what the French asked, and demonstrated, was that the offending nation put its own culprits to death in order to *avoid* war, while on the Choctaw side there was no institutionalized way to do this. Worse, since there was no such person as an executioner who could be ritually freed from responsibility for his action and no authority that could free him, whoever should undertake such a task would himself be subject to vengeance on the part of the relatives of the man executed. We shall see that the civil war did not solve this problem, since its dynamics were strongly influenced by an attempt to avoid killing Choctaws who had only been responsible for the deaths of non-Choctaws.

The history of the Choctaw during the whole of their alliance with the French is much too complex to more than summarize, but it is necessary to contextualize the events of the civil war by tracing something of this antecedent series of events. The Choctaw chose to ally themselves with the French in the first place because they were hard-pressed by gangs of Chickasaw and Creek slave catchers, armed and instigated by the English traders who had extended their activities to the Mississippi River as early as 1698. To acquire firearms and to defend themselves, the Choctaw entered eagerly into a French alliance in 1702. Thus the French gained a powerful buffer to the east and north of their infant colony, and the Choctaw, in return, acquired guns and other trade goods. By and large they stuck with the French quite loyally until the complications of the Yamassee War in Carolina took some of the slave-raiding pressure off them, and when this persecution was not continued, a large obstacle to improved relations with the English was removed.

It was not the Choctaw who first took advantage of this possibility. The Natchez, who occupied what the French considered the best agricultural land in the lower Mississippi valley, were finally induced by French land grabbing to break out in full revolt with the support of the Chickasaw and their English allies. This they did in 1729 by killing nearly all the men of the French fort and settlement at Natchez and by taking the women and children prisoner. The French called the Choctaw in to help pursue the Natchez and to recover French prisoners, and this the Choctaw did, though afterward they had a very hard time securing what they had understood as the promised reward for this action. The Natchez, however, managed to escape to take refuge among the Chickasaw, and at this point the French realized that the Mississippi River connection with the upper Louisiana colony in Illinois could never remain secure until the English-allied Chickasaw, who had been implicated in the Natchez rebellion, were subdued.

To this end Bienville pressed the Choctaw into service in two more campaigns in 1736 (via the Tombigbee River) and 1739–40 (via the Mississippi), both of them abortive. Throughout the period of the Natchez Revolt the French encouraged the Choctaw to attack the Chickasaw whenever the occasion presented itself. But these attacks, though they were favored by the young Choctaw warriors as a way to make a name for themselves, were not pursued with much enthusiasm unless Choctaw lives had been lost. And it should be noted that in the case of the Natchez rebellion and the French deaths it occasioned the French themselves took the field in considerable force no less than three times.

Meanwhile, the French had established a missionary post near the southern border of the Choctaw nation in 1728 and had built Fort Tombecbé as a supply base for the 1736 Chickasaw campaign. Both were to serve as bases for French trade activity among the Choctaw. The French colony had always, from its foundation, experienced a chronic shortage of goods from the mother country, and this presented a special problem for the Choctaw alliance because of the institution of annual presents given to the medal chiefs. This was an activity separate from the skin trade, which required merchandise within the nation throughout the year as well as on the occasion of the annual presents, when the Choctaw usually brought more skins to Mobile to trade. The shortage of trade goods became particularly acute in the late thirties and early forties as more French resources were bound up in Continental wars and French shipping began to be preyed upon by British privateers. By then, however, the Choctaw had had time to become dependent upon European goods for certain comforts and especially for the powder and ball that they needed to make their hunt successful. When French supplies failed, the English traders to the Upper Creeks and Chickasaw were ready and willing to supply the Choctaw and at lower prices than the French could offer.

It is obvious throughout the period leading up to the war and through the war itself that there was a set of several "national" priorities in operation providing the backdrop to events otherwise complicated by the conflicts of personal leadership and kinship claims among the Choctaw themselves. The Choctaw were a tribe of some fifteen thousand or more people, and to all intents and purposes they inhabited nearly the entire eastern border of the lower Louisiana colony at this period. To the French, especially in time of war with Britain, it was unthinkable that the Choctaw should be allowed to maintain a mixed allegiance, and to the French that was the import of any scale of trade with the English. To the English, who were too far away from their sources of supply in Carolina to have a realistic hope of becoming sole suppliers and allies of the Choctaw, the trade was a lucrative business with the added virtue of providing harassment of the French and keeping them too worried about events near home to intrigue with the Creek and Cherokee neighbors of the British colonies. The evidence suggests that the Choctaw themselves had no intention at all either of breaking completely with the French or of going over entirely to the English and that generally they sought to emulate the neutrality of the Alabama tribe, which had been the Alabama's key to the best of both trades and an enviable independence.[38]

The Chickasaw and their relationships with all three parties is a constant and important theme during the Choctaw civil war, as during the rest of colonial history. In spite of Adair's romantic claims, the Chickasaw had also managed a French-English balancing act from 1702 until 1729, when they took in the refugee Natchez.[39] Even then a sizeable group, perhaps as much as half the nation, was prepared to go and live with the Choctaw rather than break with the French over this issue.[40] The real break came in 1736, when, in an even more extraordinary blunder than he was later accused of committing, Bienville had his force make its first attack on the village of Ackia—the very village of which the strongest French partisan, Imayatabé Le Borgne, was chief.[41] The Chickasaw were closely related linguistically to the Choctaw, and stronger links are indicated both by the Choctaw migration legend and by some evidence of intertribal marriage alliance.[42] If they continued to pursue peace initiatives with the French, it was probably done because they wished to secure cessation of the continual Choctaw attacks urged by the French, who would not permit a treaty with the Choctaw alone. The English traders, knowing that the Choctaw trade could be more easily carried on from a safe base nearby, gave the Chickasaw such support that the French demand for their expulsion as a condition for peace would never be met.

There are several Choctaw leaders whose careers prior to the Choctaw civil war are important because they tell us much about the roles that these men played both before and during the war. Red Shoe has already been mentioned as the man whose actions led to the outbreak of the war. What we know about him is little enough. When first met with in the French correspondence, he was living in Couëchitto and serving as the *porte-parole* (presumably taska-nangouchi) for the supreme medal chief of the nation.[43] He was referred to several times as an "ordinary warrior" until in 1731 he led a highly successful raid against the Chickasaw and was rewarded with the medal, perhaps the medal of supreme war chief.[44] Beginning in 1734 he had an interest in the English trade through friends or possibly relatives through marriage alliance among the Chickasaw.[45] In 1738 his relationship with the English was formalized when he himself or an emissary speaking in his name went to Charleston and was recognized as supreme chief of the Choctaw with an English medal.[46] Doubtless he used the proceeds of both sides to build a faction, which is referred to by the French as consisting of members of his *famille* or his *race*; these expressions may refer to his moiety, since he found allies scattered throughout at least the towns of the Western Division, and one of his closest allies of this early period was the red shoe of Cushtusha village.[47] His general strategy in building power by benefiting from both French and English alliance was to make attacks on the Chickasaw during the late fall or early spring in order to secure his French present, while at other times he sought to establish peace with the Chickasaw to permit an English trade, sometimes even bringing English traders into his village of Couëchitto.[48] By 1739 he had been assigned control of ten villages by the authority of his French medal, since in that year he and the ten villages were actually cut off from the French present for his dealings with the English.[49]

Of equal importance in the politics of the Choctaw nation was the chief Alibamon Mingo of the Concha villages. His influence among the Choctaw was great, and in 1730 his harangue to the besieged Natchez Indians secured the release of the French and Negro prisoners they had taken.[50] During the next few years he was active against the Chickasaw on behalf of the French, but in 1735 he joined with Red Shoe to bring the English traders into the nation, and in the following year he was deprived of the medal chief's present along with Red Shoe.[51] After this, however, he joined with the French in the first and second Chickasaw campaigns, and although at times he was reluctant to commit his people to breaking a peace with the Chickasaw established by Red Shoe, Alibamon Mingo's loyalties were pretty steadily committed to the French.[52] He stated several times that he belonged to the Inholahta moiety; he was also the medal chief of the Concha villages, which numbered at least ten.[53] His name and other circumstantial evidence suggest that he enjoyed a special relationship with the Alabama tribe that included some sort of alliance.[54]

Another chief whose influence before his death in 1746 seems to have been greater than that of Red Shoe or Alibamon Mingo is Choucououlacta. His name contains the *holahta* element, which implies membership in the Inholahta moiety. Never mentioned in the English documents, he is portrayed in the French sources as a nearly fanatically loyal ally. In 1739 he was described as the war chief of the Choctaw nation and was said to control the ten easternmost villages nearest to Fort Tombecbé; in that year he was granted a French medal in the place of Red Shoe.[55] Also in that year and from then on he was closely allied with Alibamon Mingo in attacks on the Chickasaw, though he acted alone in leading the attack that killed a Chickasaw embassy and possibly precipitated Red Shoe's open rebellion.[56] In the year of that rebellion, 1746, he died, possibly of wounds suffered in the attack, possibly of the smallpox, which raged epidemically through the nation in the following year. Whatever the cause, the ceremonial treatment accorded his remains after death attested to his great importance in the nation, and the statement was made by a Choctaw leader that if he had lived, he and Alibamon Mingo together could have averted the civil war.[57]

A further person deserving of mention is the man frequently identified as one of Red Shoe's most trusted partisans, Mongoulacha Mingo. A member of the Imoklasha moiety, Mongoulacha Mingo was medal chief of Chickasawhay villages, with authority over the Sixtowns. He was said to have been granted the medal for support of the mission of Father Baudouin.[58] This position must have been one that he assumed after 1741, since before that date he was only listed as a subordinate to the chief of Chickasawhay and in that year the chief was killed in a quarrel.[59] His resentment of the French, very vehemently expressed, was apparently caused by what he perceived as their discriminatory treatment of the moiety to which he belonged, and he remained so intransigent in his convictions that he was eventually killed by those in his village who opposed him.[60]

It has already been suggested that the Choctaw civil war became an internecine struggle because the French demanded satisfaction from the Choctaw themselves for the deaths of three Frenchmen. The prelude to the war demonstrates vividly that the Choctaw would not find this kind of solution appropriate. In 1743 the Chickasaw had made elaborate overtures to the French to request peace, and at the annual presents at Mobile in December and January Vaudreuil announced an offer of peace to them if they would drive out the English. All the chiefs, honored men, and principal warriors of the Choctaw nation who were present agreed to this, although the Eastern Division and Alibamon Mingo of the Concha in particular were still disposed to make war on the Chickasaw for former losses, even attacking a peace embassy from the Chickasaw on its way to Fort Toulouse. Yet the Chickasaw persisted, sending a French prisoner to Mobile to plead for them. In answer the French sent him back with an old-time Chickasaw trader from pre–Natchez Revolt days, but the expected reception at the Chickasaw villages was reversed when the warriors claimed that they had no desire for peace and had been sold out by their chiefs. By July Vaudreuil was urging the Choctaw back into war with the Chickasaw, but rumors that a peace was being arranged anyway in spite of French disapproval led to a more specific request of Choucououlacta and Toupaoumastabé (war chief of the Concha and "brother" to Alibamon Mingo) to put together a party to break the peace. It took until September for the French in Louisiana to receive word of the outbreak of war with England in the spring.[61]

English documents show that in January 1745 the Chickasaw "Blind King" (Imayatabé Le Borgne, who had been so wronged by Bienville), together with the trader John Campbell, had negotiated a peace with the Choctaw through Red Shoe, who was said to have won over all but one of the Choctaw medal chiefs to the plan. But the Chickasaw had apparently continued raids against the Choctaw, since soon after that the Choctaw captain of Boucfouca village led a party that recaptured Choctaw prisoners and brought in Chickasaws for torture. At the last minute before the presents in March, Red Shoe and Mongoulacha Mingo led small parties to take Chickasaw scalps for presentation in Mobile, and Red Shoe not only was received with gratitude but was treated in the Mobile hospital for wounds and eye trouble.[62]

That Red Shoe's actions had been a facade became apparent when on July 20 at an assembly at Yanabé village he persuaded the medal chiefs to seek an English trade, doubtless aided in his persuasion by several intervening French actions: in the spring the French traders had closed a warehouse at Concha without the government's knowledge, and later the Choctaw of Chickasawhay had complained of a rape by a French soldier. After the Yanabé assembly Red Shoe sent an embassy made up of his son-in-law and two brothers-in-law (one of them possibly Mongoulacha Mingo) to negotiate with the Chickasaw. Soon afterward at an assembly held at Oni village the full support of Alibamon Mingo and his district chiefs was secured by Red Shoe, and on August 24 a Chickasaw embassy addressed a group, including all but one of the medal chiefs at Bouctoucoulou Chitto, opposed only by the Oni and Concha villages—though the character and strength of this opposition is not known.[63]

In an attempt to stiffen the resolve of the pro-French Choctaw and to gather additional intelligence on the happenings in the Choctaw nation, the French sent the interpreter Jean Baptiste Allain *dit* Roussève from Mobile into the nation with trade goods for the villages of Couëchitto, Concha, Yazoo, and Bouctoucoulou Chitto in early September. On September 15, probably as a result of this initiative, yet another assembly was held in Concha, and there Alibamon Mingo was scolded by his Concha subchiefs Toupaoumastabé and Offemeko, Red Shoe by his "brother" Tatoulimataha of Little Wood. By October 2 the village of Blue Wood had fielded a party that attacked an English convoy on its way to the Chickasaw and killed two English traders. Later on in the month the subalterns Chambly and Henri de Verbois, the latter based at Red Shoe's village of Couëchitto, were accused of rape. On December 15 an embassy from the Chickasaw, consisting of a Choctaw woman from Cushtusha and Imayatabé's nephew, came to propose an English trade and the opportunity to ransom Choctaw prisoners. The Choctaw medal chiefs decided to send a party, including the chief of Cushtusha, to ransom captives and to fetch Imayatabé to confirm the peace. In spite of the fact that the Cushtusha chief turned back at the French-inspired rumor of a trap, Red Shoe, visiting at Fort Tombecbé in late December, assured the commander that a peace among the Choctaw, Chickasaw, Alabama, Tallapoosa, and Abihka was imminent. At that time only four Choctaw villages were estimated to be loyal to the French.[64]

In late March and April the French presents were held at Mobile, and some twelve hundred Choctaws attended, although Red Shoe and Mongoulacha Mingo did not appear and Vaudreuil humiliated another medal chief known to be allied with them. The Choctaw principal men and warriors demanded that the medal chiefs' presents be taken from them for their perfidiousness and divided among the other chiefs and warriors, but Vaudreuil did not do this. By April, faced with the actual loss of his present from the French, Red Shoe sent Imataha Pouscouche (his "brother," the "Little King" to the English) to negotiate the Chickasaw peace and thereby obtain an English trade, but apparently there was trouble with those chiefs whom Vaudreuil had rewarded, because later in the spring Red Shoe once more called an assembly and argued for the English alliance. He was opposed with some success by Choucououlacta, and in late May he set off for conferences with the Abihka and the Coweta. In June, at the urging of the English trader James Adair and the chiefs Pastabe and Pahemingo-Amalahta, the Chickasaw sent presents to Red Shoe with another offer of peace, having heard through Red Shoe's allies the Chakchiuma of the accusation of rape against Verbois and the involvement of Red Shoe's wife. By that time Choucououlacta had begun to lead attacks on the Chickasaw with the support of the Eastern Division. In July Red Shoe sent an embassy to treat with Adair and offer a promise of death to several Frenchmen to avenge the deaths of the two English traders of the previous year at the hands of the Choctaw. A return embassy from the Chickasaw was attacked by Choucououlacta as it made its way from Bouctoucoulou Chitto to Couëchitto, and two important men and one woman were killed.[65]

Red Shoe and his allies, cut off from their French presents, had to have an English trade in order to maintain their influence, and to do that they had to have a Chickasaw peace. Yet two Englishmen and three Chickasaws had been killed by Choctaws, in both cases by parties composed of men of the Eastern Division. Red Shoe had to demonstrate good faith to the English and Chickasaw, but the solution he chose was to avoid vengeance on his own people, even though the responsible parties were not from his own division, were not his allies, and at least in the case of Choucououlacta were not of his moiety. What he chose to do was kill three Frenchmen; doubtless this solution was suggested by the personal injury he had suffered, but it is clear that it was not his solution alone, since two other important chiefs allied with him—Apekimataha of West Abeka and Opayéchitto of Immongoulacha, whose villages were bases for the two traders Petit and Replinque killed with Verbois —were also involved in the deaths.[66] Thus we see a corporate decision taken by a faction composed of members of a single division: that corporate decision was to repay deaths from one European group with deaths from another, even though Choctaws were responsible for the deaths to be avenged. Red Shoe and his allies may still have thought that it might be possible to make allies of the Eastern Division in a complete break with the French, and this may be taken to explain why they avoided killing their own people at this juncture; but it does not explain why this pattern continued on both sides long after such an assumption had been proved wrong.

On August 14, then, the three Frenchmen were ambushed and killed as they traveled along a path from one village to another. It is not known who killed them. Red Shoe and his two allies doubtless ordered the killings, and the suggestion is that they were carried out by men from all three towns, but the identities of these men were never known or indeed considered important either by the French or apparently by the Choctaw. Both sides treated the killings as a corporate act for which the chiefs of the three villages, at least, were responsible. Such a view was doubtless reinforced as far as the French were concerned by the fact that after the killings the French warehouses in the Western Division were plundered. And Red Shoe himself represented the killings as an action of his faction when he sent portions of the Frenchmen's scalps both to the Chickasaw and their English traders and to the Abihka and Tallapoosa.[67]

The first English response to this action was from Campbell, who sent two English traders into the Choctaw nation from the Chickasaw; apparently, the French deaths had been adequate recompense for those of the English traders. The French response, after recall of all traders from the nation and sealing of those warehouses that had not been plundered, was to send an important officer with the French demand for three Choctaw lives in payment for the three French lives. On September 16 Jadart de Beauchamp, major of Mobile, was sent to the Chickasawhay village to deliver the French ultimatum. It is unfortunate that Beauchamp was not more perceptive in his understanding of the conventions of Choctaw diplomacy, but even though his observations do betray misapprehension, his journal of the mission, covering nearly a month, offers a day-by-day account of developing loyalties in the Choctaw nation as its leaders considered the French demand. What actually went on during Beauchamp's visit was a series of meetings with groups of leading Choctaw men at which Beauchamp reiterated the French demand for vengeance and the chiefs argued the merits of the various courses they could take. In examining this account we must remember that though Beauchamp did not realize it at the time, the meetings he held were to the Choctaw a matter of external negotiation, and no real internal decisions were made in his presence. The value of the journal lies in the fact that many of the issues that were to influence Choctaw conduct in the course of the coming civil conflict did surface here.

The assemblies were held in the Chickasawhay village where Beauchamp and his party—which included Verbois's brother—stayed with Father Baudouin because they had been warned that their safety could not be guaranteed beyond that point. During the course of the meetings Beauchamp received and sent messages to and from Fort Tombecbé, Fort Toulouse, and Mobile, thereby receiving news of what was happening as the repercussions of the Choctaw act and the French response began to be considered by both the Choctaw and the Upper Creek groups to the east. The men who came to meet with Beauchamp did not all come at once but in groups probably of allies. We have no way of knowing how representative they were of the opinions and loyalties of their villages.

The first and second days of October were devoted to a meeting with the leading men of the Chickasawhay villages. All shades of opinion were offered. Mongoulacha Mingo, who appeared in an inebriated state, was virulently anti-French, partly because he had heard that the medal chiefs were to lose their medals to the red chiefs, and as medal chief of the Chickasawhays and the Sixtowns he felt himself to be aggrieved. The Choctaw captain of Chickasawhay argued that the Choctaw needed French guns and ammunition and would starve without them. The captain of Immongoulacha village and the taskanangouchi of Yowani were pro-French and felt that justice should be done, while Mingo Ouma of Chickasawhay urged that the French leave the Choctaw to solve the problem in their own way. On the second day of this conference it was reported that the Abihka had rejected the French scalps and thereby an alliance with Red Shoe against the French.

On October 3 Alibamon Mingo and his supporters from the Concha villages and the Eastern Division arrived. Alibamon Mingo spoke eloquently in favor of acceding to the French demand, but Toupaoumastabé and Quikanabé Mingo, also from Concha, argued that vengeance should be carried out by the Western Division, since the Frenchmen had been killed by their partisans. The taskanangouchi of Blue Wood urged calm deliberation to choose the best course of action. The next day the taskanangouchi of Yazoo pledged the support of the Eastern Division to Alibamon Mingo, who seems by now to have taken over the leadership of the Eastern Division in the power vacuum left by the death of Choucououlacta, and on October 5 the chiefs of Oni declared themselves pro-French.

On October 6 the chiefs of the Sixtowns arrived. The chiefs of Yellow Canes and Nachoubaouenya expressed pro-French sentiments, while the chief of Tala, Mingo Ouma of Nachoubaouenya, Imataha Pouscouche and Fanimingo Tchaa of Seneacha, the chiefs of Bouctoulouctsi and Toussana, and Pouchimataha of Toussana argued against taking the side of the French if it would mean civil war. In spite of what Beauchamp considered a very persuasive speech from Alibamon Mingo arguing the French position and the isolation of the Choctaw as a result of the horrified reaction of the Abihka, Pouchimataha of Toussana replied for all of the Sixtowns that they would refuse a civil war, though they would gladly take up the Chickasaw war again. The implication was that they felt that Chickasaw deaths should suffice as a reaffirmation of loyalty.

Meanwhile, at Fort Tombecbé, Paemingo of Cushtusha had brought in skins to trade, and though trade had been suspended for the whole nation pending restitution, he claimed a right to both trade and a reward for having led an attack on the Chickasaw. In private consultation with the fort commander he proposed to kill Red Shoe himself with the aid of a picked party consisting of Taskaoumingo of Boucfouca, Pouchimataha of Toussana, Illetaska of Immongoulacha, and Tatoulimataha of Little Wood, Red Shoe's "elder brother." It is probable that this proposal had more to do with the individual jealousies of several leading men than with any intention to comply with the French notion of justice. In any case, the proposal was reported to Beauchamp by letter, giving him what seemed to be a possible solution that he could suggest in private talks if the occasion presented itself.

On October 7 Alibamon Mingo departed to go and take part with other chiefs in mourning the death of Choucououlacta, who had died advising the

Eastern Division to support the French in opposition to the action of Red Shoe. On the same day the French-recognized supreme chief of the nation, from the village of Oulitacha of the Eastern Division, arrived along with a chief of Chichatalaya and Imataha Mingo of Ibitoupougoula. The supreme chief expressed himself as unreservedly pro-French but spoke of the very little authority he had and of an attack that had already been made on his life. He did promise to speak for the French at the tribal assembly that would be held for the ceremonies connected with the preparation of Choucououlacta's bones for interment. Imataha Mingo, on the other hand, was strongly opposed to civil war for whatever reason. The supreme chief ordered Espaninantela, the only Sixtowns representative still present, to command the Sixtowns chiefs to apologize for the rudeness of their speeches. Through subsequent days there were promises from Sonakabetaska, perhaps from Couëchitto, to avenge Verbois at the assembly for Choucououlacta and from the chiefs of Immongoulacha to avenge their trader, Petit, but these individual promises may have represented personal obligations to the dead Frenchmen rather than corporate commitment. The white chief of Okalusa proposed that the actual killers be punished but Red Shoe spared; a chief of West Abeka felt that Red Shoe should be sacrificed for the sake of the nation. The red chief of Concha—perhaps Toupaoumastabé—warned that even self-defense against the more populous faction of Red Shoe might be difficult for the Concha in case of civil war.

Meanwhile, apparently some Choctaw had gone to the Chickasaw to seek English goods, for it was reported to Beauchamp that they had found no goods there. On October 12 an embassy from the Alabama tribe arrived to address the assembly, led by Tamatlémingo, war chief of the Conchatys Alabama, and his Choctaw son, the nephew of the red shoe of Yanabé village. Tamatlémingo described the opposition of the Alabama, Tallapoosa, Abihka, and Coweta tribes to Red Shoe's action and their demand for justice for the French. He warned that English goods were in short supply and that the English never offered presents on a regular basis as the French did. He also brought news of a pan-Indian peace being promoted by the Shawnee that Choctaw actions would spoil. His Choctaw son (presumably the son of a Choctaw wife) assured the assembly that Tamatlémingo spoke the truth, and this assertion was supported by the red shoe of Tombecbé and Assetaoumastabé of Concha, who made up the rest of the accompanying party. As a result apparently of these speeches, the red shoe of Yanabé, who had argued against the killing of Red Shoe on the previous day, spoke in private with Beauchamp, proposing to kill Red Shoe along with some picked men. Beauchamp, taking this opportunity to put together such a party, suggested as members Paemingo of Cushtusha, the captain of Toussana, Illetaska of Immongoulacha, Tatoulimataha, and Taskaoumingo (captain?) of Boucfouca, the last of whom the red shoe of Yanabé rejected as untrustworthy because too ambitious.

On the following day Beauchamp spoke with Tatoulimataha, since if he were involved in the death of Red Shoe it was said that his close relationship of blood might prevent civil war. Tatoulimataha responded that he could not take part in such an action against one so nearly related and that Red Shoe should be killed, if at all, not by the Choctaw but by the Abihka or Tallapoosa. He also offered an explanation of Red Shoe's revolt: abuse of his wives by the French, jealousy of the French trader given to Pouchimataha of Toussana, and the English request for revenge for the Blue Wood attack on their traders. It is significant that Tatoulimataha clearly thought this last reason at least partly justified Red Shoe's action, at least as far as the Choctaw were concerned.

By October 16 Beauchamp had seen all the chiefs he could and departed for Mobile, to be followed by a messenger bringing Choucououlacta's medal and a message from Attachimingo and Tchioulacta pledging the loyalty of the Eastern Division. Neither Beauchamp nor his superiors were particularly satisfied with the outcome of the meetings, since apparently they had expected an actual conclusion to be reached. Beauchamp was especially nettled by the failure of the groups of chiefs to reach consensus, since he had expected them to transact serious tribal business in his presence. It seems obvious to us with hindsight that they had no intention of doing so, that the use to which the Choctaw put the meetings was to assure the French of their loyalty in order to retain their presents while presenting all the arguments available against an internal war, which they anticipated as the inevitable outcome of the death of Red Shoe. At the same time, the evidence of several chiefs speaking with Beauchamp in private shows that many of the sentiments expressed were for public consumption and that the Choctaw themselves had mostly adopted a wait-and-see attitude, waiting to see how events would develop—specifically, to see how much support would be forthcoming to Red Shoe from the English and the Creeks—and also to see how the consensus of the Choctaw nation itself would begin to shape. Beauchamp was quick to assume that sentiments were divided along moiety lines, and perhaps his assumption does reflect a strong impression that he received, but the nature of the evidence he has left us is not sufficiently unambiguous for us to accept that at this early stage such a division was completely inevitable.

The French were not prepared to await Choctaw consensus in order to obtain satisfaction. Apparently, the post commanders felt that the death of Red Shoe could bring a quick end to the problem, for on October 20 a party led by a Great Tohomé Indian long resident at Fort Tombecbé and another Indian called Broken Leg left the fort to try to kill him. On November 3 two young men not yet warriors, from Yazoo Iskitini and Chickasawhay, reported to the Tombecbé commander that in an attempt to kill Red Shoe they had burned his round house, though he had escaped. These two attempts at a solution using both non-Choctaw and uninitiated young men were irregular enough that perhaps they would have stood a chance of success without substantial consequence had they succeeded, but they did not.[68]

Instead, Red Shoe's strength seemed to be increasing. By November 9 it was reported that his "brother," presumably Imataha Pouscouche, was escorting an English convoy to the Chickasaw, and Mingo Ouma of Ibitoupougoula was sent as his emissary to the Chickasaw to announce that he was coming to fetch the English goods. On November 12, at the Chickasaws, Red Shoe concluded a peace with the Chickasaw and the English, represented by the traders Adair, Campbell, Newberry, and Chinnery, who had come to meet him there. By December 11 twenty-five towns had declared in favor of Red Shoe, probably about half of the nation, though the Chickasawhays and the Conchas were still loyal to the French. Also by that date Red Shoe had sent Imataha Pouscouche with fifteen headmen to make a treaty in Charleston.[69]

In retrospect, the first six months of 1747 were the backdrop for a race against time, as Imataha Pouscouche attempted to reach Charleston and return with a sizeable quantity of English goods before the French could persuade the Choctaw to carry out their demand for retribution against Red Shoe. By January 14 the Choctaw embassy had reached Coosa, but in late February and March Vaudreuil was meeting with deputies said to represent all forty-two Choctaw villages, promising large rewards for Red Shoe's death and securing their promise to carry out his request. On March 24 Imataha Pouscouche's party had reached Fort Moore, and by March 28 an English trader, apparently coming independently from the Creeks, reached Fanimingo Tchaa at the Sixtowns village of Seneacha with ten horse loads of goods, thus helping shore up the English allegiance of the Sixtowns. On the same day Taskaoumingo of Concha sent word to the chiefs and leading warriors to come to an assembly at Fort Tombecbé, and one of the young Choctaws who had previously attempted to kill Red Shoe set out to try it again. At the Tombecbé assembly on April 1 all the chiefs and principal men of twenty-three villages loyal to the French resolved to kill Red Shoe; the number is more than the villages of the Eastern Division plus the Conchas and perhaps includes some of the Chickasawhays. Ten days later Imataha Pouscouche had reached Charleston, and by April 18 the English treaty was concluded. Governor James Glen chose Charles McNaire to carry presents and trade goods to the Choctaw, but it took him until June 10 to prepare his train of two hundred horses, and while he was still on the road, on the night of June 22, Red Shoe was killed while escorting the Creek trader Elsley to the Choctaw. In spite of Red Shoe's death his faction was not to dissolve. Elsley's convoy continued on to Couëchitto, his village, and its contents were given out as presents to confirm Imataha Pouscouche as his successor.[70]

Meanwhile, Red Shoe's head and two English scalps were handed over to the French by their allies, clearly an attempt to answer the demand for three deaths. The French, however, not only continued to insist that two more Choctaw deaths were required, but apparently they now intended not just to have vengeance but to destroy the leadership of Red Shoe's faction: instead of the chief of Immongoulacha, they demanded that Imataha Pouscouche be killed along with Apekimataha to make up the three required Choctaw deaths. The English scalps were dismissed as having nothing to do with the satisfaction that had been demanded.[71]

McNaire finally arrived in the Choctaw nation on September 25, having left some of the goods he carried behind among the Creeks. Imataha Pouscouche called an assembly, and once again presents were given out, reportedly binding forty-two Choctaw towns to the English, though this English report seems rather optimistic in counting only four towns as still loyal to the French. In a demonstration of strength, again avoiding direct aggression against other Choctaws, the English-supported group attacked settlements on the Mobile River, killing five French people and one Negro; shortly thereafter another band attacked the Natchez fort. In similar action against Europeans in October Elsley was killed by the French-allied Choctaw while on his way back to the Creeks for more goods, and on October 25 the Great Tohomé leader and twelve Conchas attacked a convoy of five English traders carrying back sixty horse loads of deerskins, killing one Englishman and the Choctaw chief who

ESSAYS IN ETHNOHISTORY

was escorting the party. Apparently in reaction to this Choctaw death, the Western Choctaw then attacked the Concha fortifications, and two were killed on each side before the attackers were driven off. Somewhat later four English traders, possibly the four who had escaped the Eastern Choctaw attack, returned from the Creeks with powder and bullets, and in late November McNaire left the Choctaw with Imataha Pouscouche and Payamataha (Paemingo of Cushtusha?) to ask for more goods in Charleston, where they arrived at the end of the year.[72]

This sequence of events shows that the Choctaw had resisted becoming involved in internecine strife as long as it was possible to do so. The documents do not tell us who it was that actually killed Red Shoe, and it is possible that in the stealth with which it was done no one really knew. Revenge for his death was certainly inflicted upon the French, not the Choctaw. The Western Choctaw did not attack the Eastern Choctaw until after one of their chiefs had been killed by a Concha attack—a death that might well have been unintended, since it was plainly aimed at the English convoy. And even at that the Western Choctaw attack on the Concha villages was not particularly violent or determined. One explanation for this lack of enthusiasm might be sought in the smallpox epidemic that had killed one thousand to twelve hundred Choctaws by the end of 1747, since although the victims would be predominantly very young and very old and hence noncombatants, Choctaw mortuary customs would have been a distinct hindrance to concerted military activity.[73] Certainly, this massive mortality must have played a role, especially if Choucououlacta had been among the victims, and if many of the older men valued for their wisdom in council had died, then it would be more likely for impulsive decisions to be able to prevail in Choctaw councils after 1747, as was apparently the case. It is also true, however, that the Choctaw were reluctant to kill one another in payment for foreign lives when custom and the lesson of the Natchez wars licensed them to wonder why the French did not declare war to avenge their own dead.[74]

The French did not cease their demands nor the English their support. By the end of March 1748 McNaire had arrived back in the Choctaw nation, but Imataha Pouscouche had stayed back at the Creeks to await the coming of McNaire's partner Vann, who was actually bringing the convoy of goods. Using Campbell as his interpreter, McNaire gave out ammunition that he had taken from his storehouse at the Creeks. Meanwhile, Louboey, commander at Mobile, was hosting twenty-eight loyal Choctaw villages for the French presents from April 9. These villages, which included six from the Western Division, pledged vengeance on Red Shoe's party, and Vaudreuil's offer of pardon to the Western Division in exchange for the three deaths previously demanded was passed on to be communicated to them officially by Imataha Mingo of Ibitoupougoula and the second chief of Chichatalaya, who must have been the only ones with enough authority—or perhaps sufficient connection with the Western Choctaw leadership—to be convincing. But this was not done, and shortly after the presents there was another Western Choctaw attack on the French colony, this time on the German Coast below New Orleans, where a man was killed, his wife scalped, and his daughter and five Negroes taken prisoner. An abortive French attempt to catch the perpetrators encountered Pahémingo of Immongoulacha and a small party in the woods near Lake Pontchartrain with what they claimed were six black and three Indian runaway slaves but took no action; by June 15 it was reported that the leader of the raid on the Germans had been killed in his own village by his brother and chief. Also by that date Imataha Pouscouche and his Choctaw party were attacked in the vicinity of the Abihka on the way back from Charleston, and the French spread the rumor that he had been taken away as a prisoner to Carolina.[75]

The summer of 1748 seems to have been the turning point when the Choctaw finally accepted the fact that the French would indeed not be satisfied with anything less than civil war and strongly prosecuted attacks by Choctaws on Choctaw villages began. We may speculate that a more moderate course might have prevailed for even longer if the smallpox epidemic had not taken its toll of the more seasoned leadership, and it does seem to be the case that in the actions to follow some new names come to the fore. Yet neither the Choctaw perception of French determination nor a more impulsive leadership can account for the whole of the explanation for this turn of events, since there is an obvious—though not always explicable—political significance to the choice of villages attacked, and it seems to be clearly connected with prior events and loyalties. The first attack of this kind, made on July 14 by the Conchas and their allies of the Eastern Division led by Alibamon Mingo, was a raid on Couëchitto, Red Shoe's village, and Nushkobo (classified by Swanton as an Eastern Choctaw village, perhaps attacked for having deserted the eastern cause).[76] In this raid Tchicachas Ouma, chief of Nushkobo, was killed along with two honored men of Couëchitto and ten others, among them six of Red Shoe's Chakchiuma allies. At this point the Chakchiumas living at Couëchitto fled to the Chickasaw, and the two villages were abandoned.[77]

In August the second big English convoy from Charleston came as far as the accustomed waiting point on the Black Warrior River and then turned back after waiting three weeks for an escort. McNaire was forced to get ammunition from the traders at the Chickasaw, which he distributed before departing. Adair himself traveled through the Choctaw nation after this, holding a large assembly at the Sixtowns, where he gave out extensive presents that included gorgets, bracelets, and earrings. Presumably on the strength of all this English support, the western faction attacked Oulitacha, the village of the French-allied supreme medal chief, on August 16. More than a hundred were killed in this engagement, but the Western Choctaw attackers seem to have had the worst of it, losing the captain of Boucfouca, the chief of West Abeka (perhaps Apekimataha, whose death was demanded by the French), Mongoulacha Oupayé of Immongoulacha (the original third of the demanded deaths), Pahémingo of Toussana, and more than eighty more. It is worth noting that the body of the probable leader of the attack, the captain of Boucfouca, was terribly mutilated, a practice that the French said had been unknown among the Choctaw before. The Eastern Choctaw defenders lost the chief of Chichatalaya, honored men of Ibitoupougoula and Bouctoucoulou Chitto, and ten more.[78]

After this military failure the Western Choctaw sent to the Chickasaws for more ammunition, and at this juncture Vann finally arrived with Imataha Pouscouche and the pack train from Charleston. By October 4 there were sixteen Choctaws in Carolina, sent previously by Adair for more ammunition. On October 22 Red Shoe's Chakchiuma allies attacked the Natchez fort and killed a French soldier, but by October 24 Mongoulacha Mingo of Chickasawhay, the brother of Pahemingo of Toussana, and an honored man of West Yazoo had been killed by their own villages, and Red Shoe's "family" was said to have fled en masse to the Abihka or Alabama because the Western Choctaw faction was out of ammunition. This must have been a rather specious explanation, since on November 8 a party of thirteen Choctaws attacked again at the German Coast and killed five people, losing five of their own.[79]

Although Imataha Pouscouche had not been killed, by now the Eastern Division had actually satisfied the original French requirements for vengeance, since Red Shoe, Pahémingo of Toussana, and perhaps Apekimataha had been killed. When we look at what happened at the French present giving, however, something very different seems to be going on. Vaudreuil came to Mobile on November 26 and was met by a victorious party consisting of Alibamon Mingo, the chiefs of the Concha villages, the supreme chief, and all the chiefs and warriors of the Eastern Division, including Okalusa and Yanabé. They brought him more than a hundred Western Choctaw scalps and the heads of three chiefs, and obviously they thought that the French requirements would be satisfied. The heads they brought were those of chiefs from Couëchitto of the west, Nushkobo of the east, and West Abeka of the west, the first two obviously obtained purposely in their attack in July, the third won in the battle against Western Choctaw attackers in August. This point is worthy of note because it was in their power to present the other, originally demanded deaths for consideration.[80]

Yet the French still demanded that the attack on the Germans be avenged, and Alibamon Mingo handed out the weapons left behind by the attackers to the warriors of Yowani, Chickasawhay, and the Sixtowns so that they too might prove their loyalty. The war chief of Yowani used them to attack Okéou-lou, killing one man and taking three prisoners. It seemed that perhaps the violence could at last be concluded, and Vaudreuil offered a pardon to the villages of the Western Division through representatives from West Yazoo and West Immongoulacha.[81]

This much-desired conclusion was probably close to being reached if only because the Western Division was in a desperate state for ammunition, which had apparently been in short supply in the pack trains that had arrived. In December the sixteen Choctaws sent by Adair arrived in Charleston and met with the Royal Council to ask for more munitions. On January 7, 1749, twenty more Choctaws arrived in Charleston with Campbell, among them Pouchimataha of Toussana and Paemingo of Cushtusha, claiming that all the chiefs of the Western Division were dead and their cause was almost lost. Also in January an English trader was captured with a twelve-horse convoy near the Alabama; in the spring Imataha Pouscouche died, apparently of natural causes; and on March 12 the English trader in West Yazoo village was shot. Also in March Fanimingo Tchaa of Seneacha brought in four English traders from the Chickasaw and then attacked a party from the Eastern Division in the plain of Seneacha. He and eight of his kinsmen were killed, and the English traders were plundered, causing a split in the village. The pro-English group joined Oni, Tchanké, and Okéoulou villages in attacking Nachou-baouenya, killing twenty men and forcing the entire village to withdraw to

Yowani. By mid-April, however, a party made up of forces from Chicka-sawhay, Yowani, Nachoubaouenya, Bouctulouctsi, Yellow Canes, and the pro-French Seneachas attacked Oni, Tchanké, and Okéoulou, killing twenty to forty people.[82]

The split in the village of Seneacha must have been bitter, but again resent-ment was turned against the French when on July 1 ten Seneacha men killed three people near Mobile and withdrew to Seneacha. After the English trader at West Immongoulacha had been killed by the chief's nephew, an assembly was called at Fort Tombecbé by Joseph Louis Boucher de Grandpré, the com-mander, and Antoine Chauvin Des Islets, the leading French trader. At this assembly, presumably attended by the Concha, the Eastern Division, and the Sixtowns, the Choctaw agreed to end the war, and soon afterward what was supposed to be a definitive attack on Seneacha was made, during which nine of the ten men who had attacked the Mobile River settlement were killed.[83]

Since war with the French in Europe had ended, the English were no longer particularly concerned to supply the Choctaw with anything that would not be paid for. However, there was still some support to be had. By August 3, three Choctaws who had come to Charleston with some Chickasaw chiefs claimed that all ammunition was gone; the trader John Pettycrew said that they were reduced to using glass beads for bullets. This lack may have been partially provided for when Pouchimataha arrived back in the nation on September 22 with three English traders, but the French were countering with gifts to Mingo Ouma and his warriors from Nachoubaouenya for the Chicka-saw scalps they had started to bring in. Around October 6 Pettycrew left Charleston with fresh supplies of ammunition, arriving at the Chickasaw on November 25 only to be told that the Choctaw had gone to Mobile to seek peace. This report was only partly erroneous, for Des Islets brought fourteen leading men of Tchanké, Oni, Okéoulou, and Tala to New Orleans to talk peace and to see for themselves the supplies of trade goods then available. By December, however, Pouchimataha was in Caffetalaya with an English trader, and it was reported on December 20 that Caffetalaya and Cushtusha, sup-ported by the English trader and the two chiefs Pouchimataha and Mingo Ouma, were still holding out against the French allies. Further, on January 1 a Choctaw guard fetched Pettycrew from the Chickasaw to counter the influ-ence of the French interpreter Faberie (Simon Favré), who had been sent into the nation with a promise of French goods and a reward for British scalps. On January 12 Pettycrew arrived in Pouchimataha's village, Toussana, and called an assembly to distribute presents; after that he claimed to have traded in 24 towns and to have bound 1,322 men to the English alliance.[84]

On April 14 the French present giving began in Mobile, with all villages except Caffetalaya and Cushtusha represented, despite Pettycrew's claims. Now the Sixtowns made their final proof of loyalty, bringing 130 scalps from the raiders of the French settlements and their friends and relatives and claiming that they had themselves lost 30 killed and wounded. Representatives of the Western Division brought twelve Chickasaw and three English scalps, and apparently the French were willing to accept this as enough.[85]

The English supplies and resentments built up through the war continued to influence events, however. By June 24 a West Immongoulacha party killed a soldier at the Natchez fort, and by early July ten young men of the Eastern Division had been killed by the Western Choctaw in revenge for a Western Choctaw woman killed by an Eastern Choctaw man. In September fourteen English traders came to the Choctaw but were soon pillaged. The French must have realized that this kind of minor engagement could disrupt the nation indefinitely. Perhaps, too, they had grasped the fact that internal vengeance would be endless. At any rate, later in September Grandpré led a party from the Eastern Division with a detachment of French soldiers and a swivel gun from Fort Tombecbé to attack Cushtusha and Caffetalaya, burning five forts and scalping twenty-five people. This attack proved to be decisive; the French had at least symbolically taken the field in their own behalf, as the Choctaw had asked them to do in the first place. On November 15 the so-called Grandpré Treaty was entered into by the Choctaw at Tombecbé. They agreed to four points:

1. Any Frenchman killed by a Choctaw must be avenged by the Choctaw.
2. English traders and their Choctaw sponsors were to be killed by the Choctaw with no revenge obligation.
3. The Choctaw would pursue their Chickasaw war.
4. The Western Choctaw villages would destroy their forts and exchange prisoners with the Eastern Division.

This treaty was ratified by Atakabé Oulacta, referred to as the former supreme medal chief of the Choctaw, and by Alibamon Mingo in the name of the whole nation. A white feather flag and the English commissions of Pouchima-taha and Mingo Ouma were sent to Vaudreuil. From November 15 until January of the following year the Choctaw took the field against the Chickasaw several times, killing fourteen Chickasaws and an Englishman and taking ten prisoners. Although the French continued to have problems in supplying the Choctaw, and although some chiefs—notably Pouchimataha of Toussana and Mingo Oumastabé of Cushtusha—remained unregenerate in appealing to the English, this was the end of the Choctaw civil war.[86]

It is obvious from the foregoing narrative that there is no simple explanation of the patterns of loyalties that emerged during the war, since the loyalties that were appealed to during its course were not only political but also social and individual. We have, however, seen that the Choctaw did everything they could to avoid killing one another and that, in spite of European demands (and just because the English sources do not indicate that such demands from them were continuously made we cannot assume that they were not), the only times Choctaws were intentionally killed by other Choctaws were when Choctaw lives had been lost. It is true that during the second half of the war there was more fighting among the Choctaw themselves, but the French action that was required to end the war indicates that the principle of capital punishment *within* the tribe on behalf of an external complaint had not been adopted. What the Choctaw did do consistently was kill representatives of other *external* groups, and it is obvious that they expected this to serve as adequate retribution. This fact may suggest that here is an aspect of aboriginal intertribal warfare that deserves more investigation: the killing of mutual enemies as retribution for the unsanctioned death of an ally at the hands of the tribe.

Certainly, there were numerous other factors involved in the war. We have indicated that moiety affiliation was an important influence on the composition of factions, and the very character of the moiety distribution may also account for much of the confusion of loyalties that has been observed. The relative availability of European goods and the effects of the smallpox epidemic also had their influence. The full story of the several charismatic personalities that emerged during the war and their role in the conflict has not been told here either. There are a number of such issues that will repay more detailed investigation than there has been space for in this paper. The rich potential of a study of this conflict has barely yet been assayed, but the above consideration of only one aspect shows that there remains a great mine of information on the problems of culture contact and change.

Notes

1. Paape, "The Choctaw Revolt."

2. AC, série C13A. Selections relevant to French-Choctaw relations are printed in Rowland and Sanders, *Mississippi Provincial Archives*, vols. 1–3, referred to hereafter as MPA:FD.

3. Vaudreuil Letterbooks, Huntington Manuscript Loudoun (H M LO) 9:III. For a calendar see Barron, *The Vaudreuil Papers*.

4. See my "Louisiana Post Letters, 1700–1763: The Missing Evidence for Indian Diplomacy," in this volume.

5. Atkin, "Historical Account"; Adair, *History*.

6. What remains of the "Indian Books" has been edited in three volumes by William L. McDowell as *The Colonial Records of South Carolina*, series 2, vols. 1–3. Charles Lee and Ruth Green, in a series of articles in the *South Carolina Historical Magazine*, have published useful guides to the remaining South Carolina records mentioned in the text.

7. Vaudreuil to Rouillé, January 12, 1751, AC, série C13A, 35:65v.

8. Atkin, "Historical Account," 57; Adair, *History*, 330.

9. Jadart de Beauchamp, Journal, September 16–October 19, 1746, in Archives des colonies, série C13A, 30:222–40 (see 226v), translated in Rowland, Sanders, and Galloway, *Mississippi Provincial Archives*, 4:269–97.

10. Almost twelve hundred were said to have died of smallpox by the end of 1747; see Louboey to Maurepas, February 16, 1748, AC, série C13A, 32:212v. According to my count of actual numbers of Choctaw dead mentioned in the documents, a maximum of 418 Choctaws lost their lives in the actual fighting of the civil conflict.

11. This seems to be the import of the common settlement pattern of daughter villages strung out along watercourses as observed by the French: Baudouin to Salmon, November 23, 1732, AC, série C13A, 14:183.

12. See my "Choctaw Names and Choctaw Roles: Another Method for Evaluating Sociopolitical Structure," in this volume. For a discussion of these offices see Swanton, *Source Material*, 90–96. Swanton, who had access only to the French documents acquired up to that time by the Library of Congress and other American libraries (see Beers, *The French in North America*), did not recognize the titular nature of the "soulouche oumastabé" and "fanimingo" appellations. It also seems, from the frequency with which the taskanangouchi appears rather than the village chief for external negotiations, that he and not the tichou mingo was the chief's speaker.

13. Gearing, *Priests and Warriors*.

14. Beauchamp, Journal, 232v.

15. Swanton, *Source Material*, 78.

16. See my "Dual Organization Reconsidered: Eighteenth-Century Choctaw Chiefs and the Exploration of Social Design Space," in this volume; Gearing, "Priests and Warriors," 47–54; Hudson, *The Southeastern Indians*, 224–25. Compare Nassuba Mingo's statement in the 1765 Choctaw Congress with John Stuart in Rowland, *Mississippi Provincial Archives: English Dominion*, 1:241–42.

17. For the practice among the Creeks see Swanton, "Social Organization," 249.

18. In general, "red" chiefs tend to speak more often and more assertively. Examples in Beauchamp, Journal.

19. There are very few extant recorded observations even of Choctaw external negotiation. The only extant description for this period of Choctaw society in its domestic aspect that is worthy of mention is the so-called "Anonymous Relation" printed in Swanton, *Source Material*, 243–58, and even this does not describe internal political activities. James Adair, close as he was to the Chickasaws, recorded very little about such activities for them, which suggests that inclusion of Europeans was very rare.

20. Compare the lists in the various sources summarized by Swanton in *Source Material*, 58–75. This summary table gives the erroneous impression that division membership was static, but

a comparison of Régis du Roullet, Journal, 1729, in AC, série C13A, 12:67–99, translated in MPA:FD, 1:21–54, with Atkin, Treaty of Freindship and Commerce, shows immediately that this was not the case.

21. For references to dress and speech see Swanton, *Source Material*, 55–57.

22. See Galloway, "Henri de Tonti du village des Chactas." Four Choctaws came to the first negotiation with Iberville, but the Tonti documents make it clear that only three were actually sent as representatives.

23. MPA:FD, 1:194–95.

24. Red Shoe was an Imoklasha (inferred from Vaudreuil to Maurepas, February 12, 1744, AC, série C13A, 28:200–202); Alibamon Mingo was an Inholahta (see his speech in the 1765 Choctaw Congress with John Stuart in MPA:FD, 1:239); for other chiefs' moiety affiliations where known see below.

25. Beauchamp, Journal, speech of taskanangouchi of Yowani, an Inholahta (227).

26. Baudouin to Salmon, November 23, 1732, AC, série C13A, 14:184; Bienville, Memoir, August 25, 1733, AC, série C13A, 16:208.

27. For examples see Beauchamp, Journal, 231v; MPA:FD, 1:32–33.

28. Vaudreuil to Baudouin, December 19, 1745, H M LO 9:III, 185.

29. Swanton, *Source Material*, 162–64; Hudson, *Southeastern Indians*, 225; Gearing, "Priests and Warriors," 50–51.

30. The rivalry and enmities observed by the Soto expedition among the neighboring chiefdoms of the Southeast and especially of the Alabama-Mississippi area manifested themselves in concrete terms by the existence of fortified towns. Archaeological evidence shows that during the florescence of Mississippian cultures fortification was seen at small villages only when they lay at considerable distance from the protection of a larger center, while during the "Mississippian Decline" fortifications are seen on even very minor sites. See Peebles, "An Overview."

31. The first supreme chief was created by Bienville in about 1708. This was Chicacha Oulacta, who was succeeded by his nephew; see Baudouin to Salmon, November 23, 1732, AC, série C13A, 14:186v–87.

32. MPA:FD, 1:150–54; Vaudreuil to Maurepas, February 12, 1744; AC, C13A, 28:199v.

33. Beauchamp to Maurepas, October 24, 1748, AC, série C13A, 32:216.

34. Baudouin to Salmon, November 23, 1732, AC, série C13A, 14:184; Bienville, Memoir, August 25, 1733, 16:207v–8v.

35. As we have seen, "soulouche oumastabé," or red shoe killer, was a functional title. The French version of the title is *soulier rouge*, or simply red shoe. Here I will capitalize the title and use it as a name to refer only to this particular man; others will be referred to as "the red shoe of —." Red Shoe's motives will never be known with certainty, but clearly he wished to maintain neutrality and deal with both French and English. By disciplining him through cutting off his present at intervals, the French forced him to turn to the English to maintain the support of his allies.

36. Hudson, *Southeastern Indians*, 239.

37. The two young half-brothers Barthelemy, one sixteen and the other twenty-four years old, were put to death in 1738 for the murder of a Choctaw man and woman who had been employed in hunting for French settlers near Mobile. They were executed by order of the Superior Council of Louisiana, possibly under pressure from Bienville, in the presence of Choctaw witnesses. See AC, série C13A, 23:200–205, 24:115–18v, 246–49. See also my "The Barthelemy Murders: Bienville's Establishment of the Lex Talionis as a Principle of Indian Diplomacy," in this volume.

38. The Alabama, who had the French Fort Toulouse built in the midst of their lands, also

traded quite happily with the English for whatever the French could not provide. They always refused absolutely to harm either French or English allies and also to take the side of any other tribe that would. See Bienville, Memoir, 1726, 1:371.

39. Adair, *History*, categorically states on many occasions that the Chickasaws had always demonstrated unswerving loyalty to the English.

40. Régis du Roullet to Périer, February 21, 1731, AC, série C13A, 13:177v.

41. Crémont to Maurepas, December 9, 1732, AC, série C13A, 15:191.

42. Swanton, *Source Material*, 10–34; marriage alliances are indicated by several mentions of apparent wife exchanges (cf. AC, série C13A, 13:177v).

43. *MPA:FD*, 1:46, 110, 175.

44. *MPA:FD*, 1:187.

45. *MPA:FD*, 1:34.

46. *MPA:FD*, 1:371; Atkin, "Historical Account," 2.

47. *MPA:FD*, 1:371.

48. *MPA:FD*, 1:224, 232.

49. *MPA:FD*, 3:725.

50. *MPA:FD*, 1:79.

51. *MPA:FD*, 1:289.

52. *MPA:FD*, 1:299, 338, 368.

53. Noyan to Maurepas, January 4, 1739, AC, série C13A, 24:227.

54. Crémont to Maurepas, August 18, 1732, AC, série C13A, 15:191v; Noyan to Maurepas, January 4, 1739, AC, série C13A, 24:229v.

55. *MPA:FD*, 3:724–26.

56. Vaudreuil to Maurepas, November 30, 1746, AC, série C13A, 30:76v–77v.

57. Beauchamp, Journal, 229v.

58. Beauchamp to Maurepas, October 24, 1748, AC, série C13A, 32:216.

59. *MPA:FD*, 1:42; Baudouin to Louboey, May 20, 1742, AC, série C13A, 27:131(3)v–131(4).

60. Beauchamp, Journal, 225; Vaudreuil to Rouillé, March 3, 1749, AC, série C13A, 33:18v.

61. The primary sources for this narrative are AC, série C13A; H M LO 9:III; and Atkin, "Historical Account." Adair's *History* would be very helpful if events of many different periods were not inextricably intertwined, undated, in his account; here it is only used as corroborative evidence. To reduce the thicket of endnotes, references will be simplified and grouped by paragraph under a single number. Because the events related will be chronological, it will be sufficient to reference blocks of manuscript material. AC, série C13A, 28:199–211v, 260–61v, 29:196–200v; H M LO 4036; H M LO 9:II, 23v, 9:III, 4–11, 36, 42, 48–51, 62–67, 81, 89–91, 99, 117, 119, 125–28.

62. Atkin, "Historical Account," 37–38; AC, série C13A, 29:189–95v, 30:76–84.

63. AC, série C13A, 29:189–95v, 196–200; HMLO 9:III, 167, 178.

64. AC, série C13A, 29:189–95, 30:169–74; H M LO 9:III, 167, 180.

65. AC, série C13A, 30:49–56; Atkin, "Historical Account," 38; H M LO 9:III, 198, 201, 204; Adair, *History*, 313, 315.

66. H M LO 9:III, 125.

67. Beauchamp, Journal, 30:76–84. Hereafter cited by date in text.

68. AC, série C13A, 30:183–86; H M LO 9:III, 242, 247.

69. AC, série C13A, 30:183–86; Atkin, "Historical Account," 2, 5, 36, 38; H M LO 4021.

70. Atkin, "Historical Account," 3–6; H M LO 521; H M LO 9:III, 266; AC, série C13A, 19:11–12, 31:17–23, 32:122–31, 210–13.

71. AC, série C13A, 31:98–102; H M LO 9:III, 268.

72. Atkin, "Historical Account," 6–12; AC, série C13A, 32:122–31, 210–13.

73. AC, série C13A, 32:210–13; Swanton, *Source Material*, 170–93; cf. Beauchamp, Journal, 228v–29.

74. The Choctaws always asked for Frenchmen to accompany their external war parties.

75. Atkin, "Historical Account," 14–15; AC, série C13A, 32:81–87, 102–4, 33:12–27.

76. Swanton, *Source Material*, 66.

77. AC, série C13A, 32:122–31.

78. Atkin, "Historical Account," 15; Adair, *History*, 329–30; AC, série C13A, 32:122–31.

79. Atkin, Historical Account, 17–18; AC, série C13A, 32:122–31, 137–44, 215–18.

80. AC, série C13A, 33:12–27.

81. AC, série C13A, 33:12–27.

82. Atkin, "Historical Account," 21, 29; AC, série C13A, 33:49–54, 79–88.

83. AC, série C13A, 33:79–88, 34:251–58.

84. Atkin, "Historical Account," 29–33; AC, série C13A, 33:79–88, 34:251–58; H M LO 508.

85. AC, série C13A, 34:261–69.

86. AC, série C13A, 261–75, 315–17, 35:61–69, 354–60.

16. The Medal Chief's *Grosse Lettre*

*A Chapter in French Indian
Management Policy*

Tribes, Chiefs, and Prestige Goods Trade

Many of the Indian groups of the Southeast had been organized in late pre-history as chiefdoms, exhibiting a hierarchical sociopolitical organization with leadership perpetuated through inheritance as well as an elite-supported specialization in craft production. By the time Europeans came to stay, European disease had done its work in precipitating demographic loss, population movements, and reorganizations among these chiefdoms, which had fragmented and re-formed as confederations of towns. Yet less centralized groups, not organized in this way or having split off from chiefdoms long before, had also been present, and they seem to have suffered these shocks of the European arrival less seriously, even taking in refugees.[1] The reorganizations that took place, whatever the complex details of each case, eventuated in much more egalitarian arrangements across the Southeast. The leadership implications here were that although to a degree the lineage of a chief could still be important, there was now pretty much nowhere across the Southeast a surplus flowing in tribute from villages to be managed by chiefs. The chief of a town or the leader of a group of towns had to depend upon other mechanisms to consolidate his power. A chief generally chose to build a cadre of followers, a faction that would support him in competition for the office of chief with leaders of other factions.

Exchange was the most important element in status maintenance for a "tribal" chief, as it had been one of the legitimation tools of chiefdom elites. All relationships were maintained by means of reciprocity, the simple daily

---

The material in this chapter was first presented at the French Colonial Historical Society in Mackinack Island, Michigan, in 1990. It was revised for this volume.

exchanges of favors, food, marriage partners, and so on that grease the functioning of any society.[2] But for the chief, generosity was the very substance of his rank, and he was most frequently judged not by what he had but by what he gave away, not by how rich he was but by how poor.[3] This is not to say that he remained poor; by periodically distributing gifts to his followers, the chief established obligations on their part that might be redeemed in the form of services or reciprocal gifts. All of this made the tribal chief an important part of the economic system as well as a political leader. Like the more exalted leader of a chiefdom, the tribal chief was important to the redistribution of the wealth that assured the well-being of every tribal member.

Leaders must establish that they are special in some way, and in nearly all societies leaders must *look* different from their followers. Generally, there are sumptuary rules, providing for the restriction of certain visible signs of rank to the elite. The visible signs of rank themselves must be out of the ordinary, and where everyone has access to the materials and techniques that constitute the requirements of everyday life, leaders must somehow procure items of personal adornment that are unavailable to others, either because their making requires special skills that cannot be practiced part-time, because it requires materials that are not available locally, or both.[4] To obtain such items, then, the leader must maintain specialized workers and import specialized materials for them to use, or he must import the items ready-made. Participation in a trade network for the purpose of securing such items is referred to as "prestige goods trade," and it is an important aspect of the maintenance of status.[5] But it was only the most visible part of trade; it is thought that exchange of prestige goods served to establish and maintain trading and alliance relations that guaranteed access to more mundane requirements not available locally.

Prestige goods trade was the motor of long-distance communication deep in the prehistory of North America, literally going back thousands of years. The Woodland period Hopewell culture, famous for its zoomorphic earthworks in the Midwest, traded copper from the Great Lakes, mica from the Appalachians, and shell from the Gulf of Mexico to make its striking ceremonial artifacts.[6] Much later, the Mississippian chiefdoms trafficked in many of the same materials, using many of the same routes. The most visible sign of this trade and of the fact that the resulting objects functioned as prestige goods is the extraordinary distribution of objects from Oklahoma to the Atlantic Coast and from the Gulf of Mexico to Illinois referred to as the

"Southeastern Ceremonial Complex," in which a range of exotic artifacts decorated with specific motifs and emanating from specific workshops was distributed to and often buried with the leaders of the great chiefdoms of the region.[7]

Anthropologists think that such objects, particularly those meant to be worn on the body, denoted the (high) rank of the wearer and sometimes also sex or kinship affiliation.[8] During the late prehistoric period in the Southeast one of the most favored types of these objects was the gorget. Although gorgets, large medallions to be worn at the throat, had been worn for thousands of years, the Late Mississippian period saw the development of a group of gorgets that fit the discussion here especially well. They were made of shell from the Gulf of Mexico, a particularly demanding material to work. But they were not made on the coast; archaeologists have been able to localize many of the workshops to the mountain regions of Tennessee. The gorgets were engraved with a range of animal motifs—spiders, pileated woodpeckers, and rattlesnakes—as well as images of men dressed as animals and symbols of the sun that was central to the symbolic system of most of the Mississippian peoples. And although many of them are found in Tennessee, many more are found all over the region in elite burials.[9]

Although chiefdoms were effectively a thing of the past in the early colonial Southeast, and town or confederacy chiefs were no longer rich enough to maintain specialist craftsmen to create objects specific to them, yet the symbolic necessity for prestige goods trade persisted, and a chief who wanted to build power in the context of southeastern tradition had to do so by getting for himself and giving to his loyal faction things that they could not get elsewhere. European disease had damaged the system of long-distance trade with other Native groups, since Indians had come to distrust the health of strangers. The very Europeans whose diseases had so disrupted the trade, however, turned out to provide the solution to the problem of the ambitious chief.

French Presents to the Indians in the Southeast

Their experience in Canada had taught the French the value of helping chiefs to build their power through control of access to desired trade items. Using a strategy that would be referred to as "indirect rule" by the British in the nineteenth century, the French had learned how to function as the kind of well-connected trading partner the chiefs had allied themselves with in prehistory in order to maintain and build their own status, and they did this through a system of gifts and trade.

Following Immanuel Wallerstein's center-periphery discourse, work in North American history has developed a view of the Native role in such trading systems that sees Native recipients of the trade as at the extreme edge of the periphery, "underdeveloped" and "dependent" on the trade as they learned to be European Enlightenment-style rational actors in the emerging "market economy." From the perspective of the participants themselves, however, each culture views itself as center and others as periphery, and in a very real sense colonizing European elites needed the prestige goods from their colonies to consolidate their legitimacy fully as much as chiefs sought European goods to do the same. A presentist, Orientalist discourse of market revolution ignores as irrelevant the Native view of things, which saw Europeans as dwelling far indeed from Native views of the world's navel and their goods as interesting to a degree but improvable by Native modifications. The example I want to discuss here shows, I suggest, a more nuanced view of how European and Native leaders understood alliance and exchange obligations because it manifests their attitudes toward these relations in the treatment of some specific material objects meant to be representative of them. Native leaders could and did repudiate allegiances, and their treatment of the objects depended less on the characteristics with which Europeans endowed them and more upon how they fit into an established system of symbolic Native action.[10]

I will be most concerned with gifts here, but the "presents" were simply one end of a spectrum, and it is not clear where the dividing line fell. For the "presents" were not presents at all but a symbolic part of a system of reciprocity in which every item was exchanged for an item viewed by its Indian donor as of equal or greater worth—hence the scandal of French governors giving royally financed gifts to the chiefs and passing in silence over what the Natives saw as equally sumptuous gifts to the governors, gifts that governors did not report because in fact they were crucial to the prosperity and legitimacy of these ranking Frenchmen. It must be understood that some of the items that changed hands served to *establish* the conditions without which trade could not happen, while others were *objects* of the trade, and in general the first class of objects was only available to leaders.[11]

The French system of indirect rule involved the channeling of goods through a hierarchical system of "medal chiefs." Among the southeastern tribes what the French saw and described was a system of village chiefs, sometimes apparently only loosely confederated and sometimes partially subordinated to one of their number in certain circumstances. In view of a number of forty to fifty villages for the Choctaw alone, it would have been difficult to try to keep every village chief happy. The French goal was to make this system more "rational" and hence more manageable by identifying a single tribal chief for each self-recognized group through whom everything would be done, in return for which the French would enable their chosen tribal chief to aggrandize his power. This process began in earnest among the Choctaw with Bienville's choice of Chicacha Oulacta as tribal chief in 1707. As initially managed by Bienville, all the presents were channeled through this man, although he was clearly expected to reward village chiefs and their assistants for loyalty to the French as well as to himself.[12]

When Bienville was replaced by Périer in 1727, the policy changed somewhat. Eager to establish expanded trade with the Choctaw on behalf of the Company of the Indies (from which he apparently expected to profit handsomely himself), Périer gradually expanded the presents to reward the support of various chiefs until he was providing presents in a two-tiered system, to village chiefs and their assistants as well as to the so-called great chief. When Bienville returned in 1733 after the Company of the Indies had retroceded the colony to the Crown, he bemoaned the disorder that had thus been introduced and the expense that it would cause the Crown until he was able gradually to restore the former system.[13] In fact, he was unable to do this and was even forced into giving presents to individual chiefs rather than through redistribution to avoid faction building by multiple recipients.[14] This practice was then continued under his successors. But Bienville was able to limit the "special presents" to a small set of medal chiefs.

Under Périer the chiefs and their subordinates were given special presents that consisted of particularly impressive garments: military-style coats made of scarlet or blue wool material, liberally decorated with metallic or colored braid. Because most organic materials do not long survive in archaeological contexts, we only have the evidence of early explorers to tell us that Indian leaders originally wore splendid feather or pieced-fur mantles, which these coats may have replaced. Clearly, southeastern Indians had not lost their taste for gorgets, either, and were now getting them through trade, for a 1729 trade list for the Chickasaw trade mentions "round porcelain plaques, the width of two crowns and perforated in the center," but it is difficult to pinpoint when the major chiefs of the Choctaw were first distinguished with medals and commissions.[15] The earliest mention I have been able to find dates from 1729, but it clearly describes an established system, when the great chief refers to his medal and commission, or *grosse lettre*.[16] In a list of villages and chiefs made in 1732, five medal chiefs are mentioned, from Chickasawhay, Cushtusha, Concha (Alibamon Mingo), and Couechitto (Great Chief and Mingo Soulouche Oumastabe/Red Shoe).[17] This number remained fairly constant for the "great" medal chiefs, since it reflected the three divisions and the central civil and war chiefs.

What, in spite of the wishes of the French, did the chiefs do with their presents? Clearly, they retained the chiefs' presents properly so-called, the sumptuary and other items of the finest quality and greatest desirability in Indian eyes. The "present" part of the exchange was, however, not limited to such items and included all kinds of goods over and above what the French actually traded with individual Indians. A chief's present toward the end of the 1720s consisted of a whole outfit of European goods: coat, leggings, breechcloth, blanket, shirts, hat, gun, gunflints, powder, bullets, axes, tomahawk, knives, scissors, nails, awls, needles, comb, beads, vermilion, brass wire, and bells.[18] These items were used in order to build influence and persuade other men to adhere to their factions by the men the French had identified as chiefs. Both French and British Indian diplomatists alternately complained and attempted to make use of this mechanism.

The items the chiefs kept for themselves clearly functioned for them as signs of rank and preferment and were integrated into the traditional system of rank definition as such. Chiefs wore their fancy coats and hats on ceremonial occasions only (for reasons of comfort, according to the French), but the items that were closer analogues of chiefly rank symbols were apparently worn on a daily basis as they had always been and were buried with their owners as well.[19] Furthermore, what the historical documents tell us about their treatment may help expand our knowledge of the symbolic treatment of signs of rank in prehistory.

Perhaps the most interesting practice with regard to these items is the repudiation process. On at least two reported occasions chiefs who had fallen out with the French for real or imagined bad treatment indicated that they had repudiated the allegiance symbolized by the gorget and the commission by casting both into running water. In 1729 the great chief of the Choctaw complained to Régis du Roullet in a meeting in the town of Couechitto:

I know furthermore that the English, when they appoint a chief, give him all that he needs and the French, who could do the same thing, leave me poor. I have my brother, Mr. Diron, chief of Mobile, who gave me a medal and a big letter of consideration. When he gave it to me he recommended me to listen well to his word and always to reject that of the English, which I promised him to do. I hoped that that would get me out of distress, but I see that I am as poor as before, and as my brother, the chief of Mobile, sends me word that I was a woman and that he did not wish to see me any more, I said, "What is the use of this medal and of this big letter he has given me? I am still poor; my brother, Mr. Diron, is angry; he does not wish to see me any more." I threw my medal and my big letter into the water.[20]

Régis observed that indeed the great chief did not have the medal at hand. The next day, after Régis had announced the impending establishment of a trading house in the town that would be under the control of the chief and had given the chief a large number of goods as a present that he was free to redistribute, Régis was able to report:

On the twenty-fourth the Great Chief sent his son to look for his medal and his big letter that he had fished for when he learned of my arrival, but which he had not yet worn. He took it in his hand and holding his fan in the other came with ceremony to say these words to me: "It is now that I make my explanation and that I speak in my name and in the name of the entire nation. . . . I know that the French have made us men [by supplying guns for self-defense] and the English have never done us anything but evil, so I embrace absolutely the word of the French and I reject the English. If I threw away my medal it was because my brother, Mr. Diron, sent me word that I was a woman; that he did not wish to see me any more, and because, since I did not get any coat last year, I was ashamed to wear it."[21]

In 1746 Jadart de Beauchamp heard the speech of Mongoulacha Mingo of Chickasawhay, who angrily rejected the French demand for Choctaw action against Red Shoe:

He began over again to revile us with indefensible attacks, adding that he knew well that he would never return to favor with us, since he had rejected our word; that since the Indians had told him that the authority of the medal chiefs was being taken away to be given to the red chiefs, that had made him decide to cut off his medal and to throw it into a stream; that since then

ESSAYS IN ETHNOHISTORY

he had been told that it was as if he had killed ten Frenchmen; that he certainly thought that sooner or later he would be killed for having made this mistake.[22]

Beauchamp attributed the man's vehemence to liquor and reported that he then stormed out and went to his house, where he tore down his French flag as well. But evidently Mongoulacha Mingo considered that the medal and commission were important to the French, and he used Choctaw terms to measure that importance.

The southeastern Indian worldview saw water as associated with disorder and change and bodies of water as the entrance to the underworld of death, so it seems that by this action the chiefs had symbolically "killed" the obligation signified by the gorget and the commission, both of them in situations where they felt humiliated.[23] Yet interestingly, as the first example shows, simply removing the items from the water could restore the relationship to "life." This observation needs to be investigated further for its significance to the interpretation of southeastern belief, but its meaning is quite clear in this instance.

Kerlérec's Commissions and the French and Indian War

We know that in the 1740s medals had begun to be created in France specifically for the purpose of Indian diplomacy, and Governor Pierre de Rigaud de Vaudreuil had used them to some effect in his management of the Choctaw through the grueling events of the Choctaw civil war of 1746–50.[24] When Governor Louis de Kerlérec arrived in Louisiana in 1753 he inherited an established and reasonably effective system that included a new wrinkle: in 1741 the Choctaw war chief Red Shoe had attempted to redeem himself after having been denied his French present for disloyalty by handing over to Bienville both his own English commission as "king of the Choctaw nation" and an English medal that had been given to one of his faction chiefs, then dead.[25] In 1750, at the time when the Grandpré Treaty ended the Choctaw civil war, Vaudreuil had been given, by the leading French loyalist chiefs who were "victors" in this war, the English flags and commissions that had been received by the "rebellious" chiefs, together with a white feather flag and a calumet, "the usual symbol of an enduring peace among the Indians."[26] Clearly, both cases indicate that the Choctaw themselves felt that these items carried important symbolic freight, as both actions were voluntary.

Kerlérec came on station just in time to hold the fort through the French

Fig. 16.1. French commission to Mingo Ouma, 1760. From the Copping family collection, courtesy of Mrs. A. M. Copping and John Copping.

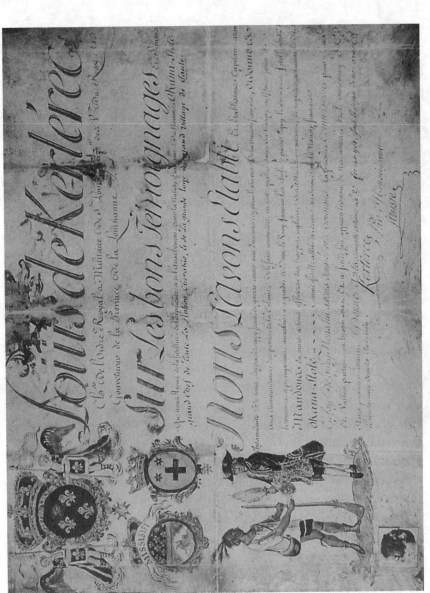

Fig. 16.2. French commission to Oconostota, 1762. National Archives and Records Administration, RG 59, General Records of the Department of State, Miscellaneous Accession 161, Item 35. Courtesy of the National Archives.

and Indian War, which broke out in 1754. France virtually ignored Louisiana during this period; Kerlérec went for years sometimes without seeing a ship from France, far less trade goods or gifts for the Indians. The governor thus had to depend upon his management skills and mother wit to maintain south-eastern Indian allegiance or at least neutrality throughout the war. The iconography of two rare surviving "commission" documents, which accompanied gorgets he gave as gifts to medal chiefs in 1760 (the Choctaw small medal chief Toupa Ouma of Caffetalaya) and 1761 (Oconostota of Chote, leader of the Overhill Cherokee), gives some idea of how he did it (figures 16.1, 16.2). The commissions, first of all, indicate that Kerlérec was formalizing the notion of a military rank granted to the chiefs, indicating that they were to be considered his subordinate officers, but officers with peculiarly privileged status relative to the authoritarian organization of the French military of the time. This, along with the naming ceremony accorded to Kerlérec reciprocally indicates that by the 1750s at least such a novel relationship had been established as a workable one and was so recognized by Indian and Frenchman.

The appearance of the commissions is important too. Physically, they are extraordinarily impressive, written on vellum, measuring 17 by 15 inches (the phrase "big letter of consideration" should be taken literally), and illuminated in full color. The left third of the commission is devoted to symbol, certainly as understandable to Indian as to Frenchman if perhaps on different terms. The arms of France are very elaborately rendered at the top. Below them are seen to the left the arms of the colony of Louisiana and to the right the personal arms of Kerlérec himself. Below the armorial images are two figures, an Indian on the left and a French officer—presumably Kerlérec—on the right. The Indian is conventionally dressed as a warrior, but he is dressed in European trade goods worn in Indian style. He wears a European trade shirt above his trade-cloth breechcloth and fancy braid garters on his bare legs. He also wears a shot bag and holds a trade gun in his left hand. With his right he shakes the hand of the Frenchman, who carries in his right hand an object of equal power to the Indian, a white feather "wing" mounted on a handle—such objects were carried and exchanged among the Indians during treaty talks to denote alliance and peace, as we have seen. The Frenchman is wearing elaborate officer's dress and the Cross of St. Louis on his left lapel.

Does this image really reproduce an actual treaty-making scene? It would seem at best to be a conventionalized one, since the two Indian images are almost identical, but the white wing Kerlérec carries is surely symbolically

Fig. 16.3. Louis XV silver Indian medal of 1740, reverse side, engraved by French royal medalist Jean Duvivier. Courtesy Library and Archives Canada, Picture Division, C-062182.

significant, as doubtless is the gun carried by the Indian, presumably supplied by the French. Further, there is no evidence in the lists of supplies sent to Louisiana that the materials for these commissions were sent, so it is not clear either where or by whom they were made, except to say that they were obviously created by a skilled penman. There is no reason why they could not have been made in France and filled in in Louisiana with names and ranks and even specific war paint for the warriors, since the whole scene is a conventionalized one of colonial dealings. It should be compared with the reverse of a Louis XV silver medal struck in 1740 to give to the Indians: a Gaulish savage on the left and a Roman soldier on the right are shown hand in hand, but each carries a spear in the other hand (figure 16.3).

The text of the commissions outlines both the privileges to which the bearer is entitled and the rank that is established for him in a fictive French-Native military service (variant expressions in brackets):

> Louis de Kerlerec, Chevalier of the royal and military Order of St. Louis, Captain of the vessels of the King, and Governor of the province of Louisiana, on the basis of good testimonies and proofs that we have of the faithfulness, experience, and attachment to the French nation of the said [Touppa Ouma, chief of the village of Kafetalaya], we have established and do establish him [Captain and small medal Chief] of all the parties that shall go to war against our enemies and for the service of the French nation. We order the commandants of the posts of the colony to have him recognized in this rank in the nation and to have him enjoy the honors and prerogatives attached to this rank and which the King promises party chiefs who serve him faithfully. We order in addition all officers of regular troops and militia and others to regard and treat the said [Touppa Ouma] as faithful ally and dedicated to the service of the French nation. In promise of which we have given and do give him the present commission to serve as a witness wherever there will be need and to that end we place the seal of our arms and the countersignature of our secretary. Done at New Orleans [the first of November 1760], Kerlerec by M. Jouisie[27]

These Indian "commissions" are not modeled on actual military commissions but are rather a mixture of military commission, military decoration, and safe-conduct language. The two extant commissions vary textually only as to name of the recipient, rank, and date. There are also a few minor scribal variations, so that the words are distributed slightly differently on the lines, but the emphasized words at line beginnings are the same formulaically. There are also slight differences in the portrayal of the figures: the Indians wear distinctive and different war paint patterns on their faces that must have been specifically chosen.

Kerlérec was uniquely successful in Indian management, extending French influence farther than any governor before him to the Lower Creeks and the Cherokee, and these two commissions are cases in point. The Choctaw commission dates from 1760, when the French and Indian War had been going on for six years and Kerlérec was particularly concerned to assure the loyalty of the Indians in Louisiana's own backyard. Toupa Ouma was a youngish chief who seems to have risen to prominence after 1750 (when Caffetalaya was destroyed and its chief killed in the Choctaw civil war) and to have remained a leader through the 1760s. The name means "red couch" and may have referred to the seats constructed in arbors around the ceremonial grounds and occupied by the red, or war, moiety of the tribe. It is not a name unique to this individual, so it may be a rank name or title.[28] The commission was drafted in November in New Orleans, so it may have been a rather hypocritically given reward delivered in the course of the following event reported by Kerlérec: "A Choctaw party came to bring me the scalp of a British trader-merchant who was in the eastern section and who had never attacked them. . . . Since I have never been in the habit of accepting British scalps, and although the British request and accept French scalps daily, I did not accept the one I was offered, but I did not fail to pay the chief of the party well for his trouble in making the trip from his village to this place."[29]

Part of Kerlérec's success in Indian diplomacy came from the fact that he was not too punctilious to make extremely effective use of the nephew of his predecessor Vaudreuil, Antoine Adhémar de Lantagnac. Lantagnac claimed that as a young ensign he had been captured by the Chickasaw when he was lost in the woods in the vicinity of Fort Toulouse, taken to South Carolina, and amused himself with establishing a Cherokee trade while under a kind of "house arrest" by Governor Glen.[30] Ludicrous as this claim sounds, Kerlérec saw that Lantagnac, who had also acquired a Cherokee wife and a wide acquaintance with the Overhill Cherokee and their allies among the Creeks, could be an invaluable agent provocateur if he was sincere in wishing to return to a French life.[31]

As it happened, Lantagnac was quite willing to do what Kerlérec wished. Supported by the commandant at Fort Toulouse, Montault de Monberaut, and by Kerlérec himself, Lantagnac proceeded to work with the Upper Creek chief The Mortar to induce the Cherokee to revolt against the British, finally winning over not only Attakullakulla but also Oconostota, the recipient of the second commission.[32] In 1760 the Cherokee attacked Fort Loudoun in the Appalachians and killed most of the inhabitants, at least partly to avenge the deaths in the previous year of loyal Cherokees killed by British colonists on their way home from supporting the British against the Canadians and their Indian allies in the Ohio River valley.[33] Oconostota's overtures of peace to Governor Lyttelton at this time were rejected, as Oconostota was taken hostage and then released to secure peace, leaving twenty-some Cherokees in English hands who would later be killed. French support from Fort Toulouse near present-day Montgomery aided Oconostota in besieging and capturing Fort Loudoun. Unable to reward Cherokee leaders as they desperately needed with adequate munitions to continue the war with the British, Kerlérec probably hoped that such honors as the medal and commission would make up for the lack of other supplies, and Oconostota received his while on a visit to New Orleans early in 1761.[34] Without military supplies, however, Oconostota had to make peace with the English within a few months, and the Cherokee War was over in the British colonies. It would not be long before the British would be victorious everywhere.

Afterlife of the French Commissions

The French may have "lost" the French and Indian War, but they did not lose it in the Southeast. When by the terms of the 1763 Peace of Paris the British came to take over the lands of Louisiana, they had to pacify the undefeated allies of a former enemy. Indian congresses were held across the region, and one feature of them was the conversion of enemies into allies. A symbolic part of this conversion was the exchange of French medals and commissions for English ones, as had gone on throughout the struggle for Indian allegiance. Toupa Ouma's commission is now preserved in the hands of a private individual (a memeber of the English family that established the Player tobacco company) and was perhaps obtained from someone involved in the 1760s with colonial tobacco farming. My best guess is that an English witness who was present managed to carry the French commission home as a souvenir from the Choctaw congress held in Mobile in 1765, at which Toupa Ouma of Caffetalaya received a small medal and commission from the British.[35]

The Cherokee commission, on the other hand, is preserved in the National Archives in Washington, among the General Records of the Department of State. How it got there may imply that Oconostota did not in fact hand over his commission in any negotiation. In 1780 it may have been captured by an American expedition that attacked his town: "We found in Okana-Stote's Baggage, which he left behind in his fright, various manuscripts, copies of treaties, commissions, letters, and other Archives of the nation, some of which shews the double game that People have been carrying on, during the present war."[36] In this accumulation of what the British observer had already learned

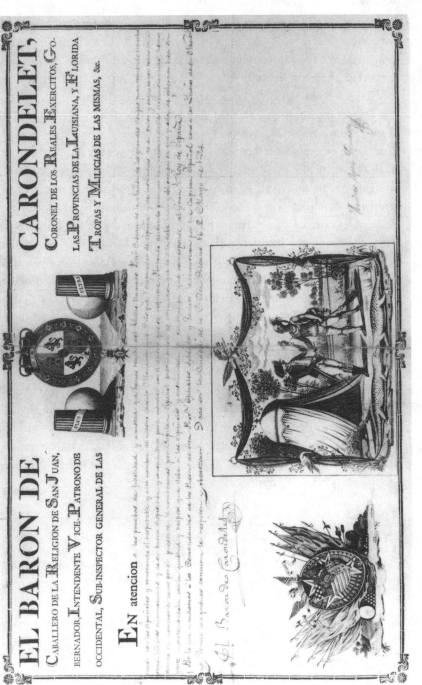

Fig. 16.4. Medal commission from Carondelet to Uamado opayé, 1794. Courtesy the Historic New Orleans Collection, Williams Research Center, New Orleans, Louisiana, accession no. 67-12-L, MSS 309.

to call "Archives" we may actually see as well a more traditional armory of symbolic power.

Remarkably, the iconography of the two Kerlérec commissions was still functional under the Spanish regime in Louisiana thirty years later. A 1794 medal commission signed by François-Louis Hector de Carondelet, the governor of Spanish Louisiana, showed the governor with a similarly conventionalized Indian warrior wearing two gorgets, a breechcloth, leggings, and garters and carrying a musket with a powder horn over his shoulder (figure 16.4). The figure of Carondelet, in full-dress uniform with a sword at his side, offers the medal in his left hand to the Indian, while the Indian places an arrow in Carondelet's right hand. The vignette is completed by a field tent behind Carondelet, while a lake in the background and a pair of alligators in the foreground conjure up Louisiana. The Spanish royal coat of arms is positioned at the top center of the document, while Carondelet's personal arms are shown to the left. To the right an area is left blank for the arms of the recipient, which are lacking except for a flourished signature.

According to the text of the treaty, the recipient was the Tallapoosa village chief Uamado opayé, who was being rewarded with the medal for his support of and loyalty to the Spanish king. In so rewarding the loyalty of the Upper Creek Tallapoosas, Carondelet, like Kerlérec, was stretching the influence of Spain deeply into a territory of presumed American hegemony, thirty years after non-Anglo Europeans had supposedly been expelled from the region. And the commission, like those of thirty years earlier, still stands witness to the symbolic importance of special recognition of southeastern Indian leaders to guarantee the trustworthiness of exchange, even in the full flush of the supposed market revolution.

Notes

1. For southeastern examples of this process see Galloway, *Choctaw Genesis*, as well as papers in Barker and Pauketat, *Lords of the Southeast*; and Hudson and Tesser, *The Forgotten Centuries*. In *Lords of the Southeast* see especially Widmer, "The Structure of Southeastern Chiefdoms," 125–55.

2. For a summary treatment of reciprocity see Sahlins, *Stone Age Economics*, chap. 5.

3. Gearing, *Priests and Warriors*.

4. See Helms, "Political Lords."

5. The locus classicus for prestige goods trade is Frankenstein and Rowlands, "The Internal Structure."

6. Seeman, *The Hopewell Interaction Sphere*.

7. See essays in Galloway, *Southeastern Ceremonial Complex*.

8. Peebles and Kus, "Some Archaeological Correlates."

9. Brain and Phillips, *Shell Gorgets*, 395–402, argued for a late development of the shell gorgets

and their continuing use into the protohistoric period. Others contest the late development but concur that the gorgets continued long in use, making it even more likely that the practice of wearing such rank badges continued too.

10. Examples like this support the substantivist position that economic exchanges are embedded in social systems rather than being universally the same everywhere in principle and kind. See James Taylor Carson's discussion of "marketplace society" among the Mississippi Choctaws from colonization to Removal (*Searching for the Bright Path*, chap. 4). Greg O'Brien, in *Choctaws in a Revolutionary Age*, divides "diplomacy" from trade and sees different values being parsed out into the two categories in the context particularly of exchanges with the British, which had to take place at long distance from the home base of the British; here I concentrate on a context where Choctaws could and did go in large numbers to carry on both ceremonial treaty renewal and trading at Mobile on (when things went well) an annual basis.

11. For especially the Canadian experience see Jaenen, "The Role of Presents." For a survey treatment of French and English present giving, with particular attention to the era of the French and Indian War with which we are primarily concerned, see Jacobs, *Wilderness Politics*. Wesson, "Prestige Goods," explores the application of Bourdieu's concept of symbolic capital to the prestige goods trade in the Southeast. That symbolic exchange often accompanies and establishes legitimate grounding for trade can be seen by comparing similar features of the Kula Ring described by Bronislaw Malinowski in *Argonauts of the Western Pacific*. High-status objects are still exchanged by heads of state to renew cordial relations that are vital for trade, as the display of sumptuous gifts to Lyndon Baines Johnson from heads of state (at the LBJ Presidential Library on the University of Texas campus in Austin) makes abundantly clear.

12. Baudouin to Salmon (from Chickasawhay), November 23, 1732, AC, série C13A, 14:186–87, translated in Rowland and Sanders, *Mississippi Provincial Archives*, 1:157–58, hereafter MPA:FD; Bienville, Louisiana, On the Indians, August 25, 1733, AC, série C13A, 16:206–17 (see 208), translated in MPA:FD, 1:193–204.

13. Bienville, Louisiana, On the Indians, August 25, 1733, AC, série C13A, 16:207, translated in MPA:FD, 1:194.

14. Bienville to Maurepas, April 28, 1738, AC, série C13A, 23:58–68 (see 64v–65), translated in MPA:FD, 3:714–15.

15. Régis du Roullet, Journal of the journey that I made in the Choctaw nation in the year 1729, AC, série C13A, 12:67–99 (see 99), translated in MPA:FD, 1:53.

16. Régis du Roullet, Journal, 1729, AC, série C13A, 12:78v, translated in MPA:FD, 1:32–33.

17. Régis du Roullet, Itinerary from Mobile to the Choctaws, April to August, 1732, Archives du service hydrographique, vol. 67², no. 14-1, portefeuille 135, document 21, translated in MPA:FD, 1:136–54.

18. Régis du Roullet, Journal, 1729, AC, série C13A, 12:90v, translated in MPA:FD, 1:44–45.

19. An example of the continuing practice of burying precious objects rather than passing them on to perpetuate status appeared in the richly accompanied burial (including a Washington Peace Medal dated 1793, uniform buttons, and an epaulet—thus presumably also a coat—and round and crescent-shaped gorgets) of Chickasaw chief Piomingo, who died around 1800. See Atkinson, "Death of a Chickasaw Leader."

20. Régis du Roullet, Journal, 1729, AC, série C13A, 12:78v, translated in MPA:FD, 1:32–33.

21. Régis du Roullet, Journal, 1729, AC, série C13A, 12:83–84, translated in MPA:FD, 1:36–37.

22. Jadart de Beauchamp, Journal, September 16–October 19, 1746, AC, série C13A, 30:222–40 (see 225), translated in Rowland, Sanders, and Galloway, MPA:FD, 4:269–97 (see 273–74).

23. Hudson, *The Southeastern Indians*.

24. See my "Choctaw Factionalism and Civil War, 1746–1750," in this volume.

25. Bienville to Maurepas, March 7, 1741, AC, série C13A, 26:55–65, translated in MPA:FD, 3:740–44.

26. Vaudreuil to Rouillé, January 12, 1751, AC, série C13A, 35:63v, translated in MPA:FD, 5:61.

27. My translation of the following French text: Louis de Kerlérec, Chevr de l'ordre Royal & Militaire de St Louis, Capn des Vaissx Dy Roy, et Gouverneur de la Province Dc la Louisiane, Sur les bons Temoignages Et preuves que Nous avons De la fidelite, De 1'Experience, Et de 1'Attachement pour la Nation francaise du Nomme [Touppa Ouma Chef du Village de Kafetalaya], Nous L'Avons Etabli et Etablissons [Capitaine et Chef a petit medaille] de tous les parties quy Iront en guerre contre nos Ennemis et pour le Service de la nation francaise. Ordonnons aux Commandants des postes de la Colonie de le faire reconnaitre en cette qualite dans la Nation Et le faire jouir ces honneurs et prerogatives attaches a ce grade et dont le Roy promise les chefs de partie qui le Servent fidellement. Mandons en outre a tous officiers des troupes regles & de la Milice & autres de regarder et traiter Ledt [Touppa Ouma]. . . . comme fidelle allié et dédié au service de la Nation francaise. En foy de qouy Nous lui avons donne et donnons la present Commission pour servir a Valloir partout ou besoin sera Et a celle fait apposa le sceau de nos armes et le contresigne de Notre secretaire. Donne a La nouvelle orleans [le 1er Novembre 1760] Kerlerec Par Monseigneur Jouisie.

28. See my "Choctaw Names and Choctaw Roles," in this volume.

29. Villiers du Terrage, The Last Years, 127.

30. Petition of Lantagnac to Kerlérec, 1755, AC, série C13A, 39:40–44, translated in MPA:FD, 5:161–66.

31. Kerlérec to De Machault d'Arnouville, October 1, 1755, AC, série C13A, 39:37–39, translated in MPA:FD, 5:159–61.

32. Note that apparently Oconostota, who had become the dominant leader of the whole Cherokee nation by 1753, had taken an interest in French alliance as early as 1736. See Kelly, "Oconostota."

33. Villiers du Terrage, The Last Years, 134.

34. Kelly, "Oconostota."

35. See my " 'So Many Little Republics': British Negotiations with the Choctaw Confederacy, 1765," in this volume. I reproduce this commission with the kind permission of Mrs. A. M. Copping and with gratitude to Mr. John Copping for information about the Player connection.

36. Campbell to Jefferson, January 15, 1781, in Boyd, Papers of Thomas Jefferson, 4:362–63, quoted in Kelly, "Oconostota," 231.

17. "So Many Little Republics"

British Negotiations with the
Choctaw Confederacy, 1765

In March 1765 the Choctaw met with British representatives in Mobile to negotiate a boundary and land cessions in that city's vicinity. It was well after the close of the French and Indian War had spelled the end of the French colony of Louisiana east of the Mississippi and thus of the long-standing alliance between the Choctaw and the French. Not only were the Choctaw adjusting to the relative disadvantage of having only one European power to deal with, "people intoxicated with their success who regard themselves as the masters of the world," but they were forced to reckon with a former enemy as well.[1] The Choctaw were not at a loss, however. The elegiac tone that we perceive today in their public utterances on this occasion stems more from our knowledge of their eventual displacement than from their attitude at the time. As they had been doing since the first encounter with Europeans, the Choctaw adapted to the world as they apprehended it and attempted to force others to accommodate them.

In this essay I am going to look at the 1765 congress for evidence that one hundred years of European contact had not made the Choctaw into what the Europeans wanted them to be—a single entity with which they could deal as such. Instead, the congress reflects the persistence and adaptability of the heterarchical, multiethnic confederacy of autonomous towns that constituted the Choctaw "nation" in the eighteenth century.[2] In particular, land rights were invested in the ethnic divisions rather than in the "Choctaw" as a single

The material in this chapter was first presented at the annual meeting of the American Historical Association in 1992 in a session titled "Surviving the Frontier." It was revised for publication as " 'So Many Little Republics': British Negotiations with the Choctaw Confederacy, 1765," in *Ethnohistory* 41, no. 4 (1994): 513–38. It is reprinted by permission of the American Society for Ethnohistory.

entity, obliging the Europeans to recognize Choctaw divisions and towns individually. Perhaps more important, the negotiations illustrate the chronic European-Choctaw misunderstandings that guaranteed the confederation's continuation.

In the early historic period the Choctaw were a multiethnic confederacy still forming out of the wreckage of prehistoric chiefdoms. A relatively small core of villages (which would become the "Western" Choctaw, closely related culturally to the Chickasaw) had lived in central Mississippi for thousands of years and had probably constituted in late prehistory a simple chiefdom with a single small ceremonial center. During the late sixteenth century and into the seventeenth century European agency altered the region demographically and technologically, causing a significant refugee population to join them: the "Eastern" Choctaw from the middle Tombigbee region (closely related to the Alabama and probably once part of the elaborate Moundville multileveled chiefdom on the Black Warrior River). Western and Eastern Choctaws formed an alliance, or confederacy, retaining separate group leadership, on two neighboring watersheds in present-day east-central Mississippi. The Natchez-related Sixtowns from the southwestern Pearl River region, the Chickasawhays from the Mobile delta, and the Conchas from the Tombigbee-Alabama forks later joined the confederacy.[3] Thus Choctaw identity, if that is the word for it at the early stages, was a composite from the beginning. It was also shaped by Spanish, French, and English pressures, influences, and definitions, which joined with those of neighboring similarly emergent Native groups to create the semipermeable membrane that would define the boundaries of Choctaw identity.

Although the timing is uncertain, this process must have started by 1675, when the Choctaw were first mentioned in Spanish documents. By 1702, when Pierre Le Moyne d'Iberville sent Henri de Tonti to invite their leaders to meet with him in Mobile for nonaggression and trade agreements, it was apparently incomplete. The people then recognized by the French as Choctaw, under attack by English-sponsored Chickasaw and Upper Creek slavers, were only too ready to take any help they could get. Three Choctaw chiefs, their identities unrecorded, went with Tonti to Mobile.[4] Iberville then took the opportunity to compose a census of their villages.[5] He writes in his logbook of "1090 huts" in "three villages"—the French frequently used the latter expression to express subdivisions of what they recognized as "nations." The list of villages he passed on to the mapmaker Claude Delisle, however, is not divided into three groups; more significantly, the Chickasawhay towns and the Six-towns are missing from Iberville's list.[6]

This omission indicates that the Chickasawhays, who would be represented by the towns of Yowani and Chickasawhay, were probably still resident in the Mobile River delta in 1702.[7] No later evidence exists on when the Six-towns joined the confederacy, but they were always considered distinctive in accent and personal ornamentation, probably because of their Natchezan antecedents.[8] It is likely that even if the Sixtowns were part of the confederacy in some sense at this time, they were not considered "Choctaw" by the other groups. Hence the towns on Iberville's list constituted what the Eastern and Western Choctaw representatives, whose towns *are* listed, recognized as "Choctaw" in 1702.

That view seems to have changed after an incident that significantly amplified Choctaw numbers at the same time that it marked an attempt to change their organization. By 1700 most of the region's Native inhabitants were already participating at least peripherally in the European-sponsored trade network, including the Choctaw.[9] The customs of prestige-goods trade, which had been the currency of power for hereditary Mississippian chiefs, were appropriated by Europeans for their own ends as they substituted metal gorgets, for example, for the prehistoric shell badges of rank.[10] All the chiefs of the region found it natural that Europeans should provide a steady supply of prestige-goods items as a sign of alliance and of the reciprocity that was the basis for trade, and the French, recognizing this fact, grew famous for Indian diplomacy.[11]

In 1708 Thomas Nairne, Indian agent of South Carolina, imagined that the French could be driven out of the lower Mississippi valley if he could engross the Indian trade east of the Mississippi or destroy the French-allied Indians militarily. To that end he traveled with the Chickasaw trader Thomas Welch deep into the Old Southwest, where he claimed to have won over what he called "Choctaws" with gifts and promised trade goods.[12] The French, who viewed this British activity as dividing "the Choctaw nation," were kept informed of it by Choctaw allies.[13] Bienville reported that Nairne had "shocked" the "chiefs of the Choctaws" when he proposed that they exterminate all the "small nations" living near the French in the Mobile delta, the Tohomes, Apalachees, Mobiles, Taensas, Chatots, Pascagoulas, and Pensacolas.[14] Clearly, Nairne had erred here, for he had doubtless listened to definitions of "Choctaw" that came from his Chickasaw-allied Western Choctaw hosts. As a result he had drawn an ethnic boundary on what turned out to be very unstable sand indeed.

Clearly, several definitions of "Choctaw" were being confused here, but there is too little evidence of actual Indian attitudes to do much more than suggest possibilities. Interestingly, Nairne did not mention the Chickasawhays and Conchas, larger groups from the same lower Tombigbee and Mobile delta region that had been suffering from the British-backed slavers, to whom they had lost "more than two thousand warriors."[15] They asked Bienville to grant them aid and asylum; under his protection they moved west across the Tombigbee to settle. At the same time, the smaller tribes mentioned by Nairne moved nearer to Bienville's improved fortifications at Mobile.

Emboldened by new French weapons, the Chickasawhays and Conchas even attacked the Western Division towns of Couechitto and Cushtusha that hosted English storehouses established by Nairne. The chief pro-British supporter, Conchak Emiko, was killed by Chicacha Oulacta and his head presented to Bienville, who chose that occasion to recognize Chicacha Oulacta as the single great chief of the Choctaw.[16] Hoping to attach Chicacha Oulacta to the French, Bienville appointed him to receive all gifts for the tribe and redistribute them to those who acted in the French interest.[17] However little success this particular plan met with in the long run, it is probably true that the contest between Nairne and Bienville actually created the canonical "Choctaws" of the eighteenth century, hastening the inclusion of Chickasawhays and Conchas and inducing them to settle closer to the Eastern Division.

Once the constituent populations had joined together, whether pushed by Europeans or not, the Choctaw confederacy was so populous (twenty to thirty thousand) and therefore powerful during the eighteenth century that neither the British nor the French could significantly control it. The French wanted a controllable hierarchy, even though their own observers frequently complained that the Indians behaved as though they were "so many little republics."[18] But among the Choctaw especially a power center had to be created, for one did not exist naturally. Power relationships in the confederacy were structured as metaphorical kinship relations, and although we cannot now be certain about the details, it is clear that they were also tightly bound to external alliances with ethnically related tribes or tribal segments. Hence the Alabama were termed "elder brothers" to the Eastern Choctaw, and the

Inholahta moiety that dominated the Eastern Division was "elder brother" to the Imoklasha moiety that dominated the Western; the Western Choctaw were "brothers" to the Chickasaw. Strong relations also persisted between the Six-towns people and the Natchez and between the Chickasawhays and the small tribes of the Mobile River delta.[19] No one division, town, faction, or leader was able to sustain coercive dominance relations, which were simply not recognized as having any existence.[20]

Bienville's scheme of a single great chief surrounded by a very few medal chiefs, each answering for the behavior of his people in exchange for gifts, never worked as the French wished to mold a single disciplined response. By endowing with gifts the very men who were leaders of ethnic divisions, the French made it possible for these men to perpetuate a limited partitive brand of power.[21] To their credit, the French did recognize the factional nature of the medal chiefs' power. At the annual Mobile present-giving ceremonies the Choctaw factions were invited in shifts, not only because it would have been nearly impossible to host the whole nation at once but because there was danger of factional jealousy.[22]

Recognition gradually settled on six medal chiefs: leaders from the Eastern, Western, Sixtowns, and Chickasawhay Divisions, the somewhat exiguous great chief, and a single, long-term war chief for the tribe.[23] This latter office was new; war chiefs had been temporary leaders whose influence lasted only as long as intertribal conflicts.[24] Warfare and diplomacy had reached new prominence in the European scheme of things, however. During their colonial presence the French offered greater reward for contract warfare than for peaceful hunting, so that the office of supreme war chief became more important as an income-producing (and therefore influence-conferring) office than that of the single "peace" chief.[25] Though unintentional, it was the most significant European creation.

The war chief who in a very real sense created the office made its "red shoe" apellation into a name Europeans identified most strongly with himself.[26] Red Shoe came to prominence during Indian wars fomented by Europeans, beginning with Choctaw participation in the French revenge for the Natchez uprising of 1729.[27] When the French called upon the Choctaw for support in besieging the Natchez and securing the return of hostage French women and children and black slaves, two young leaders emerged: Alibamon Mingo, a young (peace) subchief of Concha whose eloquent harangue to the Natchez secured the return of most of the hostages; and his contemporary Red Shoe, the village war chief of Couechitto whose exploits included the taking of Natchez scalps.

The Natchez remnant that escaped the French fled to settle among the Chickasaw, whose long-maintained alliance assured asylum. To save face the French had to pursue them and demand their return from the Chickasaw. Here the complexities of both Chickasaw and Choctaw factionalism came into play. At the same time the Natchez were being taken in, Chickasaws from four central Chickasaw villages but led by the Ackia chief Imayatabé Le Borgne came in 1731 to settle with Red Shoe's people, ostensibly because they wished to escape the blandishments of the English.[28] Initially, Red Shoe stopped the Choctaw from honoring the French request to attack the Chickasaw, yet shortly thereafter, at news of the flight of the Natchez, he sent others to raid (presumably other) Chickasaw cornfields and to take scalps.[29] When the French-Choctaw force actually marched on the Chickasaw from the south in 1736, some faction other than Red Shoe's was probably responsible for precipitating the premature attack on the potentially friendly Ackia village group.

Red Shoe's efforts to play the English off against the French to obtain trade goods and to maintain his faction at a time of French scarcity led to the intratribal Choctaw civil war of 1746–50. The Eastern Choctaw, now including the Conchas, led by Alibamon Mingo, squared off against Red Shoe's Western Choctaw and their allies the Sixtowns and the vacillating Chickasawhays. The French demanded blood restitution after several Frenchmen were killed. They apparently secured the murder of Red Shoe himself by an unknown assailant and eventually of several leading chiefs belonging to his moiety by Alibamon Mingo's Conchas and even by their own fellow villagers. The closing events of the Choctaw-prosecuted part of the war, which ended only when the French themselves took to the field to avenge their losses, included the razing of several Sixtowns villages and the murder of their chiefs.[30] Yet these events were apparently shocking to the Choctaw, and Alibamon Mingo emerged at the end of the civil war as the preeminent peace chief, the man possessed of the actual and moral authority to put an end to the fighting and to reestablish the confederacy in 1750.

Despite the sustained effort by the English and French to impose or to bribe into existence a controllable hierarchical organization favorable to themselves and the external wars and internal ethnic divisions leading to a civil war, the Choctaw were able to maintain their autonomy. They did this simply by failing to create or maintain a governmental structure that could be controlled.[31] There were fundamental structural reasons, apart from political factionalism, why the constituent groups that made up the Choctaw were never significantly submerged into the whole: marriage and residence rules perpetuated geographically localized and ethnically distinct extended matrilineal households.[32] The European presence was therefore important to the maintenance of Choctaw unity. European definitions of Native "nations" all over the region led to specific alliances, material support, and ceremonialisms that continually reinforced the European-constructed ideas of Native polities while ignoring sometimes very different ethnic faultlines.

As European conflicts shifted north and east during the French and Indian War, very little was heard from the Choctaw. They were undoubtedly amazed when without so much as a single pitched engagement or even guerrilla harassment the French gave up their settlements east of the Mississippi to the British. They were certainly displeased to discover that as a result of this action the British believed that they had somehow gained control of Choctaw people and their land. They had no intention, however, of changing their behavior. Their apparent willingness to meet with the British for treaty talks in 1765 had more to do with the initiative of two pro-British chiefs and their desire to negotiate better trade rates than with any acknowledgment of subordination to the British. British traders had, after all, been alternately (and unsuccessfully) wooing them and victimizing them for more than sixty years.

Although the records of the 1765 congress are biased and incomplete (like those of all formal meetings held by Europeans with North American Native people), they do hint at the Native political background if the speeches and actions are seen in the light of the history of Choctaw-European interaction.[33] The British participants were new to the region, but the Choctaw chiefs had spent a lifetime learning how to manage Europeans as an additional and interesting feature of their political geography. The Choctaw speeches contain much that is traditional along with much that reflects the political realities of the moment. Choctaw custom dictated the very form and sequence of the meeting, and Choctaw history dictated its content.[34] Although the British made much of the representativeness of the congress, their view was far from the case. Instead, the congress was a political drama played out by certain Choctaws who sought to gain advantage for their own faction beyond the constraints of their traditional authority. A close examination of its structure and dynamics shows that the supposed Choctaw unity was still consciously constructed and that the diversity of Choctaw political opinion was still bound to small-group loyalties.

The first part of the congress, even only on the testimony of its record preserved by Arthur Gordon, southern Indian agent John Stuart's secretary, was obviously biased in the direction of the pro-British Choctaws, who managed it throughout.[35] On November 14, 1763, the main body of the Choctaw, mostly pro-French, had met in Mobile to hear their transfer to British rule explained by French governor D'Abbadie and Robert Farmar, British military commander for Mobile. From November 5 through 10, 1763, however, another Indian congress, including pro-British Choctaws along with the Cherokee and Creek, had been held in Augusta. Two pro-British Choctaws who had received British medals at the Augusta congress and had not attended the Mobile congress—Chulustamastabe of West Yazoo and the Red Captain of Chickatalaya—played important parts, as did the Chickasaw chief Paya Mattaha, in the second Mobile congress nearly a year and a half later.[36] The two Choctaw chiefs must have been making good on promises made in Augusta, whence they had been taken to Charles Town by John Stuart and subsequently given passage by ship to Mobile by the British.[37]

In examining the 1765 congress as reported by the British it becomes clear that the voices of formerly pro-French chiefs were often silent; when heard, they were dubious. The testimony of the former French commandant of Fort Toulouse, Henri Montault de Monberaut, named by Stuart as his deputy, reveals that in Choctaw eyes the congress had been broken off by Governor Johnstone and is not complete as the British recorded it. A good part of the Eastern Division did not attend the congress at all while Johnstone was present and only appeared in Mobile some weeks later.[38] Thus this account must be amplified by reference to Montault de Monberaut's story of the rest of the congress, which will be discussed last.

The congress opened on March 26 with a calumet ceremony offered by the Choctaw and prayers offered by the British.[39] The ceremony itself, often read as simple conventional acknowledgment of friendship, was still for the Indians a formal prerequisite to interpolity negotiation, which could not proceed without recognition of the participants.[40] This step may have been especially important if we can trust Adair's observation that "the Choktah are the most formal in their address, of all the Indian nations I am acquainted with:

and they reckon the neglect of observing their usual ceremonies, proceeds from contempt in the traders, and from ignorance in strangers."[41] It would be interesting to know who conducted the ceremony, since both of the pro-British Choctaw chiefs were war chiefs and could not have done so.[42] After the opening ceremonies Governor Johnstone explained and rationalized the division of lands between the French and the British at the close of the Seven Years' War. He then spoke of the British need for land around Mobile, in return for which they were offering favorable trade terms and a commissary established within the Choctaw nation.[43]

The proceedings on March 27 began with peace overtures by Chulusta-mastabe. He verbally emphasized his sincerity and physically demonstrated his intentions by pointing out his possession of the white wings, eagle tails, and calumet of civilized peaceful talks, asserting the readiness of the Choctaw to listen. His speech is full of the fictive kinship terminology of Choctaw diplomacy, referring to the British officials as "fathers" and to the British and Chickasaw as "brothers."[44] Although the patrilineal Britons were perfectly happy to hear such terms, they probably did not realize that their matrilineal Muskogean neighbors expected indulgence from a father.[45]

Nearly the entire remainder of the day was occupied by Stuart's lengthy formal speech. As Indian agent to the Choctaw and Chickasaw, Stuart asserted that now the pro-British "great party" (the Western Division) and the pro-French "six villages and small party" (Sixtowns, Chickasawhays, Conchas, and Eastern Division) were to be treated as one, and all were to be dependent on King George. Stuart discussed the terms on which medal chiefs would continue to hold medals, promised commissaries and armorers, insisted that the Choctaw chiefs should ignore Pontiac, and asked for the grant of land that the British must have to provide trade.[46] In the British account a brief summary of Montault de Monberaut's speech to the pro-French Choctaws present is drastically abbreviated, but Montault de Monberaut's own testimony suggests that he said much the same.[47]

The congress was ostensibly delayed until April 1 because of bad weather, and the Choctaw wished to wait for clear weather to symbolize their clear talk, but it is also likely that the Choctaw took the time to hold their own councils to discuss the British proposals. Montault de Monberaut's information about the nonappearance of the Eastern Division, however, suggests that the British may also have made some effort to delay for them.[48] Whatever the reason, the Eastern Division did not appear, and it is evident in what followed that the whole of the Choctaw "nation" was not equally committed to the grant or the treaty.

When talks resumed on April 1, the order of proceeding was ostensibly left to the Choctaw. Four Choctaw chiefs spoke on the subject of the land grant. The grantors of the land spoke first and last, while in between were the speeches of the Choctaw tribal war chief (after being empowered to speak by his village peace chief) and the leading Choctaw peace chief. The British would recognize these four with "great medals."

First, Tomatly Mingo of the Sixtowns asserted his authority to speak as the most senior of the Imoklasha moiety: "It is the Custom of the Red Men to take Preceedence according to their Seniority, I am of the Race of Imongolatcha & in Consequence the Second in Rank in the Chactaw Nation, the Race of Ingholakta is before me, but on this day being Invested by the Consent of the Chiefs with the Authority of the Pipe and other enseigns of Peace, I now take place of Alibamo Mingo, Altho I acknowledge him to be my Superior." Tomatly Mingo then stated that the land grant was to be officially given by those who had the authority to give it, namely himself and Nassuba Mingo of Chickasawhays, "Altho the Land is Said to Belong to the whole Nation."[49] Clearly, the location of the grant, which was between the Chickasawhay-Pascagoula River on the west, the Mobile River on the east, and Sinte Bogue (Snake Bayou) on the north between them, was the material issue here: it was directly to the southeast of the Chickasawhays villages, which were in turn allied with the Sixtowns or Six Villages.[50] Tomatly Mingo asserted his understanding that in return the Choctaw would receive a trade house at the French Fort Tombecbé site and dignified treatment from the traders. He also explicitly mentioned the Choctaw requirement of presents: "If I am become their [the English] Son, they must Act the part of a Father by Supplying my Wants by proper presents."[51] The presents are thus plainly stated to be part of the fictive kinship relation.

Tomatly Mingo finished and then rose again to address an omission: he explicitly exempted from the agreement the lands occupied by the Choctaw-related Naniaba, Tohome, and Mobilian "small tribes" from the Tombigbee forks down into the Mobile-Tensaw delta.[52] As a Sixtowns Choctaw he could not have even pretended to speak for these groups, which although they were termed "Choctaws settled on the Mobile River" by Jean Christophe de Lusser in a 1732 census, were if anything related to the Chickasawhays and Conchas, as we have seen.[53] But Tomatly Mingo clearly believed that the British might consider their lands included in a "Choctaw" grant.

The second speaker, Tabuka of West Yazoo, asserting his own authority to speak as an Imoklasha, characterized himself as a peace chief and deputized his authority to the war chief Chulustamastabe of his village: "For my part I dont Talk much I have allways been a Man to make Union Among the Warriors, I am the Chief it is True, & in Consequence hold up this white Wand as a Sign of the peace but all the other Powers I have given to Shulustamastabe who is more Capable."[54] There was no particular reason for him to speak except to grant this authority to Chulustamastabe; despite the development of the power of the office of war chief because of European contact, this formal act by Tabuka suggests that it was not seen as ceremonially authoritative for peace negotiations. In the ensuing negotiations Chulustamastabe thus took the role of formal speaker for his peace chief. Yet the British did not seem to recognize this deputized status, and Chulustamastabe rather than his peace chief eventually received the British medal.

The third speaker was Alibamon Mingo of Concha, by then the most senior of the Choctaw chiefs.[55] It is unclear why Alibamon Mingo should have come, except to be assured of retaining his influence through the present he could expect to receive. His presence must have been an important coup for Chulustamastabe and the Red Captain. Fully and frankly pro-French, Alibamon Mingo could not be ignored or the congress proceed with any semblance of believability without him. He first bemoaned his feebleness, then asserted his seniority:

> You Favre have allways heard me Speak in every Assembly, Since you was a Boy, but now that I am Old without Teeth, half Blind, and all the Race Convened to give their Sentiments, perhaps it may not be proper for me to Speak.[56] Nevertheless I feel myself so fired with the Occasion that I cannot refrain.
>
> I am of the Great Race of Ingulacta, I am Master of the whole Chactaw Nation by Birth, by Long Employment & by Long Experience it is to me to give Instruction to the rest, I have made alliance with the other Race of Imongulacha, and we have agreed that our Talk Should be one.[57]

But Alibamon Mingo made no bones about his having been pro-French and about his wait-and-see attitude toward the British. He claimed that he was not consulted about the land grant since those who made it had the authority to do so. He was ready to accede to it, however, on condition that the British not make good on Stuart's threat to cashier the French medal chiefs and that the traders behave more circumspectly toward Choctaw women. Finally, he reminded the British that the grant was a usufruct grant, not one that would alienate the land from the Choctaw.[58]

Though formally endorsing the negotiations, Alibamon Mingo thus distanced himself from the land grant decision and even from the proceedings themselves. He was an Eastern Choctaw and the leading Inholahta, hence the leading peace chief of the Choctaw, a position he had held uncontested since the end of the civil war in 1750. The only land affected by the grant was that of the Chickasawhays, and Alibamon Mingo would not have been concerned except in a general way. Yet he stood strongly against any British attempt to manipulate Choctaw politics by depriving existing medal chiefs of their medals and access to presents; in this he was clearly speaking for at least all of the pro-French chiefs.[59] "If they wish to gain the affection of my people" as the French had, Alibamon Mingo said, the British "will be equally Bountyfull."[60]

The final speaker was Nassuba Mingo of Chickasawhay, the second of the chiefs actually making the grant.[61] He first described his career as a peace chief: "The latter part of my Days has passed near a Talker to the Great Spirit, he was a Man of Soft & Peaceable manner, instead of embroiling, he endeavoured to Conciliate. Since I saw the Beauty of his Conduct it affected my heart, & I have endeavoured to follow his Example, So that the English may depend my Talk will be for Peace."[62] He then urged the British to quiet Choctaw unease about the grant—"Some people are angry that we have given so much Land"—by performing their part of the agreement promptly and generously. Like the others, he sounded the theme of presents: "The English . . . have said they have all things in greater abundance than the French, so I expect my people will receive presents in greater abundance, and if we do not, it must proceed from want of affection, in their Father, & not from want of Ability. I do not speak for myself but for my Warriors, their Wives & their Children, whom I cannot Cloathe or keep in order without presents."[63]

This issue of the people actually empowered to make the land grant being those whose land was seen as being granted has powerful implications for the understanding of the "Choctaw" identity that we have been talking about. Scholarly literature stresses the "corporateness" of Indian landholding. Here the power to alienate land—however little alienated it may have been believed to be—clearly rested with a segment of what Europeans called the

Choctaw, this particular land probably being considered Chickasawhays-Sixtowns hunting grounds. This fact makes it clear that the Choctaw confederacy was still made up of autonomous parts.

Another important point regarding the land grant may be the terms of relationship in which it is expressed. The British speeches make much of the "father-child" relationship as modeling the British-Choctaw relation being established, but the Choctaw use different terms. When the Choctaw speak of the land grant itself they constantly refer to granting it to their English brothers to use, and they repeatedly emphasize that the British will be sharing the land with the Choctaw. Although the English treaty text certainly asserts British ownership of the land, these speeches indicate that the Choctaw understood something else by it.[64]

The Choctaw expectation of receiving presents was crucial to granting the land for use to the British. The area in question had previously been used by the French, and the Choctaw had steadily exchanged presents with them to maintain the fictive kinship-reciprocity relationship that permitted such use and removed from it the stigma of alienation. Yet the Choctaw knew full well that it was not British policy to supply their allies with presents in the same manner. In 1746, on the eve of the outbreak of the Choctaw civil war, the Alabama war chief Tamatlé Mingo had warned the Choctaw not to expect any presents from the English, who were only useful for the trade of items other than guns and ammunition.[65] He knew this firsthand because the Alabama had pioneered a "play-off" system, copied when possible by most of the southeastern tribes. The Alabama received guns and ammunition as gifts from the French, maintained free by a French gunsmith; cloth and metal items in trade from the British for most of the deerskins they had harvested with French guns; and an alliance relationship with the French maintained by presents of the rest of the skins, although the officials who profited by them seldom reported their existence.[66] And here, though certainly the Choctaw did not come empty-handed to Mobile, no mention is made of presents to the British leaders either.

On the British side, the speeches from Johnstone and Stuart carefully do not mention any future presents. Instead they adjure the Choctaw to earn their trade goods by being industrious hunters. As they tell it, British reciprocity for the use of the land will be to grow provisions on it so as to host the Choctaw when they visit. Yet they also carefully set no regular future meetings. The Choctaw chiefs were aware of these points; their explicit and frequent mention of presents in this "land grant" segment of the speeches made it plain that the food supplied to guests was the least of what they expected. The chiefs literally required the presents to maintain the very influence for which the British were honoring them. It is likely that Chulustamastabe and the Red Captain had promised a great deal to persuade the chiefs to negotiate with the British. After their good treatment in Augusta, their time as Stuart's guest in Charles Town, and their voyage to Mobile, they themselves probably believed that the presents they had promised would actually be forthcoming.

Most of the activities on April 2 were directly conducted by the three participants in the Augusta congress, the Chickasaw Paya Mattaha and the Choctaws Chulustamastabe and Red Captain. They began with a naming ceremony to "adopt" the British dignitaries as fictive Choctaws so that the British could become participants in the reciprocity arrangements the Choctaw had been talking about. As the war chief or "red shoes" Chulustamastabe conducted the ceremony. It very clearly articulated what the Choctaw saw as the political situation they confronted. Johnstone was named "Support of the Imoklashas" (Imoklasha Mataha)—the moiety that had led the pro-British faction since Red Shoe's day—by the West Yazoo peace chief, Tabuka. This fact joins with the precedence taken by the Imoklashas in general to confirm that they were here taking the lead in relations with the English because of the long-standing English alliance and the fact that the land cession being made was wholly or partially under the control of Imoklashas. Next, Indian agent John Stuart was flatteringly and perhaps hopefully named "Great Support of the Choctaws" (Chactamataha Chitto) by Chulustamastabe of West Yazoo. Interestingly, Lt. Col. David Wedderburne, the British military commander, was named "Support of the Calumet Chief" (Fanimingo Mataha) by the peace chief Nassuba Mingo.[67] Wedderburne was thus given the fanimingo task: to take the part of the Choctaw in the councils of his own people, to serve as English calumet chief.[68] Note that Nassuba Mingo's speech on the previous day suggested that he may himself have been a calumet chief.

Finally, Montault de Monberaut was named "Support of the Inholahtas" (Inholahta Mataha)—the predominantly pro-French moiety—by Appopaye of West Abeka.[69] It is interesting that the Frenchman chosen by the British as their liaison with the Indians, the man who had masterminded Creek and Cherokee attacks on the British of South Carolina during the French and Indian War, should be made a leading Inholahta and thus higher in rank than Johnstone.[70] The Choctaw gave this same name—with the addition of the honorific "Chitto"—to French governor Kerlérec in 1754.[71] It also may be significant that Appopaye gave the name: presumably he was an Inholahta himself, but his name suggests that he was also a "prophet," or shaman.[72]

Chulustamastabe then proceeded to announce himself as speaking with one voice for "his nation" in the European manner:

> I now arise to Speak for myself & people, it is the Custom of the English & other Nations amongst whom I have been, to appoint one or two persons in great Assemblies to deliver the Sentiments of the whole, in this I Chuse to follow their Example rather than that of my own Countrymen . . . I have been in many Nations where the Sentiments of the people were allways delivered by one Chosen for that purpose, the Chactaws only have the Rage of Speaking, & all want to be Orators.[73]

Leaving aside the chief's desire to impress his British patrons with what he had learned in South Carolina, we can stop for a moment and consider how closely Adair echoes this observation: "Those who know the Choktah, will firmly agree . . . that they are in the highest degree . . . ready-witted, and endued with a surprizing flow of smooth artful language on every subject, within the reach of their ideas . . . they far exceed any society of people I ever saw."[74] This Choctaw "rage of speaking" was the bête noire of the French governors, who repeatedly complained of enduring days of it at every annual present giving. Here Chulustamastabe derailed the normal practice, in which many speakers made their opinions public to form consensus, and by doing so he in some sense dictated consensus instead of listening for it. The establishment of consensus would have been especially important to the Choctaw as a coherent confederacy, probably much more important than it was to the Cherokee or Chickasaw, or to Creek subdivisions such as the Alabama, with their slighter ethnic diversity. The fact that this would-be cultural broker short-circuited the major means of reaching consensus suggests either that his claims of wide acquaintance with diplomacy were overstated or that on this occasion it might not have been to Chulustamastabe's advantage for all the Choctaw chiefs to express themselves fully.

Chulustamastabe himself nevertheless reminded his British hosts once more of the need for presents, expressing the hope that "you will not send us home empty." He then summarized Choctaw expectations of the British, agreeing to land cessions in return for favorable Creek trade rates and continued peace with the Chickasaw. He ended by presenting his own adherents with rewards, emphasizing finally in deed as well as word the necessity of presents.[75]

The next part of the ceremonies is not well defined in the document. Apparently the Choctaw chiefs handed over their French medals and commissions, led off by Mingo Houma of East Immongoulacha, who asked the British for another medal and for a present of powder and guns for the hunt in return. Presumably, the rest of the French medal chiefs made the same request.[76] After the surrendering of the medals, the Chickasaw chief Paya Mattaha spoke of the Augusta congress and the favorable terms already received from the British by himself and Chulustamastabe and the Red Captain, brandishing a copy of the written treaty. The Red Captain then spoke of his British flag and medal and urged the Choctaw to forget partisanship.[77]

The record of April 3 is rather puzzling, but it indicates how unreliable Chulustamastabe's claims of consensus were. In the compressed report by the British secretary only one chief's speech is detailed to stand for all. Poucha Houma of Concha, a pro-French chief, harped upon the importance of the grant, the fact that the land was to be shared, and the necessity for the British to repay the Choctaw for it. Oddly, he demanded rum, which he referred to as "English drink"—both Johnstone and Stuart had inveighed against the turmoil that had been introduced among the Chickasaw by the British traders with rum.[78] The day's talks, then, appear to have been given over to just the sort of lengthy opinion venting that Chulustamastabe wished to avoid, naming conditions and demands that the British preferred not to report fully, probably because they continued to express demands for presents.

The record of the last day, April 4, simply consists of the treaty text, the signatures of the chiefs present, and the agreed trade schedule, to which is appended a rather briefer British ceremony creating medal chiefs.[79] Great medals were given to the Chickasaw Paya Mattaha and five Choctaw chiefs, each chosen for an obvious reason by the British and by no means representative: Alibamon Mingo (the most powerful of the Choctaw chiefs, even though pro-French), Captain Houma (the Red Captain) and Chulustamastabe (the two pro-British chiefs who had already met at Augusta), and Tomatly Mingo and Nassuba Mingo (the two chiefs who were actually ceding the land). Small medals were then granted to five more Choctaws, even less representative: Appopaye of West Abeka, Mingo Ouma of West Immongoulacha, Toupa Houma of Kafetalaya (these three from the Western Division), Oulactopaye of

Seneacha (Sixtowns), and Poucha Ouma of Concha (Eastern Division).[80] The congress then adjourned.

As far as the British record goes, that was the end of it; they had obtained their land concessions and considered that particular negotiation complete. Such was not the case, however, for the Choctaw, as Montault de Monberaut reported in the *Mémoire justificatif*. He describes a second, perfectly symmetrical meeting between the Eastern Choctaw and John Stuart and David Wedderburne two to three weeks later, after Johnstone had departed for Pensacola.[81] Montault de Monberaut was certainly at least as biased a reporter as was Arthur Gordon, and his account is a summary of a few pages, but having examined in detail the first part of the congress, we can see that the ceremonial structure of the second part is perfectly comparable.

On the day of arrival or the following day, initial overtures took place. Stuart apparently spoke to the Choctaw and described what he wanted: the handing over of French medals, gorgets, and commissions, just as the Western and Sixtowns Choctaws had already done. The Indians, led by Mingo Emitta, first mentioned the disappointment of the Western Choctaw with the skimpy quality and quantity of the presents they had received, comparing them with the excellence of the French presents they had been accustomed to receive. Montault de Monberaut says that after this first exchange the Choctaw chiefs withdrew to discuss their response.

A three-day delay intervened (compare the four-day gap after initial presentations in the previous session), during which Montault de Monberaut and the interpreters Favré and Renochon discussed the issues with the Choctaw. Initially, the Choctaw refused to give up their French medals and commissions; the interpreters' report of their refusal sent Stuart and Wedderburne off to the country and intensified Montault de Monberaut's negotiation efforts. Yet the Eastern Choctaw could hardly have been surprised at this request, since they had already spoken with the Western chiefs. It may be that Chulustamastabe had promised them some sort of dispensation, or that they had expected Stuart to give in, or that their resistance was a negotiation ploy to secure better presents; at any rate, there was a pause for the chiefs to settle their position. In two days of persuasion Montault de Monberaut focused on the necessity of their continuing to receive presents, stressing how without them they would fall from being "dominant chiefs and the most respected of their Nation" to "objects of contempt in that Nation of which they had been the oracles."[82] If the Choctaw knew that Wedderburne had been named calumet chief, they may have expected that he was similarly arguing their side with Stuart.

The congress resumed on the fifth day with Stuart's repetition of his earlier speech, followed by speeches from individual chiefs, although Montault de Monberaut does not give sequence and subject details. On the sixth day the chiefs and captains surrendered their marks of French rank, with the lowest-ranked "captains" going first, followed by the small medal chiefs and then the three great medal chiefs, Mingo Emitta (Tiou Oulacta), Tchoukooulacta, and Mingo Ouma.[83] The actions of the latter three are described in detail: holding the insignia they had removed, they first greeted Montault de Monberaut, then placed the insignia before Stuart. And Montault de Monberaut does at least describe their speeches, revealing how they had determined to reconcile their reluctance. They would be, they said, not replacing their old French father (Montault de Monberaut) but rather adding a new one (Stuart). And they repeated their request for the presents a father should provide. This request was doomed to disappointment, as they presumably received the same kind of presents given to the Western chiefs.

Taking both parts of the congress into consideration brings the Choctaw and British aims into sharper focus. To the British the main issue was plainly the land grant, which got Johnstone's personal attention; the medal exchange was important, but secondary. To the Choctaw, on the other hand, the main issue was the shift in allegiance and the assurance of a steady supply of presents; the two segments of the congress were of a piece. For them, usufruct of land by fictive kin friends was a minor issue. The main hurdle was deciding to allow the British that fictive kinship in the first place. This decision was easy for the Western Choctaw, who had been informally allied with the British periodically for years, and they had apparently persuaded the Sixtowns and Chickasawhays to go along. But the Eastern Choctaw, always the strongest allies of the French, had a harder time in adjusting and presumably expected to be courted more assiduously rather than being left to Stuart and Wedderburne alone.

What did the congress achieve? Not much, as far as the British were concerned. British settlers came to Mobile, but the British failed to uphold their side of the reciprocity. They initially provided but soon discontinued the promised commissary and gunsmith, and although Stuart had compiled a detailed list of hundreds of Choctaws who had received presents from the

French, with their towns and ranks, the British never offered additional presents; the Choctaw accordingly began to raid settlements in the ceded area.[84] In 1771 Governor Peter Chester wrote, "I am informed that they have already said they had given us their Lands upon a promise of having congresses, and now we are in possession of them, we think no more of performing our agreements." John Stuart thus felt compelled to assemble another congress; each side upbraided the other for its bad behavior.[85] Yet constantly, despite the death of most chiefs recognized in 1765, the old theme of presents, or rather the lack of them, was heard. This time it was the Western Choctaw who declined to attend the congress, for by then the influence of the Spaniards west of the Mississippi was beginning to be felt. The Frenchman Jean de la Villebeuvre had begun his Indian diplomacy on behalf of Spanish Louisiana, giving the Choctaw once more the opportunity to maintain their autonomy by playing Europeans off against one another.[86]

The economic dependency that Richard White's analysis saw in the evolving relationship between the Choctaw and Euro-Americans certainly reflected an economic reality, and its beginnings can readily be seen even in the colonial period, as White suggested.[87] But *within* what evolved as the historic Choctaw confederacy in the eighteenth century, the political realities of small-scale, kinship-regulated social units remained alive and thus explain the confederacy's resilience. The prestige goods changed, but chiefs still expected that reciprocity would define an advantageous relationship, and they retained the power to think of the Europeans as socially poor when they failed to live up to that expectation.

The Choctaw war chief Chulustamastabe was correct in 1765 when he asserted that in speaking alone for the Choctaw nation he was doing something novel. Yet clearly he was not speaking for all the Choctaws, even on the evidence of this congress, and the British were mistaken in understanding him to have asserted a Choctaw corporate unity that could be so dealt with. In attempting to negotiate with the Choctaw on such terms they were disappointed, as the later history of Choctaw-British relations demonstrates.

Why, then, did the Choctaw choose to continue with a fiction of unity? By the end of the eighteenth century their confederacy as such remained the largest population unit in the Old Southwest, the single Native group with whom all whites were compelled to deal. Had they insisted upon segmentary sovereignty, none of the constituent divisions was large enough to demand such attention. Further, it is doubtful that they saw any particular contradiction in making tactical unity of their plurality, only political advantage. In the Choctaw civil war they had come dangerously close to pushing factional differences so far as to make such tactical unity impossible, and they did not do so again. Thus they deprived Europeans of the chance to divide and to definitively conquer.

Acknowledgments

An earlier draft of this paper was presented at the 1992 American Historical Association meeting in the session "Surviving the Frontier," organized by Daniel Mandell. I am grateful to the commentator, James Merrell, for his advice on that version and to a group of anonymous reviewers for their criticisms of a revised version for publication in *Ethnohistory*; I take full responsibility for this final version.

Notes

1. D'Abbadie to Kerlérec, November 6, 1763, AC, série C13A, 43:235–38, translated in Rowland, Sanders, and Galloway, *Mississippi Provincial Archives*, 5:293, series hereafter cited as MPA:FD.

2. This complex and cumbersome terminology reflects a social structure that defies the timeless and spaceless ideal categories defined by Service, *Primitive Social Organization*; Fried, *The Evolution of Political Society*; and Sahlins, *Tribesmen*. The divisions of the Choctaw "tribe" evident in the eighteenth century originated in a century-long process of confederation that was not complete when the Choctaw emerged into history around 1700. To call them a "tribe" is incorrect in any technical anthropological sense, although the constituent divisions, all coming from more or less destabilized chiefdoms, may have been, in effect, intact tribal segments. Nor is it appropriate to call each Choctaw town a "chiefdom," as Richard White has done (*The Roots of Dependency*, 37–38), for the coercive authority element is missing. There is no single center of power among the Choctaw anywhere but rather a "heterarchy" of many division and subdivisional segment chiefs, none of them wielding significant power, who together almost never achieved complete consensus (see Crumley, "A Dialectical Critique"). In fact, White believes that this kind of structure—or lack of it—developed as a result of eighteenth-century contact (*The Roots of Dependency*, 64–65), but there are good reasons to argue that it was instead an artifact of the historical process of confederacy formation and was simply adaptively successful for the Choctaw in the context of extended European contact.

3. The arguments for this version of Choctaw ethnogenesis are presented in a full-length monograph (Galloway, *Choctaw Genesis*). A summary of this research appears as Galloway, "Confederacy as a Solution."

4. For a close reading of the documents recording the journey and Tonti's diplomatic efforts among the Choctaw and Chickasaw see Galloway, "Henri de Tonti du village des Chacta."

5. See Le Moyne d'Iberville, *Iberville's Gulf Journals*, 174.

6. This list, transcribed from the Delisle Papers in the Archives nationales, has been printed by George Kernion in "Documents Concerning the History," 20–21.

7. The Chickasawhays indicated to the missionary Father Baudouin in 1728 that they had obtained permission from Bienville to take refuge from slave raids west of the Mobile River, most probably not long after 1702; Baudouin to Salmon, November 23, 1732, translated in *MPA:FD*, 1:156–57. The archaeological evidence of pottery typology confirms this particular population movement; see Mooney, "Migration of the Chickasawhays."

8. See Swanton, *Source Material*, 57.

9. Henri de Tonti's letter of 1702 written during his trip into the Choctaw and Chickasaw nations indicates that the Choctaws already had deerskins prepared for sale for the European market, presumably intending to sell them to the British; the British, however, were finding the Choctaws themselves the more attractive commodity. Tonti witnessed Chickasaw-Chakchiuma slaving parties led by an Englishman against the Choctaw and was actually able to free one Choctaw captive by paying a ransom to his Chickasaw captor (see Galloway, "Henri de Tonti du village des Chacta").

10. Smith, *Archaeology*, 25–26, 36–41.

11. James Adair, the most famous and certainly the best self-publicist of the British Indian traders, grudgingly admired the French understanding of Indian ways in the use of presents but misunderstood their real function. See Adair, *History*, 302.

12. Nairne's journey and his project are outlined in Nairne, *Nairne's Muskhogean Journals*.

13. Baudouin to Salmon, November 23, 1732, translated in *MPA:FD*, 1:157.

14. Bienville to Pontchartrain, October 12, 1708, translated in *MPA:FD*, 3:3.

15. Baudouin to Salmon, November 23, 1732.

16. See Father Baudouin's description in *MPA:FD*, 1:156–58.

17. Richard White has placed this incident at around 1715, but the earlier date, possible in view of Father Baudouin's assertion that the creation of the great chief happened at a date that was "twenty or twenty-five years ago" in 1732, makes more sense, since it also coincided with the Chickasawhay and Concha migration into the homeland area. (Note that in the previously published text the sense of this sentence was unaccountably and incorrectly reversed.)

18. Another of Baudouin's observations, in *MPA:FD*, 1:156.

19. These relationship terms are scattered through French reports of Choctaw diplomacy, and they are strongly correlated with the protohistoric and early historic relationships to other groups in the region as just outlined; see Galloway, *Choctaw Genesis*.

20. Given that most of the historic southeastern tribes, including the Choctaw, were the inheritors of the hierarchically organized, probably theocratic mound-building chiefdoms of late prehistory and that some of them were still carrying their chiefs around on litters in life and honoring them with human sacrifice in death at the time of European contact, it is interesting to speculate on the degree to which this determined egalitarianism was the product of the memory of chiefdom collapse.

21. As Bienville wrote in a 1733 report on the Indians after his return to Louisiana, "Each of these [by this time 111] chiefs by means of the present which he receives and which he knows how to distribute expediently forms himself a party which he has at his command independently of the Great Chief who has only the name, so that to move the mass of the nation one must win all these different chiefs who ordinarily value themselves according to the circumstances, which causes considerable expense" (*MPA:FD*, 1:195).

22. The Choctaws themselves cooperated in making such arrangements; for a 1746 example see *MPA:FD*, 4:265.

23. Later the Eastern, Concha, Western, and Sixtowns Divisions.

24. Bossu and Romans, cited in Swanton, *Source Material*, 163–66.

25. See discussion in White, *The Roots of Dependency*, 52–55.

26. This effect is so powerful in the French documents that the early translator and editor of the Mississippi Provincial Archives series believed that only one man bore this name, as the footnotes show. The name itself, variously represented in the French documents as Soulouche Ouma, Soulier Rouge, or Soulouche Oumastabé and by the English as Red Shoes, apparently represents the Choctaw *shulush* (a loanword from the French *soulier*) *humma* (red) *imastabi* (he took and killed) (see Swanton, *Source Material*, 94n120; Byington, *A Dictionary*). It seems to be connected with the practice, reported for the Chickasaws, of the war chief's conferring red moccasins on a newly initiated warrior who had killed his first man.

27. See White, *The Roots of Dependency*, 54–62, and "Red Shoes."

28. See Régis du Roullet to Périer, February 21, 1731, and March 16, 1731, in MPA:FD, 4:61–62, 65.

29. Régis du Roullet to Périer, 16 March 1731, in MPA:FD, 4:65–72.

30. See Galloway, "Choctaw Factionalism."

31. This perceptive conclusion is by Richard White: "The conflicting interests and loyalties of the various parts of Choctaw society came to be the best insurance the nation had against European domination. . . . Choctaw independence was maintained not through unity, but through divisiveness. . . . The genius of Choctaw factionalism lay in its ability to avert . . . [economic] dominance and turn the internal divisions . . . to the nation's advantage" (*The Roots of Dependency*, 64–65).

32. Choctaw descent rules were regularly noted by Europeans during the eighteenth century as reckoning through the mother, or matrilineal (see Swanton, *Source Material*, 76–90). The regularity with which female ownership of Choctaw land appears in the nineteenth-century Armstrong Roll recording Choctaw land claims suggests that residence was also matrilocal. Matrilineal-matrilocal rules tend to connect geographical stability with genealogical identity.

33. Some balance is offered by Henri Montault de Monberaut's amazing *Mémoire justificatif*. Montault de Monberaut, the erstwhile French commandant of Fort Toulouse, served temporarily in 1765 as John Stuart's deputy Indian agent among the previously French-allied southern Indians.

34. Detailed analysis of formal European-Indian meetings has not generally been concerned with the praxis of Native diplomacy, but recent work on the Iroquois shows that Native control of form and content was not unusual. See Foster, "On Who Spoke First"; Hagedorn, "'A Friend to Go between Them.'"

35. The principal source for the 1765 Choctaw congress held in Mobile is a document recording it by Arthur Gordon in the Public Record Office, Colonial Office Class 5, vol. 582, reprinted in Rowland, *Mississippi Provincial Archives: English Dominion*, 215–55.

36. "Chulustamastabe" is apparently a British spelling of *shulush humma imastabi*; although the spelling varies even in the document, this one will be used from now on to refer to this man. The "Red Captain" also bore a *humma* name in Choctaw (connected by Swanton with a warrior rank). "Captain" is a title used by Europeans to refer to a minor chief (Swanton, *Source Material*, 94). "Paya Mattaha" is Chickasaw *hopaye* (Byington defines the Choctaw equivalent, *hopaii*, as war prophet, military leader, seer [*Dictionary*]) and probably *imataha* (in Choctaw, supporter, bulwark), or "supporting (war) prophet." Swanton says that the *hopaii* epithet was conferred on war leaders whose charisma and medicine were particularly compelling and successful (*Source Material*, 94). Yet Swanton quotes Speck to the effect that the Chickasaws had a *hopaye* for each moiety "who attended to its spiritual interests" (Speck, "Notes"), and Adair refers to the conduct of peace-making ceremonies by the "old beloved man," or "magus," who wore *white* shoes (Swanton, "Social and Religious Beliefs," 237), so it seems that this *hopaye*, the leading Chickasaw

chief of his era, may have been a peace chief. Clearly, the epithet deserves more systematic investigation.

37. Alden, *John Stuart*, 183–86.

38. Howard and Rea, *Mémoire Justificatif*, 149–55.

39. Rowland, *Mississippi Provincial Archives: English Dominion*, 659.

40. Compare the specific opening exchanges of wampum meant to "kindle the fire" at Anglo-Iroquois councils in Foster, "On Who Spoke First."

41. Adair, *History*, 299.

42. Adair, *History*, 237; it may be that Paya Mattaha was qualified for this role.

43. Rowland, *Mississippi Provincial Archives: English Dominion*, 659–72.

44. Chulustamastabe's speech is in Rowland, *Mississippi Provincial Archives: English Dominion*, 672–74.

45. I have argued elsewhere that the matrilineal Choctaw understood that such a relationship entitled them to indulgent treatment by their European "fathers" and that it actually modeled quite well the affinal relationship of a father in Choctaw society. See Galloway, "The Chief Who Is Your Father."

46. See Rowland, *Mississippi Provincial Archives: English Dominion*, 674–81. The threat of Pontiac's rebellion accounts at least in part for the British motivation to win over the Choctaw at this particular time.

47. The speech is summarized in one sentence in the record of the congress (Rowland, *Mississippi Provincial Archives: English Dominion*, 681–82), but his own account of it is available in the *Mémoire justificatif*.

48. Rowland, *Mississippi Provincial Archives: English Dominion*, 682.

49. Tomatly Mingo's name is not unique either to him or to the Choctaws, but its meaning is uncertain. It may represent Choctaw *tamaha* (town) and *tali* (stone) or *tala* (palmetto), and its frequency may simply be explained by common environmental settings of southeastern Indian towns (see Byington, *Dictionary*). The two Choctaw moieties, Inholahta and Imoklasha, crosscut the confederacy and its divisions. Membership in them determined marriage rules and burial ritual, but they apparently had even greater political significance, still only poorly understood: the "senior" Inholahta moiety was "white," or apparently the "peace party," while the Imoklashas were the "red," or "war party." Swanton (*Source Material*, 78), quoting from a confused British source, transposes them, but more telling here is the fact that Alibamon Mingo was an Inholahta, while the preponderance of war chiefs seem to have been Imoklashas. See Rowland, *Mississippi Provincial Archives: English Dominion*, 683, 685.

50. This grant is clearly marked on the 1772 map of the Mobile Bay and delta region in Public Record Office, Colonial Office Class 700 America North and South, Florida 51. Recall that the region had only been inhabited by the Chickasawhays and Sixtowns for some fifty years and had not been settled, though it was used for hunting for hundreds of years before that.

51. Rowland, *Mississippi Provincial Archives: English Dominion*, 684; Tomatly Mingo reiterates the need for presents several times.

52. Rowland, *Mississippi Provincial Archives: English Dominion*, 686–87.

53. Rowland, *Mississippi Provincial Archives: English Dominion*, 117.

54. Rowland, *Mississippi Provincial Archives: English Dominion*, 687. Tabuka, frequently rendered in French as "taboka," may reflect the Choctaw *tabokoa*, "meridian, noon, highest point" (see Byington, *Dictionary*).

55. *Alibamon mingo* means "chief of/among the Alabamas," and it likely expresses the historic genealogical and diplomatic connection between the Eastern Choctaw and the Alabama.

56. This reference is to Jean Favré, longtime Choctaw interpreter under the French who had been hired by the British and was interpreting on this occasion. See Galloway, "Talking with Indians." Alibamon Mingo's action in first specifically addressing himself to the French interpreter rather than treating him as an invisible mediating device probably also has political significance and may even have been meant to be insulting: he thus foregrounds the fact that the British are receiving his talk through a Frenchman.

57. Rowland, *Mississippi Provincial Archives: English Dominion*, 688. As the leading Inholahta chief Alibamon Mingo automatically assumed the authority of the senior moiety, but his authority also stemmed from his past deeds. Without his formal statement, the negotiations probably could not have proceeded. The speech is a fine example of the rhetorical universality of the modesty topos.

58. Rowland, *Mississippi Provincial Archives: English Dominion*, 689–91.

59. According to Montault de Monberaut, this was the very complaint that made most of the Eastern Division chiefs reluctant to relinquish their French medals (Howard and Rea, *Mémoire Justificatif*, 149–53).

60. Rowland, *Mississippi Provincial Archives: English Dominion*, 688.

61. Nassuba Mingo may be from the Choctaw *nashoba* (wolf) (see Byington, *Dictionary*).

62. Rowland, *Mississippi Provincial Archives: English Dominion*, 691–92. It is intriguing to speculate upon the identity of Nassuba Mingo's "Talker to the Great Spirit"; although this person was probably a Choctaw mentor, there is also a possibility that the conduct of Jesuit Father Baudouin, who lived at Chickasawhay from 1729 to 1746, had had some effect after all (there were few conversions). See Delanglez, *French Jesuits*, 451–77. According to Delanglez, Baudouin accompanied the French governors to the annual present-giving ceremonies even after he became the superior of the Jesuit mission in New Orleans in 1749.

63. Rowland, *Mississippi Provincial Archives: English Dominion*, 692, 693.

64. See Galloway, "The Chief Who Is Your Father," for a discussion of the use of these terms of relationship in diplomacy.

65. Another chief with a similar tamaha tali/tala name. See Jadart de Beauchamp, Journal, September 16–October 19, 1746, AC, série C13A, 30:222–40, translated in MPA:FD, 4:269–97 (see 288–89).

66. Alabama neutrality was effective in preserving them through the colonial period. See Crane, *The Southern Frontier*; and Alden, *John Stuart*.

67. Rowland, *Mississippi Provincial Archives: English Dominion*, 694.

68. See Galloway, "The Chief Who Is Your Father."

69. Rowland, *Mississippi Provincial Archives: English Dominion*, 694.

70. Montault de Monberaut had been the commandant of the most eastward French post in the Southeast, Fort Toulouse near present-day Montgomery AL. See the introduction to Howard and Rea, *Mémoire Justificatif*.

71. Kerlérec to De Machault d'Arnouville, December 18, 1754, in MPA:FD, 5:155.

72. The name seems to contain the *hopaii* element discussed in note 36.

73. Rowland, *Mississippi Provincial Archives: English Dominion*, 694–95.

74. Adair, *History*, 283.

75. Rowland, *Mississippi Provincial Archives: English Dominion*, 696.

76. The French medals and commissions were not merely discarded. John Stuart later used a pile of them symbolically to impress the Creek chief The Mortar, and at least one of the Choctaws' French commissions collected on this day, that of Toupa Ouma of Kafetalaya, is preserved to this

day by descendants of the British Player tobacco family (see my "The Medal Chief's *Grosse Lettre*: A Chapter in French-Indian Management Policies," in this volume).

77. Rowland, *Mississippi Provincial Archives: English Dominion*, 698–701.

78. Rowland, *Mississippi Provincial Archives: English Dominion*, 664, 681.

79. Rowland, *Mississippi Provincial Archives: English Dominion*, 712–13.

80. "Oulactoupaye" is probably *inholahta hopaii*, "war prophet of the Inholahtas" (Byington, *Dictionary*), while Swanton interprets "Poucha Ouma" as "meal," or "one-who-pulverizes," followed by "red" (*Source Material*, 123). Another possible suggestion is that the name contains the element *pushka*, meaning "a scratcher."

81. Howard and Rea, *Mémoire Justificatif*, 150–54.

82. Howard and Rea, *Mémoire Justificatif*, 151.

83. See my "Choctaw Names and Choctaw Roles: Another Method for Evaluating Sociopolitical Structure," in this volume. Montault de Monberaut tells us that Mingo Emitta had an alternative name, Tiou Oulacta, which seems clearly to contain the *inholahta* element, as does that of Tchoukooulacta. Mingo Ouma is plainly another red chief.

84. The list is found in two places: Public Record Office, Colonial Office Class 323/23, fols. 193–201, and Class 5/73, 659–762. This extraordinary document apparently includes the names of all the Choctaw men who attended both parts of the congress, and I am indebted to John Juricek for having brought it to my attention.

85. Rowland, *Peter Chester*, 102, 135–59.

86. Holmes, "Juan de la Villebeuvre," 65–82.

87. White, *The Roots of Dependency*, 97–104.

18. The Four Ages of Alibamon Mingo, fl. 1700–1766

A person, seen from the perspective of ethnobiography, is a sequence of culturally patterned relationships, a forever incomplete complex of occasions to which a name has been affixed, a permeable body composed and decomposed through continual relations of participation and opposition.

JAMES CLIFFORD, " 'Hanging up Looking Glasses at Odd Corners' "

Biographizing the Other

In the eighteenth-century Choctaw chief Alibamon Mingo we confront someone whose personal testimony is fragmentary and filtered through the translations of interpreters. His "public life," seen through the eyes of mostly uncomprehending others from entirely different societies, is made up only of events of interest to those others, and his private life is virtually unknown. Therefore, it is presumptuous to undertake to write a biographical essay that is constructed according to the same rules as a biography written about a modern Western person whose many public acts might conceivably be well documented even if very little were known of him or her otherwise.[1] I cannot assume much of anything about Alibamon Mingo's private life or even that he had one in the sense that any modern Western person does. I do not know precisely when he was born or when he died: I am reduced to the historian's floruit when I offer life-span dates, so I will be forced to guess at his age in evaluating his actions. Assumptions I might be able to make about his having adhered to the common practices of his society are also problematic, because

This chapter was originally published as "The Four Ages of Alibamon Mingo, fl. 1700–1766" in the *Journal of Mississippi History* 65, no. 4 (2003): 321–42. It is reprinted by permission of the Mississippi Historical Society.

(1) we know disappointingly little about the common practices of Choctaw society during the eighteenth century, (2) that society was changing significantly during his lifetime, and (3) he was part of those changes. Further, we have only a reasonable idea of what Choctaw society *changed to* by the early nineteenth century but not of what it *started with* when Alibamon Mingo was a child.

Standard Western biographical practice calls for a presentation that has a moral thrust—a temporal life trajectory in which the subject is born, struggles and accomplishes his life project(s) (or fails to do so), and then dies justified or failed according to the conventional social trajectory of his time. To write such a piece, even if I considered it justifiable to assume that Alibamon Mingo had a self constructed like mine, I would have to know what he was trying to accomplish in his life and how he and his society measured his success or failure. For that I have only a few items of testimony by my subject and a few of those who knew him, and I am ill prepared to interpret what they said because I do not share their values and have no means of obtaining access to them. If I write a seamless narrative that claims to deliver a meaningful understanding of a real person, I will inevitably be writing a fiction even more distorted than the everyday fictions of better-documented modern persons.

I want to attempt, therefore, something more modest: to sketch a context for Alibamon Mingo's life and then to examine and compare not only several of the public instances in which we can more clearly hear him speak at length but also his words on those occasions as well. I will make one usual biographical assumption, which is that his life may reasonably be considered an arc from birth to death, but I will be somewhat more specific in referring to the several sequential age grades in terms of which we believe that the Choctaw of his era construed the life course.[2] I will then explore the words of Alibamon Mingo in their contexts in an attempt to understand some of the relationships and perspectives that accrued to his persona over his lifetime. I will be concerned especially with two areas in which expressed relationships could signify power: Alibamon Mingo's genealogical relations and how he might have been acting in behalf of one or several of the social entities of moiety, clan, or matriline at specific times; and Alibamon Mingo's relations with other Choctaw chiefs and the chiefs of other villages, divisions, and polities and how these relations might have been articulated.

Prologue: Choctaw Context, 1700

First, however, I am compelled to make use of historical and anthropological generalizations to reconstruct something of the context in which Alibamon

Mingo emerged to international visibility. In 1765 we know that Alibamon Mingo claimed to be suffering from the infirmities of old age, having lost his teeth and much of his eyesight, and this means that he could have been born around 1700 or somewhat before; it is safe to assume, therefore, that Alibamon Mingo's world was one that had Europeans in it from its beginning, even if only on its margins. He was born into a polity that amounted to a confederation of village groups that had come together during the seventeenth century.[3] His group, the Concha village group, would be known as part of the Eastern Division of the Choctaw confederation of some forty to fifty towns, and the division was located in east-central Mississippi (present-day Kemper and Lauderdale counties). It was probably composed of refugees who had come from the east and from the Moundville prehistoric polity on the Black Warrior River. Finally, the Choctaw Eastern Division had a sustained relationship with the Alabama polity within the Upper Creek confederation, located around the Coosa/Tallapoosa confluence in central Alabama (near present-day Montgomery).

Alibamon Mingo was born into a social environment that had already been drastically altered by the European presence. Spanish explorers had disrupted traditional life with their violence and their contagions a century and a half before. Englishmen began contacting the Chickasaw to the north in the 1680s at the same time as Frenchmen began exploring the Mississippi River to the west. By the turn of the eighteenth century the English had begun arming and paying their Chickasaw allies to capture Choctaws to be sold eastward as slaves, while the Choctaw were condemned to try to defend themselves with bows and arrows against firearms. Hence the arrival of the French on the Gulf Coast in 1699 served the Choctaw as a rescue—everyone had something to gain, as the French on their side sought a Native alliance with a powerful nation that could serve, if armed, as a buffer against an English threat from the east. The Choctaw joined a French alliance in 1702 and gained weapons to defend themselves and other useful trade goods and gifts.[4]

The Choctaw were useful allies for the French and continued to be supported by them in those ways in return for important support for the young French colony during the early years when the English colonies of the Atlantic seaboard, especially South Carolina, reconnoitered the region several times—in 1708 and 1713—to estimate the possibilities for dislodging the French.[5] In each case the Choctaw alliance was strong enough and posed enough of a threat that the English gave up the effort. The Choctaw were supplied early on with several young boys who would grow up to be interpreters and traders.[6] Although the Choctaw requested it several times, the French did not establish a government trade house among them for a long time, not even when in the wake of the Yamassee War against South Carolina they established posts among the Alabama, Natchez, and Yazoo in 1716–18.

Over time the Choctaw remained a large and powerful ally, but with the transfer of the French capital itself from Mobile to New Orleans in 1718 and with an emphasis by French colonizers upon specialty agriculture in the Mississippi valley through the 1720s, the Choctaw were too far from the center of French activity to attract focused management attention from them. Was the young Alibamon Mingo active as one of the several hundred Indians who aided the French in attacking Pensacola during the War of the Spanish Succession in 1719? What did he know of the growth of the French settlements after 1720? We do not know, but the participation of Choctaws in the back-and-forth struggles between European powers must have been instructive to all of them. During all of this time he was maturing far from official European observation; he made his status passage to manhood in some way that we can only infer, and he almost certainly married, though there was never any mention of children.[7] He would probably have been at least the same age as the century, so that by the time he became visible to Europeans he was already past the carelessness of youth.

Natchez Revolt, 1730: Alibamon Mingo as Secondary Chief

The French-Choctaw alliance potentially affected Choctaw sociopolitical organization in many ways. The French were framed in Choctaw terms as a powerful ally whose pseudokinship relation required a constant mutual flow of exchanges. At first the French sought to funnel these exchanges through a limited number of chiefs and thus to manage Choctaw politics and their own expenditures to their advantage. Doubtless there was a serious disconnect here, since, as has been recently pointed out, by the 1730s French presents— much to Bienville's chagrin—were flowing to the French-designated great chief, three divisional chiefs, leading warriors and moiety leaders, and the leaders of influential clan lineages. These presents were used not necessarily to build factions, as Bienville complained, but to maintain the internal relationships cast into relief by the very evolution of the system and to maintain a right and virtuous relationship between the French and the Choctaw.[8]

The relative French neglect of the Choctaw ended in 1729. In that year the Natchez Indians revolted against the expropriation of their land by a tyrannical local commandant and, aided by enslaved Africans who hoped to achieve freedom, killed the French Fort Rosalie garrison and the men of the agricultural settlement, taking French women and children hostage. Besieged two months later by a Choctaw-French army, the Natchez were first forced to give up 51 French women and children and 150 African men and women by capture. Finally, cornered in a fortified position, they called for a truce. At that point Alibamon Mingo, acting as spokesman for the 400–500 Choctaws in the army, addressed the Natchez:

> Do you remember or have you ever heard it said that Indians have remained in such great numbers for two months before forts? You can judge by that our zeal and our devotion for the French. It is therefore useless for you who are only a handful of people beside our nation to persist any longer in being unwilling to surrender the women, children and negroes whom you have to the French who still are good enough to spare you as you see after the treason that you have shown them, for if they had wished to shoot their big guns (speaking of the cannons) you would already be reduced to dust and we will keep you blockaded here to die of hunger, until you have surrendered the women, children and negroes who belong to the French, since we have resolved to sow here our fields and to make a village there, until you have executed what we demand of you.[9]

Alibamon Mingo's rhetoric here offers several possible indications of the character of his leadership. He argued a position that was counter to his culture's hit-and-run style of war making, emphasizing the unusual determination that the Choctaws were demonstrating through the image of actual settlement to perpetuate the siege. But although there is threat of violence in the speech, Alibamon Mingo argues in terms of acceptable expectations, of treason and meeting demands. His "harangue" was effective, to judge by the fact that the remaining French women and children and African slaves were handed over, although the Natchez then escaped and fled in several directions. For the French he had become a significant chief, not only because of his leadership of a large war party, for which in this case he apparently spoke (Soulouche Oumastabé, the red shoe, or war chief, of Couechitto, the Choctaw central town, also made his name in this Natchez war), but, significantly, because of the influence of his word and its power to settle an issue without violence.

Who was Alibamon Mingo by now? How did he arrive at the position that allowed him to play such an active role and thus emerge into the visibility of European documentation in 1730? French visitors, recording lists of Choctaw leaders at this time, observed that he was the second chief of the Concha village group, receiving a coat as a gift in the French present-giving protocol.[10] Certainly, he had attained to that position by proving himself in some way in the context of his own culture, and, as we see here, that proof had probably involved an ability to lead men and the rhetorical mastery in public speaking for which the Choctaw were noted among tribes in the Southeast.[11] By this time it is even quite possible that he was already known in some way to the Natchez leadership.

But even on the occasions when he joined with Red Shoe of Couechitto in fostering trade with the English, which had already happened by 1730, he took something of a temporizing line (or presented himself as having done so), and as time went on the two—though often linked in their actions—seemed to function as foils for one another. In 1729, on an occasion in which Red Shoe and Alibamon Mingo were both answering to the French interpreter Huché for the presence of an English trader, the former said he favored letting the more powerful of the two Europeans carry off the other, while Alibamon Mingo said he would disarm them both and cause them to eat together in peace.[12] Again Alibamon Mingo took the side of negotiated peace. On the other hand, in 1731 he was referred to as Alibamon Ajo (*ajo* probably being the same as Creek *hadjo*, meaning "mad, berserk" and referring to wild, warlike behavior), suggesting that he had some standing as a warrior.

He was listed as second to Asatchioullou as chief of Concha in 1729, but his actions in assisting the French apparently earned him the French great medal for Concha by 1732, although we do not know if he also replaced Asatchioullou as the primary leader of Concha in Choctaw terms.[13] When the Choctaw retained captured Africans in their custody pending French remuneration for their efforts, Alibamon Mingo was responsible in the end for organizing the return of several of them in 1731. At that time he was said to have asked for permission to succeed to the chieftainship of Concha, with the second place being reserved for his brother, Ité Oumastabé.[14]

In 1734 there was a false report of Alibamon Mingo's death at the hands of the Chickasaw, but a clarified report indicated that it was his brother Cougta who had been killed, along with the son of the great chief of the Choctaw.[15] Remarkably, Red Shoe turned to the English for trade in the following year and persuaded Alibamon Mingo to join him in inviting them into the nation. Alibamon Mingo and another brother (Ité Oumastabé?) even defended the English trader who came to Alibamon Mingo's village against a French attempt to arrest him, echoing the 1729 event. Both Red Shoe and Alibamon Mingo were subsequently castigated by the French for their actions and deprived of presents.[16]

As a result of the flight of the Natchez and of asylum offered them by the Chickasaw, the French were determined to prosecute war against the Chickasaw in an attempt to force them to hand over the Natchez. Alibamon Mingo participated in the planning for the war as well as joining with Red Shoe and the great chief of the Choctaw in its prosecution in 1736. In the course of the campaign the French finally built the long-desired Tombecbé post east of the Choctaw. In the actual attack French strategies were thwarted by the great chief's desire for revenge on the southernmost Chickasaw villages, and many French officers were killed. In the retreat Red Shoe tried to convince his warriors to withdraw and abandon the French, while Alibamon Mingo ordered his men to carry off the wounded French officers.[17]

Between the Two Chickasaw Wars, 1738: Alibamon Mingo as Village Chief

In 1738 Alibamon Mingo met with Bienville's nephew Gilles Augustin Payen de Noyan when the latter was sent among the Choctaw to negotiate secure relations. Reportedly, the Choctaw had resumed trading with the English through the Chickasaw, and a Choctaw couple had been murdered recently by some French youths. If the French were planning a second attack on the Chickasaw to force the relinquishment of the Natchez they still harbored, they needed to mend fences with the Choctaw.[18] Noyan sought to meet with Alibamon Mingo and the chief of the Chickasawhay village, calling Alibamon Mingo "the only man capable of offering resistance to Red Shoe." The meeting took place at Chickasawhay and included the two chiefs and Father Baudouin, the Jesuit missionary to the Choctaw who had come in 1728. Alibamon Mingo's speeches as reported by Noyan were lengthy and constituted almost a connected narrative explanation of Choctaw actions from before the Natchez revolt, or over the preceding ten years. Among other things, he informed Noyan that the English had engineered the Natchez revolt by telling them falsely that the Choctaw had agreed to a massive uprising and that Red Shoe was now lost to the French and could not be won back over. But as to his position on an English alliance, Alibamon Mingo explained it as a strategy to seek leverage within the French relationship rather than an irretrievable shift of allegiance:

> They [the English] began by asking to be received [in] the nation as traders, [promising] that they would sell us merchandise more cheaply than would the French. Red Shoe, whom they had won over by presents, declared himself their protector and even made me share his intentions, which were meant, he said to me, only to oblige the French to sell us merchandise at the same price as the English did. Is it astonishing . . . that men who are poor and who are fond of opulence should let themselves be taken in by these enticements? I entered into Red Shoe's plans on condition that when the French had granted us trade at the rate of the English we would dismiss the latter in order not to get into a quarrel with the others, whom our action [in dismissing the English] could not fail to please. The English were therefore brought into the nation. I even established one of their warehouses in my village. My policy had in part the success that I expected from it; the French traders reduced the price of their goods, but it made me lose a great deal more than it made me gain, inasmuch as it involved me in a quarrel with the French chief, who to punish me deprived me for two years of the presents that I had been accustomed to receive.[19]

This explanation seems to frame Alibamon Mingo as chagrined by his failure to understand the consequences of his actions as far as the French were concerned. Yet here he spoke of nothing outside his sphere of competence as the leading chief of the Conchas. His significant relationship with Red Shoe, sometimes alliance but more often opposition, had clearly come to occupy an important place in Alibamon Mingo's world, more important perhaps than the Europeans they were both learning how to manage. He went on to explain that Soulouche Oumastabé had subsequently set up an alliance with the Chickasaw that he was unable to thwart because he had lost influence in the nation as a result of being cut off from his French present, but that he drew on other influence that he had with Native allies in order to rid himself of even the appearance of an English alliance:

> I hesitated no longer about the course that I was to follow. I had already driven the English from my village. I sent back to the Alabamas, who consider me their chief, the flag that these traders had brought me on behalf of their governor so that they might send it back on my behalf to the one who had made me a present of it. At the same time I begged the nations of those

districts to refuse passage to the English, or at least not to furnish them any more guides to come to us, because we did not wish to have any dealings with them any longer. This declaration did not prevent two troops of them from coming under the escort of Red Shoe, who went to find them at Kaapa; but his presence did not prevent one of our young warriors from going and killing on their journey three of their horses, the finest of which belong to Red Shoe. Since that time I have opposed him on all occasions, so that we have several times been on the brink of coming to blows. The French traders, who have often attended our assemblies, will give you testimony about it.[20]

Would that we actually did have the testimony of the French traders who lived so intimately in the nation! In fact, on at least one occasion they reported stern words from Alibamon Mingo to Red Shoe in public meetings.[21] His words here in discussing the events of ten years with Noyan reveal a degree of considered strategic thinking that also discloses, if believable as his own style of thought, a maturity of understanding and an established experimental modus operandi in dealing with Europeans. Alibamon Mingo took extraordinary ceremonial measures to avoid giving offense in his handling of the English flag and his use of the Alabama as his advocates with the English: not only were the Alabama better acquainted with the English, but they were also seen as ceremonially more senior in rank than the entire Choctaw nation and therefore perhaps more appropriate actors in external negotiation.

Alibamon Mingo's statement about his relation to the Alabama is also significant to understanding his situation. The Alabama, he says, consider him their chief. What does this mean? It has been suggested that perhaps he had been adopted and was acting as a *fani mingo*, or domestic exponent, of the Alabama in the councils of the Choctaw; this ceremonial recognition would have given him additional personal power but would also have bound him to specific responsibilities.[22] I still think that it makes more sense to imagine that he was himself the son of an Alabama mother who had married into the Conchas as part of a diplomatic alliance or maintenance of a direct genealogical relationship; although such marriages were unusual, they were not unheard-of.[23] In matrilineal southeastern terms, that would make him an Alabama with the same rank and standing as his mother—hence a chief, if her family represented a chiefly lineage, and as an Alabama intrinsically of greater standing than any Choctaw chief. Whatever the truth of the case, clearly Alibamon Mingo stood in some kind of special relationship with the Alabama. The Alabama themselves enjoyed an extraordinary relationship with both French and English colonies, since they equally hosted both the French Fort Toulouse and an English trading house within their lands; in short, they effectively *did* make the French and English sit down and eat together.

In spite of Alibamon Mingo's assertion that he would be unable to break Red Shoe's peace, Bienville subsequently managed to persuade the Eastern Division war chief, a highly respected man named Choucououlacta, to join Alibamon Mingo in breaking the peace while Red Shoe was absent seeking a full-fledged trade agreement in South Carolina.[24] This was accomplished, and the Choctaws killed in the attack gave Red Shoe the excuse to turn on the Chickasaw after his return in order to secure vengeance for the deaths—and return nominally to the French fold in time for the second Chickasaw war of 1740.[25]

The route taken by the French for their second Chickasaw war was up the Mississippi River rather than the Tombigbee, which meant that the Choctaw were to be used to cut off Chickasaw escape from the southwest, joining the main French force coming overland from the Chickasaw Bluffs (modern Memphis). When the main force found itself unable to drag munitions eastward across the swampy and wooded Yazoo delta toward the Chickasaw, the decision was taken to negotiate peace with the Chickasaw and withdraw, leaving most of the Choctaw, who had held themselves in readiness for months and thereby missed the chance to hunt for food and peltries, without recompense for their trouble.[26] Some sixty Choctaws, however, had traveled northward to meet the French army and joined a party of Iroquois led by Pierre Joseph de Celoron from Canada in making a modest attack on a fortified Chickasaw position in another attempt at vengeance for their murdered men before the peace was negotiated.[27]

Choctaw Civil War, 1746–1750: Alibamon Mingo as Faction Chief

Red Shoe's English connection was only temporarily broken as a result of the abortive French campaign of 1740, but he continued his dealings with the Chickasaw and through them with the English, as European war after 1744 made it impossible for the French to supply presents and trade goods as promised and agreed. In 1746 he was responsible for the killing of three Frenchmen, one of them a trader, allegedly for their having raped one or more of his wives.[28] This action made him a major problem for the entire Choctaw confederacy, not just for individual chiefs like Alibamon Mingo. The major of the Mobile garrison, Jadart de Beauchamp, was sent to convene a large meeting at the Choctaw village of Chickasawhay to demand that the guilty parties be turned over to satisfy the French sense of justice and to reciprocate for the punishment the French had meted out to the French murderers of Choctaws in 1738. Several days after Beauchamp's arrival, Alibamon Mingo and several of his division chiefs came to meet with him. Beauchamp laid out the restitution that was being demanded, but Alibamon Mingo's reply was not as positive as he had hoped:

> This chief answered, after having stood up and made two circles, one of which symbolized the settlement of the French, and the second larger one enclosed the Choctaw nation . . . that I ought not to doubt his attachment for us; that it was not his fault that this unpleasant affair was not already finished with, since he had brought all of its consequences to the attention of the nation, and particularly to the people of his village and its dependencies; that he remembered perfectly well his former state; that it was not necessary to treat with respect people who for a long time sought nothing but the fall and the ruin of the Choctaw nation, and who had just crowned it by their heinous crimes; that all the red men ought to see clearly that all the promises of Imataha Chitto [Red Shoe] were vain and fantastic; that he regarded all these projects as impossible; that as for him he was willing, but that he could not give us the satisfaction that we justly asked, fearing to be attacked by the whole nation; that if he had some backing he would do it willingly, but that his village and that of the Chickasawhays, which had long been united, could not make this restitution, however much they wanted to, without running the risk of being slashed to pieces by the rest of the nation; that it was necessary to wait for the chiefs of the western part, who are most concerned with this affair, since the Frenchmen who were assassinated lived in their villages; that he would use all his influence to persuade them to give us reasons, and would speak loudly and boldly to convince them.[29]

Again Alibamon Mingo stressed that he would act through the power of his word but emphasized that kinship issues would decide who was appropriate to carry out the punishments demanded by the French: he could not simply act, for he had power to act only for his village and its dependencies and to ally with other leaders of his division, or he would be abusing his authority. The helplessness of the united Conchas and Chickasawhays was not only a result of their being numerically fewer than the population of the Western Division but of their being ceremonially inappropriate as avengers. The truly appropriate avengers, of course, would have been the French, as would be suggested many times.[30] It could be that this is what Alibamon Mingo meant to suggest in drawing the two circles symbolic of national "fires."

In the end, the French-allied Choctaw were compelled both to have Red Shoe murdered and to act in a drastic way in concert to counter opposition. In December 1748 Alibamon Mingo and the Choctaw great chief, together with the entire Eastern Division, brought to the French governor Pierre de Rigaud de Vaudreuil more than a hundred scalps of rebel warriors and the skulls of the chiefs of Couechitto, Nushkobo, and West Abeka. The French-allied chiefs, led by Alibamon Mingo, assured the French governor

> that the three villages of which the late Red Shoe made use in order to have the Frenchmen killed had suffered the penalty their perfidy deserved and existed no longer; that they were bringing me the heads of the chiefs and the scalps of the warriors; that if there had been so much difficulty in deciding to give me the satisfaction that I [Vaudreuil] had been demanding of them for such a long time, it was not because of any lack of attachment for the French but only because they foresaw that in order to do it in the proper way it was necessary that they renounce their own blood and decide to destroy their kinsmen, their friends, and in general all those of their nation who, having let themselves be seduced by the malicious speeches of the English, had risen against the French; that I could not doubt that it had cost them a great deal to give me such marked proof of their attachment, and that in order to succeed in it they had experienced much wretchedness, lost several chiefs and a large number of warriors, but that they hoped that in gratitude I would grant them what had been promised them at Mobile and at Tombecbé, namely: that I would give them a double present this year, pay them for the scalps that they were bringing [a price] three times as high as I had paid for those of the Chickasaws, since they had done themselves much more violence in killing their own brothers than in killing strangers, and that I would liberally compensate the families of warriors who had been killed defending our cause.[31]

In the end Vaudreuil shorted all these loyal chiefs on the promised payment, but they apparently accepted his authority and in 1750 "sent me [Vaudreuil] in the name of the entire nation white feathers worked in the form of a flag together with a calumet, the usual symbol of an enduring peace among the Indians."[32]

Was the mere mending of a trade relationship adequate recompense for the loss of the chiefs and warriors killed and the villages destroyed in the civil war? Did the loyal Choctaws really "renounce their own blood," and if so, what did that mean? I suspect that whatever was done, the Choctaw did not simply come over to the French way of thinking but that instead they reconfigured their own procedures in order to meet French requirements with the minimum of interior disruption. It is possible that there was a mixture of outcomes: in some villages people joined together to kill those long suspected of antisocial activities like witchcraft; in others perhaps elder and ailing relatives volunteered to die for guilty parties; sometimes killing may have been a result of jealousy or a rage for power. The one thing we can be sure of is that it was construed in personal and genealogical terms, not in terms of an abstract notion of justice. It is also plain, however, that in the course of the internecine struggle Alibamon Mingo emerged as far more than a village chief: in two years he had become the only leader who could finish something that nobody wanted to start.

Last Years of Louisiana, 1750–1763: Alibamon Mingo as Sole Polity Leader

After 1750 the affairs of the Choctaw mainly centered on their relations with their neighbors: an outbreak of hostilities with the Abihka in 1751 and the Tallapoosa in 1754 and a nearly constant harassment of the Chickasaw during 1757. In 1751 Alibamon Mingo and five other chiefs from the towns of Ebitoupougoula, Bouctoucoulou, and Chichatalaya, as well as fifty other Choctaws, brought in French deserters to Fort Tombecbé and asked for their pardon. Alibamon Mingo spoke first:

> I beg you [i.e., the trader Dupumeux] to write to M. de Vaudreuil, my father, that when the two first races, Inoulactas and Imongoulachas, go so far as to ask for the life of a man it is never refused them, even though the man should be fastened to the frame. I recently came down to Mobile to save the lives of two Frenchmen. I was deceived, for when I arrived these two men had already run the gauntlet twice. I hope that it will not be the same this time. I put my word with that of all the chiefs and honored men of the small faction, and I pray you to send it to M. de Vaudreuil. Explain to him carefully that these are all the chiefs and honored men of the whole small faction in general who ask for a pardon for these seven men. As for myself, I ask for it on my own part in the name of my whole village. I know well, however, that these Frenchmen have done wrong, but that will show the red men so much the more clearly

that M. de Vaudreuil, their father, has consideration for their requests. He can easily imagine the infinite pain that it would give the Choctaws to see shed the blood of people who every day bring them the things they need, and that with great difficulty. Furthermore, are not these Frenchmen, so to speak, our brothers; do we not dwell, as it were, in the same cabin? I hope therefore that the great chief of the French will not refuse his children the favor that they ask of him. You may also inform him that that will greatly increase the zeal of the red men for the French.[33]

This brief appeal emphasized Alibamon Mingo's leading position among Choctaw allies of the French by 1751, expressed openly by him without fear of contradiction in terms of moiety membership and representation of the pro-French faction. In fact, it is likely that the deserters were captured by the Ebitoupougoula villagers, since theirs was the closest village to the fort, so Alibamon Mingo was lending his authority to their request; significantly, the speakers who followed echoed his rhetoric. His words also point emphatically to the notion of a fictive kinship with all the French and thus a prohibition against allowing harm to come to them. In some sense this seems to have been the lesson of the Choctaw civil war, which was fought on the premise that the deaths of Frenchmen had to fit into the Choctaw version of the lex talionis.[34] The French now had to learn the lesson that the Choctaw would not be inconsistent in applying the principle so painfully worked out.

Yet the pleas of Alibamon Mingo and the other Eastern Choctaw chiefs had still not been answered by 1753, when they presented them once more to the new governor, Louis de Kerlérec. At the governor's arrival he gave presents to the Choctaw and the Alabama and was in turn given the ceremonial name Youlakty Mataha Tchito, anké achoukema, which Kerlérec translated as "King of the Choctaws and greatest of the race of the Youlakta, which is the finest and the oldest; all this ends with anké achoukema, which means a very good father."[35] Doubtless this ceremony was led by Alibamon Mingo as the leading Inholahta, but Kerlérec's reports name almost no Native leaders and give few ethnographic details.

Through the remainder of the 1750s the French documents contain little about the Choctaw, as Kerlérec began to concentrate on the Alabama and Upper Creek and then the Cherokee to push his buffer against the English farther eastward. Ironically, Choctaw activities began during this time to be reflected more clearly in the records of the English Carolina traders. The failure of trade goods and presents from the French from 1754 to 1758 and 1759 to 1763 forced them to turn to the English for what they needed, yet when French presents were expected, they renewed attacks on the Chickasaw and came near to decimating them by constant attacks in 1757.[36] Even the 1763 handover from the French to the English at the end of the Seven Years' War—for which the Choctaw were summoned to Mobile to meet its new commandant, Robert Farmar—was poorly documented: neither European principal knew anything of the Indians they addressed, and only the words of the Europeans were recorded, not the Indian responses.

Rapprochement with the English, 1765:
Alibamon Mingo as Elder Statesman

In 1765, however, Governor George Johnstone of West Florida held an elaborate congress with the Choctaw in Mobile to make official the new alliance with the English. As still one of the leading chiefs of the Choctaw, great medal chief for thirty-three years, Alibamon Mingo gave his last recorded diplomatic speech. To form a better idea of the force that this speech may have had, we should note that Governor Johnstone considered that the greatest threat to the English in North America was a general Indian insurrection orchestrated by "three very Superior Characters": Pontiac; The Mortar, of the Creeks; and "old Alabama Mingo, who had long led the Chactaw Nation."[37] This observation comes as something of a shock, and it is not clear where Johnstone and Stuart got this idea, but it suggests that the English took Alibamon Mingo as seriously as did the French. I give the whole of the speech, which was the third given in response to the English request for land from the Choctaw:

> You Favre have allways heard me Speak in every Assembly, Since you was a Boy, but now that I am Old without Teeth, half Blind, and all the Race Convened to give their Sentiments, perhaps it may not be proper for me to Speak. Nevertheless I feel myself so fired with the Occasion that I cannot refrain.
>
> I am of the Great Race of Ingulacta, I am Master of the whole Chactaw Nation by Birth, by Long Employment & by Long Experience it is to me to give Instruction to the rest, I have made alliance with the other Race of Imongulacha, and we have agreed that our Talk Should be one, I heard the Words of the Chiefs with great Attention, and when I really found they came here to make any Brothers happy I wished for my Eyes & my Ears & my Teeth again.

When I was Young the White Man came bearing abundance along with them, I took them by the hand & have ever remained firm to my Engagements, in return all my wants & those of my Warriors & Wives & Children have been Bountyfully Supplied. I now See another Race of White Man Come amongst us bearing the Same abundance, & I expect they will be equally Bountyfull which must be done if they wish equally to gain the affection of my people.

I and my Men have used the Guns of France these Eighty Winters Back, I wish I was Young to try the English Guns & English Powder both of which I hope will flourish & rejoice the Heart of the Hunters thro' the Land and Cover the Nakedness of the Women.

With respect to the Land I was not Consulted in it, if I was to deliver my Sentiments evil disposed People might impute it to Motives very different from those which actuate me, it is true the Land belonged chiefly to those who have given it away; that the Words which were Spoken have been written with a Lasting Mark, the Superintendant marks every word after word as one would count Bullets so that no variation can happen, & therefore the words have been Spoken and the eternal marks traced I will not Say anything to contradict, but, on the Contrary Confirm the Cession which has been made. What I have now to Say on that head is, to wish that all the Land may be Settled in four years that I may See it myself before I die.

I Listned to all the parts of the Talks and Liked them exceeding well, except that part from the Superintendant, where he reported that those Medal Chiefs who did not behave well Should be broke & their Medals given to others. The Conversation I have held with Faver, in private, has rung every Night in my Ear, as I laid my Head on the bear Skin & as I have many Enemies in the Nation, I dreamed I should be the Person, which would break my heart in my Old Age, to Loose the Authority I have so long held.

I cannot Immagine the Great King could Send the Superintendant to deceive us. In case we deliver up our French Medals & Commissions we expect to receive as good in their place, and that we Should bear the Same Authority & be entitled to the Same presents, If you wish to Serve your Old Friends you may give New Medals & Commissions & presents, but the worthy cannot bear to be disgraced without a fault, Neither will the Generous Inflict a Punishment without a Crime.

There was one thing I would mention tho' it cannot concern myself, & that is the Behaviour of the traders towards our Women, I was told of old by the

Creeks & Cherokees, wherever the English went they caused disturbances for they lived under no Government and paid no respect either to Wisdom or Station. I hoped for better things, that those Old Talks had no truth in them. One thing I must report which has happened within my own knowledge, that often when the Traders sent for a Basket of Bread & the Generous Indian sent his own wife to Supply their wants instead of taking the Bread out of the Basket they put their hand upon the Breast of their Wives which was not to be admitted, for the first maxim in our Language is that Death is preferable to disgrace.

I am not of opinion that in giving Land to the English, we deprive ourselves of the use of it, on the Contrary, I think we shall share it with them, as for Example the House I now Speak in was built by the White people on our Land yet it is divided between the White & the Red people. Therefore we need not be uneasy that the English Settle upon our Lands as by that means they can more easily Supply our wants.[38]

Obviously there are many significant elements to this speech, but I would like to point to two: its historical content and its formulation as the utterance of an elder. In reflecting over the speeches we have so far seen, it is obvious that when Alibamon Mingo spoke, he always included an historical element in his speeches; in fact, this was doubtless a significant part of Choctaw rhetoric and a fundamental element in the oral preservation of historical memory. With increasing age, however, the importance of historical precedent to the argument in Alibamon Mingo's speeches increased. Again, this is not surprising if we consider that one of the roles of an elder was to provide the wisdom of a long temporal perspective.

It is interesting to notice how he crafted his history, given that we know something of it. He spoke of the French as age-long allies and trade partners (even if the first French supply of guns to the Choctaw or some part of them took place in 1685, which is not impossible, Alibamon Mingo was unlikely personally to have seen "eighty winters" of French alliance by 1765), while he spoke of the English as though only newly met, in spite of what we know to have been a long dalliance with English trade on his part and that of the Choctaw as a whole. Further, he certainly knew that everyone present knew at least the broad outlines of this historical sequence to be mythical, so it seems to me that we must take it as intentionally stereotypical, metonymic of the translation of allegiance from one European to another.

There are specific elements in this speech that situated it as the speech of an elder, that indeed privileged it as such. He asked his hearers to indulge him as an elder, to give him the right to speak at length even in the midst of important men of more active leadership (although in fact he had not yet been eclipsed by a younger leader of similar genealogical position, making this claim read rather like a modesty topos).[39] He first sounded the theme of infirmity—the closing off of the senses of sight and hearing and perhaps with loss of teeth the attenuation of the power of speech. These sources of weakness he nevertheless contrasted with his supreme power through birthright, perhaps also alluding to the Alabama connection. With this background he was outspoken in his complaints about the potential deprivation of elder leaders by the English government and the bad treatment of Choctaw women by English traders while conceding the propriety of the usufruct grant of land that had been made and reminding the English of their obligation in fulfilling all parts of the agreement. Thus once more he spoke strongly and persuasively about negotiation and its proper outcomes, making it very clear in his own words—equally to be "written with a Lasting Mark, . . . every word after word as one would count Bullets so that no variation can happen"—what he understood the English to have promised and perhaps believing that his inscribed words would have the same force that had always attended his spoken words.

Much as he might have wanted to, Alibamon Mingo apparently did not live those four years to see the English settled upon Choctaw lands. By 1772, the next occasion on which the Choctaw attended a serious diplomatic convocation with Europeans, Alibamon Mingo had disappeared from the record and was succeeded as the leading Choctaw diplomatist by Taboca of West Yazoo, whose modest words had preceded his in 1765. I would suggest, however, that Alibamon Mingo had died earlier, in fact within a year or so of his having spoken these words. Alibamon Mingo had been a mainstay of good relations with the Alabamas and their Upper Creek allies, and I would suggest that it was his death, perhaps added to the younger chiefs' concerns with manipulating European trade, that allowed the outbreak of war with the Creeks after 1766.[40]

"Alibamon Mingo" is a public persona, a formal robe of identity worn by a specific Choctaw leader of the central third of the eighteenth century. We know nothing of his family life, what his house looked like, what tattoos he bore, whether he actually liked hominy or not. It is, however, helpful to think of his persona as a developing one, pacing the stages of a model Choctaw male life of the eighteenth century. We have seen him as a secondary chief, a village chief, a faction chief, and as preeminent leader of the Choctaw confederacy. We have seen him grow in power, but not just this: we have also seen him negotiate serious moral disaster, in anyone's terms. We see him of necessity through the eyes of Europeans who want things of him, yet in most of the words I chose (and unfortunately they are most of the words there are) he does not speak slavishly or in a way to gladden European hearts but always so as to discomfit us now with the strangeness of implications we cannot quite catch. I suggest that Alibamon Mingo was, on balance, what was thought of as a "peace chief": a leader who accomplished his goals through persuasion rather than violence, although he was unable to avoid completely the use of violence as a tool. This kind of investigation amplifies a simplistic notion of peace chief by exploring how such a leader practiced his craft in the dangerously shifting power relationships of the eighteenth century. We will never know the more intimate details of his life, for this formal identity is all that diplomatic speech can outline for us, but reading and following this kind of speech can nevertheless lead us to a more nuanced understanding—if we do not ignore the importance of cultural context and seek as much of it as we can find.

Acknowledgments

I would like to thank Greg O'Brien for inviting this paper and the National Endowment for the Humanities, whose grant no. RO-21631-88 continues to inform my eighteenth-century research, nearly twenty years later.

Notes

1. I most especially cannot speak of what Alibamon Mingo thought or why in every case he did what he did, as Richard White did when writing of Red Shoe, Alibamon Mingo's age-mate, more than twenty years ago (nor, I expect, would Richard White do so now).

2. Swanton, *Source Material*, 91, quotes the anonymous French memoir of ca. 1735 in mentioning several age grades for males, including childhood, unproven adult, proven adult (warrior), beloved man (elder). The manuscript conflates ranks and ages, but it is clear that there were at least these four and that leaders emerged from the grade of warrior and retained their leadership as elders. This study, of course, will itself add to the literature on which these assumptions rest.

3. Galloway, *Choctaw Genesis*, argues this concept of Choctaw origins.

4. Galloway, "Henri de Tonti du village des Chacta."

5. In 1708 Thomas Nairne, who primarily visited the Chickasaw; in 1713 Price Hughes, who explored the Mississippi River valley as well as Choctaw country.

6. Galloway, "Talking with Indians."

7. Greg O'Brien's recent *Choctaws in a Revolutionary Age* suggests that the male status passage to adulthood included some kind of violence, carried out in war, the hunt, or even the ballgame, but that participation could be part of a team effort and not a face-to-face encounter. I have followed this up in suggesting (in "Eighteenth-Century Choctaw Chiefs, Dual Organization, and the Exploration of Social Design Space," in this volume) that the crucial part of the passage was the successful negotiation of a situation involving the voluntary submission to chance and that direct violence was not an obligatory ingredient. Additional studies of specific biographies of Choctaw chiefs, like O'Brien's of Taboca and Franchimastabé and the present essay, may help to clarify these issues.

8. Rosecan, "Unpacking."

9. Diron D'Artaguette to Maurepas, March 20, 1730, AC, série C13A, 12:371–375, translated in MPA:FD, 1:79–80.

10. Régis du Roullet, list of chiefs and villages, in Journal, 1729, AC, série C13A, 12:67–99 (see 89–90), translated in MPA:FD, 1:21–54.

11. Adair, *History*.

12. Diron d'Artaguette to Huché, July 9, 1729, AC, série C13A, 12:167–69.

13. Régis du Roullet, list of chiefs and villages, in Journal, April–August 1732, in Archives du service hydrographique, vol. 67², no. 14-1, portefeuille 135, document 21, translated in part in MPA:FD, 1:136–54.

14. Régis du Roullet to Périer, March 16, 1731, AC, série C13A, 13:187–95.

15. Crémont to Maurepas, June 20, 1734, AC, série C13A, 19:166–70.

16. Bienville to Maurepas, January 10, 1736, AC, série C13A, 21:122–53.

17. Bienville to Maurepas, June 28, 1736, AC, série C13A, 21:168–70.

18. See my "The Barthelemy Murders: Bienville's Establishment of the Lex Talionis as a Principle of Indian Diplomacy," in this volume.

19. Noyan to Maurepas, January 4, 1739, AC, série C13A, 24:225–35, translated in MPA:FD, 4:162–63.

20. Noyan to Maurepas, January 4, 1739, 163–64.

21. Noyan to Maurepas, January 4, 1739, 165.

22. Rosecan, "Unpacking."

23. Jadart de Beauchamp, Journal, August 1746, AC, série C13A, 30:222–40, translated in MPA:FD, 4:269–97. At the meeting hosted by Beauchamp he talked with a Tamatlémingo, war chief of the Alabamas, and his son; the son was referred to as "a Choctaw settled among them and nephew of the Red Shoe [of Yanabé]" (translated in MPA:FD, 4:287)—hence Tamatlémingo was likely married to the Yanabé Red Shoe's sister, and his son was a Choctaw because she was.

24. Bienville to Maurepas, March 25, 1739, AC, série C13A, 24:35–43.

25. This in spite of the fact that his party seems to have killed more Chickasaw horses than Chickasaw men: see Bienville to Maurepas, May 28, 1740, AC, série C13A, 25:78–80.

26. Beauchamp to Maurepas, March 12, 1740, AC, série C13A, 25:245–48.

27. Bienville to Maurepas, May 6, 1740, AC, série C13A, 25:42–68.

28. According to Adair, *History*, 313–19. The French documents reveal that the situation was more complicated: the accusation of rape was made in October 1745, but the murders were not carried out until August of the following year, probably as much to make amends for the Choctaw killing of several English traders as to punish rapists. See my "Choctaw Factionalism and Civil War, 1746–1750," in this volume.

29. MPA:FD, 4:277–78.

30. Galloway, "Choctaw Factionalism and Civil War."

31. *MPA:FD*, 5:16, 61.

32. *MPA:FD*, 5:61.

33. Dupumeux to Beauchamp[?], June 18, 1751, AC, série C13A, 35:354–60.

34. Galloway, "The Barthelemy Murders."

35. Kerlérec to De Machault d'Arnouville, December 18, 1754, AC, série C13A, 38:122–29.

36. See, for example, the reports of Chickasaw traders Jerome Courtance (413–17) and John Buckles (458–60), as well as several pleas for help from the Chickasaw, in McDowell, *The Colonial Records of South Carolina: Documents Relating to Indian Affairs, 1754–1765.*

37. Johnstone and John Stuart, June 12, 1765, in Rowland, *Mississippi Provincial Archives: English Dominion*, 184.

38. From Chactaw Congress, 1765, Gage Papers, American Series No. 137, Clements Library, University of Michigan, printed in Rowland, *Mississippi Provincial Archives: English Dominion*, 239–41. For more detailed analysis of other elements of the event, see my " 'So Many Little Republics': British Negotiations with the Choctaw Confederacy, 1765," in this volume.

39. How old was he? I have suggested that his reference to "eighty winters" seems excessive and that he was probably closer to sixty-five. Johnstone referred to him as "old," but it should be remembered that Johnstone was only thirty-five years old in 1765 and would himself live to be only fifty-seven.

40. Compare O'Brien, "Protecting Trade."

19. Dual Organization Reconsidered

*Eighteenth-Century Choctaw Chiefs
and the Exploration of Social
Design Space*

Several of the main ideas that make up this paper have been lurking in my thoughts ever since I began thinking about Choctaw naming conventions as social and genealogical evidence in 1988, but they might never have come together without the catalyst of Greg O'Brien's new book on Choctaw leadership in the late eighteenth century, *Choctaws in a Revolutionary Age*, the manuscript of which he was gracious enough to share with me before publication.[1]

O'Brien framed his argument for changes in Choctaw leadership during the late eighteenth century in the context of economic changes in the colonial landscape and gender roles in southeastern matrilineal societies. He proposed a baseline definition of gender roles according to which women were symbolically whole, while men were not. Women were capable of creating life and hence naturally powerful spiritually, whereas men had to prove their grasp of spiritual power. To prove their spiritual power, all men had to be successful in war (or the hunt, or perhaps the ballgame). To achieve outstanding leadership they had to be able to retrieve magical tokens from afar; there was no fundamental differentiation between the tasks required of "war" and "peace" chiefs. Because southeastern men with leadership ambitions aspired to such demonstrations, they were vulnerable (or perhaps "preadapted") to the twin appeals of war with their neighbors and trade with Europeans, and O'Brien argued that this phenomenon played itself out through the careers of two late-eighteenth-century chiefs, Franchimastabé and Taboca. The quick adoption of the new market economy was thus a product of a kind of "mobilization of desire" not precisely intended by European merchants, since their trade goods

The material in this chapter was first presented at the American Society for Ethnohistory annual meeting in Quebec City, Quebec, in 2002.

could have been construed from the Choctaw side as directly symbolic of spiritual power and therefore literally fetishized rather than metaphorically so.[2]

Obviously, this brief paragraph does not do the arguments as much justice as the book itself, which I recommend to interested readers. This hypothesis is very interesting as an explanation of chiefly choices during the eighteenth century, and to the degree that Choctaw men had begun to adopt Euro-American habits of thought I suspect that it is correct. But I believe it raises a great many other fruitful questions by virtue of O'Brien's detailed analysis of the two chiefs' careers, and in this essay I want to ask whether some of them are applicable in the Choctaw case for several decades earlier. I am especially interested in how the behaviors of these particular chiefs can be compared with those of their predecessors, with reference especially to how they were embedded in a historical sequence of events. I think it is possible to propose that there might be a "rest of the story" that sets the behavior of Choctaw male leaders as O'Brien has described it in a larger context of traditional activities connected with dual organization, broadly (and quite heterogeneously) construed. I think not only that the participation of certain Choctaw leaders in the "market revolution" of the late eighteenth century represented an aspect of the quite traditional practices that made southeastern polities so flexible and resilient but also that the participation in question was a development that did not lessen that resilience. O'Brien's work offers the occasion for a reconsideration of what we think we know about Choctaw social organization and for a much better understanding of the "micropolitics of power" among the Choctaw of the late eighteenth century as they interacted with Europeans.[3]

Dual Organization

Along with others who have been eager to sweep away bad old structuralist excesses that tended to ignore the complexities of especially gender relationships, O'Brien has rejected dual organization and turned to the construction of gender for an explanation of the sources of power in Choctaw political leadership. But it is important to draw a distinction between the too-convenient tendency to consider that dual organization offers a single axis for organizing all aspects of distinction in a social entity (the binary oppositions list syndrome) and the real perspicuousness of the concept for recognizing in quite varied sociocultural phenomena the common theme of tension between vital elements of communal life. Even Claude Lévi-Strauss, whose name has become synonymous with binary oppositions, argued that a strictly diametric dual organization was a far too simplistic formulation for the many social phenomena that were assumed to be articulated through it, especially given the instability resulting from the frequent inequality between moieties (clearly a part of the Choctaw case), which should therefore be considered more dynamic organizational entities. More important, he pointed to dual organization as a likely product of historical processes of population amalgamation (precisely the case of the eighteenth-century Choctaw).[4] It seems, therefore, that it is still worthwhile to investigate together the dualities included in gender as well as marriage rules and practices, genealogical classifications, age sets, spatial organization, color symbolism, temporal process, and the distribution of power. Before we reject dual organization among the eighteenth-century Choctaw as a significant factor of social organization in these several domains, we should first attempt an understanding of what it actually meant.[5]

The European documents speak of two "races" or "castes" (French) or "families" (English) that were ranked and that seemed to dominate individual villages and even perhaps village groups. These two groups were known as the Inholahta and Imoklasha in order of rank. We have one piece of evidence cited by John Swanton that maps the Creek-like classifications of red and white onto the two in that order, yet this classification would conflict with the widespread southeastern preference for white/peace/civil chiefs as the more distinguished leaders, and it also conflicts with French and English evidence that is consistent in suggesting the opposite case.[6] But the point is that there is European testimony to the idea that the two Inholahta and Imoklasha groups may have played a role similar to the white and red Creek function of dominating the actions of peace and war in that order. These parallels were what interested Swanton and led to the assumption that dual organization among the Choctaw might be articulated along a single axis, but they were based more on informed speculation than solid evidence. To make a more sophisticated poststructuralist analysis of the myriad elements now understood to underlie far more complex traditional notions of dual organization, as well as to support other claims about eighteenth-century Choctaw social organization and traditional sources of power (including my suggestion that the two groups may have originally, in the seventeenth century, reflected the two dominant ingredient ethnicities of the Choctaw confederacy, the "Moundvillian" and "prairie" in that order), it is important to address several still unanswered questions about dual organization among the Choctaw:

1. Did Inholahta and Imoklasha actually function as moieties regulating marriage among *all* the people who considered themselves Choctaw in the eighteenth century? Is O'Brien right when he suggests that this function was filled by the *iksas* that were already part of the constituent ethnic groups and did not need to concern the apparent moieties?

2. Were the two great male political roles, peace and war leadership, articulated on the same moiety division, did they represent a second duality, or were they two poles of a separate axis of male leadership? Did each village and division have both a peace and a war chief, or might a village be led by one or the other?

3. How did peace chiefs manage to prove themselves spiritually powerful if they were forbidden to shed blood? Is O'Brien right in assuming that all males of whatever category were called on to prove themselves through violence against human life, or is there some other way that blood might come into the process of constructing Choctaw masculinity in the eighteenth century?[7] And does it really make sense for the male coming-of-age to be seen as a kind of mimicry of the female?

4. Did the peace/war dichotomy only map fortuitously onto an emerging discourse of traditional/progressive (or, as James Taylor Carson would have it, primordialist/cosmopolitan) as increasing commoditization began to disenchant every realm of Choctaw conduct, or is there a deeper universal principle at work here that might explain the persistence of some kind of duality as a way of describing Choctaw leadership?[8]

5. If moieties were expressed politically in peace and war leadership, were they also expressed in ceremonial practices? Did such expression reflect (as O'Brien seems to suggest) or contradict the political expression?

In this essay I will try to at least open up some of these questions, following on from issues capably raised by O'Brien and using a broadened data set drawn from Choctaw chiefly activities from roughly 1700 to 1800.

Two Cases and Their Contexts: Alibamon Mingo/Red Shoe, Taboca/Franchimastabé

The careers of these four preeminently visible Choctaw leaders of the colonial period must first be sketched in processual and life-cycle terms. Alibamon Mingo and Soulouche Oumastabé (Red Shoe) were born into the colonial context but reared far from documentary visibility during the initial colonial period when neither the French nor the English were attempting to micromanage the Choctaw. They would have been youths of the same age set at the time when Europeans across the Southeast suffered an early bout of "Indian troubles" following on the Yamassee War of 1715, but in French Louisiana there was little repercussion for the Choctaw. In the 1730s they emerged as "young" (twenty-something? thirty-something?) subordinate leaders during the Natchez and Chickasaw wars, Alibamon Mingo being the second in rank for the Concha towns and Soulouche Oumastabé as fourth in rank for the perhaps more important Couechitto town group, home of the central Choctaw leader intentionally supported by the French beginning in 1701. Circumstances and their own initiative raised both Alibamon Mingo and Soulouche Oumastabé to prominence in the French-led wars against the Natchez and Chickasaw in the 1730s. At this time Alibamon Mingo was named with a "war" appellation (Alibamon Ajo, "berserker") when he led a war party to assist the French in recovering their women, children, and African slaves held hostage by the Natchez—although it should be pointed out that his most notable act on that occasion was to negotiate successfully with the Natchez for the release of the French women and children. Meanwhile, Soulouche Oumastabé by his own testimony had performed mighty feats against the Chickasaw in client warfare for the French during the 1720s, and he also led a party against the Natchez.[9] By 1732 both Alibamon Mingo (as chief of Concha) and Soulouche Oumastabé (as war chief of Couechitto) had French medals. Both of them then remained the most visible of Choctaw leaders as the Europeans attempted to manipulate them in favor of their own colonial ends: in the middle 1730s both flirted with British trade, Soulouche Oumastabé more effectively because of his close relations with several Chickasaw leaders (and because of at least one trip he made to Carolina), but he continued to be overruled by the great chief, who committed the Choctaw to war against the Chickasaw on behalf of the French in 1736. French shortages in the 1740s, when both Alibamon Mingo and Soulouche Oumastabé doubtless depended upon French trade goods to some degree to maintain their leadership through generosity to followers, eventuated in a Choctaw civil war when Soulouche Oumastabé had French traders killed and Alibamon Mingo was eventually compelled to secure vengeance for it, in the course of which Soulouche Oumastabé was killed. It is arguable that other chiefs continued to be equally or more important until Red Shoe was dead, the Choctaw civil war was over, and Alibamon Mingo had attained to the distinguished seniority that made him preeminently authoritative in the 1760s, but certainly these two men remained extremely visible to French observers of diplomacy and warfare from 1729 to their deaths in 1747 (Sou*louche Oumastabé*) and 1766 or thereabout (Alibamon Mingo). Finally, as I have argued elsewhere, Alibamon Mingo seems to have been an Inholahta, while Soulouche Oumastabé was an Imoklasha.[10]

O'Brien has given a significant account of the lives of Taboca and Franchimastabé in his book and various articles, so I will only offer a brief summary here. O'Brien sees Franchimastabé as the seeker of power through prestige goods trade with Europeans, while Taboca sought another kind of power and authority by traveling to distant sites to carry out diplomacy. I would remark, however, that there may have been more to the remarkable Taboca than even O'Brien has suggested, since he is not the only man to have borne the name: on the 1729 lists three men were identified not only as Taboca but also as holding the office of *taskanangouchi* (according to one account, the man who "gives out offices"), suggesting that the name may have gone with the role and even perhaps that it marked lineage affiliation.[11] Both leaders were known to the English by 1763, and Taboca even played a role in the early negotiations between the English and Choctaws after the departure of the French, but as was true in at least the case of Alibamon Mingo (Soulouche Oumastabé's great chief outlived him), neither of these later chiefs could fully emerge to preeminent external leadership until elder leaders were dead. I cannot identify the specific moiety to which each belonged, but if O'Brien is right that Taboca was married to Franchimastabé's sister, then at least they had to belong to opposite moieties, as had Alibamon Mingo and Soulouche Oumastabé.

I think it is also important to observe that Red Shoe and Franchimastabé both emerged as what might be termed unmanageable local war leaders barely subordinated to elder chiefs, just as Alibamon Mingo and Taboca emerged primarily as local peace leaders initially apprenticed to elders. These facts are significant to understanding how the thematic of two primary male leadership careers might be articulated.

The Function/Meaning of Inholahta/Imoklasha

What do we actually know after all about what Inholahta and Imoklasha meant to the Choctaw confederacy in the eighteenth century and earlier? Precious little in any direct way, it turns out: just those few items cited above, plus the testimony of the Jesuit missionary to the Choctaw that each of the

ESSAYS IN ETHNOHISTORY

two groups had specific "races" grouped under it. Greg Urban's review of southeastern social organization, particularly the linguistic evidence for it, found that Choctaw social organization should be grouped with those of the core-Muskogean linguistic group: Creek, Seminole, and Chickasaw. The diagnostic feature of the core-Muskogean group was in fact the presence of matrilineal moieties, which in the case of the Choctaw were "unquestionably exogamous." Urban confirmed Swanton's claim that, in addition to the function of regulating marriage, the moieties also certainly served to structure the performance of roles in burials and may have been involved in the organization of the ballgame.[12] This litany of functions leaves the political largely to one side in favor of the ceremonial.

What did it mean for the moieties to be concerned in the provision of burial services? Anthropological studies of death contend that death, as the fundamental societal disruption, constitutes an occasion of danger and pollution. Where the "death work" of body handling and preparation is done by an Other, the practice serves to dissipate a pollution that is seen as dangerous only for Same. We know that the Choctaw also provide a model for what is referred to in mortuary studies as extended or secondary processing of the body.[13] Choctaw burial practice included the placement of the body on a scaffold for a period of months during which the flesh decomposed; preparation of the body for the next stage of transition into the otherworld by persons referred to as "bone-pickers" who removed the remaining flesh, packaged the bones in a basket, and officiated at mourning ceremonies; and preservation of bone packages in a community ossuary for a period of time, after which the entire contents of the ossuary was enclosed in a mound of earth. Swanton reported all these facts from profuse observations collected significantly from nineteenth-century witnesses (when the practice was under siege from Christian missionaries) but was not explicit about how the moiety function worked itself out in this picture.[14] If indeed the so-called bone-pickers themselves (who could apparently be male or female) also performed their offices only for decedents of the opposite moiety to their own (if, indeed, there were always at least two Choctaw bone-pickers at any one time—some testimonies indicated more than that), then by definition the opposite moiety was present at the beginning and ending of all Choctaw life and had a fundamental part in the definition of the perdurable form of an individual's identity (i.e., bone rather than flesh). It may also be important to pay attention to the fact that part of the final bone preparation process seems to have been painting the skull red, perhaps to signal the bloody crown of a head being "born" into the otherworld.

Another question that should be asked is whether the moieties had a role in other major ceremonial events. By analogy with other southeastern polities we might reasonably expect that they had such a role for the annual cycle of major ceremonials, including green corn and harvest, but we might also ask by analogy with the mortuary duty whether they also functioned similarly at other such life-cycle/status-transition ceremonies as birth, puberty, and transition to "honored" or elder status. For these latter roles, however, we have no solid evidence but only analogy.

Urban points out the anomalous position of the Choctaw with respect to the lack of totemic clans and the substitution of what Swanton called "house" or local groups that were apparently matrilineal and shared a segmentary (as opposed to structural) nature. This would mean that they were truly local groups in geographical proximity, tending to fission when growing beyond a certain size. But among the Choctaw these local groups were both exogamous and aligned with one of the moieties, which would tend to maintain the moieties as geographically distinct rather than broadly distributed. This accords well with evidence that has suggested originary geographical (east and west) and ethnic identities for the Inholahta and Imoklasha. What this means is not that there was a bewildering thicket of marriage prohibitions: a person was obliged to marry an individual from both outside his or her local group and outside his or her moiety, which merely meant that all the local groups in the opposite moiety offered possible marriage partners. Because residence was matrilocal, however, matrifocal residence groups would therefore remain geographically fixed. For the eighteenth century there is no secure evidence to assert whether married men spent most of their time in their wives' households rather than in their sisters'. There is scattered evidence, however, that when women truly married "out" (i.e., beyond the boundaries of the emergent Choctaw confederacy), they might go to live in the polity of their husband, just as a "foreign" woman might marry into a Choctaw town in order to cement an alliance (as I suspect was the origin of Alibamon Mingo's name and stated rank of chief among the Alabama Indians).[15]

Urban also emphasizes that although in the core-Muskogean tribes there is some evidence of ranking in the form of moiety ranking (Inholahta as "elder brother" to Imoklasha in the Choctaw case), emergence of chiefly clans (to the extent that chiefs had more than local power), and a control hierarchy of age grades ("stages of warriorhood to elderhood"), nevertheless, "the core-Muskhogean systems were strongly egalitarian."[16] This is a point we should not forget in considering any claims that Choctaw chiefly leadership was in any substantive sense equivalent to Mississippian chiefdom elite ranking.[17] Repeated testimony of chiefs themselves (regretting their lack of control over their turbulent young men) and the evidence of behavior (endless exhaustive public discussion of important events by people of every rank) make it abundantly clear that in the eighteenth century Choctaw chiefs led by what looked to Europeans like consensus (in the case of "peace" chiefs) and charisma (in the case of "war" chiefs), though it is probably not wrong to refer to both of their leadership qualities as partaking of a spiritual element. Over time some chiefs would consolidate considerable power, but even in the nineteenth century no single chief led the Choctaws.

The Function/Meaning of Peace/War

Does the explanation of peace and war leadership as consensus and charisma, respectively, help very much for understanding political leadership? Again, what we think is axiomatic may not be well supported by historical evidence. We think that peace chiefs had relatively permanent leadership, while war chiefs were more likely to attain to significance only in time of war and to lose influence when active war was in abeyance. One influential source for this idea is a 1714 memoir from Father Le Maire, written from Mobile:

> There are two kinds of chiefs, or two kinds of kinglets among our savages. Some are war chiefs; their courage plus the election by the tribe gives them this rank; the others are village chiefs; these only busy themselves with the internal government, but they can, nevertheless, be looked upon as real chiefs. Their power is more stable than that of the other chiefs which only holds good in time of war. The respect which certain nations show their village chiefs reaches adoration.[18]

Robbie Ethridge has argued that during the colonial period there was an increasing premium on war leadership as Europeans chose to foster inter-tribal wars for their own ends, but it is difficult to know what must have been the case before the sustained presence and observation of Europeans.[19] According to the lists of villages and chiefs assembled by French observers in the late 1720s and 1730s, most villages seem to have had at least one chief with some war-related semantic element in his name, and that chief was most frequently not the one considered by the French observers to have primary leadership.[20]

If white and red map onto peace and war symbolically, do they also map onto the moieties? I think the answer is yes, but in a more complex way than saying that the groups of one moiety were all white and the other all red. For the Choctaw there do not seem to have been truly "white" towns (sanctuaries where no violence was permitted), yet all village "peace" chiefs seem to have been able to maintain the peace most of the time within the precincts of their villages, while the powers of "war" chiefs seem to have been especially relevant to lands *external* to the village, thus implying that peace and war had a geographical mapping that crosscut that of the moieties.[21] Moiety identity with peace and war, therefore, may have been metaphorical and more closely related to the elder/younger dichotomy: the senior moiety was seen to be aligned with peace and stability, while the junior one was more like the "turbulent young men" who made the best warriors.

If O'Brien is right, and the war and peace functions were simply points along a continuum of male chiefly power, then it might be worth asking whether the Choctaw age grades might also have constituted an axis of duality in this sense. O'Brien emphasizes the rite of passage initiated by the youth's first participation in war, but he does not address the fact that the status of "beloved" or "honored" man also amounted to an age grade attained through status transition, that the greatest chiefs tended to be found among those senior ranks, and that the most respected among these elder chiefs were peace chiefs (possibly because war chiefs tended to get killed off). In fact, almost none of the chiefs reported by Europeans were young in eighteenth-century terms: they began to emerge into lesser chiefly ranks and documentary visibility only in their twenties and thirties. It is notable that the few chiefs mentioned as being so inadequate that for one reason or another their villages replaced them are invariably described as young: I suggest that it was not their disinclination for war that made them unattractive as leaders but their youth and lack of experience.

A final but I think significant consideration with respect to the expression of duality in chiefly power is the *pairing* of peace and war chiefs, both within a village and on a larger scale. It is the appearance of centralized leadership itself that most scholars have attributed to the effects of the European presence; O'Brien argues for it as one of the innovations wrought by Franchimastabé in the 1780s, using his talents in accumulating goods to build power among kin and dependents. Certainly, we see the French attempting from the beginning to find and name a manipulable single chief to serve them as the funnel for their goods to the tribe and to be held responsible for its cooperation, but it is also true that this institution was far from easy to create, since power was persistently shared in some sense between chiefs who seemed to have the characteristics of peace/Inholahta and war/Imoklasha. The careers of the two pairs of chiefs considered here seem to suggest that the social mechanism of age sets among the Choctaw tended to throw up generational groups from which such pairs could and did emerge. The mechanism of the "play-off" system fortuitously meant that pairs of chiefs could choose to manipulate external allies by working together or playing off *each other's* talents and inclinations.[22]

Blood/Semen, Blood/Milk: Blood Symbolism in the Construction of Gender and Power

O'Brien argues that the notion of dual organization, of moieties organized with a set of dualisms, including war and peace and red and white, was far less significant in his scenario of market revolution than was gender, which he argues was the most fundamental duality. He has adopted the by now standard gender complementarity discourse that has substituted for earlier concepts of gender division of labor, which in its turn replaced a discourse of gender inequality. Its importance is that it is used to hold both genders to equal symbolic standards of "power." In O'Brien's argument, as we have seen, all males, of whatever moiety or iksa, were obliged to prove themselves through violent activity of some kind (war or hunting or perhaps the ballgame—"little brother to war" that could itself eventuate in death), and all were theoretically obliged to shed blood to prove their command of the supernatural, whereas women, who already both shed blood naturally in proof of their fertility and by creating new life proved their command of the supernatural, were not obliged to do anything to prove their essential wholeness and spiritual power.

According to O'Brien and other researchers, a set of essentialist categories or "natural symbols" cluster around the dual construction of gender in the Southeast.[23] Several things are not clear here. First, although this concept seems to be conceived as a pansoutheastern one, it is presented as in some sense a "natural" or baseline concept, even though the evidence for it was not gathered until much later and the southeastern Native people of the eighteenth century were in anything but a "pristine" cultural condition with respect to gendered interaction with Europeans and especially gendered documentation by them. The documentary evidence is very sparse when it comes to actual eighteenth-century observations and is particularly thin when it comes to women. The observers' enculturation in patriarchal societies made them nearly blind to female power and agency, and most of their observations of women were additionally filtered through male Choctaw informants.[24] Further, the model suggests that women were "naturally" powerful and leaves them in a sense without any but bodily agency (anatomy is destiny?), with no evident field for the exercise of their power outside of childbirth (including the natural and symbolic birthing of Others into a Choctaw identity to assist in diplomacy) and horticulture; while men were compelled to demonstrate intellectual as well as bodily agency and were allocated the fields of war, politics, and trade for their action. This dichotomy is too fine a mirror of the documentary demographics of gender to be wholly convincing.

Clearly also, this structure, assuming that it did exist in the eighteenth century, was not likely to have been as solid and uniform as Swanton and after him Charles Hudson made it seem: if menstruating Mikasuki women today are openly served on paper plates instead of china ones in the tribal cafeteria, while Choctaw women have adopted menstrual hiding behaviors, might there not have been significant variations in the eighteenth century? In other words, there is no pristine pansoutheastern belief or practice in the eighteenth century or at any other time, only constantly revised belief and practice with local variation, fitting the specific historical trajectory of each emerging tribal entity. It is clearly hypothetical to suggest a reconstructed gender essence, especially where the gender in question is notoriously underrepresented in the documents. For example, given the widespread existence of ceremonies surrounding a girl's experience of menarche in all cultures, it would be surprising if there had not been such a significant status passage for Choctaw girls to womanhood equivalent to that for boys to manhood, and the provision of ceremonial services during such a status passage by the opposite moiety is well attested for other matrilineal societies.[25] Nor does O'Brien's scenario account for the politically significant status passage for men from active warrior status to that of "honored" or "beloved" elder and the doubtless symmetrical passage through menopause for women, both of which have clear implications for the practice of "power" in Choctaw society. In other words, the argument from gender dualism is not really needed to motivate a striving for spiritual power: it was a universal, not a gendered motivation.

When it comes to the definition of male power and its sources, it should also be remembered that most European observers had a vested interest in securing Choctaw cooperation in warfare and were more likely to value warlike skills themselves than peaceful pursuits. I am therefore not entirely comfortable with the emphasis on warlike skills being singled out as the sole route to power; I think O'Brien is on much firmer ground than other exponents of this "fight club" scenario when he emphasizes the more nuanced view that dutiful (and bloodless) participation in a war *party* that succeeded in shedding blood could suffice as proof of manhood as well, perhaps, as hunting and the ballgame: all three activities, we should note, bear strong structural similarities to one another, and all involve moiety roles in other cultures. More important, *they all represent a voluntary submission to uncertainty*, providing a mechanism by which the favor of chance could be demonstrated.[26] I submit that this is the real source of male spiritual power, whether observed by Europeans or not, but I also suggest that the favor of chance did not need to be demonstrated solely through killing or the shedding of blood and that two poles of male spiritual power were importantly twinned.

Duality and Leadership

Chance could choose a man for another fate than that of a killer of men or a shedder of blood—hence a peace chief eventually forbidden to shed blood might negotiate his manhood status passage without having shed it in the first place. His actions upon entering the liminal status of a war party member within a voluntarily accepted uncertainty could guide his personal outcome: he could emerge as primarily an instigator of open-ended situations or as primarily a restrainer of them. This would explain the widespread tendency to speak in terms of leaders who were "modern, innovating" or "traditional, conservative" that O'Brien so justifiably deplores. In fact, I would suggest, it was the nearly universal *pairing* of these two qualities, embodied in pairs of chiefs associated with peace and war or sometimes with the two moieties (at the village, division, or even tribal level), that represented the "wholeness" that women possessed (or that they achieved and perhaps that they *also* articulated in two modes), and its political correlate was the ability to explore novel situations (red, or war, leadership) while remaining safely within the restraints of specific ceremonial restrictions (white, or peace, leadership). In terms of physiological "natural symbols" this even fits, since the "blood" of chance and death would be balanced by the "semen" of established practice and nurturance, just as women alternated menstrual blood with breast milk. Both were red *and* white.

Conclusions

I would like to propose that these considerations of the various meanings of dual organization among the eighteenth-century Choctaw may permit the following conclusions:

1. The Inholahta/Imoklasha moieties probably articulated both originary ethnicity and geographic boundary definitions. They certainly did control at least acceptable marriage partnering and mortuary ritual and may have been involved symbolically in other axes of duality.

2. All chiefs could be involved variously in war when necessary, especially during youth, but war chiefs properly so called were more directly involved on a sustained basis. When a divisional or polity leader was a peace chief, he used his war chief to organize the activities of war. Peace chiefs ranked above war chiefs in the Choctaw notion of an ideal leader, and at the highest levels these two ranks probably did map most appropriately onto the Inholahta and Imoklasha moieties, as in the cases of at least the first pair of leaders I have discussed. War chiefs were symbolically "young," and peace chiefs were symbolically "elder."

3. Gender duality is not sufficient or even relevant to motivate male striving for "power." Both genders were potentially symbolically complete, and both had to perform specific status transitions adequately and fill ascribed and achieved roles competently in order to reach that completeness, although the relative invisibility of women to European male observers, and the fact that much status-transition activity took place "offstage" with respect to European observation, has masked this fact. Exceptional performance in the achievement of the appropriate variant of the gender ideal granted the individual in question what Europeans interpreted—when they saw it— as "power."

4. Both male roles were selected through various status-passage tests, during which potential war chiefs emerged as risk-takers and potential peace chiefs emerged as maintainers of order. These two categories tended to map onto the named moieties but were achieved rather than ascribed. In the context of age grades, however, a man could potentially transition through both war and peace leadership during a life course, though at a lower and less visible level of activity.

5. The dualities of white/red and peace/war did not likely map in any simple way onto ceremonial/political functions. As the named moieties were clearly involved with status passages through life stages, so they may have been involved less simply in the political arena by virtue of their symbolic mapping onto age grades. Deeper understanding of ceremonial practices and roles will be required to make sense of these relationships.

If all this is true, then it may prove to be a larger metaphor explaining some aspects of social organization and definition in the Southeast. Shmuel Eisenstadt has pointed out that the social division of labor beyond the household level of "primordial ascription" raises fundamental uncertainties about the construction of trust and solidarity, power without exploitation, and the meaning and legitimation of cultural models and has suggested that these areas of uncertainty tend to be articulated by different social actors.[27] He observes that the individual life cycle entails the deconstruction and reconstruction of trust at several transition points to achieve the extension of trust into instrumental and power relations. This insight is clearly reflected in the variation in historically visible male Choctaw roles over the life cycle. On a larger metaphorical scale it is also reflected in O'Brien's argument that the progressive commoditization of the "market revolution," to the extent that it began to alter relations of control over material resources among the Choctaw, could alter the workings of Choctaw society itself and, reflexively, leadership (and even gender) roles.

But I would argue that this does not mean that this kind of fundamental "dual organization" or dual expression of a range of social phenomena must disappear under the pressure of European market forces. It is worth considering that dual war/peace leadership articulates in an operationalizable manner the human will to reach into the unknown. In the mechanism of paired war and peace chiefs we see how this curiosity may be harnessed as the will to explore social design space while establishing appropriate regulatory mechanisms to avoid "fatal" decisions. For the Southeast we may observe that it was probably active prior to the arrival of Europeans, possibly even explaining the alternations between welcome and bellicosity experienced by the earliest European observers.[28] Neo-Darwinians argue that evolution is the problem-solving activities of life; Popper refers to history as the problem-solving activities of societies. Without straying into such analogies, I think it is not far-fetched to suggest that there is something Darwinian here: without having been explicitly designed in any way, the emergence and persistence of dual organization suggest that because it maintains this controlling tension it may represent a frequently achieved local maximum (or a peak on a "rugged fitness landscape") for accomplishing innovation without danger of complete collapse.[29] This advantage may explain its persistence along with that of the southeastern tribes themselves.

Acknowledgments

I want to thank Greg O'Brien for sharing his work with me and for participating in the 2002 American Society for Ethnohistory symposium "New Approaches to Southeastern Indian Social Organization and Power in the Eighteenth Century," along with Robbie Ethridge and me; I would also like to thank Regna Darnell for stepping in to comment at the last moment. I am indebted to Jason Jackson for comments on the original version of this paper, although it's not his fault that I didn't revise it much.

Notes

1. See my "Choctaw Names and Choctaw Roles: Another Method of Evaluating Sociopolitical Structure," in this volume; O'Brien, *Choctaws in a Revolutionary Age*.

2. The expression "mobilization of desire" is from Baudrillard and refers to the capitalist incitement of the desire to possess; for a useful overview of commoditization and its relation to fetishization see Kopytoff, "The Cultural Biography of Things."

3. The phrase is built on Michel de Certeau's recognition in *The Practice of Everyday Life* of the possibilities for local problematization of Michel Foucault's "microphysics of power" that constituted the minute disciplinary practices making up and reproducing specific behaviors (see Foucault, *Discipline and Punish*, 139).

4. See Lévi-Strauss, "Do Dual Organizations Exist?" For a collection of recent and more processual essays on dual organization see Maybury-Lewis and Almagor, *The Attraction of Opposites*.

5. See Galloway, "Choctaw Names."

6. Classic discussions of leadership and chieftainship in the Southeast can be found in Gearing, *Priests and Warriors*; Reid, *A Law of Blood*. For the French and English evidence see Galloway, *Choctaw Genesis*; O'Brien, *Choctaws in a Revolutionary Age*.

7. Slotkin, *Regeneration through Violence*.

8. Carson, *Searching for the Bright Path*.

9. I must remark here that Richard White's picture (in "Red Shoes") of the rise of Soulouche Oumastabé as an exceptional career for a "commoner" is much exaggerated: he was not only not the only "Red Shoe" of his time, but he was not the only one who held a medal, and where other war chiefs were also the first chiefs of their villages, Soulouche Oumastabé was always formally subordinated to the man the French recognized as the great chief of the nation, who happened to be his village chief as well.

10. See my "Four Ages of Alibamon Mingo, fl. 1700–1766," in this volume.

11. See Galloway, "Choctaw Names," and Moore, "Mvskoke Personal Names," for the Creeks.

12. Urban, "The Social Organizations," 173, 175–76.

13. Hertz, *Death and the Right Hand*.

14. Swanton, *Source Material.*

15. See especially the evidence for another ("Conchatys") Alabama intermarriage in the case of Tamatlémingo and his Choctaw son: my "Choctaw Factionalism and Civil War, 1746–1750," in this volume.

16. Urban, "The Social Organizations," 178.

17. Especially since the whole notion of "chiefdom" is a synthetic theoretical construction by anthropologists working within a cultural evolution paradigm; see Kehoe, "When Theoretical Models," who quotes William Sturtevant saying in 1979 that "American chiefdoms are an artifact of postmedieval European preconceptions."

18. Delanglez, "M. Le Maire on Louisiana," 144–45; the document is a letter written from Pensacola (where Le Maire served as priest to the Spanish garrison briefly) on January 15, 1714.

19. Robbie Ethridge, in a paper presented at the Southeastern Archaeological Conference annual meeting, 2000, discussed warfare as a result of European presence.

20. Galloway, "Choctaw Names."

21. Compare the Natchez Deer Festival in Swanton, *Indians,* 111–12.

22. For a description of the "play-off" system see Gearing, *Priests and Warriors.*

23. Douglas, *Natural Symbols.*

24. Several writers have tackled the issue of biased observation of women: Paper, "The Post-Contact Origin"; Churchill, "Understanding"; Perdue, *Cherokee Women.*

25. See Rosman and Rubel, "Dual Organization."

26. The fundamental importance of the management of chance is broadly recognized cross-culturally at a far more granular level; on the poison oracle as a guide for daily life see Evans-Pritchard, *Witchcraft.*

27. Eisenstadt, "Dual Organizations."

28. See my "The Unexamined Habitus: Direct Historical Analogy and the Archaeology of the Text," in this volume.

29. Stuart Kauffman articulates the model of evolution in a "rugged fitness landscape" in *At Home in the Universe.*

IV. *Ethnohistory and Ethics*

Defining the Situation

20. Mississippi 1500–1800

Revising the South's Colonial History
for a Postcolonial
Museum Audience

Every generation, our own included, will, must inevitably, understand the past and anticipate the future in the light of its own restricted experience, must inevitably play on the dead whatever tricks it finds necessary for its own peace of mind.

CARL BECKER, "Everyman His Own Historian"

Efforts to replace the Mississippi state historical museum's 1961 exhibits covering the colonial period have cast into sharp relief the new role of museums as forums for the discussion and contesting of community identities. The 1961 exhibits spoke with one white male voice to tell the community, in effect, how inevitably its colonial past supported a segregated Mississippi, and the educated white audience whose story was thereby legitimated had become very comfortable with that version of the past, though it had become an embarrassment to the museum staff. The story of how those exhibits have been revised is worth reviewing because of what it tells us about the reception of revisionist history and its significance to communities.

Given the fact that funding for the museum, which is a unit of the Mississippi Department of Archives and History, can only come from legislative, grant, or private funding, the fact that it took twenty years for the full range of 1961 exhibits to begin to be replaced is indicative in itself of the priorities of power brokers in several venues with respect to history. The museum staff decided to begin with the most recent period for its ready relevance and then to work backward: the Twentieth Century Room was redone from 1982 to 1986

The material in this chapter was first presented at the March 28–31, 1996, annual meeting of the Organization of American Historians in Chicago.

and garnered national recognition for the civil rights exhibit that had attracted extraregional grant funding. Next the museum staff undertook to revise the Civil War and Reconstruction Room from 1986 to 1991. While hesitating to decide how to deal with the antebellum period, the museum took advantage of the National Endowment for the Humanities' Quincentenary initiative to seek grant funding to tackle the colonial period.

There was no specific colonial period expertise within the museum staff itself, and the discourse of the 1961 exhibits was not very helpful in suggesting new themes:

1. Great White Explorers (Soto, La Salle, Iberville, and Bienville) were shown triumphantly Discovering everything.
2. French and Spanish failure at colonization was crowned by Anglo-American success with cotton: Spanish-British Natchez, Andrew Jackson, and the War of 1812 were featured.
3. Indians were portrayed on the fringes of the colonial story, being instead relegated to "ethnographic" atemporal exhibits that stressed the Natchez massacre, Chickasaw loyalty to Britain, the Choctaws pining for civilization.
4. There were no Africans in the 1961 vision of Mississippi's colonial past.

When the work began on the colonial exhibits in 1988, they were viewed as traditional object-driven exhibits, meant to embody "the latest historical research": while museum staff made lists of colonial period holdings, a group of advisory scholars, including archaeologists and ethnohistorians for the Native American side of the story, was drawn up and contracted to produce essays that would sum up the most recent scholarship in their areas of expertise.[1]

As the list of objects was completed and the scholarly input started to be received, two things became obvious. First, the museum's holdings of objects dating from the period 1500–1800 were woefully small, except for archaeological artifacts from the prehistoric Late Mississippian period and for materials originating with the Anglo settlement of the Natchez region at the end of the eighteenth century. Second, colonial history had since 1961 been affected by the revisionist influences of social history and microhistory, and the story would no longer be one of a perhaps unfortunate but nevertheless smooth displacement of Native people in a majestic translation of empire.

In fact, a lengthy list of very complex issues began to emerge, promising at least as much controversy as the other two recent efforts had elicited. The new exhibits would need to

ETHNOHISTORY AND ETHICS

1. address the "denial of coevalness" to Native Americans in the portrayal of the precolonial past as an "ethnographic present";[2]
2. problematize the Black Legend of Spanish cruelty;
3. assimilate modern evidence of the massive demographic disaster suffered by Native Americans as a result of European disease and aggression;
4. discuss openly the African side of the slave trade;
5. assimilate new evidence for the agency of African slaves under the French regime and its slave laws (the so-called Code noir);
6. evaluate the effects of Native American hegemony and African resistance on colonial strategies.

Not one of these issues had even been mentioned in the previous exhibits, yet it was clear that they would be central to new ones unless we ignored the work of our scholars. It should also be said that with a sizeable African American caucus in the Mississippi legislature and a Choctaw Indian tribe that is one of the state's largest employers, the Eurocentrism of 1961 was no longer tolerable in any case. But the shortage of artifacts remained a nagging worry. Museum staff members were made uneasy by the need to use reproductions to make up for errors of omission in a historical collections policy based primarily on the generosity of wealthy old families, yet it was too late and the museum was too poor to initiate a major collecting effort to remedy the lack with examples of "the real thing."

A new "master story" emerged from the work of the scholars (and not coincidentally echoed some of the "cultural encounters" discourse of the contested 1992 Quincentenary celebrations): taking 1500 as the beginning of the time line, it would show three civilizations, Native, European, and African, meeting on widely differing terms on the land of Mississippi; stories of the forging of a common culture would be embodied in the presentation of the stories of seven selected individuals, most of them cultural brokers; this would be set against an event history of colonial Mississippi under the French, English, and Spanish flags, ending with 1798, the beginning of the territorial period, which would mark the end of the exhibit; several "lifestyle" exhibit units would explore the mixing of cultures through the examination of the survival today of foods and linguistic elements derived from all the constituent cultures of the colonial period (cultural mixing as "tossed salad" rather than "melting pot").

The effects of the problematic 1992 commemoration struck this project directly when the application for an implementation grant with this construction of the story was denied by NEH, apparently at least partly for excessive political correctness. But as the exhibit project was put on hold for a year awaiting the glacial NEH cycle and a new review committee, several things happened that committed the team to sticking with its revisionist intentions and indeed to go even farther. First, the museum mounted a temporary exhibit on the history of the cotton gin that led to acrimonious response from the African American community, including one of the department's own board members. Second, it became clear that the public was ahead of its culture czars on these subjects as films, documentaries, and other media successfully raised many of the painful issues about Native American displacement and African American slavery that many official venues were avoiding or were "gentling down." Finally, in 1990 the Native American Graves Protection and Repatriation Act, which mandated the repatriation of skeletons, grave goods, and items of cultural patrimony from museums accepting federal funding, raced through Congress with barely a dissenting voice, and by 1993 its first requirements were being met by museums, including ours. Some of the artifacts we had blithely planned to use were likely to be subject to repatriation.

The year 1992 had seen another election and subsequently a very changed NEH. Once again the museum applied for a grant; this time a planning grant for the development of a design proposal was obtained. Then finally in the following year an implementation grant was sought and obtained, and I was asked to direct the project beginning in the summer of 1994. In preparation I began reading the critical museology literature, which has been profoundly affected by the postmodern debate. A tentative consensus has emerged that preserves the museum's privileged position by adopting the Habermasian concept of museums as part of the "public sphere" where rationality emerges through communicative action.[3] The implications of this concept are that the museum as public space remains an important part of community life, but instead of being a place for the imposition of hegemonic discourses about official versions of the past, about culture as fetishism, and even about proper behavior in public space, the museum can and should become a place where community identities are debated and forged. Just as there is tension in the critical theory versus postmodern theory debate, there is a variety of opinion on whether the goal of exhibition should be to encourage consensus or to celebrate coexistence in diversity.[4] Working museum staffs, on the other hand,

ETHNOHISTORY AND ETHICS

can get very upset about the threat that community participation in decision making poses to their professional expectations; these themes emerge repeatedly in discussions in professional journals (e.g., *Curator*), on the Internet (e.g., MUSEUM-L; a 1995 thread on this issue evolved from "for whom do we do our work" to "Visigoths at the gates" in the space of two weeks), and within individual museum walls. The American Museums Association has addressed such issues somewhat indirectly through its Excellence and Equity initiative, which calls for affirmative action in hiring and enhanced efforts to reach out to communities that museums serve while retaining the highest standards of scholarship.[5]

I found the basic museum-as-agora concept a persuasive working assumption for the exhibits to be developed. But since the exhibit team and its external contractors were all white and middle class, and there were no apparent options for increasing staff diversity during the grant period, it was clear that we needed to form an advisory committee that would bring diversity to the process. We decided to constitute a committee consisting of descendants of the communities whose history we were going to tell.

This move was somewhat daunting to the exhibit team but was accepted because it was seen as possibly "inoculating" the exhibit against the controversy meted out to so many of the Quincentenary programs and our own recent cotton gin exhibit. That latter exhibit had produced a good deal of bad feeling within the larger department staff; though the museum had no African American staff members in positions to influence exhibit decisions, the department as a whole had a significant minority of African American professional staff in its archives division, yet their opinion had not been solicited or heard in advance of the public outcry. The team was therefore also persuaded to form an advisory group among the department's nonmuseum staff that could offer advice both as history professionals and as community members. Finally, we resolved that neither committee would be window dressing: both would be listened to and taken seriously as participants in the process.

The exhibit team had already decided to be revisionist because we had accepted the authority of professional historical discourse. But in making the "consultative turn" we also accepted that history has other stakeholders than historians, that in the process of museum exhibit construction the stakeholders whose identities were most at risk and who deserved an opportunity to participate included

1. ourselves: the exhibit team consisted entirely of upper-middle-class whites of liberal persuasion, only one of whom was male; the exhibit team had concerns of professional reputation and institutional integrity and was looking toward a pending reaccreditation by the American Museums Association;
2. our historical advisors, only one of whom was minority; the historians also had professional reputations to consider, based upon research quality;
3. the design firm we hired, consisting of upper-middle-class whites living in New York; the design firm was not so much concerned with historical accuracy as it was with professional reputation, based upon success in creating a spectacle that would attract visitors and incorporate enough novelty, in the context of a restrained house style, to receive favorable notice in the design world;
4. the remaining staff of the department of which we were a part, consisting of mostly college-educated whites and blacks; these colleagues were concerned that the institution of which they were a part not represent them with a presentation that their own communities would find offensive;
5. the community of people whose history we were going to tell, consisting of whites, blacks, and Indians; we did not know at the outset what would be the dominant concerns of these groups, but we guessed that a fair presentation of their past would be a first requirement.

Finding a workable paradigm for museum-community consultation is not easy. In our case we had not begun our exhibit development process with consultation, and because so much was already invested in preliminary design, consultation was not entirely open-ended. Further, because as a state historical museum we occupied such a hegemonic position (the museum in fact occupied a prominently located antebellum state capitol with a full complement of neoclassical columns across the front), we could not seek out just any community representatives. Political considerations required us to go through existing institutional gatekeepers in seeking committee members; for example, we had to take a government-to-government approach in contacting Native American tribal chairmen and chiefs. Within those constraints, however, we attempted to do as much as we could to create an open forum, offering the committees organizational support and urging them to communicate apart from our common meetings. In addition, we took a presentation on the road and visited community gatherings convened by community representatives in Mississippi, Louisiana, and Oklahoma in a further search for input.

I confess to having had my own curiosity about this process. Because I am a colonial period ethnohistorian interested in the negotiations of power that took place during the colonial period, I was interested in observing a sort of level playing field rerun of those same negotiations: the committee membership we planned would echo both the demographics of today (in the relative numbers of representatives) and those of the colonial period (in the communities represented). Hence the following committee representation of colonial period descendants:

1 French
1 Spanish
1 English
3 African
3 Choctaw
1 Chickasaw
1 Tunica-Biloxi

While the Native American community did not quite have the majority (as had been the case during the whole of the 1500–1800 period), both blacks and whites would have to stand solidly together to oppose their views; and if blacks sided with Native Americans (as they frequently did in the colonial period), whites could not prevail. I knew that the committee members would not hold the same opinions about many of the issues addressed in the exhibit, but I hoped that they would be willing to discuss and reach rational compromise. At the least, I hoped that all would come to realize how difficult it is to satisfy everyone.

In the event, I was wrong and right. In our officious anxiety to "do things right" we offered the committee the use of a "multicultural trainer," and they quickly made it plain that they were ready to talk without intermediary if we were. The first request from the committee was a request for veto power over exhibit elements. We took a deep breath and said yes. But when we all began our discussions, the very reasonable possibilities became clear:

1. I don't accept your view of my past
   a. I want my view or nothing at all
   b. I can tolerate your view if mine is presented too

2. I accept your view of my past
   a. I have additional information
   b. Your view is too painful as is and must be softened

What was the real issue after all? That the communities' importance in the past be recognized and that their existence in the present not be ignored; that we overtly recognize that all presentation of the past is about the creation of present community identities. People wanted their stories told, and they didn't want to see something completely unrecognizable represented as "their story." But if it was possible to tell their story, they were quite prepared to accord the same privilege to others. The following negotiated emphases emerged from our discussions.

European Colonial Story

1. In fairness to Spaniards, we would counter the so-called Black Legend of Spanish cruelty with a presentation of the efforts of people like Bartolomé de Las Casas to stop the violence of the sixteenth century and a clear portrait of the relatively tolerant eighteenth-century Spanish colonial regime.

2. Frequently neglected for their long-term contributions, the French would be spotlighted for their relatively insightful Indian policy and comparatively liberal slave code.

3. Usually spotlighted, the British heritage would be somewhat played down, but stress would be placed on pioneering and initiation of cotton agriculture.

4. All Europeans would be shown as working toward their own success, willing to use violence and cruelty against non-Europeans to succeed.

Native American Story

1. Exhibits would stress the precontact civility and complexity of Native societies.

2. Emphasis on variety instead of homogeneity would show that North America had already been a "nation of nations" before Europeans and Africans arrived.

3. European disease would be highlighted as the source of loss of Native power, not stupidity, bloody-mindedness, or liquor.

4. The role of Indian tribes in intertribal slave catching would be honestly portrayed.

5. The relative success of modern tribes in recovering from European disease disaster and their dominance of the region through the whole of the colonial period would be stressed.

African Story

1. Lacking artifacts, we would use video to portray complex African civilizations.
2. African participation in the early slave trade would be discussed in the light of African practice.
3. The losses of the Middle Passage (material culture, freedom) would be highlighted as the source of loss of power, not stupidity or weakness.
4. The importance of African skills to early colonial success would be stressed, along with African resistance modes to coerced labor.
5. African agency would also be stressed through examining African collusion with Indians.

All three communities accepted compromises. Europeans had a tough time of it, being deposed from the central place in the story. Indians would now dominate; Africans would be portrayed as strong, intelligent, and skilled; Indian and African heroes would be named and made prominent; European heroes would be made less prominent. Native Americans, finding consensus among a variety of opinions held by modern tribes, agreed that pottery, shell, and metal items that had been discovered with burials might be shown in replica so that their workmanship could speak to the sophistication of their culture; and the Choctaws allowed a mortuary scaffold to be reproduced to serve as a striking symbol of Indian losses by European disease. African Americans allowed the representation of a place symbolizing social death—the onboard cubbyhole for a slave on a slave ship—and the open discussion of degrees of oppression. Both Native Americans and African Americans were satisfied that the famous Europeans of the colonial period whom people expected to hear about would be represented, as long as they were not dominant. Finally, the museum had to make its own compromises by forgoing complete control and settling for the use of reproduction objects.

After compromise had made itself felt, the new story line became clearer. It would show three civilizations, Native, European, and African, portrayed as of equal value to their people. They would meet on the land of Mississippi as a result of European imperialism; Native people would be devastated by European disease, while Africans would be stripped of possessions and coherent social structures by the process of enslavement. There would be a struggle for autonomy, characterized by Indian wars and slave revolts, during the colonial period, and Native people would have great power to control events, while

Africans would win freedom in previously unrecognized numbers. In the end market forces and gang-style field agriculture would seal white European hegemony, which would clearly be on the way to triumph by 1798.

Overall, this story would raise few objections from a modern historian of the period. For the museum, too, it was much harder to adjust to using new sources to tell the story than to the story itself. And the gains were enormous. The communities involved took on tasks in the work on the exhibit that were invaluable as an overburdened museum staff struggled to complete an enormous piece of work on an inflexible schedule. The Chickasaws of Oklahoma videotaped seven auditions to facilitate the choice of a Chickasaw woman to portray Molly Gunn. French descendants from the Gulf Coast assisted by providing authentic reproduction artifacts and costumes for both videos and static displays. Anglo descendants from Natchez lent furniture for a video, while Tunica-Biloxi descendants offered to prepare reproduction ironwork. Museum efforts to find actors for the videos drawn from the communities themselves received consistent assistance, and the plan to use the original languages with subtitles in the videos was accepted and supported by intensive linguistic research among Native elders for authenticity.

Some issues could not be addressed directly. Miscegenation was treated very delicately, for it is a subject with which the modern community is still explosively uncomfortable. There are asides referring to it, accommodated in the individual videos: the free black entrepreneur speaks of purchasing his wife, who already has children by her white master, his employer; the Chickasaw woman tells her story of Chickasaw origins to children who are half-Cherokee, and later she marries a white man.[6] But direct presentation in the exhibits was avoided. Instead, a "food table" showing the multicultural origins of the foods now characteristic of southern cuisine stands in for the mixed genetic heritage of the people who consume it.

Nor was this account the end, of course. The original essay was written months before the exhibit opened. That event—which took place with the participation of all the communities involved, who together invented their own ceremony of dedication, drawing upon the Native American calumet ceremony—was capped with a multicultural festival. The video segments of the exhibit have proved to be the most popular element for the communities; of the seven individual videos that the museum originally proposed, three were rejected by the committee and replaced with others, and many addi-

ETHNOHISTORY AND ETHICS

tional candidates for presentation were suggested. The communities assisted actively with the videos' creation, from providing artifacts and costumes to training actors in proper comportment to recovering Chickasaw-language text for one actor to speak. The exhibit had, in short, ceased to be just another enunciation from on high of another authoritative Euro-American presentation of the past. It became a story in which all three communities could find themselves and recognize the stake that this past gives them in this present.[7]

Notes

1. These essays were published as *Natives, Europeans, and Africans in Colonial Mississippi*; copies were distributed to social studies teachers throughout Mississippi.

2. For the notion of "denial of coevalness" see Fabian, *Time and the Other*.

3. See "Social Action and Rationality" and "The Public Sphere," in Seidman, *Jürgen Habermas on Society and Politics*.

4. There is a great deal of debate here. Theorists lean toward a multiperspectival view of the museum's future. For two excellent collections of this literature see Karp and Lavine, *Exhibiting Cultures*, and Karp, Kreamer, and Lavine, *Museums and Communities*.

5. See American Association of Museums, *Excellence and Equity*.

6. We did discuss this issue openly at least once: at an on-site presentation of exhibit plans at the Smith-Robertson Museum of African American history in Jackson, our discussions made all of those present realize that both blacks and whites in Mississippi are related to one another through large numbers of each community being related to Indians.

7. Twelve years later the power of this new story continues as plans for a completely new museum include a broadly expanded community committee representing all the people of Mississippi over its history.

21. Blood and Earth

*Native Bodies in the North
American Landscape*

The first European explorers of North America found that many of its indigenous people preserved the remains of their dead in elaborate ways and participated in mortuary rituals that looked very exotic. They also reported activities in which rival Native groups apparently destroyed their enemies' mausolea for political ends. As in many other aspects of the earliest contact between European and American, however, Spaniards, Frenchmen, and Englishmen fitted themselves into the Native sociopolitical landscape in their behavior toward what they certainly perceived were rites of considerable significance for the Native peoples and did not themselves generally desecrate burials except as allies of other Native groups.

Somewhere along the line that behavioral restriction was discarded, such that nineteenth-century soldiers on the Great Plains practiced a lucrative sideline in the exhumation of newly dead Indian bodies to be sent to anthropologists on the East Coast for study; such that Euro-American archaeologists still assert a natural right to the study of long-dead Indian bodies; such that poor marginal farmers of the Mississippi River valley today dig up Native graves dating from the thirteenth to the nineteenth century to sell to art connoisseurs (not [usually] the bones but the pottery and other artifacts found with them). In this paper I will carry out a historical examination of European and Native American death practices and some consequences of those practices in the present status of Native burials.

The material in this chapter was first published as "Blood and Earth: European Use of North American Native Remains from Contact to the Present," in *Rediscovering America, 1492–1992: National, Cultural and Disciplinary Boundaries Re-examined* (111–31), selected proceedings of the Louisiana Conference on Hispanic Languages and Literatures, which was held in Baton Rouge, February 27–30, 1992. The article was substantially updated and revised for this volume.

Ways of Death

Death is the ultimate non sequitur, and for all peoples at all times it has been one of the most significant of the rites of passage. While the variety of details of mortuary practices is limitless, there are several constants that seem to be universal, some of them pertaining to the individual and some to the community.

Because human beings are reluctant to face the idea of termination of life, all human communities have developed some notion of the survival of an individual spiritual essence after death, and special tasks have to be carried out by the living to deal with it. This essence or "soul" is often thought to hesitate in its journey to the otherworld, reluctant to leave. Its presence is deemed dangerous and "polluting," and the living must both protect themselves from its baleful influence and encourage it to depart. What people believe about the structure of the otherworld influences their behaviors in this aspect of mortuary ritual.[1]

Because death threatens the continuity of the community, other tasks have to be carried out to ensure that the threat of discontinuity cannot be realized. The social roles, interests, and obligations of the deceased have to be transferred to others or extinguished. Material matters must be dealt with, such as the disposition of personal and real property.[2] Social, political, and especially economic factors influence strongly how this side of mortuary ritual is carried out, so much so that the archaeologist Lewis Binford enunciated the rule that an individual's importance in life would influence significantly the material investment made in his treatment in death.[3]

The otherworld/this-world dichotomy comes together in the details of mortuary ritual in a way that is importantly correlated with the form a culture takes, leading to the generalization that people seek to structure the society of the dead in the otherworld in such a way as to mirror and ensure the reproduction of their society in this world. This fact is significant to our enquiry here because it affects the placement of remains in the earth and the significance that placement has to the people who put them there.

The simplest form of burial is what archaeologists refer to as a "primary" burial, where the body is simply placed on or in the earth and left there to decompose without further human intervention. Cultures that practice primary burial exclusively do not usually wait long before carrying out the burial, and one purpose of their practice seems to be to hasten the dissolution of the remains; furthermore, they usually believe that the decedent's journey to the otherworld is a short one. They tend to be egalitarian and sometimes only semisedentary, depending for at least part of their subsistence on hunting and/or herding, so the locations of their burials are usually distributed among their households and mark direct claim to only a central locality. The dissolution of the body is left to the forces of nature and is not observed by the living, while the location of the burial itself is usually unmarked and is therefore only known through the memory of the living. Presumably, there is a correlation between the dissolution of the body and the eventual failure of memory as to its resting place.

When people choose to "process" a dead body, they may choose any one of a number of methods to attain two principal results: whole-body preservation through evisceration and mummification or reduction to a preservable mineral form through rotting, boiling, flaying, or cremation. It has been argued that these results may have something to do with kinship principles, but the significance of both is that they take some time—usually correlated with a belief in a long and difficult journey to the otherworld—and that the result is a set of preserved material remains. Peoples who practice this "secondary" form of burial are usually fully sedentary and depend primarily on agriculture for their subsistence. Their societies are not strictly egalitarian but are more often hierarchical, and indeed this secondary processing may be limited to only the higher echelons of the society. The resulting remains are used to constitute what are often major monuments on the land, marking significant claims to the subsistence base.

These anthropological generalizations do not apply only to "primitive" peoples, although they appear thus starkly generalized in the descriptions of such peoples made by Western anthropologists. They lack the dimensionality of the participant's experience of mortuary practice because so few descriptions of such practice have been recorded by or with the assistance of indigenous peoples.[4] Literate cultures have cloaked their own mortuary practices in the flourishes of literary and religious meditations, but their practices are no less correlated with their construction of their worlds.

Deathways of European Colonizers

The Europeans who claimed to have discovered a "new world," already known to its inhabitants through millennia of custom, had their own millennia of mortuary practice behind them, long enough for them to have begun noticing the remains of their distant ancestors and wondering reflexively about them.

ETHNOHISTORY AND ETHICS

At least the late end of the "prehistoric" era of European cultural evolution had gone in for mortuary monuments on the landscape in a big way: people of the Bronze Age built the megalithic tombs known as dolmens in France and passage graves in Ireland; people of the Iron Age built earthen mounds known as barrows. All of them buried in those monuments the most important of their people, to mark a claim on the land. Most of the population, however, had come to be buried in cemeteries related to settlement sites.[5]

The rise of the Roman Empire made barbarians of the rest of Europe, but neither Rome nor the Christian hegemony that followed did much to change mortuary practices beyond substituting flesh burial for cremation among the northern Germanic peoples. Prehistoric European custom had not in general included the lengthy processing of dead bodies that would indicate a belief in a long journey for the soul. Clearly, the notion of confining the dead, as in a churchyard, was already established among barbarians; what was new was the injunction that all were equal in death. But feudal endowments of churches and the privileged treatment of the nobility through burial under those churches' very floors—coupled, in the special case of kings, with lengthy secondary processing of their bodies—effectively negated the asserted principle of equality.[6] The world of the dead was now a part of the network of Christian monuments encompassing Europe, but as such it continued to be structured so as to stake claims upon the land: the dead bodies of its most important leaders were co-opted to add accretions of power to Christian centers, while the heaven, purgatory, and hell of the otherworld reinforced the feudal structures of this one. Thus by the end of the medieval period

> the fate of the soul was now linked to that of the corpse in all classes, not just among saints. The same spatial relationships are evident. The "holy" were entombed within the church, the holiest at the east end; but the common folk, most of whom supposedly began their otherworldly existence in purgatory, were buried outside the churchyard. Excommunicates lay beyond the holy bounds of the cemetery altogether, their souls banished to hell. They had chosen to cut themselves off from Christian society. Pagans, Jews and unbaptized infants were also excluded because they never joined it. Consequently they too were banished to the wilderness of unconsecrated ground. Finally . . . the active rejection of the Church by the relapsed or impenitent heretic was punished by denial of burial whether inside or outside consecrated ground: far from being preserved in an aura of holiness, he was literally cast to the winds.[7]

What we are interested in here is to bring European traditions of death down to the seventeenth and eighteenth centuries so we can understand the behavior of Europeans toward the obsequies of the American Other. Recent scholarship in Europe has been very active in examining early modern attitudes toward death, spurred by the scholarship of Philippe Ariès and his theories about an evolution in western European attitudes toward death from the twelfth century until modern times.[8] Criticisms of Ariès's synthesis have affirmed the patterns he saw but have argued that they were less chronological than overlapping.[9]

Ariès thought that a "tame" death, in which the dying person accepts death calmly as a natural process and dies surrounded by his community, affirming and strengthening its values, began to be superseded in Europe in the twelfth century as notions of individualism among the elite class began to emerge and the fate of the individual began to be of concern.[10] It is during this period that the Catholic Church began to elaborate church-mediated otherworldly progress through purgatory, requiring masses for the dead and prayers drawn out over years, which Ariès saw as the "ecclesiastic colonization of death." This process slowly trickled down to the more ordinary people by the fifteenth and sixteenth centuries. By the seventeenth and eighteenth centuries, with the emergence of the nuclear family as the support of the individual, mourning and a concern with death had become private.

It is also worthy of remark that in the second half of the eighteenth century graveyards began to be removed beyond city walls for reasons of public health.[11] This says something about advances in medicine, certainly; and it means that Europeans had to develop new rituals first for the task of reburial (which had already been required as graveyards within the cramped confines of city walls had been filled, emptied into ossuaries, then refilled) and then for corteges to the distant graveyard.[12] But it also means that population growth in cities was leading to a more and more symbolic relation to the land as city dwellers first gave up their dead to a cemetery near their homes and eventually gave them up to a cemetery belonging to the larger collective and situated on its border with the Outside, or the farming land for which the growing cities were now service centers rather than residences. The French historian François Lebrun referred to the "divorce of the village of the living from the village of the dead."[13]

At the same time all this was happening, a kind of proto-archaeology was being born of an interest in the legitimation of power. Certainly, all along

ETHNOHISTORY AND ETHICS

the way it had been common to treat with respect the more obvious marks upon the landscape constituted by large earthworks and monuments, and among ordinary people they bore a reputation for mystery and fear, just as they do today. But this was all the more reason for emerging nation-states to try to take advantage of the implied awe as with the Renaissance came a nationalistic interest in history and the legitimation of existing regimes and cultures through links with antiquity. The civilizations of ancient Egypt and Greece had collected and revered relics of what they viewed as more ancient golden ages. Although during medieval times Europeans had concerned themselves mostly with the relics of saints, still the monks of Glastonbury claimed to have dug up the bodies of Arthur and Guenevere in 1191, either to quash popular rumors of Arthur's reincarnation in Arthur of Brittany or to raise money for new buildings, while Geoffrey of Monmouth tried to tie both Arthur and the victorious Normans to Stonehenge.[14] In the same spirit one of the narratives of Hernando de Soto compared his funeral to that of Alaric the Goth to flatter the Spanish monarch, who traced his lineage from the Visigoths.[15] Yet until Europeans encountered the Native Americans of the Western Hemisphere, they had no idea of the real antiquity of the European stone tools they had been attributing to magical or natural sources for hundreds of years; it was, in fact, contact with "primitive" people that made them begin to wonder about their own preliterate origins.

Deathways of Eastern North American Indians

The notion of using burials as a settlement charter had clearly been an important feature of the cultures of prehistoric inhabitants of eastern North America as they became sedentary farmers during the last two undisturbed millennia of their tenure. The people of the Hopewell culture of the Ohio valley, which had widespread influence on cultures all across the East, built log charnel houses, often related to the spectacular earthworks that characterized their culture, and subjected the bodies of their elites to lengthy processing before final interment within them. Although Hopewell peoples did not depend upon a single staple crop to support their settlements and were often only semisedentary, archaeologists now think that they did support a relatively complex social organization and did intend to structure their relationship with the land by their earthwork construction.[16]

The maize-based Mississippian culture that developed after ca. AD 800 in the major river valleys of central and eastern North America, organized in ranked lineages, also used the bodies of elites to punctuate the landscape,

burying them at least temporarily in or near one or more of the large substruc-
tural mounds that characterized Mississippian ceremonial centers. Chiefs and
priests (or perhaps they were one and the same) were buried with the skulls of
their enemies and the bodies of children and servants killed to honor them and
serve them in the next world. Bodies of elites were also processed at greater
length than those of commoners, which were most frequently buried either in
cemeteries related to the ceremonial center (in the case of those who served the
elites at the center) or in graves on the outskirts of associated hamlets or
farmsteads, but toward the end of the period, in the fifteenth and sixteenth
centuries, there was a trend toward increased use of secondary processing of
bodies.[17]

Scholars have discussed the possible form and meaning of Mississippian
mortuary ritual at great length but have been limited by the fact that the
accompanying ceremonial and hence much of the meaning cannot be observed in the patterning of material remains. For that they have been forced to
use the several funerals among the mound-using Natchez of the lower Mississippi valley as observed in the early eighteenth century by French colonists.[18] As more archaeological evidence has come to light, however, it seems
that what the colonists were allowed to see or were told does not tally with
what the actual practice was: the French were told that commoners were
subjected to secondary processing as well as elites, but this now seems not to
have been the case, and the Natchez, like most mound-building societies of
the region, buried their common people more simply. Still, all the evidence
shows that Mississippian practice included both emphasis upon ceremonial
pomp marking a ceremonial center and the burial of ordinary people out
across the landscape where they lived their lives, in effect structuring the
world of the dead as the world of the living was structured.

Colonial Period

Since the most immediate effect of the first contacts with Europeans was
contagion and death, and since European disease continued to make horrific
inroads that made decimation seem mild, death must have assumed a tremendous metaphysical significance for Native peoples at the same time that the
enormous numbers of dead must have made it impossible to maintain traditional mortuary practices. We know a great deal about the objective effects of
these large numbers of deaths: sixteenth-century North America was in a state
of political ferment as enormous death rates dismantled societal structures

ETHNOHISTORY AND ETHICS

and forced the survivors to migrate and consolidate in entirely new group-ings.[19] The value of each individual would have been very great and his or her loss a correspondingly great loss to the newly constructed societies; mortuary ceremonies, which we know from material remains became very protracted in many cases, must have become much more important for the perpetuation of roles and the strengthening of group solidarity.

It is hard to say how beliefs were affected by this holocaust, because we still know very little of beliefs after the great disruption of European dis-ease and nothing of them before it. And there is no real alteration in the *range* of funerary practices: after as well as before, people practiced everything from whole-body interment to cremation to separation of flesh from bone to mummification. Different people did different things after reorganizing their groupings, even though they regrouped with their ethnic relatives or their close neighbors, but in spite or perhaps because of having to pass through terrible death rates that may have forced them to leave corpses strewn about unburied, they continued to treat their dead with veneration, and the treat-ment of the dead remained crucial to the structure of the society of the living.

How did the European colonizers treat the dead of the Indians they met? Their behavior, not surprisingly, was not uniform, but, perhaps surprisingly, it was generally restrained at first, as I have already observed. Bruce Trigger would argue that this restraint was probably connected to the widespread belief of the time in psychic unity and common humanity, which emphasized the civilizing mission of the Europeans and the perfectibility of the Indians. Since the Indians were simply at the most primitive level of human life, there was thought to be no particular necessity of learning anything about their past by digging up burials, since it had nothing of value to teach Europeans.[20] Also, it should be noted that only where Native people practiced elaborate mortu-ary ceremonial, particularly extended secondary processing of the remains, were the remains likely to come to the special attention of Europeans.

The first Europeans to make extended enough contact with the Native people of the interior Southeast to be concerned with their burials were the members of the Hernando de Soto expedition. First, when Soto and his men landed they found the castaway Juan Ortiz, who had been captive among the Indians of the Florida peninsula for ten years. In the first year of his captivity he had been set to guarding from wild beasts the corpses of the dead that had been exposed to the elements in the first stage of secondary processing. The account given of this task in the two narratives that mention it does not indicate undue squeamishness with the concept of secondary processing on the part of the Spaniards, nor does the account of the charnel house in the village of Talomeco, where the elite dead of the Cofitachequi province were said to be placed. Soto and his men, directed to this charnel house by the ostensible ruler of Cofitachequi and invited to help themselves to the pearls placed with the bones of the dead, did not hesitate to take them, but unless the accounts of this episode represent an agreed-upon lie, the Spaniards did not simply plunder and carelessly disturb the burial place. It is certainly also possible that the remains in the charnel house were those of a rival group, somehow ritually taboo to the Cofitachequi people, who were using the Spaniards to despoil it.[21]

On later occasions among the prosperous chiefdoms of the Mississippi valley Soto's army also supported "allies" who were taking revenge on their enemies by sacking their ossuaries and deliberately desecrating burials. The Spanish accounts imply that the Native peoples of the valley considered the plundering of charnel houses a fundamental part of warfare and a requisite sign of conquest and subjugation. Clearly, the Spaniards had no qualms about taking part in these activities, but clearly also they did not share their allies' motivations—or at least those who described the events did not. It is obvious throughout that they appreciated a serious if heathen treatment of the dead and did not find unusual the idea that extended and complex treatment of remains should be associated with elites.[22]

The British were much more cavalier in their behavior toward Indian dead, apparently according no respect at all to the remains of Indians known to have been buried with rich accompaniment. James Axtell documents numerous seventeenth-century incidents of grave robbing from Virginia to New England, so frequent that they may have led the Native people of the region to begin to hide the graves of their dead, forcing them to cease the practice of outward differentiation of elite burials. In spite of pressure by missionaries, however, it did not force them to cease burying the dead with the necessities for their journey to the otherworld, and accordingly the robbing of graves for their contents continued.[23]

The French colonists of New France and Louisiana met with many examples of rather spectacular mortuary treatment among the tribes they encountered, always connected with secondary processing. The most striking of these was certainly the Huron Feast of the Dead, during which bodies that had been scaffolded to decompose on the borders of a village were bundled up and interred in a large mass when a village was due for abandonment because of exhaustion of soils, thereby leaving the village for the habitation of the dead until its lands should return to fertility.[24] The psychologically savvy Jesuits who took charge of French missionary efforts in Canada from earliest days did not attempt to make their Native converts give up traditional practices, feeling as they did that reverence toward the dead meant that the Indians believed in an afterlife and that such belief should be encouraged. The general practice in Canada of treating Native peoples in such a way as to respect their sovereignty, too, must have influenced a generally hands-off approach that does not seem to have been very readily transgressed in the case of burials.

This was not for want of French observation of Native burials. Pierre Le Moyne d'Iberville at his earliest exploration of the Gulf Coast observed an ossuary mound on what he was thus pleased to call "Massacre Island."[25] Antoine Simon Le Page du Pratz observed details of Natchez mortuary ritual, and Father Charlevoix described intermediate deposition treatment of Natchez elites in the middle 1720s. Although both decried the sacrifice of retainers on the death of the elite person, neither disapproved or appeared not to understand the reverent treatment of remains.[26]

These variant behaviors on the part of European colonists may be less attributable to a Latin reverence for Native burials versus British overwhelming greed and more the result of their respective security with regard to the tribes that were their neighbors. Although the British were always very insecure about the safety of the frontier region, Indians died off and were "reduced to civility" in great numbers along the eastern seaboard, where most of the grave robbing went on, but Britons rarely disturbed the burials of tribes like the Iroquois or Cherokee that remained strongly situated in the fastness of mountain or distant valley. Except for the several Spanish mission towns established in Florida in the sixteenth and seventeenth centuries, most of them destroyed by British slave raids by the first quarter of the eighteenth century, the Spaniards were too few to exert much influence upon the way the Indians of the interior chose to bury and would not have dared to disturb existing burials. The same was true of the French, who were far less numerous in the Indian-dominated interior and who even occasionally participated in or observed Native funerary rites.[27]

American Period, Nineteenth Century

With the final victory of the new American confederation and its subsequent acquisition at the turn of the nineteenth century of the lands of North America that Europeans had presumed to control, the Puritan/Protestant mindset of moral superiority over the savage spread out of the Northeast and the eastern colonies in general and metamorphosed into the irritated desire for Indian Removal to clear space for a growing agricultural population.

As the new America was pushing its first inhabitants out onto the Plains, anthropology was making its debut as a discipline worthy of respect and academic recognition. Europeans had been fascinated for centuries by "cabinets of curiosities" and the peculiar habits of savages, which had led them to investigate by excavation what were seen by the late eighteenth century as the romantic tombs and obsequies of Druids and Saxons.[28] When nineteenth-century colonialism made it necessary to manage savages, anthropology emerged as a systematic study of savage societies whose inferiority to European societies was now—not coincidentally—being explained as a result of intrinsic defects; anthropology received official support in exchange for its promise of control.[29] Because anthropology, in the full bloom of scientific racism, was making a systematic study of racial groupings, it was interested in the physical characteristics of human beings, and especially savages, who promised to provide the ground for the dominant figure of the European.

Taught by the eighteenth-century anatomists and pursuing activities similar to theirs that led to body snatchings and grave robbings throughout Europe and even in New England, the early physical anthropologists needed the bodies of savages to complete their studies of them and to prove them racially inferior to Europeans.[30] Since they believed that American savages' cultures had not changed significantly in the whole time they had inhabited the lands of the Americas, there was no need to go to the trouble of finding old burials, particularly since most often they were not intact. It was far easier to rob a freshly made burial, and that is exactly what took place, to such a degree that throughout the second half of the nineteenth century "the collecting of Indian crania appears to have been a cottage industry on the frontier."[31] The grisly details are sparse, but they do indicate that the predominant attitude toward Indian burials was that they were the remains of zoological specimens. Neither the greedy soldier who dug them up nor the eminent doctor or professor who paid for it to be done seems to have given a second thought to the sentiments of the Indians, except to be careful to protect themselves from Indian anger by carrying out their depredations under cover of darkness.[32]

A link with the activities of the French anatomists and clinicians that Foucault studies in *Birth of the Clinic* is real, since leading craniologist Samuel

Morton, a physician, had taken some of his medical training with the clinicians in Paris in the 1820s as medicine began to focus upon the disease rather than the patient and turned to the autopsy/dissection as the ultimate opportunity for an exhaustive investigation of its pathology.[33] This attitude was clearly becoming a commonplace of clinical medicine in the Euro-American world of the nineteenth century, and it conduced to a general subjection of any ailing Other to the demands of medical science, but in practice it was the bodies of the powerless—the poor and indigent in Europe, who had to depend upon the charity of the clinics for treatment and the potter's field for burial when treatment failed, and the non-European colonized peoples outside of Europe—that were subjected to such dissection. This connects directly with the parallel triumph of social Darwinism during the same period, which relegated the poor and powerless in Europe and non-European societies elsewhere to the losing position in the evolutionary sweepstakes.[34]

Morton's position as both the "father of American physical anthropology" and the leading researcher in the study of racial differences in crania was attained significantly as a result of his efforts in collecting crania to study. This he did by establishing a network of doctors in the opening West to send him Indian crania, both from historic burial sites and from recent burials. Recent burials of known individuals were preferred, offering the opportunity to check phrenological theories about intelligence and leadership qualities against data on the living person. Morton was not alone as a collector of crania; other physicians also exhibited such an interest, and the study of crania became widespread, such that Louis Agassiz, teaching anatomy at Harvard, received skulls and even whole bodies from the secretary of war (who controlled the Bureau of Indian Affairs) in the late 1840s, and Franz Boas, certainly the founder of academic anthropology in the United States and later notable for his opposition to racism, was shipping skeletons to the Smithsonian in the 1880s.[35] These researchers played no favorites: they were equally interested in the skulls of other colonized peoples. But their work had the effect of confirming the attitude of Euro-American whites that Indians were not only doomed to extinction but deserved to be. This research justified Removal and treaty breaking on a massive scale, and it remains an integral part of many popular ideas about the Indian today. But the point here is the likelihood that this research line developed because it was needed to provide just such a justification, and it remains a matter of popular belief because the

Indians are still disturbingly present in their burials even on land they have long vacated.

Meanwhile, where Indians were being encroached upon and preached to by Europeans, they made some changes in at least the external form of their mortuary practices. We have already seen that Indians on the East Coast had had to cease marking elite burials in order to avoid having them robbed. The English missionaries also tried to stamp out the use of grave offerings and to confine burials to a churchyard, but by and large they were not successful except among the minority of Indians who made up the few "praying towns." Similar success by Spanish missionaries in Florida was restricted to Indians settled in mission communities. The Canadian Jesuits, on the other hand, did not attempt to alter Native practices except to substitute religious medals and other such items as grave offerings and to insist that converts be buried separately from others.[36] Where there were few converts, as in colonial Louisiana, no substantive alterations were made except that European trade goods came to be included in grave offerings.[37]

The real push for change in mortuary practice came only in the nineteenth century, when Indians east of the Mississippi were literally overrun by Euro-Americans and were pressured and coerced to adopt white ways. The Choctaws, for example, pleased their Presbyterian missionaries in the early nineteenth century by ceasing to place the dead person upon a scaffold next to his house to decompose before being packaged as bones in a charnel house for eventual burial. Instead, they buried him next to his house and built an empty scaffold over the grave, and at the end of the period when formerly the flesh should have rotted from the exposed bones they dismantled the scaffold and held the same sort of ceremony they had held before over the prepared bones to be taken to the ossuary.[38] Thus they succeeded in creating a ceremonial sequence that was structurally almost exactly the same as the one the missionaries disapproved, and in some places this sequence is still practiced, although in a cemetery. Wherever they now live, Indians, like Europeans, continue to structure the land actively with their burials.[39]

Landownership and Burial

The situation that exists today with respect to noncontemporary burials can be clearly seen in the eastern United States, where the former Native inhabitants have been most effectively Removed, both physically and politically, from control of the land. Land was what both rich and impoverished Euro-

ETHNOHISTORY AND ETHICS

peans quickly came to prize in North America, and free "government" land, acquired in usually fraudulent treaties with Indians, became the foundation of most landholding in the United States today. From the beginning the Puritan party line had said that Indians did not deserve to hold land because they had not "improved" it, and by that they meant—being ignorant of the vast ecological changes that the Indians had wrought on the lands of North America—that Indians had not reduced the land to the kind of submission required to support large populations dependent on mixed agriculture.[40] Because northeastern Indians had died out so apparently quickly, the myth of Indian sparseness across all of North America took root quickly, and it was reinforced by the missionaries' failure to persuade Indians to become European farmers, which conveniently implied that they had always been too indolent to work the land.

This attitude was enshrined in American land grant laws, which were intended to tame the land quickly, to "Euroform" it.[41] These laws—which were similar to colonial requirements for land grants that preceded them—usually specified that the recipient of free government land had to "improve" it in specific ways within a specific period of time or forfeit claim to it. Once the land was "improved" by the claimant, however, assuming that he was willing and able to pay the continuing taxes that supported the machinery of the law, he (and I use the pronoun advisedly, for women had limited property rights in the early Republic) was able to enjoy (and continues to enjoy) complete sovereignty over that land and everything on or under it (with some exceptions for valuable natural resources like water and, especially, minerals). This sovereignty is so fundamental a part of landholding in the United States that landowners resent being told that they cannot desecrate prehistoric (or even historic) graves, especially when those graves lie directly in the path of agricultural land alteration. One newspaper report of a land-leveling contractor in the Mississippi delta demonstrates the typical attitude: "Most of the sites were obvious knots, and they were the first to go. . . . It's just like a dent in your car—after a while you can't stand it."[42] Like New England farmers' famous tenacity at grubbing out stones from their fields, the farmers of the rich Mississippi valley have been intent on grubbing out the bodies of the prior inhabitants. One cannot help feeling that one ingredient of this abiding resentment is the dismaying ubiquity of the mortuary expression of Indian claim upon the land.

To understand the extent to which this practice is intentional, one has only to examine the burial laws for the states. It is clear that when those laws were framed, generally in the nineteenth century, there was no consideration at all for the rights of Native people to protection for the burials of their ancestors—or even of their contemporaries, if they had not buried according to white standards. State burial laws as originally conceived in the nineteenth century, concerned both with public health and the prosperity of the undertaking industry, generally envisaged specific dedicated cemeteries with marked graves, imported as a practice from Europe.[43] They also tended to structure the land of the Euro-American dead as the land of the living was structured: palatial settings for white burials, segregated places for black burials, and legal erasure of Indian burials. As states have aged, laws covering the protection of abandoned cemeteries and the removal of cemeteries lying in the way of development have had to be devised, and it should be pointed out that these phenomena created their share of anguish among Euro-Americans whose relatives were disturbed. But none of these accommodations of the dead were originally conceived to apply to Indian burial grounds or individual Indian burials. Although in many places such laws have been so construed, in many other places decomposed Indian skeletons were not considered to fit technical "dead body" definitions in the laws (partly because the laws did not envisage having to deal with decomposed skeletons at all), and unmarked Indian burial grounds were not considered to fit the "cemetery" definition.[44] Furthermore, although the sanctity of Euro-American burials is almost universally respected even if they lie on private land, the superior sanctity of landholding and property rights continues to stand in the way of protection of Indian burials in situ on private property, while marked white burials on private property are often spared because of "desecration" laws that apply everywhere. The best that can be hoped for when Native burials are discovered is usually a report to the coroner, subsequent excavation of the burial, and its reinterment in a different place, as many state laws handed over authority over Indian burials to the State Historic Preservation Offices when these were set up in the 1960s.[45]

Surprisingly little was changed by the passage of the Native American Graves Protection and Repatriation Act (NAGPRA) in 1990, which specifically applies only to federal lands and federally funded institutions and projects; in most eastern states, state law still covers the vast majority of the lands in the state. And as far as legal definitions are concerned, NAGPRA does little more than finally define Indian burials as the burials of dead *people*.[46] By 1991, only twenty-five states required reburial of prehistoric aboriginal remains, although excavation of such remains by authorized institutions was required or allowed. (Contrast this with the fact that in only a handful of states was the reburial of non-Indian remains *not* required.) By 1997, thirty-eight states had actually revised their laws or introduced new reburial and repatriation laws.[47]

An especially interesting point to be addressed for our purpose here is *where* the bodies are to be reinterred. Although Marcus Price's study of reburial did not specifically note where reburials would take place, the frequent requirement that it be at the expense of the descendants would argue that the least expensive option would be reinterment in a modern cemetery on Indian land—which usually means a reservation, especially in the West. Only Massachusetts and Arizona specified reburial as close as possible to the original site.[48] At least three states have mandated the provision of state-owned cemeteries for the reburial of ancient remains (Iowa, Kansas, and New Hampshire), and one state, Delaware, mandates reburial in airtight and exhumable containers. Most states, however, have been moving in the direction of scientific excavation followed by reburial by or with the consultation of Indian people, but their ability to regulate what is done on privately owned land will remain limited as long as public values continue to favor private property over the sanctity of the (Other's) grave.

Archaeology and the Death of the Other

In the considerable changes that have taken place in the discipline of archaeology since the turn of the twentieth century and before about the 1980s there was little introspection about the treatment of the Indian burials that have been an important part of archaeological research. Archaeologists, like anthropologists, served the Bureau of American Ethnology from the beginning as gatherers of additional information on Indians that would enable the government to better deal with its charges, and in 1906 the federal Antiquities Act put the emerging archaeological profession in control of at least the federally owned part of the American archaeological record, including Native American burials and the Indian lands under the control of the federal government.[49] At the beginning archaeology shared with anthropology the so-called short chronology that implied that Indians had only been in the Americas for a few thousand years, if that long, and that during that time their cultures had changed so little that the ethnology of living peoples offered valid commentary upon the meaning of their ancestors' buried artifacts and settlement patterns.

Worldwide, archaeologists active today in the discipline look back on more than a hundred years of tradition that sees the graves of "prehistoric" people as valid and even central subjects for study. To be fair, it should be recognized that this is nowhere more true than in Europe, except that there it is generally their own ancestors that archaeologists dig up. Having secularized and attenuated their own burial rituals, as Ariès has suggested, having cast their lot with a universalizing science that privileges their own secular worldview, archaeologists find it very hard to understand why there should be any objection to their treating the burials of Others the world over as simply a source of information. Yet clearly archaeologists' attitudes are measurably different when applied to what are undeniably their "own" people (there are only a handful of Indian and black archaeologists in the United States): Euro-American whites buried within the last hundred years in marked graves—the same population covered by American burial laws.

Evidence that archaeological practice is constrained by the exercise or threatened exercise of political power comes from the changing treatment of African American burials in the United States. Vulnerable throughout the nineteenth century to grave robbing for anatomical study, such burials have become especially sensitive with the success of the civil rights movement, such that events like the near destruction of parts of the African Burial Ground in New York by expansion of a federal office building have raised public and civic outcry. Significantly, the seventeenth- and eighteenth-century burials rescued there from development activities (around two hundred burials remained undisturbed), after analysis by physical anthropologists (including DNA studies to confirm connections with African homelands) at Howard University, were reinterred on the site in 2003 together with grave-associated artifacts, which were replicated for later study; finally, a memorial is to be erected at the site and an interpretive center provided.[50]

The African Burial Ground is also evidence that grouped unmarked graves may be respected differentially, but additional examples of individual unmarked graves are not far to seek. Indian mounds in the Mississippi valley were used by plantation owners for private cemeteries because of the danger of flooding, though of course in itself this practice represented the colonization of an already sacred space. The archaeologist Jeffrey Brain, after having excavated without question multiple Mississippian mound-builder burials from the Winterville site near Greenville, Mississippi, which had also been the site of a plantation in the nineteenth and early twentieth centuries, was advised to avoid one mound because it was known to have recent graves in it, "so recent, in fact, that many local residents still knew about them although there were no markers or any other indication." Brain then undertook to test another mound in which a modern disturbance was encountered in the form of postholes and pits: "One of the latter . . . was observed to have a suspiciously regular outline, and discreet probing brought up nails and fragments of wood. When more such evidence was found . . . it became quite apparent that we were in the middle of a nineteenth-century plantation graveyard," and this area of the mound was excluded from further excavation.[51]

Archaeologists and especially physical anthropologists have argued long and vehemently against being deprived of the ability to excavate Indian burials on scientific grounds: without written records, they say, it is impossible to learn many things about prehistoric lifeways unless bones are subjected to analysis. This is even more true as exotic analytical methods like bone collagen analysis are brought into play to determine the contents of the person's diet in life and DNA analysis is invoked as the grail of establishing "true" genetic relationships among "skeletal populations." In addition, it should be observed that burials have long enjoyed a special theoretical status in archaeology as "closed finds," in which all the objects found with the skeleton can be dated to the same deposition event and thus correlated chronologically to help in the building up of chronological sequences, which is why the associations of specific objects with specific burials are of such great importance. This kind of nondestructive observation of groupings and patterns has proved to be an approach on which Indians and archaeologists have cautiously agreed, at least in circumstances where archaeologists work with—or for—Native people to structure research designs by Native concerns with their own unwritten history, where they do not excavate except to mitigate destruction, where they treat remains with the same consideration they would accord the remains of their own people, and especially where all these questions are relatively moot because the archaeologists themselves are Native people or are employed and directed by Native people.[52]

The stumbling block is reburial. The imperfect nature of archaeological research tools is a familiar trope of processual archaeology, in view of the assumed progress being offered by new techniques supposedly being devised by scientists every day. Archaeologists are also habituated to talking in terms of a time squeeze, as development destroys literally hundreds of ancient sites every day and archaeologists are supposedly powerless to stop it. They argue that they therefore need to proceed with rescue excavations of what will be destroyed otherwise, and they want to preserve for future study everything they dig up: careful curation is a central value of the discipline.[53] If they are to be compelled to rebury, they want to study at length before they do so, and often there is not enough money available to make this an expeditious procedure. When they study, they want to be able to study destructively—by pulverizing a sample of bone—as well as nondestructively, although the fact that destructive testing prevents the later study of bone pathology keeps it to a minimum. It is not impossible for archaeologists to come to a rational compromise with Native people that could conceivably benefit both, but not as long as archaeologists insist upon the primacy of their "scientific" discourse.

Both parties are at least publicly united in their opposition to the looting of Native burials that takes place worldwide in the service of the international "art" market. Indians see burials as objects of veneration, their disturbance unthinkable unless unavoidable; archaeologists see burials as sources of information, their disturbance a matter of scientific enquiry justified when unavoidable; looters of burials see them as sources of wealth, their disturbance justified because of a number of rationalizations: the Indians abandoned them and didn't appreciate the value of the burial goods, the sites will be destroyed anyway because of development and farming practices. These looters are often (but not by any means always) poorly educated and semiskilled at best when measured by professional archaeological standards but far from either when it comes to finding and looting artifacts. They have little concern for the disturbance of a grave, and when they can do so they often simply lease a site from a landowner and systematically destroy it and any burials that are part of it for the artifacts.[54] The artifacts in turn are sold to wealthy collectors, most of them quite aware of the dubious source of their collections.[55] Yet although American law considers that a purchaser of stolen property does not obtain title to his purchase, the burden of proof is upon the complainant, who must prove that a given pot came from a given burial. The great auction houses like Sotheby's and Christie's deal in such materials without a qualm because such provenience cannot be proved, even though everyone may know perfectly well that certain kinds of artifacts have never been found except in mortuary contexts.

ETHNOHISTORY AND ETHICS

NAGPRA as Removal

In the past fifty years, all over the world indigenous peoples have begun to reassert their claims to cultural autonomy and human rights. In the United States this has manifested itself most insistently in the demand that historic and prehistoric Native burials and their accompaniments be accorded the same protection that American law accords to burials in general, culminating a century-long struggle for repatriation.[56] Not surprisingly, the concerns of Native people vary considerably: most on principle object to the abuse of their ancestors' remains, considering it the final unsupportable indignity; but motivation toward militancy against the study of the remains of their own people is related significantly to both traditional and current beliefs about death and the journey to the other world. Navajos, who fear possible pollution expressed as the ghost of the dead, do not want to take remains into custody and use non-Navajo archaeologists to carry out researches on Navajo land. Choctaws, whose traditional ritual was lengthy processing and reduction to bones, then burial in a communal mound, are aware that handling of bones was acceptable after a certain period; they have consented to limited dignified treatment of bones for scientific research. Tribes like the Chickasaws that practiced flesh burial feel that the remains ought to be allowed to disintegrate naturally to dust in the ground without being disturbed and object to any unnecessary handling of bones.

As this human rights issue became a central and undeniable concern of Native Americans, the U.S. government took symbolic action to defuse these concerns by creating a national Museum of the American Indian to absorb and thus legitimate the enormous collections made in the nineteenth and early twentieth centuries by some of the methods we have already discussed. A second action that was taken prior to the passage of NAGPRA was to promise funding to Native tribes that took responsibility for their own historic preservation activities on tribal lands.[57] The 1990 *Keepers of the Treasures* report, which summarized the results of meetings with Native representatives sponsored by the Department of Interior, came up with a number of suggestions, including putting in place efforts to train Native spiritual leaders as museum conservators and supporting tribal efforts to preserve their Native languages and crafts. And although the report recommended that tribal governments be treated the same as state governments in the national historic preservation structure, all the recognized tribes in the United States were forced to compete for the tiny sum of $100,000 per year for all of their projects, while each state was funded at several times that amount. Angered by this clearly meaningless sop, the tribes founded their own Keepers of the Treasures organization to help one another with preservation problems and to put pressure on Congress to make a more meaningful commitment.

But where Congress would not provide money, it could eventually agree to a grand symbolic gesture. Hence NAGPRA raced through Congress in 1990 in spite of the objections of archaeologists and physical anthropologists, who had visions of their entire professions going down the drain if Native concerns were actually to be taken literally. They need not have worried significantly, however, for although repatriation and reburial of skeletons and grave goods are required under the act, and all federally funded programs with such materials in their custody from the past had to make an inventory of such goods and attempt to identify them as to ethnic source, the burden of proof and claim lies with Native people, and proving claim to very old burials and objects according to objective scientific standards is difficult and costly unless the destructive technique for extracting DNA from bone can be applied effectively. The National Park Service took so long to craft regulations under the act that deadlines were missed, and Indian tribes without any historic preservation staff were suddenly burdened with hundreds of inventories to evaluate. Meanwhile, dissident archaeologists began to work with wealthy collectors to create private museums, which are not affected by the act, for privately owned artifacts and human remains.

Even more ironically, this means that Euro-Americans are now taking the lofty moral position of refusing to allow tribes access to remains on the argument that they may be those of their enemies, at the very time when indigenous peoples of former colonies worldwide are beginning to identify common concerns and North American Indians are in the process of forging a common cause in rejecting the right of former colonialists to decide how to dispose of the inconvenient burials of their ancestors. The reaction of Indians themselves to these issues has only in the 1990s begun to be articulated in such a way as to be heard and acknowledged by mainstream culture. The violent reactions of Indians to grave desecration from the sixteenth through the nineteenth centuries certainly never left their wishes in doubt, but only in the twentieth century have they taken to the tools of political power to secure the human right to undisturbed burial by shaming the dominant culture with its blatantly unequal treatment of burials. Simply on principle, Indian people are demanding that they not be hounded even to their graves.[58]

Nevertheless, most Indian people accept that repatriation and reburial are the best they can hope for given their continuing relative powerlessness. And this comes back around to the point I started with, the uses of bodies, the placement of bodies in the landscape. Reburial on tribal lands where remains can be protected is coming to be the most satisfactory final resting place for the remains of people who once marked the whole continent with their bodies. This issue of symbolic structuring of the world of the dead is of great importance to understanding many issues that remain problematic in this process. It may be said that what is going on here is a fundamental clash between ontologies of dead bodies.

Cultural bias permeates all the rites of passage, and death is certainly no different. One of these kinds of bias is Cartesian dualism's discreteness bias. The "scientific" view is that the ontological status of the physical remains is different and separate from that of the metaphysical remains: that even if anyone believes in a soul, it has certainly departed from a dead body, and the physical remains are just matter like all other nonliving materials studied by scientists. Yet if that view were carried to its logical end, then anthropologists would have to admit to believing that it is not possible to desecrate material human remains at all. U.S. burial laws, however, imply that human physical remains are somehow "haunted" by enough of the metaphysical part of the person that they should not be disturbed, such that the denial of applicability of the laws to Indian burials is equivalent to a denial of personhood to Indians themselves. Because there has really been no serious consideration of what Euro-Americans believe about the relation between body and soul over extended periods (and there are obviously issues of interest here, including a belief in resurrection, that would require a guarantee of permanent sanctity for human burials in order to serve the religious convictions of many Americans), it is clear that laws protecting all burials (e.g., from looting for patentable genetic material) are still insufficient and still suffering from the short temporal perspective of the establishment period of Euro-American communities in North America.[59]

Yet there is an even more serious unstudied issue here, especially important in view of recent interests in landscape anthropology and literal situatedness. The federal government, by passing legislation decreeing the repatriation and reburial of Native American remains, has at a stroke, merely by sacrificing the concerns of the archaeological profession, ironically managed to set in motion a process that will eventually extinguish even the symbolic Native American claim to the lands of North America forever, constituting a kind of final Removal. Repatriation, as long as it means returning remains not to the place whence they were taken but to the place where Native Americans now live, the relatively small enclaves officially left to them, will have the effect of carrying out the ultimate kind of ethnic cleansing: washing the very earth clean of any Native American presence. Instead of forming a vast and multidimensional web covering the land and inscribing it with many layers of meaning, the remains of three hundred generations of the continent's First Nations will be confined to the reservations that are all that is left to their descendants, as Euro-American land alteration rewrites the very landscape in its own image.

It is interesting to compare to this effect the work that was done in the early 1980s to decide how the federal government would mark nuclear waste repositories so that populations to come for 10,000 years would be warned away from them and would not dig them up. Semioticians, archaeologists, and anthropologists brought a number of suggestions to the table, most of them very familiar: nonlinguistic symbols, megalithic constructions—passive methods to suggest that people should keep away and respect the awe and danger of the places. Led by semiotician Thomas Sebeok and financed by Atomic Energy Commission contractor Bechtel Corporation, the final report concluded that given language and culture changes there could be no universal passive way of conveying such a message and called for the establishment of a living tradition carried by an "atomic priesthood."[60] A 1991 Oslo conference went further and concluded that a literal priesthood—world religions—would be the only likely way to so transmit such information.[61] Yet none of the archaeologists involved raised the issue of how they had been treating the sacred in their pursuit of evidence during the first widespread rage of digging on the North American continent. In spite of religious and other tradition-borne concerns expressed repeatedly and earnestly, in spite of the emotional suffering of living people, through the several processes discussed in this paper Euro-Americans have unearthed enemies dead thousands of years and concentrated their remains in the very centers of American political power. What if all those remains had embodied lethal radiation? Can scientists always be sure that they will read correctly and ignore safely messages from the past?

Notes

1. For details on this notion see Hertz, *Death and the Right Hand*; for a further development of Hertz's ideas see Huntington and Metcalf, *Celebrations of Death*.

2. This idea is developed through detailed examination of death among an African tribe in Goody, *Death, Property, and the Ancestors*.

3. Binford, "Mortuary Practices." Critics of Binford's "law-like generalization" have pointed out that as far as the material record is concerned the reverse might be true, and great respect might be marked by great simplicity in the disposal of remains. Nevertheless, it remains true that *differential* treatment in death correlates with phenomena within the social system of those who bury the decedent.

4. A recent exception, reflecting on the experiences of the senses in the extended processing accorded to dead bodies in Madagascar, is Kus, "Toward an Archaeology."

5. For a standard outline of pre-Roman European archaeology see Piggott, *Ancient Europe*; for a revision of same see Renfrew, *Before Civilisation*. A useful recent summary of many of the issues so far discussed from a scientistic point of view is Parker Pearson, *The Archaeology of Death and Burial*, esp. chap. 6.

6. Kantorowicz, *The King's Two Bodies*, 409–36, discusses some of the elaborate medieval funerary practices for kings and their significance in perpetuating the political structure.

7. Finucane, "Sacred Corpse," 60.

8. Ariès, *The Hour of Our Death*.

9. For the revision of Ariès presented here I refer to McManners, "Death and the French Historians."

10. Ariès's "tame" death is seen by anthropologists as the "natural," "rite of passage" death (for the use of this term see Morris, *Burial and Ancient Society*, 36) practiced by "traditional" societies, which in this case seems to mean "nonstate" societies. It is not obvious, however, that dying people in traditional societies do actually accept their fates, since anthropologists cannot of necessity gather the thoughts of such dying people. The process of distancing from death that Ariès describes for Western societies is probably happening in different ways for other societies that seem to be maintaining "traditional" forms (cf. Bayly, "From Ritual to Ceremony") as they move toward universal literacy and improved health care, but Western commentators understand so little of the emotions connected with the traditional form that they are unlikely to perceive such changes.

11. This was true even in the North American colonies; in the 1730s the burial ground of the Nova Scotia seaport/fortress of Louisbourg was shifted outside the town walls in what was its third move since the foundation of the settlement in 1713 (Johnston, "From *port de pêche*"). In the town of Old Mobile, founded in 1702, the burial ground was sited from the start at the edge of the planned settlement (Gregory Waselkov, personal communication, 1992).

12. See Ariès, *The Hour of Our Death*, 51–61.

13. Quoted by Whaley, "Introduction."

14. For Glastonbury see Alcock, *Arthur's Britain*, 73–80; for Stonehenge and Geoffrey see Trigger, *A History*, 45.

15. This is, of course, the highly literary Garcilaso de la Vega in *La Florida*; see Garcilaso, *The Florida of the Inca*, 504–5.

16. For a useful outline of the prehistory of southeastern North America that can serve to support the generalizations asserted here see Smith, "The Archaeology."

17. For a summary of the temporal and geographical distribution of mortuary practices across southeastern North America during the period in question see Galloway, *Choctaw Genesis*, chap. 7.

18. For the classic description of funerary retainer and infant sacrifice as observed among the Natchez by the French in the eighteenth century see Du Pratz, *Histoire de la Louisiane*, 3:23–57.

19. See Dobyns, *Their Number Become Thinned*; Ramenofsky, *Vectors of Death*; and Smith, *Archaeology*. Although it now seems that death rates were not uniformly high everywhere, still they were serious enough in enough places to restructure North American indigenous societies.

20. See Trigger, *A History*, 57–59.

21. For Garcilaso's version of both incidents see *The Florida of the Inca*, 65–67 (Ortiz) and 312–15 (Talomeco).

22. Garcilaso, *The Florida of the Inca*, 438–39, 445, for the sack of Capaha by Casquin. Garcilaso's Inca background, of course, may have colored this matter-of-fact treatment of secondary mortuary processing.

23. Axtell, "Last Rights."

24. Trigger, *The Children of Aataentsic*, 85–90.

25. Le Moyne d'Iberville, *Iberville's Gulf Journals*, 38.

26. For reports from Du Pratz and Charlevoix see Swanton, *Indians*, 138–49.

27. I infer this from the description of the activities surrounding a Choctaw flesh-stripping ceremony reported by the French in 1746. See Rowland, Sanders, and Galloway, *Mississippi Provincial Archives*, 4:282.

28. Trigger, *A History*, 66.

29. Trigger, *A History*, 125.

30. This practice was not strange in the context of medical anatomy practice and the acquisition of bodies to supply it. See Foucault, *The Birth of the Clinic*, 124–48, for a background on surgical autopsies and the study of anatomy; see Schama, *Dead Certainties*, for a fictionalized portrayal of the atmosphere in which the "resurrection men" operated in the United States. Richardson, *Death, Dissection, and the Destitute*, shows how the poor were exploited for anatomical study in nineteenth-century England, while Sappol, *A Traffic of Dead Bodies*, outlines the same situation in nineteenth-century America.

31. Bieder, *Science Encounters the Indian*, 67. For a good deal of the story that follows I am indebted to Bieder's chapter on Samuel G. Morton (55–103).

32. As we shall see shortly, this attitude survives today among greedy looters and the wealthy collectors (very frequently and ironically doctors) who pay them to destroy Indian graves for the sake of what the international art market has made the very valuable artifacts to be found in them.

33. Foucault, *The Birth of the Clinic*; also see Warner, *Against the Spirit of System*.

34. Trigger, *A History*, 114–18.

35. Bieder, *Science Encounters the Indian*, 67 n. 24.

36. Axtell, "Last Rights," 120–22.

37. Brain, *Tunica Treasure*, documents an extravagant example.

38. Swanton, *Sources*, 170–94, provides accounts of the Choctaw ceremony of the eighteenth century and the changes that took place in the nineteenth century under white pressure.

39. Choctaws have placed the burials of children around the official marker at the site of the treaty of Dancing Rabbit Creek in Noxubee County, Mississippi; see McKee and Schlenker, *The Choctaws*, 81, pl. 6.

40. Jennings, *The Invasion of America*, 82–83. Jennings draws the line of continuity between the appropriation of Indian lands and the elite enclosure and appropriation of common lands in feudal Europe. Clearly, most of the "yeoman farmers" who were so glad to have land of their own in North America had few problems with seeing the same confiscatory practices applied to others.

41. The expression is inspired by the concept of science-fiction "planetary engineering" or "terraforming" of extraterrestrial planets by colonizing humans and by Alfred W. Crosby's "Neo-Europes" in *Ecological Imperialism*, in which Crosby quotes the French archaeologist François Bordes on general human expansion on the planet: "There can be no repetition of this until man lands on a hospitable planet belonging to another star" (17).

42. Tom Charlier, "Progress."

43. See Laderman, *The Sacred Remains*.

44. For state laws referring to these matters and their inconsistency see Trope and Echo-Hawk, "The Native American Graves Protection and Repatriation Act," 130–31. In my own experience I saw how Native American political pressure—contact from the governor of the Chickasaw Nation to the governor of Mississippi—could lead to a ruling by the state's attorney general in 1981 that such definitions *did* so apply. It should also be observed that in some cases state laws were prompted by nineteenth-century anatomical grave robbing aimed not only at Indians but at blacks and poor whites; see Sappol, *A Traffic of Dead Bodies*, 98–135.

45. The pre-NAGPRA situation outlined in this section is based largely upon the data collected by Marcus Price III in his study *Disputing the Dead*. Although some changes have been made to state burial laws in the interim, by and large the legal situation remains the same.

46. Thomas, *Skull Wars*, 214.

47. Schamel, "Update." This source does not consider specific opinions that may have been rendered by state attorneys general or courts with reference to pre-NAGPRA laws, however. See also Fine-Dare, *Grave Injustice*, 97–108, for the significant contributions of state laws in western states to the formulation of NAGPRA.

48. The Arizona law was passed in 1990; see Trope and Echo-Hawk, "The Native American Graves Protection and Repatriation Act," 135.

49. Thomas, *Skull Wars*, 142.

50. See the website for the ABG at http://www.africanburialground.gov/ABG_Main.htm.

51. Brain, *Winterville*, 44, 46. This practice is not unusual, but Brain's frank description of what happened is, and it is also a good example of how avoidable in practice grave excavation is. It is interesting that in the report we are not explicitly told who gave the warning, especially since Brain used African American plantation laborers in the work. This graveyard might have held black as well as white bodies (the reported evidence provided only a rough chronology), so the excavator's caution is a stark example of the distinction being made in practice between pre-historic Indians and everyone else by the 1960s, when the excavation was carried out under the aegis of Harvard's Lower Mississippi Survey. It was not, however, just the chance of recent burials that urged this caution. Access to private land and permission to excavate depends upon land-owners who might be descendants of those buried in plantation graveyards, and even though the Winterville site was by that time state owned, future excavation opportunities had to be considered.

52. Dongoske, "NAGPRA."

53. Because there is never enough funding to excavate everything that will be destroyed, archaeologists generally only excavate a sample, leading amateurs to argue the virtue of their own efforts to "rescue" the rest.

54. One of the most dramatic examples of this in North American archaeology is the system-atic looting of the Spiro site in eastern Oklahoma, where an extraordinary concentration of artifacts stemming from the Spiro elites' control of trade between the Plains and the Mississippi valley was literally mined from the mounds on the site in such a way that it has been impossible

for archaeologists to reconstruct the complex structure of the main burial find. See Peterson, "A History of Excavations."

55. Most of the artifacts in Roy Hathcock's *The Quapaw and Their Pottery* come from such collections; the collectors are not named, but their knowledge of the source of the materials is proclaimed in the attribution of a geographical provenience to almost every pot.

56. Fine-Dare, *Grave Injustice*.

57. Parker, "Keepers of the Treasures."

58. Fine-Dare, *Grave Injustice*.

59. For a brief consideration of these matters that compares the treatment of white and Indian burials see McGuire, "The Sanctity of the Grave."

60. Sebeok, *Communication Measures*. See also Eco, *The Search*.

61. The conference was arranged by Scandpower under contract from the Swedish Radiation Protection Institute (ssi) as a part of a Nordic Nuclear Safety Research project (kan 1.3) and held at Oslo Military Society, September 26 and 27, 1991. Information gathered on August 29, 2004, from http://www.coopcomm.org/nonukes/w28relig.htm.

Bibliography

Archival Sources

Anonymous. Mapa del Golfo y costa de la Nueva España. 1544[?]. Seville, Archivo General de Indias, Indiferente General, est. 145, caj. 7, leg. 8, ramo 272. Map no. 1 in Cumming, *The Southeast in Early Maps*.

"Anonymous Relation." Ayer ms. 530. Newberry Library, Chicago.

Anville, Jean-Baptiste Bourguignon d'. Carte de la Louisiane, 1732 [1752]. Mississippi Department of Archives and History, MA/A04/0.07.

Archives des colonies (AC). Centre des archives d'Outre-Mer, Aix-en-Provence, France, Série C9, correspondance générale, Saint-Domingue. Copies of the following series are in the Library of Congress, Washington DC; Mississippi Department of Archives and History, Jackson; and Center for Louisiana Studies, University of Southwestern Louisiana, Lafayette: série B, correspondence originating in France; série C13A, correspondance générale, Louisiane; and série C13C, reports and memoirs.

Atkin, Edmond. "Historical Account of the Revolt of the Chactaw Indians." 1753. Lansdowne MS 809. British Library, London.

———. Treaty of Friendship and Commerce, July 18, 1759. Lyttelton Papers. Clements Library, University of Michigan.

Barnwell, John. Untitled manuscript map of southeastern North America. 1722[?]. Public Record Office, Colonial Office, North American Colonies, General 7. Map no. 184 in Cumming, *The Southeast in Early Maps*.

Crenay, Baron de. Carte de partie de la Louisianne qui comprend le Cours du Missisipy depuis son embouchure jusques aux Arcansas celuy des rivieres de la Mobille depuis la Baye jusqu'au Fort de Toulouse, des Pascagoula de la riviere aux Perles . . . 1733. Ministère des colonies no. 1, Louisiane, Paris. Map no. 215 in Cumming, *The Southeast in Early Maps*.

Crisp, Edward/Nairne, Thomas. Crisp, A Compleat Description of the Province of Carolina . . . ; Nairne inset, A Map of South Carolina Shewing the Settlements . . . 1711. Map no. 151 in Cumming, *The Southeast in Early Maps*.

De Brahm, William Gerard. A Map of the Indian Nations in the Southern Department. 1766. Clements Library, University of Michigan. Map no. 352 in Cumming, *The Southeast in Early Maps*.

——. A Map of the Southern Indian District. 1764, 1774[?]. Additional MS 14,036.8, British Museum. Map no. 341 in Cumming, *The Southeast in Early Maps*.

Delisle, Guillaume. Carte de la Louisiane et du Cours du Mississipi. 1718. Map no. 170 in Cumming, *The Southeast in Early Maps*.

——. Carte des environs du Missisipi. 1701. Recueil 69, carte 4, Service historique de la marine, Vincennes. Map no. 131 in Cumming, *The Southeast in Early Maps*.

——. Carte du Canada et du Mississipi. 1702. Service géographique, Ministère des affaires étrangères, Paris. Map no. 134 in Cumming, *The Southeast in Early Maps*.

——. Carte du Mexique et de la Floride . . . 1703. Map no. 137 in Cumming, *The Southeast in Early Maps*.

Mobile Church Records. Catholic Diocese of Mobile.

Ortelius/Chiaves. La Florida, 1584. Map no. 5 in Cumming, *The Southeast in Early Maps*.

Rapalje, George. Rapalje/Rapalji (George) Notebook. Mississippi Department of Archives and History, Private Manuscript Collection Z0580.000.

Régis du Roullet. Carte du cours de la Riviere aux Perles, 1732. Archives hydrographiques 4040c, no. 42, Archives nationales, Paris.

Romans, Bernard. A Map of Part of West Florida . . . 1772. Gage Papers, Clements Library, University of Michigan. Map no. 441 in Cumming, *The Southeast in Early Maps*.

——. Map of West Florida containing Mr. Romans and Mr. Taitts observations and the different established boundary lines. Manuscript map of Choctaw and Chickasaw country, 1772[?]. Gage Papers, Clements Library, University of Michigan.

Vaudreuil Letterbooks. Huntington Manuscript Loudoun (H M LO) 9:I–III. Huntington Library, San Marino CA.

Published Sources

Aberle, David F. "Matrilineal Descent in Cross-Cultural Perspective." In Schneider and Gough, *Matrilineal Kinship*, 655–727.

Adair, James. *Adair's History of the American Indians*. Ed. Samuel Cole Williams. 1930. Reprint, Johnson City TN: Watauga Press, 1971.

——. *History of the American Indians*. London: Edward and Charles Dilly, 1775.

Adorno, Rolena. "The Discursive Encounter of Spain and America: The Authority of Eyewitness Testimony in the Writing of History." *William and Mary Quarterly* 49, no. 2, 3rd series (1992): 210–28.

Alcock, Leslie. *Arthur's Britain: History and Archaeology, AD 367–634*. Harmondsworth: Penguin, 1971.

Alden, John. *John Stuart and the Southern Colonial Frontier: A Study of Indian Relations, War, and Land Problems in the Southern Wilderness, 1754–1775*. Ann Arbor: University of Michigan Press, 1944.

Alexander, Christopher. *The Timeless Way of Building*. New York: Oxford University Press, 1979.

American Association of Museums. *Excellence and Equity: Education and the Public Dimension of Museums*. Washington DC, 1992.

Ammerman, Albert J., L. L. Cavalli-Sforza, and Diane K. Wagener. "Toward the Estimation of Population Growth in Old World Prehistory." In Zubrow, *Demographic Anthropology*, 27–61.

Anderson, David. "The Paleoindian Colonization of Eastern North America: A View from the Southeastern United States." In *Research in Economic Anthropology, Supplement 5*, 163–216. New York: JAI Press, 1990.

Anderson, David, Ken Sassaman, and Christopher Judge, eds. *Paleoindian and Early Archaic Period Research in the Lower Southeast: A South Carolina Perspective*. Columbia: Council of South Carolina Professional Archaeologists, 1992.

Ariès, Philippe. *The Hour of Our Death*. Trans. Helen Weaver. New York: Knopf, 1981.

Arthur, S. C., and G. C. Huchet de Kernion, eds. *Old Families of Louisiana*. New Orleans, 1931.

Atkinson, James R. "Death of a Chickasaw Leader: The Probable Grave of Piomingo." *Mississippi Archaeology* 35 (2000): 124–72.

——. "A Historic Contact Indian Settlement in Oktibbeha County, Mississippi." *Journal of Alabama Archaeology* 25, no. 1 (1979): 61–82.

Atkinson, James R., and Crawford H. Blakeman Jr. *Archaeological Site Survey in the Tallahalla Reservoir Area, Jasper County, Mississippi*. Mississippi State University, 1975. Submitted to the National Park Service.

Avellaneda, Ignacio. *Los sobrevivientes de la Florida*. Gainesville: P. K. Yonge Library, 1990.

Axtell, James. "Last Rights." In James Axtell, *The European and the Indian: Essays in the Ethnohistory of Colonial North America*, 110–28. Oxford: Oxford University Press, 1981.

Badger, R. R., and L. A. Clayton, eds. *Alabama and the Borderlands: From Prehistory to Statehood*. Tuscaloosa: University of Alabama Press, 1985.

Barker, Alex W., and Timothy R. Pauketat, eds. *Lords of the Southeast: Social Inequality and the Native Elites of Southeastern North America*. Archaeological Papers of the American Anthropological Association 3, 1992.

Barron, Bill. *The Vaudreuil Papers: A Calendar and Index of the Personal Records of Pierre de Rigaud de Vaudreuil*. New Orleans: Polyanthos, 1975.

Basso, Keith H. *Wisdom Sits in Places: Landscape and Language among the Western Apache*. Albuquerque: University of New Mexico Press, 1996.

Bayly, C. A. "From Ritual to Ceremony: Death Ritual and Society in Hindu North India since 1600." In Whaley, *Mirrors of Mortality*, 154–86.

Beers, Henry Putney. *The French in North America: A Bibliographical Guide to French Archives, Reproductions and Research Missions*. Baton Rouge: Louisiana State University Press, 1957.

Bender, Barbara. "Subverting the Western Gaze: Mapping Alternative Worlds." In Ucko and Layton, *The Archaeology and Anthropology of Landscape*, 31–45.

Berkhofer, Robert F., Jr. *The White Man's Indian*. New York: Vintage Books, 1979.

Bieder, Robert E. *Science Encounters the Indian, 1820–1880*. Norman: University of Oklahoma Press, 1986.

Binford, Lewis. "Mortuary Practices: Their Study and Their Potential." In James Brown, ed., *Approaches to the Social Dimensions of Mortuary Practices*, 6–29. Memoirs of the Society for American Archaeology 25. Society for American Archaeology, 1971.

Binford, Lewis R., and W. J. Chasko Jr. "Nunamiut Demographic History: A Provocative Case." In Zubrow, *Demographic Anthropology*, 63–143.

Bintliff, John, ed. *The Annales School and Archaeology*. Leicester: Leicester University Press, 1991.

Blitz, John. *An Archaeological Study of the Mississippi Choctaw Indians*. Mississippi Department of Archives and History Archaeological Report 16, 1985.

Booker, Karen, Charles Hudson, and Robert Rankin. "Place Name Identification and Multilingualism in the Sixteenth-Century Southeast." *Ethnohistory* 39, no. 4 (1992): 399–451.

Boserup, Ester. *The Conditions of Agricultural Growth: The Economics of Agrarian Change under Population Pressure*. Chicago: Aldine, 1965.

Boston, Barbara. "The 'De Soto Map.'" *Mid-America* 23 (1941): 236–50.

——. "The Route of de Soto: Delisle's Interpretation." *Mid-America* 21 (1939): 277–97.

Bourdieu, Pierre. *Outline of a Theory of Practice*. Trans. Richard Nice. Cambridge: Cambridge University Press, 1997.

Bourne, Edward G., ed. *Narratives of the Career of Hernando de Soto*. 3 vols. New York, 1922.

Brain, Jeffrey P. "The Archaeology of the Hernando De Soto Expedition." In Badger and Clayton, *Alabama and the Borderlands*, 96–107.

——. *The Archaeology of the Tunica (cont'd): Trial on the Yazoo*. National Geographic Society Research Report. Cambridge MA: Peabody Museum, Harvard University, 1975.

——. "Late Prehistoric Settlement Patterning in the Yazoo Basin and Natchez Bluffs Regions of the Lower Mississippi Valley." In Smith, *Mississippian Settlement Patterns*, 331–68.

——. "The Natchez 'Paradox.'" *Ethnology* 10 (1971): 215–22.

——. *Tunica Treasure*. Papers of the Peabody Museum of Archaeology and Ethnology 71. Cambridge MA: Peabody Museum, Harvard University, 1979.

——. *Winterville: Late Prehistoric Culture Contact in the Lower Mississippi Valley*. Mississippi Department of Archives and History Archaeological Report 23, 1989.

Brain, Jeffrey P., and Philip Phillips. *Shell Gorgets: Styles of the Late Prehistoric and Protohistoric Southeast*. Cambridge MA: Peabody Museum Press, 1996.

Brain, Jeffrey P., Alan Toth, and Antonio Rodriguez-Buckingham. "Ethnohistoric Archaeology and the De Soto Entrada into the Lower Mississippi Valley." *The Conference on Historic Site Archaeology Papers* (1972): 7, (1974): 232–89.

Brasseaux, Carl. *A Comparative View of French Louisiana, 1699 and 1762: The Journals of Pierre Le Moyne d'Iberville and Jean-Jacques-Blaise d'Abbadie.* Lafayette LA: Center for Louisiana Studies, University of Southwestern Louisiana, 1979.

Bright, William. "What IS a Name? Reflections on Onomastics." *Language and Linguistics* 4 (2003): 669–81.

Brown, A. J. "Antiquities of Newton County, Mississippi." *Publications of the Mississippi Historical Society* 6 (1902): 441–48.

Burke, Peter. *The French Historical Revolution: The Annales School 1929–89.* Stanford CA: Stanford University Press, 1990.

Burkhart, Louise. " 'Here Is Another Marvel': Marian Miracle Narratives in a Nahuatl Manuscript." In Nicholas Griffiths and Fernando Cervantes, eds., *Spiritual Encounters: Interactions between Christianity and Native Religions in Colonial America,* 91–115. Lincoln: University of Nebraska Press, 1999.

Butzer, Karl. "An Old World Perspective on Potential Mid-Wisconsinan Settlement of the Americas." In Dillehay and Meltzer, *The First Americans,* 137–56.

Byington, Cyrus. *A Dictionary of the Choctaw Language.* Ed. John R. Swanton and Henry S. Halbert. Bureau of American Ethnology Bulletin 46. Washington DC: Government Printing Office, 1915.

Cabeza de Vaca, Álvar Nuñez. *La relación que dio Álvar Nuñez Cabeza de Vaca de lo acaescido en las Indias en la armada donde iva por governador Pánphilo de Narbáez* . . . Zamora: Augustín de Paz and Juan Picardo for Juan Pedro Musetti, 1542.

Capers, Charlotte. "Foreword." In Rowland, Sanders, and Galloway, *Mississippi Provincial Archives,* 4:xi–xiii.

Carleton, Kenneth. "Eighteenth-Century Trails in the Choctaw Territory of Mississippi and Alabama." MA thesis, Department of Anthropology, University of Georgia, 1989.

Carson, James Taylor. "Horses and the Economy and Culture of the Choctaw Indians, 1690–1840." *Ethnohistory* 42 (1995): 495–518.

——. *Searching for the Bright Path: The Mississippi Choctaws from Prehistory to Removal.* Lincoln: University of Nebraska Press, 1999.

Certeau, Michel de. *The Practice of Everyday Life.* Trans. Steven Rendall. Berkeley: University of California Press, 1984.

Charlier, Tom. "Progress Scrapes Heritage off Map: Part III." *Commercial Appeal* (Memphis), November 26, 1989.

Cherry, John. "Investigating the Political Geography of an Early State by Multidimensional Scaling of Linear B Tablet Data." In John Bintliff, ed., *Mycenaean Geography: Proceedings of the Cambridge Colloquium, September 1976.* Cambridge: British Association for Mycenaean Studies, University Library Press, 1977.

Churchill, Mary. "Understanding the Oppositional Paradigm in Charles Hudson's *The Southeastern Indians.*" *American Indian Quarterly* 20 (1996): 563–93.

Claassen, Cheryl, and Rosemary Joyce, eds. *Women in Prehistory: North America and Mesoamerica.* Philadelphia: University of Pennsylvania Press, 1997.

Clifford, James. "'Hanging up Looking Glasses at Odd Corners': Ethnobiographical Prospects." In Daniel Aaron, ed., *Studies in Biography*, 41–56. Cambridge MA: Harvard University Press, 1978.

Cody, Janice. "Natchez Social Structure: Anomaly or Variation." Paper presented at the American Society for Ethnohistory, 1985.

Cohen, Sande. *Historical Culture: On the Recoding of an Academic Discipline*. Berkeley: University of California Press, 1986.

Collins, Henry B. "Potsherds from Choctaw Village Sites in Mississippi." *Journal of the Washington Academy of Sciences* 17, no. 10 (1927): 259–63.

Crane, Verner. *The Southern Frontier, 1670–1732*. Durham NC: Duke University Press, 1928. Reprint, New York: Greenwood, 1981.

Crawford, James. *The Mobilian Trade Language*. Knoxville: University of Tennessee Press, 1978.

Cronon, William. *Changes in the Land: Indians, Colonists, and the Ecology of New England*. New York: Hill & Wang, 1983.

Crosby, Alfred W. *Ecological Imperialism: The Biological Expansion of Europe, 900–1900*. Cambridge: Cambridge University Press, 1986.

Crumley, Carole. "A Dialectical Critique of Hierarchy." In Thomas C. Patterson and Christine W. Gailey, eds., *Power Relations and State Formation*, 155–69. Salem WI: American Anthropological Association, 1987.

——, ed. *Historical Ecology: Cultural Knowledge and Changing Landscapes*. Santa Fe: School of American Research Press, 1994.

——. "Three Locational Models: An Epistemological Assessment of Anthropology and Archaeology." In Michael B. Schiffer, ed., *Advances in Archaeological Method and Theory*, 2:141–73. New York: Academic Press, 1979.

Cruzat, Heloise H., Henry P. Dart, and Walter Prichard. "Records of the Superior Council of Louisiana, LXXV." *Louisiana Historical Quarterly* 21, no. 2 (1938): 564–609.

Cumming, William P. *The Southeast in Early Maps*. Princeton NJ: Princeton University Press, 1958.

Custred, Glen. "Oral Traditions and Rules of Evidence." *Mammoth Trumpet* 16 (June 2001). http://www.centerfirstamericans.com/mt.html?a=48. Accessed March 24, 2004.

Dávila Padilla, Agustín. *Historia de la fundación y discurso de la provincia de Santiago de México*. Facsimile of 1625 ed., 1 vol. Mexico City: Editorial Academia Literaria, 1955.

Debo, Angie. *The Rise and Fall of the Choctaw Republic*. Norman: University of Oklahoma Press, 1961.

Deevey, E. S. "The Human Population." *Scientific American* 201 (1960): 3.

Delanglez, Jean. *French Jesuits in Lower Louisiana*. Washington DC: Catholic University of America, 1936.

——, ed. and trans. "M. Le Maire on Louisiana." *Mid-America* 19 (1937): 124–54.

DeMallie, Raymond. "'These Have No Ears': Narrative and the Ethnohistorical Method." *Ethnohistory* 40 (1993): 515–38.

DePratter, Chester B., Charles Hudson, and Marvin T. Smith. "The Hernando de Soto Expedition: From Chiaha to Mabila." In Badger and Clayton, *Alabama and the Borderlands*, 108–27.

DeVille, Winston. *Gulf Coast Colonials*. Baltimore MD: Genealogical Publishing Company, 1968.

DeVorsey, Louis, Jr. "Early Maps as a Source in the Reconstruction of Southern Indian Landscapes." In Hudson, *Red, White, and Black*, 12–30.

Dillehay, Tom, and David Meltzer, eds. *The First Americans: Search and Research*. Boca Raton: CRC, 1991.

Dincauze, Dina. "Pioneering in the Pleistocene: Large Paleoindian Sites in the Northeast." In James Stoltman, ed., *Archaeology of Eastern North America: Papers in Honor of Stephen Williams*, 43–60. Mississippi Department of Archives and History Archaeological Report 25, 1993.

Dobyns, Henry. *Their Number Become Thinned: Native American Population Dynamics in Eastern North America*. Knoxville: University of Tennessee Press, 1983.

Dongoske, Kurt E. "NAGPRA: A New Beginning, Not the End, for Osteological Analysis —A Hopi Perspective." In Mihesuah, *Repatriation Reader*, 282–93.

Douglas, Mary. *Natural Symbols: Explorations in Cosmology*. New York: Vintage, 1973.

Dowling, Lee. "*La Florida del Inca*: Garcilaso's Literary Sources." In Galloway, *The Hernando de Soto Expedition*, 98–154.

Doyle, Don H. *Faulkner's County: The Historical Roots of Yoknapatawpha*. Chapel Hill: University of North Carolina Press, 2001.

Drechsel, Emanuel. *Mobilian Jargon: Linguistic and Sociocultural Aspects of a Native American Pidgin*. Oxford: Oxford University Press, 1997.

——. "Mobilian Jargon: Linguistic, Sociocultural, and Historical Aspects of an American Lingua Franca." PhD dissertation, University of Wisconsin, 1979.

Dreyfus, Hubert L., and Paul Rabinow. *Michel Foucault: Beyond Structuralism and Hermeneutics*. Chicago: University of Chicago Press, 1982.

Dumont de Montigny. *Mémoires historiques sur la Louisiane*. 2 vols. Paris: Cl. J.-B. Bauche, 1753.

Dye, David, and Ronald Brister, eds. *The Protohistoric Period in the Mid-South: 1500–1700*. Mississippi Department of Archives and History Archaeological Report 18. Jackson, 1986.

Dyson, John. "Kettles, Metals and Killing: A Spanish Source for a Chickasaw/Choctaw War Title." *Journal of Chickasaw History and Culture* 8, no. 3, series 31 (2002): 24–32.

Eco, Umberto. *The Search for the Perfect Language*. Oxford: Blackwell, 1987.

Eggan, Fred. "Historical Changes in the Choctaw Kinship System." *American Anthropologist* 39 (1937): 34–52.

Eisenstadt, Shmuel N. "Dual Organizations and Sociological Theory." In Maybury-Lewis and Almagor, *The Attraction of Opposites*, 345–54.

Elliott, Jack. "Mississippi State Plan for Archaeology: Historic." Historic Preservation Division, Mississippi Department of Archives and History, Jackson, n.d.

ESRI. "Rubber Sheeting." In *ArcEdit Users Guide*, chap. 14. ESRI, 1987.

Evans-Pritchard, E. E. *Witchcraft, Oracles and Magic among the Azande*. Oxford: Oxford University Press, 1937.

Fabian, Johannes. *Time and the Other: How Anthropology Makes Its Object*. New York: Columbia University Press, 1983.

Falk, Eugene. *Types of Thematic Structure: The Nature and Function of Motifs in Gide, Camus, and Sartre*. Chicago: University of Chicago Press, 1967.

Field, Steven, and Keith H. Basso, eds. *Senses of Place*. Santa Fe: School of American Research Press, 1996.

Fine-Dare, Kathleen S. *Grave Injustice: The American Indian Repatriation Movement and NAGPRA*. Lincoln: University of Nebraska Press, 2002.

Finucane, R. C. "Sacred Corpse, Profane Carrion: Social Ideals and Death Rituals in the Later Middle Ages." In Whaley, *Mirrors of Mortality*, 40–60.

Fischer, J. L. "Solutions for the Natchez Paradox." *Ethnology* 3 (1964): 53–65.

Flannery, Kent, ed. *The Early Mesoamerican Village*. New York: Academic Press, 1976.

Flinn, Michael W. *The European Demographic System, 1500–1820*. Baltimore MD: Johns Hopkins Press, 1981.

Fogelson, Raymond D. "The Ethnohistory of Events and Nonevents." *Ethnohistory* 36 (1989): 133–47.

Ford, James A. *Analysis of Indian Village Site Collections from Louisiana and Mississippi*. Louisiana Department of Conservation Anthropological Study 2. New Orleans, 1936.

Foster, Michael K. "On Who Spoke First at Iroquois-White Councils: An Exercise in the Method of Upstreaming." In Michael K. Foster, Jack Campisi, and Marianne Mithan, eds., *Extending the Rafters: Interdisciplinary Approaches to Iroquoian Studies*, 183–207. Albany NY, 1984.

Foucault, Michel. *The Archaeology of Knowledge and the Discourse on Language*. Trans. A. M. Sheridan Smith. New York: Pantheon Books, 1972.

——. *The Birth of the Clinic*. Trans A. M. Sheridan Smith. New York: Vintage, 1975.

——. *Discipline and Punish*. Trans. Alan Sheridan. New York: Vintage, 1979.

——. *The Order of Things: An Archaeology of the Human Sciences*. New York: Vintage, 1973.

Frankenstein, S. M., and M. J. Rowlands. "The Internal Structure and Regional Context of Early Iron Age Society in Southwestern Germany." *Bulletin of the Institute of Archaeology* 15 (1978): 73–112.

Frawley, William, Kenneth C. Hill, and Pamela Munro. "Making a Dictionary: Ten Issues." In William Frawley, Kenneth C. Hill, and Pamela Munro, eds., *Making Dictionaries: Preserving Indigenous Languages of the Americas*, 1–22. Berkeley: University of California Press, 2002.

Fried, Morton. *The Evolution of Political Society*. New York, 1967.

Friederich, Werner P. *Outline of Comparative Literature: From Dante Alighieri to Eugene O'Neill*. Chapel Hill: University of North Carolina Press, 1954.

Froger, D. J. *La critique des textes et son automatisation*. Paris: Dunod, 1968.

Fulbert of Chartres. *The Letters and Poems of Fulbert of Chartres*. Ed. and trans. Frederick Behrends. Oxford: Clarendon Press, 1976.

Fuller, Richard. "The Bear Point Phase of the Pensacola Variant: The Protohistoric Period in Southwest Alabama." *Florida Anthropologist* 38, nos. 1–2, pt. 2 (1985): 150–55.

———. *The Swan Lake Canoe*. Baton Rouge: Coastal Environments, 1992.

Galloway, Patricia. "The Barthelemy Murders: Bienville's Establishment of the *lex talionis* as a Principle of Indian Diplomacy." In E. P. Fitzgerald, ed., *Proceedings of the Eighth Annual Meeting of the French Colonial Historical Society, 1982*, 91–103. Lanham MD: University Press of America, 1985.

———. "The Chief Who Is Your Father: Choctaw and French Views of the Diplomatic Relation." In Wood, Waselkov, and Hatley, *Powhatan's Mantle*, 254–78.

———. "Choctaw Factionalism and Civil War, 1746–1750." *Journal of Mississippi History* 44 (1982): 289–327.

———. *Choctaw Genesis 1500–1700*. Lincoln: University of Nebraska Press, 1995.

———. "Choctaw Names and Choctaw Roles: Another Method of Evaluating Sociopolitical Structure." Paper presented at the American Society for Ethnohistory meeting, 1988.

———. "Clustering Variants in the *Lai de l'Ombre* Manuscripts: Techniques and Principles." *ALLC Journal* 3 (1982): 1–8.

———. "Confederacy as a Solution to Chiefdom Dissolution: Historical Evidence in the Choctaw Case." In Hudson and Tesser, *The Forgotten Centuries*, 393–420.

———. "Conjoncture and Longue Durée: History, Anthropology, and the Hernando de Soto Expedition." In Galloway, *The Hernando de Soto Expedition*, 283–94.

———. "Eighteenth-Century Choctaw Chiefs, Dual Organization, and the Exploration of Social Design Space." Paper presented at the 2002 meeting of the American Society for Ethnohistory, Quebec.

———. "The Four Ages of Alibamon Mingo, *fl.* 1700–1766." *Journal of Mississippi History* 65 (2003): 320–42.

———. "Henri de Tonti du village des Chacta, 1702: The Beginning of the French Alliance." In Patricia Galloway, ed., *La Salle and His Legacy: Frenchmen and Indians in the Lower Mississippi Valley*, 146–75. Jackson: University Press of Mississippi, 1982.

———, ed. *The Hernando de Soto Expedition: History, Historiography, and "Discovery" in the Southeast*. Lincoln: University of Nebraska Press, 1997.

———. "Louisiana Post Letters, 1700–1763: The Missing Evidence for Indian Diplomacy." *Louisiana History* 22, no. 1 (1981): 31–44.

———. "The Medal Chief's *grosse lettre*." Paper presented at the Sixteenth Meeting of the French Colonial Historical Society, Mackinac Island MI, May 18, 1990.

——. "Mississippi State Plan for Archaeology: Protohistoric." On file at the Historic Preservation Division, Mississippi Department of Archives and History, n.d.

——. "Multidimensional Scaling for Mapping Ethnohistorical Narrative: Choctaw Villages in the Eighteenth Century." In *Proceedings of the Xth Congress of the UISPP, Comisión IV: Coloquio manejo de datos y metodas mathemáticas de arqueología*, 1981, 158–75.

——. "Narrative Theories as Computational Models: Reader-Oriented Theory and Artificial Intelligence." *Computers and the Humanities* 17 (1983): 169–74.

——, ed. *Native, European, and African Cultures in Colonial Mississippi*. Jackson: Mississippi Department of Archives and History, 1991.

——. "Note on Terminology for Comb Descriptions." *Medieval Archaeology* 20 (1976): 154–56.

——. "Producing Narrative Maps with Multidimensional Scaling Techniques." *Computers and the Humanities* 13 (1979): 207–22.

——. "Restoring the Map of Medieval Trondheim: A Computer-aided Investigation into the Nightwatchmen's Itinerary." *Journal of Archaeological Science* 5 (1978): 153–65.

——. " 'So Many Little Republics': British Negotiations with the Choctaw Confederacy, 1765." *Ethnohistory* 41 (1994): 513–38.

——, ed. *Southeastern Ceremonial Complex, Artifacts and Analysis: The Cottonlandia Conference*. Lincoln: University of Nebraska Press, 1989.

——. "Talking with Indians: Interpreters and Diplomacy in French Louisiana." In Winthrop Jordan and Sheila Skemp, eds., *Race and Family in the Colonial South*, 109–29. Jackson: University Press of Mississippi, 1987.

——. "Testing a Theory of Narrative Analysis by Computer." In D. E. Ager, F. E. Knowles, and J. M. Smith, eds., *Advances in Computer-Aided Literary and Linguistic Research*, 53–57. Birmingham: University of Aston in Birmingham, 1979.

——. "The Unexamined Habitus: Direct Historical Analogy and the Archaeology of the Text." In Gardin and Peebles, *Representations in Archaeology*, 178–95.

——. "Transaction Units: An Approach to the Structural Study of Narrative through the Analysis of *Percyvelle of Galles, Li Contes del Graal,* and *Parzival*." PhD dissertation, University of North Carolina–Chapel Hill, 1973.

——. "Where Have All the Menstrual Huts Gone? The Invisibility of Menstrual Seclusion in the Late Prehistoric Southeast." In Claassen and Joyce, *Women in Prehistory*, 47–62.

——. "Yngve's Depth Hypothesis and the Structure of Narrative: The Example of Detective Fiction." In Maxine MacCafferty and K. Gray, eds., *The Analysis of Meaning: Informatics* 5, 104–10. London: ASLIB, 1979.

Galloway, Patricia, and Clara Sue Kidwell. "Choctaw Land Claims in Mississippi." Grant proposal submitted to the National Endowment for the Humanities, 1988.

Galloway, Patricia, and Mark Newcomer. "The Craft of Comb-Making: An Experimental Enquiry." *Bulletin of the Institute of Archaeology of the University of London* 18 (1981): 73–90.

Garcilaso de la Vega. *The Florida of the Inca*. Trans. John and Jeannette Varner. Austin: University of Texas Press, 1951.

Gardin, Jean-Claude, and Christopher S. Peebles, eds. *Representations in Archaeology*. Bloomington: Indiana University Press, 1992.

Gatschet, Albert S. *A Migration Legend of the Creek Indians*. Vol. 1. Philadelphia: D. G. Brinton, 1884.

Gearing, Fred. *Priests and Warriors: Social Structures for Cherokee Politics in the Eighteenth Century*. American Anthropological Association Memoir 93, 1962.

Gero, Joan M. "Genderlithics: Women's Role in Stone Tool Production." In J. M. Gero and M. W. Conkey, eds., *Engendering Archaeology: Women and Prehistory*, 163–93. Oxford: Basil Blackwell, 1991.

Giraud, Marcel. *Histoire de la Louisiane français: Le règne de Louis XIV, 1698–1715*. Paris: Presses universitaires de France, 1953.

——. *History of French Louisiana: The Reign of Louis XIV, 1698–1715*. Trans. Joseph C. Lambert. Baton Rouge: Louisiana State University Press, 1974.

Goody, Jack. *Death, Property, and the Ancestors: A Study of the Mortuary Customs of the LoDagaa of West Africa*. Stanford CA: Stanford University Press, 1962.

——. *The Domestication of the Savage Mind*. Cambridge: Cambridge University Press, 1977.

Gould, Peter, and Rodney White. *Mental Maps*. Harmondsworth: Penguin, 1974.

Gunn, Joel. "Analysis of Modern Climate Data." In G. Muto and J. Gunn, eds., *A Study of Late Quaternary Environments and Early Man along the Tombigbee River, Alabama and Mississippi*, 2:19–26. Atlanta: National Park Service, 1982.

Gunn, Joel, and Richard E. W. Adams. "Climate Change, Culture, and Civilization in North America." *World Archaeology* 13 (1981): 85–100.

Guttman, L. "A General Nonmetric Technique for Finding the Smallest Coordinate Space for a Configuration of Points." *Psychometrika* 33 (1968): 469–506.

Haag, William G. "Choctaw Archaeology." *Southeastern Archaeological Conference Newsletter* 3 (1953): 25–28.

Haas, Mary R. "What Is Mobilian?" In James Crawford, ed., *Studies in Southeastern Linguistics*, 257–63. Athens: University of Georgia Press, 1975.

Hagan, William T. "Archival Captive—The American Indian." *American Archivist* 41 (1978): 135–42.

Hagedorn, Nancy L. "'A Friend to Go between Them': The Interpreter as Cultural Broker during Anglo-Iroquois Councils, 1740–70." *Ethnohistory* 35 (1988): 60–80.

Halbert, Henry S. "Bernard Romans' Map of 1772." *Publications of the Mississippi Historical Society* 6 (1902): 415–39.

Hall, Edward T. *The Hidden Dimension*. New York: Doubleday, 1966.

Hall, Gwendolyn Midlo. *Africans in Colonial Louisiana: The Development of Afro-Creole Culture in the Eighteenth Century*. Baton Rouge: Louisiana State University Press, 1992.

Hally, David J., Marvin T. Smith, and James B. Langford Jr. "The Archaeological Reality of de Soto's Coosa." In David Hurst Thomas, ed., *Columbian Consequences*, 2:121–38. Washington DC: Smithsonian Institution Press, 1990.

Hanke, Lewis. *The Spanish Struggle for Justice in the Conquest of America*. Philadelphia: University of Pennsylvania Press, 1949.

Hann, John. *Apalachee: The Land between the Rivers*. Gainesville: University Presses of Florida, 1988.

Hart, C. W. M. "A Reconsideration of the Natchez Social Structure." *American Anthropologist* 45 (1943): 374–86.

Harvey, Mark. "Land Tenure and Naming Systems in Aboriginal Australia." *Australian Journal of Anthropology* 13 (2002): 23–45.

Hassan, Fekri A. *Demographic Archaeology*. New York: Academic Press, 1981.

Hathcock, Roy. *The Quapaw and Their Pottery*. Camden AR: Hurley Press, 1983.

Heidegger, Martin. "Building Dwelling Thinking." In *Poetry, Language, Thought*. Trans. Albert Hofstadter. New York: Harper Colophon, 1971.

Helms, Mary. "Political Lords and Political Ideology in Southeastern Chiefdoms: Comments and Observations." In Barker and Pauketat, *Lords of the Southeast*, 185–94.

Henige, David. *The Chronology of Oral Tradition*. Oxford: Oxford University Press, 1974.

——. "The Context, Content, and Credibility of La Florida del Ynca." *Americas* 43 (1986): 1–23.

——. *Oral Historiography*. London: Longman, 1982.

Hertz, Robert. *Death and the Right Hand*. Trans. Rodney and Claudia Needham. Glencoe: Free Press, 1960.

Hillier, Bill, and Julienne Hanson. *The Social Logic of Space*. Cambridge: Cambridge University Press, 1984.

Hirsch, Eric, and Michael O'Hanlon, eds. *The Anthropology of Landscape*. Oxford: Oxford University Press, 1995.

Hodder, Ian, ed. *Reading the Past*. Cambridge: Cambridge University Press, 1986.

——. *The Spatial Organization of Culture*. Pittsburgh: University of Pittsburgh Press, 1978.

Hoffman, Paul. *A New Andalucia and a Way to the Orient: The American Southeast during the Sixteenth Century*. Baton Rouge: Louisiana State University Press, 1990.

Holmes, Jack D. L. *Honor and Fidelity: The Louisiana Infantry Regiment and the Militia Companies, 1766–1821*. Birmingham, 1965.

——. "Juan de la Villebeuvre: Spain's Commandant of Natchez during the American Revolution." *Journal of Mississippi History* 37 (1976): 97–129.

——. "Spanish Policy toward the Southern Indians in the 1790s." In Charles Hudson, ed., *Four Centuries of Southern Indians*, 65–82. Athens: University of Georgia Press, 1975.

Howard, Milo, and Robert Rea, eds. and trans. *The Mémoire Justificatif of the Chevalier Montault de Monberaut*. Tuscaloosa: University of Alabama Press, 1965.

Hoxie, Frederick. "Ethnohistory for a Tribal World." *Ethnohistory* 44 (1997): 595–615.

Hudson, Charles. *Conversations with the High Priest of Coosa*. Chapel Hill: University of North Carolina Press, 2003.

——, ed. *Red, White, and Black: Symposium on Indians in the Old South*. Athens: University of Georgia Press, l971.

——. *The Southeastern Indians*. Knoxville: University of Tennessee Press, 1976.

——. "The Uses of Evidence in Reconstructing the Route of the Hernando de Soto Expedition." Alabama De Soto Commission Working Paper 1, Tuscaloosa, 1987.

Hudson, Charles, Marvin T. Smith, and Chester B. DePratter. "The Hernando de Soto Expedition: From Mabila to the Mississippi River." Paper presented at the conference "Towns and Temples along the Mississippi," Memphis TN, 1987.

Hudson, Charles, Marvin T. Smith, Chester B. DePratter, and Emilia Kelley. "The Tristán de Luna Expedition, 1559–1561." *Southeastern Archaeology* 8 (1989): 31–45.

Hudson, Charles, Marvin Smith, David Hally, R. Polhemus, and Chester DePratter. "Coosa: A Chiefdom in the Sixteenth-Century Southeastern United States." *American Antiquity* 50 (1985): 723–37.

Hudson, Charles, and Carmen Tesser, eds. *The Forgotten Centuries: Indians and Europeans in the American South, 1521–1704*. Athens: University of Georgia Press, 1994.

Huntington, Richard, and Peter Metcalf, eds. *Celebrations of Death: The Anthropology of Mortuary Ritual*. Cambridge: Cambridge University Press, 1979.

Illich, Ivan. "A Plea for Research on Lay Literacy." In Olson and Torrance, *Literacy and Orality*, 28–46.

Jacobs, Wilbur, ed. *Indians of the Southern Colonial Frontier: Edmond Atkin's Report and Plan of 1755*. Columbia: University of South Carolina Press, 1954.

——. *Wilderness Politics and Indian Gifts: The Northern Colonial Frontier, 1748–1763*. Lincoln: University of Nebraska Press, 1950.

Jaenen, Cornelius. *Friend and Foe*. New York: Columbia University Press, 1976.

——. "The Role of Presents in French-Amerindian Trade." In Duncan Cameron, ed., *Explorations in Canadian Economic History: Essays in Honor of Irene M. Spry*, 232–50. Ottawa: University of Ottawa Press, 1985.

Jenkins, Keith. *Refiguring History: New Thoughts on an Old Discipline*. London: Routledge, 2003.

——. *Why History? Ethics and Postmodernity*. London: Routledge, 1999.

Jennings, Francis. *The Invasion of America: Indians, Colonialism, and the Cant of Conquest*. New York: Norton, 1976.

Johnson, Jay, and John Sparks. "Protohistoric Settlement Patterns in Northeastern Mississippi." In Dye and Brister, *The Protohistoric Period in the Mid-South: 1500–1700*, 64–81.

Johnston, A. J. B. "From *port de pêche* to *ville fortifiée*: The Evolution of Urban Louisbourg, 1713–1758." In Patricia Galloway, ed., *Proceedings of the Seventeenth Meeting of the French Colonial Historical Society, 1991*. Lanham MD: University Press of America, 1993.

Kantorowicz, Ernst H. *The King's Two Bodies: A Study in Medieval Political Theology.* Princeton NJ: Princeton University Press, 1957.

Karp, Ivan, Christine Mullen Kreamer, and Steven Lavine, eds. *Museums and Communities: The Politics of Public Culture.* Washington DC: Smithsonian Institution, 1992.

Karp, Ivan, and Steven Lavine, eds. *Exhibiting Cultures: The Poetics and Politics of Museum Display.* Washington DC: Smithsonian Institution, 1991.

Kauffman, Stuart. *At Home in the Universe: The Search for the Laws of Self-Organization and Complexity.* Oxford: Oxford University Press, 1995.

Kehoe, Alice. "When Theoretical Models Trump Empirical Validity, Real People Suffer." *Anthropology News* 45 (April 2004): 10.

Kelly, James C. "Oconostota." *Journal of Cherokee Studies* 3 (Fall 1979): 221–38.

Kendall, D. G. "Construction of Maps from 'Odd Bits of Information.'" *Nature* 231 (1971): 158–59.

——. "Maps from Marriages: An Application of Non-Metric Multidimensional Scaling to Parish Register Data." In Roy Hodson, D. G. Kendall, and P. Tautu, eds., *Mathematics in the Archaeological and Historical Sciences*, 303–18. Edinburgh: Edinburgh University Press, 1971.

——. "Review Lecture: The Recovery of Structure from Fragmentary Information." *Philosophical Transactions of the Royal Society of London: Mathematical and Physical Sciences* 279, no. 1291 (1975): 547–82.

Kernion, George. "Documents Concerning the History of the Indians of the Eastern Region of Louisiana." *Louisiana Historical Quarterly* 8 (1925): 38–39.

King, Grace. *Jean Baptiste Le Moyne, Sieur de Bienville.* New York, 1892.

Kniffen, Fred, Hiram Gregory, and George Stokes. *The Historic Tribes of Louisiana: From 1542 to the Present.* Baton Rouge: Louisiana State University Press, 1987.

Koehler, Lyle. "Earth Mothers, Warriors, Horticulturists, and Chiefs: Women among the Mississippian and Mississippian-Oneota Peoples." In Claassen and Joyce, *Women in Prehistory*, 211–26.

Kopytoff, Igor. "The Cultural Biography of Things: Commoditization as Process." In Arjun Appaduri, ed., *The Social Life of Things: Commodities in Cultural Perspective*, 64–91. Cambridge: Cambridge University Press, 1986.

Krech, Shepard, III. *The Ecological Indian: Myth and History.* New York: Norton, 1999.

Kruskal, J. B. "Multidimensional Scaling by Optimizing Goodness of Fit to a Non-Metric Hypothesis." *Psychometrika* 29 (1964): 1–27.

Kus, Susan. "Toward an Archaeology of Body and Soul." In Gardin and Peebles, *Representations in Archaeology*, 168–77.

Laderman, Gary. *The Sacred Remains: American Attitudes toward Death, 1799–1883.* New Haven CT: Yale University Press, 1996.

Layton, Robert. "Relating to the Country in the Western Desert." In Hirsch and O'Hanlon, *The Anthropology of Landscape*, 210–31.

Layton, Robert, and Peter Ucko. "Introduction." In Ucko and Layton, *The Archaeology and Anthropology of Landscape*, 1–20.

Lee, Charles, and Ruth Green. *South Carolina Historical Magazine* 67 (1966): 187–202, 68 (1967): 1–3, 85–96, 165–83.

Lee, Richard. *The !Kung San: Men, Women, and Work in a Foraging Society*. New York: Cambridge University Press, 1979.

Le Moyne d'Iberville, Pierre. *Iberville's Gulf Journals*. Ed. and trans. Richebourg G. McWilliams. University: University of Alabama Press, 1981.

Le Page Du Pratz, Antoine Simon. *Histoire de la Louisiane*. 3 vols. Paris: De Bure, 1758.

———. *The History of Louisiana, or of the western parts of Virginia and Carolina: Containing a Description of the Countries that lie on both sides of the River Mississippi: With an Account of the Settlements, Inhabitants, Soil, Climate, and Products*. Anonymous translation. London: T. Becket, 1763 (1st ed., 2 vols.) and 1776 (2nd ed., 1 vol.).

Lévi-Strauss, Claude. "Do Dual Organizations Exist?" In *Structural Anthropology*. Trans. Claire Jacobson and Brooke Schoepf, 128–60. Garden City NY: Anchor Books, 1967.

———. *Structural Anthropology*. Trans. C. Jacobson and B. Schoepf. New York: Doubleday Anchor, 1967.

Lewis, G. Malcolm, ed. *Cartographic Encounters: Perspectives on Native American Mapmaking and Map Use*. Chicago: University of Chicago Press, 1998.

Lienhardt, Godfrey. *Divinity and Experience: The Religion of the Dinka*. Oxford: Oxford University Press, 1961.

Lingoes, J. C., and E. Roskam. *A Mathematical and Empirical Study of Two Multidimensional Scaling Algorithms*. Psychometrika Monographs 38 (1973).

Livingood, Patrick. "Investigation of Mississippian Mounds on the Middle Pearl River, Mississippi." Paper delivered at the Southeastern Archaeological Conference, 1999.

Lockhart, James. *The Men of Cajamarca*. Austin: University of Texas Press, 1972.

Lynch, Thomas. "The Peopling of the Americas—A Discussion." In Dillehay and Meltzer, *The First Americans*, 267–74.

Maduell, Charles R., Jr. *The Census Tables for the French Colony of Louisiana from 1699 through 1732*. Baltimore MD: Genealogical Publishing Company, 1972.

Malinowski, Bronislaw. *Argonauts of the Western Pacific*. 1922. Reprint, New York: E. P. Dutton, 1962.

Marshall, Richard. "Lyon's Bluff Site (22 OK 1) Radiocarbon Dated." *Journal of Alabama Archaeology* 23, no. 1 (1977): 53–57.

Martin, Calvin. "Introduction" and "Epilogue." In Calvin Martin, ed., *The American Indian and the Problem of History*, 3–26, 192–220. Oxford: Oxford University Press, 1987.

———. *Keepers of the Game: Indian-Animal Relationships and the Fur Trade*. Berkeley: University of California Press, 1978.

Mason, Carol. "Natchez Class Structure." *Ethnohistory* 11 (1964): 121–33.

Maybury-Lewis, David, and Uri Almagor, eds. *The Attraction of Opposites: Thought and Society in the Dualistic Mode*. Ann Arbor: University of Michigan Press, 1989.

McDermott, John Francis. "Some Recent Books about Louisiana and Some Books to Come." *Louisiana History* 8 (1967): 53–65.

McDowell, William L., ed. *The Colonial Records of South Carolina: Documents Relating to Indian Affairs, 1750–1754.* Series 2, vol. 2. Columbia: South Carolina Department of Archives and History, 1958.

——. *The Colonial Records of South Carolina: Documents Relating to Indian Affairs, 1754–1765.* Series 2, vol. 3. Columbia: South Carolina Department of Archives and History, 1970.

——. *The Colonial Records of South Carolina: Journals of the Commissioners of the Indian Trade, 1710–1718.* Series 2, vol. 1. Columbia: South Carolina Department of Archives and History, 1955.

McGahey, Samuel O. "Mississippi State Plan for Archaeology: Preceramic." On file in the Historic Preservation Division, Mississippi Department of Archives and History, n.d.

——. "Paleoindian and Early Archaic Data from Mississippi." In Anderson, Sassaman, and Judge, *Paleoindian and Early Archaic Period Research*, 295–321.

McGuire, Randall. "The Sanctity of the Grave: White Concepts and American Indian Burials." In Robert Layton, ed., *Conflict in the Archaeology of Living Traditions*, 167–84. London: Routledge, 1994.

McHugh, Peter. *Defining the Situation: The Organization of Meaning in Social Interaction.* Indianapolis: Bobbs-Merrill, 1968.

McKee, Jesse, and Jon Schlenker. *The Choctaws: Cultural Evolution of a Native American Tribe.* Jackson: University Press of Mississippi, 1980.

McLuhan, Marshall. *The Gutenberg Galaxy.* Toronto: University of Toronto Press, 1962.

McManners, John. "Death and the French Historians." In Whaley, *Mirrors of Mortality*, 106–30.

McNeill, William. "Mythistory, or Truth, Myth, History, and Historians." In William McNeill, *Mythistory and Other Essays*, 3–22. Chicago: University of Chicago Press, 1986.

Menier, Marie-Antoinette, Étienne Taillemite, and Gilberte de Forges. *Inventaire des archives coloniales: Correspondance à l'arrivée en provenance de la Louisiane.* 2 vols. Paris: Archives nationales, 1976–83.

Mereness, Newton D. *Travels in the American Colonies.* 1916. Reprint, New York: Antiquarian Press, 1961.

Merrim, S. "The Castle of Discourse: Fernandez de Oviedo's *Don Claribalte* (1519) or 'Los correos andan mas que los caballeros.'" *Modern Language Notes* 97 (1982): 329–46.

Mihesuah, Devon, ed. *Repatriation Reader: Who Owns American Indian Remains?* Lincoln: University of Nebraska Press, 2000.

Millares Carlo, Agustín. *Cuatro estudios biobibliográficos mexicanos.* Mexico City: Fondo de Cultura Económica, 1986.

Miller Surrey, Nancy M. *Calendar of Manuscripts in the Paris Archives and Libraries Relating to the History of the Mississippi Valley to 1803*. 2 vols. Washington DC: Carnegie Institution, 1926–28.

Millhouser, Paul. "A Map Method for Investigating Settlement Patterns: The Choctaw Case." BA honors thesis, Department of Anthropology, Harvard University, 1988.

Milling, Chapman J. *Red Carolinians*. Chapel Hill: University of North Carolina Press, 1940.

Minsky, Marvin. *The Society of Mind*. New York: Simon & Schuster, 1985.

Mooney, Timothy. "Migration of the Chickasawhays into the Choctaw Homeland." *Mississippi Archaeology* 27 (1992): 28–39.

Moore, John H. "Mvskoke Personal Names." *Names* 43 (1995): 187–212.

Morgan, David. "Mississippi State Plan for Archaeology: Ceramic Prehistoric." On file in the Historic Preservation Division, Mississippi Department of Archives and History, n.d.

Morphy, Howard. "Landscape and the Reproduction of the Ancestral Past." In Hirsch and O'Hanlon, *The Anthropology of Landscape*, 184–209.

Morris, Ian. *Burial and Ancient Society: The Rise of the Greek City-State*. Cambridge: Cambridge University Press, 1987.

Nagel, Thomas. *The View from Nowhere*. Oxford: Oxford University Press, 1986.

Nairne, Thomas. *Nairne's Muskhogean Journals: The 1708 Expedition to the Mississippi River*. Ed. Alexander Moore. Jackson: University Press of Mississippi, 1988.

Náñez Falcón, Guillermo, ed. *The Favrot Family Papers: A Documentary Chronicle of Early Louisiana*. 3 vols. New Orleans: Howard-Tilton Memorial Library, Tulane University, 1988.

Nelson, William. *Fact or Fiction: The Dilemma of the Renaissance Storyteller*. Cambridge MA: Harvard University Press, 1973.

Novick, Peter. *That Noble Dream: The "Objectivity Question" and the American Historical Profession*. Cambridge: Cambridge University Press, 1988.

O'Brien, Greg. *Choctaws in a Revolutionary Age, 1750–1830*. Lincoln: University of Nebraska Press, 2002.

——. "Protecting Trade through War: Choctaw Elites and British Occupation of the Floridas." In Martin Daunton and Rick Halpern, eds., *Empire and Others: British Encounters with Indigenous Peoples, 1600–1850*, 149–66. Philadelphia: University of Pennsylvania Press, 1999.

Olson, David R., and Nancy Torrance, eds. *Literacy and Orality*. Cambridge: Cambridge University Press, 1991.

O'Neill, Charles E. "The Death of Bienville." *Louisiana History* 8 (1967): 363–69.

Ong, Walter. *Orality and Literacy: The Technologizing of the Word*. London: Methuen, 1982.

Paape, Charles William. "The Choctaw Revolt: A Chapter in the Intercolonial Rivalry in the Old Southwest." PhD dissertation, University of Illinois, 1946.

Paper, Jordan. "The Post-Contact Origin of an American Indian High God: The Suppression of Feminine Spirituality." *American Indian Quarterly* 7, no. 4 (1983): 1–24.

Parker, James A. "Archaeological Test Excavations at 1-Su-7: The Fort Tombecbe Site." *Journal of Alabama Archaeology* 28 (1982): 1–104.

Parker, Patricia L. "Keepers of the Treasures: Protecting Historic Properties and Cultural Traditions on Indian Lands." Report on tribal preservation funding needs submitted to Congress by the National Park Service, United States Department of the Interior, 1990.

Parker Pearson, Mike. *The Archaeology of Death and Burial.* College Station: Texas A&M University Press, 2000.

Parkhurst, Helen. "Don Pedro Favrot: A Creole Pepys." *Louisiana Historical Quarterly* 28 (1945): 679–734.

Peacock, Evan. "Twenty-five Years of Cultural Resource Management on the National Forests of Mississippi." *Mississippi Archaeology* 29 (1994): 72–81.

Pease, Theodore Calvin, and Ernestine Jenison, eds. *Illinois on the Eve of the Seven Years' War, 1747–1755.* Springfield IL, 1940.

Peebles, Christopher. "An Overview of Research in the Lubbub Creek Archaeological Locality." In Peebles, *Prehistoric Agricultural Communities,* 70–129.

——. "Paradise Lost, Strayed, and Stolen: Prehistoric Social Devolution in the Southeast." In Miles Richardson and Malcom Webb, eds., *The Burden of Being Civilized: An Anthropological Perspective on the Discontents of Civilization,* 24–40. Athens: University of Georgia Press, 1986.

——, ed. *Prehistoric Agricultural Communities in West Alabama.* 3 vols. Ann Arbor, 1981.

——. "The Rise and Fall of the Mississippian in Western Alabama: The Moundville and Summerville Phases, A.D. 1000 to 1600." *Mississippi Archaeology* 22 (1987): 1–31.

Peebles, Christopher, and Susan Kus. "Some Archaeological Correlates of Ranked Societies." *American Antiquity* 42 (1977): 421–48.

Pénicaut, André. *Fleur de Lys and Calumet: Being the Pénicaut Narrative of French Adventure in Louisiana.* Ed. and trans. Richebourg Gaillard McWilliams. Baton Rouge: Louisiana State University Press, 1953.

Penman, John T. *Archaeological Survey in Mississippi, 1974–1975.* Mississippi Department of Archives and History Archaeological Report 2, 1977.

——. "Historic Choctaw Towns of the Southern Division." *Journal of Mississippi History* 40 (1978): 133–41.

Perdue, Theda. *Cherokee Women: Gender and Culture Change, 1700–1835.* Lincoln: University of Nebraska Press, 1998.

Peterson, Dennis. "A History of Excavations and Interpretations of Artifacts from the Spiro Mounds Site." In Galloway, *Southeastern Ceremonial Complex,* 114–21.

Phillips, Philip. *Archaeological Survey in the Lower Yazoo Basin, Mississippi, 1949–1955.* 2 vols. Papers of the Peabody Museum of Archaeology and Ethnology 60. Cambridge MA: Peabody Museum, Harvard University, 1970.

Phillips, Philip, James A. Ford, and James B. Griffin. *Archaeological Survey in the Lower Mississippi Alluvial Valley, 1940–1947.* Papers of the Peabody Museum of

Archaeology and Ethnology 25. Cambridge MA: Peabody Museum, Harvard University, 1951.

Piggott, Stuart. *Ancient Europe: From the Beginnings of Agriculture to Classical Antiquity*. Edinburgh: Edinburgh University Press, 1965.

Pitt, David C. *Using Historical Sources in Anthropology and Sociology*. New York: Holt, Rinehart and Winston, 1972.

Plog, Fred. "Demographic Studies in Southwestern Prehistory." In Alan Swedlund, ed., *Population Studies in Archaeology and Biological Anthropology: A Symposium*, 94–103. *American Antiquity* 40, no. 2 (2), memoir 30, 1975.

Price, Marcus, III. *Disputing the Dead: U.S. Law on Aboriginal Remains and Grave Goods*. Columbia: University of Missouri Press, 1991.

Priestley, Herbert I., ed. and trans. *The Luna Papers*. 2 vols. Deland: Florida State Historical Society, 1928.

——. *Tristán de Luna, Conquistador of the Old South: A Study of Spanish Imperial Strategy*. Glendale IL: Arthur H. Clark, 1936.

Quimby, George I. *The Bayou Goula Site, Iberville Parish, Louisiana*. Fieldiana: Anthropology 7, 1957.

——. "The Natchezan Culture Type." *American Antiquity* 7 (1942): 255–75.

Ramenofsky, Ann F. *Vectors of Death: The Archaeology of European Contact*. Albuquerque: University of New Mexico Press, 1987.

Reid, John Phillip. *A Law of Blood: The Primitive Law of the Cherokee Nation*. New York: New York University Press, 1970.

Renfrew, Colin. *Before Civilisation: The Radiocarbon Revolution and Prehistoric Europe*. Harmondsworth: Pelican, 1976.

Ricard, Robert. *The Spiritual Conquest of Mexico: An Essay on the Apostolate and the Evangelizing Methods of the Mendicant Orders in New Spain, 1523–1572*. Trans. Lesley Byrd Simpson. Berkeley: University of California Press, 1966.

Richardson, Ruth. *Death, Dissection, and the Destitute*. London: Routledge and Kegan Paul, 1987.

Robinson, A. H., and B. B. Petchenik. *The Nature of Maps: Essays toward Understanding Maps and Mapping*. Chicago: University of Chicago Press, 1976.

Romans, Bernard. *A Concise Natural History of East and West Florida*. 1775. New Orleans: Pelican Press, 1961.

——. *A Concise Natural History of East and West Florida*. Ed. Kathryn E. Holland Braund. 1775. Tuscaloosa: University of Alabama Press, 1999.

Rosecan, Stephen. "Unpacking Early Eighteenth-Century French and Choctaw Relations." Paper presented at the 2002 Annual Meeting of the American Society for Ethnohistory, Quebec.

Rosenzweig, Roy, and David Thelen. *The Presence of the Past: Popular Uses of History in American Life*. New York: Columbia University Press, 1998.

Rosman, Abraham, and Paula Rubel. "Dual Organization and Its Developmental Potential in Two Contrasting Environments." In Maybury-Lewis and Almagor, *The Attraction of Opposites*, 209–34.

Rowland, Dunbar, ed. *Mississippi Provincial Archives: English Dominion*. Vol. 1. Jackson: Mississippi Department of Archives and History, 1911.

Rowland, Dunbar, and Albert Godfrey Sanders, eds. and trans. *Mississippi Provincial Archives: French Dominion, 1729–1740*. Vol. 1. Jackson: Mississippi Department of Archives and History, 1927.

———. *Mississippi Provincial Archives: French Dominion, 1701–1729*. Vol. 2. Jackson: Mississippi Department of Archives and History, 1929.

———. *Mississippi Provincial Archives: French Dominion, 1704–1743*. Vol. 3. Jackson: Mississippi Department of Archives and History, 1932.

Rowland, Dunbar, Albert Godfrey Sanders, and Patricia Galloway, eds. and trans. *Mississippi Provincial Archives: French Dominion, 1729–1748*. Vol. 4. Baton Rouge: Louisiana State University Press, 1984.

———. *Mississippi Provincial Archives: French Dominion, 1749–1763*. Vol. 5. Baton Rouge: Louisiana State University Press, 1984.

Rowland, Eron, ed. *Peter Chester*. Jackson: Mississippi Historical Society, 1925.

Sahlins, Marshall. *Historical Metaphors and Mythical Realities: Structure and Early History of the Sandwich Islands Kingdom*. Ann Arbor: University of Michigan Press, 1981.

———. *Islands of History*. Chicago: University of Chicago Press, 1985.

———. *Stone Age Economics*. New York: Aldine, 1972.

———. *Tribesmen*. Englewood Cliffs NJ: Prentice-Hall, 1968.

Said, Edward. *Orientalism*. New York: Pantheon, 1978.

Sappol, Michael. *A Traffic of Dead Bodies: Anatomy and Embodied Social Identity in Nineteenth-Century America*. Princeton NJ: Princeton University Press, 2002.

Saussure, Ferdinand de. *Course in General Linguistics*. Trans. Wade Baskin. New York: Philosophical Library, 1959.

Schama, Simon. *Dead Certainties (Unwarranted Speculations)*. New York: Knopf, 1991.

Schamel, Kathleen. "Update of Compilation of State Repatriation, Reburial, and Grave Protection Laws (July 1997)." Report prepared for the Natural Resources Conservation Service under order number 40-3A75-7-102. http://www.arrowheads.com/burials.htm. Accessed July 31, 2004.

Schank, Roger C. *Dynamic Memory*. Cambridge MA: MIT Press, 1982.

Schank, Roger C., and R. Abelson. *Scripts Plans Goals and Understanding: An Inquiry into Human Knowledge Structures*. Hillsdale NJ: Lawrence Erlbaum Associates, 1977.

Schneider, David M., and Kathleen Gough, eds. *Matrilineal Kinship*. Berkeley: University of California Press, 1961.

Sebeok, Thomas A. *Communication Measures to Bridge Ten Millennia*. Technical report for the Office of Nuclear Waste Isolation. Columbus: Batelle Memorial Institute, 1984.

Seeman, Mark F. *The Hopewell Interaction Sphere: The Evidence for Interregional Trade and Structural Complexity*. Indiana Historical Society Prehistory Research Series 5 (2), 1979.

Seidman, Steven, ed. *Jürgen Habermas on Society and Politics: A Reader*. New York: Beacon, 1989.

Sellar, Walter Carrithers, and Robert Julian Yeatman. *1066 and All That: A Memorable History of England, Comprising All the Parts You Can Remember, Including One Hundred and Three Good Things, Five Bad Kings, and Two Genuine Dates*. New York: E. P. Dutton, 1931.

Serrano y Sanz, Manuel. *España y los indios Cherokis y Chactas en la segunda mitad del siglo XVIII*. Seville, 1916.

Service, Elman. *Primitive Social Organization*. 2nd ed. New York: Random House, 1962.

Shea, John Gilmary. *Early Voyages up and down the Mississippi*. Albany: Joel Munsell, 1861.

Sheldon, Craig Turner. "The Mississippian-Historic Transition in Central Alabama." PhD dissertation, University of Oregon, 1974.

Sheldon, Craig Turner, and Ned Jenkins. "Protohistoric Development in Central Alabama." In Dye and Brister, *The Protohistoric Period in the Mid-South, 1500–1700*, 95–102.

Silver, Timothy. *A New Face on the Countryside: Indians, Colonists, and Slaves in South Atlantic Forests, 1500–1800*. Cambridge: Cambridge University Press, 1990.

Simpson, Lesley Byrd. *The Encomienda in New Spain: The Beginning of Spanish Mexico*. Berkeley: University of California Press, 1966.

Slotkin, Richard. *Regeneration through Violence: The Mythology of the American Frontier, 1600–1860*. Middletown CT: Wesleyan University Press, 1973.

Smith, Bruce. "The Archaeology of the Southeastern United States: From Dalton to de Soto, 10,500–500 B.P." *Advances in World Archaeology* 5:1–91. New York: Academic Press, 1986.

——, ed. *Mississippian Settlement Patterns*. New York: Academic Press, 1978.

Smith, Marvin T. *Archaeology of Aboriginal Culture Change in the Interior Southeast: Depopulation during the Early Historic Period*. Gainesville: University Presses of Florida, 1987.

——. *Coosa: The Rise and Fall of a Southeastern Mississippian Chiefdom*. Gainesville: University Press of Florida, 2000.

——. "Depopulation and Culture Change in the Early Historic Period Interior Southeast." PhD dissertation, University of Florida, Gainesville.

Speck, Frank. "Notes on Chickasaw Ethnology and Folk-Lore." *Journal of the American Folk-Lore Society* 20 (January–March 1907): 57.

Spoehr, Alexander. *Changing Kinship Systems*. Field Museum of Natural History Anthropological Series 33 (4), 1947.

Stahle, David, Edward R. Cook, and James W. C. White. "Tree-Ring Dating of Baldcypress and the Potential for Millennia-Long Chronologies in the Southeast." *American Antiquity* 50 (1985): 796–802.

Stannard, David E. *American Holocaust: Columbus and the Conquest of the New World*. New York: Oxford University Press, 1992.

Steward, Julian H. "The Direct Historical Approach to Archaeology." *American Antiquity* 7 (1942): 337–43.

Stoianovitch, Traian. *French Historical Method: The Annales Paradigm*. Ithaca NY: Cornell University Press, 1976.

Stowe, N. Read. "The Pensacola Variant and the Bottle Creek Phase." *Florida Anthropologist* 38, nos. 1–2, pt. 2 (1985): 144–49.

Swanton, John R. *Early History of the Creek Indians and Their Neighbors*. Bureau of American Ethnology Bulletin 73. Washington DC: Government Printing Office, 1922.

——. *Final Report of the U.S. De Soto Expedition Commission*. Washington DC: Government Printing Office, 1939.

——. *The Indians of the Southeastern United States*. Bureau of American Ethnology Bulletin 137. Washington DC: Government Printing Office, 1946.

——. *Indian Tribes of the Lower Mississippi Valley and Adjacent Coast of the Gulf of Mexico*. Bureau of American Ethnology Bulletin 43. Washington DC: Government Printing Office, 1911.

——. "Social and Religious Beliefs and Usages of the Chickasaw Indians." In *Bureau of American Ethnology Forty-fourth Annual Report*. Washington DC: Government Printing Office, 1928.

——. "Social Organization and Social Usages of the Indians of the Creek Confederacy." In *Bureau of American Ethnology Forty-second Annual Report*. Washington DC: Government Printing Office, 1924–25.

——. *Source Material for the Social and Ceremonial Life of the Choctaw Indians*. Bureau of American Ethnology Bulletin 103. Washington DC: Government Printing Office, 1931.

Tanselle, G. Thomas. "The Editing of Historical Documents." *Studies in Bibliography* 31 (1978): 1–56.

Teute, Frederika J. "Views in Review: A Historiographical Perspective on Historical Editing." *American Archivist* 43 (1980): 43–56.

Thomas, Daniel H. *Fort Toulouse: The French Outpost at the Alabamas on the Coosa*. Tuscaloosa: University of Alabama Press, 1989.

Thomas, David Hurst. *Skull Wars: Kennewick Man, Archaeology, and the Battle for Native American Identity*. New York: Basic Books, 2000.

Thompson, Stith. *The Folktale*. New York: Holt, Rinehart and Winston, 1946.

Thornton, Russell. *American Indian Holocaust and Survival: A Population History since 1492*. Norman: University of Oklahoma Press, 1987.

Thwaites, Reuben G. *The French Regime in Wisconsin, 1634–1760*. 3 vols. Madison: State Historical Society of Wisconsin, 1902–8.

——, ed. *The Jesuit Relations and Allied Documents . . .* 73 vols. Cleveland: Burrows Brothers, 1896–1901.

Tobler, W. R., and S. Weinberg. "A Cappadocian Speculation." *Nature* 231 (1971): 39–41.

Todorov, Tzvetan. *The Conquest of America: The Question of the Other*. Trans. Richard Howard. New York: Harper & Row, 1984.

Tooker, Elisabeth. "Natchez Social Organization: Fact or Anthropological Fancy?" *Ethnohistory* 10 (1963): 358–72.

Trigger, Bruce. *The Children of Aataentsic: A History of the Huron People to 1660.* Kingston: McGill-Queen's University Press, 1976.

——. *A History of Archaeological Thought.* Cambridge: Cambridge University Press, 1989.

Trope, Jack, and Walter Echo-Hawk. "The Native American Graves Protection and Repatriation Act: Background and Legislative History." In Mihesuah, *Repatriation Reader*, 123–68.

Turner, Victor. "Social Dramas and Stories about Them." *Critical Inquiry* 7 (1980): 141–68.

Ucko, Peter, and Robert Layton, eds. *The Archaeology and Anthropology of Landscape.* London: Routledge, 1999.

Urban, Greg. "The Social Organizations of the Southeast." In Raymond DeMallie and Alfonso Ortiz, eds., *North American Indian Anthropology: Essays on Society and Culture*, 172–93. Norman: University of Oklahoma Press, 1994.

Usner, Daniel. *Indians, Settlers, and Slaves in a Frontier Exchange Economy: The Lower Mississippi Valley before 1783.* Chapel Hill: University of North Carolina Press, 1992.

Vansina, Jan. *Oral Tradition: A Study in Historical Methodology.* Trans. H. M. Wright. Harmondsworth: Penguin, 1973.

——. *Oral Tradition as History.* Madison: University of Wisconsin Press, 1985.

Villiers du Terrage, Marc de. *Les dernières années de la Louisiane française: Le chevalier de Kerlérec, d'Abbadie-Aubry, Laussat.* Paris, 1903.

——. *The Last Years of Colonial Louisiana.* Trans. Hosea Phillips, ed. Carl Brasseaux and Glenn Conrad. Lafayette: Center for Louisiana Studies, 1982.

Voss, Jerome A., and C. Baxter Mann. "Stylistic Variation in Historic Choctaw Ceramics." *Mississippi Archaeology* 21 (1986): 43–58.

Ward, Rufus A., Jr. "English Earthenwares Associated with Early 19th Century Choctaw Sites." *Mississippi Archaeology* 18 (1983): 37–45.

Ware, John D. "Introduction." In P. Lee Phillips, *Notes on the Life and Works of Bernard Romans.* Gainesville: University Press of Florida, 1924.

Warhus, Mark. *Another America: Native American Maps and the History of Our Land.* New York: St. Martin's Press, 1997.

Warner, John Harley. *Against the Spirit of System: The French Impulse in Nineteenth-Century American Medicine.* Princeton NJ: Princeton University Press, 1998.

Watson, J. Wreford. "The Role of Illusion in North American Geography: A Note on the Geography of North American Settlement." *Canadian Geographer* 13 (1969): 10–27.

Weddle, Robert. "Soto's Problems of Orientation: Maps, Navigation, and Instruments in the Florida Expedition." In Galloway, *The Hernando de Soto Expedition*, 219–33.

——. *Spanish Sea*. College Station: Texas A&M University Press, 1985.

Weeks, Charles. *Paths to a Middle Ground: The Diplomacy of Natchez, Boukfouka, Nogales, and San Fernando de las Barrancas, 1791–1795*. Tuscaloosa: University of Alabama Press, 2005.

Welinder, Stig. *Prehistoric Demography. Acta Archaeologica Lundensia* Series Minore 8. Lund: Gleerup, 1979.

Wesson, Cameron. "Prestige Goods, Symbolic Capital, and Social Power in the Proto-historic Southeast." In Cameron B. Wesson and Mark A. Rees, eds., *Between Contacts and Colonies: Archaeological Perspectives on the Prehistoric Southeast*, 110–25. Tuscaloosa: University of Alabama Press, 2002.

Whaley, Joachim. "Introduction." In Whaley, *Mirrors of Mortality*, 11–12.

——, ed. *Mirrors of Mortality: Studies in the Social History of Death*. New York: St. Martin's Press, 1981.

White, Douglas R., George P. Murdock, and Richard Scaglion. "Natchez Class and Rank Reconsidered." *Ethnology* 10 (1971): 369–88.

White, Hayden. *The Content of the Form: Narrative Discourse and Historical Representation*. Baltimore MD: Johns Hopkins University Press, 1987.

——. *Metahistory: The Historical Imagination in Nineteenth-Century Europe*. Baltimore MD: Johns Hopkins University Press, 1973.

——. *Tropics of Discourse: Essays in Cultural Criticism*. Baltimore MD: Johns Hopkins University Press, 1978.

White, Richard. *Land Use, Environment, and Social Change: The Shaping of Island County, Washington*. Seattle: University of Washington Press, 1980.

——. "Red Shoes: Warrior and Diplomat." In David G. Sweet and Gary B. Nash, eds., *Struggle and Survival in Colonial America*, 49–68. Berkeley: University of California Press, 1981.

——. *The Roots of Dependency: Subsistence, Environment, and Social Change among the Choctaws, Pawnees, and Navajos*. Lincoln: University of Nebraska Press, 1983.

Widmer, Randolph J. "The Structure of Southeastern Chiefdoms." In Barker and Pauketat, *Lords of the Southeast*, 125–55.

Williams, Stephen. "On the Location of the Historic Taensa Villages." *Fifth Conference on Historic Site Archaeology Papers, 1965–1966* 1 (1967): 2–13.

——. "Some Historic Perspectives on Southeastern Ceramic Traditions." In Frederick H. West and Robert W. Neuman, eds., *Traces of Prehistory: Papers in Honor of William C. Haag. Geoscience and Man* 22 (1981): 115–22.

Williams, Stephen, and Jeffrey P. Brain. *Excavations at the Lake George Site, Yazoo County, Mississippi, 1958–1960*. Papers of the Peabody Museum of Archaeology and Ethnology 74. Cambridge MA: Peabody Museum, Harvard University, 1983.

Willis, William. "Divide and Rule: Red, White, and Black in the Southeast." In Hudson, *Red, White, and Black*, 99–115.

Wolf, Eric R. *Europe and the People without History*. Berkeley: University of California Press, 1982.

Wood, Peter. "The Changing Population of the Colonial South: An Overview by Race and Region, 1685–1790." In Wood, Waselkov, and Hatley, *Powhatan's Mantle*, 35–103.

Wood, Peter H., Gregory A. Waselkov, and M. Thomas Hatley, eds. *Powhatan's Mantle: Indians in the Colonial Southeast*. Lincoln: University of Nebraska Press, 1989.

Works Progress Administration. Historical Records Survey. *The Favrot Papers, 1695–1803*. Vols. 1–7, 9. Transcriptions of Manuscript Collections of Louisiana, no. 1. New Orleans, 1940–41.

Worster, Donald. "Transformations of the Earth: Toward an Agroecological Perspective in History." *Journal of American History* 76 (1990): 1087–1110.

Wylie, Alison. *Thinking from Things: Essays in the Philosophy of Archaeology*. Berkeley: University of California Press, 2002.

Yaukey, David. *Demography, the Study of Human Population*. New York: St. Martin's Press, 1985.

York, Kennith. "Mobilian: The Indian *lingua franca* of Colonial Louisiana." In Galloway, *La Salle and His Legacy*, 139–45.

Zubrow, Ezra B. W., ed. *Demographic Anthropology: Quantitative Approaches*. Albuquerque: University of New Mexico Press, 1976.

Index

Buckles, John (English trader), 356n36
Bureau of American Ethnography, 403
Bureau of Indian Affairs: and Native American archival records, 19; supplying Native American remains for study, 399
burial practices: American laws for, 402–3, 409; and beliefs about the soul, 389, 391; and cemetery location, 392; Christian, 391; and desecration, 388, 396, 400, 406; European, 390–93; and European disease, 394–95; and French colonial cemeteries, 411n11; and "Massacre Island" ossuary, 397; and missionaries, 400; precontact Native American, 393–94; primary, 389–90; and reburial practices, 392; and repatriation of burials, 407; and retainer sacrifice, 397; Saxon, 398; secondary, 390–91, 393–97; and settlement charter and land claims, 400–403, 409–10; spousal sacrifice and, 101; structuration of the world and, 389, 391–92; Visigoth, 393; and Winterville mound, 405
Bush, George H. W., 20
Byington, Cyrus, 206

Cadillac, Antoine Lumet de La Mothe de, 234
Caffetalaya Choctaw village, 184, 216, 220, 285–86, 302, 303, 306
Cahokia mound, 135
Cajamarca, Peru, 61, 63
calumet ceremony: Chitimacha, 103; and fictive kinship, 231; as model for museum exhibit dedication, 386; Natchez, 104; as sign of peace, 347; mentioned, 318
Campbell, John (English trader), 272, 274, 279, 281, 284
Canelle (French officer-interpreter), 36–37, 45, 52n10, 53n13, 236
Carleton, Kenneth, 166, 174
Carnegie Institution, 3
Carondelet, François-Louis Hector de, 308
Carson, James Taylor, 184, 360
cartography: Casa de Contratación, 69; and cognitive space, scales, and functions, 178; coordinate systems in, 165; and European bias, 69, 183; European observations in, 164; geographical information systems and, 14, 114, 165, 172; and hydrography, 169; instruments for, 59, 164; itineraries as evidence for, 13, 68, 148, 155; origins of modern, 164; and photogrammetry, 165; and portolan charts, 69; and rectification of images, 165; rubber sheeting for, 14, 165; and wayfinding, 68, 180, 199. *See also* Anville; Barnwell, John; Crenay, Baron de; De Brahm; Delisle, Claude; Gauld, George; Régis du Roullet; Romans, Bernard; Santa Cruz, Alonzo de

Castellan, Tomás, 84
Cavalli-Sforza, L. L., 132
Caxiti town, 88
Celoron, Pierre Joseph, 345
Center for Editions of American Authors, 5
Central America, 60
ceramics: Addis fabric type, 143; Bayou Goula Incised type, 13, 138–39, 141, 143–44; Chickachae Combed type, 13, 138–46; for cultural identification, 12–13; for dating, 121; Fatherland Incised type, 142–43
ceremonial centers: Mississippian, 124–25
Chactamataha Chitto (John Stuart's Choctaw name), 324
Chakchiuma Indians, 183, 229, 230, 263, 273, 283
Chambers, Moreau, 114
Chambly de Rouville, 48, 272
Chaouacha Indians, 237
Charleston (Charles Town), 269, 279–85, 318, 324
Charlevoix, Father Pierre François-Xavier de, 397
Chasko, W. J., 134
Chatot Indians, 313
Chauvin Deléry, Marguerite, 54n33
Cherokee Indians, 50, 107, 207, 237, 268, 304–5, 306, 324–25, 352, 386, 397
Cherokee language, 237
Cherokee war, 306
Chester, Peter, 329
Chicacha Oulacta (Choctaw chief), 296, 314
Chicasa polity, 227
Chichatalaya Choctaw village, 277, 282, 283, 348
Chickasaw Bluffs, 345
Chickasawhay Choctaw village: as host to French missionary, 267; as site of Beauchamp assembly, 275; mentioned, 49, 52n5, 159, 160, 187, 193–94, 196–97, 203–4, 206, 215, 217, 220, 232, 297–98, 313, 342, 346
Chickasawhay Choctaw village group: in Choctaw civil war, 263, 265, 271–72, 274–75, 279–80, 284–85; in Mobile congress, 312, 314–16, 319, 322, 328; mentioned, 252
Chickasawhay River, 169, 184, 194, 320
Chickasaw Indians: and attitude toward human remains, 407; in Choctaw civil war, 45–48, 263, 265, 267–68, 271–74, 276–77, 279, 283, 285–86, 345, 348, 350, 363; colonial population in Mississippi of, 112; language of, 226–27, 229, 230–33, 237; and loyalty to Britain, 378; at Mobile congress, 312–16, 325–26; and museum exhibits, 383, 386; in wars with French of, 50, 247–48, 250, 253, 267, 316, 361; mentioned, 16, 35–37, 107, 147–48, 160, 183–185, 194, 215–16, 246, 248, 252, 296, 305, 342–43

chiefdom: as social organization, 56–57, 292–93

children, French: taken captive in Natchez revolt, 185, 237, 267, 270, 315, 340

Chinnery, Nicholas (British trader), 279

Chitimacha Indians: kinship, 105; mentioned, 10, 102

Chitimacha (slave) woman: as informant on Native culture, 105; as interpreter for Du Pratz, 103, 104; related to Natchez by marriage, 103; mentioned, 102–10

Choctaw civil war: and Alibamon Mingo, 345–48, 349; casualties, 261, 283; causes, 45–49; history, 259–91; and lex talionis, 254–56, 316; smallpox during, 261, 281, 287; mentioned, 16–17, 40, 148, 194, 204, 210, 232, 252, 299, 305, 322–23, 330, 361

Choctaw Indians: and attitude toward human remains, 407; burial practice of, 363, 385, 400; ceramics of, 138, 140–42, 145, 148, 151–52; history of, 177, 337–39, 266–69; kinship of, 210; language of, 206, 226, 229, 230–33, 237, 240, 245; and lex talionis, 245–58; lists of chiefs and place-names of, 153, 188, 190–92, 195–96, 365; location and ethnicity of, 147, 165–66, 169–71, 177; marriage and residence rules of, 317; medal chiefs of, 296, 315; migration legend of, 269; at Mobile congress, 311–35; and museum exhibits, 378–79, 383; origins of, 204, 311–14, 330n2; and place-names, 175–201; population, 112, 312–13, 314, 329; "prairie" people as constituent population of, 359; respect for elders among, 353; slave-raiding against, 265–67, 338; and sociopolitical organization, 46, 148, 159, 261–65, 202–3, 206; status of, in modern Mississippi, 379; and trade relations with French, 339, 348; mentioned, 13–17, 239, 35–37, 39

Choctaws in a Revolutionary Age, 357

Chote (Cherokee village), 302

Choucououlacta (Choctaw chief): biography, 270; in Choctaw civil war, 271, 273–74, 276–78; mentioned, 46, 328, 345

Christie's auction house, 406

Chulustamastabe of West Yazoo (Choctaw chief): at Augusta congress, 318, 326; as chief negotiator at Mobile congress, 319, 321, 324–25, 327, 329

Coça Indians: complaining of encroachment, 89; similes for behaviors in war of, 90–91

Coça province: archaeological views of, 60, 93, 94; description of, 89; as goal of Luna expedition, 79, 81, 82, 88

Code Noir, 384

Cofitachequi province, 396

cognitive science: as model for culture contact, 62–65

Collins, Henry B., 138, 148

Columbus Quincentenary, 18, 111, 378–79

combs: and ceramic decoration, 139–46; European boxwood, 13, 140–41, 144; indigenous, 140

commissions: exchanging of, to switch allegiance, 286, 299, 306; and formalizing quasi-military rank, 302; giving of, to chiefs by European powers, 297, 299, 302–308; iconography of, 302; and text, 304; and treaty scene, 302, 306–8

Commons House of Assembly (of South Carolina colony), 260

Company of the Indies, 107, 296

comparative literature, 1, 6

Conchak Emiko (Choctaw chief), 314

Concha Oumanstabe (Choctaw chief), 217

Conchatys Alabama Indians, 277

Concha villages: in Choctaw civil war, 270–72, 276–77, 279–82, 284–85; as home of Alibamon Mingo, 338, 341, 343–44, 346; at Mobile congress, 312–16, 319–21; mentioned, 153, 160, 215, 232, 297, 361

confederation, 292

consensus: in Indian decision-making, 325

contract hunting: by Choctaws for French, 248, 249

Cook, James, 65

Coosa chiefdom. *See* Coça Indians; Coça province

Coosa River, 338

Coosa village, 227, 279

Coronado, Juan Vásquez de, 79

"corsair war" (Spain and French pirates), 79

Cortés, Hernando, 61, 65

Couechitto Choctaw village: in Choctaw civil war, 261, 269, 272–73, 277, 280, 282–84; as home of Red Shoe, 340–41, 347, 361; mentioned, 45, 48, 153, 156, 160, 216–17, 220, 297, 314, 316

Cougta of Concha (brother of Alibamon Mingo), 341

Counter-Reformation, 85

Courtance, Jerome (English trader), 356n36

Coweta Indians, 273, 277

Crawford, James, 225, 226–28, 230, 232, 234

Creek Indians: war with Choctaw, 194, 196; mentioned, 50, 101, 107, 147, 246, 248, 264, 268, 305, 324–25, 352, 363

Crenay, Baron de: and map of Choctaw country, 148–51, 155–57, 159–60, 187, 194, 197, 210

Creole (Louisiana) language, 244

Cronon, William, 179

Crosby, Alfred, 179

Cross of St. Louis, 302

Crumley, Carole, 136

Fort Nogales, 201
Fort Rosalie, 16, 280, 283, 286, 339, 340
Fort St. Pierre, 16, 201, 339
Fort Tombecbé, 16, 37, 45, 47–49, 52n5, 53n11, 54n28,
    138, 160, 203, 233, 236, 253, 267, 270, 273, 275–76,
    279, 285–86, 320, 339, 342, 348
Fort Toulouse, 16, 49, 54n28, 236–37, 271, 275, 305,
    318, 345
Foucault, Michel, 28n15, 398
Franchimastabé (Choctaw chief), 355n7, 357, 362,
    366
Franciscan order, 85, 92
French and Indian War, 50, 183, 193, 302, 304–5, 311,
    317, 324. *See also* Seven Years' War
Friederich, Werner P., 6
Froger, D. J., 5

Garcilaso de la Vega, 61, 66, 73–74, 226
Gatschet, Albert, 227
Gauld, George, 166
Gaulish barbarian, on Indian medal, 304
Gearing, Fred, 207, 262
gender: and power, 370; roles, 357, 367
Geoffrey of Monmouth, 393
Georgia, 227
German Coast: Choctaw attacks on, 282–84
Gilfoil, Anne, 95n20
Giliberti, Joe, 119, 136
Glastonbury: monkish archaeology at, 393
Glen, James, 237, 280, 305
Gordon, Arthur, 318, 327
gorget: as badge of rank, 294; as present, 296–97
Grandpré, Carlos de, 54n33
Grandpré, Joseph Louis Boucher de, 54n33, 285–86
Grandpré Treaty, 255, 286
Grand Turk, 74
Great Chief of Choctaw, 284, 297, 342, 347
Great Lakes, 293
Great Plains, 388
Great Sun (Natchez chief), 104, 105
Great Tohomé chief, 279–80
Greenville MS, 405
Grevemberg (Quapaw interpreter), 40, 42n22
Griffin, James B., 59, 60
Grigra Indians, 106
Guadalquivir River, 68
Gulf Coast, 152, 227, 338, 386, 396
Gulf of Mexico, 69, 78, 293–94
Gunn, Joel, 134
Gunn, Molly: portrayed in museum exhibit, 386
Guttman-Lingoes smallest-space analysis, 151

Haag, William G., 138
Haas, Mary R., 225–26
Habermas, Jürgen, 380
habitus, 11, 62–64
Halbert, Henry, 148, 169, 206
Hall, Gwendolyn Midlo, 112
Hanson, Julienne, 179
Harvard University, 166–67, 399, 405
Harvey, Mark, 181–82
Haskell Indian Nations University, 19
Hassan, Fekri A., 122–23
Hazeur, 53n11, 54n28
Henige, David, 22
Hermon Dunlap Smith Center for the History of
    Cartography, 76
Herodotus: quoted by Du Pratz, 100
Hillier, Bill, 179
Histoire de la Louisiane, 102
*Historia de la fundación y discurso de la provincia de
    Santiago de México*, 83–86
historical editing: annotation, 34, 38; and loan trans-
    lations, 40; and orthography, 38; rendering pho-
    netic systems in, 39; and translating documents, 1–
    3, 9, 35; mentioned, 33–42
historiography: Annales school, 7–8, 11, 15, 25–26,
    60, 94; of Choctaw name lists, 207; and codicol-
    ogy, 5; diplomatics, 5, 27n9; and documentary evi-
    dence, 2, 9–10; of eighteenth-century South, 43;
    German positivist, 94; and historiology, 22–23, 26;
    and intertextuality, 6; and mythistory, 20, 23, 26;
    of oral sources, 6, 21–23, 64; and prosopography
    of conquest expeditions, 60; and recordkeeping,
    24–25, 35–36, 43–45, 52n4, 203; Renaissance, 85,
    93; and temporal telescoping, 21–25; mentioned, 1,
    7, 55, 72
history: and authorial intention, 70–71, 74–75; and
    Choctaw conventions, 352; context and, 66, 72, 74;
    environmental, 179; ethnocentrism and, 34;
    genres, 6, 61, 74, 86; as ideology, 71–72, 74; indige-
    nous, 19; and moral discourse, 8, 19; narrative, 55,
    61, 70–75; Natchez Indian, 105; and objectivity, 83;
    oral, 20–22; and plot, 71; providential, 85, 90; pub-
    lic, 18; social, 7, 94; structure of, 66
History of the American Indians, 37, 48
Holahta. *See* Inholahta Choctaw moiety
honored men, 262
hopaii mingo title, 215, 220, 262
Hopewell culture, 293, 393
Hordes, Stanley, 27n5
Houma Indians, 239
Houma language, 231

museums: collections and policies of, 379; and community identities, 377, 379, 380, 383–84; *Curator* and Museum-L discussion of community participation in, 381; historical, 18; and objects, 378–79, 385; and public sphere, 380; and scholarship, 378; and stakeholders, 382. *See also* Mississippi 1500–1800

Muskogean people, 363

Nachoubaouenya Choctaw village, 217, 276, 284–85

Nairne, Thomas, 215, 231, 313–14

naming in Choctaw practice: according to Swanton, 204; action contexts of, 207; ceremony for, at Mobile congress, 324; as evidence, 13–14; and function titles, 205, 207, 213–14; genealogical, 217–20; and *iksas*, 219–20; and lists, 208–9, 212–13; and moiety designations, 207, 218–19; personal, 205, 213; sources for, 204, 210–11

Naniaba Indians, 230, 315, 320

Nanih Waiya mound, 147, 177

Nanipacana town, 81, 82

Napochie Indians: alleged foes of Coça, 88, 93; expedition against, 90–92; surrender of, to Spanish threat, 91

Narváez, Panfilo de, 148

Nassuba Mingo of Chickasawhay (Choctaw chief), 320, 322, 324, 326

Natchezan culture, 142, 144–45, 192, 230

Natchez Indians: burial practices of, 394, 397; kinship system of, 99–100, 106–7; rank/class among, 99, 204; as representative of moundbuilders, 98; revolt of, 50, 107, 149, 182, 185, 210, 237, 265, 267, 315, 340; and spousal sacrifice, 101; and temple guardian, as tutor for Du Pratz, 104; war against, 361, 378; mentioned, 10, 35, 143, 147, 156, 160, 183, 232–33, 235, 268, 270, 312–13, 315–16, 339, 342

Natchez post, 127, 236, 252, 280, 378, 386. *See also* Fort Rosalie

Natchez Trace, 114

National Archives and Records Administration, 19, 307

National Endowment for the Humanities, 14, 111, 136, 165, 174, 221, 354, 378, 380

National Historical Publications and Records Commission, 4–5

National Park Service, 408

National Science Foundation, 151

Native American Graves Protection and Repatriation Act, 18, 20, 380, 402, 408

Native Americans: as archivists, 19; displacement of, 16, 138, 260, 380; hegemony of, during colonial period, 9, 379, 384; as historians, 18–19; as mapmakers, 164, 172, 178; and partnership with Africans, 385; and variety and complexity of cultures, 384

Navajo Indians: attitude toward human remains, 407

Neshoba County MS, 147

Newberry, Mr. (British trader-interpreter), 279

Newberry Library, 76

New England, 396, 401

New Laws: and Spanish rules of exploration, 79, 85

New Orleans, 16, 43, 102–3, 107, 145, 152, 238, 250–52, 282, 285, 305, 339

Nicaragua, 61

Nicklas, Dale, 240

Nieto, Alvaro (Soto survivor), 79, 81–82, 88

Noyan, Gilles Augustin Payen de, 211, 250, 252, 342–44

Nunamiut Indians, 134

Nushkobo Choctaw village, 261, 282, 284, 347

O'Brien, Greg, 354, 357–58, 362, 367, 371–72

Ochuse. *See* Pensacola Bay

Oconostota (Cherokee chief), 302, 305–6

Offemeko (Choctaw chief), 272

Ohio River, 50, 305

Okalusa Choctaw village, 194, 215, 277, 284

Okeloussa. *See* Okalusa Choctaw village

Okéoulou Choctaw village, 284–85

Oklahoma, 138, 294

Olacta. *See* Inholahta Choctaw moiety

Onachiqui town, 88

Oni Choctaw village, 272, 276, 284–85

Opayéchitto of Immongoulacha (Choctaw chief), 274

Oquechiton River, 91

Organization of American Historians, 18

Ortiz, Juan (castaway-interpreter), 395

Oskelagna Choctaw village, 153, 156, 160, 215

Oulactopaye of Seneacha (Choctaw chief), 326

Oulitacha Choctaw village (home of Great Chief), 277, 283

Overhill Cherokee Indians, 302, 305

Oviedo y Valdés, Gonzalo Fernández de, 61

Paape, William, 259

Paemingo of Cushtusha (Choctaw chief), 276, 278, 284

Pahemingo-Amalahta (Chickasaw chief), 273

Pahémingo of Immongoulacha (Choctaw chief), 282

Pahémingo of Toussana (Choctaw chief), 283

pakana: as iksa name, 220

Pardo, Juan: expedition of, 58, 60

Régis du Roullet: as observer of Choctaw chiefs, 210–11; as observer of Choctaw villages, 148–50, 152, 155–56, 160, 184, 187, 189–94, 197–98; poor language skills of, 39; mentioned, 297

Reid, John Philip, 16

Reinhardt, Stephen G., 257n31

Renochon (interpreter), 327

Rentería, Juan de, 79

Replinque (French trader killed by Choctaw), 274

Ricard, Robert, 84

River of the Holy Spirit, 91

Rochette, Gamon de la, 53n11

Roman Empire, 391

Romans, Bernard, 14, 140, 148–49, 166, 172, 194–98

Rossard, Michel, 54n35

Rowland, Dunbar, 2, 3, 4, 35, 40, 245

Royal Council (of South Carolina colony), 260, 284

Salazar, Domingo de, 88

Salmon, Edmé Gatien, 211, 232, 249–51

San Agustín, 92

Sanders, Albert Godfrey, 2, 4, 35, 245

Santa Cruz, Alonzo de, 69

Santa Elena: as goal of Luna expedition, 79, 82

Santo Domingo, 51, 85, 107

Saussure, Ferdinand de, 7

Sauz, Mateo del, 81, 88

Scanapa Choctaw village, 217

Scardaville, Michael, 27n5

Scollar, Irwin, 174

Sebeok, Thomas, 410

Sellar, Walter Carrithers, 23

Seneacha Choctaw village, 215, 285

Senegal-Gambia River region, 239

Sepúlveda, Juan Ginés de, 80, 92

Seven Years' War, 319, 350. See also French and Indian War

Shawnee Indians, 277

Shulashhummashtabe. See Red Shoe

Silver, Timothy, 179

Sinte Bogue, 320

Siouan culture and language, 229

Sixtowns division: in Choctaw civil war, 263, 271, 275–77, 279, 283–86; at Mobile congress, 312–13, 315–16, 319, 328; mentioned, 155, 159–60, 192, 207

slavery: laws regulating, 379, 384; and raids on Choctaw Indians, 147; revolts against, 385; and trade in slaves, 379, 384–85

Smith, Bruce, 123

Smith, Neal, 174

Smith-Robertson Museum of African American History, 387

Smithsonian Institution, 399

Social Darwinism, 399

Society of American Archivists, 29n35

Sonakabetaska (Choctaw chief), 221n14, 277

Sotheby's auction house, 406

Soto, Hernando de: burial of, 393; Florida expedition, 58–60, 65, 67–70; and Native American burial practices, 395–96; texts and evidence, 66–70; mentioned, 56, 61, 78, 147–48, 160, 226, 378

soulouche houma title, 216, 262

Soulouche Oumastabé. *See* Red Shoe

South America, 60, 72

South Carolina, 49, 237, 246, 248, 252, 260, 268, 305, 313, 324–25, 338–39, 345, 361

Southeastern Ceremonial Complex, 57, 294

Southern Cult. *See* Southeastern Ceremonial Complex

Spiro site: burials mined from, 413n54

Spoehr, Alexander, 202

Starkville MS, 127

State Historic Preservation Office: authority over unmarked burials, 402

St. Cosme, Jean-François Buisson de, 103

St. Denis, Louis Juchereau de, 236

Steward, Julian, 59

St. Louis River. *See* Mississippi River

St. Michel (cabin boy-interpreter), 231

Stowe, Read, 145

structural pose, 207, 209, 262

Stuart, John, 166, 318–19, 323–24, 326–29, 350

Stuart-Purcell map, 166

Stubbs, John, 126

Sucarnoochee Creek, 177

Sun King (Louis XIV), 204

Superior Council (of Louisiana colony), 54n35, 236, 250–52

Swan Lake canoe, 111

Swanton, John R.: and gender roles, 368; and Soto expedition, 67; and southeastern Indian ethnography, 3, 14–15, 40, 99, 152–53, 202, 206–7, 213, 217–18, 227, 262–63, 282, 359, 363–64; and use of Dávila Padilla for evidence, 86–87, 93

symbolic action, 15, 17, 294

symbols, natural, 367

Taboca of West Yazoo (Choctaw chief), 321, 324, 353, 355n7, 357, 362

taboka: as iksa name, 220

Tachka oumma (Choctaw chief), 217

Taensa Indians: and ceramic decoration, 142–45; mentioned, 313

Taitt, David, 166

Tala Choctaw village, 276, 285

Talis town, 88

Tallapoosa Indians, 232–33, 273–74, 277–78, 308, 348

Tallapoosa language, 233

Tallapoosa River, 338

Talomeco town, 396

Tamatlémingo (Alabama chief), 232, 277, 323, 355n23

Tanselle, G. Thomas, 4–5

Taskanangouchi Arta (Choctaw chief), 214

Taskanangouchi Atlako (Choctaw chief), 214

Taskanangouchi Chaoulacta (Choctaw chief), 214

taskanangouchi title, 202, 214, 262

Taskaoumingo of Boucfouca (Choctaw chief), 276, 278

Taskaoumingo of Concha (Choctaw chief), 280

Tatoulimataha of Little Wood (elder brother of Red Shoe), 46–47, 254, 272, 276, 278

Tattooed Serpent (Natchez chief), 104, 105

Taxcaluça province, 88

Tchanké Choctaw village, 284, 285

Tchioulacta (Choctaw chief), 278

Tchoukooulacta. *See* Choucououlacta

Tennessee, 294

Tennessee-Tombigbee Waterway archaeology, 114, 127, 131

Tensaw River, 81, 177, 229, 320

Teotihuacan effect and site discovery, 114

Ternan, Terisse de, 54n35

Texas, 239

The Mortar, 305, 350

Thicachas Ouma of Nushkobo (Choctaw chief), 282

Thompson, Stith, 6

Thornton, Russell, 16

tichou mingo title, 203, 214, 262

time: in archaeology, 12; in history, 12, 21–26

Tiou Indians, 106

Tiou Oulacta. *See* Mingo Emitta

Todorov, Tzvetan, 61, 65–66

Tohome Indians, 218, 230, 313, 315, 320

Tomatly Mingo of Sixtowns (Choctaw chief), 320–21, 326

Tombecbé village, 216, 277

Tombigbee River, 68, 144, 147, 160, 166, 169, 177, 194, 197, 227, 229, 233, 263, 312, 314, 320

Tonti, Henri de, 142, 189, 227, 265, 312

Torre, Alvaro de la, 81

Toupa Houma of Kafetalaya (Choctaw chief), 302, 304, 306, 326

Toupaoumastabé of Concha (brother of Alibamon Mingo), 271–72, 276–77

Toussana Choctaw village, 276, 278, 285

Tozzer Library, 167

trade: control of by Louisiana government, 238; in market economy, 17, 294, 358, 371. *See also* presents for Indians; prestige goods

traders: English, 45, 272, 274, 279, 280–81, 283–86, 313, 322, 338, 343–44, 349–53, 356n36; French, 46, 237, 274, 277, 348; as source of cartographic data, 151

treaties, 14, 16

Treaty of Paris, 193

tribe: as unit of social organization, 56

Trigger, Bruce, 395

Tumbikpe. *See* Fort Tombecbé

Tunica Indians, 59, 239, 252, 383, 386

Tunican culture and language, 229

Tuscaloosa AL, 229

Uamado opayé (Tallapoosa chief), 308

Ulibahali town, 88

Upiache town, 88

Upper Creek Indians, 233, 261, 268, 275, 308, 312, 338, 349, 350, 353

Upper House (of South Carolina colony), 260

Urban, Greg, 363

U.S. Army Corps of Engineers, 68

U.S. Department of State, 306

U.S. Department of the Interior, 407

U.S. Forest Service: archaeological survey, 131

Usner, Daniel, 112

Vann (British trader), 281, 283

Vansina, Jan, 21–22

Vargas, Juan de (Soto survivor), 79

Vaudreuil, Pierre de Rigaud de: and conduct of Indian affairs, 46–47; letterbooks, 36, 37, 44–45, 49, 52n4; as observer of Choctaw civil war, 259–61, 264, 271, 273, 279, 282, 284; papers of, 10; mentioned, 233, 237, 299, 305, 347–49

Vauparis (cadet-interpreter), 233

Vazquez, Rodrigo (Soto survivor), 79, 82, 88

Velasco, Luis de, 79, 81, 89

Verbois, Dominique de, 45–47, 53n13, 54n33, 275

Verbois de Baussière, Henri de (subaltern killed by Choctaw), 45–48, 272, 274, 277

Villafañe, Angel de, 82

Villebeuvre, Jean de la, 329

Villiers du Terrage, Marc de, 51

Virginia, 396

Voss, Jerome, 126

Wagener, Diane K., 132
Wallerstein, Immanuel, 295
Ware, James, 136
War of 1812, 378
War of the Austrian Succession, 253
War of the Spanish Succession, 339
Washington Peace Medal, 309n19
Wedderburne, David, 324, 327, 328
Weddle, Robert, 84
Weeks, Charles, 221
Welch, Thomas (British trader), 313
West Abeka Choctaw village, 261, 274, 277, 283–84, 347
Western Apache Indians. *See* place-names
Western Choctaw division: in Choctaw civil war, 263–64, 269, 274, 276, 281–84, 286; in Mobile congress, 312, 314–16, 319, 326, 328–29; mentioned, 192, 346
Western Muskogean language family, 226, 228, 230, 239
West Florida, 350
West Immongoulacha Choctaw village, 284–86
West Yazoo Choctaw village, 45, 283–84
White, Hayden, 8, 71
White, Richard, 179, 329
Winston County MS, 147
Winterville mound, 405
Wolf, Eric, 21
women: as captives in Natchez revolt, 185, 237, 267, 270, 315, 340; and differential fertility by class, 100; as diplomats, 272; excluded from European observations, 207; and flight from Spanish explorers, 88; as informants for Europeans, 10, 104; and population models, 133; and rape by French soldiers, 37, 45–46, 48, 272–73, 278, 345; and rape during Choctaw civil war, 253; and roles in matriliny, 98; rude treatment toward, by English traders, 322, 351–53; scalped by Choctaws, 282; status passages for, 368; as wives of interpreters and traders, 237
Wood, Peter, 16, 112
Woodland period, 293
Wright, Alfred, 215

Yamassee War, 267, 339, 361
Yanabé Choctaw village: in Choctaw civil war, 272, 277–78, 284; mentioned, 194, 216, 232
Yazoo Choctaw village, 214, 272, 274
Yazoo delta, 227, 345
Yazoo Indians, 149, 185, 339
Yazoo Iskitini Choctaw village, 279
Yazoo River, 183
Yeatman, Robert Julian, 23
Yellow Canes Choctaw village, 276, 285
Yoknapatawpha, 183
York, Kennith, 240
Youlakty Mataha Tchito, anké achoukema (Gov. Kerlérec's Choctaw honorific), 40, 349
Yowani Choctaw village, 152, 156, 159, 193–94, 215, 220, 263, 275, 284–85, 313

Zimmerman, Larry, 19